GOVERNING AND RULING

CHINA UNDERSTANDINGS TODAY

Series Editors: Mary Gallagher and Xiaobing Tang

China Understandings Today is dedicated to the study of contemporary China and seeks to present the latest and most innovative scholarship in social sciences and the humanities to the academic community as well as the general public. The series is sponsored by the Lieberthal-Rogel Center for Chinese Studies at the University of Michigan.

Resisting Spirits: Drama Reform and Cultural Transformation in the People's Republic of China
   Maggie Greene

Going to the Countryside: The Rural in the Modern Chinese Cultural Imagination, 1915–1965
   Yu Zhang

Power over Property: The Political Economy of Communist Land Reform in China
   Matthew Noellert

The Global White Snake
   Liang Luo

Chinese Netizens' Opinions on Death Sentences: An Empirical Examination
   Bin Liang and Jianhong Liu

Governing and Ruling: The Political Logic of Taxation in China
   Changdong Zhang

GOVERNING AND RULING

The Political Logic of Taxation in China

Changdong Zhang

UNIVERSITY OF MICHIGAN PRESS
Ann Arbor

Copyright © 2021 by Changdong Zhang
All rights reserved

For questions or permissions, please contact um.press.perms@umich.edu

Published in the United States of America by the
University of Michigan Press
Manufactured in the United States of America
Printed on acid-free paper
First published October 2021

A CIP catalog record for this book is available from the British Library.

Library of Congress Cataloging-in-Publication data has been applied for.

ISBN 978-0-472-07501-0 (hardcover : alk. paper)
ISBN 978-0-472-05501-2 (paper : alk. paper)
ISBN 978-0-472-12940-9 (e-book)

To my father, 张炳亮
In memory of my mother, 张仙艳

Contents

List of Figures	ix
List of Tables	xi
List of Abbreviations	xiii
Acknowledgments	xv

Introduction		1
ONE.	A Fiscal Sociological Theory of Regime Resilience	14
TWO.	Tax-State Transition	43
THREE.	Fiscal Decentralization, Bureaucratization, and Economic Growth	92
FOUR.	Explaining Regional Variations in Governance Quality	123
FIVE.	Representation through Taxation?	149
SIX.	Forbearance and Rule by Fear	181
SEVEN.	Conclusion and Theoretical Implications	209

Notes	245
References	289
Index	321

Digital materials related to this title can be found on the Fulcrum platform via the following citable URL: https://doi.org/10.3998/mpub.11945851

Figures

Figure I.1. Relationships among governance and ruling, governance problems, and taxation mechanisms — 7

Figure 1.1. Relationships among governance problems and regime resilience — 21

Figure 1.2. Relationships among governance problems and dilemmas — 32

Figure 1.3. Dilemmas and mechanisms for how taxation matters for authoritarian resilience — 41

Figure 2.1. Changes in two ratios, 1978–2017 — 54

Figure 2.2. National revenue breakdown by type of income, 2014 — 57

Figure 2.3. National revenue breakdown by type of taxes, 2014 (percentage of general budgetary income) — 57

Figure 2.4. County Warm River's fiscal income, 2014 — 58

Figure 2.5. County Warm River's tax revenue breakdown, 2014 — 58

Figure 2.6. County Warm River's government fund revenue breakdown, 2014 (%) — 59

Figure 2.7. Rise and decline of land-transfer fee, 1998–2017 — 63

Figure 2.8. Citizens' perception of tax burden, 2014 (compared to peer group) — 71

Figure 2.9. Citizens' perception of tax burden, 2014 (compared to public services received) — 72

Figure 2.10. Half-tax state as double-edged sword for authoritarian resilience — 74

Figure 2.11. Organizational structure of tax administrations in China before 2018 — 79

Figure 3.1. Coevolution of the bureaucracy and market — 98

Figure 4.1. Deaths from coal-mining disasters in China since 1990 — 130

Figure 5.1. Nominal local power relationships — 155

Figure 5.2. Real local power relationships — 156

Figure 6.1. Under-institutionalized taxation system and
    authoritarian resilience   183
Figure 6.2. Deeper institutional explanation of
    authoritarian resilience   207
Figure 7.1. From institutional origins to political outcomes   224
Figure 7.2. A model of endogenous institutional change   227
Figure 7.3. Endogenous causality between taxation and
    CCP resilience   228
Figure 7.4. Comparison of nominal GDP, real GDP, and
    national tax growth rates, 1978–2019   239

Tables

Table I.1. Two primary and five secondary cases	10
Table 2.1. Stages of market and tax-state transitions in the PRC	46
Table 2.2. Governance problems under three political economic systems	48
Table 2.3. Two dimensions of tax-state transition and implications for two taxation dilemmas	49
Table 2.4. Governance problems under three types of tax state	50
Table 2.5. Stages of the fiscal system in the PRC	51
Table 2.6. Share of national tax revenue in 2014, by enterprise type	56
Table 2.7. Composition of industrial output and tax by enterprises of different ownership, 1998 and 2004, percentages	60
Table 2.8. Land-related revenue and relative value to local government tax revenue	63
Table 2.9. Major revenue breakdown for County Warm River, Zhejiang Province, 2008	64
Table 2.10. Land-transfer fee expenditure in China, 2015	67
Table 2.11. Major revenue breakdown for County Cold Mountain, Shanxi Province, 2008	69
Table 3.1. Stages of bureaucratization	96
Table 3.2. Dividing the case into subcases	99
Table 3.3. Industry output and growth rate	104
Table 3.4. Discipline of bureaus through elimination of small private coffers	112
Table 3.5. Sizes and value of land in County Warm River, 2015	117
Table 4.1. Role of industries in regional variation of bureaucratization	126
Table 4.2. Comparison of County Warm River and County Cold Mountain, late 2000s	127

Table 4.3. Number, ownership, and production of coal mines in County Cold Mountain — 129

Table 4.4. Time line of coal-mine regulation in County Cold Mountain — 134

Table 4.5. Separating the cases into subcases — 138

Table 4.6. Complementary cases — 139

Table 5.1. Entrepreneurs at different political levels and size of enterprises — 166

Table 5.2. Empowering the LPC — 171

Table 5.3. Comparison of LPCs in three counties — 171

Table 6.1. Private-sector capital's demand for democracy — 184

Table 6.2. Taxation and bureaucratization — 193

Table 6.3. Summary of four indicators of tax burden — 196

Table 6.4. Tax revenue structure of County Cold Mountain's LTB, 1994–2003 — 198

Table 6.5. Ratio of coal-resource-related taxes to resource tax in County Cold Mountain — 199

Table 6.6. Summary of resource dependence — 199

Table 6.7. Summary of political status (membership as independent variable) — 200

Table 6.8. Summary of political status (membership as ordinal variable) — 200

Table 6.9. Summary of political status (membership as nominal variable) — 200

Table 6.10. Summary of control variables — 202

Table 6.11. Summary of district and party membership — 202

Table 6.12. LSR model of governance quality (four types of tax and nontax burdens) — 203

Table 6.13. LSR model of robustness check of governance quality (overall tax burden) — 204

Table 7.1. Comparison of agricultural and business taxation — 222

Table 7.2. Comparison of three informal practices/institutions — 223

Table 7.3. Revised trajectories of Barrington Moore — 235

Table 7.4. Typologies of states — 236

Abbreviations

AIC	Administration for Industry and Commerce
CCDI	Central Commission of Discipline and Investigation
CCP	Chinese Communist Party
CDI	Commission of Discipline and Investigation
CPPCC	Chinese People's Political Consultative Conference
FCS	Fiscal contracting system
GTP	Golden Tax Project
LPC	Local People's Congress
LPPCC	Local People's Political Consultative Conference
LTB	Local Taxation Bureau
NPC	National People's Congress
PC	People's Congress
SAT	State Administration of Taxation
SOEs	State-owned enterprises
TSS	Tax-sharing system
TVEs	Township and village enterprises
VAT	Value-added tax

Acknowledgments

Writing this book was a very long journey. Fortunately, I was not alone. This book grew out of my PhD dissertation, "Good Governance through Taxation: Business Politics in Authoritarian China," which I began in 2009 for the Department of Political Science at the University of Washington, Seattle. I finished the final revision of this book in July 2020 at Peking University. During this long journey, I received much support from, and I am grateful to, many people and organizations.

I owe most to my dissertation committee members, Susan Whiting, Joel Migdal, and Margaret Levi. They taught me not only in classes and via supervising the dissertation but also by personal example. Both the dissertation and book were deeply inspired by their works. Susan, the committee chair, had full confidence in me from the beginning but also set high standards for me. She read through each chapter at the dissertation stage and the book manuscript stage and kept challenging me to improve the quality of my research. She also taught me how to do fieldwork, cross-validate data, and more important, go back and forth between data and theory. Joel is also an ideal mentor. He is always inspiring and encouraging, and his state-in-society theory illuminated my intellectual exploration during the whole journey. Joel provided valuable comments and advice through the last round of revision. Margaret influences me not only through her masterful studies on taxation politics and institutional analysis but also by pushing me to think and write in a clear, consistent, and coherent way. I still remember feeling enlightened when she told me to reframe the dissertation as providing "a non–Robert Putnam answer to the Robert Putnam question" during the hardest stage of writing.

The journey began as early as 2006. Even before I departed for graduate study in Seattle, Xu Wang advised me to study regional governance through the perspective of government-business relationships, which eventually became the topic of my dissertation; however, I used taxation and asset mobility, not enterprise size, as the variables. Xu also taught me what an intellectual should do in a changing society.

I am grateful to the individuals who helped me navigate the longer journey from dissertation to finished book. I owe special thanks to Mary Gallagher and Dan Slater. In April 2013, I attended Mary's talk on her manuscript on authoritarian legality in China at the Stanford Center at Peking University, which helped me reframe this book. In November 2017, I met Mary again at a workshop, and she gave me advice for revision and kindly invited me to submit it to this book series. Mary also organized a book workshop in September 2018 at the Lieberthal-Roger Center for Chinese Studies at the University of Michigan and again provided valuable advice for revision. Dan Slater, at a conference at Fudan University in May 2014, was the first to provide comments, advice, and encouragement for my article that lays out the theoretical framework of this book (published in 2017 in *Sociological Theory* as "A Fiscal Sociological Theory of Authoritarian Resilience"). Dan later also offered valuable critique and advice during a personal conversation in Beijing.

Two book workshops made the long journey of exploration endurable, and I am very grateful to the participants for their valuable insights and suggestions. The earlier book workshop was organized by Tianbiao Zhu at the Institute for Advanced Studies of Humanities and Social Sciences (IAS) of Zhejiang University on June 2, 2016. Tianbiao, Gregory Chin, Lynette Ong, Qi Zhang, and Yi-wen Yu provided many suggestions for further writing. At the September 2018 book workshop at the University of Michigan, Mary, Susan, Dan, Mark Dinccceco, Yuming Sheng, and Mike Thompson provided advice and comments, including restructuring the book to make it more reader-friendly.

I am also grateful to Gary Hamilton and other professors at the University of Washington for training me to be a political scientist; and I thank my colleagues in the Political Science Department and China Program, John Buchanan, Spencer Cohen, Chris Heurlin, Yuting Li, and Man Wang, among many others, for their suggestions and friendship.

I also thank others who provided comments, suggestions, and help at various stages of this project: Bruce Dickson, Hualing Fu, Dongya Huang, Yan Long, Xiao Ma, Adam Przeworski, Liang Tang, Yutaka Tsujinaka, Eric (Haixiao) Wang, Wei Xiong, Xiaojun Yan, Xuan'ge Yao, and Feizhou Zhou. I am grateful for Bruce's generosity for allowing me to use his data set in the book. I also had opportunity to present the book project at a number of universities during different stages. I presented the whole project at

University of Hong Kong (October 2015), the IAS of Zhejiang University (May 2016), and Institute of Humanities and Social Sciences of Peking University (December 2016). I presented part of the project at the University of Washington (October 2017), University of Michigan (April 2018), Sun Yat-sen University (March 2018), Xiamen University (May 2018), University of Waseda (October 2018), and Oxford University (November 2019). I thank the organizers and participants for their valuable comments and suggestions.

I am also grateful for my informants, whose names I cannot reveal, for their help and support; without them this book would not have been possible.

The School of Government at Peking University provided a supportive academic environment where I started my study of political science and developed my career. I thank Yuan Ruijun, my master of arts supervisor in the early 2000s, who led me to study new political economy and encouraged me to do high-quality research. I am also grateful to Shen Mingming, Wang Puqu, Xu Xianglin, and Yan Jirong, who were my teachers then and now my colleagues, for their instruction and support. The IAS of Zhejiang University provided an environment for me to finish most chapter drafts in three very productive months, from March to early June 2016.

I thank four anonymous reviewers for their valuable critiques, comments, and suggestions that helped improve this book. I thank Dr. Kate Epstein for helping a nonnative speaker thoroughly edit the manuscript. I also thank my editorial and production teams for shepherding this book to publication.

Certain portions of this book were previously published as Changdong Zhang, "A Fiscal Sociological Theory of Authoritarian Resilience: Developing Theory through China Case Studies," *Sociological Theory* 35, no. 1 (2017): 39–63; and Changdong Zhang, "Reexamining the Electoral Connection in Authoritarian China: The Local People's Congress and Its Private Entrepreneur Deputies," *China Review* 17, no. 1 (2017): 1–27. I thank these journals for allowing me to reprint portions of my work.

During this long academic journey, I also experienced many changes in my life. I married Xiaohong in October 2012, and our children, Yunzhong and Yunning, were born in 2014 and 2019. I thank them for their love and understanding when I was not able to spend much time with them. My mother passed away in March 2011. I wish she could share all this happiness. I dedicate the book to my parents because, without their sacrifice and support, a peasant's son could never imagine writing such a book.

Introduction

> The public finances are one of the best starting points for an investigation of [a] society, especially though not exclusively of its political life. The full fruitfulness of this approach is seen particularly at those turning points.... This is true both of the causal importance of fiscal policy (insofar as fiscal events are an important element in the causation of all change) and of the symptomatic significance (insofar as everything that happens has its fiscal reflection).
> —Joseph Schumpeter, "The Crisis of the Tax State"

> The most important political distinction among countries concerns not their form of government but their degree of government. The differences between democracy and dictatorship are less than the differences between those countries whose politics embodies consensus, community, legitimacy, organization, effectiveness, stability.
> —Samuel Huntington, *Political Order in Changing Societies*

> Fiscal and taxation system is the foundation and an important pillar of state governance. Good fiscal and taxation systems are the institutional guarantee for improving resources allocation, maintaining market unity, promoting social equity, and realizing enduring peace and stability.
> —CCP Central Committee, "Decision of the Central Committee of the Communist Party of China on Some Major Issues concerning Comprehensively Deepening the Reform"

On March 4, 2016, Xi Jinping, the Chinese Communist Party's (CCP) general secretary and president of the People's Republic of China (PRC), met with members of the industry and commerce sector of the Chinese People's Political Consultative Conference (CPPCC),[1] China's National Democratic Construction Association (CNDCA),[2] and the All-China Federation of Industry and Commerce (ACFIC).³ It was the second day of the twelfth CPPCC annual session and the day before the Twelfth National People's Congress (NPC) annual session—that is, during the politically symbolic Two Sessions (两会). Xi remarked at the meeting, "China should stick to its basic socialist economic system (under which state ownership and private ownership coexist)." At the same time, he acknowledged that private enterprise is very important to China. The CCP, he claimed, respects private ownership and entrepreneurship and will build a better environment for private enterprise. He criticized collusive government-business relationships that had existed in China in recent decades and emphasized the need to build healthy government-business relationships. Officials and businessmen "should follow a principle of treating each other with respect instead of forming cliques or factions. It is necessary to set boundaries between private and official affairs." He outlined an ideal for these relationships:

> Sincerity (亲) and honesty (清) succinctly summarize the focus of government-business relations. Sincerity highlights the connotation of officials' offering contacts and service for people, dismissing many officials' concerns about keeping contacts with businesspeople. Honesty highlights the bottom line of the law, drawing a red line on anticorruption, which clarifies specifications for officials' actions in strict accordance with the law. (*Xinhua* 2016)

Xi also emphasized that private entrepreneurs should keep in mind that "they should adhere to socialism and that therefore they should 'strengthen self-learning, self-educating, and self-improving' as the party's leadership would recommend instead of feeling 'uncomfortable with these demands.'" The speech concluded by arguing that private entrepreneurs should also have a role in the Local People's Congress (LPC), Local People's Political Consultative Conference (LPPCC), CNDCA, and ACFIC (*Xinhua* 2016).

On the same day of Xi's speech, CCP's Central Commission of Discipline and Investigation (CCDI), which handles its anticorruption investigations, announced a new investigation (双规) of a powerful minister-level official: Wang Min, an NPC deputy and vice-director of the NPC Standing Committee's subcommittee. More important, Wang was a former party secretary of Liaoning Province and Jilin Province (Y. Yan 2016). During Xi's high-profile anticorruption campaign, CCDI had investigated 169 ministers or higher-level party, military, and government officials from 2012 to October 25, 2018 (*Economic Daily* 2021); the number increased to 196 on June 2, 2020 (*Economic Daily* 2020), and the number keeps growing.

These events show that a ruler needs to be able to rule and govern at the same time. The juxtaposition of these events on a single day raises many questions that I take up in this book: Why can some authoritarian regimes be sustained while others fail? Specifically, how do authoritarian rulers monitor and discipline their local agents? How do they elicit compliance and cooperation from the ruled (especially the resource-rich capitalists), therefore achieving economic growth and regime resilience? What are the institutional tools of repression, concession, and co-optation? Are there any tensions between these goals and tools?

We find that a number of authoritarian regimes around the world have collapsed while transitioning to a market economy (Centeno 1994; Saxonberg 2001, 2013), usually associated with a fiscal crisis. Even the liberalization of an economy (e.g., structural adjustment in Latin America in the 1980s and 1990s) can topple a regime (Haggard and Kaufman 1995; Greene 2007). Certainly, several nations have transitioned to democracy while successfully developing their economies (Lipset 1959; Przeworski 2000). But the Chinese authoritarian party-state has been able to hold on to power through a market transition and almost four decades of continuous rapid economic growth since 1978, which makes the society highly pluralized and changes the old pattern of domination. Scholars, journalists, and others thus consider why and how the CCP sustains its power without serious domestic challenge to be a crucial question for both comparative political studies on democratization or authoritarian resilience and real-world policy implications.

As Samuel Huntington demonstrated half a century ago, "the most important political distinction among countries concerns not their form of government but their degree of government" (1968, 1). In other words, regimes vary in terms of stability (and effectiveness); a regime's stability is a question of degree (or an ordinal variable), which varies from resilience to survival, to instability, to breakdown whether it is democratic, authoritarian, or hybrid. Democracies could be broken down, unstable, or consolidated, because waves of democratization have low and high tides.[4] For authoritarian and hybrid regimes, regime instability and breakdown may or may not lead to democratization. Authoritarian resilience differs from authoritarian survival:[5] "Survival is simply a matter of maintaining power over an extended period of time. Resilient regimes, however, not only survive but also thrive and adapt while fostering the growth of national military and economic power. They remain the unchallenged authority during periods of significant social and economic change" (Gallagher and Hanson 2013, 187). "Authoritarian resilience" also meets Dan Slater and Sofia Fenner's definition in that it avoids or resolves crises in a way that is decisively in the regime's favor (2011, 17).[6] I use "authoritarian resilience" and "authoritarian durability" interchangeably in this book. By this definition, the PRC under the CCP's single-party rule may be the most resilient modern authoritarian regime because it has successfully managed a (partial) market transition, promoted rapid economic growth, undergone two world financial crises, and improved people's living standards and welfare in the last four decades.

The factors that determine differing degrees of stability among authoritarian regimes and drive regime change have attracted much academic attention and effort in the last decade, known as the "institutional turn of comparative authoritarianism" (for comprehensive reviews of the literature, see Art 2012; Brancati 2014; Brownlee 2002; Morse 2012; and Pepinsky 2014). Barbara Geddes (1999) pioneered this area with her seminal work on typologies of authoritarianism. In contrast to scholars who study democratization theories that focus on either structural factors or agencies (elite conflict; e.g., O'Donnell, Schmitter, and Whitehead 1986; Treisman 2020),[7] scholars studying authoritarian resilience have addressed the role of different institutions in sustaining authoritarian rule, which I review in chapter 1. Scholars who critique this explanation in particular include David Art (2012), Carl Knutsen and Håvard Nygård (2015), Yonatan Morse (2012), and Thomas Pepinsky (2014). While these institutional explanations of authoritarian resilience significantly enrich our understanding of authoritarian politics, they have weaknesses. Specifically, many scholars provide only exogenous or functionalist explanations and neglect the autocrat's dilemma. For example, Art points to "an overly simplistic view of how institutions and organizations matter" in this body of literature, resulting in underspecification of a variety of causal mechanisms (2012, 363). Therefore, critiques of the way of attributing resilience to "democratic-looking institutions" call for a focus on state institutions rather than legislatures or elections (Slater and Fenner 2011; Knutsen and Nygård 2015). This book reveals that an important state institution, taxation, explains the CCP's resilience without the problems other explanations have encountered and provides implications for general questions of regime resilience.

The Argument in Brief

Following classic writers such as Niccolò Machiavelli, recent scholarship generally recognizes the challenges or governance problems authoritarian rulers face in their quest to retain power. Built on pioneer works by Kung-chüan Hsiao (1967), Milan Svolik (2012), and Jennifer Gandhi (2008), among many others, this book addresses three governance problems: social control (to achieve compliance), cooperation, and discipline of local agents. In other words, a successful authoritarian ruler governs to discipline agents and elicit cooperation and rules to achieve social control. Many authoritarian rulers rule well but govern badly, and failed authoritarian rulers do not rule or govern.

How do authoritarian rulers resolve these governance problems and sustain their rule? How does the CCP resolve these problems during a tax-state transition associated with a market transition? Joining the recent institutional turn of comparative authoritarianism literature, this book, though a mechanism-based study, tries to shed light on these questions and tackle the three governance problems by examining a neglected state institution, taxation, as an important "regime characteristic" or state institution, as well as how it influences authoritarian resilience through resolving the three governance problems. I argue that taxation complements the other institutions in resolving these problems and sustains authoritarian rule, but in many ways taxation is more fundamental and more significant than other institutions.[8]

I reframe the general question of authoritarian resilience into more specific ones through the perspective of the institution of taxation: How does the institution of taxation resolve the three governance problems? What role does taxation play in shaping the resource-rich economic elites' (capitalists') strategies of survival? Why will the current taxation system sustain authoritarian rule rather than lead to democratization? In addressing these questions, I follow the tradition of fiscal sociology of Joseph Schumpeter, Alexis de Tocqueville,[9] and Max Weber, arguing that taxation may play an important role in sustaining authoritarian rule by addressing the three governance problems. Schumpeter (1991) suggested the importance of the taxation system in "the state's nature, form and fate" and noted that a transition from a domain state to a tax state provides a good opportunity for democratic transition.[10] However, given taxation's theoretical and substantial importance, most existing research in fiscal sociology uses taxation as a dependent variable but rarely focuses on its "*causal* significance" or its impact on politics and economy (i.e., an independent variable) (Martin, Mehrotra, and Prasad 2009, 2).[11]

I agree with Slater and Fenner's (2011) idea that taxation's mechanisms of infrastructural state power sustain authoritarian regimes. However, I argue that to study those aspects of the institution of taxation that bolster resilience, we need to examine two specific taxation dilemmas for authoritarian regimes that are generated by increasing infrastructural state power: the representation dilemma and the growth dilemma. Only when an authoritarian regime can successfully resolve or alleviate these dilemmas will it achieve resilience. I argue that the taxation system has three important mechanisms to resolve or alleviate taxation dilemmas in the short term; however, in the long term, these mechanisms can counteract each other, forcing the autocrats to make trade-offs. These mechanisms reflect three dimensions of the taxation system.

The first mechanism, de facto fiscal federalism, refers to how regional taxation competition constrains local governments' predatory behavior, promotes regional economic growth, and improves the level of bureaucratization, which I call "coevolution of market and bureaucracy." It also causes local governments to co-opt private entrepreneurs into the local legislature and therefore elicits cooperation and promotes economic growth.

The second mechanism is China's still being a half-tax state that has a high dependence on nontax revenues (which compose more than one-third of fiscal revenue), indirect taxes (about two-thirds of tax revenue), and state-owned enterprises (SOEs). This structure can reduce both the citizens' perception of their tax burden and the costs of tax collection while increasing government autonomy, which relieves the social-control problem.[12]

The third mechanism is an under-institutionalized taxation system that sets very high tax rates while allowing many taxpayers to evade taxes, gives tax officers great discretionary power, and sets the annual tax target. On the one hand, this contributes to resolving the growth dilemma by reducing effective tax rates and promoting economic growth. On the other hand, it makes taxpayers vulnerable to the authoritarian state by creating incentives for them to act illegally to evade taxes. Their illegal behavior makes them vulnerable to state censure, thus weakening their political bargaining power.

Figure I.1 illustrates the relationships among governance and ruling, the three governance problems, and the three taxation mechanisms.

The half-tax state, especially its high dependence on indirect taxes, makes businesses the major taxpayers. Therefore, this book focuses

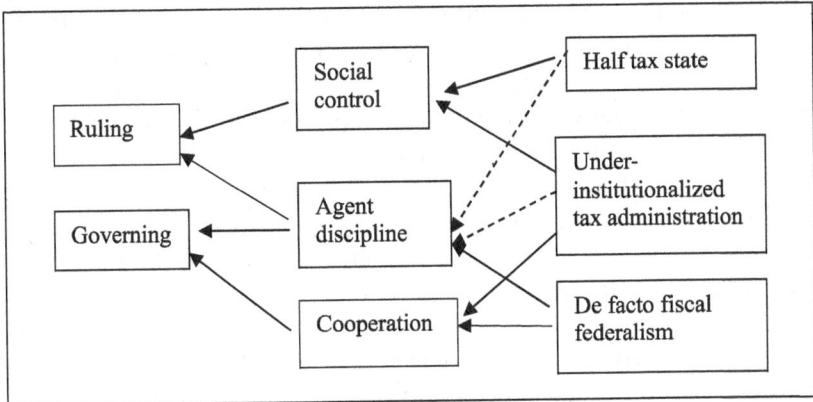

Figure I.1. Relationships among governance and ruling, governance problems, and taxation mechanisms. Solid arrows refer to positive effects, and dashed arrows refer to negative effects.

mainly on private enterprises and private entrepreneurs and discusses how the other two mechanisms affect their economic and political behavior. On the one hand, de facto fiscal federalism empowers private enterprises that have high asset mobility with bargaining power and promotes economic growth and quality of governance. On the other hand, under-institutionalized taxation drives private entrepreneurs to pursue patron-client relationships with the state, seeking to be co-opted by the party-state for protection (e.g., seeking to become an LPC deputy) rather than challenging it. However, this weakens local government responsiveness and accountability—that is, the quality of governance. I call this "co-optation via deterrence." Therefore, this book also contributes to the literature on government-business relationships.[13] I elaborate on the argument, two dilemmas, and three mechanisms by developing a fiscal sociology theory of authoritarian resilience in chapter 1 and discuss the mechanisms of de facto fiscal federalism and the under-institutionalized taxation system in detail in the rest of the book.

Research Design and Data Sources

The multiple-method research design employed here combines cross-regional comparison, process tracing, and Large-N studies. The process began by building theories with causal mechanisms based on a theory-guided case study. The case study includes both a historical and a comparative dimension. Hypotheses are developed based on the case study. Then I use quantitative data to test the external validity of the hypotheses.

My use of a mechanism-oriented and theory-guided case study as the basis for my hypotheses responds to Morse's proposal that "studies of electoral authoritarianism need to start engaging in more midrange, case-based research" (2012, 163).[14] China is an ideal case to study the importance of taxation for authoritarian resilience. First, China exemplifies authoritarian resilience: the CCP has been in power since 1949, and scholars regard it as an adaptive and flexible authoritarian party-state (Dimitrov 2013; Nathan 2003; Shambaugh 2008).[15] Second, China's double transition and rapid economic growth are testing that resilience. Third, international forces driving democratization in China are limited, and domestic drivers are more prominent (Levitsky and Way 2010). Fourth, many existing institutional explanations for authoritarian resilience, including elections and a legislature, can be excluded because election in China is limited to the self-governing village, and, as I demonstrate, the economic elites' fear of the authoritarian regime's predatory power drives the co-optation of the economic elites in the legislature.

China's vast size presents a methodological challenge as well as opportunity. I use cross-regional comparison and quantitative methods to deal with this challenge. In the last decade, studies of comparative politics and Chinese politics have taken a "subnational turn" that focuses on the regional variations within one country (Rithmire 2014, 166). I examine two major cases (counties) and five complementary cases to build the causal relationship between taxation and governance quality, developing hypotheses based on cross-regional comparison. I use micro-level comparisons and carefully look through the macro-level analysis to examine the causal mechanisms that link taxation and authoritarian resilience.

The county government is the basic unit used to analyze Chinese political economy: it incorporates most of the government functions of the central government (except national defense and diplomacy), and it has its own budgetary power; it directly governs the people. The county- and township-level governments directly implement policies, while higher-level governments make policies and monitor their implementation. At the same time, county governments have great discretionary power in making policies. Therefore, the county is regarded as the foundation of stability; as an old Chinese proverb says, "When the counties are well governed, the country is stable and peaceful [郡县治，天下安]." Chinese president Xi Jinping has referenced this point on many occasions, including at a commendation meeting for one hundred county party secretaries on June 30, 2015. Xi emphasized that party committees and governments at the county level are of great importance in promoting economic growth, providing public services, and maintaining stability (Xi 2015). In other words, he sought to address two governance problems, social control and cooperation, mostly at the county level.

I selected the two primary and five complementary county cases based on variations of the independent and dependent variables. Table I.1 provides an overview of these variations. The most important case, County Warm River in Zhejiang Province in East China, has had the most vibrant private economy in China since the 1980s and is dominated by export-oriented light industries with high asset mobility. It is examined in great detail through process tracing of its development trajectory since 1980. The other primary case, County Cold Mountain, experienced similar development levels in 2010, based mainly on coal mining with very low asset mobility. But local governance institutions in County Cold Mountain are performing much more poorly than those in County Warm River. County Cold Mountain actually had higher development levels than its counterparts in Zhejiang at the beginning of reform in the late 1970s and early 1980s because of its coal-mining industry. However, County Warm River overtook County Cold Mountain in the 1990s during rural industrialization. But with the coal boom in the mid-2000s, County Cold Mountain has regained good economic performance in terms of gross domestic product (GDP) per capita in the last several years. But unlike what occurred in County Warm River, improved economic performance in County Cold Mountain has not brought better governance. The institutional performance of local governments in these regions differs significantly. Comparing institutional performance and tracing its evolution provide a useful opportunity to study institutional variations and change, especially of representative institutions and institutions of taxation in an authoritarian state.

To test the external validity of the argument, another five secondary cases are introduced with different focuses: County Wenling is a complementary case for comparing LPCs, and the other four are complementary cases for implicit bargaining. I use the method of difference to reflect and explain regional variations and the method of agreement to capture similarities within the country. The analysis addresses the economic and (limited) political reform since the early 1980s. A methodological challenge for this book (as for most social science research) is the endogeneity problem. Taxation relates to both the symptoms and causes of market transition, evolution of governance, and social change, as Schumpeter (1991) suggests. To use the terminology of state-society relationships, there is a "mutual transformation" (Migdal 2001, 100) between taxation and market transition, between taxation and governance, and between taxation and authoritarian resilience. I use process tracing to deal with the endogeneity problem, through which I also build an endogenous institutional explanation of authoritarian resilience. Accessibility to data is a major barrier since both political and taxation issues are somewhat sensitive in China. I rely on various sources: official statistical data, secondary data, and my fieldwork. The fieldwork includes three sources: my interviews, government and LPC archives (both published and unpublished; for reasons of anonymity, some published and most unpublished archives are referenced

Table I.1. Two primary and five secondary cases

County	Province	Economic development (2009 GDP per capita)	Industry	LPC	Level of bureaucratization: governance quality
County Warm River	Zhejiang	28,200 (390,000)*	Light industry (high asset mobility)	Active	High: good services and infrastructure, less corrupt and responsive
County Cold Mountain	Shanxi	28,035 (490,662)*	Coal mining (low asset mobility)	Inactive	Low: predatory, bad infrastructures, rampant corruption and unresponsive
County Wenling	Zhejiang	Very high (40,893)	Light industry	Active	High
County D	Shanxi	Medium (21,544)	Coal mining	Inactive	Low
County X	Hunan	Low (14,424)	Agriculture	Inactive	Low
County Yiwu	Zhejiang	Very High (41,933)	Light industry	Active	High
County Z	Chongqing	Low (9,820)	Light and heavy industry	Inactive	Medium

* Population in 2009.

without more detailed sources), and media reports. From 2007 to 2014 (a few interviews were conducted more recently), I interviewed dozens of tax officers and other government officers, private entrepreneurs, trade association leaders, and tax scholars in the seven case-study counties as well as in universities in Beijing, Wuhan, Taiyuan, and Xi'an. I read the unpublished LPC archives from 1980 to 2011 and the Local Taxation Bureau (LTB) archives from 2004 to 2012 of one county in Zhejiang Province and conducted several interviews with two officers of the State Administration of Taxation (SAT). I consulted the unpublished LTB archives from 2001 to 2010 of a county in Shanxi Province, as well as the Shanxi provincial LTB's journal, *Theory and Practice of Taxation* (*Shuishou Lilun yu Shijian*). I stayed in a guesthouse of a county tax bureau for two weeks, interviewing and chatting with tax officers and reading their documents and archives. Given that tax evasion is a very sensitive topic, I used different sources to cross-validate the data to ensure the reliability and validity of the research. Since most of China's taxes are directly collected from businesses, the social actors whom I focus on in this book are private entrepreneurs, who pay a large share of taxes in China.

The book also uses two quantitative data sets. The first draws on three sources: a nationwide private-enterprise survey (PES) conducted by ACFIC and the Chinese Academy of Social Sciences in 2007 and 2013 (see All-China Federation of Industry and Commerce 2007a, 2014); the nationwide county-level fiscal data from 2007; and the county-level GDP and population data for 2006 (for time-lag effects). I also collected county-level data for the counties in the data set. The economic development level measured by GDP per capita and some fiscal data were added. Resource dependence, measured by the resource tax's share of tax revenue, is calculated based on the fiscal data. I used both the individual and aggregated data (at the county level for the year 2007) to test the hypotheses drawn from case studies. The second data set is a nationwide random sample of Chinese urban residents' evaluation of public services and local government trust conducted by Research Center for Contemporary China of Peking University in 2014.

Chapter Overview

While this introduction raises the question of authoritarian resilience and briefly introduces the argument, chapter 1 builds a fiscal sociological theory of authoritarian resilience. The chapter critically reviews existing institutional explanations of authoritarian resilience and taxation's infrastructural power mechanisms for authoritarian resilience. Based on that, I introduce two taxation dilemmas (growth and representation) and elaborate on the three taxation mechanisms of authoritarian resilience: de facto fiscal federalism, under-institutionalization, and the half-tax state as causal mechanisms that resolve or alleviate the two taxation dilemmas in contemporary China.

Chapter 2 discusses China's partial transition from a communist state to a tax state. It includes three dimensions. The first is a brief history of intergovernmental fiscal relationships since the early 1980s, with a focus on the fiscal contracting system (FCS) and tax-sharing system (TSS), which lays out the institutional foundation for regional tax competition. Second is the under-institutionalized taxation administration; that is, it sets unreasonably high nominal tax rates, grants tax officers a high degree of discretionary power, and collects taxes based on targets set by supervisors rather than taxpayers' tax liabilities. Third is the half-tax state, which refers to the structure of fiscal revenue: Chinese local governments rely heavily for revenue on highly regressive indirect taxes, taxes paid by SOEs, land-transfer fees, and other nontax revenue. The half-tax state increases the state's autonomy and alleviates the representation dilemma by reducing compliance (social-control) cost. However, the half-tax state may exacerbate the growth dilemma because it generates inefficiency and high levels of inequality and contributes to the serious local government debt crisis.

Chapter 3 builds a revised coevolution model of market and bureaucracy via a process-tracing study of County Warm River while undergoing a double transition. Borrowing an idea from mutual transformation of state and society, I argue that the FCS somehow destroyed the bureaucracy system while motivating bureaucrats to raise fiscal revenues by exploiting and running township and village enterprises (TVEs). However, TVEs and private enterprises promoted economic growth and drove the local government to work hard to discipline predatory bureaus. Therefore, the market and bureaucracy coevolve. The chapter elaborates on the theoretical basis of de facto fiscal federalism and critically discusses two popular theories for explaining China's economic growth: market-preserving federalism and local state corporatism.

Chapter 4 uses the method of difference to explain variations in local governance quality and test the external validity of the causal argument developed in chapter 3. I argue that regional competition for tax revenue under de facto fiscal federalism incentivizes local political leaders to improve quality of governance to attract investment and therefore confers higher quality of governance on regions with high asset mobility. I find that both physical and institutional factors shape asset mobility in that local government sets trade barriers to protect local industries, most of which local governments own. Then I explain how this provides a new answer to the Robert Putnam question—that is, variations in regional governance quality of governments with the same formal institutions.

Chapter 5 examines the role in local governance and authoritarian resilience of two democratic-looking institutions: the LPC and its direct election. I find that about one-third of county-level LPC deputies are private entrepreneurs. At the same time, the local government depends heavily on their tax payments for revenue. While this coincidence suggests a representation-through-taxation mechanism, my fieldwork reveals that the LPC's function of co-optation and organization of clientelist platforms plays a stronger role than representation in the CCP's resilience.

Chapter 6 uses method-of-agreement analysis to capture similarities in local governance. I find that the under-institutionalized taxation system generates both forbearance and fear, therefore resolves the representation dilemma by weakening private entrepreneurs' bargaining power: instead of demanding institutional change and representation in the LPC, private entrepreneurs seek patron-client ties. Therefore, the representation dilemma is resolved and authoritarian resilience is strengthened. A quantitative study of private entrepreneurs' political title and regional asset mobility's influence on private enterprises' overall tax burden is also conducted to test the external validity of conclusions I draw in earlier chapters.

Chapter 7 summarizes the findings of the book and discusses some general theoretical implications. I discuss taxation's implications for economic development, state capacity, state and society relations, and authoritarian resilience. I also build an endogenous institutional explanation for authoritarian resilience.

CHAPTER 1

A Fiscal Sociological Theory of Regime Resilience

> There is one which is of particular interest to us: the view of the state, of its nature, its form, its fate, as seen from the fiscal side.
> —Joseph Schumpeter, "The Crisis of the Tax State"

> Since there is almost no issue of public interest which does not derive from taxes or end up in taxes, from the moment when the two classes [the aristocracy and the bourgeoisie] were no longer equally subject to taxation, they had almost no further reason to meet together again, no more reason to experience common needs and feelings; it no longer required any effort to keep them apart: in a sense the motive and desire to act together had been taken away from them.
> —Alexis de Tocqueville, *The Old Regime and the Revolution*

> Though the emperor conquered the country by violence (riding on the horse), it is impossible to rule/govern the country on the horse. Great emperors use both generosity and bureaucrats to rule, which is the strategy for long-term stability (居马上得之,宁可以马上治之乎?且汤、武逆取而以顺守之，文武并用，长久之术也).[1]
> —Lu Jia, in Sima Qian, *Shiji*

At the G20 meetings of finance ministers and Central Bank governors in Chengdu, Sichuan Province, on July 23, 2016, China's finance minister, Lou Jiwei, pledged to go to great lengths to introduce a property tax. Lou thought that promoting the reform of income tax and property tax would ensure fairer income distribution. However, effective policies for income redistribution would definitely face obstacles: "This is a challenge, and this is our next task. We are devoted to carrying it on. . . . Information collection, taxation capacity building and vested interests are the major challenges," Minister Lou remarked (Wang and Jing 2016).

Minister Lou's remarks coincided with the CCP Politburo's meeting on July 27, 2016,[2] which emphasized the importance of inhibiting asset bubbles for China's sustainable economic growth. On December 20, 2017, Minister of Finance Xiao Jie published an article in *People's Daily* and briefly mentioned that the property-tax proposal should be sent to the legislature no later than 2019 and then be implemented step by step (J. Xiao 2017). These three important messages immediately led to hot discussions among both policy analysts and academic researchers.[3] People suspected that the timing of pushing forward the property tax reflected the CCP Politburo's concern about inhibition of asset bubbles, primarily the housing bubble. Some economists suspected that it was related to addressing the great economic inequality in China, which is a major challenge for increasing the domestic market and promoting sustainable economic growth. Some fiscal experts regarded it as a way to find a solution for local governments' lack of reliable tax revenue and a substitute for the land-transfer fee. Some law scholars and political scientists, however, debated the legitimacy of a property tax in China. Since Chinese urban citizens do not own the land that their houses and apartments are built on and most of them paid huge land-usage fees when they bought their properties, there is no reason that they should pay a tax based on a property price that includes a land-usage fee.

For the purposes of this book, I find that the two earlier events, which are a continuation of the CCP Politburo's "Overall Plan on Deepening Fiscal and Tax System Reform" passed in June 2014, reflect the CCP's efforts to deal with the three governance problems and the problems of China's current taxation system. During tax-state transition, the CCP can extract about 38 percent of GDP as its fiscal revenue, but its taxation capacity is still limited (20 percent of GDP is tax revenue), and any further reform may bring huge administrative and political costs. The following event, however, shows the urgency of pushing forward further taxation reforms regardless of potential costs. Recent reform efforts, particularly merging two independent taxation bureaus (SAT and LBT) into a new SAT in June 2018, redeviding value-added tax (VAT) shares between central and local governments in October 2019,[4] and substantially reducing the tax target since 2018, demonstrate the CCP top leaders' determination to deal with challenges.

Just one day before Minister Lou's remarks, *21st Century Business Herald*, a prominent commercial business newspaper, reported that one of the "Top 100 Counties" (百强县), Fugu County in Shaanxi Province, could meet only about half of its fiscal expenditure in 2015 (3.99 billion yuan), though the budgetary fiscal revenue maintained growth of 0.25 percent. This means that the county government could pay only salaries and part of its administrative costs and was unable to cover its rapidly increasing social-welfare expenditures (H. Wang 2016). Though Fugu is an extreme case that relied heavily on the coal-mining industry, many other county governments also suffered severe fiscal difficulties when economic growth slowed in recent years, especially in Central, Western, and Northeast China, according to a report by the Ministry of Finance's Chinese Academy of Fiscal Science.[5]

As the epigraphs in the introduction and at the beginning of this chapter demonstrate, both academia and policy makers, whether ancient or modern, Western or Chinese, believe that taxation provides a very good perspective to examine "the view of the state, of its nature, its form, its fate," which includes authoritarian rule and resilience. But a fiscal sociology theory of authoritarian rule, unfortunately, is underdeveloped. This book tries to develop such a theory based on the China case, with a focus on private entrepreneurs as major taxpayers.[6]

A brief introduction to fiscal sociology is needed before we move ahead. In "The Crisis of the Tax State," Joseph Schumpeter (1991) defines fiscal sociology as the study of the social processes behind taxation and public finances and regards it as one of the best starting points for an investigation of society, particularly its political life. It is a multidisciplinary field that covers at least economics, sociology, political science, history, and law. Fiscal sociology differs from other approaches to the study of taxes and public finances "because it considers how these things affect and are affected by a wide range of political, economic, cultural, institutional, and historical factors . . . by focusing explicitly on the complex social interactions and institutional and historical contests that link state and society in ways that shape fiscal policies and their effects" (J. Campbell 1993, 164). As Richard Swedberg (1998, 2009; Schumpeter and Swedberg 1991) claims, great thinkers, especially Alexis de Tocqueville, Max Weber, and Joseph Schumpeter, have important ideas and insights concerning fiscal sociology even though they had not developed systematic theories that laid out the foundation for the rediscovery and renaissance of fiscal sociology since the 1970s.[7]

Some comprehensive summaries of the literature on taxation in sociology discuss either the consequences of taxation for other aspects of politics and society (Block 1981; J. Campbell 1993; Martin and Prasad 2014) or the causes of the origins and development of tax systems defined as tax revenue, tax structure, and tax administration (Gould and Baker 2002; Kiser and Karceski 2017). Scholars from various disciplines "have begun to recognize the central importance of taxation to modernity and produce innovative comparative historical scholarship on the sources and consequences of taxation," which is an emerging field known as the "new fiscal sociology" (Martin, Mehrotra, and Prasad 2009, 2).

While fiscal sociology studies both expenditures and taxes, there are many more studies on expenditures than on taxes. Among studies of taxation, more studies treat taxation as a *symptom* or *consequence* than as a *cause* or *engine* of social change. This book contributes to fiscal sociology by treating taxation as a cause of social change while recognizing the reciprocal relationships.

In this chapter, I first introduce three governance problems (especially for authoritarian governance and ruling) and then critically review the existing explanations of authoritarian resilience through the perspective of the governance problems. Then I discuss the existing theories of the institution of taxation's infrastructural power mechanisms and introduce the growth and representation dilemmas. I next elaborate on the three taxation mechanisms and how they resolve some of the taxation dilemmas, followed by a discussion of their limitations, and then draw a conclusion.

The Governance Problems

To achieve regime resilience, rulers face four main governance problems (or challenges),[8] three of which this book addresses: social control, cooperation, power sharing (not discussed in this book), and discipline of local agents. These challenges differ under different regimes because of two intrinsic features of authoritarian regimes: the lack of an independent third party to enforce agreement (therefore lack of credible commitment and thus widespread betrayal) and the use of violence as an ever-present and ultimate arbiter of conflicts (Svolik 2012, 2). In other words, a successful authoritarian ruler governs (to discipline agents and elicit cooperation) and rules (to achieve social control or compliance), while many authoritarian rulers rule well but govern badly (Cook 2007; Taylor 2013). This book focuses on three of the problems because they are closely related to taxation under authoritarian regimes. The problem of power sharing is of less interest to the current analysis because the institution of taxation has limited bearing on this problem, but it is referenced when relevant.

Milan Svolik defines authoritarian control in this way: "All dictators face threats from the masses, and I call the political problem of balancing against the majority excluded from power the problem of authoritarian control" (2012, 2). Jennifer Gandhi also defines it in a similar way: "As rulers who hold power without the legitimacy of having been chosen by their citizens, they must prevent attempts to undermine their legitimacy and usurp power. In other words, they must thwart challenges to their rule" (2008, xvii). Authoritarian control, or social control under authoritarianism, differs from social control under established democracy in many ways, including particularly lack of rule of law and the absence of an independent third party (e.g., an independent judiciary system) to enforce rules to constrain the behaviors of both citizens and government. Authoritarian control uses multiple strategies: repression (coercion), legal repression, ideological inculcation, and co-optation. Authoritarian regimes use such strategies more frequently and intensively than democracies do, whereas democracies rely more on eliciting "quasi-voluntary compliance" (Levi 1988, 52) and rule of law.

However, dictators must do something beyond seeking social control of citizens, or their *passive* compliance; dictators also need their citizens' *positive* cooperation. Like democratic rulers, autocrats must achieve economic and fiscal-revenue growth to retain power in the long run.[9] Unlike democratic rulers, authoritarian rulers need economic growth to achieve performance legitimacy and fiscal-revenue growth to buy insiders' loyalty through distributing spoils (Reuter and Szakonyi 2019), co-opt elites, purchase popular support through providing public services, fund repressive institutions, and so on. Other goals that require cooperation include implementation of policy and provision of public goods.[10] Thus, the second challenge is for dictators to solicit the cooperation of outsiders, capitalists, professionals, workers, and peasants to ensure that individuals have incentives to make investments and engage in productive activities that promote economic and revenue growth (Gandhi 2008, xvii–xviii).

The power-sharing problem stems directly from the authoritarian control problem, as controlling the citizenry requires a ruling coalition to support the dictator (Bueno de Mesquita, Smith, and Siverson 2003; Svolik 2012). Unlike democratic leaders, authoritarians face potential violent betrayal from people within the ruling coalition; therefore, the authoritarian governance problem is "a separate political conflict [that] arises when dictators counter challenges from those with whom they share power" (Svolik 2012, 2). Sharing power among factions at the national level poses a significant risk of lack of coherence among top elites, which may lead to authoritarian breakdown through coup or democratization (O'Donnell and Schmitter 1986). Power sharing goes beyond sharing power within the ruling coalition; because the situation is continuously changing, the ruler should share power with potential rivals from the ruled and co-opt them into the ruling coalition. This process of co-optation could take place in democratic-looking institutions such as the legislature (Gandhi 2008, xix) and party (Svolik 2012) or in the form of patron-clientelism.

Power sharing also goes beyond national political elites; local government officials or party cadres are also part of the ruling coalition, especially in a large country where the rulers have to delegate power to local agents or elites. Nobles or bureaucrats thus have some share of power (see Weber 1968, especially chaps. 11, 12). In China local government officials consist of low-level party and government officials. Though they cannot directly threaten the power of an authoritarian ruler, they can indirectly influence authoritarian stability because they have discretion in how they implement policies made by the central government. These local agents also have the ability to initiate regional policies, so they influence state capacity (including extractive capacity), "the ability of state leaders to use agents of the state to get people in the society to do what they want them to do" (Migdal 1988, xiii); quality of governance; policy implementation (Holland 2016; O'Brien and Li 1999); corruption (Treisman 2007); and economic growth (Shleifer and Vishny 1998).[11] Some scholars suggest that the party is an important institutional instrument for co-optation of agents and note that an effective party system has the following features: hierarchical assignment of services and benefits, political control over appointments, and selective recruitment and repression (Svolik 2012, 163). All three are features of the CCP and play an important role in promoting regional economic growth and sustaining one-party rule. However, agents also must be disciplined and co-opted to support authoritarian control. This involves a central-local government relationship problem in which the central government must discipline its local agents,[12] and local agents' discipline of their apparatus, which is a bureaucratization problem (Evans 1995). In democracies, election, the legislature (McCubbins and Schwartz 1984), and free media play a monitoring role and provide accountability, but authoritarian regimes lack these mechanisms, which can be a serious problem, as Steven Solnick (1998) found in the Soviet Union. I call this aspect of the power-sharing problem the "(local) agent-discipline problem." Authoritarian regimes need institutional instruments, such as undemocratic elections (Gandhi and Lust-Okar 2009), a judiciary system (Ginsburg and Moustafa 2008), and free media to discipline their low-level officials, preventing them from exploiting society.[13] But these instruments, including the party (Cai 2015), are not effective enough to discipline powerful local agents in China.[14] The local agents and their apparatus need to be motivated as well as monitored and disciplined;[15] otherwise, they will tend to selectively implement policies that serve their own interests (O'Brien and Li 1999).

Another aspect of the power-sharing problem is that the agent-discipline problem intersects with the social-control and cooperation problems in that eliciting societal compliance and cooperation requires state coherence, as suggested by Peter Evans (1995) and others.[16] State coherence could be built through a process of bureaucratization (Weber 1968; Kohli 2004).[17] Figure 1.1 illustrates these relationships.

While all authoritarian regimes face these governance problems, the problems vary in different contexts. Chapter 2 presents three of the problems in the context of China's undergoing dual transitions: a market transition associated with a tax-state transition, which make these problems much more challenging. Before proposing a fiscal sociological explanation of authoritarian resilience, I first critically evaluate other institutional explanations.

Institutional Explanations for Authoritarian Resilience

How do authoritarian rulers tackle governance problems? In this section, I critically review the role of coercive institutions, China's unique stability-maintenance system (the judiciary system as part of it), democratic-looking institutions, public-goods provision, and the party's organization as sources of the CCP's resilience. Other institutional explanations, including the role of propaganda and censorship (especially internet censorship),[18] and noninstitutional explanations such as culture and nationalism are addressed in other chapters as relevant.[19]

Coercive Institutions

Scholars have long attributed authoritarian resilience to coercive institutions (e.g., Albertus and Menaldo 2012; Bellin 2000; Greitens 2016; Lev-

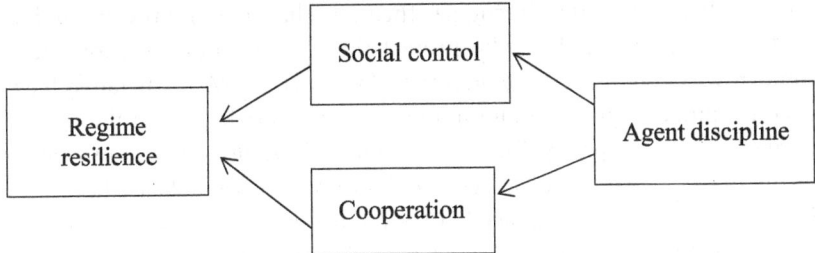

Figure 1.1. Relationships among governance problems and regime resilience.

itsky and Way 2010). Juan Linz (1975, 2000) finds that rulers of totalitarian regimes use state-sponsored domestic terror, mass coercion, human rights abuses, and repression to threaten and even eliminate real and potential rivals.[20] While totalitarian rulers use terror, which is unpredictable and arbitrary, authoritarian rulers use repression. As many scholars have described, police play an important role in maintaining social control in China (Wang and Minzner 2015; Zhou and Yan 2014), and the CCP has learned how to use targeted repression to minimize negative effects.[21] Going back to Mao Zedong's embrace of what he called "power from the gun," the CCP continued to term the military the state's "gun" (枪杆子). Jiang Zemin, Hu Jintao, and Xi Jinping, who together have made up the CCP's key leadership since 1989, emphasize the importance of controlling the "knife" (刀把子) of the Commission of Politics and Law (CPL; 政法委) (*People's Daily Online* 2015).[22] In a recent comprehensive study, Xuezhi Guo argues that coercive institutions in China are the "CCP's ultimate instruments of state control, and they have been instrumental to the survival of the regime" (2012, 3). Effectively, Guo argues that repression is crucial to the survival of the regime largely because of the substantial commitment the CCP has made to it, and it does appear to play a crucial role. Yet there are three reasons that terror and repression undermine resilience even as they appear to solidify it.

Yongshun Cai summarizes the first problem with terror and repression: "[It] not only causes the opposition to gain allies: it may also leave the opposition little alternative but to revolt, or it can produce a radicalization of collective action and a more effective organization of opponents" (2008, 413).[23] Repression may also cause some supporters to lose trust in the regime and weakens its legitimacy. The CCP combines concession with repression to address these problems, and the taxation system combines both. Second, rulers recognize the moral hazard of repression in that soldiers or (secret) police who protect them today could turn on them tomorrow (Greitens 2016; Migdal 1988; Svolik 2012). Many dictators have used purging, or simple rotation, to mitigate this risk, even at the cost of weakening state capacity. But military forces have nonetheless proven to be out of the state's control, as coups in Latin America and Africa have suggested. Even the CCP has faced crises controlling its military and armed police force in recent years.[24] Third, though terror and repression create a high level of social control in the short term, they cannot elicit cooperation from social actors. They generate insecurity that weakens incentives for investment in a country.

The Stability-Maintenance System

President Hu Jintao called for the creation of a "harmonious society" shortly after he came to power in 2002. He stated that improving "social management" and promoting social harmony were basic conditions for building a prosperous and harmonious socialist society and thus required a social-management strategy that could coordinate social relationships, regulate behavior, promote social justice and stability, and manage social risk. His administration assigned the CPL and the Ministry of Civil Affairs to lead the creation of a social-management system, dubbed the stability-maintenance (维稳) system. The administration describes it as a "people-centered" (以人为本) and "services-centered" program to resolve rising discontent following decades of economic growth that has paved the way for expressions of grievances and discontent, even riots, which pose a threat to the regime's stability.[25]

Stability maintenance is a particularly Chinese institution distinct from pure repression and terror. With this new idea about governing, the CCP experienced a strategic shift from "strike-hard campaigns" (严打) targeting "criminals, vice, and cults" in the 1980s and 1990s to a coordinated effort among the courts, bureau of justice, state security, bureau of civil affairs, and propaganda department (Liao 2009, 44). In contrast to repression, stability maintenance includes a petition system that allows citizens to voice complaints to party and government organizations through different methods, including both coercion and soft coercion. Yanhua Deng and Kevin O'Brien (2013) find, for example, that local officials sometimes utilize their personal influence and social networks to demobilize protesters and halt popular action without deploying outright violence and that it effectively quells dissent.

However, through cadre evaluation, in which one failure such as a riot could lead to economic or political punishment, cadres began to combine repression and bargaining (Lee and Zhang 2013) or repression and concession (Cai 2008) to absorb social tensions at the grassroots level to keep riots local. Cai (2008) argues that China's highly decentralized state structure, in which the central and local and grassroots governments have different preferences and responses to dissent, explains why widely spread social protests do not lead to regime collapse (see also Hess 2013).[26] This is a process of "institutional conversion," which refers to the use of institutions in ways that deviate from their intended purpose (Thelen 2004, 36).

Other problems have also made stability maintenance unsustainable.[27] While independent courts can play an important role in sustaining authoritarian rule, the court is also marginalized. On the one hand, the party wants to promote rule by law to carry out the five functions proposed by Tamir Moustafa and Tom Ginsburg (2008). On the other hand, the party's goals may sometimes conflict with rule by law. The pursuit of economic growth and stability maintenance by local officials, for example, may lead the very authorities charged with enforcing laws to violate those same laws (see C. Lee 2007 on labor law). Under certain conditions, therefore, the pursuit of rule by law fails. Judicial independence could also threaten authoritarian rule (Moustafa 2007). Therefore, the CCP maintains the courts' dependence on the party or intentionally implements laws with high "flexibility and state discretion" that demobilize collective representation and push forward no social changes (Gallagher 2017, 49).

Democratic-Looking Institutions

In the last two decades, scholars have been addressing the power of democratic-looking legislative institutions under authoritarian regimes as sources of resilience. These researchers argue that legislatures under authoritarian regimes are not simply symbolic or window dressing. Instead, they play important roles in resolving authoritarian governance problems: achieving social control via co-optation of various social groups and classes and soliciting the economic elites' cooperation to achieve economic growth (Gandhi and Przeworski 2007; Gandhi 2008). Gandhi (2008) argues that when authoritarian rulers need to raise revenue but face strong opposition, they tend to have co-optative legislatures that provide institutionalized bargaining between the ruler and opposition forces, deliver policy compromise, and therefore achieve social compliance (see X. Yan 2011 for its implication in China). Other researchers describe the role of legislatures in eliciting cooperation and promoting economic growth by providing a credible commitment to private property rights protection. Chapter 5 provides a thorough review of scholarly applications of this theory to explain the CCP's resilience; this chapter presents a summary of the weaknesses of these arguments.

The first weakness is that rulers must make trade-offs among different goals when using and manipulating these institutions—what political scientists have described as "autocrat's paradoxes" or "politician's dilemmas."[28] For example, as Mancur Olson describes, giving too much privilege to certain groups will lead to "distributional coalition(s)" or special-interest groups that harm economic growth (1982, 44),[29] so buying support and sustaining economic growth are in conflict. Unfortunately, few scholars who attribute the CCP's resilience to institutions address this paradox (except Dickson 2016), which is addressed in this book.

The second weakness is that explanations attributing resilience to democratic-looking institutions do not take institutionalism theories seriously and tend to be exogenous. David Art finds that they "adopt an overly simplistic view" (2012, 363), underspecifying a range of causal mechanisms. He suggests that these explanations will not be convincing until they unpack exactly how institutions influence resilience. Some scholars such as Gandhi (2008) rely on rational choice institutionalism, which tends to be functionalism and even tautology, and therefore overestimate these institutions' functions (Art 2012).[30]

Public-Service Provision

Authoritarian rulers also use what Peter Flora and Jens Alber propose: "social welfare as authoritarian defense against (full) political citizenship and as consequence of a competition for loyalty" (1981, 46), later on termed the "authoritarian welfare state" (Beck 1995). This is a subtype of co-optation with private transfer. Otto von Bismarck of Germany famously pioneered the strategy in the late nineteenth century (Flora and Alber 1981). Hu Jintao's "harmonious society" incorporated similar measures in the 2000s, increasing services to citizens and expanding peasants' access to services. As Bruce Dickson notes, the policy aligns with the CCP's "traditional ideology to 'serve the people'" (2016, 16). The 1994 Tax-Sharing Reform (TSR) generated rapidly increasing fiscal revenue in the late 1990s, which made it affordable for the CCP to spend more money on social-welfare programs.

Scholars have debated whether increased social-welfare expenditure wins citizens' support. Kevin Morrison (2014) finds an association between government spending and regime stability across democratic and authoritarian states. The authoritarian welfare state theory also endorses this argument (Beck 1995; Forrat 2012). However, as general theoretical debates suggest, the effects of social policy on mass political attitudes and regime support are mixed (A. Campbell 2012). The literature on co-optation by means of cash, price controls, subsidies, or redistribution policy is relevant here (Svolik 2012). Scholars find the strategy of co-optation with immediate private transfers does not produce stability, which is another weakness of co-optation via public-services provision. Co-optation via transfers, which frequently takes the form of cash, price controls, subsidies, and redistribution, according to Svolik (2012), has only a short-term stake in the regime's survival. Regimes are easily destabilized if authoritarian rulers stop providing public services during economic crises (Greene 2007; Magaloni 2008). As Niccolò Machiavelli warned, rulers cannot only rely on the love of the ruled because it is not enduring.

Welfare state authoritarianism increases support for China's central government but not for local governments (Dickson 2016; Lü 2014). Jeremy Wallace (2014) argues that the historical emphasis on services to urban residents has helped reduce collective resistance to the CCP because urban residents are more likely to be organized than rural residents who were excluded from social-welfare programs (see X. Huang 2015 for inequality of social welfare in China). Jennifer Pan finds that social-assistance programs (最低生活保障) could be used as a tool for "repressive assistance—by facilitating repeated interactions as well as relationships of dependence and obligation that constrain the autonomy of targeted persons" (2020, 21) and therefore contribute to authoritarian stability, but with some backlash.

However effective it is to co-opt the majority of the population through public service points to the importance of revenue generation and thus supports my overall argument that taxation is fundamental. Providing such services is very expensive; thus, as Morrison (2014) argues, systems that provide a large amount of revenue are the basis for any system of authoritarian welfare.

The Single-Party System

Samuel Huntington (1968) argued that parties played an important role in institutionalizing politics and improving government capability (i.e., state capacity) in developing countries (see also Huntington and Moore 1970). More recent scholarship has addressed the single or dominant party's role specifically in sustaining authoritarian resilience. Barbara Geddes (1999), for example, finds that one-party and dominant-party regimes are less likely to break down or democratize than authoritarian regimes that are personalist, military based, or hybrids not solely based on a particular party. A number of scholars have followed Geddes, finding different empirical evidence and causal mechanisms for the contribution of institutionalized single-party regimes to authoritarian resilience, including co-optation of the opposition, credible power sharing, exchange (especially patronage), and punishment (Slater 2003; Smith 2005; Magaloni 2006; Magaloni and Kricheli 2010; Brownlee 2007). Steven Levitsky and Lucan Way (2010) suggest that organizational power,[31] in which party cohesion is a key element, explains authoritarian stability in the face of international and domestic challenges. A party's origin can explain the institutionalization of the party and its durability (Smith 2005). The CCP is a classic case of a party built up through decades of intensive military struggles; therefore, it is highly institutionalized.

Svolik argues that three organizational features make parties effective sources of regime resilience through co-optation and direct political control: hierarchical assignment of services and benefits, political control over appointments, and selective recruitment and repression (2012, 11). The CCP's nomenklatura system, the system of performance-based cadre evaluation,[32] conforms to his description.[33] The taxation bureaus are also under party leadership. CCP national leaders could reform the taxation system under certain conditions, and the nomenklatura system shapes tax officers' incentives. I build an endogenous institutional change theory of taxation and authoritarian resilience to further discuss the party's role in chapter 7.

Andrew Nathan argues that four aspects of the CCP's institutionalization drive its resilience: "1) the increasingly norm-bound nature of its succession politics; 2) the increase in meritocratic as opposed to factional considerations in the promotion of political elites; 3) the differentiation and functional specialization of institutions within the regime; and 4) the establishment of institutions for political participation and appeal that strengthen the CCP's legitimacy among the public at large" (2003, 2–3).[34] In other words, he claims that it addresses the power-sharing problem through the first and second aspects, the agent-discipline problem through the third, and social compliance through the fourth. But Nathan does not elaborate on the last two aspects.

The CCP is no doubt the key institution of authoritarian resilience, which is defined as the CCP's base of power. In China, the CCP as the government is also a bureaucratic institution and has branches at all levels with full-time staffs leading, monitoring, supervising, and coordinating the government, military, and other state organs (including People's Congresses [PCs] and People's Political Consultative Conferences [CPPCCs]). Therefore, the party itself faces serious agent-discipline problems. While an anticorruption campaign and daily party discipline could reduce corruption, rationalization and bureaucratization could be a more effective and fundamental solution.[35]

Besides the weaknesses pointed out earlier, all the abovementioned institutions require a lot of fiscal resources; therefore, the taxation system is the foundation of state power. Using coercive organizations and stability maintenance as examples, how the military is funded is an important issue for the military's political role and professionalism.[36] The cost of buying off protesters or pacifying them through concession is very high. Spending on internal security already outstrips military spending.[37] Many riots and protests have fiscal causes.[38] Eliciting compliance and cooperation for a party requires substantial fiscal resources (Magaloni 2006; Greene 2007; Slater 2010b). But fiscal resources are scarce for most authoritarian regimes in developing countries; repressive and stability-maintenance institutions can crowd out other areas of economic investment or be used in a very unproductive way. Thus, they could harm the growth imperative.

The logical extension of the most convincing institutional arguments for authoritarian resilience is that, while resilience may depend on various institutions, in China those institutions reliably depend on and complement the taxation system. Thus, I build on the arguments of other scholars in relating the role of the important state institution of taxation to the question of the CCP's remarkable resilience and authoritarian resilience in general. I use terminology of state capacity (or infrastructural state power) popular in the state-centric (e.g., Evans, Rueschemeyer, and Skocpol 1985) and state-society-relation (e.g., Migdal 1988) literature of the 1980s and 1990s to argue that the state's extractive capacity is the foundation of its other capacities, including penetrative, regulatory, and distributive functions. However, a fiscal sociological theory of authoritarian resilience needs to go beyond taxation's infrastructural power mechanisms and discuss the growth and representation dilemmas associated with improved taxation capacity.

Taxation's Infrastructural State-Power Mechanisms

While taxation and war as the engines of modern state building have attracted extensive attention (Dincecco 2011; Elias 1994; Ertman 1997; Kiser and Kane 2001; Kiser and Schneider 1994; Levi 1988; M. Mann 1993; Schumpeter 1991; Tilly 1990; Weber 1968),[39] literature on comparative authoritarianism has paid limited attention to taxation. Since international war has not been a threat for most developing countries since World War II, taxation plays a crucial role in shaping state-society relationships in developing and transitional countries: it rebuilds the state as well as society (Brautigam, Fjeldstad, and Moore 2008; Martin, Mehrotra, and Prasad 2009). Scholars who have acknowledged the role of taxation in authoritarian resilience include Benjamin Smith (2007) and Dan Slater (2010b; Slater and Fenner 2011), all of whom focus on taxation's infrastructural power.

Drawing on Michael Mann's (1986) description of infrastructural power as the capacity of the state to penetrate civil society and to use this penetration to enforce policy throughout its entire territory, Dan Slater and Sofia Fenner (2011) attribute the power of institutions of taxation to four infrastructural power mechanisms.[40] First, it coerces rivals by funding the coercive apparatus. Second, it extracts revenue to support other government functions, including public-service provision; as well as co-opting supporters, it demands that a cohesive tax agency be built.[41] Third, it registers information on enterprises and individuals, which in turn requires a coherent and capable bureaucracy and helps build the state's capacity to penetrate society. Fourth, it cultivates dependence by patronizing followers.

As the first infrastructural power mechanism reveals, taxation is fundamental to other institutional mechanisms reviewed previously. Modern states need huge fiscal resources to maintain coercive power, provide public goods, and co-opt. For example, Eva Bellin regards taxation capacity as the foundation of a robust coercive apparatus:

> First, the robustness of the coercive apparatus is directly linked to maintenance of fiscal health. The security establishment is most likely to give up when its financial foundation is seriously compromised. When the military can no longer pay the salaries of its recruits and the security forces cannot guarantee supplies of arms and ammunition, the coercive apparatus disintegrates from within. (2003, 144)

To some degree, taxation's infrastructural power mechanisms explain the China case well. China has experienced almost four decades of rapid economic and tax-revenue growth. The CCP benefits from rapidly increasing tax revenue in many ways. The central government was able to abolish agricultural taxes in 2004, which significantly reduced rural tax riots.[42] And huge expenditures on public-goods provision, including social-welfare programs and education (Shue and Wong 2007), have helped the central government maintain stability and political support (Dickson 2014; Lü 2014). Expenditures for coercive institutions such as the military and domestic police also increased rapidly. The government has been able to hire large numbers of internet police to strengthen its censorship (King, Pan, and Roberts 2013). Increased government revenue also provides local governments with the fiscal resources to buy off troublemakers to sustain the regime (X. Chen 2013; Lee and Zhang 2013).

In fact, taxation is an important institution for all states, and the infrastructural state-power mechanisms are regime neutral. Both democratic and authoritarian regimes are easier to sustain when they have high taxation capacity. But the process of improving taxation capacity can be dangerous to different regimes, just as the process of modernization is dangerous for traditional rulers, as Huntington (1968) warned. Morrison claims, "While higher levels of taxation may indeed lead to representation by destabilizing authoritarian regimes . . . it can also lead away from representation by destabilizing democracies" (2014, 3).

Two Taxation Dilemmas

To study the aspects of the taxation system that bolster resilience, we need to examine two specific taxation dilemmas for authoritarian regimes: the growth dilemma and the representation dilemma. Only when an authoritarian regime can successfully resolve or alleviate these dilemmas will it achieve resilience. Bruce Dickson identifies measures that generate short-term benefits for the CCP's survival but can create challenges in the long run: "Rising living standards may produce a desire for more accountability from the Party and government. Relaxing controls over society to encourage economic growth and reduce the costs of repression may create demands for even greater openness" (2016, 3). A similar dynamic applies to taxation in that measures that resolve the representation and growth dilemmas can have negative consequences in the long term.

Morrison finds that "increased taxation destabilizes both democracies and dictatorships, and that government spending stabilizes them" (2014, 9). While government spending can have stabilizing effects, increasing taxes to increase spending can have destabilizing effects. Overtaxation can lead to economic stagnation or even crisis, which I call the "growth dilemma." In the "representation dilemma," increasing infrastructural power typically weakens despotic power, foments resistance, and may lead to democratization.

The Growth Dilemma

Economic growth is crucial for an authoritarian government's performance legitimacy (Zhao 2001), whereas democracies enjoy procedural legitimacy, and economic crisis could be the major cause of authoritarian breakdown (Pepinsky 2009). Thus, an authoritarian government's taxation system cannot be predatory (Acemoglu, Johnson, and Robinson 2002; Levi 1988; North 1981, 1990; Olson 1993). It should be able to meet the need for revenue in the short term without harming economic growth in the long run or causing tax riots and revolution.[43] While democracies also face this challenge, in the absence of checks on tax legislation and a reliance on performance legitimacy instead of procedural legitimacy, authoritarian rulers have more difficulty facing it. Indeed, most Chinese dynasties in history failed to address the growth dilemma in their taxation policy and therefore experienced a period of expanded government and improved, but predatory, extractive capacity, which led to economic stagnation and financial crisis, thus triggering rebellion and dynasty breakdown.[44]

The growth dilemma is related mainly to the cooperation problem. To elicit mass cooperation for investing capital and labor in productive activities, rulers must provide a credible commitment that the government will not prey on investors and will protect private property rights. Because capitalists are the owners of capital, their cooperation is of crucial importance in a developing country that lacks capital and entrepreneurship. In turn, the growth dilemma also complicates the agent-discipline challenge: one reason the central government must enact agent discipline is to prevent predatory behavior by local agents and to promote regulatory or developmental behavior.

The Representation Dilemma

The representation dilemma poses as serious a challenge as the growth dilemma to authoritarian rulers' tax policy. A number of scholars provide historical institutional explanations of the representation dilemma, such as Joseph Schumpeter (1991). He argued nearly a century ago that the transition from a feudal-domain state to a tax state may lead to the emergence of a modern democratic state. Charles Tilly (1990) and Michael Mann (1993) both find that when Western European countries made this transition, the state penetrated society to extract more fiscal and human resources, but society also penetrated the state because eliciting cooperation of the social actors required opening the state to social demands. Like Scott Gehlbach, I describe this as representation through taxation, which Gehlbach defines as "bargaining between politicians and organized sectors over the provision of collective goods" (2008, 61). Therefore, the state's infrastructural power will increase as despotic power decreases. The logic of representation through taxation reflects the mutual transformation of state and society proposed by Joel Migdal: "In the midst of such struggles [for social control] and accommodations, the boundary between the state and other parts of society may continually shift, as powerful social forces in particular arenas appropriate parts of the state or as the components of the state co-opt influential social figures" (2001, 128; see also Migdal 1994).

There are also rational choice institutional explanations of the representation dilemma. For example, Margaret Levi provides the microfoundation for the coevolution of infrastructural power and despotic power. She argues that in addition to coercion, governments elicit citizens' "quasi-voluntary compliance" typically by democratic reform (Levi 1988, 52).[45] In a similar line of thought, Morrison denies the existence of the representation dilemma, saying that high taxation is always destabilizing, and since

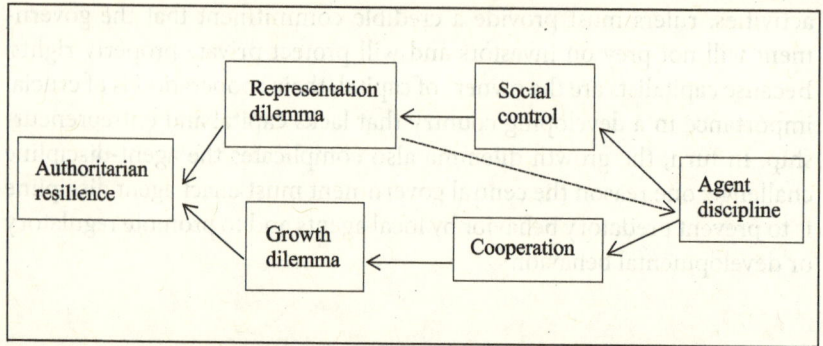

Figure 1.2. Relationships among governance problems and dilemmas.

it can destabilize democracies as easily as authoritarian regimes, it does not inherently make representation more likely (2014, 3, 15–16).

The representation dilemma is related mainly to the social-control problem: achieving taxpayers' compliance without inciting them to demand political power, which would weaken the authoritarian regime.[46] It is also related to the agent-discipline challenge, as Levi's quasi-voluntary compliance theory suggests: taxpayers will not comply with taxes unless they are confident that rulers will keep their bargains and that other constituents will keep theirs (1988, 53). Both of these require a coherent bureaucracy that delivers public goods effectively and prevents tax favoritism by not treating different taxpayers in different ways. I add these two dilemmas into the analysis and illustrate their relationship to the three governance problems in figure 1.2.

Whether authoritarian rulers are able resolve these two dilemmas reveals their capacity to tackle the three governance problems and is crucial for authoritarian resilience. I argue that within the context of a partial tax-state transition in China, the CCP has resolved, or at least partially alleviated, these dilemmas through a pressure-based fiscal federalism, an under-institutionalized taxation system, and a half-tax state that relies heavily on nontax revenue, indirect taxes, and SOEs.[47] However, these three tax institutions have generated some negative consequences (e.g., high inequality, huge local government debt, and clientelism) that threaten sustainable economic development and therefore authoritarian resilience.

Three Taxation Mechanisms

Both David Art (2012) and Thomas Pepinsky (2014) suggest that theorists should fully address causal mechanisms between institutions and authoritarian resilience.[48] The institution of taxation includes both the formal institutional arrangements and the practice of tax administration, which has both formal and informal dimensions.[49] Important dimensions of institutions of taxation include whether the state imposing them is a domain state or a tax state (Schumpeter 1991), its degree of decentralization, the level of rule of law of tax legislation and administration, the overall tax burden, and the degree of progressiveness. Most studies of taxation systems use taxation as the dependent variable to be explained, such as focusing on the legislation of tax categories (Ardanaz and Scartascini 2013; Steinmo 1993) and intergovernmental fiscal relationship. Scholars have also described the important role nontax revenue plays in developing and transitional countries (Turley 2006), including China (Wong 2009). However, little effort has been made to consider the institution of taxation as a cause of social and political change, as Schumpeter argued nearly a century ago. Moreover, few scholars have addressed tax administration, or the on-the-ground practice of taxation,[50] especially as an independent variable for authoritarian resilience.[51] This book uses Evan Lieberman's definition of tax administration, "the registration of taxpayers, calculation of liabilities, and actual collection of taxes" (2003, 50–52), while focusing on potential leakages and the informal practices that lead to these leakages.[52]

Intergovernmental fiscal relations, tax administration, and types of tax state have significant impact on regime stability and authoritarian resilience, especially in relation to the growth and representation dilemmas. I argue that the taxation system has three important mechanisms to resolve or alleviate the taxation dilemmas. However, these mechanisms may work well only in the early stage of industrialization; as China becomes a middle-income economy, these mechanisms will not work as well and further reforms are needed.

De Facto Fiscal Federalism under a Pressure-Based System

The first mechanism, de facto fiscal federalism, refers to how regional taxation competition constrains local governments' predatory behavior (agent-discipline problem) and causes local governments to co-opt private entrepreneurs into the local legislature to elicit cooperation and promote economic growth. A well-disciplined Weberian bureaucracy is crucial for economic growth (Evans and Rouch 1999). Yuen Yuen Ang (2016) finds the current literature trapped in a chicken-and-egg problem: developmental state theory uses the existence of Weberian bureaucracy as the independent variable to explain economic growth, and modernization theory uses level of economic development to explain the existence of Weberian bureaucracy. Historical institutionalism argues that the acquisition of Weberian bureaucracy is exogenous—that is, a function of unique historical experiences such as colonialism.

I argue instead that de facto fiscal federalism provides incentives for solving the agent-discipline problem (and building a modern bureaucracy) under certain conditions and therefore solves the cooperation problem. Agent discipline is important not only because it provides a credible commitment but also because a well-disciplined Weberian bureaucracy is a precondition for both regulatory state and collaborative government-business relationships.[53] When the growth dilemma is resolved or alleviated, the regime can achieve performance legitimacy. Economic growth also makes revenue increases possible without leading to tax resistance and contributes to the infrastructural power mechanism by coercing rivals and making revenue extraction possible.

Scholars have provided various theories to explain market transition and economic growth in China. Some scholars focus on local government officials' incentives and development strategies. Puzzled by the decision of some local government officials not to block economic reform, Jean Oi (1992) argues that fiscal decentralization, specifically the FCS in the 1980s, empowered local cadres with a residual claim of economic growth. This in turn drove them to spearhead economic reform in the 1980s, leading to rural industrialization and the emergence of collectively owned township and village enterprises (TVEs). She terms this "local state corporatism." From a bottom-up perspective that focuses on the daily interactions among grassroots actors, Kellee Tsai finds that "adaptive informal institutions" reduced the risk of investment for the citizens (2006, 118; 2007), producing a win-win solution for both grassroots government officials and citizens. Despite their value, neither perspective examines the agent-discipline problem, and the top-down perspective does not examine the cooperation problem. Yet failure to address the agent-discipline problem makes economic growth almost impossible, which leaves the state unable to provide a credible commitment to solve the cooperation problem.

Other literature explains market transition and economic growth in China by directly applying market-preserving federalism theory to the agent-discipline problem. Recognizing that the government must constrain its power to resolve the credible-commitment problem, adherents argue that institutionalized decentralization in China is a substitute for constitutional government, which provides a credible commitment to protecting private property rights by constraining the power of both the central and local governments (Montinola, Qian, and Weingast 1995). However, both empirical and theoretical objections have been raised (Cai and Treisman 2006). For example, as Margaret Levi (1988) and Mancur Olson (1993) theorized, revenue-maximized governments could be either developmental or predatory. Such states may promote economic growth only under certain conditions, through either structural or institutional constraints. In other words, fiscal decentralization could lead to either market preservation or market thwarting (K. Tsai 2002).[54]

And yet other literature describes local government officials as sources of both fiscal decentralization and a centralized political institution. Recognizing the importance of fiscal decentralization, Susan Whiting (2001) finds that political centralization, especially the CCP's evaluating cadres by their economic performance, plays a crucial role in promoting regional economic growth and is critical to China's many decades of rapid economic growth. Li'an Zhou's "Tournament for Promotion" likewise emphasizes the importance of the cadre evaluation and promotion system's role in motivating and monitoring local officials to promote economic growth and achieve a tax-revenue increase.[55] As Hongbin Li and Li'an Zhou point out, the system constrains local governments' predatory behavior and motivates them to spend resources on economic growth (2005; see also C. Xu 2010).

Among the explanations for how fiscal decentralization works to promote economic growth, few address the conditions that support regional competition and discipline of local government (except Cai and Treisman 2005; Yuhua Wang 2015; Whiting 2001). Regional economic and tax competition was limited until the mid-1990s because of low asset mobility under a limited market economy.[56] However, as this changes, fiscal decentralization could lead to a predatory local government,[57] regional protection, and market fragmentation rather than regional economic competition and development (e.g., Lou 2008; Wedeman 2003; Steinfeld 1998). Market transition and economic growth in China reflect the evolution of asset mobility; both natural and institutional factors shape its evolution in market transition. Higher asset mobility leads to a higher degree of bureaucratization. Fiscal federalism partially resolves the agent-discipline problem at the local level. As the Tiebout (1956) model suggests, when there is asset and labor mobility, local governments compete with each other to improve regional public-service provision and therefore attract more investment and (high-quality) labor. By resolving the agent-discipline problem and co-opting some private entrepreneurs into the local legislature and as honorable consultants to conferences (LPPCC), de facto fiscal federalism elicits cooperation from the capitalists. Chapters 3 and 4 examine the fiscal federalism mechanism and discuss its implications for the agent-discipline problem through bureaucratization, therefore contributing to resolving the cooperation problem and growth dilemma. They also discuss the limits of China's fiscal federalism. Fiscal federalism could empower capitalists and give them some representation power, therefore alleviating the representation dilemma, as demonstrated in chapter 5. However, as chapter 6 describes, capitalists have limited representation power because of the under-institutionalized taxation system.

The Half-Tax State

The second mechanism is that China is still a half-tax state, which means high dependence on nontax revenues (more than one-third of fiscal revenue), indirect taxes (about two-thirds of tax revenue), and SOEs for state revenue. This structure can reduce both citizens' perception of their tax burden and costs of tax collection while increasing government autonomy, which relieves the social-control problem.

Many scholars have studied the various types of tax state (the composition of a state's tax revenues) and their implications for regime stability. Morrison (2014) argues that taxation destabilizes regimes and spending stabilizes regimes, so nontax revenue is the best option for rulers to use to maintain power because it reduces taxation and increases spending. He identifies two mechanisms by which nontax revenue could stabilize a regime: a "substitution" effect and a "wealth" effect. Substitution refers to reducing individual tax burdens by replacing them with nontax revenue.

The wealth effect refers to the increased government spending that theoretically follows increased revenue (Morrison 2014, 33). Many scholars have addressed the rentier state in the last decade, but conclusions about its political consequences have been elusive. Some essentially concur with Morrison that windfall revenue helps authoritarian rulers maintain power via public-service provision (Morrison 2009).

Scholars who focus on institutionalization find that the rentier state has a resource curse. That is, countries with abundant natural resources or who receive significant foreign aid cannot extract revenue from their domestic populations. Rentier states fail to build viable institutions that are crucial for fostering state capacity, democratic regimes, and long-term economic growth. Some suffer civil conflicts or even civil wars. Scholars provide several explanations for the resource curse attached to the rentier state. James Robinson, Ragnar Torvik, and Thierry Verdier (2014) argue that there are four reasons that resources' impact on economic and political consequences depend on politicians' incentives to build accountability and competence: (1) Politicians tend to overextract natural resources relative to the efficient extraction path because they discount the future too much, and (2) resource booms improve the efficiency of the extraction path. However, (3) by raising the value of being in power and by providing politicians with more resources to influence the outcome of elections, resource booms increase resource misallocation in the rest of the economy. (4) The overall impact of resource booms on the economy depends critically on institutions, which determine the extent to which political incentives map into policy outcomes. I argue that these insights also apply to other nontax sources of revenue. A state will not invest in institutional building that may strengthen state capacities and build accountability institutions if it relies too heavily on any nontax source of revenue. Therefore, such reliance undermines rather than promotes resilience.

Kenneth Greene finds that access to public resources is also crucial for authoritarian durability: "Dominant parties win consistently because they generate resource advantages from the public budget that fundamentally skew the partisan playing field in their favor. To be sure, dominant parties employ earmarks and pork barrel projects like advantage-seeking politicians in all competitive systems" (2007, 811). John Waterbury (1997) found a similar phenomenon in the Middle East: the incumbents benefited from a large sector of SOEs.

China's transition from communist state to tax state is still under way.

In the midst of this transition, until recently, the Chinese state (especially the central government) relied heavily on SOEs for tax revenue, most of which was from indirect taxes; local governments relied heavily on non-tax revenue, especially land-transfer fees, which have composed one-third to one-half of local governments' fiscal revenue in the last decade. Individual income tax contributes 6 percent of total tax revenue. Thus, China is a half-tax state (Ma 2011). Indirect taxes, taxes paid by SOEs, and various types of nontax revenues improve the state's extractive capacity without demanding citizens' direct compliance. By reducing the state's direct engagement with citizens, the half-tax state improves state autonomy and reduces citizens' tax consciousness (Gilley 2017). Thus, it partially resolves the social-control (tax-compliance) problem and alleviates the representation dilemma.

As an adversary tax state,[58] the half-tax state also has some negative effects on authoritarian resilience. SOEs are inefficient (Slemrod and Yitzhaki 2002) and even corrupt. Indirect taxes are regressive rather than progressive and therefore increase inequality, which undermines the Chinese government's redistributive capacity (Gao 2010; Benjamin et al. 2008). China has therefore become a highly unequal society with a 0.474 official Gini coefficient in 2012.[59] A high level of inequality harms regime resilience because it generates social discontent, impairs the regime's moral legitimacy, and may block long-term economic growth.[60] Thus, it can exacerbate the growth dilemma (C. Zhang 2017a; see also Gilley 2017).

Future reforms may change the half-tax state: the minister of finance's recent announcement that China will seek to increase direct taxes as a share of government revenue and decrease local government's reliance on land-transfer fees (by implementing a real estate tax) suggests such a shift (Ministry of Finance of the People's Republic of China 2013), but the tax reforms in the last decade have increased the national tax revenue share of indirect taxes.

The Under-institutionalized Taxation System

As mentioned earlier, institutionalization moderates the impact of sources of revenue on governance and authoritarian resilience. In other words, modes of collection matter in terms of a taxation system's effect on resilience. The first paragraph of an article by Richard Bird identifies the importance of how the state collects taxes:

> Money alone is not enough; but it is necessary for any state to function, and the most reliable way to get it is with an effective tax administration. How countries tax affects the allocation and distribution of resources and the rate of economic growth. In addition, however, the tax system constitutes one of the major interfaces between citizens and state in any country so how taxes are administered may affect not only the political future of the government of the day but also, more fundamentally, public trust in government. Tax administration may thus play a critical role not only in shaping economic development but in developing an effective state. (2015, 23)

Tax administration is under-institutionalized in China.[61] This addresses the growth dilemma by reducing the effective tax, as under-institutionalization combined with very high tax rates leads to rampant tax cheating and evasion. Cheating makes taxpayers vulnerable to the strong authoritarian state,[62] which does not hesitate to use tax investigation as an effective legal-repression tool.[63] Therefore, major taxpayers, especially private entrepreneurs, pursue patron-client relationships with the state, seeking to be co-opted by the party-state for protection rather than challenging it.

The 1994 Tax-Sharing Reform improved the effectiveness and efficiency of tax administration significantly, and several rounds of taxation reforms since have achieved some degree of success in institutionalizing the taxation system, improving both its autonomy and capacity.[64] However, it still suffers from several weaknesses, including the domination of bureaucratic legislation, unreasonably high nominal tax rates, tax officers' high level of discretionary power, and a tax-target system that violates rule of law. China's tax-legislating process is dominated by the bureaucracy. The State Council and its ministries (especially the Ministry of Finance and the State Administration of Taxation), rather than a legislature, draft tax laws. The central authority set unreasonably high nominal tax rates: VAT is 17 percent, and the corporation income tax rate is 33 percent.[65] Indeed, adhering to high tax rates would make it difficult for private entrepreneurs, most of whom are in low-profit-margin industries, to make any profit at all. At the same time, tax officers have a high degree of discretionary power. A third driver of under-institutionalization is that higher levels of government set tax targets for lower-level governments. Like other components of local government, the tax-administration system is thus what Jingben Rong et al. (1998) have deemed a "pressure-based system"

(压力型体制).⁶⁶ As a result, tax officers collect taxes based on targets set by supervisors rather than taxpayers' tax liabilities (依法征税，应收尽收). The law enforcer becomes a lawbreaker.

However, private enterprises, as well as other taxpayers, have many opportunities to influence the assessment of tax liabilities and collection of taxes and therefore to significantly reduce the real tax rate. Tax evasion is rampant. Companies build patron-client connections with tax officers and/or party/government officials to enable this evasion as well as to realize other business benefits. This is a situation Alisha Holland defines as forbearance, "intentional and revocable government leniency toward violations of the law" (2017, 13). Tax evasion drives these political connections because the authoritarian state severely punishes evasion. The threat of an audit thus effectively negates any bargaining power private entrepreneurs have with the party-state for any politically sensitive issues, which addresses the representation dilemma. Thus, it is easy for the government to repress entrepreneurs, whose economic resources might otherwise empower them to demand political reform, which addresses the social-control problem. This is a mechanism of co-optation via deterrence. The patron-client connections that entrepreneurs build to protect themselves effectively reduce predation by local governments but at the same time worsen the agent-discipline problem.

In summary, three taxation mechanisms affect authoritarian resilience through two taxation dilemmas. Figure 1.3 illustrates the relationship between the three mechanisms and the two taxation dilemmas that the authoritarian state faces. Between the dilemmas and the mechanisms, a solid line indicates a positive effect in resolving the dilemma; the dashed line indicates a negative effect. It is clear that there are self-contradictions within it; therefore, the current institution of taxation is not a sustainable solution for the dilemmas.

Conclusion

Many institutions help dictators maintain power. However, dictators incur costs in accepting their help. Taxation (broadly defined) provides needed government revenue, but its tendency to increase representation and its complicated relationship with growth can also threaten authoritarian resilience. The design of a taxation system can either heighten or impair these mechanisms by solving, alleviating, or exacerbating the two taxa-

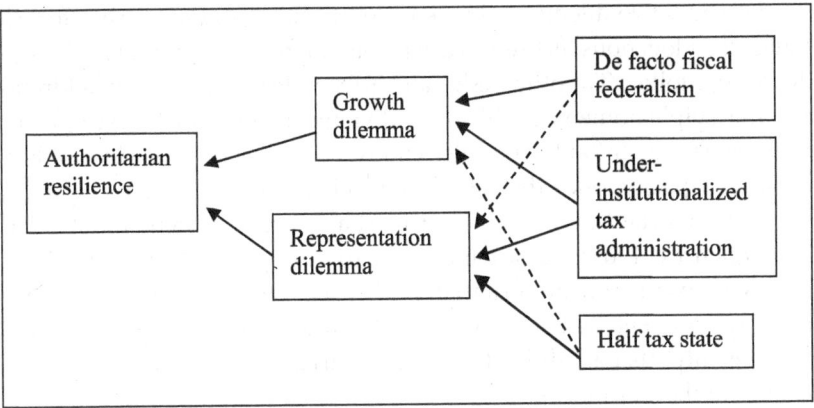

Figure 1.3. Dilemmas and mechanisms for how taxation matters for authoritarian resilience. Solid arrows refer to alleviating the dilemma, and dashed arrows refer to worsening the dilemma.

tion dilemmas, which in turn are related to the three governance problems. Addressing the inherent questions in these insights, I build a fiscal sociological theory of authoritarian resilience based on the China case in this chapter and elaborate the theory in subsequent chapters. Therefore, this book contributes to an emerging literature on taxation politics/fiscal sociology. Considering the institution of taxation as the cause rather than consequence of social changes, I reveal its key role.

The China case suggests that taxation's infrastructural power mechanisms, including the spending effects that Morrison (2014) emphasizes, contribute to authoritarian resilience. However, my examination of the growth and representation dilemmas that the authoritarian rulers face reveals that the CCP alleviates two dilemmas by fiscal federalism, a half-tax-state,[67] and an under-institutionalized taxation system. By weakening taxpayers' bargaining power while eliciting their compliance and cooperation, under-institutionalism reduces taxpayers' tax burden and bolsters the state's autonomy. In this way the authoritarian regime improves its infrastructural power without weakening its despotic power.[68] However, a half-tax state generates high inequality and is inefficient, and it consequently blocks sustainable economic growth. The negative effects of the current taxation system on sustainable economic growth are mounting, but the system has effectively protected the CCP's power thus far.

In addition to discussing the role of the taxation system in addressing the autocrat's two dilemmas, I seek to contribute to the scholarly effort to build an endogenous institutional explanation for authoritarian resilience. To do so, I follow Timothy Besley and Torsten Persson (2014) in addressing the epiphenomena problem by dividing institutional development into two stages. Initially, the ruler chooses whether to invest in building taxation capacity; once the ruler has decided to invest, taxation systems become important because of their inertia, generating some unintended consequences. I use quasi-parameters to endogenize the institutional effects of taxation on authoritarian resilience.[69] Once established, the taxation system generates some structural consequences (e.g., contributing to inequality) that are difficult for authoritarian rulers to manipulate and change in the short term.

By proposing that taxation plays a key role in authoritarian resilience, I challenge some conventional institutional explanations of authoritarian resilience. Specifically, I demonstrate that the local legislature (LPC) and its direct elections play a minimal and epiphenomenal role.[70] Related to this, the book reexamines capitalists' role in sustaining authoritarianism or promoting democratization by placing capitalists within the framework of double transitions as well as the institutional framework of democratic-looking institutions and taxation systems.

Governing and Ruling makes contributions to general theories of authoritarian resilience and fiscal sociology. It also contributes to our understanding of some topics of contemporary Chinese politics: government-business relationships, political economy of development, and the LPC.

CHAPTER 2

Tax-State Transition

> In a State, pecuniary gain is not to be considered prosperity, but its prosperity will be found in righteousness [国不以利为利, 以义为利也].
> —Confucius, *The Great Learning* (大学)[1]

> The reform we are now carrying out is very daring. But if we do not carry it out, it will be hard for us to make progress. Reform is China's second revolution. It is something very important that we have to undertake even though it involves risks.
> —Deng Xiaoping, *Selected Works of Deng*

> You know, also, as well as I do, what is the great aim of all the governments of the earth: obedience and money. The object is, as the saying goes, to pluck the hen without making it cry out; but it is the proprietors who cry out, and the government has always preferred to attack them indirectly, because then they do not perceive the harm until after the matter has become law.
> —Anne-Robert-Jacques Turgot, *Reflections on the Formation and the Distribution of Riches*[2]

In early April 2011, the State Council proposed an amendment to the Individual Income Tax (IIT) Law. The draft suggested increasing the minimum threshold for taxable income from 2,000 yuan to 3,000 yuan per month and reducing the number of income tax brackets from nine to seven. Instead of directly approving or rejecting the State Council's amendment, the NPC Standing Committee publicized the draft and asked for feedback online. Individuals and social organizations submitted more than one hundred thousand suggestions in the first three days, and by the time the website had been open for comment, the committee had received more than two hundred thousand suggestions, which exceeded the number of suggestions the NPC had received for all other twenty laws since 2009.[3] Additional suggestions continued to flood the NPC website. The *China Daily* reported:

> A survey of 282,000 Internet users showed more than 90 percent supported lifting the threshold to 4,000 yuan or even 5,000 yuan, as they believe the tax burden for low- and middle-income earners is heavy.... China's total tax revenue surged 22.6 percent in 2010 and soared 32.4 percent in the first quarter of 2011, two or three times the gross domestic product growth. The amendment is estimated to cut the country's IIT revenue by about 120 billion yuan, said Finance Minister Xie Xuren. (*China Daily Online* 2011)

Six years earlier, in September 2005, the NPC Standing Committee held a public hearing on the emendation of the old IIT Law in the Great Hall of the People. It was the first public hearing on legislation in NPC history. The law was amended, and the minimum threshold of IIT, which had been set in 1980, was increased from 800 to 1,600 yuan per month. Thus, IIT was once more restricted to a tiny minority of earners.

In 2018, the NPC Standing Committee again asked for public comments and suggestions for the seventh-round adjustment of the IIT Law, made a more comprehensive revision in September, and immediately implemented the amendment in October. The minimum threshold of IIT was increased to 5,000 yuan per month, and other income besides salary would be included, while some deductions, such as children's education, were allowed. But other expected revisions, such as tax based on annual family income, were not made because, as acknowledged by Lou Jiwei, a comprehensive IIT includes many deductions, which require "complete information on individual incomes and properties and revisions of relevant laws [beyond the taxation bureau's capacity]" (*Caixin* 2016). In 2019, individual income tax was collected based on an individual's annual income, many tax exemptions (such as children's education, provision for the aged, apartment rent,[4] and mortgage interest) were introduced, and taxpayers were also required to apply for a tax refund in 2020.

The party describes the process of soliciting comments, which it terms "open-door legislation" (Y. Jiang 2012), as an opportunity for citizens' participation in an orderly fashion (有序政治参与, terminology created by the CCP). Taxation also attracted intensive attention from NPC deputies and CPPCC members. According to an SAT leader, SAT headquarters had submitted three NPC bills (议案) for comment and received 244 suggestions (建议) and 102 proposals (提案) in response. Citizens' active engagement with democratic and open-door legislation and NPC deputies' advocacy suggest their concern for people's interests and willingness to participate in politics. Given that taxation is directly related to citizens' income, it is not surprising that the committee's call for comments would spur more participation than other issues. However, this particular event was an outlier because it is not the NPC and its Standing Committee that determine most taxation issues but the Ministry of Finance and/or SAT headquarters, and they do so without public comment (discussed in detail later). The solicitation of public comment for a tax law reflects the fact that although China's tax-state transition, like its market transition, is still under way, it has significant impact on how the CCP governs and rules the country.

Since 1978, a transition from state socialism, characterized by a planned economy and state ownership, to what Barry Naughton and Kellee Tsai (2015) call state capitalism has generated rapid economic growth and the emergence of a large number of private enterprises and capitalists in China. The market transition is associated with the tax-state transition, a neglected topic in studying market transition. The dual transitions led to and were associated with rapid economic growth and generated "social and economic change—urbanization, increase in literacy and education, industrialization, mass media expansion—extended political consciousness, multiple political demands, [and] broaden[ed] political participation." Therefore, the transitions may weaken or destroy the old authority and lead to political instability (Huntington 1968, 5). Dual transitions can also change the distribution of power in a country, giving capitalists, among others, more resources and independence and weakening the state's social control in many ways (Walder 1996); it even provides opportunities for regime change. As Douglass North, John Wallis, and Barry R. Weingast argue, "The rise of a new source of wealth from commerce and trade caused a series of political problems, including new sources of economic and political power" (2009, 106). They further argue that this may lead to collapse of the natural state (authoritarian rule). Xianglin Xu (2020) conceptually distinguishes transition crisis from governance crisis and proposes that to deal with transition crisis and stop it from becoming governance crisis, the CCP needs to reform its state governance system. Joseph Schumpeter argues that "the full fruitfulness of this [fiscal sociology] approach is seen particularly at those turning points" (1991, 101) and emphasizes the tax-state transition's political significance by arguing that it drove the rise of democracy in Europe. China is experiencing tax-state and market transition in a very short time period. These dual transitions change the three governance problems substantially,[5] which in turn change the CCP's governing and ruling strategies.

The next section describes market transition and a brief history of the tax-state transition. Following are discussions of the evolution of intergovernmental fiscal relationships and de facto fiscal federalism, as well as the evolution of revenue composition (a narrowly defined tax-state transition) at both the national and regional levels. Also included is an in-depth discussion of three elements of the domain or rentier state—SOE revenue, land revenue, and indirect tax. A discussion of the third dimension of the half-tax state, the under-institutionalized taxation administration, is followed by a summary and discussion of a half-tax state's implication for the three governance problems.

Dual Transitions

Table 2.1 defines the three stages of China's dual transitions, which are discussed in detail here.[6]

Market transition began in China in the late 1970s. In the 1950s, the newly established party-state had faced a hostile international environment as a late developer in the immediate aftermath of World War II and a four-year-long civil war. Like some other late developers, the CCP used catch-up industrialization strategies through the state's direct mobiliza-

Table 2.1. Stages of market and tax-state transitions in the PRC

	Economic system	Type of tax state
Before 1980	Underdeveloped planned economy (M-form economy)	Communist state: unitary remittance and unitary expenditure
1980–1993	Partially liberalized market, rapid development of TVEs	Feudal state: FCS, tax farming, and rampant extra-budgetary fund
1994–present	Toward a socialist market economy (or state capitalism)	Half-tax state: TSR, high reliance on nontax revenue and indirect taxes; efforts to monitor extra-budgetary fund; SAT and LTB merged in 2018

tion of capital and other resources to SOEs,[7] which in turn built up the planned economy and communist political system (Gerschenkron 1962; Kornai 1992).[8] China thus achieved significant progress in industrialization before the late 1970s. However, the CCP began to transit to a market economy thereafter, as further improving industrial innovation and people's living standards had proven impossible under a planned economy; the political chaos of the Cultural Revolution was also a factor driving new leaders after Mao to reform the economic and political system (Naughton 1995, 2007; Shirk 1993). Such a market transition is a multidimensional phenomenon, with economic reform depending on vast, interdependent changes. They involve institutional changes, including decollectivization, fiscal decentralization, tax reform, enterprise reform, and legal and regulatory reform. Political institutions have a significantly different role in market economies, and even informal norms and social networks change (Nee and Matthews 1996). All of these effects have been felt in China, although the country has not reached and may never reach a liberal market capitalism or coordinated market capitalism economy. However, non-state-owned industry has accounted for 55–65 percent of the economy's share of GDP since 2000. In 2005, the most recent year for which statistics have been reported, it employed 84.1 percent of China's labor force and contributed more than half the national tax revenue.[9] Naughton and Tsai describe this system as "a distinctive form of 'state capitalism' in which state-owned enterprises remain central to its evolving model of political economy," noting that "the state retains direct control of strategic sectors, engages in industrial policy, and holds a dominant position in the banking sector and equity markets" (2015, 2–3).[10]

About four decades of rapid economic growth have followed China's transition. Private entrepreneurs have become an important "new social strata" (新阶层), if not a capitalist class.[11] As Samuel Huntington (1968) demonstrates, the social-economic changes raise many new challenges to the old authority. While economic growth solves some problems for the CCP, the rise of this "new social strata" intensifies its challenges. First, the CCP has become highly dependent on resource-rich capitalists to pay taxes, make efficient investment, hire, and innovate. This mutual dependence explains why Xi Jinping made the high-profile speech on November 1, 2018, trying to send a signal of credible commitment to elicit capitalists' cooperation.[12] Second, market transition may weaken the power of the party and government officials, who had control over resources under the planned economy (as resource distributors) and may therefore resist the party's plan for market transition. Without discipline by the CCP, local governments could degenerate into a predatory autocracy (Pei 2006). The third challenge stems from the first and intensifies the second. To encourage investment, the CCP must credibly commit to protect private property rights, which requires disciplining local agents. A fourth challenge arises because of the management of the first three: as citizens acquire more autonomy from the state and society becomes more and more pluralized, the problem of social control intensifies. The fifth challenge relates to increased inequality, which harms sustainable economic development by generating a middle-income trap and social instability.

Meeting these challenges requires reforming many old institutions and establishing new ones to achieve balance between political institutionalization and social mobilization, as Huntington proposed. The CCP has managed some challenges better than others. Table 2.2 summarizes the relationship of a planned economy, state capitalism, and a liberal market economy to each of the three governance challenges. By putting the China case under these three general governance problems, we have some analytical leverage of comparative studies of authoritarianism, even a comparison with democratic regimes because they also face similar governance problems, though they may deal with them in different ways.

The tax-state transition is also under way simultaneously with the market transition.[13] Under the communist (tax) state there was essentially no

Table 2.2. Governance problems under three political economic systems

	Agent discipline	Social control	Cooperation
Planned economy	Soft budgetary constraint, low incentive	Patron-clientelism* and repression	Socialist developmental state;† forced/mobilized "cooperation," low incentive
State capitalism	Soft budgetary constraint, predatory or developmental local state	Patron-clientelism and selective repression	Elicit cooperation, state also directly invests
Liberal market economy	Modern bureaucracy; rule of law, electoral representation under democracy	Rule of law	Regulatory state, self-motivated cooperation

* See Walder 1986 on urban working units; and Oi 1989 on rural areas.
† White and Gray 1988.

taxation for the almost nonexistent private sector.[14] Under state capitalism, however, the government relies on taxing its citizens for a major share of its expenditures. Thus, it requires the cooperation of nonstate actors to secure the revenue it needs to run and perform its functions. After decades of economic reform, the Chinese government continues to rely heavily on indirect taxes,[15] SOEs, and nontax revenue for fiscal income, which makes it a half-tax state. This reduces both the administrative and political costs that a full-tax state requires. Associated with the tax-structure change, the tax-state transition has required changes to tax administration. Under the communist (tax) state, no professional tax administration was needed, and the Taxation Bureau, which was staffed by nonprofessionals, was even abolished during the Cultural Revolution. But a tax state requires professional and highly institutionalized tax administration. Table 2.3 illustrates two dimensions of tax-state transition.

Contemporary China is essentially an adversarial tax state (type IV)—a half-tax state with an under-institutionalized administration, evolving from a communist state with a low institutionalized tax administration

Table 2.3. Two dimensions of tax-state transition and implications for two taxation dilemmas

		Tax state		
		Full	Middle/half	Low
Institutionalized tax administration	High	I. Cooperative tax state: representation (economic development and democratization)*	II. Bureaucracy-led tax administration,† bargaining under de facto fiscal federalism	NA
	Low	III. Adversarial tax state: patron-clientelism and hidden bargaining (economic growth and authoritarian resilience)	IV. Adversarial tax state: patron-clientelism, hidden bargaining (economic growth and authoritarian resilience, but high inequality harms sustainable economic growth)	V. Feudal domain state, communist state, rentier state, or skeleton state (economic stagnation and regime collapse)

* See Besley and Persson 2014 for the development cluster.
† See Kiser and Schneider 1994.

since the late 1970s. This reflects a partial market transition—one reason that China is a half-tax state is that under state capitalism it is halfway to a market economy. It is an adversarial tax state in the sense that it is overall regressive: it has a heavy reliance on regressive indirect taxes and SOE taxes. It is hard to tax the richest people, who do not rely on income from salaries, which is well monitored by the Taxation Bureau. Local governments are like rentier local states because of their heavy reliance on land-related revenue.

Alongside tax structure and taxation administration, the third dimension is intergovernmental fiscal relationships, especially the central-local fiscal relationship, which has experienced decentralization and recentralization in the last four decades and achieved some institutionalization but still suffers many problems. The tax-state transition changed the nature of the three governance problems in that social control came to include achieving tax compliance. The government had to respond to tax riots that rural taxation had spurred in the 1990s and early 2000s. After agricultural taxes were abolished, land seizure took the place of rural taxation as a major source of social disorder in the last decade (Whiting 2011; Zhang and Heurlin 2014). Table 2.4 summarizes the distinctions between the governance problems taxation brings about under the three types of tax state.

Table 2.4. Governance problems under three types of tax state

	Agent discipline	Tax compliance and social control	Cooperation
Communist state (Soviet Union, China before 1978)	Ideological bureaucracy	Limited taxes, coercive taxation	State-planned economy, workers' low incentive
Half-tax state (contemporary China)	Decentralization, federalism under pressure-based system, improving but limited bureaucratization	Legal repression, patron-clientelism	Weak property rights, collusive relationship
Tax state: adversary (Brazil)	Limited bureaucratization	Legal repression, patron-clientelism	Low incentive, collusive relationship
Tax state: cooperative (US)	Bureaucracy and legislature control	Legal-rational domination: quasi-voluntary compliance	Self-motivated

Creating De Facto Fiscal Federalism: A Brief History of Tax Reform

To promote economic growth and build a socialist market economy, the CCP Central Committee has initiated a series of taxation reforms since 1978, which eventually led to a tax-state transition associated with market transition;[16] it also intensified the challenges the market transition presents to the CCP.[17] This section briefly reviews tax reform in China since 1978 with a focus on intergovernmental fiscal relationships, especially the central-local fiscal relationship.[18] Table 2.5 illustrates the three stages of the fiscal system in the PRC.

From the mid-1950s to 1978, the CCP treated taxation as an issue of political struggle between classes.[19] The fiscal system associated with the planned economy, known as "unitary remittance and unitary expenditure" (*Tongshou tongzhi* 统收统支), was also a highly centralized and redistribution-oriented system, leaving local governments little autonomy in tax collection and spending and therefore with incentive to promote economic growth. Since 1978, the Chinese government has gradually rebuilt the tax system, enacting two rounds of substantial reforms. China is experiencing a multidimensional tax-state transition. Both the formal

Table 2.5. Stages of the fiscal system in the PRC

Fiscal system	Time period	Characteristics
Unitary remittance and unitary expenditure (*tongshou tongzhi*)	Before 1980, but with several rounds of adjustments	Lower-level government submits all revenue income to the highest level, which in turn transfers fiscal resources back to lower level according to expenditures made by the highest level
Fiscal contracting (*fenzhao chifan*)	1980s–1993	Lower-level government can retain (part of) the revenue that exceeds the quota but is responsible for all its expenditures
Tax sharing (*fenshuizhi*)	1994–present	Central and local governments have different tax sources and shared taxes; fiscal transfers from central to local; two independent tax administrations (merged in June 2018)

taxation system and the informal practice of taxation have experienced significant but limited reform since the reform and opening up in 1978. The fiscal-contracting (*Caizheng baoganzhi* 财政包干制 or *Fenzao chifan* 分灶吃饭, eating from separate stoves) reform moved both the power of tax collection and expenditure obligations from the central government to local governments, aiming to motivate and empower them to develop regional economies. The local governments were required to sign fiscal contracts with higher-level governments to submit a given amount of tax revenue and keep (all or a large share of) the rest. These contracts recognized projected growth in each region and differentiated quotas based on these projections.[20]

Before 1984, tax reform focused on merging tax categories and simplifying tax collection while keeping the tax burden unchanged. The goal was to maintain tax increases throughout the reemergence of the market economy in rural areas and the new economic activities and sectors. Whereas the government had previously taken all profits from SOEs (or compensated for the loss) and allocated funds for production, SOEs now began to pay taxes instead.[21] There were nine types of taxes between 1972 and 1984: industrial-commercial tax (rates varied by industry), industrial-commercial income tax (for private and collective enterprises and those that were state-owned but not included in the economic plan), slaughtering tax, urban real estate tax, livestock trade tax, license tax, open fair-transaction tax, customs tax, and agricultural tax.

Tax provided the major income for local government at that time, but nontax income from corporations, including SOEs and collective enterprises, was also significant; in one municipality it amounted to 20 percent of the local government's budget from 1969 to 1983. Several new taxes were introduced in 1984 as part of the "tax-for-profit" reform (*ligaishui* 利改税): corporation income tax, product tax, VAT, business tax, SOE bonus tax, and SOE adjustment tax.[22] These taxes were designed to replace SOE profit remittances incrementally as part of the SOE reform, especially to separate SOEs from government. The share of corporation income that made up fiscal income decreased steadily thereafter.

While it drove rapid economic growth, fiscal decentralization also led to increased tax revenue in absolute terms. However, measured in relative terms, the state's taxation capacity weakened in that the tax revenue share of GDP and the central government's share of total tax revenue decreased. Shaoguang Wang and Angang Hu (1994) described this as a signal of a weakened state and central government's capacity, as well as a threat to regime stability, and called for centralization of fiscal power.[23] Fiscal decentralization worsened the agent-discipline problem. At the same time, however, it also substantially loosened both the central government's disciplinary capacity over its local agents and local government's decreased capacity to discipline its branches. The FCS led to greater fragmentation in the bureaucratic system. As Kenneth Lieberthal (1992) argues, local governments and government agencies gained access to funds outside the central budget and therefore gained some autonomy in terms of policy.[24] Government predation and corruption became rampant, leading to social instability (including students' movements in the late 1980s).

The 1994 Tax-Sharing Reform (TSR) was the most comprehensive reform the CCP Central Committee introduced as part of the economic reform of the last quarter of the twentieth century. TSR built the foundation of the current taxation system. The principle, according to the Ministry of Finance, was "to reform and improve the taxation system in line with the principles of unifying tax law, fairness of tax burden, simplification of the tax system, rational division of power and set an appropriate (fiscal) distribution between the central and local [governments], standardize the redistribution manner, and achieve fiscal revenue growth."[25] This section addresses two aspects of tax policy resulting from this reform: resetting tax categories so they were simpler and redefining (specifically, recentralizing) the fiscal relationship between the central and local governments. TSR also reorganized the institution of taxation and tax-collection methods. Changes to tax policies after 1994 include turnover-tax reform, corporation and IIT reform, and reform of resource taxes. As illustrated in figure 2.1, TSR effectively improved the Chinese government's taxation capacity and the central government's share of national tax revenue.

The 1994 tax system was revised several times in response to economic development. The major revisions included the "tax-for-fee" reform (*feigaishui* 费改税) in rural areas, unification of the corporate income tax rate for domestic and foreign companies, and VAT revision (in 2009) and "VAT for business tax" (*yinggaizeng* 营改增, fully implemented in 2016). However, TSR also has had negative consequences, chiefly that it provides insufficient revenue for local governments to meet their expenditure obligations even after receiving a fiscal transfer from the central government, called "unfunded mandates." The abolition of agricultural taxes in 2006, following severe rural tax riots and other forms of resistance (Bernstein and Lü 2003), worsened the problem for Central China. Local governments must rely heavily on nontax revenue. Since local government bud-

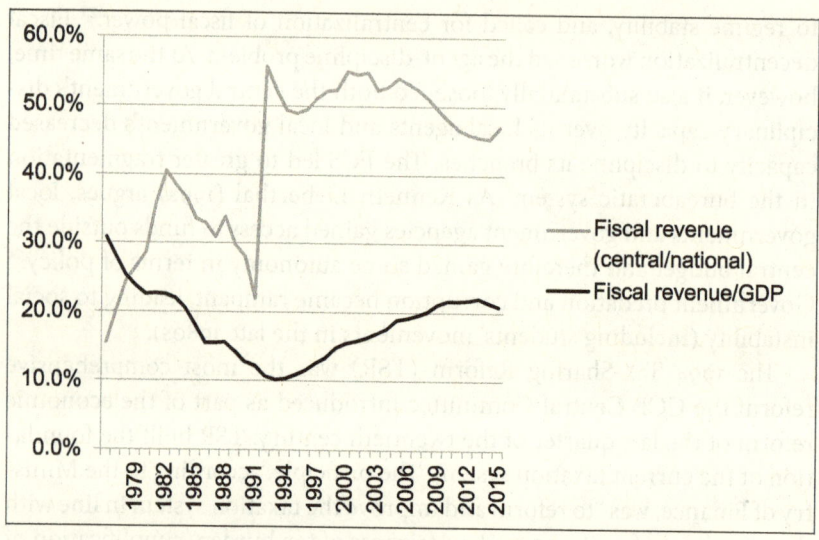

Figure 2.1. Changes in two ratios, 1978–2017. Source: Author's calculation based on Ministry of Finance of the People's Republic of China 2018.

gets do not list most nontax revenue, these are called extra-budgetary funds; consequently, local governments became half-tax local states. Some local governments charge high fees and fines that deter development of the private sector. Heavy reliance on extra-budgetary funds also worsens the agent-discipline problem because they are harder to monitor than budgetary funds.

The Half-Tax State

The tax reforms help build a socialist market economy and promote economic growth, as well as change China from a communist to a half-tax state. Compliance from private-sector businesses was minimal before the rapid nationalization of private enterprises in the 1950s. Thus, in 1950, private enterprises paid 56.6 percent of the total industrial and commerce tax (equals 2.6320 billion yuan),[26] while SOEs paid 31.2 percent (collective enterprises paid 0.7 percent, and public-private partnerships [PPP] paid 1.5 percent).[27] By 1959, however, private enterprises paid only 1.9 percent of total tax, SOEs paid 88.3 percent, and collective enterprises (no PPP remained) paid the other 9.7 percent. For most of the years between 1959 and 1981, with few exceptions, private enterprises paid about 1 percent of total tax, while SOEs paid more than 80 percent of total fiscal revenue (through taxes and profit remittance). During this period, tax revenue rose from 16.467 to 54.748 billion yuan (State Administration of Taxation 1993). Besides fiscal revenue, price scissors and state-owned rural credit cooperatives helped the government extract revenue and low-interest funds from rural areas.[28]

But the profit remittance from SOEs almost disappeared between 1984 and 2006, although they still paid a huge amount in taxes. Thus, the state now had to rely on tax revenue as its major fiscal revenue source.[29] Since the early 2000s, the Chinese state has collected more than 20 percent of GDP and 6 percent of government fund revenue as taxes. At the same time, the state's dependence on private enterprises for revenue has increased since 1978 from almost zero to about two-thirds of its tax revenue. As reported by the SAT, from 1982 to 1993, while national tax revenue rose from 62.317 to 397.052 billion yuan, the share SOEs paid decreased from 76.8 to 65.7 percent. Collective enterprises' share decreased from 21.4 to 17.5 percent, and private enterprises' share rose from 1.0 to 8.2 percent.[30] However, the changing categorization of enterprises after 1994 made it difficult to distinguish SOEs from private enterprises, and the SAT stopped reporting these numbers.[31] Yongjie Chen, a senior research fellow who had working experience in drafting private enterprise reports for the CCP Central Committee and the State Council, provided the estimates for 2014 shown in table 2.6. The state's tax dependence on private enterprises has continued to increase. A half-tax state forms after decades of market reform: the central government continues to rely heavily on SOEs for tax revenue, while local governments rely heavily on nontax revenue, especially land-transfer fees. Thus, both levels of government depend on indirect taxes, which reduce both the administrative and political costs that a full-tax state requires.

Figures 2.2 to 2.6 show the dependence of the Chinese government and County Warm River on SOEs, land-transfer fees, and other forms of indirect taxes for their annual revenue in 2014. Though more than 20 percent of GDP is taxed, China's transition from a communist to a tax state is still in its early stages.

State-Owned Enterprises and Government Revenue

Article 6 of the PRC constitution (2003) states:

Table 2.6. Share of national tax revenue in 2014, by enterprise type

Ownership	Tax revenue (billion yuan)	Percentage	Notes
National total	13,602.148	100.0	
SOE and state held	4,318.552	31.7	
Broadly defined private enterprises		68.3	Excludes SOEs and state-controlled joint-stock enterprises
Foreign-related enterprises	2,476.296	18.2	
Domestic private enterprises		52.3	Non-SOEs, excluding foreign-related enterprises
Narrowly defined private enterprises		~51.0	Non-SOEs, excluding collective enterprises and foreign-related enterprises
Individually owned private enterprises	1,952.973	14.3	Non-SOEs held by individuals (only this amount is reported officially)
Public enterprises		~34.0	SOEs and state-held enterprises, collective and collective enterprises
Nonpublic enterprises		~66.0	Excluding public enterprises

Source: Revenue amounts from SAT's *Tax Monthly Report* (Shuishou tongji kuaibao); percentage estimates from Y. Chen 2016.

The basis of the socialist economic system of the People's Republic of China is socialist public ownership of the means of production, namely, ownership by the whole people and collective ownership by the working people. The system of socialist public ownership supersedes the system of exploitation of man by man; it applies the principle of "from each according to his ability, to each according to his work."[32]

Qiushi Magazine, the CCP Central Committee's mouthpiece, stated in 2015 that SOEs are crucial for "improving social justice, people's welfare, and national security, and consolidating the party's rule."[33] SOEs employed the vast majority of Chinese urban residents until the early 1990s, providing for the welfare, health, and political indoctrination of their workers (Naughton 2007, 299–300). They were, and many of them still are, "work

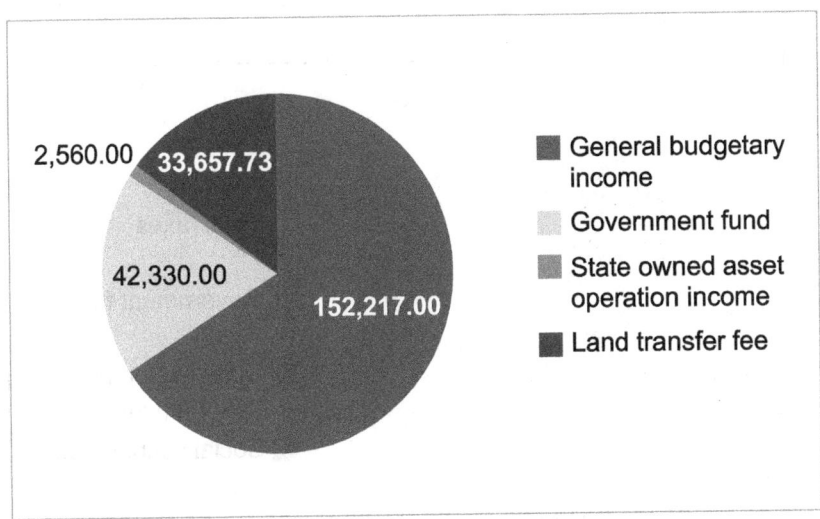

Figure 2.2. National revenue breakdown by type of income, 2014 (unit: 0.1 billion yuan). Source: Chinese government website (Zhongguo zhengfu wang), at http://www.gov.cn/guoqing/2015-02/09/content_2816639.htm.

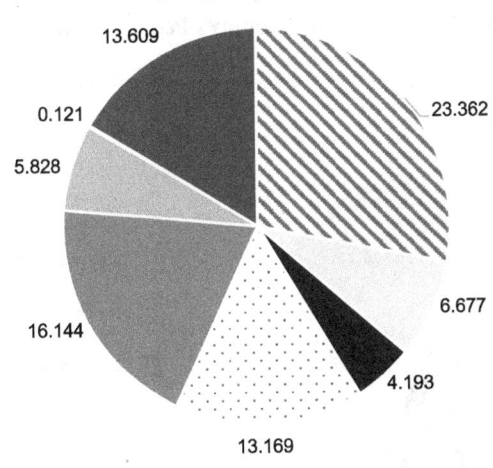

- Domestic value-added tax
- VAT and sales tax collected by customs
- Enterprise income tax
- Others
- Consumption tax
- VAT and sales tax returned by customs
- Individual income tax
- Non-tax revenue

Figure 2.3. National revenue breakdown by type of taxes, 2014 (percentage of general budgetary income). Export tax return shares = −8.45%. Source: Chinese government website (Zhongguo zhengfu wang), at http://www.gov.cn/guoqing/2015-02/09/content_2816639.htm.

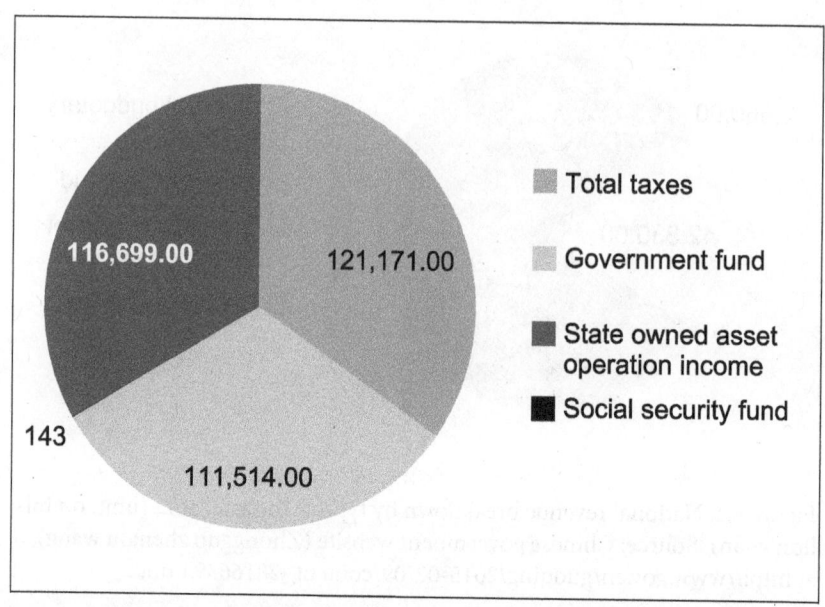

Figure 2.4. County Warm River's fiscal income, 2014 (unit: 10,000 yuan). Source: Data from County Warm River's Report on Fiscal Budget Implementation of 2014 and draft for 2015 to the County's People's Congress.

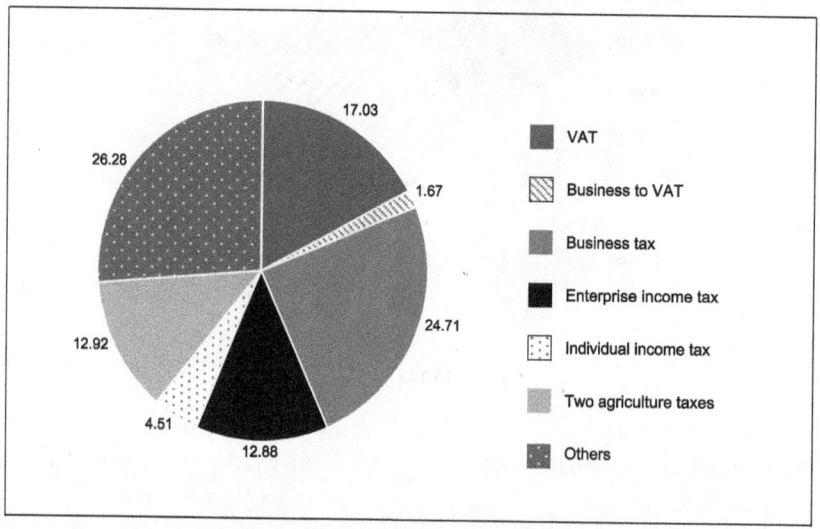

Figure 2.5. County Warm River's tax revenue breakdown, 2014 (%). Source: Data from County Warm River's Report on Fiscal Budget Implementation of 2014 and draft for 2015 to the County's People's Congress.

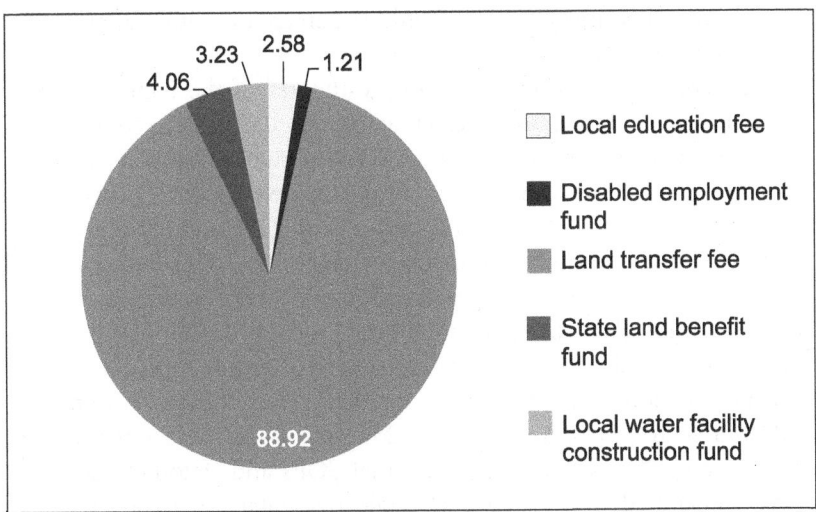

Figure 2.6. County Warm River's government fund revenue breakdown, 2014 (%). Source: Data from County Warm River's Report on Fiscal Budget Implementation of 2014 and draft for 2015 to the County's People's Congress.

units" (*Danwei* 单位) integrated into the government bureaucracy rather than independent enterprises. The mission of SOEs has changed over time, from catch-up industrialization in the 1950s, to stability (by preventing unemployment) in the early 1990s, to improvement of efficiency and profitability in late 1990s, and then reached national economic heights. More recently, SOEs have been charged with being centers for national innovation (Naughton and Tsai 2015). All of these functions are directly or indirectly related to governance. About sixty-four million Chinese citizens worked for SOEs in 2013 and continue to receive political indoctrination as well as crucial benefits such as housing through them (Sheng and Zhao 2013).

The decline of SOE profit remittance and tax payments as a share of total fiscal revenue began in 1979 with the initiation of reform and opening up.[34] SOE share of total industrial output was 77 percent in 1978 and declined to 49.6 percent in 1998. Industrial SOE profits were 15 percent of GDP in 1978 but fell below 2 percent in 1996 and 1997 (Li and Putterman 2008). Change has been more gradual since the 1990s, and the Chinese government changed how it categorized enterprises in 1992. But SOEs and corporations held by the state (the majority of whose shares were owned by government entities) produced only 38 percent of industrial output by 2004 (see table 2.7).

Different sources provide different estimates of the contribution of SOEs to state revenue. According to official data, their contribution peaked at 92 percent in 1960. In 2006, SOEs (excluding publicly held joint enterprises) paid only 24.8 percent of total tax revenue (M. Huang 2008). Jun Ma's pioneering study of how relying on SOEs and "hidden taxes" has limited political change in China estimates that SOEs and state-held enterprises contributed 44.82 percent of national tax revenue in 2001 but steadily decreased to 35.27 percent in 2007. In contrast, IIT, private enterprises, and individual enterprises in the mixed economy contributed 42.59 percent to national tax revenue in 2007, while the rest came from foreign and Chinese overseas enterprises (Jun Ma 2011, 21–24). Ma's figures accord with Yongjie Chen's; Chen estimates that SOEs and state-held corporations contributed 31.7 percent, and collective enterprises and collective holdings contributed about 34 percent of national tax revenue. The fact that the two scholars generated these estimates independently suggests they are reliable.

Yongjie Chen (2016) points out, however, that SOEs collect the cigarette consumption tax (536.093 billion yuan) and gasoline tax (399.59 billion yuan) and that together these direct taxes composed 58 percent of

Table 2.7. Composition of industrial output and tax by enterprises of different ownership, 1998 and 2004 percentages

	1998		2004	
	Industrial output of above-scale firms*	Tax 1999	Industrial output	Tax
SOE and state-controlled corporations	49.6	49.5	38.0	27.2
Joint-stock corporations	6.4		42.1	
Collective enterprises	24.7	11.8	5.3	3.6
Foreign-invested enterprises (including Hong Kong, Taiwan, and Macau)	19.6	15.7	30.8	21.3
Private and individual		8.5		12.7
Mixed economy		14.4		35.2

Source: Naughton 2007, 303; and Ma 2011.
* Firms with an annual output value of more than 5 million yuan.

SOE tax, or 88 percent of the national consumption tax, in 2015. Therefore, he reduces the significance of the tax contribution of SOEs. The gasoline tax grew by 44 percent in 2015, and the securities transaction stamp tax grew by 282 percent as the result of the government's increase in the tax rate and encouragement of stock transactions. But these tax increases were not driven by SOEs' performance improvements. This further supports Chen's contention that these types of taxes should not be considered SOE tax, although SOEs collect them on the government's behalf.

Besides their tax contribution, SOEs contributed to government fiscal revenue by submitting profits before 1993 and after 2007. SOE profit remittance was a major source of national fiscal revenue. Though SOEs are regarded as owned by the people, SOEs have not submitted their profits to the people and its representative, the State Council or its local agents, since 1994, when most SOEs were losing money. SOEs started submitting up to 30 percent of their profits in 2007, but the government reinvests most of them. The profits were 1.98706 trillion yuan in 2010, reflecting a growth rate of 37.9 percent over 2007. The government's portion was 44 billion yuan. Numbers in 2013 could be expected to be analogous, except that fees paid to SOEs engaged in providing electricity increased. A report calculated that for each kilowatt-hour of electricity that citizens use, they would be paying 4.8 cents in extra fees (*dianli fujiafei* 电力附加费, under four to five different names in different regions), about 28 billion yuan (S. Wang 2012).

The Ministry of Finance deemed 963 entities central or government run, encompassing SOEs and state-held corporations in 2011. It classified them into four categories (and one subcategory) and set the percentage of profits to be submitted according to these classifications. Monopolized resource enterprises, which encompass the subcategory of cigarettes, gasoline, electricity, telecom, and coal mining, were to pay 15 percent of profits; competitive industries such as iron, transportation, trade, and construction, 10 percent; military enterprises and the *China Post*, 5 percent; and policy enterprises were exempt. These numbers were increased by an extra 5 percent after 2014.

The CCP benefits substantially from SOE profits. Kenneth Greene's (2007) study of Mexico's hegemonic Institutional Revolutionary Party (PRI) identifies four ways in which SOE profits can benefit such parties, which are typically illicit. While the fourth, harvesting SOE resources for electoral campaigns, is irrelevant to the CCP, the other three apply directly. First, the state can divert funds from SOE budgets, which can be substantial. Second, party operatives can reward supporters with patronage jobs. Third, by enforcing the state's dominance of the economy, SOEs promote conditions that encourage domestic enterprises to provide kickbacks in exchange for government contracts or other advantages. Greene asserts that SOEs are thus the backbone of single-party rule (2007, 811–812). While both are dominant parties in their respective countries, the CCP and PRI differ in several ways; for example, there are factions within the CCP while the PRI needs to compete with other parties.[35] When different factions control different SOEs and compete for advantage by deploying patronage,[36] they may weaken the CCP's overall resilience.

While they improve state autonomy and resolve the representation dilemma, SOEs are also inefficient and corrupt,[37] which impairs authoritarian resilience.[38] SOEs rely on the power of monopoly to extract rent rather than innovation to gain profit, enjoy privileged access to land and bank loans that inflate their revenue, and generate inequality between industries (Xiaolu Wang 2013, chap. 5). Some economists also describe SOEs as hindering China's economic growth (Sheng and Zhao 2013). Nonetheless, they have a powerful effect in offsetting the government's dependence on tax revenue.

Local Rentier States

Land-transfer fees have contributed from one-third to one-half of local government revenue in East China for a decade.[39] If we combine land-transfer fees and land-related taxes and fees, the land's contribution to fiscal revenue is much higher. As shown in figure 2.7, land-related revenue income was even higher than local government tax revenue in 2010. If we deduct land-related taxes from local government tax revenue, the ratio of land-related revenue to the rest of local government tax revenue would be 1.47.[40] While some land-related taxes pertain to productive efforts, most can be regarded as land rents. Therefore, many local governments in China are local rentier states.

Table 2.8 provides national data on land-related revenue and its importance for local government fiscal revenue. Table 2.9 shows County Warm River's reliance on land-transfer fees. Even as it decreased land-transfer fees by 48 percent in 2014, they amounted to 36 percent of the county's revenue that year.

Two institutions are responsible for the rise of land revenue in China.

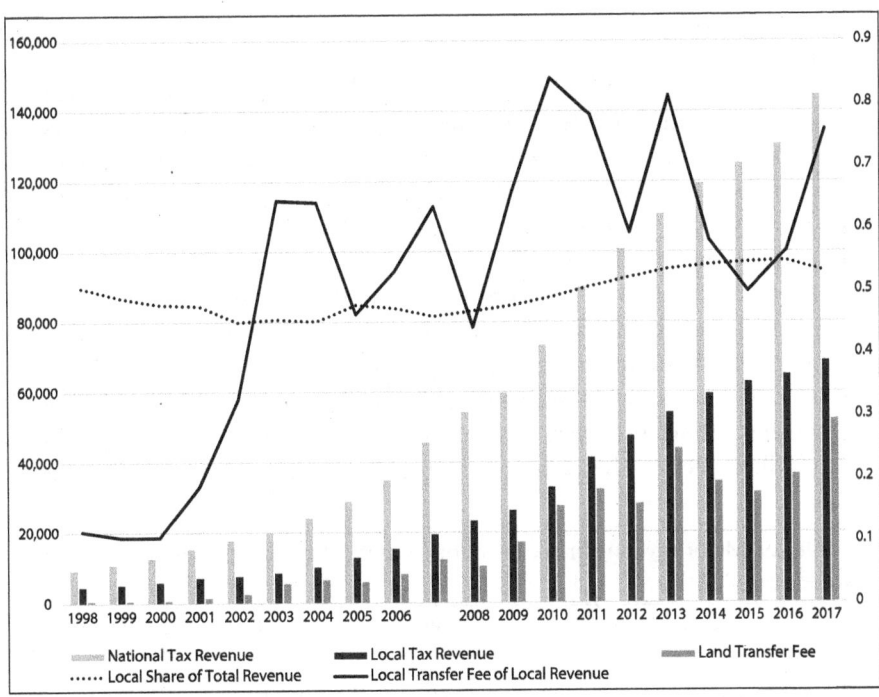

Figure 2.7. Rise and decline of land-transfer fee, 1998–2017 (unit: 100 million yuan, %). Source: Data from Ministry of Finance of People's Republic of China, various years; Ministry of Land Resource *Annual Report*, various years; Ministry of Land Resource of People's Republic of China, various years.

Table 2.8. Land-related revenue and relative value to local government tax revenue

	Amount (100 million yuan)	Relative to local government tax revenue (%)
Local government tax revenue	40,613.00	100.00
Land-transfer fee	29,110.00	69.49
Land-related taxes: land VAT, tax on use of arable land, city maintenance and construction tax, urban and township land-use tax, house property tax, contract tax, business taxes of construction and real estate industries	12,171.59	29.05
Land-related fees (incomplete): urban infrastructural fee	611.01	1.46
Total land-related revenue	41,892.60	100.00

Source: Chen and Chen 2012, 64.

Local governments in East China have relied on such revenue since 1994, when China implemented land laws and regulations and diminished other revenue sources as part of TSR (see figure 2.7). Local governments' share of national tax revenue decreased from 78 percent in 1993 to 44.3 percent in 1994, while share of expenditure remains around 70 percent. Local governments therefore rely heavily on the 30 percent of taxes transferred from the national government and nontax revenue to fund a variety of mandated expenditures. They have increasingly turned to the land they monopolize, a revenue source first used in 1987. At that time total land-transfer fees nationwide were only 3,250 million yuan. By 1992, driven by a housing bubble, these fees were 52.5 billion yuan, and in 1994, they were 63.9 billion. Before the 1994 TSR, the total amount of land-transfer fees

Table 2.9. Major revenue breakdown for County Warm River, Zhejiang Province, 2008

Types of taxes	Revenue (10,000 yuan)	Share of tax revenue (%)	Share of total fiscal revenue (%)
Total tax revenue	124,071	100.0	67.80
Local tax revenue	67,386	54.3	36.82
VAT (25% rebate)	13,633	(20.2)	(7.45)
Business tax	16,624	(24.7)	(9.08)
Enterprise income tax (40% rebate)	7,176	(10.6)	(3.92)
Individual income tax (40% rebate)	3,385	(5.0)	(1.85)
City maintenance and construction tax	3,607	(5.4)	(1.97)
Other	9,620	(14.3)	(5.26)
SOE deficit compensation	−1,000	(−1.5)	(−0.55)
Two agricultural taxes	7,412	(11.0)	(4.050)
Central revenue	56,685	45.7	30.98
VAT (75%)	40,899	(33.0)	(22.35)
Enterprise income tax (60%)	10,674	(8.6)	(5.83)
Individual income tax (60%)	5,077	(0.4)	(2.77)
Total nontax revenue	58,926		32.2
Land-transfer fee	35,028		(19.14)
Social security fund	21,251		(11.61)
Agriculture fund (mainly water conservation)	2,121		(1.16)
Other	526		(0.29)
Total fiscal revenue	182,997		100.00

Source: Bureau of Finance and Local Taxation of County Warm River: Report of 2008's Fiscal Revenue and Budget to the County PC.

collected nationally was about 200 billion, even less than collected in the single year of 1999 (China Land Surveying and Planning Institute 2006). After the turn of the century, land-transfer fees rose quickly, as shown in figure 2.7. In addition to land-transfer fees and other land-related sources of funds, local governments gain financial leverage to make investments by borrowing money from government-owned banks, using the land they own as deposit.

As compensation for local governments' loss of taxation power, TSR granted all land-transfer fees from the state's land holdings to local governments. A variety of land-related laws and regulations influence land's role in generating revenue. Article 10 of the 1982 PRC constitution claims that all urban land became the property of the state.[41] While collectives own a good deal of land in rural and suburban areas, including home sites and private plots of cropland and hilly land, this is no longer true in urban areas. Additionally, in rural and suburban areas, the state may take over land for its use in accordance with the law. According to Article 10, "All organizations and individuals who use land must make rational use of the land." The 1988 constitutional amendment expanded on this limitation, stating that "no organization or individual may appropriate, buy, sell or otherwise engage in the transfer of land by unlawful means. The right to the use of land may be transferred according to law" (PRC Constitution 2003). Then in 1990 the State Council enacted a regulation on transfer of urban land-use rights that further clarified rights such as transfer, rent, and deposit. The Land Management Law, enacted and revised in 1998 and 2004, further clarifies that the central government manages landownership on the people's behalf. The law requires local government to submit 30 percent of land-transfer fees to the central government for state-owned land converted from collectively owned land, most of which was arable, and keep the rest.[42]

Before 2002, local governments' most commonly used method for pricing land was bargaining (*Xieyi dingjia* 协议定价), most of which was backroom and case-specific. As a result, most land was sold cheaply. The Ministry of Land Resource issued "Regulations on Bidding, Auction, and Listing of State-Owned Land's Usage Rights" and other relevant policies in 2002, requiring local governments to use bidding, auction, and listing rather than backroom bargaining to price land. As a result, listing became the dominant mode of land transfer. This increased competition caused land prices to rise rapidly.

The evolution of the land-management institution, especially the land-transfer fee management institution, reflects the central government's approach to the agent-discipline problem. To motivate local governments, the central government should delegate some power, but power delegation may lead to local governments' abuse of power. So the central government keeps adjusting rules and policies, trying to motivate local agents while maintaining monitoring and disciplinary capacity. Responding to local governments' illegal use of land, the central government initiated many new policies and regulations and established the position of supervisor of state land in 2004, filled by the Ministry of Land Resource, which sets nine monitoring branches nationwide, to supervise and monitor land use.

Land-transfer fees and land-related taxes and fees are only part of local government finance; an equally important element of financing local government's huge amount of infrastructural investment and commercial endeavors is based on local government financing platforms (*Difang zhengfu rongzi pingtai* 地方政府融资平台).[43] Land finance was crucial for the CCP as it sought to sustain economic growth rates in the short term and help local governments meet the gap between expenditure obligation and taxation capacity. Especially in East China, land revenue and land finance became the most important sources of funds to sustain a government investment-led growth model (Chen and Chen 2012; Whiting 2011; F. Zhou 2012, chaps. 12, 13, 14).[44] This model has been effective: China has sustained a national GDP growth rate above 8 percent from 2006 to 2013 and above 6 percent afterward, even during the 2008 world financial crisis.[45]

But the model has downsides. First, economic growth based on land supply cannot continue indefinitely. The Ministry of Land Resource has set a limit on the urbanization of arable land as a means to guarantee China's food security, and most governments will reach this limit in the near future if they have not already. Second, unlike real estate taxes, land-transfer fees are an irregular or one-time revenue that cannot be collected every year.[46] Land-transfer fees make property tax illegitimate because the fees grant land-usage rights (S. Zhang 2012). Third, the housing bubble raises labor costs, which enterprises may need to pass on to consumers, weakening the comparative advantage of Chinese products. This threatens the government's stability by worsening the growth dilemma (Liu et al. 2020). In regions where the housing bubble collapsed, land-transfer fees also decreased significantly (e.g., County Warm River's land-transfer fees decreased 48.8 percent in 2014).[47] Fourth, riots over land seizure as it has replaced rural taxation have become a major source of social riots in the last decade,[48] increasing the regime's difficulty in maintaining social control.

While land-transfer fees grew at a rate of 3.1 percent in 2014, they decreased substantially, by 21.6 percent, in 2015. Most provinces experienced substantial decreases in land-transfer fees: East China, 23.6 percent; Middle, 17.3 percent; and West, 21.2 percent. Some extreme cases include Dalian, −56.4 percent; Ningbo, −54.1 percent; and Inner Mongolia, −51.8 percent. The few exceptions reported very minor gains: Tibet, 1.8 percent; Xiamen, 1.2 percent; and Gansu, 0.2 percent; however, Shenzhen, which experienced a rapid rise in housing prices, reported a gain of 36.9 percent (Ministry of Finance of the People's Republic of China 2015).

Seizure of land is a self-subverting mechanism: more land revenue leads to higher land-seizure costs. An important consequence of resistance to land seizure is rapidly increasing land compensation. In some regions, the price of land compensation is very high and makes land transfer less profitable for the government than in the 2000s. According to a recent report, expenditure on compensation for peasants who lost their land in 2015 was 1.79 trillion yuan, plus land-development and other related costs. The total costs of land seizure was 2.68 trillion, or 80 percent of total land-transfer fees (3.37 trillion) in 2015 (Ministry of Finance of the People's Republic of China 2015). Table 2.10 provides detailed information of the costs.

The unexpected rise in land-transfer fees also worsens the agent-discipline problem by offsetting the government's efforts to rationalize fiscal income and expenditure. This reliance on nontax revenue gives local government more autonomy and in effect lessens the representation dilemma. Reliance on nontax revenue weakens the local governments' efforts to discipline the government bureaus. Local governments' heavy reliance on land-transfer fees brings new challenges to the effort to ratio-

Table 2.10. Land-transfer fee expenditure in China, 2015

Item	Amount (billion yuan)	Percentage of total
Total	3,372.778	100.00
Costs	2,684.459	79.59
Peasant compensation	1,793.582	(53.18)
Land development	653.390	(19.37)
Urban compensation	237.487	(7.04)
Non-cost expenditure	688.319	20.41
Rural development	252.817	(7.50)
Public housing	82.349	(2.44)
Urban construction	353.153	(10.47)

Source: Ministry of Finance of the People's Republic of China 2016.

nalize fiscal income and expenditure. According to media reports on the anticorruption campaign, a number of government corruption scandals in the last decade have involved land-transfer issues.

This conclusion is also supported by the Ministry of Finance, which summarizes three problems related to land transfer. The first is serious illegal seizure and use of land. The Ministry of Land Resource found 81,420 cases of illegal land seizure involving 40,900 hectares in 2014. Local governments exceed the amount of land the national government permits and resell lands at a lower price (to attract investment). Second, land-transfer-fee management is dysfunctional in some regions. Local governments may discount, remit, postpone, or return land-transfer fees, either because of investment recruitment or personal favoritism. Some local governments do not submit land-transfer fees to the state treasury for budgetary management; therefore, monitoring and expenditure of land-transfer fees are arbitrary and inefficient. Some local governments have not been punctual in paying peasants who lost their land or paid them less than promised, and some spent land-transfer fees on illegal or forbidden items, such as luxury cars, buildings, and bonuses (Ministry of Finance of the People's Republic of China 2015).

Overreliance on land finance also worsens the agent-discipline problem in terms of central-local fiscal relationships. Zhu Rongji's market-oriented reform associated with the 1994 TSR achieved some progress in setting hard budgetary constraints on local governments by cutting off their administrative connection with state-owned commercial banks. However, local governments and banks found that land is reliable as collateral to obtain loans. Local government financing platforms flourished in many regions as a result, achieving significant leverage to borrow and make investments. However, this led to a large increase in local government debt (Ma 2013), which makes economic growth unsustainable. Yu You (2012) provides an in-depth analysis of the situation in Chongqing, the strongest city in China economically in the last several years. You argues that the economic growth model based on land finance is unsustainable and risky for Chongqing because the government investment cannot generate enough profit to pay the principal and interest.

Indirect Taxes and Citizens' Tax Consciousness

If taxation hurts regime stability, citizens' tax perception and behavior should reveal this instability. Indeed, tax riots and other forms of resistance followed the institution of agricultural taxes and related rural taxation in the 1990s and early 2000s.[49] After many rounds of reform, the CCP Central Committee and the State Council decided to abolish agricultural taxes nationwide in 2006. However, the half-tax state that relies heavily on indirect taxes reduces citizens' perception of their heavy tax and nontax burdens. The Chinese government has taxed more than 15 percent of GDP since 2003; the figure reached 20 percent in 2010. Direct taxes in China include IIT, company income, and real estate taxes, which have constituted about 30 percent of all tax revenue since 2006. In 2014, for example, IIT and company income taxes made up 28.62 percent of total tax revenue and 15.48 percent of total government revenue. Because tax revenue amounts to only about 60 percent of government fiscal revenue and most taxes are indirect, taxpayers find it difficult to perceive their tax burden. Further, individuals do not typically recognize the role of company income tax. Real estate tax for individuals is still in its pilot stage, with no clear schedule of implementation in the future. The local government tax structure is also dependent on indirect taxes, as shown in previous figures. Table 2.11 is another example.

Table 2.11. Major revenue breakdown for County Cold Mountain, Shanxi Province, 2008

Type of taxes	Revenue (10,000 yuan)	Share of total local tax revenue (%)
Total tax revenue (incomplete)	174,040	100
Tax revenue collected by county LTB	72,948	42
Business tax	9,801	
Enterprise income tax	45,635	
Individual income tax	5,508	
City maintenance and construction tax	3,092	
Resource tax	4,068	
Real estate tax	622	
Stamp duty	649	
Urban and township land-use tax	2,693	
Land-appreciation tax	109	
Vehicle and vessel tax	171	
Tax collected by county SAT office (incomplete)		
VAT (25% of which is assigned to the county government)	101,092	58

Source: Municipal J LTB Office: *Tax Statistics of Municipal J 2008*; *County Cold Mountain Yearbook* 2008.

Note: The county government's tax revenue is higher than the tax collected by LTB (72,948) plus 25% of the VAT collected by the SAT office (25,273), which is 98,221. Therefore, it is close to the tax revenue of County Warm River.

In recent years, there has been more discussion of citizens' tax burden in the media and on the internet. A number of newspaper articles have tried to calculate the tax burden white-collar workers bear at different income levels.[50] For example, taxes on steamed bread (*mantou*), North China's staple food, were hotly debated online.[51] The discussion led to further discussions of citizens' tax burden, especially the invisible tax burden that people pay through consumption, which is much heavier than direct taxes. Many people realize that China's income tax system is quite regressive, in part because rich people earn most of their income from investments, on which they pay minimal tax. IIT is now a payroll tax. Citizens are also now more aware of taxation because of the greater transparency of the NPC. In addition to permitting citizens to publicly comment on legislation, the SAT headquarters made a public announcement of the "taxpayer's rights and obligations" in November 2009 as part of its avowed attempt to build a transparent government and to disseminate information on tax compliance (State Administration of Taxation 2009). It lists fourteen types of taxpayer rights, including the right to information, the right to supervise tax collection (by reporting abuse of tax-collection power), and the right to a hearing if accused of tax evasion.

Citizens, who ultimately pay heavy indirect taxes through their purchases, rarely perceive them. Scholars and journalists describe this as the underdevelopment of a citizen's "taxpayer's rights consciousness" (W. Li 2011) and attribute it to the difficulty of developing a "political rights consciousness" in China, which naturally benefits authoritarian resilience. This view is also supported by survey data. A nationwide random sample survey conducted by the Research Center for Contemporary China of Peking University in 2014 shows that citizens are generally clueless about the appropriateness of their tax burden relative to that of their peer groups or the public services they receive from the government.[52] As figures 2.8 and 2.9 reflect, more than one-half to two-thirds of respondents report that they "do not know" whether their tax burden is too high or fair. Less than one-tenth report that their tax burden is too high compared to that of their peers (6.8 percent) or to the public services they receive (9.7 percent). Among those with an opinion, most respondents considered their tax burdens fair. Relying on indirect taxes reduces citizens' tax perception, therefore alleviates the representation dilemma.

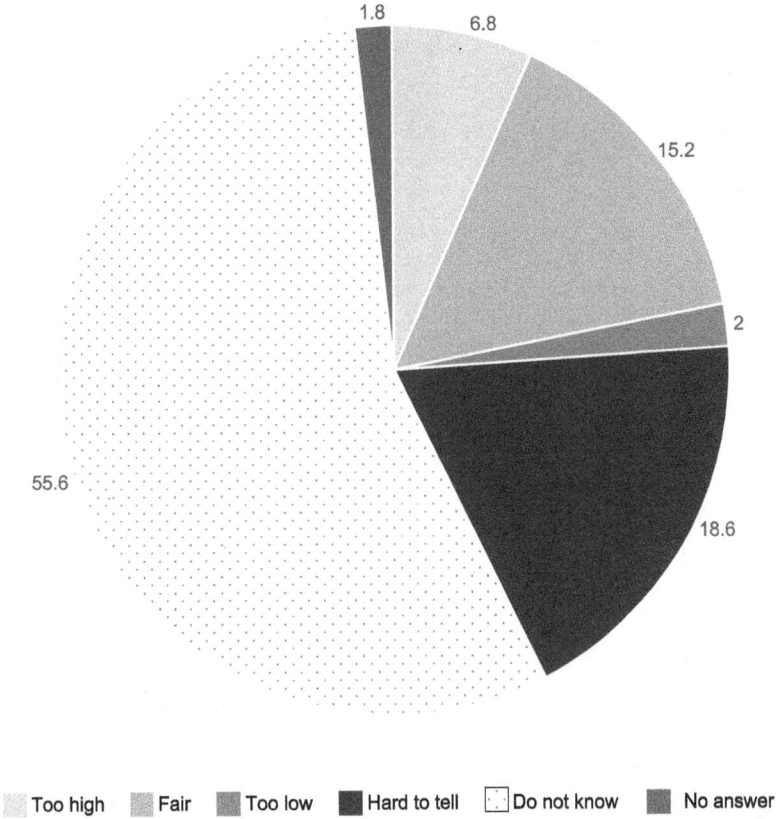

Figure 2.8. Citizens' perception of tax burden, 2014 (compared to peer group). $N = 4{,}128$. Source: Data from "Public Service and Government Support Survey 2014," Research Center for Contemporary China, Peking University.

Half-Tax State as a Double-Edged Sword

More than twenty-six hundred years ago, a famous Chinese politician and founding thinker of legalism (*fajia*, which proposes rule by law, whereas Confucianism proposes rule by a moral code), Guan Zi, proposed to the king of Qi:

> People are happy when they receive something [from the government]; people are angry when they are deprived [by the govern-

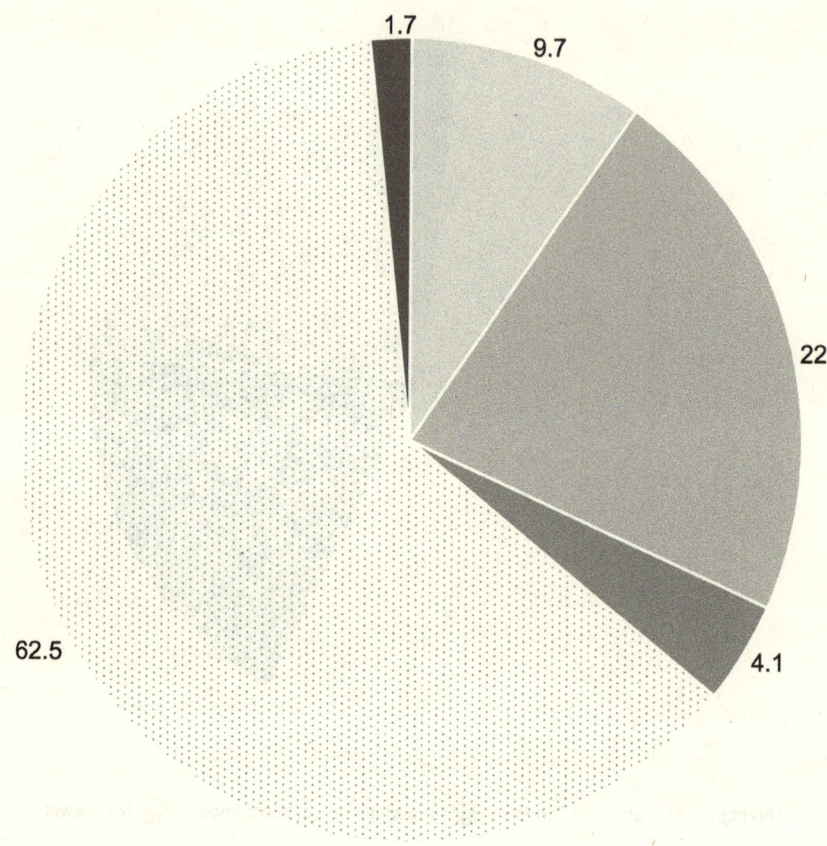

■ Too high   ■ Fair   ■ Too low   ■ Do not know   ■ No answer

Figure 2.9. Citizens' perception of tax burden, 2014 (compared to public services received). N = 4,128. Source: Data from "Public Service and Government Support Survey 2014," Research Center for Contemporary China, Peking University.

ment]. A smart king knows this human nature; his gifts are visible, and his extractions are invisible. Therefore, his people love him. Some taxes are visible while others are invisible; a smart king abolishes the visible and increases the invisible, so people are happy to follow him. (Guan, 1998, 857)

This is similar to Anne-Robert-Jacques Turgot's metaphor of plucking the hen but goes beyond it. China's tax-state transition has been associated with decentralization and recentralization of fiscal power. Thus, it has become to some extent a system of de facto fiscal federalism. The tax-state transition interacted with fiscal (de)centralization, changing the three governance problems and making them more difficult to deal with.

China's reliance on indirect taxes has minimized the crying out of its citizens because they do not recognize that the feathers in the state's hands are their own. The CCP is a good student of Guan Zi. The half-tax state requires minimal direct compliance by citizens and therefore improves the state's extractive capacity. Thus, it alleviates the representation dilemma. However, continuing as a half-tax state will exacerbate the growth dilemma because of high levels of inequality and limits on sustainable growth. Christine Wong and Richard Bird point out that "[China's tax] revenues are overly dependent on productive activities rather than income, which distorts resource allocation as localities compete to attract industry and businesses; and the heavy dependence on turnover taxes and small share of income taxes means the tax structure lacks progressivity" (2008, 200). High dependence on indirect taxes and fees also impedes authoritarian resilience. It is inefficient (Slemrod and Yitzhaki 2002), and it weakens a taxation system's ability to reduce inequality by redistributing wealth.[53] Compared to direct taxes such as income and property taxes, indirect taxes are regressive rather than progressive, and China has seen rising inequality (Gao 2010; Benjamin et al. 2008; *Xinmin wanbao* 2013). Various scholarly sources suggest inequality is actually far higher due to underestimation of household income among wealthier people.[54] A high level of inequality harms authoritarian resilience because it generates social discontent, impairs the regime's moral legitimacy, and blocks long-term economic growth by limiting domestic demand.

Figure 2.10 depicts the contradictions inherent in the half-tax state. It depoliticizes taxation and alleviates the social-control problem because citizens do not perceive indirect taxes (Gilley 2017; Ma 2011; Yingyao Wang 2017). Peasants who lose their land present a problem, which the CCP

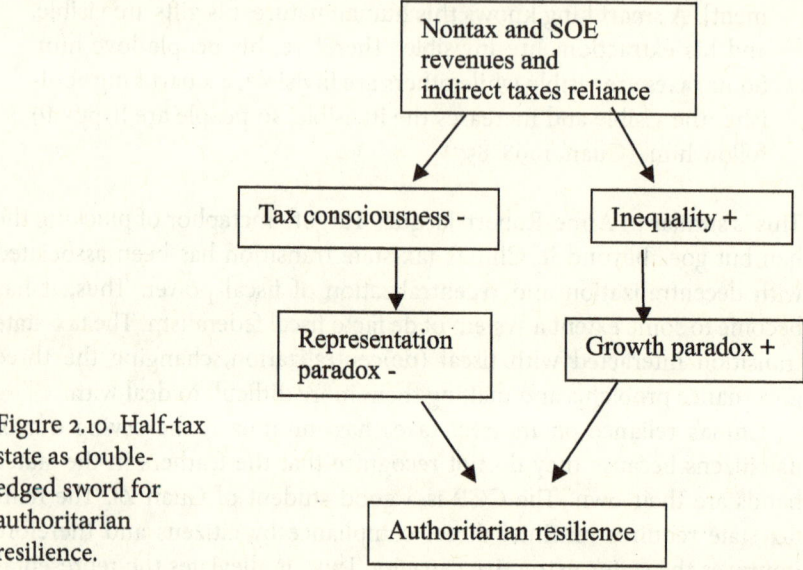

Figure 2.10. Half-tax state as double-edged sword for authoritarian resilience.

has addressed by a combination of repression and co-optation.[55] Nonetheless, government expenditure in investments (both for infrastructure and industry) and public services, made possible with revenue collected through indirect taxes, has driven impressive economic growth. As Kevin Morrison (2014) and Kenneth Greene (2007), among many others, find, abundant nontax revenues and the dominant party's access to them have contributed to authoritarian resilience.

The half-tax state also reduces the need for cooperation from social actors. Under state capitalism, China still runs many SOEs and makes a huge investment in them. This investment is targeted to improve innovation in technology and dominate the world market (Brandt and Thun 2015). It also alleviates the power-sharing problem because patronage jobs pacify political elites.[56] However, SOEs suffer from inefficiency generated by too much construction and therefore excessive production capacity. Local governments have taken on huge debt to keep them functioning. The economic growth model is unsustainable under these circumstances. The half-tax state worsens the agent-discipline problem. Dependence on land finance makes it impossible for the central government to set hard budgetary constraints for local governments. Thus, local governments' efforts to discipline their agents have also been weakened. Land revenue is a major source of corruption and social instability.

The government faced a hard choice concerning whether to enact the property tax (房产税, or real estate tax), an important direct tax, as a local tax. In 2003, the third session of the CCP's Sixteenth Central Committee proposed to enact a property tax "when conditions permit" and abolish the relevant charges and fees. The third session of the Eighteenth Central Committee again proposed to facilitate legislation of a property tax. The NPC also approved the State Council's five-year plans that proposed to "reform real estate taxes" in 2006, 2011, and 2016. The Property Tax Law had been listed as a "preparatory project" (预备项目) for the NPC's annual legislature plan since 2015, and in 2019 it was upgraded to a "primary deliberation project" (初次审议项目). The minister of finance's announcement in March 2016 that China would enact and implement the real estate tax to increase local governments' reliance on direct taxes instead of land-transfer fees again led people to predict that a property tax would be enacted in 2020 (*People's Daily* 2012b). However, Premier Li Keqiang did not mention property tax in the government's annual report to the 2020 NPC annual conference, which is regarded as a signal of retreat from "steadily promoting" (稳步推进) and "properly promoting" (稳妥推进) property tax legislation in 2019 and 2018, respectively. All of these reflect the CCP leadership's paradoxical attitude toward the property tax.

Two municipalities, Shanghai and Chongqing, were selected as pilot cities for property tax collection in 2011. Two municipal party leaders, Yu Zhengsheng of Shanghai and Bo Xilai of Chongqing, volunteered for the pilot program because both wanted to "obtain competition-specific capital by launching bold policy reforms" in their race for the CCP Central Committee Politburo's Standing Committee membership (Y. Zhang 2020, 670). The pilot municipalities used different models of taxation and have achieved limited success in collecting property taxes. Scholars' concerns for enacting property tax include legitimacy,[57] capacity to pay (because of very high housing prices), equality, and high political and administrative collection costs.[58] However, if the CCP does enact property tax law and implement it nationwide, it will provide a good opportunity for studies of fiscal sociology.

An Under-institutionalized Taxation System

The tax-state transition has also required changes to tax administration. Under the communist (tax) state, no professional tax administration was needed, and the Taxation Bureau, which was abolished during the Cultural Revolution, was staffed by nonprofessionals. A tax state requires professional and highly institutionalized tax administration, using the most up-to-date technologies to collect information and calculate taxes. China's tax-state transition reflects changes in taxation administration as well.

Scholars have not given much attention to tax administration or the on-the-ground practice of taxation, especially as an independent variable. Studies on rural taxation and tax riots are exceptions (Bernstein and Lü 2003; Takeuchi 2014), but China abolished agricultural taxes in 2006. There is a need to study tax administration and its implication for capitalists' political preference, strategy of survival and bargaining power, and regime durability. Evan Lieberman finds that "the registration of taxpayers, calculation of liabilities, and actual collection of taxes are the most significant steps in the administrative process" (2003, 50–52). This chapter uses Lieberman's definition of tax administration with a focus on potential leakages and informal practices that lead to leakages. I argue that the Chinese taxation system has three characteristics: very high nominal tax rates, high discretional power of tax officers, and a tax-target system that violates the rule of law.[59] I elaborate on these characteristics later and also discuss dimensions of the institution of taxation that have a significant impact on regime stability and authoritarian resilience, especially in relation to two dilemmas that increased taxation and infrastructural capacity can generate.

High Nominal Tax Rates and Rampant Tax Evasion

China's central government, the State Council and its ministries, rather than the NPC, the legislature and nominal highest authority, dominates tax legislation. In 1985, the NPC Standing Committee delegated the power of tax legislation to the State Council and has not reclaimed it.[60] Tax legislation is a closed process, and taxpayers have limited opportunity to lobby it.[61] Officials at the headquarters of the SAT and the Ministry of Finance draft national tax codes, which the NPC Standing Committee enacts. At the provincial level, the LTB may also draft local tax statutes, regulations, and policies, but it levies only small taxes, such as a slaughtering tax or feast tax, and sets the rates for the urban land-usage tax within guidelines determined by the central authorities. China's taxation structure warrants further research, but my scope here is its impact on representation—policy implementation, not policy making.

High dependence on indirect taxes leads to a narrow tax base and a high nominal tax rate. Most taxes come directly from private enterprise, though individuals and families are the final recipients of the tax burden. Reflecting a narrow tax base, China's nominal enterprise tax rates (a VAT of 17 percent and corporate income tax of 33 percent) are too high for most enterprises, especially corporations, who also need to contribute to a social security fund for employees. During my fieldwork, private entrepreneurs from different sectors admitted, implicitly or explicitly,[62] that the nominal tax rates are too high for them to fully comply. Many told me that full compliance would bankrupt them. A US citizen who runs a medium-sized company in China and has lived in China for more than twenty years explained that he had no choice but to evade taxes, making this analogy: if the speed limit on a highway is too low (say, sixty kilometers per hour), then drivers will exceed the speed limit if possible.[63] A private entrepreneur in Beijing told me that he asked his friend who works at the SAT headquarters whether the SAT intentionally sets high nominal tax rates just for rents, because he could not think of any other explanation.[64] Many government officers that I interviewed, including tax officers who implement tax policies, explicitly or implicitly admitted that nominal tax rates were unreasonably high. A senior tax officer told me that in his thirty years of tax administration in two counties in Hunan Province, he came across only one enterprise in which he could not identify any tax evasion.[65]

The reason the state set high but unattainable tax rates in the early 1990s was that policy makers were concerned mainly with increasing revenue in the face of limited tax-collection capacity and a narrow tax base. To reach the tax target under these constraints, the SAT had to set tax rates high, which led to rampant tax evasion.[66] Tax rates have not decreased significantly in the last two decades,[67] even though China's tax-collection institutions have been strengthened and collection capacity has greatly improved.[68] There is a vicious cycle between high nominal tax rates and tax evasion. Besides criticizing high tax rates and rampant tax evasion, my informants criticize the current tax system for its complexity, lack of transparency in collection, and unfair classifications of enterprises into different brackets according to ownership, type of industry, and region. Some informants state that political connections affect these classifications and therefore tax rates.

Tax Administration: Institutional Framework of the Current Taxation Regime

Before the 1994 TSR, the Tax Administration, under the direct leadership of local government at the corresponding level, was in charge of tax collection in its jurisdiction. Combined with the TSR that asked the local government to submit fiscal revenue at a given growth rate to the higher-level government and keep the rest, this Tax Administration gave the local government too much power to retain tax revenue and failed to collect enough tax revenue for the central government to fulfill its tasks.[69] Reform addressed the problem by creating two parallel and independent tax administrations. Both the SAT and LTB are vertically managed as a way to minimize the intervention of local governments, which had caused the central government's tax revenue to decrease in the 1980s and early 1990s. The SAT is institutionally independent from the local government,[70] while the LTBs are under dual leadership of the higher-level LTB and the local government. However, the higher-level LTB (or SAT for the province-level LTB) holds most of the power, such as appointing and supervising directors and determining the size and organization of lower-level LTBs. In some provinces, such as Zhejiang, the LTB and Bureau of Finance are a single institution. Since the Bureau of Finance is responsible mainly to the local government rather than the higher-level Bureau of Finance, merging it with the LTB weakens the autonomy of the LTB. Figure 2.11 illustrates the organizational structure in provinces with separate institutions.

The independent structure of the SAT and LTB helps improve the autonomy of tax bureaus. In an interview, a senior tax officer told me several stories about the tax bureau's autonomy and its limits. In County X, where he had worked in the Tax Bureau for twenty-eight years and as the director of the Inspection Bureau for eight years, an owner had lost his paper factory because he had complained that the newly appointed SAT office director had forced him to buy the SAT's abandoned office at a very high price. The entrepreneur had made the complaint at a meeting where the county party secretary met with private entrepreneurs and government officers, and the SAT office director, whom the officer described as young, energetic, and politically well-connected, was embarrassed. He asked the officer I spoke with to check the tax records and impose fines to the limit of the law. The manufacturer had to sell his factory to pay them.[71] The story illustrates the autonomy of tax bureaus, which operate with little interference from local government, although local government retains

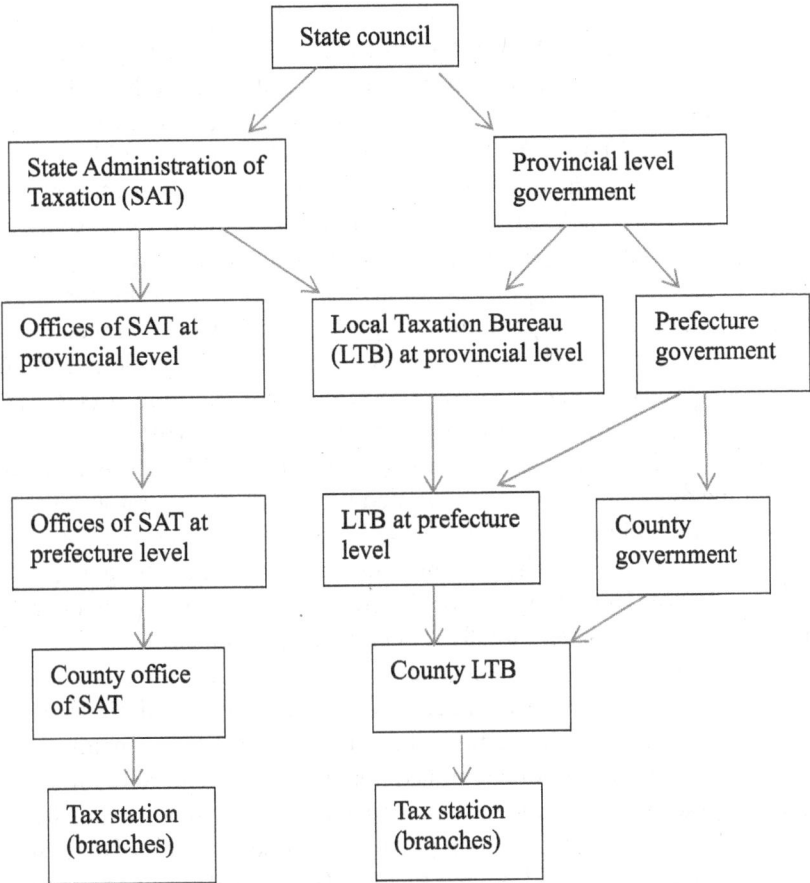

Figure 2.11. Organizational structure of tax administrations in China before 2018. SAT headquarters has vertical leadership over its offices across China and assists governments at the provincial level by a system of dual leadership over the local tax bureau. Local tax bureaus below the provincial level are under the dual leadership of both the higher LTB and governments at the same level, with the higher LTB as the predominant one.

some influence. The tax bureaus' autonomy has helped increase the central government's tax revenue significantly. The percentage of tax revenue in relation to GDP and the percentage of the central government's tax in relation to total government taxes started to increase in 1995, and gains have accelerated since.[72]

The taxes assigned to the SAT and LTB are different. The SAT is responsible for the major and easy-to-collect taxes, including the VAT and sales tax. The LTB is responsible for the small and hard-to-collect taxes, such as the business tax and personal income tax. One of the tax officers I spoke with told me that "the SAT gets the watermelon [big and sweet, easy to collect] and the LTB gets the sesame [small and hard to collect]."[73]

The 1994 TSR left local governments in China with insufficient tax sources, thus driving local governments to rely on other revenue sources, such as hundreds of types of fees and fines, bank loans, and, later, land-transfer fees, to meet expenses. Research suggests that the mismatch of budgetary power and expenditure obligation, or the unfunded mandates, have caused many local governance problems, including underprovision of public goods (Wong 2009), overtaxation, and social unrest (see Bernstein and Lü 2003 for a discussion of overtaxation in rural areas). The (in)sufficiency of fiscal revenue strongly correlates with, and is actually caused by the political power associated with, the administrative level of government, as illustrated in a saying: "The fiscal revenue of the central government is jubilant, the province government is flourishing, the prefecture government barely works, the county government is crying, and the township government totally suffers" (Zheng 2006, 99).

The second negative consequence is high costs and low efficiency of taxation for both the tax collector and the taxpayers.[74] One tax-administration organization can collect the taxes, but now there are two organizations with different staffs, buildings, and equipment that do not share information with each other.[75] Though some local governments have tried to build a network of "protecting and supporting tax collection" (*Hushui xieshui* 护税协税), they have had limited success. The Road Administration, the state-owned Electronic Corporation, and some other related government agencies have coordinated to gather systematic information about coal mines to improve collection of the resource tax; however, such coordination has been rare and only marginally effective because different organizations have their own interests. Citizens also bear the cost directly, as they must deal with two independent tax-gathering agencies. Neither tax bureau has significant budgetary check on its power, which increases costs for the state. My informants told me that the LTB and SAT offices are the "best" government bureaus to work for: workers receive high salaries and benefits (housing, children's education, bonus for holidays). The 2007 annual report of the National Audit Office, based on an audit of costs of taxation of 236 tax bureaus in eighteen provinces, states:

The cost of collecting 100 yuan tax revenue has been reduced since 2002, but there are still some problems of managing tax-collection costs because of lack of a department budgetary system for the tax bureaus and loose implementation of fiscal rules [*caizheng jilv*]. The problems are (1) the personal expenditure is too high; [for example,] in 2006, the average personal expenditure for the tax bureau staffs of the eighteen provinces was 58,300 yuan (USD [US dollars] 7,300), and 90,600 yuan (USD 11,200) for the 236 tax bureaus we audited; (2) oversized office use: they use 58 percent more office space than needed; (3) purchasing cars without quotas approved, which happens in 90 tax bureaus out of 162; (4) overspending on expenditures of receiving guests, conferences, training, and visiting foreign countries. The 236 tax bureaus spent 1.055 billion last year on these items, which is much too high. (J. Liu, 2008)

From On-Site Collection to Separation of Collection, Auditing, and Inspection

The 1994 TSR changed tax collection in China, substituting the concentrated administration system (*jizhong zhengguan zhidu*) for the so-called one-person-in-charge-of-all system (*shuishou zhuanguanyuan zhidu*). The tax-administrator system (*shuishou guanliyuan zhidu*) replaced them both in 2001. In the system in place from the 1950s to 1993 in most regions,[76] a single tax officer in a specific area took care of collection (征), monitoring and assessing (管), inspection (查), and keeping records of all taxpayers in her or his jurisdiction. A tax officer I spoke with describes the system as "[one person with] one bag, one receipt book, one document. [He] gives people a receipt if they pay and gives people a ticket if they refuse to pay. Just very simple" for taxpayers.[77] In rural areas the village committee, aided with records, and in urban areas the subdistrict administrative office (*jiedao banshichu*) have this role. Under this system developed in the 1950s, there was no division of labor and no check on the tax officer's power. It was easy to administer, low cost, and flexible. But taxpayers tried to bribe tax officers with varying degrees of success. The "personal relationship tax" (关系税) and "favor tax" (人情税) were very common. Citizens who bribed tax officers received various exemptions, and tax revenue share of GDP was quite low.[78] Prior to 1994, tax administrations tried to minimize tax evasion by frequently switching the tax collectors to different jurisdictions. This raised the cost of bribing taxpayers and discouraged familiarity. It also set rules and regulations for tax officers. But these rules were hard to enforce.

Market reform in the late 1980s led to emergence of many small and medium-sized enterprises, which essentially made the system unworkable. Mr. Zhang of Wenzhou Prefecture in Zhejiang Province described his work as a tax collector in the 1980s to the *China News Weekly* (*zhongguo xinwen zhoukan*). He was responsible for more than seven hundred individual and family workshops (*getihu*) and was supposed to collect taxes from them door to door every day, in amounts ranging from 5 to 7 yuan per household.[79] He began requiring the taxpayers to bring payments to the tax office and to fine people who paid late. The article states:

> The only instrument [Mr. Zhang] had was an abacus, and it signified his prestigious status. . . . [He admitted], "A tax collector was even more powerful than a party secretary; he makes the final decision on how much [exemption he can give to someone] and when [tax was due]." (*China News Weekly* 2011)

Mr. Zhang's innovation was considered significant, and the Tax Administration in Zhejiang Province invited him to speak publicly to other tax collectors about it.

The management of tax administration was similarly chaotic in County Warm River prior to reform. At a special meeting of the county PC in 1992, the deputies generated a list of desired improvements to the Tax Administration:

> First, the tax officials should strengthen studies to improve their ideology and professional ability. If you look around and listen to how people are talking about them, you will agree that the problems of low professional ability and unhealthy/wrong thoughts are serious. Second, we should improve the supervision of tax collection [as law enforcement]. The rampant tax evasion and tax dodging are caused not only by the low taxation consciousness of the taxpayers but also by the problems within tax collection: some tax officers take personal relationships too seriously; they reduce taxes for the taxpayers they know well or do not inspect their tax account. The supervision during the process of tax collection [before, during,

and after] is too weak to deter the taxpayers from tax dodging. The punishment for tax dodging and evasion is unfair; if you know the tax officer or other government officers, you get no punishment. Otherwise, you receive severe punishment. All of these make people unwilling to pay taxes according to the law and cause popular dissent [against the Tax Administration]. Only when we improve supervision can we collect more taxes for the state. Third, some tax officers are too doctrinaire in collecting taxes; they do not consider the feasibility of policies set by higher-level government (for example, [they fail to] collect taxes for tea, watermelons, and silk).[80]

The 1994 TSR separated the responsibility to assess taxes from collection. Subsequent regulation separated inspection from collection and assessment. In this new centralized administration system, according to item 11 of the 1992 Tax Administration Law (*Shuishou zhengshou guanli fa* 税收征收管理法), "tax collection, management, audits, and administrative review should be clearly assigned to different staffs, and they should be separated and mutually monitored."[81] The widespread small taxation offices were abandoned and merged into larger ones, each with a Tax Service Hall where taxpayers pay taxes. The law called on tax-inspection officers to inspect the taxpayers selectively, and the inspection function was strengthened to deter tax evasion. Initially a tax-inspection team (*shuishou jicha dadui*) served as a subunit of the Tax Administration; this was later upgraded to the Tax-Inspection Bureau (*shuishou jicha ju*), the most powerful subunit in the Tax Administration. The leader of the bureau was second only to the head of the Tax Administration, the most powerful figure in the LTB.

A nationwide survey of unregistered taxpayers in 1998 revealed flaws in the system. With no specific tax officer responsible for monitoring a given jurisdiction, information on new enterprises and significant changes to existing enterprises was difficult to collect and report. The survey revealed 1.2 million unregistered taxpayers who owed 1.2 billion yuan in taxes and fines as a result of poor monitoring and enforcement (Ma 2011). Another reform in the early 2000s brought the tax officer back to the enterprises; he could no longer wait for payments in the Tax Service Hall. This tax officer was now responsible for management only: monitoring the tax base, checking daily, cross-validating accounts, and evaluating tax, but not collecting taxes. Tax officers know the taxpayers within their jurisdictions well, which improves monitoring, but this specialization lessens the officer's access to bribes and entrepreneurs' ability to evade taxes by this means.

My fieldwork suggests that administrative reform has curtailed the power of tax officers in relation to pre-1994 levels,[82] but tax officers who allow tax evasion face minimal consequences, which weakens the effectiveness of the institutional design and taxation capacity. Moreover, tax officers are embedded in a network in the local society and will sacrifice the state's revenue for personal benefits when institutional monitoring is not effective. I took a one-hour drive to a private entrepreneur's office with a senior tax officer in County Cold Mountain during which he told me, "Of course, we should work for the state. But what is the state? After all, the state is composed of individuals. Every individual has his interests. Why should I sacrifice my interests to serve the state?" He mentioned that he could not make ends meet on his salary, given the rapidly rising housing price in County Cold Mountain,[83] even though tax officers in the county earn more than most government officers in other government branches (2,000 to 3,000 yuan per month for a junior officer): "We should have some gray income."[84] The tax officer was generally defensive in his responses in the course of this interview, which I took as a signal that taxation is a really sensitive topic.

Assessing tax liability is difficult for many enterprises because of the common use of cash transactions, incomplete or even absent accounting systems, intentional false accounting, and other defects. Large enterprises are easier to monitor since they have better accounting systems, but medium-sized and small enterprises do most transactions in cash, and some do not have any transaction records; others keep records for their own reference and a fake one for the tax officer, with the tax officers' tacit complicity.

The Taxation Bureau requires tax officers to assess the tax liability of small enterprises that do not have accounting systems or for which it is difficult to calculate the profit and costs; thus, no reliable records result in estimation (*heding zhengshou* 核定征收) of taxes. Assessors typically use records considered reliable and base tax liability on them. For example, a restaurant's tax will be calculated based on the tables (and seats) it has, its number of employees, its location, and other factors. A family-owned hotel will be assessed based on the rooms and beds it has, its location, and so on. A family-owned workshop may be assessed based on how many machines it has or its power consumption. Assessors set an industry-specific tax rate for the gross income, if it can be calculated or estimated. For example, a small retail shop should pay 4 percent of its sales income as tax. The advantage of using such an assessment method is that it is easy to implement; the disadvantage is that it gives too much discretionary power to tax officers.

Assessing through auditing is a more advanced method, but it can be applied only to those large and medium-sized enterprises that have good accounting systems. Different types of taxes, such as the VAT, enterprise income tax, IIT, and business tax, are collected based on accounting information. Tax administrations in most regions have developed computer-based technology to assess tax, which reduces tax collectors' discretionary power slightly, but loose management makes the effect small. Enterprises often falsify their accounts. Several accountants I spoke with told me that false accounting is a required skill for an accounting job in most enterprises; they also acknowledge that the tax officers are aware of this. The implementation of tax policies, rationalization of the Taxation Bureau, and constraints on officers' discretionary power have had limited success in creating an effective taxation system.

A very important and powerful tool to improve tax collection is the adoption and upgrading of the Golden Tax Project (GTP, 金税工程), a nationwide VAT-monitoring system using the most advanced IT technology. GTP was first introduced in 1994 to resolve serious tax fraud and evasion problems. After two rounds of upgrading, GTP III currently consists of one network and four software systems. It is legally required for businesses to issue GTP invoices using government-certified tax software (known as the Golden Tax System [GTS]), a centralized monitoring system under the control of the tax authorities to reduce the incidence of fraud. All businesses must issue VAT invoices through the GTS. Invoice information is entered into the GTS and then printed on the preformatted form through a special printer. Taxpayers must submit written applications for invoice printing from the tax authority. This means it is not possible to self-bill. Invoices submitted electronically must be completed via machines bought from the tax authority. GTP was very highly evaluated by many officials and scholars.[85] For example, Xu Shanda, then vice-director of SAT headquarters, claimed that GPT substantially improved monitoring capacity of both taxpayers and tax officials in a five-level hierarchy organization. Xu Shanda (2003) even argued that GTP is a project for further administrative and even political reform.

The Tax-Target System

The tax-target system reminds us of the historical legacy of a planned economy, under which targets were planned at the central and lower-level governments. As the ruling party of a unitary authoritarian state, the CCP has developed an effective nomenklatura system; that is, the party committees select and manage officials of any importance, including those who are elected rather than selected. Under a decentralized system without elections to make officials accountable to the local residents, the party needs an effective way to motivate and monitor its agents at different levels. The Party Committee, with the assistance of the party's Organization Department, evaluates the cadres' performance and punishes or rewards them accordingly. The higher-level party and government set criteria to evaluate the main party and government leaders (or the Party Committee) at the local level, including economic growth, tax revenue, social stability, environmental protection, and population control. The criteria can be adjusted according to the party's political priorities—for example, the CCP has increasingly emphasized social stability and environmental protection in the last decade.[86] After the overall targets are set, they are broken down and assigned to lower-level government organizations or individuals. Organizations and individuals who accomplish or exceed the target will be rewarded both economically (bonus) and politically (better opportunities to be promoted). However, there is neither procedure nor scientific method for setting targets; what matters is the local government leaders' will. The rule of law of taxation is violated by the tax-target system.[87]

Some Chinese scholars at the CCP's Central Compilation and Translation Bureau, a national-level official think tank, call this performance-driven system the pressure-based system (*yalixing tizhi*) (Rong et al. 1998). Based on intensive fieldwork in Xinmi County in Henan Province, Jingben Rong and colleagues describe the pressure-based system as follows:

> To achieve the economic "catch-up" plan and meet the targets set by the higher-level party and government, the county- and township-level political organizations (the party and government as the core) assign these targets, which can be measured quantitatively, to lower-level organizations and individuals, asking them to achieve their targets in a given time. Ability to meet these targets will be rewarded or punished both economically and politically. Some of the targets are so important that if one of them is not met, you get vetoed for promotion [*yipiao foujue*]. (1998, 28)

This pressure-based system also applies to tax administration, called the tax-target system, which is regarded as the worst element of the institution of taxation.[88] In practice, taxes are not collected according to the law (*yifa zhengshui*) or tax liability but according to tax targets set by tax bureaus' supervisors. All the tax-collection agents (tax office and tax officials) have specific targets (*shuishou renwu*), which normally keep increasing at some specific rate.

In the CCP's cadre management system, economic development and taxation are two important, if not the most important, indicators of cadre evaluation. Given that officials tend to overreport the GDP growth rate, tax revenue is a more reliable indicator of growth (Lü and Landry 2014). Tax revenue is also important not only because it reflects economic performance but also because it is the money that can be used by local government. Therefore, meeting the taxation target is an important political task for both tax officials and other government officials. The higher-level tax bureau and county government set specific tax targets for both the county SAT office and LTB. Although the tax bureaus are vertically managed, county governments still try to intervene and are effective in most cases. Since county governments do not have the power to appoint and supervise tax bureau directors, a common method to motivate the tax bureaus to collect more taxes (i.e., by setting a higher tax target) is to share the "extra" taxes with the tax bureau.[89] Another reason that tax officials cooperate with local government is that tax bureau officers live in the county and may have many chances to get favors from the county government. Therefore, they protect their relationships. As County D's LTB director told me, "I want my kid to go to the best primary school [later, the best high school] there; how can I reject the county head's requirement? It [more taxes] is good for both the LTB and county government."[90] A tax officer in County Cold Mountain (a neighbor of County D) said, "My daughter will graduate from college very soon; I am thinking about getting a job for her in some school in the county. I need to find someone [who is powerful enough in the county] to help me." He admits the formal rules are typically sacrificed for personal relationships: "After all, the state is composed of real people [cadres]; the state is the people. So, after all, we are working for these people."[91]

After the supervisors set the target, the tax bureaus set targets for their branches and, later on, for every tax officer. In most counties, even the Tax-Inspection Bureau has a target.[92] But the Tax-Inspection Bureau of County Warm River in Zhejiang does not have targets because the county government wants to build what two different tax officers described as an "enterprise-friendly environment."[93] The bureau director is responsible to his supervisors for the overall performance of the bureau and sets targets for his staff. How bureaus determine tax targets is crucial and makes a difference for long-term development trajectories. Other things being equal, if a county can keep the tax-target growth rate lower than the economic growth rate, local economic development will be sustainable. If the tax-target growth rate is higher than the economic growth rate, this will harm the local economy.

The tax-target system works if the tax target (or tax growth rate) keeps pace with economic growth, which, fortunately, has been the case for most regions in China for the last thirty years.[94] However, since most local governments want the tax growth rate to stay constant or increase to cover increasing public expenditure, any economic fluctuation will bring hard times for enterprises in regard to both their economic performance and their tax burden. Besides overreporting, many local governments deal with it by collecting tax revenue in advance (预征税款) and lending fiscal funds to organizational taxpayers (税收空转). Some local governments even borrow money to meet their tax target (借款交税) or just purchase tax (买税) from other regions to meet their target.[95]

Many local governments have collected taxes in advance in hard times. The *Economic Observation* (*Jingji guancha*, a weekly newspaper and one of three national leading newspapers on economic and financial issues) reported in 2009:

> On September 9, 2009, a local newspaper in Ouhai County of Wenzhou [which is famous for the swift rise of a private economy after reform] published the county LTB's "List of Tax Arrears Enterprises." The highest amount is 0.5 million yuan (USD 74,000), and the lowest is only 54 yuan (USD 8). This list signals that the tax bureaus are serious about improving tax collection in this era of economic crisis, and it is just a good example of a nationwide movement of improving tax collection.
>
> Some presidents of trade associations [also business leaders] in Wenzhou express concern about increased taxes when the economy is declining, while the government says the increased tax growth rate is an indicator of economic recovery. The enterprises are required to self-check and report first and will be inspected by the tax bureau if they don't meet the bureaus' expectation. (Z. Chen 2009)

Two government officers mentioned to me that the tax bureaus of County Warm River also required the enterprises to pay much more in taxes in 2009 than in 2008 because otherwise the economic crises would threaten their tax targets. As one said, "The enterprises must pay the extra taxes because they had benefited from the loose tax-collection practices in the past years [that is, the tax officers tolerated their tax evasion]. Now it's time for them to pay back and help the tax officers [meet the tax target]. They cannot complain but must comply."[96]

In County Cold Mountain and County D, Shanxi Province, in which 70 percent of taxes come from coal mining, the situation was even worse in 2009 and 2010 because of the impact of economic decline and the provincial government's closure and merging of coal mines in both counties. The economy is declining to a great degree, one tax officer complained:

> Two years ago, if you came to this county, you saw long lines of heavy trucks waiting for the coal and running on the road. But now, [you can see] very few of them. Most small and medium coal mines are closed; the price of coal also decreased because of the economic decline. In the last few years, almost all the taxes come from coal in my jurisdiction. But there is only one coal mine still operating now. How can I increase tax revenue?[97]

This informant did not explain why the county LTB can still achieve the tax target; he just said he can do nothing but improve monitoring of other small businesses, which is useless for meeting the target.[98] The director of the county LTB told me how his officers would achieve the target:

> I moved to County D from a neighbor county in late 2008 [when the provincewide movement to rectify corruption in the coal-mining industry started]. Then, according to the provincial government's requirement to rectify the corruption and tax evasion by coal mining, we started a comprehensive inspection of all coal mines. My target is about 80 million yuan, but it ended with 180 million. Of course, I would not collect all of them in 2009; I asked the big coal-mine bosses to keep the money and pay it later and collected those from the small ones since they would be closed off [and don't want to pay] soon. That's how we met the tax target last year and this year, but I don't know how we can meet the target for

the next year. You know, we should keep a tax growth rate around 25 percent every year.[99]

A tax official in County Warm River told me that after several years of economic downturn, the county SAT and LTB are having difficulty meeting the tax targets. "We have some tax reservoir, just as the water reservoir that saves water on rainy days and is used for dry days. But I have to admit that we have no more water reserved in the reservoir this year." As a result, they were forced to change the tax-assessment method for some industries, which helped them meet the target last year.[100]

The National Audit Office reports that because of the great discretional power of tax bureaus, tax evasion is rampant: in an audit for 2007–2008, 54 percent of taxes from 214 enterprises in eleven provinces were delayed. Another sixty-two county SAT offices in thirteen provinces pretaxed and overtaxed 23.4 billion yuan from 169 enterprises to meet the tax target. The tax-break policies were incorrectly implemented and caused a 36.31 billion yuan tax loss as well as other problems (J. Liu 2008).

Under the regional economic competition, overreporting tax revenue to meet or exceed the tax target is another tactic to cheat the higher-level government, referred to as "local fiscal budgetary receipts fulfilled by fabricated taxes" (*shuishou kongzhuan*) (Sun and Yu 1999; Tan and Zhou 2009). A local government borrows money from the bank or even the private sector to pay extra taxes to the LTB, which are then submitted to the Bureau of Finance. The LTB reports the real tax and this borrowed "tax" to the higher-level government and then pays interest to the borrower. Sometimes the local government pays high interest rates (usury rates, which could be ten or even one hundred times more than the official interest rate). "The powerful officials and those well-connected borrowers benefit substantially from this practice, at the cost of the government and taxpayers," a tax officer in Jiangsu Province told me at a conference held in Beijing.[101]

Recent Reforms

The CCP is very adaptive and flexible (Heilmann and Perry 2011); it responds to changing environments, although there are some lags. Some of the recent reforms during 2018 to 2020 include the merger of the SAT and LTB, tax reduction, and central-local fiscal-relationship readjustment.

A major reform is merging the SAT and LTB into the new SAT and moving SAT offices at local levels under the dual leadership of SAT headquarters (with more influence) and local government.[102] Though it has been implemented for only a short time, the merge has achieved many direct positive effects, including improved efficiency through organizational reform and integration, reduction of transactional costs for taxpayers, and improved autonomy from local government (L. Yu 2018).[103]

With the establishment of a new SAT, collection for the social security fund was also assigned to it as a new task to improve collection. Compared to bureaus of human resources and social security administration at different levels, the SAT has much more ability to collect fees. But the reform was implemented at the wrong time; with economic slowdown, many enterprises complained that the rising social security burdens would drive them to bankruptcy. The central government responded by reducing the social security rate as part of its program of reducing taxes and fees.

Responding to the high tax and nontax burdens for private enterprises, referred to as the "death tax rate" by some scholars and private entrepreneurs (*Best China News* 2016); the US tax cut; and economic slowdown from the trade war between China and the United States, the central government requested several rounds of reduction in taxes and fees (减税降费) and reduction in structural taxes (结构性减税) to stimulate the economy.[104] In 2019, the central government requested tax and fee reduction of 2 trillion yuan: 1.3 trillion for 2018 and 1 trillion for 2017.[105] In response to the problem of local governments' unmatched fiscal capacity and obligations, the central government took on some expenditure obligations and redivided the VAT, the most important tax, between the central and local governments in October 2019. Local government's share of the VAT increased from 25 percent to 50 percent, which may improve its fiscal capability to meet expenditure obligations.

All these reforms and policy adjustments may have long-term effects, including stimulating economic growth, institutionalizing taxation administration, tightening budgetary constraints for local governments, and reducing local governments' discretionary power of investment recruitment, and therefore change the intergovernmental fiscal relationship, but it is too early to evaluate these effects.

CHAPTER 3

Fiscal Decentralization, Bureaucratization, and Economic Growth

> Taxes not only helped to create the state. They helped to form it. . . . If the finances have created and partly formed the modern state, so now the state on its part forms them and enlarges them—deep into the flesh of the private economy.
> —Joseph Schumpeter, "The Crisis of the Tax State"

> The history of state revenue production is the history of the evolution of the state.
> —Margaret Levi, *Of Rule and Revenue*

> A constitutional king, whenever he is in agreement with a socially important part of the governed, very frequently exerts a greater influence upon the course of administration than does the absolute monarch since he can control the experts better because of the at least relatively public character of criticism, whereas the absolute monarch is dependent for information solely upon the bureaucracy.
> —Max Weber, *Economy and Society*

In early March 1996, County Warm River's party secretary and the PC Standing Committee's director visited two enterprises in the county. The first, an SOE, paid 2 million yuan in taxes in 1995, and the second, a township-owned TVE, had paid 5.5 million. The managers presented reports on their achievements and challenges the businesses faced in a changing market environment. Afterward, the county's leaders asked government bureaus to solve some of the problems the enterprises faced. Later on, the county Party Committee established a "major leader contact enterprise" system in which such meetings would be regular and the major political leaders would help selected large enterprises solve problems.[1]

Nineteen years later, in late August 2015, County Warm River's government head spent two afternoons visiting twelve of the county's top hundred major taxpayers (*nashui baiqianghu*). Most were private enterprises doing business in the county's industrial park. He listened to the entrepreneurs' suggestions and comments concerning policy, their various complaints, and the difficulties they encountered. He emphasized that talents and technology are the most important resources for industrial upgrading and thanked them for their diligence. He took their feedback for further discussion with his colleagues and in some cases required government bureaus to make changes to address their problems immediately.[2]

Such meetings occur in most counties in China, and reports of them frequently appear in Chinese media, indicating that local governments are working hard to promote regional economic growth. They contrast starkly with reports made in the 1970s, when Revolutionary Committee directors, who replaced party secretaries during the Cultural Revolution, were busy with the class struggle and local governments treated private entrepreneurs as class enemies. The state openly disregarded private property rights from the mid-1950s to the late 1970s and had no legal provision to protect them until 2004.[3] When Deng Xiaoping began the reform and opening up in the late 1970s, Chinese citizens still had vivid memories of the state seizing personal belongings of the rich, which marked them as class enemies, and sometimes beating them. Party and government officials directly controlled the public budget on investment, public enterprises, and state-owned banks, which gave them a vested interest in the planned economy and a reason to block market reform.[4] The FCS, which gradually evolved in the early 1980s, changed local officials' incentives by empowering them with residual claim rights. This led local governments to implement economic reforms (Oi 1992; Blecher and Shue 1996). However, the FCS also further fragmented the bureaucratic system by decentralizing fiscal resources (Lieberthal 1992).

Charles Fairbanks finds that the Russian government became "feudalized" in the early 1990s because rapidly decreased state revenue could not pay government officials enough salary, so they had to find income from other sources:[5] "Almost every Russian official has both an impersonal bureaucratic role and a personal profitmaking role; almost every Russian official serves and profits from two masters" (1999, 49). Following Fairbanks, Qiang Li (2001) describes China's bureaucratization in 1990s as "refeudalization": Government agencies needed to gather revenue and therefore used public power to collect different types of taxes, fines, and fees; they selectively provided those public services for which they could charge fees and crowded out private-market actors for those services. Government became predatory rather than a public organization that provided public services.

Extensive academic discussion has addressed how the CCP worked to resolve the agent-discipline problem and elicited citizens' cooperation for investment; why and how government-business relationships have changed; how China initiated market transition and achieved rapid economic growth; and specifically, the FCS's impact on economic growth. However, because the FCS's impact on bureaucratization has been little studied, this chapter and the next add further explanation. I argue that regional tax competition plays an important role in motivating local governments to discipline predatory government agents (as a process of bureaucratization) and improve public services. However, it depends on asset mobility of the region's major industries. My argument has both a historical and a cross-regional dimension. This chapter focuses on the historical dimension by reexamining fiscal federalism theory with a focus on the coevolution of the market and modern bureaucracy. I study County Warm River in detail to process-trace the evolution of asset mobility (as marketization) and its impact on bureaucratization. Chapter 4 presents the cross-regional comparison.

Coevolution of Market and Bureaucracy

While scholars disagree about whether China has a system of fiscal federalism, they agree that its highly centralized political system creates regional economic competition. While some call it a "promotion tournament" (e.g., Li and Zhou 2005; L. Zhou 2007, 36), Chenggang Xu describes the Chinese political system as "regionally decentralized authoritarianism" in which political centralization combines with economic regional decentralization and characterizes this system thus:

> On the one hand, the national government's control is substantial in that the Chinese political and personnel governance structure has been highly centralized. Subnational government officials are appointed from above, and the appointment and promotion of subnational government officials serve as powerful instruments for the national government to induce regional officials to follow the cen-

tral government's policies. . . . On the other hand, the governance of the national economy is delegated to subnational governments. Regional economies (provinces, municipalities, and counties) are relatively self-contained, and subnational governments have overall responsibility for initiating and coordinating reforms, providing public services, and making and enforcing laws within their jurisdictions. (2010, 1078)

State rebuilding happens under regionally decentralized authoritarianism, which generates a relatively well-disciplined Weberian bureaucracy in some regions, a crucial condition for economic growth. Bureaucratization includes three attributes: fiscal, functional, and personnel, but the first two are the most important. Both Max Weber (1968) and Norbert Elias (1982) emphasize the importance of centralization of taxation power as a key characteristic of modern states that distinguishes them from feudalism. Modern bureaucratization requires revenue to pay government officials to separate public office from private gains and officials from the means of administration, whereas in a feudal administration key administrators control the means of administration and patrimonialism is associated with benefices.[6] Rapidly increasing tax revenue based on rapid economic growth has made modern bureaucracy possible in some regions since the early 2000s.[7] The state's functional separation from the market and society is very important for a post-totalitarian state under which the boundaries of state and society were blurred and the market barely existed.[8] As marketization and industrialization proceed, bureaucratization typically involves functional division among government organizations (what modernization theory terms "differentiation"), while being effectively monitored and coordinated by political leaders. Personnel bureaucratization involves requiring job candidates to take qualification exams to test their skills and uses merit-based promotion. Based on the changes in these three aspects of bureaucratization, which occurred with fiscal system reform, I divide China's process of bureaucratization into three stages, shown in table 3.1: command administration, refeudalization, and modern bureaucracy.

Table 3.1 points out that the bureaucracy system became disciplined after the late 1990s, but why and how did it happen? Dali Yang (2004) provides a full description of the distinction between the refeudalization stage and the modern bureaucracy from a top-down perspective but does not explain how it happens. Based on a study of investment recruitment bureaus in three Chinese cities, Yuen Yuen Ang proposes a coevolutionary theory of the development of Weberian bureaucracy and capitalist markets. Specifically, in China, she writes, "It is the adaptive refashioning of preexisting 'weak' institutions that first built markets. Weberian bureaucracies serve to preserve markets" (Ang 2017, 283). Capturing the "reciprocal" dimension, the coevolutionary theory provides a good explanation of bureaucratic and market development. However, I find that this explanation has some pitfalls, mostly because of Ang's limited horizon: she focuses on investment promotion/recruitment, which creates three key weaknesses. First, modern bureaucracy has many legal-rational attributes, such as eradication of corruption, functional specialization, reliance on technical expertise, and meritocratic recruitment, all of which Ang discusses. However, equally important, it also refers to separation of public office from private gains. While the FCS and local state corporatism promoted rural industrialization, they harmed or even destroyed the bureaucratic system by pushing local officers to raise funds for the bureaucracy's operation and salaries. Second, it neglects the fiscal dynamic of the bureaucratization process, which Weber (1968) and Elias (1982) credit for

Table 3.1. Stages of bureaucratization

	Fiscal	Functional	Personnel
Before 1980: command administration	Unitary remittance and unitary expenditure; very limited revenue	Undifferentiated: no boundary between government, enterprises, and social organizations	No recruitment exam, revolutionaries
1980–mid-1990s: refeudalization	Fiscal contracting: tax farming and extra-budgetary fund, very limited public services; increased revenue	Separation of government from enterprises to some degree, local governments as corporations, predatory behaviors	No recruitment exam, patron-clientelism; recruiting some educated people to government; overstaffed with temporary workers
Mid-1990s–present: modern bureaucracy	Tax-sharing system, toward budgetary management, more public services	Further separation of government from enterprises, more differentiated	Recruitment exam; maintaining presence of temporary workers

the transition from patrimonialism to a modern bureaucracy. Third, Ang uses geography, entrepreneurial histories, and natural resources to explain local variations. I find that asset mobility (also a dynamic and evolving object) plays a fundamental role, but it is not limited to natural resources.[9]

No market except the black market existed under socialism. While studies of transitional economies focus on protection of private property rights and privatization, price liberalization, contract and transactional costs, all of which are crucial for building a market, asset mobility is neglected in most studies, especially as the intermediate variable. Although most studies understand asset mobility as physical characteristics, under transitional economies, it is also shaped by institutions.[10] Government regulations and restrictions, including but not limited to trade barriers, industry access, and market access, also determine asset mobility. Therefore, asset mobility's institutional characteristics reflect well the process of marketization.

By reviewing the economic history of County Warm River since 1978, this chapter develops a revised coevolutionary model of bureaucracy and market as illustrated in figure 3.1, based on the idea of mutual transformation, which is

> the recursive relationship between state and society, the mutually transforming interactions between components of the state and other social forces. Conflicts flare up over specific thrusts and parries: attempts by the state to increase tax collection, efforts by local figures to gain control over particular state offices and resources, initiatives by state agencies to regulate certain behavior, attempts by local strongmen to extend the area of their own dominance, and more. The struggles that follow in the scattered settings end up reshaping both the state and the other social forces. (Migdal 2001, 100)

In the next section, I describe and analyze the economic history of County Warm River in Zhejiang Province. I describe three stages to make a within-case comparison to examine the coevolution of bureaucracy and market. The following discussions describe the effects of different fiscal systems on local governments' incentives and constraints, which also influence asset mobility. I present comparative case studies in chapter 4 and a quantitative study in chapter 6 to explain regional variations and test the external validity of the argument.

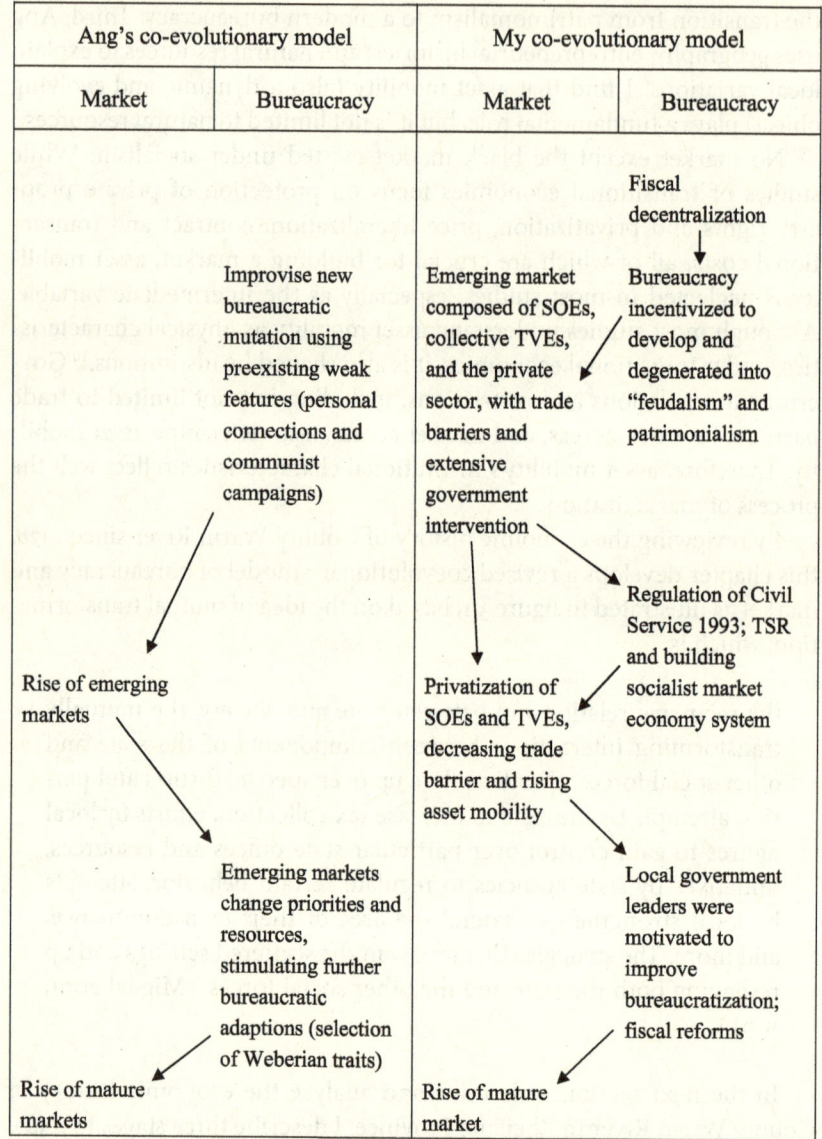

Figure 3.1. Coevolution of the bureaucracy and market.

Three Stages of Coevolution in County Warm River

This section briefly reviews County Warm River's market transition and economic development over the last forty years. Table 3.2 outlines the three major stages in which the taxation system interacted with asset mobility, shaped the government's influence in promoting (or blocking) economic development, and played a role in the coevolution of market and bureaucracy.

The county government employed different strategies to promote economic development and deal with the agent-discipline and cooperation

Table 3.2. Dividing the case into three stages

Time/policy period	Industry	Asset mobility	Government's development strategy	Private entrepreneurs' bargaining power	Bureaucratization
Stage one: early 1980s to 1990s	From agriculture to light industry	Low to medium	Monopolize the market and build collectively owned enterprises; set market barriers for different regions	Medium	Feudalism and patrimonialism
Stage two: after mid-1990s	From agriculture to light industry	High	Keep capital within the jurisdiction and invite outside investment by creating good investment environment	High	Emergence of modern bureaucracy
Stage three: after mid-2000	Rise of real estate industry; light industry keeps growing	Low	Invite investment; government-led investment based on land finance	Medium	Some decline of modern bureaucracy

problems. In stage one (1980 to mid-1990s), under the FCS, the government began by directly establishing collective enterprises. At this point it acted both developmentally (running TVEs) and predatorily (toward private enterprises). Asset mobility was low at the beginning because the trade barriers set by laws and policies made goods and production factors difficult to move. In the mid-1980s, the county government began to recognize that keeping and encouraging local private investment would foster long-term economic development without causing a tax loss in the short term, because the private sector was almost unable to tax. Thus, the county government started to discipline the predatory government bureaus. It also started to build industrial development parks (工业开发区) to generate good business environments for private enterprises. However, these efforts were not systematically designed and were badly implemented.

In stage two, an incomplete market economy emerged gradually because the central government initiated TSR and other market-oriented reforms. Asset mobility became higher thanks to reduced trade barriers.[11] The county government therefore switched development strategies. Instead of the direct operation of enterprises, it began building a good business environment to keep local investment and attract outside investment. The county government took more effective measures to generate a positive business environment that could compete with that in other regions. The central government's Temporary Regulation for State Civil Service issued in 1993, along with increased regional competition, brought about significantly improved economic development, and fiscal revenue income made it possible to promote bureaucratization, which in turn promoted marketization.

Stage three began in the mid-2000s as the local government began to rely on land-related revenue, including land-transfer fees, real estate industry taxes and fees, and land finance. Asset mobility decreased as a result, and the agent-discipline problem worsened to some degree. However, in County Warm River, institutionalization efforts prevented this windfall revenue from causing much decline in bureaucratization, unlike a similar change in resource-abundant countries after World War II (Smith 2007).

Stage One: Government as Corporation

In the early 1980s, County Warm River was an agricultural county with a few medium-sized SOEs that produced textiles and gears. The FCS imposed fiscal pressure on the county government to feed employees and meet unfunded obligations.[12] Rural industrialization (re)started nationwide, and County Warm River encouraged the rise of TVEs, the major agent of rural industrialization at the time, in the county. As in many other counties, the county government, its bureaus,[13] township governments and villages, and even public hospitals and schools (all hospitals and schools were public at the time) created their own enterprises. By 1987, County Warm River's famous TVEs included a lock-making factory, a silk factory, a cording factory, a cigarette factory, a yellow-wine-bottling plant, and a chemical fertilizer factory. County government bureaus owned the bulk of them, and township governments owned the smaller ones.

As many other studies of TVEs have documented,[14] the government had several goals in building them, but promoting economic development and increasing fiscal revenue were chief among them. Building new enterprises can promote economic development in two ways. First, investment is an important part of GDP and has a multiplier effect.[15] Second, new enterprises further economic growth by creating new demand. Some county TVEs in this period competed with private enterprises—these produced labor-intensive products such as locks and cording and silk products, which require sericulture—while others had government-imposed monopolies. Besides paying taxes, these enterprises served as the "private coffer" of local government and its bureaus, which were short of fiscal resources under the FCS.

Monopolizing the cigarette, wine, and fertilizer industries allowed the government to gain easy revenue by barring competition from the private sector and TVEs from neighboring counties.[16] These industries had low barriers of technology and capital, high sales tax rates, and government-controlled stores to support them.[17] Market monopolization made it easy to exclude external competing products that would be hard to tax.[18] County Warm River's neighboring local governments also produced cigarettes, wine, and fertilizers, but they could not legally sell them in County Warm River, and vice versa.

In addition to market regulatory power that permitted them to exclude other providers from certain industries, some powerful government bureaus could get raw materials at a price much lower than the market price for their enterprises under the dual-track price system.[19] Some government-owned enterprises could carry out speculation by forcing private enterprises through regulations to buy low-quality products at higher prices sold by companies owned by the officials or their family members and relatives: "If you don't buy these products, you will have trouble when you [are] dealing with these powerful bureaus."[20] Other bureaus lacked market regulation power and were, therefore, unable to monopolize industries. Most of the monopolized TVEs were badly managed. While they contributed to government revenue, they caused a lot of problems for a functioning market. A member of the county PC Standing Committee recognized these problems in a 1991 meeting:

> We should readjust [整顿] the economic order and screen and rectify [清理] various kinds of companies according to the central government's policies. We also should punish the illegal companies. As we saw in the audit report yesterday, the county's Economic and Technology Cooperative Company made some illegal speculations: 633.8 tons of cement were sold at a price of 156 yuan per ton instead of 112 (the planned economy price), diesel at 1,375 yuan per ton instead of 970. And this company had a tax exemption for the last few years (and I don't know why!). There are other companies doing similarly illegal business, but only this one has been punished. All of them are government-speculation companies [官倒] and governmental enterprises [官商]. We should build up and strengthen the audit system and the accounting system (to supervise these companies); otherwise, many cadres will be corrupted.[21]

At the same meeting, another Standing Committee member complained of corruption among companies owned by government officials or their relatives: private enterprises that did not purchase from these companies would experience differential treatment by the officials who owned or ran them. Self-enrichment was not the only incentive; government bureaus had tax targets. Once they met those targets, they would have to share the excess with the county government, but some of the money stayed with the bureau, which might use it without monitoring. Classic forms of local state corporatism and the local developmental state also applied, but predatory government bureaus that used TVEs to generate rent for both the bureau and the officials that worked in it were more prevalent in County Warm River in the 1980s.

The county's market became more competitive in the early 1990s as a greater number of private and individual enterprises began to compete with the collective TVEs. Privately owned retail outlets also emerged. The once monopolizing Supply and Marketing Cooperative (供销合作社)

gradually lost its market share and started to contract out and even close some of its branches in the township and villages beginning in the early 1990s. Government monopolies slipped into market competition.[22]

The liberalization of the market also made it more difficult for collective TVEs to survive. Born into a transitional economy with an underdeveloped market and too much state involvement, collective TVEs suffered many of the same problems as SOEs. Like their SOE cousins, many TVEs were inefficient and had distorted both the managers' and workers' incentive structures, insider control, overextraction (including fees, surtaxes, and government charges) by the government (both as tax collector and owner), and cronyism. Similar to the bankruptcy and subsequent privatization of the county's SOEs in the late 1990s, which government subsidies could not prevent, TVEs began to lose money. They were no longer able to function as cash cows for the local government and its organs.

Crony capitalism was a particularly serious problem: Government bureaus, as investors, appointed their cadres and/or their family members and relatives (七大姑八大姨) to important positions in the TVEs. Many of these appointees lacked the skills or knowledge required to run an enterprise. While the owners of private enterprises that competed with them also lacked good education or professional training, they had at least strong incentives to make the enterprises profitable. TVE managers and employees were more interested in sharing rents generated from their regulatory power or spending on their consumption and entertainment than working hard to make the business succeed. Some of them even claimed the collectively owned enterprises as their own property and took what they wanted. As one county PC Standing Committee member put it:

> In order to readjust the economic order, the county [party and government] leaders should take responsibility and establish a leading group [*lingdao xiaozu*] to deal with it. The conflation of government and business is bad for building a clean government. But now we have many government bureaus building their own enterprises, with very chaotic personal management, staffed with wives and sisters-in-law. These enterprises make plenty of profit by transferring the within-system material into out-system material.[23] They distribute these extra profits by giving employees luxurious bonuses and gifts to improve their quality of life. Besides, their average monthly salary is 380 yuan [more than a government official or high school teacher's salary].... They are turning the government

money into personal benefits! . . . What I will say is the collectively owned [and some state-owned] enterprises are becoming private enterprises; maybe they will change the ownership [make it their own] soon.[24]

Like private enterprises, collective TVEs also tried to evade taxes, but only to benefit the insiders (especially the managers) rather than the enterprise and its owner.

Some collective TVEs went bankrupt in the mid-1990s, while others were privatized. Those in competitive industries became profitable after privatization. They retained their competitive advantages because of their larger size, better equipment, and market access. The lock-making and cording industries would become two of County Warm River's four major industries.[25] Those that had been state monopolies simply went bankrupt, as they had no ability to compete without barring competition by the government. However, the county economy grew rapidly, contributing to tax revenues. Table 3.3 compares the growth rate of county government bureau-owned TVEs with rural private enterprises in both 1986 and 1992. County bureau-owned TVEs did not perform as well as private enterprises; some even declined. The private sector accounted for 65 percent of the county's industry production in 1992, up from 54 percent six years earlier.

The decline of collectively owned TVEs and the rapid emergence of private enterprises changed the county government's tax base, with private enterprises becoming the new major tax sources. The county government

Table 3.3. Industry output and growth rate

	1986 (%) (10,000 yuan)	1992 (%) (10,000 yuan)
Total	23,510 (44.0)	116,000 (15.7)
Enterprises of the Bureau of Economics and Trade	5,528 (14.9)	3,500 (0)
Enterprises of the Bureau of Fiscal and Trade	1,906 (14.3)	19,000 (12.8)
Enterprises of the Bureau of Second Light Industry	3,176 (23.6)	17,500 (21.0)
Rural (private) enterprises	12,675 (79.7)	75,000 (18.0)
Township enterprises		27,800 (26.9)

Source: County Warm River's PC's documents 1992.
Note: Real data for 1992 are not available; the table reflects government planned data, which usually occurs.

Fiscal Decentralization, Bureaucratization, and Economic Growth 105

thus faced a dilemma during the early 1990s: Taxing too heavily would hinder private enterprises' ability to make profits, which might prompt them to cease operations or move to a neighboring county with lower tax rates. This would slow down economic growth and result in the long-term loss of tax revenue. But letting enterprises evade taxes would result in not meeting the tax target. One county PC Standing Committee member expressed this dilemma clearly:

> The privately or individually owned businesses have a hard time making money. Most of their profits come from tax evasion [偷税] and tax dodging [漏税]. But at the same time, they have a headache of paying very heavy arbitrary charges and "donations" [to other government bureaus]. We need to take action and reorganize the tax administration to increase tax revenue. We need to make the enterprises pay taxes according to the law. The first thing we need to do is to begin auditing the enterprise account and taxes, to rectify improper economic behaviors. When we collect taxes, we need to balance two things: don't tax too heavily [i.e., strictly follow the law] to make the enterprises unable to make a profit, but also don't tax too lightly. We need to set up some private entrepreneur models that pay taxes actively [to reward them] and that violate tax law [to punish them]. No accommodations for government policies are allowed, and everyone is equal before the law. The key for meeting the annual tax target is that we should have clean cadres [tax officers] and strengthen the ideological and thought work [思想政治工作] to prevent them from corrupt behavior.[26]

The county government set high tax rates for some industries in the late 1980s, including the county's clothing industry, which was well developed at that time and had a nationwide reputation. Because of government hostile policies toward private enterprise and lack of capital,[27] most cloth-manufacturing "companies" were family workshops and were relatively easy to move. The county government started to tax the clothing industry heavily; the Bureau of Commerce and Industry Administration (Gongshang guanliju) and other bureaus also started to collect more fees and fines. As a result, the overall tax and nontax burden was so high that many enterprises moved to neighboring counties where tax rates were much lower. Others moved their factories to another province to be close to their market, which reduced transportation costs significantly in a country with an underdeveloped transportation system. The county government recognized that it was bleeding tax revenue, so it lowered its tax rate—a practice referred to as "letting in water to raise the fish" (放水养鱼). It set the lowest rates for industries new to the county, such as glass artwork, with relatively low tax rates for the industries with a firm foothold in the county. Private enterprises began to return or reversed their plans to depart, and the county's revenues from private enterprises began to grow in the late 1980s and early 1990s.

Low tax rates were only one aspect of the "letting in water" policy. The county PC held several meetings at which they encouraged private-entrepreneur deputies to air their concerns about doing business in the county. The deputies complained that villagers were picketing their businesses, charging them with polluting the land, water, or air with harmful chemicals and/or noise. They said that construction companies had threatened to block their projects and harass their workers if they did not receive factory construction contracts and that they offered low quality at a high price. The county government provided police protection, as did a countywide movement to combat harassment of private enterprises. In 1994 the county created several industry zones and put them in special jurisdictions to prevent harassment.

Private entrepreneurs also asked the PC for protection from the government itself in the late 1980s. Because of the FCS, the local government bureaus needed to find their own income resources to make state and county tax targets and cover their own costs. They were driven to extract fiscal resources from the emerging market economy through fees, surtaxes, and fines and by running some enterprises themselves to make profits. These government bureaus met their revenue targets with different degrees of success: the bureaus with regulatory power were the most successful, while those without regulatory power could not even pay staff salaries.[28] Besides building their own collective TVEs and using their regulatory power to make money, these bureaus took every opportunity to collect different types of fees, surtaxes, and fines. A county PC Standing Committee member complained:

> The central government repeatedly orders the local governments to stop all the arbitrary charges, but it seems no one is listening to it. To meet their revenue targets [or raise additional funds], some government bureaus keep on harassing the enterprises for money. Some of them even get support from certain county leaders, which makes their arbitrary charges hard to avoid. All

of these add to the enterprises' fiscal burden and reduce their profits. In the last eight months, the county's department store has paid twelve types of charges, with an amount of 21,398 yuan, or 4.3 percent of its profit. Another company's charge is higher than its profit! The enterprises can't stand so many types of heavy charges.[29]

The police department and its police stations across the county received many critiques about their predatory behavior and low incentive to provide for the public good (the crucial task for a night-watchman state: enforcement of law and social order). Many problems were pointed out by county PC deputies in an "examination of law enforcement" (执法检查):[30] ineffective in deterring criminals and enforcing judgments, very serious problems in charging fines and fees, frequent cases of the police violating the law and regulations, bad management of unofficial policemen (联防队),[31] and underfunded and badly equipped police stations.[32] This is just one case; in the PC documents, we can see that most government bureaus had similar problems of charging fines and fees, which were kept in their extra-budgetary account (小金库).

To deal with predatory government bureaus, the county PC and government decided to create an official Association for Protecting Private Enterprises in the early 1990s. The party's Commission of Discipline and Inspection (CDI) secretary was appointed president of the association, with some members of the board of directors from related government bureaus (such as the Tax Administration, Administration of Industry and Commerce [AIC], and the prosecutor) and some large enterprises (规模以上企业).[33] This official association asked its private-enterprise members to report any abuse (unreasonable charges) they faced, and the association would investigate and possibly correct it. The association was the earliest such organization in Zhejiang Province, according to a retired CDI cadre. It achieved some degree of success in circumscribing the government bureaus' predatory behavior.[34]

The county government also made great efforts to help enterprises grow and strengthen, recognizing that large enterprises play an important role in upgrading industry and are easier to tax than smaller ones. Enterprises that had over 5 million yuan in annual sales were regarded as large enterprises and received special attention and greater access than small and medium-sized enterprises to cheap land, tax breaks, and bank loans, as well as political titles for the owners. As the 1994 county government annual report outlined it:

If the TVEs get developed well, then we can get a revenue increase. Therefore, we need to focus on the important products and leading enterprises to help them expand and upgrade. Both the County Warm River and township government should serve the enterprises well and help them solve all difficulties.

One county PC Standing Committee member admitted that the county government "cares too much for the large enterprises [锦上添花, icing on the cake] but too little for the small ones [雪中送炭, to lend them a hand in hard times]."[35] In a light-industry county where asset mobility is high, large enterprises get special representation channels to gain access to specific government help (including industry policies, land, and bank loans), while small and medium-sized enterprises get relatively low tax rates but no specific channels of representation. The county government has good reason to do this since most of the tax revenue comes from the larger enterprises.

As do any kind of government policies, implementation of policies created to encourage government bureaus to support larger private enterprises came with discretionary power, which widens the officials' opportunities to abuse their power. Some enterprises ineligible for tax breaks nonetheless received tax breaks if they treated tax officers to banquets, gifts, or other bribes. Eligible enterprises were also denied breaks if they failed to please the tax officers.

To summarize, given the institutional barriers, asset mobility was low in the 1980s, and the government built enterprises directly and treated private enterprises relatively poorly (taxing them highly or preventing them from entering certain markets). Government bureaus, especially those relevant to the market and industry, acted predatorily both by establishing TVEs as monopolies and victimizing private and individual enterprises, all of which made the market a highly distorted one.

While the market was underdeveloped, we also find a refeudalized state that required government agents to collect different sources of revenue. Eager to raise more fiscal revenue to feed government officials and other public employees,[36] the county government delegated revenue-collecting power to its branches and township governments. Tax revenue under budgetary control was not included in this system, but it enabled government agents to raise and keep funds themselves without effective monitoring.[37] The government bureaus were not real government; they were more like hybrid organizations that combined both predatory administrative power and corporate behavior. Thus, it conformed to Weber's description of patrimonialism to some degree.

Fortunately, this patrimonialist bureaucracy and distorted market did not reinforce each other and trapped in a vicious circle. There were subverting forces, mainly emerging private enterprises, that developed. The emergence of a competitive market economy and regional competition made the light industries' capital/assets in County Warm River increasingly mobile, which forced the local government to take measures to create an investment-friendly environment (including disciplining government bureaus)—a public good that all private entrepreneurs preferred but could not achieve. However, the county government did not start to make comprehensive reform until the mid-1990s, when the market economy became more and more competitive.[38]

Stage Two: Competition for Investment by Disciplining Bureaucracy

Marketization-oriented reforms initiated by the central government had taken away many of local government's powers, including mandated monopolies and control of bank loans.[39] The pro-development county government could not directly intervene in an enterprise's operation as it once had. Private enterprises grew larger and had greater autonomy from the government. They also achieved greater mobility, thus opening the possibility of moving to other regions. No longer able to establish and run collective TVEs, the county government had lost an effective tool to directly promote regional economic development and increase fiscal revenue. The county party and government leaders tried to improve the business environment, primarily to further discipline predatory bureaus via mobilizing LPC deputies to deliberate and evaluate government bureaus' performance (人大评议), which is discussed in chapter 5.

More important, County Warm River switched its development strategy to promote development through its control of land, which was monopolized by the government, by building industrial parks (工业园区, industry development zones).[40] Thus, the county government shifted from operating enterprises to operating the city (经营城市) but still guided enterprises (Cao and Shi 2009).

County Warm River was ahead of a nationwide trend of building industrial parks; it built several industry zones in the early 1990s to encourage and promote the development of industry clusters. The largest and most advantageous industry zone was located fifteen kilometers from the county seat but close to the railway station. The county government hoped the zone would attract investment and promote economic development. Success was mixed in that it attracted investment, but largely from local businesses located in the county prior to its creation rather than outside investors the policy makers had hoped for. The government also created another three smaller industrial parks in different townships for existing industries. Ultimately, without comprehensive policy supports, the early stage of developing industry zones achieved limited success overall, attracting only some local enterprises and very few outside enterprises.

In 1994, during the provincewide wave of building industry zones that anticipated the nationwide wave, the county government started to build a province-level industry development zone close to the county seat. It also determined that attracting investment would require a four-lane road connecting the industrial parks, the county seat, and the railway station. To fund road construction, in 1996 the county required every resident to pay a fee of 50 yuan (a significant amount when a primary school teacher's monthly salary was about 100 yuan). The road was built but generated significant resistance, which attracted the attention of a national newspaper. A two-page story discussed the conflict between the need for development and overtaxing the peasants in County Warm River.[41] The road, however, did contribute to economic growth in the coming years.

Though the central government's policy toward the private economy had become friendlier in the late 1990s, private enterprises still faced many constraints. Building an industry zone addressed the problems of the government's strict administration of land use by making land available and cheap.[42] However, the problem of predatory government bureaus and organized crime's harassment remained. Entrepreneurs were reluctant to report harassment for fear of retaliation. To address this problem, the county created an independent government organization, the Industry Development Zone Administration Committee (开发区管委会), to administer affairs related to the industry zone. The committee's head was also a deputy county government leader, and the committee had its own bureaus that were independent of the township and county government bureaus. The objective was to keep township bureaus from harassing businesses.[43] In other words, the industry zone became a county-level "special economic zone."

At first, despite providing cheap land and good infrastructure, the industry zone had not built a reputation and comparative advantage so could not attract many outside investors. Through a combination of administrative orders and selective incentives, the county government invited the county's large enterprises to move into the new zone. It also prioritized making the industry zone more attractive to outside investment in the early 2000s and pushed several administrative reforms to improve the "soft" business environment, just as building the industry zones had been "hard" investments.

One important reform was to simplify company registry, a process that involved many government bureaus. Many had power to approve or veto business licenses, which brought them fees and even bribes, so that higher-level government would have difficulty canceling them. The county government tried to simplify the licensing process. Whereas licensing took an average of 508 days prior to the 1996 reform, forty-five items proceeded in an average of 276 days after reform. Fifteen approvals from different government bureaus were canceled, and another six were merged, which represented a marked improvement. In 1998, the county government also asked all relevant bureaus to set up spaces in the Government Business Hall (政府办事大厅) so that entrepreneurs could get all approvals done in one building. Rules and codes of government behavior were also posted to regulate officials. Another change was that companies were now allowed to begin operations even before approvals. The county allowed companies to hire agents with good political connections who could get things done quickly to facilitate registration. Another initiative was launched to discipline government officials whose actions were deemed as "harm[ing] the business environment [破坏投资环境]" by violating government policy and arbitrarily using power over enterprises.[44]

In part because of the county government's campaign to increase investment, thirty-two joint ventures moved into its industrial zone in 2003, bringing a cumulative investment of 385 million yuan (USD 46.86 million), and ninety-two domestic enterprises from outside the county, an investment of 170 million yuan (USD 13.96 million). These investments, combined with the government's huge expenditure to build industry zone infrastructure, pushed the county's GDP growth rate to 14.8 percent, the highest growth rate of the last seven years. The enterprises in the new industry zone generated tax revenue of 0.17 billion yuan, or 34 percent of the county's tax revenue. The county government also initiated a nationwide government-sponsored program for county party and government leaders to contact major enterprises and drivers of technology innovation in their county. The program assigned leaders to particular enterprises and required them to build a relationship to help them make development plans and address their difficulties (Sheng 2004). This program provided certain enterprises with effective channels of representation in the county government.

Industry zones also had another purpose: to promote industrial upgrades. Though they had played a crucial role in promoting regional economic development, increasing tax revenue, and improving family income, private enterprises in County Warm River were too small and too deconcentrated to be competitive in the coming years, especially in the world market. Most of these private enterprises belonged to four major industry clusters and were spontaneously formed without active government guidance in the 1980s and 1990s. Apart from the low tax-rate policy, government policies in the 1990s changed frequently as county leaders changed and brought their own policy agendas. The government encouraged the enterprises to grow and strengthen by providing subsidies and/or tax breaks for the largest businesses in their industry. The enterprises spent a lot on research and development, especially those in new but promising industries. Results were mixed; many that received large government subsidies went bankrupt or did not become more competitive.

During this process, the county government played a crucial role; it not only implemented higher-level governments' reform programs relatively honestly,[45] but it also initiated other reforms earlier than higher-level governments. It implemented many measures to build a modern bureaucracy to improve its business environment, for example. Table 3.4 demonstrates that government organizations' independent revenue (小金库,

Table 3.4. Discipline of bureaus through elimination of small private coffers

	1995 (million yuan)	2001 (million yuan)
General fiscal revenue	37.20	176.88
High-level government subsidy	51.68	67.56
Extra-budgetary	3.08	13.19 (year 2000)
Government organs' special savings (private coffer)	87.68	
Special fund	0.21	
Land sale	19.06	199.00
Net land revenue	(4.74)	—
Total	198.91	456.63

Source: County Warm River's PC's documents 1996, 2002.
Note: Data from only these two years are available.

private coffer) was almost abolished in the early 2000s. However, extra-budgetary funds still existed and increased as the economy grew. Before 2000, administration expenditures consumed most of extra-budgetary revenue; in stage three, most of it would be used for government-led investment. The county government, however, made an effort to separate revenue collection from expenditure (收支两条线), which improved its ability to monitor its bureaus.

In 2007, the county government decided to push forward budgetary reform by putting the extra-budgetary funding sources under unitary control and making a comprehensive budget. The government bureaus were required to cancel their independent bank accounts,[46] to separate the power of implementation (setting fines and fees) from collection (submitting directly to the banks), and to put all their fiscal revenue in a unified budget. This reform was limited in both scope and effectiveness, however: though the goal was to constrain government bureaus from overcollecting and using the extra revenue for employees' personal incomes, separating the power of implementation and collection actually served to demotivate the implementing government bureau and caused a decrease in nontax revenue. Therefore, these government bureaus still have more privileges (through sharing some percentage of the nontax revenues they collect) than other powerless bureaus (County Warm River Committee of Finance and Economics 2007).

All these reforms led to further economic growth. In 2009, in the context of the worldwide financial crisis, the county government proposed to use 1,000 mu (66.7 hectares) of land to attract "large" enterprises: large and leading enterprises and high-tech enterprises. The investment recruitment team was further professionalized and located offices in major cities. The county head reported that USD 20 million and 0.7 billion yuan in investment were utilized in that year. However, the year 2012 was hard for China's industrial economy. The county government spent more money than in 2011 and took additional measures to support industry. Nationwide, the state developed about 2,000 mu of land to be used for industry and invested 1.96 billion yuan (USD 3.57 million) in promoting industry. The county government also asked local enterprises that had removed their businesses from County Warm River since the mid-1990s to return.

Enterprises faced a credit crisis and industrial upgrading in 2014. The county government organized nine "above-scale enterprise service teams" and "consultancy and resolution mechanisms of enterprises' difficulties" to help businesses tackle the challenges.[47] The county created a fund to provide financial loans to enterprises; it made 1,258 loans that amounted to 6.38 billion yuan. Some industries received funds to upgrade. About 3,000 mu of land were taken from inefficient, or zombie, enterprises. All these factors contributed to the county government's being named the province's "exemplary county for industry upgrading." Fourteen Alien Chambers of Commerce of [County Warm River] (异地商会) were built outside the county as offices for investment recruitment, serving residents who ran businesses in the county. This helped attract 1 billion yuan in investment in 2014 that had left the county in previous years. In total the county recruited 2.83 billion yuan (USD 13.38 million) in new or returning investment that year.

Many of my informants questioned the numbers provided here, which are based on government reports. Some said the overstatement might be five- or even tenfold. One informant told me that the county had required him to report his enterprise's size as ten times larger than its actual size. He was concerned that he could be taxed based on this exaggerated number, but officials assured him that most other investors also overreported their size and that higher taxes would not be imposed.[48]

To summarize, an increasingly competitive market and mobile capital drove the government to retreat from intervening in the market directly to provide regulation and public services. The rapidly growing economy and increasing tax revenue made it possible to discipline government bureaus by cutting off their right to raise revenue. Since the early 2000s, after two decades of fiscal difficulty, the county government was able to collect enough tax revenue to fund a big government. To borrow local government terminology, it was able to transition from "payroll finance" (吃饭财政) to "economic construction finance" (建设财政), which means the county government has fiscal revenue to pay salaries and make investment in economic development.[49] The county government also required its bureaus to submit revenue from the fees and fines they collect to the county's fiscal account and to be used in the general budgetary fund, which returned a small portion to the bureaus.[50] A modern bureaucracy emerged, with some limitations. Government bureaus are better disciplined than before, and bureaucratization continues.

Stage Three: Land Finance and Real Estate Development

The third stage is a substage of stage two. Land transfer (leasing) started as a complementary institution for investment recruitment, but it evolved into local government's urbanization strategy after the mid-2000s. Rural industrialization was not associated with urbanization before the late 1990s. Because TVEs were located mainly in rural areas and peasants "left the farmland without leaving their hometown" (离土不离乡), many local governments have considered urbanization to be as important as industrialization in promoting economic growth and extracting revenue since the early 2000s. Jinchuan Shi, a leading expert on economic development in the private sector of Zhejiang Province, describes urbanization of the province:

> The urbanization process in Zhejiang Province could be divided into two stages: (1) the "strengthen the county" strategy [强县战略] from reform to the late 1990s, which could be further divided into two stages: (i) rural industrialization and (ii) rural industrialization plus urbanization; (2) a shift toward urbanization in which both industries and people started to concentrate in large and medium cities, or small-medium city clusters surrounding big cities, which became the engine and carrier of economic growth. (Shi and Qian 2006, 195–196)

With the shift toward urbanization after the mid-2000s, land seizure and transfer became an important strategy for urbanization. As a result, land became an important source of local governments' revenue. County Warm River's political leaders started to "operate the city" (经营城市). Lynette Ong finds that "fiscal incentives propel subnational governments to engage in land expropriation and leasing—and urbanization ensues. Rather than being a by-product of economic development, urbanization in recent decades has become an entrepreneurial and profiteering enterprise actively pursued by the government in order to augment revenue" (2014, 164).

County Warm River's history conforms to Ong's description. In the late 1990s and the first few years of the 2000s, the county government's major strategy of promoting economic development was creating industrial parks/zones and investment recruitment. In a very competitive market, providing cheap land for industry use and tax breaks was a commonly used strategy. The government requisitioned land not used for industry, mostly farmland near the county seat, from the peasants at a low price. The industrial park was built on this land after completion of necessary infrastructure. The transfer fee was very low, sometimes even lower than the costs of land requisition and infrastructure investment. Though selling or renting land in the industrial park did not generate enough income to cover costs, the county government used cheap land to attract investment, which contributed to further economic and revenue growth.

At the same time, as more and more rural residents moved to towns in the 1990s, especially the county seat, the county government and some township governments found it profitable to sell land for real estate development. In the early stages, land was sold as homesteads (*Zhaijidi*) and the buyers built the houses themselves. To encourage sales of such land, the county government gave buyers household registration status as urban residents, which gave them access to many public services, including education for their children, that rural residents could not obtain. In 1995, the county's Bureau of Land Management's land sale income was 19.06 million yuan, and land expenditure was 14.32 million yuan, generating net income of 4.73 million yuan.

Several years after the State Council issued the "Decision on Deepening Urban Housing System Reform" (1994) and "Notice on Further Reform of the Urban Housing System and Improvements in Real Estate Construction" (1998),[51] which commercialized the houses and apartments in urban areas throughout China, the housing market emerged in County Warm River. The county government realized that housing land was a valuable source for generating revenue. It has a transfer fee higher than the costs of land conversion and generates different types of local taxes and fees. At its peak, land-related fiscal revenue made up more than half of the county government's total fiscal revenue. For example, in 2014, while County Warm River's general budgetary revenue was 1.34 billion yuan, its land revenue was 1.41 billion (extra-budgetary). And of the 1.34 billion, more than 35.6 percent is related to land and the real estate sector. The transfer fee for commercial and residential land is much higher than for industrial land, which means the government still uses cheap industrial land to attract investment and uses commercial and residential land to generate revenue. Table 3.5 shows the increase of land revenue in the county.

The land means more than direct and indirect revenue; it is also a valuable deposit that gives local government the financial leverage to obtain loans from the independent central-government-owned commercial banks and the local banks it owns. While local governments are not allowed to borrow money or issue local government debt, many of them, including County Warm River, have established local government–owned SOEs (called city investment corporations [Chengshi touzi gongsi] or local government financing platforms [*Difang zhengfu rongzi pingtai*]), to

Table 3.5. Sizes and value of land in County Warm River, 2015

	Size (square meters)	Value (yuan)	Average (yuan/ square meters)	Method	Usage
1	161	2,601,720	16,200.00	Auction	Commercial and residential
2	13,330	11,357,160	852.00	Listing	Transportation
3	508	3,705,480	7,300.00	Auction	Commercial and residential
4	460	2,796,800	6,080.00	Auction	Commercial and residential
5	1,600	26,509,595	16,568.50	Auction	Commercial and residential
6	6,337	3,821,211	603.00	Listing	Industrial
7	6,811	4,100,222	602.00	Listing	Industrial
8	35,172	28,302,783	804.70	Listing	Industrial
9	10,004	4,051,620	405.00	Listing	Industrial
10	11,000	3,960,000	360.00	Listing	Industrial
11	97,556	1,019,460,200	10,450.00	Listing	Commercial and residential
12	11,459	53,880,218	4,702.00	Listing	Commercial and residential
13	39,488	225,160,576	5,702.00	Listing	Commercial and residential
14	4,983	2,756,560	553.22	Auction	Industrial
15	4,998	4,848,080	970.00	Auction	Industrial
16	104	3,013,970	29,000.00	Auction	Commercial and residential
17	9,213	11,650,650	1,264.59	Auction	Industrial
Total	253,183	1,411,976,845	5,576.90		

Source: Data from County Warm River's Bureau of Land Resources website.
Note: As an informant working in a relevant bureau told me, these numbers are incomplete and badly underreported. Interview by the author, Zhejiang, August 20, 2016. The last row in the table are data collected via media report, which shows that year's largest land auction in County Warm River.

obtain bank loans to build infrastructure and make direct investment.[52] Therefore, local government gains financial leverage to fund its ambitious infrastructural projects, which makes it possible for the government to drive growth through infrastructural investment while accumulating a huge amount of government debt.

However, commercial and residential land does not always generate revenue for local governments, mainly because landowners have asked for substantially increased compensation in recent years. Local governments have realized that they cannot use coercion to get cheap land from residents, especially urban ones.[53] My fieldwork in County Warm River reveals that the former county party secretary spent a great amount of money, most derived from bank loans, to demolish houses in the county seat's downtown area between 2008 and 2011. While no official data describe the county's compensation to the people who lived in these houses, my informants told me that the compensation for the last twenty households was enormous. Conjoined with the stagnation in housing prices in small and medium-sized cities since 2013, the high land price led to the land remaining in the county government's hands for four years after it meant to sell it. Government officials told me that they had not received an annual bonus in years because the county government had paid so much interest on its bank loans. The county sold part of that land (item 11 in table 3.5) at the end of 2015 for a much lower price than it had planned. While many of my informants doubt that the developer who purchased it can make a profit from it, they were happy that the sale meant they would be receiving an annual bonus again starting in 2017.[54]

Reliance on nontax revenue weakens local governments' efforts to discipline government bureaus, as the 2006 County Warm River audit report shows: though other government bureaus have good fiscal discipline (i.e., use the budgetary and extra-budgetary fiscal revenue according to the county government's rules), the Management Committee of the Industry Zone (开发区管委会) did not follow the county government's rule and spent 6.71 million yuan, almost eight times its allotted 860,000 yuan.[55] Fortunately, the negative outcome of this spending is limited to industry zones, some related bureaus,[56] and some related township governments.

County leaders, who serve only three and a half years on average, have strong incentives to achieve short-term economic growth. Real estate has been a ready source of such growth. The County Warm River Party Committee took a leading role in developing the real estate industry; the party secretary led the land-acquisition work team, and capable cadres and officials from different bureaus were assigned to the work team to improve its effectiveness and efficiency. Once the land is taken, the county auctions it on the market. However, insiders in the government told me that not all parcels of land are audited, and the auction could be manipulated to some degree. They suspect that government-business relationships in real estate and construction are very collusive. One informant said, "Real estate development is very different from other industries. After all, the government controls the land and has very strong regulation power. It is difficult to get a piece of land without close connections, [unless you] offer a much higher price."⁵⁷ A media report on an auction County Warm River held in 2016, which suggests a nationally well-known developer lost the bid to a local developer even though the national developer offered a higher price, validates his comments. The loser's staff complained that the audit procedure was unfair and not transparent.⁵⁸ Another instance of corruption is that developers took a parcel of land several times the size approved by higher-level government, which would require the county government and relevant bureaus to turn a blind eye at a minimum.

To summarize, the local government tried to take the leading role in promoting economic development through a variety of different strategies: first through building and running enterprises directly and later through improving the business environment and building industry zones. As private enterprises became simultaneously more important for the regional economy but also more mobile, the authoritarian state (via its local agents) incrementally yielded to the demands of private entrepreneurs to promote economic development and increase tax revenue. As a result, governance quality has improved significantly:⁵⁹ government bureaus are under more strict constraints and cannot act predatorily; the government and its bureaus' extra budget is under unitary control, and local government employees' payments have been leveled to some degree. Industry policies have shifted to make industry development and regional economic development a priority. But in stage three, easy land revenue somehow demotivates the county's political leaders' efforts to improve governance quality. As Xiaoyi Sun and Ronggui Huang summarize, "Chinese local governments are instigators, regulators, and participants (profit makers) of urban growth, and this state-led growth is accompanied by the violation of property rights and related conflicts, instead of being neutral and harmless" (2016, 918–919).⁶⁰ This state-led urbanization model reflects the immaturity of China's market system, in that the state still controls many resources (e.g., land). It also generates many negative effects on local governance, including government-business collusion and rising social resistance.

Conclusion

In post-totalitarian China, redefining the boundaries between the state and market, state and society, is a big challenge. In Chinese, officials and scholars refer to this power of deconcentration as *Fenquan* (分权), the same as decentralization.[61] Deconcentration focuses on the horizontal level—the retreat of the state from economic and social spheres. The bureaucratization process also reflects the struggle of separating power from the government so it can focus on public services. Government agents wanted to maximize revenue income (and power); therefore, they did not want to retreat from profitable activities, which in turn blocked market formation. How the CCP managed to discipline its agents and build a modern bureaucracy is an important challenge related to the emergence of the market.

As illustrated in figure 3.1, I incorporate into this coevolution theory some elements of theories that political scientists have applied to explain economic growth in China in the 1990s, such as local state corporatism and market-preserving federalism. I do so to build a more dynamic understanding of the mutual transformation of state and market. Based on a longer time period and a within-case comparison, my coevolution model also differs from Yuen Yuen Ang's in three important ways, both empirically and theoretically: it provides (1) a broader definition of bureaucratization, especially the separation of public and private as Weber (1968) emphasizes; (2) a broader definition of marketization; (3) and a fiscal dynamic or causal mechanism and also explains regional variations.

Besides borrowing ideas from state-society mutual transformation, this coevolution model borrows some insights from Kellee Tsai's adaptive informal institution theory:

> Formal institutions comprise a myriad of constraints and opportunities that may motivate everyday actors to devise novel operating arrangements that are not officially sanctioned. With repetition and diffusion, these informal coping strategies may take on an institutional reality of their own. In contrast to deep-rooted, "primordial" informal institutions, which tend to resist change, the resulting norms and practices can be called *adaptive* informal institutions because they represent creative responses to formal institutional environments that actors find too constraining. (2006, 117–118)

I find that grassroots actors, local government officials, and citizens developed cooperative strategies under fiscal decentralization that weakened the constraints over local government officials from above.[62] Empowered local government officials and ordinary people collaborated to convert formal institutions that opposed private ownership, and the adaptive informal institution (private ownership and market exchange) emerged. However, Tsai neglects the power asymmetry: the revenue-eager local state used its power to exploit ordinary people, who had limited bargaining power, through monopolization and heavy taxes and fees. Later on, even constrained by limited institutional taxation capacity, local officials found that they could meet the tax target easily. Therefore, a smart strategy was to encourage the growth of private enterprises at first and then tax them later. At the same time, government officials could benefit from the development of the private sector in many ways.[63] This is stage one in this chapter's case study.

In stage two, as the emerging private sectors and foreign enterprises became more and more competitive, SOEs and collective TVEs started to lose money. The FCS did not give the central government enough fiscal revenue sources, causing a fiscal crisis. TSR was implemented to recentralize fiscal power and serve as an important institutional foundation for building a socialist market economy,[64] and many SOEs and most collective TVEs were privatized. Local governments switched to investment recruitment from running TVEs as regional economic development strategies, improving asset mobility. Fiscal recentralization, ironically, helps build fiscal federalism because of its efforts to institutionalize the fiscal system. With rising asset mobility and the central government's clear attitude toward the private sector, private enterprises got more bargaining power against the local government and could constrain its predatory power to some degree. At the same time, economic growth also empowered local government with sufficient revenue to build a modern bureaucracy. As a result, a modern bureaucracy (though with many limits) and a modern market emerged.

As noted in stage three, while providing local government with a huge amount of fiscal revenue, abundant land revenue also generates many social and economic problems. With local agent discipline resolved (to some degree), the cooperation problem is also resolved (to some degree). As a result, the economy grows and government can extract more fiscal revenue to improve a modern bureaucracy and provide more and better public services, and the authoritarian regime achieves performance legitimacy and popular support.

Chapter 4 addresses the external validity of this chapter's findings in another four counties with different levels of economic development. Chapter 6 uses a quantitative study to test its generalizability across China.

122 GOVERNING AND RULING

I also further investigate other aspects of mutual transformation in the rest of the book: "attempts by the state to increase tax collection, efforts by local figures to gain control over particular state offices and resources, initiatives by state agencies to regulate certain behavior" (Migdal, Kohli, and Shue 1994, 9–10), and how the party-state and private entrepreneurs keep changing each other.

CHAPTER 4

Explaining Regional Variations in Governance Quality

> How do formal institutions influence the practice of politics and government? If we reform institutions, will practice follow? Does the performance of an institution depend on its social, economic, and cultural surround?
> —Robert Putnam, Robert Leonardi, and Raffaella Nanetti, *Making Democracy Work*

> The unique features of a local environment always give special characteristics to its inhabitants [一方水土养一方人].
> —Chinese proverb

> Underlying this contention is the recognition that robust institutions are the product of both supply and demand. Governments must have an incentive to supply them and societal actors must have both the interest and ability to make a credible demand for them.
> —Pauline Jones Luong and Erika Weinthal, "Rethinking the Resource Curse"

In early March 2010, immediately after the Chinese Spring Festival, hundreds of people from different villages and sectors gathered in the township hall in Zeguo, Wenling County, in Zhejiang Province, to discuss the township government's budget. After government officials had explained the structure of the budget and a list of projects, people were divided into groups to discuss whether some specific expenditure items were appropriate and which project should get priority. Some political science scholars—including the author—were invited to observe and give suggestions. Though the township government set a strict agenda, people still engaged in heated discussion. This "democratic deliberation meeting" (民主恳谈会) or participatory budgeting with "Chinese characteristics" originated in Zeguo and Songmen townships in Wenling and has since been adopted widely around the county. Four months later, at an academic conference in Wenling, the director of the county PC proudly announced the successful adoption of the county government's budget and the approval of projects totaling 200 million yuan that had been proposed by the county party secretary. Such significant change would have been unimaginable three years ago. The private-entrepreneur LPC deputies and meeting representatives, some of whom do business in other regions but return to attend these meetings, actively participated in the discussions. Later on I learned that meetings with democratic deliberation were the result of private entrepreneurs' resistance to some government policies because the township government realized that more communication and deliberation help in making good policies. While Wenling could be an extreme case, Xi Jinping regards Zhejiang Province as leading reform in China (走在前列，改革排头兵).

In 2008, the Shanxi provincial government enacted a strict plan to close off, merge, reorganize, and/or integrate several small and medium-sized coal mines. The plan was prompted by the high number of coal-mine disasters that had occurred in the previous five years, leading to the resignation of two provincial governors—an extremely rare occurrence in China.[1] Many believe that private coal mines experience disasters because private companies invest little in safety equipment and are plagued by corrupt government officials who squabble over money instead of actually regulating the mining. The high number of disasters and the powerful influence of coal-mine bosses (煤老板) have made being a government official related to coal mining a high-risk career.[2] After being arrested for corruption, one county party secretary explained, "I had no choice [but to accept bribes]. The first day I went to my office, a coal-mine boss went to my office and asked me to choose one of two bags he brought. One was full of money, and another had a knife in it."[3] About five years later, under Xi Jinping's anticorruption campaign, Shanxi was regarded as a province of "landslide corruption" (塌方式腐败), and many cadres, from provincial leaders to rank-and-file officials, have been arrested.[4]

These two stories illustrate the increasingly significant relation between government and business in China and the very different ways in which this relation can play out: in Zhejiang we see more public participation and transparency in local government; in Shanxi many government officials were bribed by the businessmen, and the government regulations become ineffective.[5] The government-business relationship reflects the broader governance qualities in these regions, reflecting the business environment in general.⁶ In contrast to many other theories, I find that asset mobility has a profound impact on regional governance quality. This chapter builds on the insights of my earlier in-depth historical study of County Warm River through a comparative regional study of five counties. Thus, it joins the "subnational turn" of both comparative politics and Chinese politics to examine how local-level variables determine different local economic and political realities (Putnam, Leonardi, and Nanetti 1993; Rithmire 2014).

China is a unitary country but is also highly decentralized. Under such a regionally decentralized authoritarianism (C. Xu 2010), local governments compete with each other on economic performance, including economic growth and fiscal revenue.⁷ The effective way to achieve these two goals since the mid-1990s has been to increase investment by keeping local investment and attracting outside investment to their jurisdictions. In most cases, a region can outperform other regions in economic growth and tax revenue only if the local government supports local investment and attracts more investment. Therefore, local government leaders have a strong incentive to improve the business environment: to secure private property rights, to rationalize and restrain government bureaus from acting predatorily, and to provide better infrastructure and government service, all of which will lead to higher quality of governance. But the sources of regional economic development determine the nature of this relationship. For resource-abundant regions, economic growth and increase in tax revenue are a by-product of rising resource prices rather than government's efforts to attract investment. Because natural resources are immobile, local political leaders do not need to improve the business environment.

In contrast, in regions with high asset mobility, local political leaders have strong motivation to keep local investment and attract outside investment. Because of low asset mobility, private entrepreneurs need to build strong patron-client ties with government officials at different levels to protect themselves and have weak incentives to supervise the government. A new local party or government leader, even with high motivation to rationalize the local government bureaus and improve monitoring capacity, may face vigorous resistance from the strong alliance between coal-mine bosses and local government officials, some of whom may also have strong political connections to higher-level officials. Therefore, it is much harder to create an investment-friendly environment in coal-mining regions.

Table 4.1 summarizes how the competition among different regions empowers private entrepreneurs with bargaining power and gives local political leaders the incentive to improve the business environment in regions dominated by industries with mobile assets.[8] This chapter aims to further elaborate on the causal mechanisms identified earlier and test the external validity of findings with respect to County Warm River. I begin by examining the case of County Cold Mountain in Shanxi Province, which differs significantly from County Warm River, thereby creating a very different case study. I next discuss four complementary cases as further tests of external validity of the findings in chapter 3 and then summarize and discuss the implications of the results of these tests.

County Cold Mountain under Coal Mining's Curse

County Warm River and County Cold Mountain have been at the same economic development level (in terms of GDP per capita) for several years, but the degree of bureaucratization in the two counties differs markedly, as table 4.2 shows.

Table 4.1. Role of industries in regional variation of bureaucratization

Industry	Natural resource mining	Light industry
Asset mobility	Low	High
Local party government leaders' incentive and strategy	Weakened incentives to create an investment-friendly environment because of easy revenue	Strong incentive to keep local investors and attract outside investors so seek to rationalize government bureaus, provide better public infrastructure to create an investment-friendly environment, and ally with private entrepreneurs to achieve these goals
Private entrepreneurs' bargaining power	Low	Medium to high
Private entrepreneurs' strategies	Evade tax, build personal connections, achieve more prestigious political titles	Evade tax, build personal connections, achieve more powerful political titles, sometimes collectively lobby for better infrastructure and government service
Bureaucratization	Low	High

It might seem odd that governance quality, especially level of bureaucratization that lays the foundation for that quality, would differ sharply in two counties with similar levels of economic development. But the histories of these two counties differ. Government reform was common in the light-industry counties of Zhejiang Province in the 1990s and early 2000s as a means to create investment-friendly environments. The enterprises were potentially mobile, and government had an interest in attracting additional investment. Governance quality declined during the same period in counties with abundant natural resources in Shanxi Province, as well as elsewhere in Central and Western China, as the industries generating revenue were immobile. In 2008 the Shanxi provincial government determined to close off and merge its small coal mines to reduce the number and frequency of mining disasters, improve quality of governance,[9] and attract further investment;[10] County Cold Mountain received limited benefits from these measures because of the decades-long rampant and deeply rooted corruption. In 2012, the county PC's director was charged

Table 4.2. Comparison of County Warm River and County Cold Mountain, late 2000s

	GDP per capita, 2009 (yuan)	Population, 2009	Industry (asset mobility)	Governance quality
County Warm River	28,200/49,499 (2015)	390,000	Light industry (high asset mobility)	Medium to high: high level of bureaucratization, good government services and infrastructure, less corruption, and responsive government
County Cold Mountain	28,035/43,816 (2014)	490,662	Coal mining (low asset mobility)	Low: low level of bureaucratization, predatory government, bad infrastructure, rampant corruption, and unresponsive government

Source: County Warm River and County Cold Mountain government reports.
Note: Because most fieldwork was conducted in 2010, the comparison is based mainly on that time period with some updated data from 2014 and 2015.

with corruption and sent to jail. In the following few years, the next three county heads (who served from 2006 to 2014) were charged with serious corruption and other illegal behavior and sent to jail later.

In the early 1980s, to develop the regional economy, improve family income, and increase the coal supply, the central government under the leadership of Hu Yaobang, the CCP's general secretary, called for a policy of "let the small stream flow quickly" (*youshui kuai liu*) for resource-abundant areas (L. Zhang 2010, A4). Hu also paid a personal visit to County Cold Mountain in 1981. Two years later, the Ministry of Coal Industry issued an announcement that it would "support the masses to mine coal":

> Since China has such widely distributed coal resources and limited mining capacity [of state-owned coal mines], it is important to mobilize the mass [of workers] to mine the coal to improve industrialization and the peasants' income. We need to emancipate our mind[s] and lose our overly strict policies. All work units [including government organs, hospital workers, schoolteachers], industries, and villages should be allowed to mine coal. (Ministry of Coal Industry 1983)

Because the plan was easily mobilized, so many people got involved in coal mining that even the schools and hospitals became short-staffed. People who had suffered poverty for a long time responded to this policy change with great enthusiasm. The barrier to entry was very low; coal is easy to extract using tools commonly available in China, such as garden hoes. Small productive teams built up their own coal mines, no matter how simple the mines were. At the peak, there were more than eighty thousand coal mines nationwide in 1994. Shanxi Province contained more than ten thousand mines, and more than six hundred of them were in County Cold Mountain. Small coal mines bloomed like wildflowers. In a research report, Ren Chu (2009), a senior research fellow from Shanxi Academy of Social Sciences who had studied the coal-mining industry for decades, described the mines of Shanxi: "many of them, but small and dispersed, with chaotic management" (多小散乱). In 2006, more than two decades after Hu's policy was implemented, only 8 percent of these mines had a production capacity of more than 0.3 million tons per year.

The policy of "let the small stream flow quickly" led to regional economic growth and increased average family income in County Cold

Table 4.3. Number, ownership, and production of coal mines in County Cold Mountain

Year	County owned*	Township and village owned	Private†	Production (10,000 tons)‡
1970	4	16	0	
1980	5	72	0	274.60
1985	6	218	8	397.98
1990	6	201	9	538.01
1998	—	—	222	—
2007	7	90	0	1,129.63

Source: Annals of County Cold Mountain.

Note: Many township- and village-owned coal mines were owned only nominally by the "collective"; in reality, individual investors owned and controlled them and reaped the profits. The decline in the total number of coal mines resulted from the central government's policy to close coal mines, reduce production, and ban private ownership of coal mines from 1999 onward. An em dash indicates that data were not available.

* The Second Industry Bureau (*erqingju* 二轻局) controls the county-owned coal mines.

† There were 222 privately owned but unregistered (with no permission) coal mines closed in 1998.

‡ The numbers for annual production are also underreported, both because coal mines wanted to evade taxes and fees and because the local government colluded with owners of the coal mines to "meet" the higher-level government's regulatory requirements designed to limit production.

Mountain and other coal-mining counties. Some of the country's poorest counties benefited from the policy. Table 4.3 shows the official data on the change in coal-mine numbers and production in County Cold Mountain between 1970 and 2007. The private mine statistics are probably unreliable and do not include illegal coal mines; anecdotal evidence suggests there were many (as the number of coal mines closed in 1998 suggests). However, the numbers in the county-owned and township- and village-owned columns are probably reasonably accurate.

The coal boom also had negative consequences for County Cold Mountain. First, the proliferation of mines flooded the market, which led to low prices in the 1990s. Many coal mines, especially the state-owned ones with high operating costs, ran deficits. Some mines relied on bank loans to pay workers' salaries in the 1990s. Second, primitive mining methods resulted in irresponsible and excessive extraction of coal resources,[11] which destroyed the environment and generated significant waste.[12] Third, the exuberance led to some serious mining disasters. Figure 4.1 suggests why

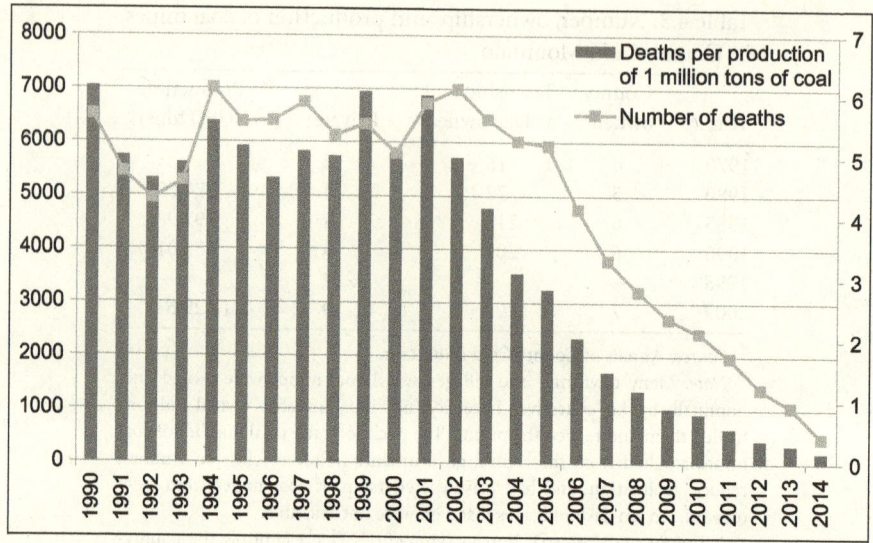

Figure 4.1. Deaths from coal-mining disasters in China since 1990. Source: Chu 2009.

coal had been called black gold with blood on it. The death rate related to coal mining in China is the highest in the world, constituting 80 percent of the total, even though China provides only 35 percent of world coal production.

Because of low prices, bad management, and frequent disasters, running a coal mine became unprofitable and even very risky in the late 1990s. Safety improvements were out of the reach of most coal-mine owners, however. Like other collectively owned TVEs in China, most coal mines have been privatized since the mid-1990s,[13] although their registrations still list them as collectively owned. According to law, coal resources belong to the state, so individuals and private collectives could not claim the property rights of a coal mine. Yet powerful and well-connected people benefited from privatization of collectively owned coal-mining TVEs, just as they did in other areas in China and other postcommunist countries.[14] The village cadres, who are jointly backed by clans within and government officials outside the village, obtained contracts for several years at a time that allowed them to keep all profits for the price of a contract fee. SOEs used this practice in the 1980s to obtain similar benefits.

The most successful coal-mine bosses had close and strong political connections that depended on giving officials stock and bribes,[15] entertaining them with fancy dinners, and even occasionally hiring sex workers for them. My informants explained that coal-mine bosses who did not please officials would lose their contracts, and those with stronger political connections might use violence to obtain control of a mine.[16] After decades of fieldwork, Chu (2009) describes five types of government-business collusion in the coal-mining industry: government officials own stock in the coal mine, sell certificates and permits to unqualified coal mines,[17] take bribes, install their relatives to run the mines, and/or fail to implement regulations.

State-owned banks supported state-owned coal mines throughout the 1990s, even as other SOEs were privatized or opened to outside investors (both private and SOEs). Because most local people in County Cold Mountain lacked the capital to run the money-losing coal mines in the 1990s, local government officials and village leaders invited outside investors to run them. They sold or contracted some of them to investors from other provinces.[18] These privately owned or contracted coal mines were still registered as collectively owned because it was (and still is) illegal for individuals to own coal mines. Like the local coal-mine bosses, these outside investors had to bribe politicians, but they had fewer options to prevent organized crime from attacking mines if they did not pay "protection" money. Common strategies of dealing with these hooligans included bribing the police for protection, buying them off, or arming coal miners to fight them. While County Warm River's government formed an official trade association that protected industry from such attacks by organizing the police, prosecutors, and courts, County Cold Mountain did not provide any institutionalized protection for investors. The coal-mine bosses were forced to rely on extra-institutional or even illegal means to maintain operations.

Since the price of coal was low in the 1990s, the mine owners' strategy to boost profits was to increase production and reduce costs. Increasing production meant overextraction—for example, extracting one hundred tons a week from a coal mine designed to produce only thirty to fifty tons a week. Bosses also tried to reduce operational costs by minimizing investment in coal mines, including investment in safety equipment. Both of these practices are illegal. More important, low investment in safety equipment and overextraction together led to a rash of mining disasters. A mining disaster can bankrupt mine bosses and lead to their imprisonment if they do not bribe government officials to allow them to maintain operations. Thus, there is a vicious cycle between the opportunistic coal-mine bosses and corrupt government officials, which only got worse when the price of coal rose.

The economic difficulties of coal mining suddenly ended in the early 2000s, as the price of coal increased rapidly beginning in 2002, boosted by a nationwide economic boom. Coal mining became very profitable, and increasing amounts of investment capital moved into coal-mining areas, including County Cold Mountain. The competition for contracting a coal mine became more intense, and investors needed to invest much more in both the coal mine and the people involved in the coal mine to win contracts. The villagers who legally own coal mines and the government officials who owned the coal resources and regulatory power could demand more than before. In an in-depth report, a journalist described a coal-mine boss who won a contract in 2003 in County Cold Mountain by promising to pay every villager 4,000 yuan a year if he won the contract.[19] He prevailed and continued to pay 2 million yuan every year to five hundred villagers until 2010.[20]

The price of investing in political support has risen with the coal price. A study of the coal-mining industry conducted by Ren Chu (2009) described a coal-mine boss who said, "I am not afraid of the government officials who come to talk to me; I am afraid of those who don't come to talk to me because I can use money to buy him off only if he comes to talk to me." Similarly, a senior official of County Cold Mountain told me that "strong political connections" are "the most important thing" and that without them "you will unable to run a coal mine."[21] Another official told me, hesitantly, that the brother and uncle of the assistant county government head (*xianzhang zhuli*) ran the two largest coal mines in his jurisdiction. He said this was "very politically sensitive" information:

> A coal-mine boss in the township [where] I work is the cousin of a county leader [assistant county head, or *xianzhang zhuli*]; his family also runs another two medium-sized coal mines around the township. There is another guy who owned a medium-sized coal mine, but many people thought he was too arrogant. He claimed that he had good connections in Taiyuan [the provincial capital], but we are not sure whether it is true. We were sent to his coal mine several times to audit his account and taxes, and he refused to show us the account at first. His arrogance also offended someone in the neighborhood who was able to mobilize the villagers to block the

only road to his coal mine. As a result, that coal-mine boss couldn't sell his coal when the price was at the peak, and he had to close the coal mine.[22]

I believe the reference to arrogance actually referred to an unwillingness to give bribes, as a well-connected coal-mine boss would not find the road on which he relied blocked. In fact, this boss may have gotten off easy; rumor suggests that coal bosses who did not nurture political relationships could lose their coal mines, be sentenced to jail, or have a hit taken out on them.

A media report that my informants confirmed suggests what paid-off politicians might allow and the fact that bribes did not equate to permanent support. In the 1990s, a Mafia organization led by a man known as "Black Pig" took some coal mines from others and used violent means to monopolize coal transportation within County Cold Mountain.[23] Black Pig was able to maintain operations until 2001. At the time a nationwide movement against criminal organizations began, and the head of the provincial Public Security Bureau decided to get rid of Black Pig. The mob leader was given a death sentence, and some of his associates were sentenced to jail. A prefecture leader and some county leaders as well as others who had accepted Black Pig's bribes were arrested and sent to jail.[24] Some former Black Pig operatives eventually reestablished control over coal mines after their release from prison. Another case in another prefecture (Yangquan) of Shanxi involved a police officer, Guan Jianjun, who ruthlessly acquired many coal mines. He arrested the boss of a mine he wanted to take over and tortured the man until he confessed to being a drug user. The boss was sent to a drug-addiction treatment center for several weeks, and Guan took his coal mine during this period. Guan bribed officials so that he could become patrol captain. He was arrested in February 2011, and it was reported that the province would be investigating higher-level officials in connection to the case (Hu 2011).

Reports of coal-mine-related corruption pervades this resource-abundant region. In the Chenzhou Prefecture of Hunan Province, the party secretary; the party's disciplinary committee secretary, Zeng Jinchun; and other high-level government officials have been arrested for coal-mine-related corruption. Several coal-mine bosses lost their mines to people Zeng had backed, who threatened to kill them if they did not leave Chenzhou. Zeng himself received tens of millions of yuan in bribes and dry stocks in coal mines.[25] He was sentenced to death in 2010.

Rampant corruption led to lack of regulation, which in turn led to frequent disasters. Responding to the increasing frequency of disasters and under pressure from the central government, the provincial government started to strengthen regulation of coal mines in the late 1980s. Table 4.4 lists the major actions taken by the County Cold Mountain government during the last three decades.

Government regulations to reduce coal-mining disasters began in 1994 but had no noticeable effect until 2007 because government officials colluded with mine owners to resist policies to manage overextraction and require safety equipment. China's minister of safety production, Li Yizhong, said in 2006: "There are many causes of industry accidents, but the trading power for money [权钱交易], government business collusion [官商勾结], [and] dereliction of duty and malpractice [失职渎职] are the deep causes"

Table 4.4. Time line of coal-mine regulation in County Cold Mountain

Year	Action
1984	Establishment of a coal-mine rescue team
1985	Establishment of a county coal school to train the manager and technicians and certify the coal-mine manager
1988	Establishment of a deputy township head of safety and one full-time official in charge of coal mines in every township
1989	Rectification (close and merge) of coal mines countywide
1996	Establishment of certificate of permission to mine coal, a county Office of Small Coal-Mine Rectification, and a picket for coal-mine safety
1997	Establishment of the Administration of Coal Mines in the county government
1998	Enactment of strict coal-mine rectification and closure of 222 coal mines that lacked certification
1999	Establishment of a Leading Work Team to Reduce Production and Close Small Coal Mines; closure of forty-four coal mines
2001	Investment of 100 million yuan by the county to improve production conditions following a coal-mine disaster that caused six deaths in 2000
2002	Establishment of the County Warm River Administration of Work Safety
2003	Enactment of several policies and bylaws to improve safe production and establishment of a network to monitor coal mining
2004	Introduction of Certification of Coal Safety Production
2005	Creation of thirteen offices of Administration of Work Safety at the township level after a coal-mine disaster that caused nine deaths and a nationwide campaign to address corruption
2008	Establishment of provincewide movements to close small mines and merge medium-sized ones and to eliminate corruption in the coal-mining industry

Source: County Cold Mountain Yearbook, various years; and China Coal Mine Annals editorial team 1999.

(*Xinhua* 2006). The head of the Ministry of Supervision, Chen Changzhi, pointed out that corruption was found to be a root cause in five of the eleven coal-mining disasters that caused more than thirty deaths each in 2005. Li Tieying, deputy director of the NPC Standing Committee, suggested that this number underestimated the role of corruption, claiming that all serious industry accidents were related to corruption (Chu 2009).

I did not collect systematic information on government-business collusion in County Cold Mountain in my 2010 field research because my informants thought the topic was too politically sensitive to talk about; however, they did share examples informally, and some said that media reports on coal mines in Shanxi also applied to County Cold Mountain. Professor Ren Chu told me that he experienced great difficulty in examining state-business relationships in Shanxi related to coal mining because of the sensitive nature of the information. Chu spent three years and mobilized all his personal connections as a resident of Shanxi to do his research but acknowledged its limitations.

The anticorruption campaign has revealed significant hidden information about state-business relationships in County Cold Mountain since 2013. Four mayors and two party secretaries (both of whom had served as mayors before promoted to this position) were charged with corruption for having collusive relationships with coal-mining bosses. The CCP's CDI report described the county's party government as "systematically corrupted" (系统性腐败) with "landslide corruption" (塌方性腐败),[26] the latter term used by the CCP to describe only extreme corruption.[27] The coal-mining industry has some spillover effects on other government services, especially the economic regulation of government bureaus, which are inefficient and corrupt. One informant described a situation very similar to that of County Warm River's bureaus in the 1980s and early 1990s:

> If you want to establish a new company, you need to go to the relevant government bureaus to get registered. But they will not handle your application for a long time. If you come to their office to ask, they will give you excuses and postpone it for another several weeks [until you pay them some money or gifts]. This is very common.[28]

The provincial LTB has effected administrative reform in the county LTB, including standardizing and publicizing procedures and the time line for various functions (Mao and Lu 2009), but it is the only bureau that has made such improvements.

A county-level government official in Prefecture J, where both Counties Cold Mountain and D are located, told a journalist that the government officials in Shanxi have

> old-fashioned ideas about managing [the economy], not service-oriented ones. How can we attract good investment projects if we can't improve the business environment? . . . . There are very serious problems with the [party and government officials] in Shanxi: [the political leaders] promote cadres who don't work, and these cadres also promote cadres who don't work and disregard the capable cadres; this is the vicious circle. (*Oriental Outlook Weekly* 2011)

Since the elimination of Black Pig and the reshuffling of the county political leaders, new leadership has made efforts to attract investment to the county, including building an industrial park. The county government report publicly recognized estimations that the town's coal mines would be exhausted by 2021 and the need to create a sustainable economy. These efforts achieved limited success, and some nonmining private enterprises were built in the county's industrial park. Yet coal continued to dominate, and its immobility decreased the government's incentive to constrain the predatory government bureaus and improve the business environment. Also, the close government-business collusion made it more difficult and risky for political leaders, who are appointed by the higher-level government from other regions, to push for reform. Local government officials, especially deputy county leaders and middle-level officials (i.e., bureau directors, township leaders) who are natives (born and live in the county) had a stake in maintaining corruption, and they had good connections with higher-level government officials and local social elites. Political leaders in County Cold Mountain also focused on attracting large investors, but unlike County Warm River's leaders, they did not reform the system in such a way as to achieve this goal.[29] Had they sought smaller investors, they might have succeeded, and the cumulative weight of multiple small investors in mobile industries might have incentivized reform and created a more sustainable economy.

The county government's incentive to build other industries was strengthened at the end of 2008 when the provincial government required all county governments in Shanxi to close and merge the small and medium-sized coal mines. This reduced the county's tax base significantly.

The government decided to attract outside investment and initiated some reform to do so. The coal-mining industry's negative effect on the government bureau extends also to the provincial level. After two provincial governors resigned after mining disasters, the new governor, Wang Jun, described four problems of provincial government bureaus and officials: lack of trustworthiness (because of frequently changing policies and contracts), greater concern for officials' and bureaus' individual interests than interest in the overall health of the government and citizenry, indifference to providing public services (some outside investors are bullied by the officials), and inefficiency (some government service centers do not work at all) (*Worker's Daily* 2006). On May 31, 2010, the new party secretary of Shanxi Province, Yuan Chunqing, took over from Zhang Baoshun, who had ruled Shanxi since 2004.[30] Yuan Chunqing enacted a provincewide movement to rectify problems in the bureaucracy, requiring government officials to work in the office during working hours and preventing them from collecting gifts or gambling with enterprise owners (another way of collecting bribes). A reform of the personnel system was enacted. The province removed 306 prefecture-level party and government officials and moved some to other positions. Candidates outside Shanxi who were seen as disruptive to an ineffective system were brought in (F. Zhang 2010; *Oriental Outlook Weekly* 2011). While these reports are striking, revelations four years later make this seem to be the tip of the iceberg. Since 2013, after Xi Jinping initiated the national anticorruption campaign, Shanxi turned out to be one of the most corrupt provinces in the country.

Table 4.5 compares County Warm River and County Cold Mountain in different time periods to reveal how changes of asset mobility changed both governments' development strategies and private entrepreneurs' bargaining power, and therefore bureaucratization.

Some analysts argue that insecure private property rights of coal mines causes most of the problems with bureaucracies in coal-mining regions of China (e.g., Chu 2009). Insecure or even illegal property rights increase coal-mine bosses' discount rate and drive them to overextract the coal and underinvest in safety equipment, thus leading to mining disasters. Insecure property rights also drove mine bosses to build strong political connections for protection. However, I argue that insecure property rights are a consequence of asset immobility. The private property rights of other industries were also insecure in County Warm River before the late 1990s, but the credible threat of moving industry to other counties secured these "illegal" property rights. This is the key point Yingyi Qian and Barry

Table 4.5. Separating the cases into two stages

County	Time/policy period	Industry	Asset mobility	Government's development strategy	Private entrepreneurs' bargaining power	Bureaucratization
Warm River	Early 1980s to 1990s	Agriculture to light industry	Low to medium	Monopolize the market and build collectively owned enterprises, set market barriers for different regions	Low	Low to medium
	After mid-1990s	Agriculture to light industry	High	Keep capital within the jurisdiction and invite outside investment by creating good investment environment	High	High
Cold Mountain	Early 1980s to late 2000s	Coal mining	Low	Rely on coal mining	Low	Low
	Recent years	Trying to develop other industries		Try to build new industries to prepare for the exhaustion of coal mines	High (investors for new industries)	Improving but still below medium

Weingast (1997) make when they describe market-preserving fiscal federalism. My findings reveal that fiscal federalism is not a sufficient condition for market preservation if local power captures the government or the government acts predatorily. Government officials' incentives do not always support development, unless discipline prevents them from seeking personal gain. Thus, we also need to examine structural factors such as asset mobility and the relationships between vertical governments—how higher-level governments intervene selectively to correct or redirect lower-level governments' behavior—as well as the importance of the performance-driven cadre evaluation system.

Comparative Case Studies

Table 4.6 shows a cross-sectional comparison of the economic development, industries, activity level of LPCs and NGOs, and level of bureaucratization of four counties in four different provinces. The table suggests that asset mobility is associated with level of bureaucratization, even if we control level of economic development. This confirms findings from chapter 3, and we also examine the possible mechanisms. Chapter 8 conducts a quantitative test.

County D

County D and its neighbor County Cold Mountain share many similarities. On a weekend day in mid-June 2010, an LTB official in County D in Shanxi accompanied me on a visit to a coal mine. We drove for more than two hours from the county seat on a road badly damaged by overloaded coal trucks. I saw eight or nine people, two in uniforms, guarding the gate to the coal mine. Some were smoking. One of them stopped and

Table 4.6. Comparison of four counties

County	Province	Economic development (2009 GDP per capita)	Industry	LPC/NGO	Bureaucratization
County D	Shanxi	Medium (21,544)	Coal mining	Inactive LPC and NGOs	Low
County Yiwu	Zhejiang	Very high (41,933)	Light industry	Active LPC and NGOs	High
County Z	Chongqing	Low (9,820)	Light and heavy industry	Inactive LPC and NGOs	Medium
County X	Hunan	Low (14,424)	Agriculture	Inactive LPC and NGOs	Low

asked us who we were and whom we were looking for. My informant told them, proudly, that he was a tax officer, but the guard said we could not come in unless he called his contact, who works in the mine, to confirm we were approved. The company's chief financial officer came to the gate and welcomed us, then led us to the manager's office. The manager treated each of us to a pack of good cigarettes but was very reserved about my visiting. My informant reassured them that I was a PhD student (which was accurate at the time). Eventually they became comfortable enough to complain about their high tax and fee burden and about rapid changes in regulatory policies:

> Everyone says the Shanxi coal-mine bosses are super rich, purchasing Land Rovers or Hummers and expensive apartments in Beijing without any hesitation. But that's not true; the owners of this coal mine are from Beijing. We work for them. The profits go to Beijing (and Zhejiang in some cases), and we [in County D] get the damaged environment. . . . The government's regulatory policies keep on changing very rapidly, and we can't adapt to them [so we try to evade the regulations instead of meeting the requirements].[31]

After two hours of talk, we declined their invitation for lunch and left for the county seat. The tax officer explained that the mine managers regularly feed visitors:

> Today is a weekend day, so we are the only visitors; on weekdays they get four or more groups of visitors, from different government bureaus and related organizations, with different tasks of investigating and checking. But they end up going back to the county seat [or provincial capital] with some expensive gifts and even red packets [envelopes with money], after getting a very good lunch or dinner. . . . The golden days of coal-mine owners are gone [with the strict implementation of the provincial government policy regarding closing small and merging medium-sized mines]. The county government should find some new revenue sources, not based on coal mining but on industry. But it is hard to build and run an "on-the-ground enterprise" [a term for any enterprise that does not involve going underground, as coal mining does] here.[32]

As in County Cold Mountain, strong political connections are a prerequisite for running a coal mine, which is very profitable, is not competitive, requires no or little entrepreneurship, and, most important, is immobile. Therefore, a coal-mine owner needs to protect his mine from predatory government bureaus and people who want to take over the mine in coercive ways. I was speaking with a mine owner, an officer, and his friends about the business. The officer's friend said that he had a friend who wanted to invest in coal mining. The owner, who had drunk several cups of very strong alcohol, said, "I don't encourage your friend to invest in a coal mine if he has any other choices. Coal mining is an industry that totally depends on your ability to build and maintain political connections [for success]."[33] As in County Cold Mountain, County D gained windfall wealth and fiscal revenue in the 2000s through abundant coal resources. And, as in County Cold Mountain, this immobile industry has not improved governance.

County Yiwu

In a government-sponsored meeting in County Yiwu of Zhejiang, a county-level city famous for its large-scale and specialized wholesale markets, I spoke to a Mr. Yu, a local private entrepreneur. He owns an enterprise producing and selling iron security doors and is a county PPCC member, president of the county's Trade Association of Security Doors, and village party secretary. He told me, "It's illegal to evade taxes [so I will not do it], but it is legal and appropriate to get favorable tax policies [for my company]." I asked him whether his title as the president of the trade association was part of how he got elected (knowing in fact he had been selected) as a city PPCC member. He indicated that being the village party secretary was probably key. "My village is a large one and close to the county seat, and there have been a lot of land-seizure issues in recent years, so the township government leaders value me a lot and recommended me to the city's PPCC." But Mr. Yu admitted that his enterprise helped him get the job as party secretary, as he built his reputation on his success. But he submits policy proposals (*ti'an*) to the PPCC only on village issues, rather than industry issues, because he thinks he has been selected to represent the village. He said the trade association ensured self-governance of industries, and he did not think it was "appropriate" to talk about industry at PPCC meetings. His trade association works closely with government bureaus to set industry standards and regulations, but he also maintains distance from the government for both the trade association and his company. "It is a competitive industry, and your success depends on your business talents [not your political connections]. The government cares about and values you because you are doing something good, contributing to society."[34]

Like most private entrepreneurs I met in Yiwu, Mr. Yu runs a small to medium-sized private enterprise in a competitive market, and he tries his best to evade tax but also pays his dues to keep from being identified as a tax evader. He tries to keep a reasonable distance from the government and to work with the government on industry self-governance issues with some degree of independence. The local government values private enterprises such as his because they support economic growth and provide tax revenue and also because the city government lacks enough personnel and fiscal resources to regulate industries.

In 2009, Yiwu was ranked twelfth among China's one hundred most economically competitive counties, with a GDP of 51.95 billion yuan (104.6 in 2015), urban resident average annual income of 30,841 yuan (49,351 in 2015), and rural resident average annual income of 12,899 yuan (28,433 in 2015). Its thriving commodity market has attracted hundreds of thousands of businesses to open shops and even build factories there. Thirty years earlier, Yiwu was a very poor county with limited arable land, and GDP per capita was 235 yuan. In the 1970s, residents operated illegal private businesses, selling wares such as brown sugar or needles in other counties.

An informal market arose in the county seat in the early 1980s, and consumers began to come to Yiwu to purchase the goods vendors had previously brought to them. The AIC regarded the market as illegal at first and tried to break it up, but vendors had few options and little to lose, so the county government began to recognize the market as a source of economic growth. It began to permit and eventually support development of the wholesale markets with the backing of higher levels of government.

In 1984, the county government decided to develop commerce as the county's main industry. Yiwu's markets gained a nationwide reputation. Market development in turn promoted the development of rural industrial enterprises. The government provided political, financial, and technical support, including tax breaks and legal protection from the Mafia. The government also played a leading role in upgrading the wholesale market by getting higher-level government permission for the development of the market, which included establishing the first county-level customs office and investing in infrastructure to support the market.[35] These efforts helped build a wholesale market with a nationwide reputation. Enterprises from throughout the country and later the world established branch offices in Yiwu.

The trade associations in Yiwu are well developed, compared to those in other counties in China, and most are independent from the government and very active. County leaders have mobilized the trade associations to supervise the government bureaus and sometimes regulate industry. For example, the Association of Hotels and Restaurants acted collectively to resist some government bureaus that were collecting high fees arbitrarily in the late 1990s. The association's resistance got the attention of the head of county government, who called a meeting between the relevant bureaus and the trade association to ask the bureaus to cancel the fees. Meanwhile, the Association of Hotels and Restaurants in a neighboring county collectively resisted the arbitrary fees but got no attention (or support) from government leaders. Ultimately, therefore, it failed. The presidents of these two associations know each other, and both of them told me that Yiwu government leaders had strong incentives to discipline the predatory bureaus to create a good business environment.[36]

Zhou Xiaoguang, a famous private entrepreneur (of jewelry and accessories), president of a very successful trade association, and an NPC deputy who has a PC deputy's office (*renda daibiao gongzuoshi* 人大代表工作室) that helps her fill her NPC deputy obligations, believes that the Yiwu government does the best job in the country of developing a service-oriented government and public-service system: "I got very good responses from the government for my proposals on the LPC. I also deliberately consult with county government when I make proposals for the NPC" (Tian 2008).

Yiwu has made some institutional innovations: it is the first county to have a migrant worker as a township-level PC deputy who speaks for migrant workers, it empowers the labor union to negotiate with government and business,[37] it has enacted comprehensive department budgeting that shows very detailed items of government bureaus and township governments, and it empowers the county PC to monitor government bureaus.

County Z

As East China develops rapidly, local governments in Western and Central China are trying to learn from the eastern regions in an attempt to catch up. Attracting investment is a major strategy for these areas. Interior county governments have tried to create good business environments by disciplining government bureaus and providing good service, as well as using cheap labor and land to their advantage. County Z of Chongqing in Western China is a good example. In the summer of 2009, the officials of the county Investment Promotion Bureau (zhaoshang yinzi ju) told me they have done a pretty good job so far and have successfully attracted billions in investment each year. For example, in November 2008 during the "Week of Investment Promotion of Year 2008," they signed sixty-eight agreements with outside investors (from the United States, Hong Kong, Beijing, and provinces in East China) worth 13.5 billion yuan. I asked how they convinced outside investors from East China and even foreign countries to make investments in their badly located county. They told me that the addition of a highway and railway the next year would improve their location and that they could build a good business environment if they worked hard.

The county party committee and government regard investment promotion as the most important work for the cadres and set targets for them in a program called "all people take part in investment promotion." The county government has an official document that promises a series of policies favorable to outside investors, which include significant tax (and fee) breaks, low-priced land, convenient financial services, a focus on four industry clusters in which they have the competitive advantage and scale economy, "one-stop service" for all administrative registrations,[38] and a system in which "leaders contact large outside investors" (*lingdao lianxi daqiye zhidu*),[39] which seeks to alleviate the problem of potential outside investors facing uncertainty without the social networks they build closer to home. These social networks help entrepreneurs obtain market information, build reliable supply and demand networks, and deal with problems with others (including the government). Without a well-developed system of rule of law, networks serve a vital purpose (Greif 2006; Hamilton and Biggart 1988), and some of my private-entrepreneur respondents told me that they prefer to invest in regions where they have personal connections. The government's promise to keep a good business environment (especially to keep predatory government bureaus from interfering) is important, but only when it is credible. By directly contacting outside investors, government officials raise their confidence of a lasting commitment to creating a hospitable environment.[40]

In spite of the success of this system and other measures, County Z's efforts to attract outside investment has hit obstacles that Counties Warm River, Yiwu, and Wenling did not. County Z's efforts to reform government bureaus and provide good public services mostly apply only to outside investors, and some apply only to large investors, so small local businesses suffer. Also, the government is ready to help capitalists restrain the power of labor, including not allowing the establishment of a legal aid center for laborers,[41] which limits individuals' access to the benefits of economic growth.[42]

County X

Mobile capital presses the local government to work to create a good business environment. But under certain conditions, local political leaders with high discount rates may not be willing to improve government services. This is very challenging and even risky, and it does not provide revenue in the short term.[43] However, officials in County X of Hunan Province in Central China have been offered incentives to make these improvements. Like others, County X government implemented a series of policies to attract investment in the late 1990s, including the construction of an industrial park. But the only big enterprise it attracted uses raw material produced in County X. This enterprise has a significant role in the county's economic health and provided many employee opportunities and generated a great deal of revenue. The county party secretary was promoted because of his success in attracting this enterprise in the early 2000s.

His successors faced a difficult situation because they were unable to attract more good investments, even if they provided zero-price land and very substantial tax breaks. However, under the performance-driven cadre evaluation system, local political leaders set high quotas for government officials to attract investment.[44] A senior local officer told me the story of the industrial park in County X. Instead of making an effort to create a good business environment, government officials collude with fake "investors" to meet quotas that are impossible to meet: the investors get low-priced land and tax breaks, make a minimum investment, and receive large sums in bank loans that far exceed the amount they invested. The investors pocket the amount they invested and use the rest of the loan to build factory buildings that then stand empty. They do not generate any GDP for the county and pay little if any taxes. And they have good political connections, so they do not need to pay the bank loans on time, although they can always sell the improved land to repay the loan. This leaves the county government with a huge amount of debt spent on building the industrial park.[45] Another senior government official also complained to me, "The industrial park does not generate much GDP or local fiscal revenue; it serves only to benefit the local political leaders, and everyone knows that. The new enterprises only bring pollution to the county."[46]

Conclusion

Through comparative case studies and process tracing, I provide a different answer, with different mechanisms based on taxation and asset mobility, to Robert Putnam's questions in the epigraph to this chapter: "How do formal institutions influence the practice of politics and government? If we reform institutions, will practice follow? Does the performance of an institution depend on its social, economic, and cultural surround?" Unlike authors of existing theories such as modernization theory, which focuses on level of economic development,[47] and social capital theory (Putnam, Leonardi, and Nanetti 1993; L. Tsai 2017), I find that under a pro-development regime with de facto fiscal federalism, private entrepreneurs' increasing economic resources—especially their tax resources—empower them in the local political arena, which, in turn, affects governance quality. The dominant industries in a specific region, especially the asset mobility of said industries, affect regional governance quality greatly by shaping actors' preferences and bargaining power.

Rapid economic growth and improved governance quality helped the CCP achieve legitimacy and sustain power. Chapter 3 reveals the coevolution of market and bureaucracy under the institutional arrangement of fiscal decentralization and political centralization, and this chapter adds cross-regional evidence. Therefore, I also enrich the infrastructural state-power mechanism by discussing the relationship between taxation and bureaucratization. Because China is a post-totalitarian state, the government should be able to discipline its bureaus (or resolve the agent-discipline problem) before it can penetrate society to extract resources effectively and distribute resources as it desires. Otherwise, government bureaus will act predatorily and harm long-term economic development by worsening the institutional environment for investment, therefore worsening the cooperation problem.[48] This occurred in Russia in the 1990s and in some low-asset-mobility regions in China. In other words, a vicious cycle emerges. With the increase of local government's fiscal revenue, local government begins to be able to fund its bureaus with its budget and, therefore, can discipline its bureaus' behaviors.

Disciplined bureaucracy does not come naturally but requires government effort. In the 1980s, local governments did not have enough fiscal revenue to fund government bureaus and left them to fund themselves by running companies and collecting fees and fines. These revenue-eager bureaus acted predatorily in grabbing revenue but did not provide the necessary public goods; therefore, they became a major threat to the development of private enterprises. Only when local political leaders have the willingness and capability to discipline predatory government bureaus to generate a good business environment can they promote regional economic development through promoting more investment. With economic development, fiscal revenue increases and the local government can improve the level of bureaucratization and have strong disciplinary power. This is a *virtuous* circle but is hard to achieve. I argue that a reliance on mobile industries is vital for this virtuous circle to develop.

But in regions with low asset mobility, especially where most fiscal revenue comes from natural resources, it is difficult to find such a virtuous coevolution. The logic of lack of institution building in the rentier state identified by Pauline Jones Luong and Erika Weinthal could be applied:

> The most prevalent explanation for the lack of institution building [in the rentier state] is that a reliance on external revenue creates a disincentive for state leaders to invest in strong institutions because it induces myopia and risk aversion. . . . Another common explanation is that mineral wealth encourages state leaders to resist building institutions, especially institutions that promote transparency and accountability, because they prefer to maximize their discretion over both the policy-making process and the distribution of export rents—even going so far as to weaken preexisting institutions "that restrict windfall use." (2006, 245)

With regard to how society can constrain the government's despotic power, our cases suggest that under an authoritarian state in which the representative institution has many deficiencies, structural power (asset mobility) constrains the government. The major taxpayers, private entrepreneurs, are unable to challenge or constrain the state individually because of the under-institutionalized taxation system (among other institutions), which makes them vulnerable to the state. However, as an industry,[49] entrepreneurs can constrain the local government that aims to promote regional economic development to some degree. Therefore, I provide a mechanism to explain why local political leaders and private entrepreneurs may have incentives to discipline bureaucracy in high-asset-mobility regions. In chapter 6, I conduct a quantitative study to test the external validity of the causal relationships identified here and in chapter 5.

Under a regionally decentralized authoritarianism there are two types of government-business bargaining: implicit and explicit. Implicit bargaining is the more influential of the two because the performance-driven local governments try to encourage local, within-county, and foreign investment locally. A good business environment means good government service and infrastructure and a noncorrupt and responsive government. The government bureaus are constrained from acting predatorily, which guarantees low and predictable tax rates (including surtaxes and fees) and transparent and easy procedures for registration. This implicates restructuring and rebuilding of the local states, cutting off local government bureaus' extra-budgetary revenue, and disciplining them through a unified and comprehensive budget.[50] The quality of the business environment thus provides a significant measurement of governance quality.

Given the institutional defects of the LPC and the under-institutionalized taxation system, explicit bargaining has minimal influence on regional tax competition. Private entrepreneurs do have increased opportunities to express their point of view to government through formal and informal channels. More and more private entrepreneurs have positions in LPCs, LPPCCs, and local party committees. The co-optation of private entrepreneurs elicits investment locally and improves the performance of these nominally representative institutions. Government officials are more responsive because of the participation of private entrepreneurs.

CHAPTER 5

Representation through Taxation?

> Tax bill in hand, the state penetrated the private economies and won increasing dominion over them. . . . The kind and level of taxes are determined by the social structure, but once taxes exist they become a handle, as it were, which social powers can grip in order to change this structure.
> —Joseph Schumpeter, "The Crisis of the Tax State"

> There [England] the aristocracy had assumed all the [tax] burdens in order to enjoy the power of governing; here [France] they steadily refused to pay taxes, as their only consolation for the loss of political power.
> —Alexis de Tocqueville, *The Old Regime and the Revolution*

> As a forum through which dictators can make policy concessions, nominally democratic institutions are instruments of co-optation.
> —Jennifer Gandhi, *Political Institutions under Dictatorship*

Mr. Liu is the chairman of a large private bedding company based in County Warm River in Zhejiang Province. He has many titles on his business card: chairman of Bedding Company X, member of County Warm River's LPPCC Standing Committee, deputy of the prefecture PC, and president of the Provincial Trade Association of Bedding. Pennants hanging on his office wall read "County Warm River's top 10 taxpayer [纳税大户] of 2008," and "Top 20 taxpayer of 2009."[1] He proudly told me that he was going to be selected as the municipal-level "Model Worker" (劳动模范) very soon, which is more valuable than a title such as "Prefecture PC Deputy."[2] He also talked a lot about proposals he had made to the county PPCC, most of which the county government had adopted. The most recent was a comprehensive plan to redesign the county's industrial park by building a Logistics Center to serve the three main industries of the county. He said that the county PPCC had selected the plan as an important project. "I believe the county party committee and government will adopt it soon," he said proudly. During the interview, he answered many phone calls. On one, I heard him say to a government official that he had heard about the meeting from a deputy county head, whose car license number is 0005, and would go there with him. Later I was told that license number 0005 indicates the number-five political figure in the county, the vice-head of county government, who is also a member of the county PC Standing Committee.[3]

There are many Mr. Lius in China. Many successful businessmen's business cards list multiple titles, including PC deputy or PPCC member at the top. After more than three decades of market transition, private entrepreneurs are becoming more important in local social-economic affairs: they promote regional economic growth, employ a large number of workers, pay a large share of local revenue, and donate money for public services. Using their socioeconomic influence, some private entrepreneurs become increasingly politically active and join the LPC, LPPCC, or even the local Party Committee. As a result, private entrepreneurs who are deputies have become the second-largest group in the LPC after the party and government cadres in many regions, especially developed regions.[4] According to various sources, including my own interviews, about 30 percent of county-level LPC deputies in many regions are private entrepreneurs.[5] While some regions in China may have lower formal participation by entrepreneurs, high involvement of private entrepreneurs may heavily influence a region, especially given the growing importance of the LPC in China. Politically active private entrepreneurs may bring something to China's local politics previously absent. The report of the third session of the party's Eighteenth National Congress released in November 2013 addresses LPC reform and improvement of its supervision power over local governments' budgeting: the party's major political reform in the coming years, which may have a conspicuous effect on the influence of entrepreneurs as a major deputy group in the LPC.[6]

Modernization theory suggests the presence of entrepreneurs in LPCs may promote democracy, as it posits that the emergence of a middle class, especially the bourgeoisie, will promote democratic governance, if not democracy (Lipset 1959).[7] The class theory of democratization proposed by Barrington Moore (1966) and developed by his followers also proposes that capitalists are the driving force for democratization.[8] More modestly, institutionalism theory argues that new social forces, as de facto power, can change the functions of formal institutions (as de jure power) without formally changing the institutions (Putnam, Leonardi, and Nanetti 1993; Acemoglu, Johnson, and Robinson 2005). According to these theories, as the composition of LPC deputies' socioeconomic background has changed significantly over time with the rising presence of private-entrepreneur deputies in low-level LPCs, the functions of LPCs will change. This chapter directly addresses whether these entrepreneur deputies are likely to strengthen the LPC's representation function and promote a more responsive and accountable local government, which could contribute to or weaken authoritarian rule.

In recent decades, under the "institutional turn" of comparative authoritarianism, some scholars have reexamined these "democratic-looking" institutions, such as legislatures (Gandhi 2008) and elections (Gandhi and Lust-Okar 2009), under authoritarian regimes. They have found that they play a role more substantial than window dressing, that in fact they play an important part in authoritarian resilience. Jennifer Gandhi argues:

> For autocratic rulers, institutions help in addressing two basic dilemmas of governance. First, dictators must secure their position in power, neutralizing any threats to their rule. Second, nondemocratic incumbents must solicit the cooperation of outsiders to ensure that individuals have incentives to engage in productive activities. (2008, 181)

To reframe the argument, ideally, a legislature and its direct election can co-opt resourceful private entrepreneurs, neutralize their threat to the state, and therefore solve the social-control problem. The LPC also helps local political leaders discipline the bureaucracy's predatory behavior under certain circumstances. This provides credible commitment that the state will protect private property rights to encourage investment to promote economic growth, through which the agent-discipline and cooperation problems are alleviated.

I argue that under the current LPC institutional arrangement characterized by the party's domination of the LPC, weak LPC power, and controlled election procedures, the presence of private-entrepreneur deputies in the LPC leads to clientelism and co-optation rather than representation and government responsiveness. Commercialization of elections may corrupt the LPC and weaken its representation function, therefore alleviating the representation dilemma. This chapter examines the LPC and its direct election and discusses whether these two democratic-looking institutions sustain authoritarianism as proposed by studies of other developing countries (Art 2012; Gandhi and Lust-Okar 2009).

I first provide a brief review of the existing literature on private entrepreneurs' political role and the LPCs' representation and inclusion functions in China. I then examine the institutional background and evolution of the LPC in local politics and the process of electing LPC deputies and provide an empirical study of private entrepreneurs' incentives to be LPC deputies. I next discuss three cases to provide evidence that LPCs could be mobilized to monitor and discipline predatory government bureaus under certain circumstances and then discuss implications of the findings.

The LPC: Representative or Inclusive?

Since the 1990s, the LPC has emerged as an important player in local politics and been strengthened as an organization; for example, it has more staff, including better-educated younger people; more differentiated and professionalized committees; institutionalized procedures for election; and standardized deputy training and learning programs.[9] Some scholars argue that the LPCs are becoming more capable, active, and effective in lawmaking and supervising local governments (O'Brien 2009, 131). As Kevin O'Brien (2009) and Melanie Manion (2009) found a decade ago, the existing research on LPCs focuses on their rationalization aspect, how their institutionalization affects the division of power within the party-state. However, the representation function of the LPC is understudied, as are the elections of the deputies, deputy-constituent ties, and deputies' behavior at plenary sessions. That is, rationalization, a top-down process driven by the central government to push rule by law (or legalization), has been far more studied than representation, a process of constraining the despotic power of the local government. Research on the NPC and LPCs also suffers from using the structural-functional analytic framework, which emphasizes the structures and functions of the PCs at different levels. While this framework is valuable for description, its explanatory power is limited.[10]

However, some recent works study the representation aspect of the LPC deputies (Manion 2016; Truex 2016), and some focus on the increasingly important role of private-entrepreneur deputies in the LPC and their representation role or lack of (Hou 2019; Sun, Zhu, and Wu 2014;

C. Zhang 2017b). The studies that address this issue diverge significantly. Young Nam Cho (2010) finds that both the rationalization and representation aspects of LPCs vary in different localities, but, unfortunately, his primary examination of the representation aspect is both unsystematic and sometimes misleading (O'Brien 2009 agrees with me). O'Brien (1994a), however, finds that LPC deputies are more like regime regents—that is, they diffuse societal pressures and provide a rationale for policy—than remonstrators, who also have little power to make change but can still offer advice to an administration and thereby create change that citizens desire. Jigang Guo (2007) argues that most deputies are not active in LPCs because they are nominated by and compliant with the party. He argues that only those deputies whose elections were contested and those with a sense of social responsibility are active. According to Guo, the legislative institutional arrangement makes the mechanism of electoral accountability unworkable in China: deputy candidates do not have an incentive to attract constituents' votes because the election is a top-down rather than bottom-up process.[11] Where Guo, O'Brien, and Cho find assertive LPC deputies, they typically find their evidence in media reports, which tend to report extreme rather than typical cases. Manion (2016, 2017) presents quantitative and qualitative data suggesting that LPCs, especially lower-level LPCs, are becoming more representative. Rory Truex (2016) finds that PCs at different levels do have "representation within bounds" because advocacy strategies potentially associated with contestation are discouraged. However, the measurement of representation in this quantitative research lacks internal validity for reasons discussed later in the chapter.

A spate of recent research has focused on the inclusive or co-optation function of legislative institutions in authoritarian states rather than their representation function. A good example is Xiaojun Yan's study of an LPPCC, in which he finds that "overall, the PPCC helps to consolidate the Communist regime's social base, improve the quality of public services and strengthen the regime's control over society" (2011, 55). Yan also admits that the patron-client networks between the party-state and social elites are built through the PPCC, "which allocates preferential treatment and consolidates its ties with elites and leaders in society" (73). Yan finds several differences between the LPPCC and the LPC: "As a representative institution with a role in regime inclusion, the [L]PC has less institutional flexibility and relatively limited room for political manipulation of the party-state" (75). In another such study, Xin Sun, Jiangnan Zhu, and Yiping Wu (2014) argue that LPCs are organized platforms of clientelism, and Ying Sun (2014) argues that the indirect election of members of the PC at the prefecture level plays a co-optation role. This chapter complements as well as revises some of Sun, Zhu, and Wu (2014) and Yan's conclusions on inclusive institutions, including both the LPPCC and LPC, and discusses implications for authoritarian resilience.

Rationalization of the LPC

Scholars and observers find that the LPC has experienced more progress in rationalization than in representation. This section discusses the LPC in the local political system and the space for a more active LPC, as well as its evolution in the last three decades.

The LPC in Local Governance: The Institutional Arrangement

The PRC's constitution describes China's polity as a combination of the legislative and executive powers,[12] best known as "the dictatorship of the proletariat." As the legislative organ, the PCs at different levels are the institutions with the greatest power: they vote to elect government and deputy government leaders, and government leaders nominate bureau heads who need the votes of the majority of PC deputies to get appointed. Other mechanisms to keep the government responsive and accountable to the PCs are power of legislation (at the provincial and national levels [立法权]), supervision (监督权), and authority to make important decisions (重大事项决策权).[13] There is no administrative leadership relationship (领导关系) between LPCs at different levels, but there is a professional leadership relationship (业务指导关系). There are parallel PPCCs at all levels of government except the township; these PPCCs are consultative institutions and, therefore, more honorable and symbolic than the PCs.[14] The PC, PPCC, and government at the same level have the same administrative level. Figure 5.1 illustrates the nominal power relationship at the local level.

However, this figure misrepresents the real power relationship in local politics. As in other modern states ruled by parties, the CCP plays an important role in organizing the government. However, China has no checks and balances from opposition parties.[15] Before the reform era, the

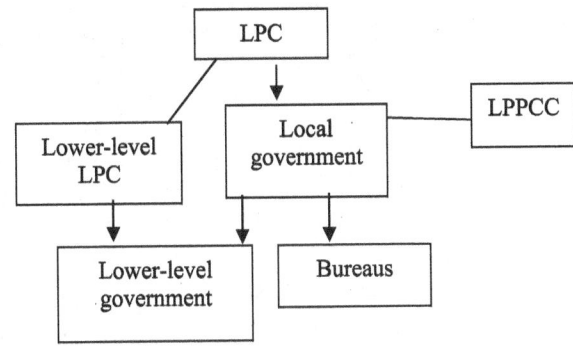

Figure 5.1. Nominal local power relationships. Arrows indicate power relationships, while plain lines indicate other types of relations (advisory or consultant).

party penetrated into all corners of society, and the LPC and LPPCC are not exceptions. The local party committee Standing Committee is above all institutions at the same level because it monopolizes the power to appoint and remove personnel,[16] party disciplinary power, and specific committees in charge of some important issues.[17] The Party Committee and LPC have similar institutions but have different roles. Therefore, the division of power and division of labor between them are important: the party's role is to lead the government, while the LPC's role is to supervise the government.

The relationship between the party and the LPCs also follows the principle of party leadership. Institutionally, there are three important ways for the party to lead and control the LPC: the party secretary may take a position as director of an LPC; the party can control the LPC's personnel through its Organization Department; and a "party team" (党组) can be set up within the LPC and placed under the direct leadership of the local Party Committee's Standing Committee at the same level. The first method is very common at the provincial but not the county level. In most cases, when the party secretary is not the director of the LPC, the county PC may have a director who is a senior local and has been the deputy government head and/or deputy party secretary for many years within the county, with several (four to seven) deputy directors who are also local and senior. These people have intensive networks within the county since they have been working there for most of their lives. This is a potential source of LPC power, especially because the party secretary and government head are not local.[18] However, the party's personnel power and the "party team" within the LPC enable the party to control the LPC effectively. The LPC directors and its Standing Committee members know that well, so they emphasize this principle: "The LPC helps the party and government but

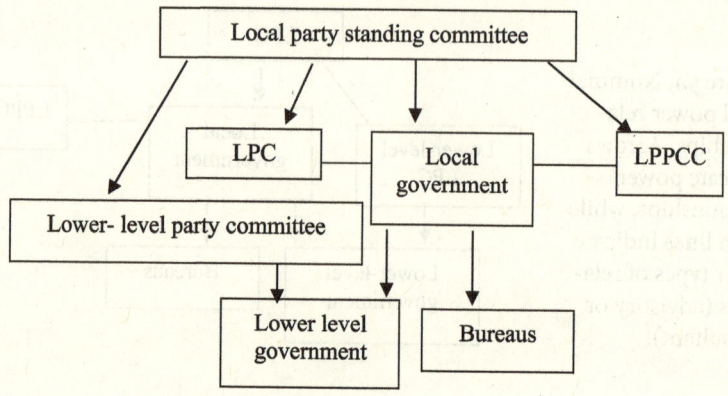

Figure 5.2. Real local power relationships.

does not make any trouble for them" (帮忙不添乱).[19] In sum, the principle of party leadership reshapes the landscape of power relationships in local politics, as illustrated in figure 5.2.

The local government is also more powerful than the LPC, both because the government heads have higher political status within the party (even when they are at the same administrative level) and because it has more fiscal and personal resources. The local government head is the deputy party secretary and the second most-powerful person in local politics. Also, there are two or more deputy government heads who are members of the Local Party Standing Committee (LPSC).[20] At the same time, the director of the LPC and the president of the LPPCC are not members of the LPSC. Though they are at the same administrative level as the party secretary and government head and they can audit the LPSC, they have no voting power there. Therefore, their political status is lower than that of the government leaders they are supposed to supervise. As a result, the supervision of LPCs depends on the support of the party.

The fuzzy boundary between the party and government makes it even more difficult for LPCs to supervise the government, because they are not supposed to supervise the party, which, in effect, leads them. For example, LPCs may want to supervise the court, but the court can say that it made its decision according to the party's Committee of Politics and Law, which is a party organ that the LPC is not supposed to supervise. Both the staff number and the budget of the LPC and LPPCC are like those in a regular government bureau, which makes the LPC and LPPCC relatively powerless. The government also determines the LPC's budget, although the LPC nominally has the final decision-making power to revise and pass the government budgetary plan. The LPC's role is really to listen to the government rather than supervise it. Or the LPC could choose the strategy of embedding with the party to make an alliance to supervise the government (O'Brien 1994b).

Another important factor that makes the LPC and LPPCC weak institutions is that their leaders are old officials "retired" from the party and government positions. The LPC and LPPCC are referred to as the "second line," and their leaders and staffs describe themselves as "retreating to the second line" (退居二线), a military phrase that reflects the imprinting of the CCP's military history. My informants repeated common sayings about the powers of different institutions that vividly capture the power relationships between different government organs. One of them explained: "The LPSC members use mouth [to discuss and make decisions], the government uses hands [to implement the decisions], the LPC deputies raise hands [to pass the party decisions], and the LPPCC members applaud hands [to support the party and government's decisions]."[21]

These institutional arrangements leave the LPC with limited power. However, as Deng Xiaoping (1993) said decades ago, if the party wants to retreat and redefine the LPC's role, there are also large institutional spaces in which the LPC might develop.[22] Some scholars argue that the institutional space is large enough to accommodate democracy without significant changes in formal institutions, which are even harder to change. There is empirical evidence that the LPC can be strengthened. As one LPC director said in a meeting of County Warm River's PC Standing Committee in the early 1990s:

> When we [the LPC Standing Committee] do a good job, we can build LPC's authority; if we abuse our power, we will lose our authority; and if we don't use our power, we will never get authority. We need to take the initiative to get the LPSC's attention [and support to do some meaningful work]. Our comparative advantage [to the party and government] is only that we can maintain social stability, because we can improve the relationships between the government and the people through listening to their voices and demands. Also, the market economy is a rule by law economy; the LPC can supervise the government through the law. We have a lot of things to do, and we are important.[23]

One of my informants, who has been working for a district-level LPPCC in Beijing for several years, told me that "under the current institutional arrangements, the LPC director can make different decisions to challenge the party secretary if he or she will and wants to take the risk"—that is, of being later removed from the position as a result.[24] County Warm River's PC meeting records support and cross-validate this informant's point.

When the new county party secretary came to County Warm River in 1991, he realized that the environment for promoting economic development, especially the private economy resulting from rapid economic development in Zhejiang Province, was not as good as that in its neighboring counties. The reasons, he found, are the predatory behaviors of the business-related government bureaus. In particular, the AIC did a bad job. So he decided to remove the heads of three bureaus (including the AIC) after deliberation and going through the procedure of cadre evaluation (the heads received less than 50 percent "satisfactory" ratings in the evaluation).[25] But the party secretary needed the LPC Standing Committee to support his decision to make it legal.

However, some of the county PC Standing Committee members (including the director), who were local people who had worked in County Warm River for decades before being moved to the LPC, had good connections with these bureau heads. So they did not want to carry out the party secretary's request. Therefore, there was a conflict between the party's power of cadre management and the LPC's power to appoint and remove government officials according to the law. To solve this conflict, the party secretary asked for a special LPC Standing Committee meeting to explain why he wanted to remove these bureau heads and called for the members' understanding and support. He said, "I am new to County Warm River and have no personal interests involved or any dislike of these people. But it is necessary to readjust (remove and change) the bureau heads to motivate the cadres to work hard, and we need to improve our work to promote the development of private economy."

The LPC Standing Committee held another meeting after the party secretary's speech. The director disagreed with the party secretary and implicitly suggested vetoing his request. He said that even though the party manages cadres (*dangguan ganbu*), the LPC has the legal authority to appoint and remove them. But some members were very concerned about violating the principle of party leadership. The party secretary's request passed with a margin of one vote (eight in support and seven against).[26]

The presence of retired party and government officials can also be a source of power, given these actors' dense networks in the county. If the LPC director's will to get something done and the LPC deputies' social and economic characteristics are sufficient, the LPC can play a more important role. As two county PC directors told me, local politics can have LPC power, but achieving respect and power (*Youwei cai youwei* 有为才有位) requires hard work.²⁷ Indeed, the LPCs in some regions are playing an increasingly important role in local politics.²⁸ My research suggests that LPCs are becoming more and more powerful and that there are some local variations in LPCs' institutional performance. Why have LPCs become more powerful, and why are there significant regional variations? The evidence presented in chapters 3 and 4 suggests that performance-driven local political leaders, facing mobile assets, are forced to work hard to discipline predatory bureaus. Mobilizing the LPC to deliberate and discuss (评议) government bureaus' work is an effective strategy. Therefore, asset mobility of a region's major industries can partially explain the regional variation of LPC rationalization and representation. However, the LPC's power can be manipulated; its role in improving governance and sustaining an authoritarian regime is exogenous to some degree, as Thomas Pepinsky (2014) suggests in a review article regarding the institutional turn of authoritarian resilience literature.²⁹

The Evolution of LPCs

The LPC has increasingly emerged as an important player in local politics since the reform and opening up of China, especially in the 1990s when the Chinese government started to build a market economy based on rule by law, if not rule of law (A. Chen 1999; Cho 2002, 2010; Xia 2008).³⁰ However, it is not an "iron stamp" with strong power; nor is it a "rubber stamp," as it was before the 1990s (Cho 2002).³¹

The major difference between the rationalization and representation aspects of LPCs is that rationalization is a top-down process driven by the central government to push rule by law (or legalization). It is more a process of state (re)building than representation—the central government uses LPCs to rationalize government bureaucracy, thus strengthening the infrastructure power of the party-state. Representation is a bottom-up process that can be changed from the bottom and by the voters. It is a process of constraining the despotic power of the state. A rationalized legislature can become an effective representative institution when socioeconomic elites penetrate it but need not.

The LPC has been strengthened in many ways since the reform era. It has far more staff, and better-educated, younger therefore motivated and energetic, people have entered the ranks. LPCs have more differentiated and professionalized committees, institutionalized procedures for election, standardized deputy training and learning programs, and other trappings of democratic bodies.[32] As a consequence, some scholars argue that the LPCs are becoming more capable, active, and effective in lawmaking and supervising local governments. Some LPCs have started to reject the candidates the party nominates in favor of independent candidates (A. Chen 1999; Cho 2009). However, local party and government organs have grown even faster than LPCs. For instance, while the office of the LPC Standing Committee in County Warm River has grown from five to twenty full-time staff members, the office of the LPSC has grown from five to twenty-five. And the officials who work in the LPSC office have much better opportunities for promotion than those who work in the LPC office. To examine whether LPCs have become representative or inclusive institutions, I link the formal institution with the deputies to examine how deputies, especially private entrepreneurs, get "elected" into the LPC.

The LPC Election Process

County Warm River provides a case study to examine how private-entrepreneur deputies have became the second-largest deputy groups in many regions in recent years. The county's private economy became increasingly important in the early 1990s. Private entrepreneurs got more attention from the county Party Committee and government. The local government began to focus on encouraging private entrepreneurs to expand their businesses and contribute to society, while also regulating them (collecting taxes, deterring them from producing and selling low-quality products, etc.). Selecting the "honest" private entrepreneurs and giving them honorable titles such as "LPPCC member" or "LPC deputy" was a solution. In theory, the exemplary private entrepreneurs assigned to these roles will influence other private entrepreneurs to act like them.[33] An LPC official who described this strategy to me regarded the title "LPC deputy" as honorable. County Warm River was one of the first to embrace it, but it has become a nationwide practice, as O'Brien (1994a) finds. The party-state expects private-entrepreneur deputies, like other LPC deputies, to explain policies to their constituencies and compel their compliance. Like other types of political participation under an authoritarian (and postcommunist) state, the LPCs' political participation is mobilized participation, and LPCs serve as the bridge between the party-state and the people. As O'Brien (1994a) argues, the deputies' state regent role dominates their remonstrator role.

My interviews reveal that private entrepreneurs found something more valuable than a symbolic title. They saw value in the opportunity to build political connections, obtain political privileges, and make policy proposals. Therefore, they had strong incentives to get "selected" or "elected" into the LPC. The manner by which they enter the LPC has important consequences.

Controlled Direct Election and Its Implication

Direct election is the institutional mechanism that generates political representation and accountability when elections are free and competitive.[34] While higher-level (from prefecture to national) PC deputies are elected by the lower-level LPC, over which the party has effective control, the constitution gives voters the right to directly elect LPC deputies at the township and county levels. As in democratic countries, China's counties and townships have many electoral districts, the parties nominate candidates, and independent candidates are also allowed to compete with the officially nominated candidates and sometimes even win the election. The formal institutional practice of direct elections suggests that there should be some, even limited, degree of political representation and accountability at the township and county levels.

However, the informal practice of LPC election, or election manipulation, weakens the representation and accountability of LPC deputies. The local party committee Standing Committee, the LPC Standing Committee, and local government work together to control the election in various ways. The most effective method is to control the nomination of candidates. Electoral law permits either "mass organizations" (人民团体)[35] or ten or more voters to nominate candidates.[36] However, in reality, the party makes the final nomination list through the Election Committee by means of a nontransparent and highly centralized decision-making process that makes the nomination easy to manipulate.[37] The county PC Standing Committee delegates its Organization Department (*zuzhibu*组织部) to work with the LPC Standing Committee to organize an Election Committee to direct and control the election of deputies. But the Election Committee's power is limited because it needs to report to the PC Standing Committee, which makes the final decision.

The party's Organization Department is in charge of nomination of LPC deputy candidates who are party members.[38] The party's United Front Work Department (*tongzhanbu* 统战部) is responsible for managing the non-party-member candidates, in consultation with the Association of Commerce and Industry, a government-sponsored social organization that organizes both private and public entrepreneurs. These party organizations try to assign quotas to different social groups (cadres, peasants, workers, entrepreneurs, intellectuals, etc.) to define their role in the LPC, even though electoral law prohibits the practice.[39] As a result, urban areas (often the county seats) have many more deputies than rural areas do, even though this is not proportional to their populations.[40] The party then assigns some of these candidates to rural townships and requires the township government to elect them.[41] As a result, a township that has eight seats might have one or two that the county government assigns and another two or three candidates the party requires to be elected (the party's secretary, the township PC's president, and sometimes the township government head). Only three to five seats remain to be filled by real candidates who depend on votes, and the township government manipulates those. County leaders may require the township government to have certain people elected as part of the commercialized elections described later.[42]

A deputy county LPC director from County C in North Zhejiang also described the existence of this informal institutional arrangement. When I asked whether the change in electoral law in 2011, which gives rural residents the same voting rights as urban voters, will change the deputy compositions in his county, he replied:

> I don't expect significant changes. You know, we need to guarantee that the important government officials will get elected as before. We also need to have deputies from different social groups. This is a political task [i.e., something must be done regardless of the costs] for the township governments [which organize and monitor the elections]. The change is there should be more deputies elected

from the rural area; we need to give the rural electoral districts more quotas, but the candidates will be the same types of people. We just assign more candidates to the rural area.... I have been to many other counties in Zhejiang [to communicate with and learn from other county PCs]. What I can tell you is that this practice is common [throughout the province].⁴³

All these informal institutional arrangements are only part of the story. The nomination of nongovernment LPC deputy candidates is even more informal and personalized. Each county political leader (of the party, government, and LPC) has a quota for nominating LPC candidates. As a senior tax officer in County Cold Mountain in Shanxi repeatedly told me during an interview: "We collect taxes for the state, but what is the state? After all, the state is the people [cadres] who compose the state."⁴⁴ This applies not only to taxation but also to other aspects of government practices, including elections of LPC deputies. Like an election in a democracy in which a party boss can use his nomination power to build patron-client ties, the party-state elites in an authoritarian state also use it as a way to patronize their clients. The county political leaders can use this political resource in exchange for private entrepreneurs' investment, which contributes to their performance and sometimes even personal benefits (such as bribes). A good example is a prefecture party secretary in Anhui Province who promised two private entrepreneurs that he would make them deputies of the provincial PC and, later, deputies of the NPC if they would make large investments in his jurisdiction, in which they were born and are registered voters, though they made their fortunes in Beijing. Eventually, this party secretary was arrested and charged with corruption, and the two NPC deputies were also put on the list of bribery offenders that includes seventeen government officials and nineteen private entrepreneurs. Though some government officials on the list were punished, these two NPC deputies were not.⁴⁵ While this is a very sensitive topic for most of my informants, a senior LPC official of County Wenling in Zhejiang Province told me explicitly that "the major leaders have their quotas [for nominating LPC deputy candidates]; our job is to balance their interests by distributing the quotas."⁴⁶

After receiving all the nominations, the township governments implement the LPC election, which is a contested election by design: the Election Law calls for 25 to 50 percent more candidates than there are seats. The township government's tactics make sure the official candidates get elected by "appointing" or nominating as their competitors weak (e.g., junior) candidates who have no chance of being elected, persuading the self-nominated candidates to give up, funding campaigns for the officially nominated candidates, and strategically assigning the electoral districts to eliminate the self-nominated candidates.[47] While these tactics now face stronger challenges than previously, they continue to be successful.

As long as the party and government control nominations, deputies have little reason to represent their constituents over the party's will. My findings suggest that O'Brien's (1994a) findings from twenty years ago remain in force: the most active LPC deputies are state regents; only a few would risk being remonstrators. The LPC is an inclusive rather than a representative institution. The corporatist institutional arrangement degenerates into a patron-client relationship. In recent years, the commercialization of elections has worsened this situation.

There are elections not obviously determined by party control. Both candidates may have backing from party or government officials who fail to negotiate an agreement about who should win. In theory, such competitive elections could make deputies more accountable to their constituents. However, evidence suggests that money, not policy proposals, drives the results in these few cases. A few independent candidates—typically in urban areas such as Beijing and Shenzhen—intellectuals rather than businessmen, have won elections by emphasizing that they would be better-qualified LPC deputies and that they represent real policy ideas. In these cases, money was not an important factor.[48] Urban voters are better educated than rural voters, and their incomes are higher, so buying their votes would be much more expensive. Whereas the close society in rural areas makes vote buying easy to organize, this would be difficult in urban areas where residents in the same apartment building do not know each other. However, evidence does not suggest this is a prevalent or growing phenomenon.

The Commercialization of Elections

Buying votes to get elected, with or without the party-state's nomination, has become a common practice in the eastern coastal areas in the last decade and shows signs of spreading elsewhere.[49] Private entrepreneurs find value in political titles, and those who cannot get patronage within the party-state use money to get elected, as a means either to build connections or to strengthen and expand their connections. In rural areas, as in my field research in Zhejiang Province, independent candidates tend to be private entrepreneurs who can afford to spend hundreds of thousands or even millions of yuan on votes. One of my informants explained:

> The practice of buying votes was very rare and regarded as a crime in the last LPC deputy election [in 2003]; the party's disciplinary committee investigated it but didn't get evidence [because the villagers who accepted the money wouldn't report it for fear of losing the money]. But in this new round of LPC deputy elections, it is such a common practice that no one bothers to investigate it, just like the village committee election.⁵⁰

Another informant added:

> The cadre deputies don't buy votes because they don't have so much money, or even if they have [some of them do have], they don't dare do it because the competitors will report to the party's disciplinary committee [and they will get punished]. The private entrepreneurs who are not well educated and not afraid of the party's disciplinary committee [they have no official position to lose] spend lots of money to buy votes.⁵¹

In most cases, private-entrepreneur deputies are recognized and endorsed by the party-state, sometimes because some officials back both parties. However, there are exceptions. In the 2011 municipal LPC election in County Warm River, Mr. Wang, a famous private entrepreneur and a senior county PPCC member, spent more than 3 million yuan (close to half a million US dollars) to buy the votes of county PC deputies and get himself elected as a municipal PC deputy.⁵²

In rural areas independent candidates are largely private entrepreneurs and have mixed influence on LPCs. They have become more independent and less willingly take direction from the LPC Standing Committee (especially compared to LPPCC deputies); therefore, they dare to act relatively independently. However, this independence does not necessarily refer to representation although it could; it refers to weakening LPC rules. As an informant told me, "The county party secretary criticized openly at the LPC annual conference that many LPC deputies do not even show up at most LPC sessions; some of them even stay in the hotel playing cards."⁵³

At the same time, they corrupt the LPC: as some of my informants put it, the LPC is never a congress of the people; it is "the congress of the cadres and rich."

Inclusion, Representation, or Clientelism?

Although capitalists' personal connections have both social and political causes, the level and intensiveness of personal political connections, as measured by the administrative level of the PC or PPCC they serve, are in general correlated with the enterprise's size and tax contribution, as table 5.1 demonstrates. It seems that there is a "representation-through-taxation" mechanism: the more taxes you pay, the more likely you are to be an LPC representative and the more likely you are to serve in a higher-level PC.

However, my informants generally believe that the quality and motivations of private-entrepreneur deputies are suspect. Yet it is possible that

Table 5.1. Entrepreneurs at different political levels and size of enterprises

PC and PPCC levels		Enterprise's sales in 2011 (10,000 yuan)	Enterprise's tax paid in 2011 (10,000 yuan)
Without any title	Mean	9,229.88 (161,062.57)	219.90 (2,408.94)
	N	2,827	2,847
Township (PC only)	Mean	8,476.37 (13,045.27)	332.41 (860.01)
	N	98	97
County	Mean	14,868.76 (57,097.46)	653.67 (2,536.50)
	N	1,103	1,113
Prefecture	Mean	26,872.80 (70,886.93)	1,425.75 (4,418.00)
	N	583	593
Province	Mean	96,099.83 (233,133.63)	3,240.36 (5,057.90)
	N	70	70
National	Mean	153,834.50 (288,472.53)	1,204.86 (1,782.33)
	N	8	7
Total entrepreneurs	Mean	14,277.74 (134,628.15)	521.81 (2,849.28)
	N	4,689	4,727
F-test		8.820*	32.784*
Correlation	Eta	0.097	0.183

Source: National Private Enterprise Survey 2012 by the All-China Federation of Industry and Commerce.
Note: Numbers in parentheses are standard deviations.
* Significance level = 0.000.

private-entrepreneur deputies in LPCs represent their constituencies' interests and therefore might strengthen the LPC and make the local government more responsive and accountable. This section addresses their incentives in joining the LPC and whether the authoritarian state purchases their loyalty and co-opts them completely by sharing spoils such as rents and privileges. The institutional arrangements, including but not limited to the LPC electoral procedures, the LPC's political role within the government system, and the lack of rule of law to protect private property rights in China shape deputies' incentives and behavior.

In my fieldwork and according to independent interviews of two senior LPC officers in County Warm River, I have identified four types of incentives for a private entrepreneur to run in an election, which may cost them hundreds of thousands or even more yuan (even more to be an LPC deputy): (1) to get political privilege, for example, protection from harassment by government officials, especially police and tax officers, or exemption from some traffic violation; (2) to get economic privileges such as tax breaks;[54] (3) to get to know more government officials and build connections, which is good for business; and (4) to gain fame.[55] These incentives are consistent with those of other empirical studies,[56] and a number of media reports support them, including a national-level party journal, *Oriental Outlook Weekly* (*Liaowang Dongfang Zhoukan*) of the Xinhua News Agency, which reported that private entrepreneurs (and some government officials) spent money to buy votes to get elected as prefecture PC deputies in Hunan Province (Z. Huang 2008). If we use this perspective to reinterpret table 5.1, owners of larger enterprises, especially those who are major taxpayers, can build connections with local political leaders or even higher-level government officials. For example, being a province-level PC deputy brings good opportunities to know and build connections with prefecture-level officials, which in turn provides bargaining leverage with county officials. The owners of smaller enterprises try to build connections with tax officers or simply to evade taxes; if they fail, the government may charge them predatory taxes and fees.

Interviews with nondeputy private entrepreneurs provide additional insights into their peers' incentives to be a deputy. One of my informants asked me whether a deputyship is worth an investment of half a million yuan: "If it is worth that much, I will make that investment."[57] Another informant, who gave me a ride in his Porsche SUV, told me, "I am not that interested in being an LPC deputy because I don't think the government can help me. You know, if your business is good, they will tell you that you are a good businessman and tax you. If your business fails, they will just say, 'Poor guy, he can't run a company.' So why should I bother to run the election to be a deputy?" But even he did not deny the benefits and privileges of being an LPC deputy.[58] Having heard me ask an official in his car why private entrepreneurs spend so much money to get selected or elected to the LPC and LPPCC, a driver for County Warm River's PPCC told me the following:

> A political title is very valuable. [Being an] LPC deputy is more valuable than [being an] LPPCC member, but even the latter is pretty useful. Let me tell you an example. Several years ago, a private entrepreneur who was a county PPCC member got into some trouble because the tax officers were inspecting his company and found some serious illegal tax evasion. He asked the president of the PPCC for help, and the president called the Tax Bureau head and claimed that they tax too much and would drive all the enterprises to other counties. The tax officers stopped the inspection because they knew the PPCC president was very powerful.[59]

LPC deputies told me they want money and gifts from those who need their votes to get elected as a LPC Standing Committee member or higher-level LPC deputy. One intellectual LPC deputy told me: "If you spend so much money to be a deputy, you are expecting to get money for your vote.... Of course, this is limited to the private-entrepreneur deputies who want to get elected for a higher position." Like my informants from the LPC, he also complained that the quality of private-entrepreneur deputies is very low: "They don't care about the broad social interests; they only care about their business. They are political whores!"[60]

With more and more government expenditures going to rural infrastructural construction in recent years, some LPC deputies use their connections to win government contracts. In three townships of County Warm River, villagers complained that the three county PC deputies won all government projects, including road constructions. One informant told me:

> A bridge near my village was almost broken, so the government blocked the road. A county PC deputy won the contract to rebuild it. However, the county PC deputy has neither a construction team nor the certificate for building a bridge [which requires some pro-

fessional training and equipment]. Besides, he wanted to save the cost, so he did not even purchase enough cement. This would be very dangerous in the future, so some villagers reported it to the government. The project is stopped now, but the PC deputy gets no punishment; we think he will still get new contracts in the future.[61]

Another case shows a more fearless LPC deputy:

> A prefecture PC deputy in County Warm River who is also a village party secretary joined with two other businessmen—one of the latter has a brother working as a senior bureau head in the county government—to win the contract to provide the quarry and stones for road construction. The contract says that all the stones from the quarry are only to be sold to that specific road construction. But these three people did not comply with the contract and sold some stones to other companies. When the county government investigated this issue, they even told the government officers that they were afraid of nobody. When it was reported to the county party secretary, he was so angry that he asked the police to investigate.[62]

With such bad behavior, LPC deputies got a bad reputation. One informant, who runs a company that plants fruit trees and had served two tenures as county PC deputy and village party secretary, told me:

> I was elected in the 1990s because I was the party secretary of that village and I did a lot to help others get rich [Deng had asked the people who have become rich to help others get rich], as well as improved the infrastructure in the village to help the enterprises. The entrepreneurs returned some of their profits to the village to further improve the village infrastructure. All the villagers knew I did a pretty good job, so most of them vote for me [to be the LPC deputy]. I was tired of being the village secretary after three tenures, so I retired.... But the situation is becoming worse and worse; those who get rich spend money to buy votes. So the deputy quality decreases. I think the deputies of my era are better than today's.[63]

How can these very self-interested private-entrepreneur deputies strengthen the LPC? One LPC official complained to me:

The deputy quality is very low now, which leads to low quality of their proposals. They don't even go to the LPC annual meeting [which is the most important chance they have to get together to listen to and vote for the government, court and prosecutor's annual report, the budget, and so on]. Yes, most of them go to the opening ceremony because they need to get registered and the county party secretary will be there. But the attendance at other sessions is very low, so how can they fill their obligations without being present? You may laugh if I told you where these deputies are during the sessions. They are in the county's best hotels, booked by the county government and guarded by the police, just gambling![64]

Of course, private-entrepreneur LPC deputies vary. Before the NPC Standing Committee banned deputy offices in 2010, some more public-interest-oriented deputies had PC deputy's offices where they or their staff regularly met with constituents. But this was the exception rather than the norm, and the practice no longer exists (Yuan 2005).[65]

Comparing the LPC in Three Counties

As discussed earlier, the county PCs in different regions have some similarities and differences. The similarities include the formal institutional arrangements, party dominance, and, very interestingly, the composition of deputies (cadres and private entrepreneurs as the two largest groups). The differences include how active LPCs are and how effective they are in monitoring government bureaus, or the role of the LPC in the local party government system.[66] Some scholars, such as Cho (2009), argue that an LPC leader's willingness explains these differences but does not answer why some LPC leaders are more motivated than others to strengthen the LPC or why some of them get more support than others from the party leaders. Cho (2009) also argues that the social background of LPC deputies matters in terms of their behavior but does not discuss the institutional effects of the changing composition of LPC deputies; that is, more private-entrepreneur LPC deputies should be able to change the LPC's political role. As discussed earlier, O'Brien (1994a) is more conservative concerning the LPC deputies' political role. Yue Hou (2019) finds that private entrepreneurs join the LPC to secure their property rights.

In contrast to both Cho and O'Brien, I argue that the nonofficial LPC deputies matter, not just because of their numbers but also because of their independence from the party government. Further, private entrepreneurs' independence from the party government is, in turn, determined by the industries in which they work. Competitive and mobile industries have more independent private entrepreneurs who are willing to make aggressive proposals and monitor the government, while monopolized and immobile industries have more dependent entrepreneurs.[67] However, since private entrepreneurs are constrained by the LPC's institutional arrangements to be active deputies and they are relatively weak and vulnerable to the state (mostly because of lack of rule of law), their political role is conditional on the will of local political leaders, who are motivated to create a good environment of economic development and need to ally with the private entrepreneurs to discipline the predatory bureaus. Table 5.2 outlines the general logic, and table 5.3 uses my two primary cases and a supplementary case to provide a more in-depth analysis.

Table 5.2. Empowering the LPC

		Political leaders	
		Highly motivated to discipline government bureaus	Low motivation
Private entrepreneurs	Willing to challenge the state	High governance quality (Warm River and Wenling)	Low or medium
	Prefer personalized connections	Low or medium governance quality	Low (County Cold Mountain)

Table 5.3. Comparison of LPCs in three counties

			LPC's role	
County	Industry asset mobility	GDP per capita 2009 (yuan)	Extra-budgetary control	Monitoring government bureau
Warm River	High	28,200	Medium	Medium to high
Cold Mountain	Low	28,235	Low	Low
Wenling	High	40,893	High, and budgeting participation	High

County Warm River

County Warm River's PC Standing Committee offices are located in a new building, along with the county Party Committee and government. I went there several times for interviews, and each time I saw most, if not all, of the staff (officials) of the LPC working in the offices or having meetings. This surprised me because I had thought the LPC was busy only before and during the annual meetings and elections.[68] My informant told me they have a lot to do because the county PC Standing Committee director asks them to work hard to improve the PC's work. The director demands that the county PC should strengthen its work in three ways: build capacity through strengthening institution building and studies and changing the work style, educate and monitor PC deputies to strengthen their functions, and use its supervision power according to the law. The deputies should go to the people to find out the important issues they care about and to find causes and solutions; they should also supervise government bureaus on implementation of policies. The county PC also innovated practices to ask the LPC deputies and its Standing Committee members (especially private-entrepreneur deputies) to at least attend meetings and contribute to the discussion and fulfill other obligations such as making inquiries and contacting their constituencies.

Many LPC deputies, especially the private-entrepreneur deputies, do not attend LPC annual meetings. There are two reasons for this low attendance: the LPC annual meeting is more symbolic and procedural than substantive—all the deputies can do is raise their hands to vote or support things; and LPC deputies are more independent than the LPPCC members because of elections—the title "PPCC member" can be easily taken away, whereas taking away a deputy title requires going through very strict procedures.[69] But the positive side is that group discussions become more active and the active deputies are debating local government policies and bringing good proposals for the government bureaus to consider. The county PC Standing Committee and government also require government bureaus to respond to these proposals, and the responses should satisfy the LPC deputies. These institutional innovations empower the LPC deputies against the government bureaus.[70]

Most of the LPC's power lies in its Standing Committee, both because it has regular monthly meetings to discuss important issues and because it is staffed with senior government officials retired from government organs and highly influential local social-economic elites. The six members of the LPC Standing Committee who are private entrepreneurs bring questions related to the development of the county's private economy to the LPC agenda, and they are more likely to play a role in the Party Committee's agenda. The LPC Standing Committee (including these entrepreneur deputies) also works closely with the county PC Standing Committee in monitoring extra-budgetary funds and leveling the payment for different government bureaus, leaving less space for corruption for some government bureaus.[71] Even in the early 1990s, the county PC was mobilized by the party secretary to discuss and criticize several economy-related bureaus. The deputies, some of whom were private entrepreneurs as well as village cadres, criticized these bureaus severely for corruption and other misbehavior. This "campaign" lasted for several years and helped discipline predatory government bureaus, provided a credible commitment, and created a good business environment.

County Cold Mountain

During my two-week stay in County Cold Mountain in June 2010, I went to the PC Standing Committee office twice during working hours, and no one was in the office. My informant asked me to stay for one more week, but later he told me the PC officials were going to the Shanghai Expo the next day, so I might as well give up my plan to interview them that time. However, I was fortunate to interview officials working in the PPCC office, which is located close to the PC Standing Committee office, as well as two county PC deputies to obtain data on how the county PC performs. I was also able to obtain published information on the topic.

Compared to the LPC deputy elections in County Warm River and village committee elections in both Counties A and C, the LPC deputy election in County Cold Mountain is not competitive. A senior county PC deputy, Mr. Shu, who is also chairman of a large casting enterprise and a prefecture PPCC member, told me that "the government nominates the candidates based on the candidates' contribution to society and willingness to participate in politics," and "[the election] is to meet the procedural requirements; people [the voters] don't care about it." So there is no vote purchasing for LPC deputy elections in County Cold Mountain.[72] He thinks the competition will be more intensive in the future and make the LPC a more effective one, but "it takes time." Asked about political participation in the LPC, Mr. Shu elaborated:

I don't think there are any changes since I became a county PC deputy about twenty years ago. I can't understand the government report, and it is hard to read the numbers on the reports. [Political participation] is meaningless, and I am not capable of doing it. We discuss some social economic problems at the meetings, but it's the government [not the LPC] that can really fix the problems. I would say the function of the LPC is to legitimate the party and government's intentions through "democratic procedure." I don't think a deputy has the power and right to vote against government policies and personnel issues, and it will not bring any benefit for you.[73]

Mr. Shu has submitted several proposals—on education, river pollution, and the bad implementation of court judgments—but most were not well received by the government. But he still added: "I should say that the LPC is making progress."[74]

A county PPCC official told me that both the county PC and PPCC provide opportunities for the private-entrepreneur deputies to interact with other entrepreneurs and government officials, but the effectiveness of their political participation is "hard to say." The low quality of deputies and PPCC members also limits their political participation: private entrepreneurs were originally peasants who were audacious enough to take advantage of flaws in the law. He also validated that most of the coal-mine bosses were the most audacious people, including some who were released prisoners.[75]

According to the 2009 official county yearbook, the county PC's work in the last few years has focused on coal-mining safety and promotion of economic restructuring (building new industries instead of relying only on coal mining). However, according to the county party secretary, it is hard to implement the provincial government's policy on strengthening safety regulations, and the LPC can play only a limited role.[76]

County Wenling

Wenling provides a good example to illustrate how well a county PC can do in China today and how it does so.[77] Every spring since 2005, many scholars and journalists have come to Wenling city, a county-level city in eastern Zhejiang Province, to observe the "democratic deliberation meeting" (民主恳谈会, also translated as "deliberately polling") or "participatory budgeting" experiment there. The participatory budgeting experiment, which is held during the annual meeting of the LPC (including both the township and county levels), asks participants (composed of LPC deputies and local residents) to discuss the very detailed budget and possible government projects. The participants have very lively discussions and do have a significant impact on the government budget. At a conference in early July 2010, Zhang Xueming, the county PC Standing Committee director and a former deputy county party secretary,[78] proudly announced that the PC had successfully reallocated 2 billion yuan to the budget,[79] including 1 billion proposed by the county party secretary[80]—something unimaginable in any other county.[81]

During an interview, Zhang told me that the participatory budget also helps effectively reduce the township fiscal deficit (a reduction of 5 to 8 million yuan every year). The deficit can be reduced because the township leaders' power has been effectively constrained by the township PC deputies and other participants, who not only discuss the budget but also elect the township leaders. Before the democratic deliberation meeting was introduced, the budget was put together by a small group: the party secretary, the township government leader, and the head of the township Bureau of Finance. Therefore, budgetary power was not supervised and was easily corrupted—indeed, many so-called achievement projects were built that generated serious government deficits. The unchecked budgetary power led to not only cadre corruption but also serious investment waste, even more wasteful than that associated with corruption.[82] Zhang says that "budgeting is the key in local governance, and closed budgetary making caused a serious government debt problem and other conflicts. Once we improve the budgetary process, we can solve these problems."[83]

Besides the scientific and democratic decision-making functions,[84] the democratic deliberation meeting has democratic educational effects for both citizens and government officials. Citizens became more active and confident in participation; some whose businesses were not in the county even spent thousands of yuan to go back to Wenling for the meeting. Citizens who participated began to make more aggressive and "professional" suggestions. The county PC also invited scholars (including several foreigners) to improve the procedure and technique of participatory budgeting. Local government officials learned to respect citizens' opinions and to accept even severe critiques, for they realized that even though the people's participation constrained their (the officials') power, it also reduced their risk of making wrong policies and actually made policies easier to implement.[85]

The democratic deliberation meeting was initiated in the township of Zeguo in 1999,[86] and it developed steadily in the following years. In 2004, the Wenling Democratic Deliberation Meeting won a national honor, China's Local Government Innovation Award, cosponsored by the party's Central Compilation and Translation Bureau and the Ford Foundation.[87] There are three stages in the development of a democratic deliberation meeting. In the first stage, the local government meets for "ideological and political work" (*sixiang zhengzhi gongzuo*), an opportunity to talk to local residents and persuade them to accept government policies. In the second stage, as this informal institutional arrangement showed some advantages in bringing public opinion into government decision-making and made government policies more acceptable for the people, the township government decided to strengthen the arrangement and made it a routine type of meeting when there was something important to discuss. The third stage is to bring the democratic deliberation meeting into the township PC and thus link it with formal institutions to legitimate it. Now the county government has decided to spread this practice countywide (in July 2010, only two township-level "street office" [街道办] did not have democratic deliberation meetings).[88] Zhang Xueming also explained that the Taizhou Prefecture government leaders decided to spread this practice to other counties in Taizhou, and the Zhejiang Province PC also sent high-level officials to do research on and appraise this practice.

Wenling also developed the "LPC deputy work station" system: deputies are asked to stay in a work station (an office) every month to talk to residents and learn their concerns. The county PC director and vice-directors are all required to contact several work stations. This institutional arrangement makes the LPC deputies more responsive to voters.

But the most important question is, Why was Wenling was able to develop this democratic deliberation meeting and, later, participatory budgeting? Zhang and another senior government official argued that it occurred because there are many private entrepreneurs there with a strong incentive to participate in local politics:

> Wenling is a well-developed county and has more than thirty thousand private enterprises, which means an enterprise for every forty people.[89] Some private entrepreneurs are village cadres and have a strong willingness and capacity to participate [in local politics].

Besides, they also dare to challenge the government. Most government policies have an important impact on citizens, especially where there is more government expenditure on rural areas [building socialist new villages], so they have good reasons to participate actively.[90]

But this cannot answer another question raised by a scholar at the Wenling conference: Why have there been no democratic deliberative meetings in Wenling's neighboring counties in Taizhou or Wenzhou? Mr. Jiang, a county PC Standing Committee member and then a township head of Zeguo, told the real story, which was not reported by many journalists. Jiang admitted that he and his colleagues were actually forced to try this new practice to solve a serious conflict between the township government and the small business owners in a local market. In 1999, the Zeguo township government tried to demolish a local market to build a new one. Government officials thought it was a good policy and would be welcomed by the people. However, the small business owners in the market refused to move out and even staged riots. Trapped in a deadlock, Jiang and his colleagues decided to have a meeting with representatives of the business owners in an effort to ease the owners' anger and to discuss how to make the market a better one. The meeting was very successful, so they decided to use the meeting method as a regular means of "ideological and political work," as well as decision-making. As outlined by Jiang:

> The reasons why Wenling has democratic deliberation meetings are, first [the government's] wrong decision-making led to social instability and people's unrest; second, the political leaders and the cadres in Wenling dared to borrow new thoughts from the intellectuals and apply them in solving real problems.[91]

Therefore, the origins of the democratic deliberation meetings were structural and actors' choices. An official who works in the county PC admitted that there was vote purchasing in Wenling (and obviously in other counties in Zhejiang) because private entrepreneurs highly value the title "LPC deputy," and he argued this means deputies in the LPC are motivated. But he would not tell me how common this purchasing behavior is.[92]

During and after the 2010 conference, Zhang Xueming proudly announced that Wenling democratic deliberation will be spread to other counties in Taizhou and then to other regions in Zhejang because both the

NPC and provincial PC leaders had visited Wenling and gave its democratic deliberation a good evaluation. But no such spread will happen in the next ten years, even though some party documents call for the PCs' active role in budgeting and monitoring at all levels.

I found that the role of the representative institution, the LPC, differs in different regions because both the local political leaders and the private-entrepreneur deputies have varying degrees of incentive to promote economic growth (or make a profit) through generating an investment-friendly environment. I also proposed that their incentives are shaped by the regions' major industries (especially their asset mobility). Therefore, the structural factor, asset mobility, is a deeper cause of LPC deputies' representation or lack of it.

Conclusion

The LPC is becoming more important in local politics in many regions. However, though private-entrepreneur deputies have become the second-largest deputy group in the LPC, and their role within LPCs and their ability to make the LPC a responsive and functional institution has also increased to some extent, institutional defects, including limited LPC power, and the defects of election procedures circumscribe this ability. On the one hand, the increasing importance of private entrepreneurs for local economies, in addition to their significant presence in LPCs, makes them an important group that local political leaders cannot neglect when making policies. Therefore, they help generate more responsive government and better economic policies. As a democratic-looking institution, the LPC plays an important role in providing credible commitment for investment and promoting economic growth in some regions. Therefore, the agent-discipline and cooperation problems, and the growth dilemma as result, are alleviated to some degree.

On the other hand, direct elections of the township- and county-level LPC deputies are under the party's strict control. Even when there is a change from "selection" to "election" for some LPC deputies,[93] the election either degenerates from an inclusive arrangement into a patron-client relationship or commercialization and corruption limit the private entrepreneurs' willingness and ability to represent constituents,[94] improve government responsiveness, or demand other institutional reform. Instead, the LPC is an inclusive regime institution that co-opts the rising private entrepreneurs into the authoritarian regime, allowing private-entrepreneur deputies to obtain privileges in exchange for their support and cooperation. As a result, the representation dilemma is resolved.

Why do authoritarian regimes have nonrepresentative legislature institutions that do not legislate? Gandhi (2008) argues that autocratic rulers who face opposition benefit from democratic-looking institutions and that they solidify their power, but her insights relate only to the institutional choices of national leaders and cannot explain local officials' responses to the LPC in China.[95] Her theory does anticipate that local governments provide some degree of credible commitment for encouraging investment and productive activities. However, what Gandhi fails to address is that the formal rules of incorporating private entrepreneurs into LPCs could degenerate into a patronage practice and both government officials and private-entrepreneur deputies gain specific benefits (Hou 2019).[96] The idea that LPCs and LPPCCs are representative and inclusive tends to assume a high level of institutionalization of local politics. However, my findings suggest that formal rules tend to degenerate into patron-client relationships that benefit the individuals within and outside the party-state, at the cost of formal rules and the party-state. While most studies of patron-clientelism of electoral politics focus on the candidate-voter relations, my fieldwork suggests that under a strong authoritarian regime in which the party-state tightly controls even direct elections,[97] the patron-client ties could be built between the patrons within the party-state and the candidates as clients. This type of patron-clientelism cannot be regarded as contributing to authoritarian resilience; rather, it is a signal of authoritarian decay.[98]

Besides engaging with the literature on legislative institutions under authoritarian, this chapter makes contributions to the electoral institution under authoritarianism (Gandhi and Lust-Okar 2009). Most studies of elections in China focus on the village committee election, an election for a nongovernmental self-governing organization, and neglect PC deputy elections at township and county levels. The few studies of LPC elections focus mainly on the formal process but neglect the informal practices that this chapter tries to reveal, or they focus on campaign strategies of independent candidates without describing the illegal use of money in campaigns.[99] Under the communism era, the state mobilized voters and achieved very high turnouts. After decades of market transition, turnout has declined; voters become rationally ignorant because candidates have no accountability to them. As political entrepreneurs, candidates pay for votes with money or other material benefits instead of policy promises;[100] in some cases they also bring an "extra-legislative variant of pork-barrel politics," public services that make them more popular (Manion 2014, 311).

Though the LPC and its direct election have many defects, the formal institution has plenty of room to accommodate democracy. However, the party shows no sign of retreating or redefining its role (O'Brien 2009). In addition, the corruption of the LPC may block its functional transformation, trapping it in a dependence trajectory, when real reforms arrive. The anticorruption campaign has significantly reduced vote buying but has been unable to reduce other institutional defects and empower the LPC.

This chapter provides new evidence concerning how asset mobility relates to the answer to Robert Putnam's question concerning quality of governance through the mechanism of representation through taxation, while recognizing the limits of governance quality, especially on dimensions such as collusion, responsiveness, transparency, voice, and accountability.[101] Chapter 6 begins to address the factors that shape private-entrepreneur deputies' incentives to join the LPC and their behavior in the LPC. This is an important question since it is related to the endogeneity problem of institutional explanation of authoritarian resilience (Pepinsky 2014).

CHAPTER 6

Forbearance and Rule by Fear

> Upon this a question arises: whether it be better to be loved than feared or feared than loved? It may be answered that one should wish to be both, but, because it is difficult to unite them in one person, is much safer to be feared than loved, when, of the two, either must be dispensed with. . . . And men have less scruple in offending one who is beloved than one who is feared, for love is preserved by the link of obligation which, owing to the baseness of men, is broken at every opportunity for their advantage; but fear preserves you by a dread of punishment which never fails.
> —Niccolò Machiavelli, *The Prince*

> Keep close with the government but keep distance from politics [亲近政府, 远离政治].
> —Wang Jianlin, public speeches and interviews

> Eight Chinese characters well illustrate the private entrepreneurs' strategy of survival: tax evasion and bribing [偷税漏税, 行贿受贿].
> —SOE manager, interview by the author, Beijing

In the 2011 prefecture PC election,[1] Mr. Wang, a famous private entrepreneur in County Warm River and a county PPCC senior member, successfully spent more than 3 million yuan (about half a million US dollars) to buy the votes of county PC deputies and get himself elected as a prefecture PC deputy. His success violated the county PC Standing Committee's plan, which was to have a deputy from the public hospitals "represent" the health sector (doctors and nurses).[2] So the county PC Standing Committee director asked Wang to resign, but he refused. The next day the county PC director and the SAT county's office head talked to Wang. They told him that he had two options: resign or have his enterprise's accounts audited. Wang resigned without hesitation.[3]

This example reveals the importance of broader institutions that affect private entrepreneurs—specifically the taxation system, which shapes private entrepreneur's preferences, strategy for survival (including joining the democratic-looking institutions such as the LPC and LPPCC), and bargaining power. Liu Chuanzhi, founder of Lenovo and "China's godfather of entrepreneurs," called for a strategy of "businessmen only talk business [在商言商]; do not talk politics" in a closed-door meeting in June 2013. In December of that year, Liu responded to critics by emphasizing that as an entrepreneur, he has no capability to talk macropolitical issues and regards this as irresponsible; instead, entrepreneurs should do business honestly and carry out their social responsibilities (*Sina* 2013). Jack Ma, chairman and founder of Alibaba, said on his inauguration of the China Entrepreneur Club in May 2016 that "President Xi Jinping calls for sincerity and honesty in relationships between government and business. My principles are don't bribe, pay full wages on time, no tax evasion, and no rights violation. . . . Entrepreneurs are the most important group in economic development" (*Huaxia* 2016). However, it is hard for many if not most enterprises to stick to these four principles, especially no tax evasion.

I argue that in the under-institutionalized taxation system, characterized by very high nominal tax rates, tax officers' great discretional power, and a tax-target system that violates rule of/by law, generates both forbearance and fear. On the one hand, the system implicitly allows for rampant tax evasion, therefore reduces effective tax rates and contributes to resolving the growth dilemma. On the other hand, illegally evading taxes also generates fear of punishment; the motivation for private entrepreneurs to build political patron-client ties is strong and to represent their collective interests (and therefore reduce the state's despotic power) is weak. The system thus resolves or at least alleviates the representation dilemma; that is, improved infrastructural state power (measured by taxation capacity) may lead to decreased despotic power. This model could sustain rather than challenge authoritarian regimes. Figure 6.1 illustrates the mechanisms.

Fear, Social Control, and Authoritarian Rule

Rapidly increased revenue resources, partially through nontax revenue, allow an authoritarian ruler to improve bureaucratization and provide public services to purchase support. However, the CCP also substan-

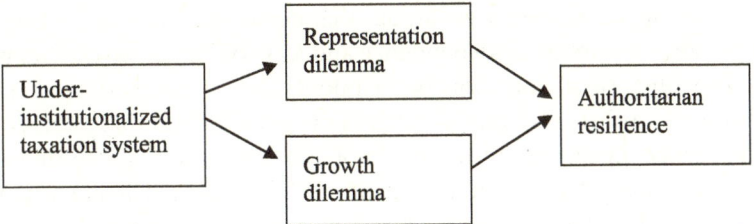

Figure 6.1. Under-institutionalized taxation system and authoritarian resilience.

tially increased taxing its citizens (more accurately, its enterprises), but it did not destabilize authoritarian rule, contrary to what Kevin Morrison (2014) predicted. As Niccolò Machiavelli (2005) proposed, to stay in power, a ruler should choose to be feared rather than loved if he or she could not do both at the same time. Co-optation through the LPC, LPPCC, and public-service provisions helps make private entrepreneurs and citizens love and therefore embrace the authoritarian regime, but that process is expensive and will convert only a limited number of people and can cause a backlash. Democratic-looking institutions also suffer the problems of endogeneity and can be manipulated by rulers (Pepinsky 2014; Slater 2003). Fear, however, has wide coverage and human nature on its side. Machiavelli rightly identifies the "dread of punishment which never fails" as the productive consequence of fear. He further writes, "I conclude, then—returning to being feared and loved—that since men love at their own pleasure and fear at the pleasure of the prince, the wise prince should build his foundation upon that which is his own, not upon that which belongs to others: only he must seek to avoid being hated, as I have said" (Machiavelli 2005, 59). Authoritarian rulers never hesitate to use fear to maintain control (L. Tsai 2017). However, coercive organizations are counterproductive (and thus incur the growth dilemma) and therefore undesirable for many authoritarian rulers in most situations. Selective and targeted repression is a good substitute.

There are two views of capitalists' political role: unilinear and contingent. Following Barrington Moore's famous slogan of "no bourgeois, no democracy" (1966, 418),[4] the role that capitalists (private entrepreneurs) play in promoting democratization has attracted substantial academic attention. Moreover, modernization theory also considers the middle class a driving force for democratization (Lipset 1959). This is the unilinear view. The contingent view argues that democratization is contingent on private entrepreneurs' dependence and fear. While some scholars find that capitalists (as major actors of the middle classes) demand democracy (Dahl 1998), others find they are conservative and afraid that democracy will generate redistribution-oriented policies that are not in their interests (see, for example, Boix 2003; Rueschemeyer, Stephens, and Stephens 1992). Eva Bellin describes the relationship between capitalists and democracy by juxtaposing fear of social unrest and redistribution with dependence on the state for profitability (2000, 180), as shown in table 6.1.[5]

While coercive authoritarian institutions generate fear throughout a population, resource-rich capitalists face structural sources of fear. The fear of redistribution (Rueschemeyer, Stephens, and Stephens 1992), for example, affects entrepreneurs. Some scholars argue that a high level of inequality prevents democratic transition that would lead to redistribution (Acemoglu and Robinson 2006), while others reject this causal relationship for various reasons (Haggard and Kaufman 2012; Slater, Smith, and Nair 2014).[6] Ben Ansell and David Samuels (2014) disagree with the redistributivist theory and suggest that capitalists fear autocrats' predatory power much more than the poor's demand for redistribution. Capitalists also fear social unrest, which makes it impossible for them to run their businesses. Both Evan Lieberman (2003) and Dan Slater (2010) argue that this fear leads economic elites to comply with tax law and support state building in South Africa and some Southeast Asian countries.

Scholars of China studies also find that capitalists in postcommunist countries have little or no interest in promoting democracy (Dickson 2008; K. Tsai 2007; Pearson 1997). Rather, they tend to collude with the party-state rather than demand democracy under "commercialized com-

Table 6.1. Private-sector capital's demand for democracy

		State dependence	
		High	Low
Fear	High	Antidemocracy	Leaning democratic or opportunism (patron-clientelism)
	Low	Ambivalence	Pro-democracy

Source: Based on Bellin 2000, 185.
Note: Opportunism (patron-clientelism) is my concept; it differs from Bellin's "leaning democratic."

munism" (Wank 1999), "crony communism," or "integrated wealth and power" (Dickson 2008, 22–23). Some scholars examine the party-state's preferences and strategies in regard to private entrepreneurs and their impact on the party-state. Bruce Dickson argues that the party's survival strategy is a combination of strategic co-optation and corporatist-style links with the private sector (Dickson 2008; Chen and Dickson 2008).[7] Recognizing the diversity of private entrepreneurs' interests and identities, Kellee Tsai builds a typology of private entrepreneurs' coping strategies that varies by their willingness and ability to challenge the state: entrepreneurs are assertive, are grudgingly acceptant, are loyally acceptant, or use avoidance strategies. Tsai also defines different patterns of local development and finds that they are associated with different dominant private entrepreneurs' coping strategies. Tsai's typology is very insightful; however, it remains largely descriptive, as she does not discuss the structural and/or institutional causes behind them or their consequences.[8] This book links the strategies Tsai proposes to the impact of the double transitions to analyze the preferences and strategies of survival embraced by private entrepreneurs and discusses the implications for authoritarian resilience.

I agree with Bellin that fear and dependence are important sources for capitalists' preferences and strategies, but I argue that besides structurally generated fear, there is institutionally generated fear. Private entrepreneurs in China and many other developing countries also fear an under-institutionalized taxation system. Most if not all private enterprises evade taxes to make a profit, which means that private entrepreneurs are vulnerable and fear potential punishment from the government. Significantly, the taxation system does not generate widespread hatred in the same way that terror and repression do because the punishment is selectively applied. Furthermore, under-institutionalization effectively reduces tax burdens, which permits economic growth and therefore contributes to authoritarian resilience.

I also argue that the combination of high fear and low dependence exists and leads to opportunism: private entrepreneurs in China act as free riders and take advantage of the current system instead of acting collectively to push for democratization or even limited-scope institutional change. I examine how the under-institutionalized taxation system resolves the representation dilemma by generating fear and patron-clientelism.

Under-institutionalized Taxation Administration and Social Control

The under-institutionalized taxation system's embedding in de facto fiscal federalism—an authoritarian party-state system with a high degree of decentralization—also profoundly affects its functioning: local governments compete with each other to attract investment and effectively reduce the real tax burdens via various tax breaks and loose enforcement. I identify three crucial consequences of these characteristics for private entrepreneurs and their political participation: rampant tax evasion by enterprises (as forbearance), rampant rent seeking by the tax officers and some other government officers, and the deinstitutionalization of taxation as a system of rule by law.

Chinese private enterprises suffer nominal heavy tax and nontax burdens, although the real burden could be much lower; during hard times for the macroeconomy, they suffer heavy burdens. Zhou Dewen, president of Wenzhou Private and Individual Enterprise Association and a famous "representative" of the private economy, estimates that the tax burden for small and medium-sized enterprises (SMEs) is far more than 37 percent, and they pay seventy different fees and charges imposed by thirty government organs. The tax and nontax burdens make SMEs uncompetitive in the world market (*China Times* 2015). As a result, tax evasion is a very common practice. Many entrepreneurs and some tax officers told me outright (the frankness is surprising culturally) that following the law and paying all their taxes would destroy all private enterprises in China. In low-profit industries, 2 percent more tax means losing half or more of the profit. In high-profit industries, rampant tax evasion means that an enterprise that pays all its taxes will lose its competitive advantage to its competitors who evade taxes. A senior tax officer who has thirty years of working experience at the county level told me that he has seen only one enterprise that was fully tax compliant. This extraordinary enterprise was a foreign supermarket and had branches nationwide; my informant suspected that it could not afford to build patron-client ties everywhere that it operates and its size gave it strength in the marketplace to overcome the low-marginal-profit disadvantage. Thus, it was rational for it to comply with the tax administration to reduce the risk of penalty.[9]

Rampant tax evasion provides tax and other government officers with many opportunities to get rent from enterprises. A private entrepreneur in Beijing told me that he asked a tax officer he was familiar with, "All of you know that the current tax rate is too high for compliance. Why don't you lower the tax rate to make it workable?" The tax officer did not answer him, and my informant said he answered his own question: "I know the reason. If the tax rate is low and everyone complied with the law, you guys never get any rents, right?"[10] Of course, officers who collect the taxes do not set the tax rates, but the high rates do create many opportunities for rent seeking. High discretional power on tax evaluation and punishment for tax evasion also feed rent seeking (the fine varies from 50 percent to five times the amount of tax evaded).

Rampant tax evasion could be a win-win game for government (with a low discount rate), government officers, and private entrepreneurs. Tax evasion, of course, reduces the government's fiscal income in the short term but promotes economic growth in the long term, therefore increasing fiscal revenue in the long term. In other words, local governments with low discount rates could benefit from tax evasion. Private entrepreneurs also benefit in that they can reduce the effective tax rates and therefore make more investments, which in turn promotes economic growth. Tax evasion also benefits local officers who receive bribes, gifts, and other advantages from private entrepreneurs for providing patronage. In Kellee Tsai's terminology, tax evasion is an "adaptive informal institution" described "as regularized patterns of interaction that emerge as adaptive responses to the constraints and opportunities of formal institutions, that violate or transcend the scope of formal institutions, and that are widely practiced" (2006, 125–126). This situation is also close to forbearance: "intentional and revocable government leniency toward violations of the law" combined with weak enforcement (Holland 2017, 13).[11]

However, tax evasion is not "apolitical low politics of grassroots adaptations to formal institutions," as Kellee Tsai argues (2006, 141); it is an ideal legal repression tool that could be used for political goals as demonstrated earlier in Mr. Wang's case. Tax evasion is not a free lunch for private entrepreneurs; by evading taxes, they become criminals and can be charged by the government at any time, which reduces their bargaining power with the party-state. Articles 201 and 211 of China's Criminal Law set very severe punishment for tax evasion.[12] In this context, private entrepreneurs would rather build personal connections to protect their tax evasion, and perhaps gain some business benefits, than challenge the government or demand institutional reform.

Mr. Zheng's story is illustrative. He owns several medium-sized glass-manufacturing companies in County Warm River. Like most other manufacturers in that industry, he applied for business registration but never contacted government officials for tax assessment. He also never paid any taxes, even though he made a profit of about 0.5 million yuan (USD 72,000) for years. In 2005 someone he knows well reported him to the tax administration. His evasion could carry heavy fines and three to five years in jail. The county LTB gave him two weeks for negotiation.[13] He searched everywhere he could think of for a connection to a government official who could help and finally found out that a student of his father's decades earlier now worked with someone at the provincial Taxation Bureau. Mr. Zheng told me that this connection called the county LTB head and took care of the problem. "The tax officials who treated me badly in the last few months began to make me a friend. I treated them with good banquets and KTV many times, though they are very expensive. Now I am going to ask them to help me in my business." Later on I was told that Mr. Zheng started a transportation company, and the LTB officers helped him by asking other companies to use his services.[14]

The broader context in which the tax administration is embedded limits the tax bureaus' independence. Like other state institutions in China, the taxation regime is embedded in the political institution: the party-state complex. The actual practice of the taxation regime is, thus, different from its design of independence. Not only do personal networks limit the tax officers' autonomy, but so do other institutions with which the Tax Bureau must work. While the county SAT office director acted independently in the case of the paper manufacturer in County X who had to sell his factory to pay his taxes after he embarrassed the director, this is exceptional. My informant explained that this happened because the director "was young and had a strong background; he also wanted to build his authority because he had just been appointed and was too young to be trusted by his subordinates." My interviews suggest that his story about the limits of tax bureaus' autonomy reflects a more typical dynamic:

> Several years ago, I moved to the SAT office of County Z, which is in the top one hundred developed counties [*bai qiang xian*] in China, and the economy is much better than in County Warm River. I have a friend who is also from County X and runs a real estate enterprise. You know their profit rate is very high in recent years, but they pay little taxes. One day, the director of the Tax-Inspection Bureau asked us to go to my friend's office to check his company's account. I didn't even get a chance to send him a message before we arrived at his office because it was so sudden (the

director asked us to turn off our cell phones). I managed to talk to my real estate friend for one minute and told him to call his friend in the county government who could help, because otherwise he would be in danger. He called the county's CDI secretary asking for emergency help. The secretary went to the SAT office right away and asked to have lunch with the directors [including the director of the inspection bureau]. The director had to come because everyone fears the CDI. The inspection ended after the director left, and my real estate friend treated us to a nice lunch and gifts. I guess the director didn't really want to make trouble for my friend because he knows that every real estate enterprise has some big guys backing it. He just wanted to let the bosses know that they should visit their director of the Tax-Inspection Bureau to show respect [by bringing a bribe].[15]

Though the Tax Bureau is vertically managed rather than horizontally integrated (into the local government), it still faces serious horizontal constraints. The Tax Bureau has to work with other government bureaus to meet its tax target, and the Party Committee and its departments and subcommittees (especially the CDI) can check the Tax Bureau's power. In addition, like any individual, tax officers are embedded in social networks that shape their interests. Especially in a small county, tax officers have many concerns beyond simply collecting more taxes for the state. Most tax officers are "corrupt" in that they have allowed tax evasion; this makes them fear the party's disciplinary power.[16]

Rampant tax evasion and rent seeking lead to deinstitutionalization of the tax regime and capitalists' weakened bargaining power. When an entrepreneur is a criminal (because of tax evasion), how can he dare challenge local politicians? Mr. Wang's story that begins this chapter is very telling. The best strategy for private entrepreneurs is not to demand building a good institution of taxation but to build a good relationship with the tax officers and/or find a patron in the government.

One good way to build patron-client ties is to join the LPC and LPPCC. Motivated by achieving personal privileges, the LPC is the "organizational clientelism platform" where private-entrepreneur deputies can obtain many privileges, including tax breaks (Sun, Zhu, and Wu 2014), rather than a representative institution, though some deputies do try to represent their constituents (Manion 2016). However, holding a political title in the LPC and LPPCC does not empower a private entrepreneur to gain advantage over the local government. While knowing a low-level tax officer's supervisors very well can confer an advantage, this does not translate to challenging higher authority. The CCP selectively punishes those who try to challenge its authority. Another private entrepreneur told me that no one would "dare" be serious [about representing collective interests] in the LPC: "You have a weakness [tax evasion], and they know it. The most effective way to keep you quiet is to send tax officers to your company and check your accounts."[17]

Ai Weiwei's case illustrates this dynamic as well. In this widely reported case, Ai, internationally recognized as an outspoken artist, blogger, filmmaker, architect, and famous political dissident who also runs an art company, was imprisoned:

> [Ai] was on his way to Hong Kong in April 2011 when he was taken into custody at Beijing's international airport and detained for 81 days.... Ai's studio in Beijing was raided, and his wife and several employees were taken into custody for questioning. The government campaign was attributed to fears of a potential Arab-Spring-style uprising, following online calls for a "Jasmine Revolution." Seven weeks after Ai was taken into custody, state news agency Xinhua reported that Beijing police said his company evaded a "huge amount of taxes" and "intentionally destroyed accounting documents." He was released on one year's probation the following June, with heavy restrictions imposed on his movements. (Lai 2012)

On September 27, 2012, Chinese authorities rejected Ai Weiwei's second and final appeal against a USD 2.4 million tax fine, a ruling he said is the product of a "barbaric and backward legal system" (Associated Press 2012). The artist and his supporters have interpreted the penalty as official retaliation against his activism. This case reflects the CCP's preference for legitimated repression over brutal repression, especially for those who have good connections or attention abroad.

Wang Jianlin, the richest person in Asia in 2015 according to the *Forbes* China Rich List and a member of National Committee of CPPCC, says, "To run a company in China, you should keep close with the government but keep distance from politics. The key is work according to the market rule, but I think it is nonsense to say that you keep distance from the government or party in China" (J. Wang 2015). This captures the key to government-business relationships in China. Many capitalists try to get close to the government. Besides joining the LPC and LPPCC, there are many illegal ways of building patron-client ties, including bribery. During my fieldwork, a number of informants mentioned this, but most did not want to go into detail, given the sensitivity of the issue. An entrepreneur in Shanxi told me that "people with power want money, and people with money want power, which is human nature."[18] After talking with me for hours, a senior tax officer in Shanxi said:

> To summarize [the government-business relationship in China]: the on-table [formal, such as the LPC and LPPCC] channels are badly undersupplied and ineffective, but the under-table [informal, such as bribery] channels are more than needed. The private entrepreneurs enjoy too much power and privilege in local politics, though their voice is too limited to be heard by the central government.[19]

The consequence is a form of what Bruce Dickson (2008) calls "crony communism": "a system of interaction between economic and political elites that is based on patrimonial ties and in which success in business is due more to personal contacts in the official bureaucracy than to entrepreneurial skill or merit" (2008, 22–23). This is for the mutual benefit of the party-state and private entrepreneurs, but patron-client ties harm other social groups that are excluded. After Xi Jinping initiated an anticorruption campaign in 2013, many reports on government-business collusion revealed the exchange of power and wealth in China, covering some cases in my field counties in Zhejiang and (most seriously) in Shanxi, even including the former CCP Standing Committee member Zhou Yongkang, who is charged with being involved in many government-business collusions.

Private entrepreneurs, vulnerable before the party-state, embrace it by establishing patron-client ties and joining democratic-looking institutions, because they fear challenging the party-state. To deter others, the party-state has long made examples of punishing entrepreneurs with political ambitions.[20] The taxation system sets up the situation in which private entrepreneurs join the legislature mainly to build patron-client ties rather than demand representation of their collective interests or institutional reform. The under-institutionalized taxation administration has similar implications for different regions with different major industries. The conclusion seems to be very simple: private entrepreneurs prefer personal benefits to demanding representation even though they pay more than half the taxes received by local governments. Instead, they are eager to build patron-client ties with government officers. As a result, capitalists, no matter how resourceful, have not challenged authoritarian rule.

Quantitative Study of Structural and Institutional Causes of Tax and Nontax Burdens

The comparative case studies in earlier chapters provide the causal mechanisms with internal and primary external validity to test how business's bargaining power, shaped by asset mobility under a regionally decentralized authoritarianism and under-institutionalized taxation system, influences the process of state rebuilding, with special reference to bureaucratization and the social-control problem. Table 6.2 illustrates these causal mechanisms. Given that China is such a large and diversified country, the following question arises: Does taxation's causal effect apply to regions other than the counties that I have covered? This chapter uses quantitative data analysis to test the external validity of taxation's causal effect.

Based on the comparative case studies, we make two hypotheses:

- H1 (regional level): The higher the asset mobility of a region's major industries, the higher the region's governance quality. Therefore, the enterprises in that region have lower tax burdens (as an important indicator for bureaucratization) than regions with lower asset mobility, and vice versa.

H1 is based on the argument developed in chapters 3 and 4: performance-driven local political leaders have strong incentives to try to discipline predatory government bureaus and improve government service, but their incentives and the effectiveness of the efforts depend on the asset mobility of the region's major industries.

- H2 (enterprise level): Private entrepreneurs with political titles (which reflect political connections) can reduce more of their enterprises' tax burden than those who do not have such titles.

H2 is based on the discussion of private entrepreneurs' political participation in local representative institutions (LPCs and related

Table 6.2. Taxation and bureaucratization

	Natural resources and mining	Light industry
Asset mobility	Low	High
Practice of tax administration	High nominal tax rates, high discretionary power, and tax-target system, all leading to rampant tax evasion	
Local party government leaders' incentives and strategy	Easy revenue generation weakens incentive to create an investment-friendly environment	To retain local investors and attract outside investors, need to rationalize the government bureau, provide better public infrastructure to create investment-friendly environment, and ally with private entrepreneurs to achieve these goals
Private entrepreneurs' bargaining power	Low	Medium to high
Private entrepreneurs' strategies	Evade tax, build personal connections, achieve higher political status/titles	Evade tax, build personal connections, achieve higher political status/titles, sometimes collectively lobby for better infrastructure and government service
Bureaucratization	Low	Relatively high
Overall tax and nontax burdens	High	Low

institutions) and institutions of taxation in chapters 5 and 6: because of institutional defects, many if not most private entrepreneurs invest in political connections to protect themselves and get new business opportunities. Political titles such as "LPC deputy" and "LPPCC member" are valuable for building political connections while also bringing some economic and political privileges.

The Data

The data set has three sources: a nationwide private-enterprise survey (PES) of the year 2007, nationwide county-level fiscal data for 2007, and county-level GDP and population data for 2006 (for time-lag effects).[21]

The PES was conducted in April 2008 by the Research Team of Private Enterprise, composed of scholars and government officials from various ministries in charge of private enterprises: the CPC Central Committee Department of the United Front, All-China Federation of Industry and Commerce, State Administration for Industry and Commerce, and the official Research Center for China's Private Economy. Some research institutions, including the Institute of Sociology of the Chinese Academy of Social Science, also participated for survey design and implementation. The PES has been conducted nationwide every two years since 1991 to collect information on the development of private enterprises in China. I chose the 2007 data because they are the most recent publicly available data (from the University Service Centre for China Studies at the Chinese University of Hong Kong). Another reason is that the Chinese government's 4 trillion yuan stimulation package in 2008 changed the national macroeconomic situation substantially, especially in terms of "the advance of the public sector and the retreat of the private sector" (国进民退) (Qian 2010); therefore, it is likely that the 2007 data represent the "golden days" of the private sector better than more recent survey data.[22]

On the questionnaire, the respondents (private entrepreneurs) were required to answer questions on their enterprises' characteristics and their own personal information for the year 2007. The survey was conducted by the local Federation of Industry and Commerce and the local AIC. Therefore, the survey may have some deficiencies: for example, the sampling is not a strict random sample;[23] the private enterprises with connections to the local Federation of Industry and Commerce and the local AIC are overrepresented; and the questionnaire was not designed to be analyzed in the manner in which we are doing so here, so we cannot build comprehensive measurements for some variables. Fortunately, however, we can still build good measurements for the important variables, with some limits.

My research assistants then added the regional-level fiscal data for 2007 to the PES data set. The county-level fiscal data come from *Nationwide Fiscal Statistics of Prefectures, Cities, and Counties 2007* (*Quanguo dishixian caizheng tongji ziliao* 全国地市县财政统计资料), edited by the Ministry of Finance of the People's Republic of China (2010). My assistants and I also added the regional-level economic development data for the year 2006. Since there are no systematic data at the county level, we collected data from the province, prefecture statistic yearbooks, and the regional *Economic and Social Development Statistic Report* (国民经济和社会发展统计公报) to the LPC annual conference. Data from Beijing,

Shanghai, and Tianjin are excluded from the data set because these three municipalities have only two levels of local government, while the provinces and autonomous regions (and Chongqing, another municipality) have three,[24] and these three municipalities have much greater urbanized economy and society that make them different from other regions.

Measurement

Dependent Variable(s)

The dependent variable is the level of bureaucracy's predatory behaviors, an important indicator of local governance quality measured by the private enterprises' tax and nontax burdens. Governance quality has many aspects, including whether the bureaucracy acts predatorily or developmentally, whether the quality of government service and infrastructure is good, and whether the government is clean (not corrupt) and responsive. If we use the World Bank's list of indicators, there are even more aspects. However, limited by the PES data set, we cannot measure government service, cleanness, and responsiveness;[25] we can measure only the *degree* of government predatoriness. The degree of government predation is well correlated with government service quality and responsiveness because there needs to be a coherent and capable bureaucracy to perform all these functions. A predatory government cannot provide good government service; it may be able to provide good public infrastructure by spending the revenue it collects though predatory actions, but it is not a sustainable strategy. A predatory government also has low inner coherence; therefore, it cannot distribute resources as it intends to. This indicator of government predatoriness can thus measure the overall governance quality, though admittedly with some limits.

In the PES questionnaire were questions regarding how much the enterprise paid in the year 2007: taxes, fees, apportionment (*tanpai*),[26] donations,[27] and public relation and reception fees. I build four indicators by dividing the following by the sales figure: (1) overall tax and fee burden (measures quality of governance); (2) tax burden (measures quality of tax administration); (3) nontax burden (sum of fees, apportionment, donation, and public-relation and reception fee, which measures predatory government behavior); and (4) apportionment, donation, and public-relation and reception fee.

These four indicators vary slightly in measuring different aspects of governance quality. (1) The overall tax burden, which includes taxes, fees, and other irregular burdens, measures how much the local government takes away from the enterprise overall. (2) The tax rate is the best institutionalized extraction system regulated by unitary laws, but at the same time the nominal tax rate is too high for sustainable economic development; given the great regional variations, it is hard to estimate what the optimal tax rate is, especially at the enterprise level. (3) Different types of fees are the second best regulated because they are based on government regulations but with a higher level of discretion. (4) The apportionment, donation, and public-relation and reception fee reflects the predatory behaviors of local government, but its effect should be shown in the non-tax and overall burdens (even the tax rate): more expenditure in donations, public relations, and reception means more investment in building political connections, which in turn reduces tax and fee burdens proportionally. For example, if an entrepreneur spends 10,000 yuan per month to build good relationships (gifts, bribes, and "wining and dining") with tax officials, he can possibly reduce his tax burden by 30,000 (a net benefit of 20,000) yuan. Since these four indicators have both strengths and weaknesses, I use all of them as a more comprehensive measurement of governance quality. Table 6.3 summarizes the descriptive statistics of four variables.

Independent Variables

Based on the hypotheses, we have two independent variables: asset mobility of the region's major industries at the regional level and the private entrepreneur's political status (party membership, LPC or LPPCC mem-

Table 6.3. Summary of four indicators of tax burden

	Overall burden rate	Tax rate	Nontax burden	Other burden rate
N valid	1,512	1,516	1,516	1,516
N missing	1,971	1,967	1,967	1,967
Mean (%)	11.81	6.31	5.48	5.48
Median (%)	7.00	4.53	1.93	1.93
SD (%)	14.08	7.12	10.23	10.23
Minimum (%)	0.00	−8.86	4.39	4.39
Maximum (%)	98.91	66.67	93.33	83.33

bership) at the enterprise level. It is hard to measure the asset mobility of the major industries within the region because of the limits of available data. I use resource dependence as a proxy for asset mobility. Resource dependence is measured by the percentage of resource tax in total fiscal revenue (to cross-validate this measure, I also use resource tax/total tax revenue).

We need to be aware that the resource tax's share of tax/fiscal revenue determined here is lower than the real total tax and nontax revenues that come from resource-related enterprises. Since the resource tax rate was low in 2007 (3 yuan per ton of coal in Shanxi), the resource tax was very limited; therefore, the value of our indicator is low and cannot fully reflect the exact degree of resource dependence, which may be several times the resource tax, depending on the coal price. However, since many other related taxes (corporate income tax, VAT, etc.) and fees (many types of fees are collected, including the environment protection fee) also come from resources and are highly correlated with the resource tax, this is still a good indicator to measure resource dependence, though the value is underestimated.

The following example estimates how the resource tax/total tax revenue measures the local government's resource dependence. Table 6.4 provides the tax revenue data for County Cold Mountain during 1994 to 2003.

As we find in table 6.4, even when the most important tax—the VAT, which is collected by the SAT but shared between the central and local governments—is not included, resource mining was a more important source for local government tax revenue because of the rising price of coal (and other natural resources). As we can see in table 6.5, in 2003, when coal prices started to rise, the ratio of resource and mining corporate taxes to the resource tax reached 2.61. In 2007, when the coal price was much higher than in 2003, the ratio reached 9.01.

Table 6.6 presents a summary of resource dependence.

Another independent variable is the private entrepreneur's political status—measured by membership in the PC, PPCC, or local Party Committee[28]—an important variable relevant to this discussion. Unlike other studies that use party member as a sign of political status, I use it as a control variable to test my hypotheses more accurately.

Memberships in these three organizations, which are different representative institutions with different levels of power, empower the private entrepreneurs with some bargaining power: the Party Committee is the most powerful, the PC is the second most powerful, and the PPCC is

Table 6.4. Tax revenue structure of County Cold Mountain's LTB, 1994–2003

	1994	1995	1996	1997	1998	1999	2000	2001	2002	2003
Total tax revenue (10,000 yuan)*	2,721	3,074	4,145	4,799	5,200	5,597	5,786	7,434	8,901	12,248
Resource tax (10,000 yuan)	633	600	618	641	673	811	847	809	1,361	2,033
Resource tax / total tax (%)	23.26	19.52	14.91	13.36	12.94	14.49	14.64	10.88	15.29	16.60
Corporate income tax (10,000 yuan)	688	683	740	673	606	1,012	1,079	2,872	3,159	4,643
Mining corporation contribution (%)	59.48	48.89	51.74	46.93	47	43.31	46.69	37.96	62.49	70.65
Resource tax and mining corporate tax / total tax (%)†	38.30	30.38	24.15	19.94	18.42	22.32	23.35	25.55	37.47	43.38
Share of resource tax and mining corporate tax / share of resource tax	1.65	1.56	1.62	1.49	1.42	1.54	1.59	2.35	2.45	2.61

Source: Prefecture J Local Taxation Bureau: Statistics of Prefecture J's Local Taxation, 1994–2003.

* This includes education fee (nontax revenue).

† This is calculated based on the data above. It is not a comprehensive statistic of the share of resource-related tax revenue because the taxes collected by the SAT office (158.63 million yuan in 2002, mostly as VAT) are not included, given the limits of the data. If we take VAT into consideration, the percentage of the resource and mining corporate taxes' share of total tax would be double.

Table 6.5. Ratio of coal-resource-related taxes to resource tax in County Cold Mountain

	2005	2006	2007
Coal-mining and coal-washing corporation income tax (10,000 yuan)	18,234	25,279	33,455
Resource tax (10,000 yuan)	4,240	3,249	4,141
(Corporate income tax + resource tax) / resource tax	5.30	8.78	9.08

Source: County Cold Mountain's LTB statistics (not publicized), multiple years.

Table 6.6. Summary of resource dependence

	Resource dependence (divided by total fiscal revenue)	Resource dependence (divided by total tax revenue)
N valid	3,483	3,483
N missing	0	0
Mean (%)	1.43	1.92
Median (%)	0.20	0.24
SD (%)	2.93	3.95
Minimum (%)	0.00	0.00
Maximum (%)	19.90	25.08

Note: As I find in the regression models, resource dependence (divided by total fiscal revenue) is not a good measurement. Thus, I have not included this in the results.

mostly seen as an "honorable" institution.[29] To simplify, I first recoded these, as seen in table 6.8, as ordinal variable(s) (highest-level of political title) and then to nominal variable(s) (with or without a political title). I use the nominal variable as the independent variable in the regression models and keep the other two here for descriptive purposes only. Table 6.7 gives a detailed description with level and institutions, table 6.8 provides the simplified description with only levels, and table 6.9 further simplifies to whether the private entrepreneur has such a political status.

As the tables demonstrate, many private entrepreneurs have political titles such as "LPC or NPC deputy," "PPCC member," or "Party Committee member." Though the percentages are overestimated due to a biased sample, the findings are still consistent with those in chapter 5.

Table 6.7. Summary of political status (membership as independent variable)

	PC		PPCC		Party Committee	
	Frequency	%	Frequency	%	Frequency	%
No membership	2,684	77.06	2,428	69.71	3,128	89.81
Township	96	2.76	—	—	110	3.16
County	390	11.20	698	20.04	193	5.54
Prefecture	237	6.80	299	8.58	31	0.89
Province	59	1.69	54	1.55	14	0.40
National	17	0.49	4	0.11	7	0.20
Total	3,483	100	3,483	100	3,483	100

Note: Political status is indicated by membership in the PC, PPCC, and/or Party Committee, which is considered separately as a nominal variable.

Table 6.8. Summary of political status (membership as ordinal variable)

	Frequency	%	Cumulative %
No membership	1,803	51.77	51.77
Township	103	2.96	54.72
County	933	26.79	81.51
Prefecture	509	14.61	96.12
Province	107	3.07	99.20
National	28	0.80	100.00
Total	3,483	100	

Note: Political status is indicated by membership in the PC, PPCC, and/or Party Committee, which is considered separately as an ordinal variable.

Table 6.9. Summary of political status (membership as nominal variable)

	Frequency	%
No	1,803	51.77
Yes	1,680	48.23
Total	3,483	100

Note: Political status is indicated by at least one membership in the PC, PPCC, and/or Party Committee, which is considered as a nominal variable.

Control Variables

The control variables include both regional-level and enterprise-level variables. Two regional-level variables are the economic development level and district. The enterprise-level variables include the enterprise size (sales, employee number), tax contribution (large tax contributors have stronger bargaining power, used for the regression model only when the overall tax burden is the dependent variable), industry (asset mobility and competition), and years of operation.

Economic development level is a regional-level variable that measures the economic development of a county (or county-level district) by GDP per capita in 2006. According to Thomas Bernstein and Xiaobo Lü (2003), because of fiscal pressure and lack of alternative tax sources, local governments in poor counties tended to overtax peasants more than in wealthier counties before the agricultural taxes were abolished. Based on their research, we can say that private enterprises' tax burden will be higher in poor counties because the local governments there have narrow(er) tax bases.

District (*qu*, a county-level administrative unit in a prefecture, given a value of 1) or not (which means it is a county and given a value of 0) is a regional-level dummy variable that measures whether the enterprise is located in a more urbanized district and under the stricter control of the prefecture-level government. Enterprises in a district may have higher tax burdens than those in the county because it is easier to monitor them within a more urbanized region.

Enterprise size is measured by its sales and number of employees. Other things being equal, a large enterprise is more influential than a small one in local politics and may have stronger bargaining power with the local government and therefore have a lower tax burden. Conversely, it is also easier to monitor a large enterprise for tax compliance. It is thus hard to predict whether the size is positively or negatively correlated with tax burden.

A private enterprise's tax contribution to the local government also affects its bargaining power with the local government: large tax contributors have stronger bargaining power. To avoid the endogenous problem, this variable is not used in the regression models, except the overall tax-burden model.

The main industry of the enterprise's business measures the asset mobility and competition; therefore it may also affect the enterprise's tax burden. In this discussion, I use two dummy variables, the manufacturing and resource-mining industries.

Years of operation may also affect the tax burden because the private entrepreneur may build a standardized accounting system for taxation and build good connections with tax and other government officials who collect tax and nontax revenue.

Party membership is another control variable, as discussed in relation to political status (1 = CPC or other party membership, and 0 = nonparty membership).

The description of these control variables is summarized in tables 6.10 and 6.11.

Table 6.10. Summary of control variables

	GDP per capita 2006 (100 yuan)	Sales (10,000 yuan)	Employees	Tax (10,000 yuan)	Years of operation
Mean	227.34	5,857.41	182.01	245.87	8.12
Median	168.82	730	40	21	7
SD	176.08	25,548.95	610.55	798.48	4.89
Minimum	22.48	0.2	0	−7	2
Maximum	1,115.23	850,000	20,000	13,800	30
Missing	2	298	122	331	0

Note: N = 3,483.

Table 6.11. Summary of district and party membership

	District	Party membership	Industry	
			Coal mining	Manufacturing
No	1,486 (42.66%)	2,068 (59.4%)	3,411 (97.9%)	2,256 (64.8%)
Yes	1,997 (57.34%)	1,415 (40.6%)	72 (2.1%)	1,227 (35.2%)

Note: N = 3,483.

Findings

I use a least-squares regression model that includes four types of tax and nontax burdens to test the hypotheses: governance quality (different measurements of tax and nontax burden) = f (resource dependence, political status, GDP per capita 2006, district, sales 2007, employee numbers 2007, years of operation, party membership, manufacturing, and coal mining). Table 6.12 illustrates the findings.

Table 6.12. LSR model of governance quality (four types of tax and nontax burdens)

Dependent variable/ independent variable	(1) Overall tax burden	(2) Tax rate	(3) Nontax burden	(4) Other non-tax burden
Constant	13.511***	6.099***	6.999***	4.203***
	(1.091)	(.389)	(.778)	(.420)
Resource dependence	.230*	.006	.169*	.082*
	(.127)	(.046)	(.092)	(.049)
GDP per capita, 2006	.004*	−.001	.003**	.000
	(.002)	(.001)	(.002)	(.001)
Political status	−1.892**	.092	−.504**	−.346**
	(.807)	(.111)	(.223)	(.120)
District	1.067	.544*	.865	.527*
	(.775)	(.278)	(.558)	(.301)
Sales, 2007	−2.643E-5	−2.511E-5***	−.00001	.00000
	(.000)	(.000)	(.000)	(.00001)
Employees, 2007	−.001	.000	−.001*	−.001**
	(.001)	(.000)	(.001)	(.000)
Years of operation	−.173*	−.003	−.132**	−.077**
	(.076)	(.028)	(.055)	(.030)
Party member (ordinal)	.358	.345	−.224	−.185
	(.764)	(.274)	(.548)	(.296)
Coal mining	2.516	3.397	−.265	−.458
	(2.544)	(.918)***	(.550)	(.993)
Manufacturing	−3.253***	−.179	−2.7947***	−1.406***
	(.779)	(.280)	(.5618)	(.303)
N	1,510	3,105	1,514	1,832
F value	8.002	3.978	7.859	9.545
Adjusted R-squared	.040	.010	.048	.043

Note: Standard errors are in parentheses; missing data use pairwise deletion method.
* $p < .10$, ** $p < .05$, *** $p < .01$.

For the robustness test, I use different measurements of two independent variables, resource dependence (a proxy of asset mobility) and political status, measuring both by two indicators: RD is resource dependence—resource tax/total fiscal revenue; RD1 is resource dependence—resource tax/total tax revenue; PS is political status measured as a nominal variable; while PS1 is an ordinal variable that measures different levels of PC and PPCC. Considering the space limitations, table 6.13 illustrates only four models for overall tax burden. For the other three indicators of tax and nontax burdens, I obtain similar outcomes. As seen in table 6.13, regardless of how we measure the two independent variables, the outcomes are

Table 6.13. LSR model of robustness check of governance quality (overall tax burden)

Dependent variable/independent variable	(1) RD + PS	(2) RD1 + PS	(3) RD + PS1	(4) RD1 + PS1
Constant	13.511***	13.500***	13.231***	13.222***
	(1.091)	(1.094)	(1.079)	(1.083)
Resource dependence	.230*	.170*	.227*	.166*
	(.127)	(.095)	(.127)	(.095)
GDP per capita, 2006	.004*	.004*	.004**	.004**
	(.002)	(.002)	(.002)	(.002)
Political status	−1.892**	−1.908**	−.525*	−.531**
	(.807)	(.807)	(.309)	(.309)
District	1.067	1.105	1.187	1.224
	(.775)	(.778)	(.773)	(.776)
Sales, 2007	−2.643	−2.639	−2.579	−2.574
	(.000)	(.000)	(.000)	(.000)
Employees, 2007	−.001	−.001	−.001	−.001
	(.001)	(.001)	(.001)	(.001)
Years of operation	−.173*	−.173*	−.181**	−.182**
	(.076)	(.076)	(.077)	(.077)
Party member (ordinal)	.358	.367	.221	.229
	(.764)	(.763)	(.760)	(.760)
Coal mining	2.516	2.547	2.458	2.490
	(2.544)	(2.544)	(2.458)	(2.547)
Manufacturing	−3.253***	−3.261***	−3.319***	−3.327***
	(.779)	(.779)	(.779)	(.779)
N	1,510	1,510	1,510	1,510
F value	8.002	5.626	8.011	5.615
Adjusted R-squared	.040	.038	.040	.038

Note: Standard errors in parentheses; missing data use pairwise deletion method.
* $p < .10$, ** $p < .05$, *** $p < .01$.

robust, with only minor changes in the coefficients and levels of statistical significance.

Interpretation

Except for model 2 in table 6.12, both hypotheses are supported by the data analysis in the nontax burden models (models 3 and 4) and the overall tax-burden model (model 1): the higher the asset mobility (higher dependence on resource tax) a region has, the better governance quality (a less unregulated no-tax burden and better disciplined bureaucracy) it may have; and political status helps reduce overall and nontax burdens for enterprises (higher-level political status reduces the level of burden).

For the tax rate model (model 2 in table 6.12, tax rate as dependent variable), none of the two independent variables are statistically significant; only the enterprise size (sales in 2007), district, and coal mining are significant. This implies that tax administration is relatively institutionalized compared to the situation for nontax revenues and that local government cannot violate it in formal ways.[30] Coal-mining enterprises paid 3.4 percent more taxes because coal mining was a very profitable industry. Enterprise size matters because larger enterprises are easier to monitor and transaction costs of taxation are lower.

Other variables important in reducing these burdens are enterprise size (employee number) and manufacturing industry, which partially supports the bargaining-power proposition. The manufacturing industry is more mobile; therefore, it partially supports the asset-mobility hypothesis but at the enterprise level. Another structural factor, level of regional economic development, is also statistically significant in models 1 and 3, suggesting that the submechanism of economic development helps bureaucratization work to some degree. These results are robust when we use different measurements of the respective independent variables.

As the regression models show, the political-title hypothesis is well supported. Political titles are valuable because they help build political connections that protect enterprises from government bureaus' predatory behavior and help enterprises obtain economic and political privileges. In the regression model, we find that tax administration is relatively institutionalized compared to the situation for nontax revenues. Political connections do not reduce the tax rate. This is somewhat inconsistent with the qualitative analysis in chapters 3 and 5. But this may reflect the limit of quantitative analysis—specifically, the lack of internal validity in measurement, especially when respondents may not provide the correct information for sensitive questions such as those regarding tax evasion. Political titles are valuable because they essentially mean that private entrepreneurs can obtain economic privileges. The under-institutionalized taxation system makes private entrepreneurs vulnerable to the government, so their strategy for survival is to build their political connections (sometimes through obtaining political titles). This prevents private entrepreneurs from acting collectively to achieve institutional reform, which can also improve governance quality.

A manufacturing private enterprise has lower burdens except for the tax rate. It may reflect that manufacturing industries are more competitive and have lower profit rates, but it also possibly means that the high-asset-mobility enterprises have stronger bargaining power with the government, which reduces their overall burden and nontax burden.

Conclusion

Going beyond taxation's infrastructural state power mechanisms proposed by Benjamin Smith (2007) and Dan Slater (Slater 2010; Slater and Fenner 2011), I argue that to sustain an authoritarian regime, rulers should increase its infrastructural power without decreasing its despotic power by strategically using ambiguity and uncertainty. I also argue that an under-institutionalized taxation system helps the CCP alleviate, if not resolve, the representation dilemma through generating fear among capitalists, who are the major taxpayers and potential regime challengers. Capitalists prefer to build patron-client ties as their strategy of survival; they embrace the authoritarian regime and fear challenging it.

Besides resolving the representation dilemma, an under-institutionalized taxation system helps resolve or alleviate the growth dilemma by forbearance: reducing effective tax rates and therefore encouraging investment. Different from coercive institutions that are counterproductive, this taxation mechanism of sustaining authoritarian regime encourages production. In this chapter, I build a deeper institutional explanation for authoritarian resilience based on the institution of taxation. After analyzing the democratic-looking institutions (the LPC and its direct election) and the taxation system, I argue that while the democratic-looking institutions could be exogenous to some degree, as Thomas Pepinsky (2014) argued, the taxation system is a more fundamental institution and serves as the deeper cause for authoritarian resilience.

As figure 6.2 illustrates, through an under-institutionalized taxation system, the CCP successfully created a situation in which private entrepreneurs have to evade taxes to be profitable. To evade taxes, private entrepreneurs need to build patron-client ties to protect them from the government. By claiming that illegal tax evasion would be punished, and punishing some evaders, the CCP also generates widespread fear among private entrepreneurs.[31] Whether or not a private entrepreneur depends on the state for resources, he or she fears the authoritarian state, and this

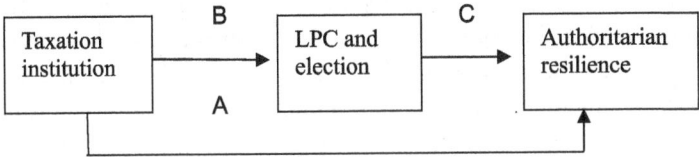

Figure 6.2. Deeper institutional explanation of authoritarian resilience.

fear differs from terror and repression in that it is not counterproductive. At the same time, the under-institutionalized taxation system also effectively reduces the tax burden and creates preconditions for economic growth. Therefore, two dilemmas are resolved or at least alleviated in the short term, and the authoritarian regime is sustained. This is how causal mechanism indicated by arrow A works to sustain authoritarian regimes.

For private entrepreneurs, there are many ways to build patron-client ties. One important and legal way is to join the LPC and LPPCC (see also Hou 2019). They benefit greatly, therefore, from the current political system and support it. Arrows B and C represent these mechanisms. Because of the existence of arrow B, arrow C has a positive role in sustaining an authoritarian regime; otherwise, private-entrepreneur deputies, along with some independent deputies, might demand institutional change and make the LPC a representative institution rather than an inclusive one. This resolves, or at least alleviates, the representation dilemma—not, or not only, because of the institutional defects of the LPC but because of the institutions in which the LPC deputies are embedded.

While the earlier qualitative chapters use both method of agreement (especially chapter 5 and the qualitative sections of this chapter) and method of difference (chapter 4) to build the causal mechanisms and primarily test their external validities, this chapter's quantitative analysis of enterprise-level data, with some regional-level variables, further tests their external validities to avoid possible biases based on limited cases. It reveals that, while asset mobility explains regional variations of bureaucratization and governance quality, an under-institutionalized taxation system generates unregulated fees and fines and the legislature provides protection and privileges for its members from state extraction. These findings are consistent with existing research; for example, Yuhua Wang (2015) finds that asset mobility, measured by FDI, helps discipline local government, as measured by the level of rule of law.

208 GOVERNING AND RULING

However, this is just the first step in testing external validities. There is still much work to be done to fully test the propositions I make in earlier chapters. Given the limitations of the data, both the dependent and independent variables (especially asset mobility) are only partially measured. Further studies would benefit from using more complete measurements of these variables.

CHAPTER 7

Conclusion and Theoretical Implications

If the state household lacks sound foundations, every private household is by the same token not only economically but morally undermined. We can go even further and say that the degree of soundness of the public household determines the level of public morality.
—Rudolf Goldscheid, "A Sociological Approach to Problems of Public Finance"

The spirit of a people, its cultural level, its social structure, the deeds its policy may prepare—all this and more is written in its fiscal history, stripped of all phrases. He who knows how to listen to its message here discerns the thunder of world history more clearly than anywhere else.
—Joseph Schumpeter, "The Crisis of the Tax State"

Whenever we move a step forward in economic reform, we are made keenly aware of the need to change the political structure. If we fail to do that, we shall be unable to preserve the gains we have made in the economic reform and to build on them, the growth of the productive forces will be stunted, and our drive for modernization will be impeded.
—Deng Xiaoping, *Selected Works of Deng Xiaoping*

This chapter addresses the questions raised in the introduction and chapter 1 by summarizing the empirical findings in other chapters: What are some of the factors that account for the resilience of authoritarian rule in China? Specifically, while the three governance problems have been changed under a double transition, how does the party leadership monitor and discipline its agents? How does the party elicit compliance and cooperation from the ruled (especially resource-rich capitalists) to maintain economic growth and authoritarian resilience? What are the institutional tools of repression, concession, and co-optation? Are there any tensions between these goals and tools? Answering these questions can also shed light on understanding possible political development in the future and theoretical understanding of taxation politics, authoritarian rule, and state-society relationships in general.

Given their functions that contribute to the three governance problems (social control, cooperation, and agent discipline), taxation systems are good institutional tools to both govern and rule. In this study, I examine the tax-state transition and its role in sustaining authoritarian rule in China. Joseph Schumpeter focuses mainly on changes in the tax structure and its implication for regime change, Alex de Tocqueville focuses on tax structure and its implication on different classes' interests and political participation (though both of them propose that taxation has an overall impact), and Max Weber focuses on tax administration and its implication for bureaucratization. I posit that the institution of taxation consists of three dimensions: the intergovernmental fiscal relationship, tax structure, and tax administration. Tax-state transition, in turn, includes transitions of all three dimensions, has substantial impact, and is affected by the emergence of the market and private entrepreneurs, bureaucratization, and governance quality.

China's tax-state transition brings new challenges to the three governance problems, which in turn are embodied in two taxation dilemmas. I discuss three taxation mechanisms that resolve the growth and representation dilemmas for authoritarian resilience in the short term. First, de facto fiscal federalism drives local governments to compete with each other and discipline once-predatory government bureaus and elicits cooperation (investment) to promote economic growth, therefore improving taxation capacity and governance quality. The market and a Weberian bureaucracy coevolve. Second, an under-institutionalized taxation system keeps effective tax rates relatively low by permitting tax evasion (as forbearance), thereby encouraging investment. Yet tax evasion keeps entrepreneurs fearful of selective punishment and motivated to build patron-client ties rather challenge the party-state or demand representation. Third, a half-tax state prevents taxpayers (including private entrepreneurs and citizens) from perceiving many tax and nontax burdens, therefore keeping governments at different levels relatively autonomous with respect to the private sector and citizens. However, in the long term, I also acknowledge that these mechanisms may be unable to resolve the governance problems simultaneously, and these dilemmas may in fact counteract each other in the long term and thereby weaken the authoritarian regime.

This book contributes to the literature of both fiscal sociology (taxation politics) and authoritarian resilience studies. It extends the meaning of the institution of taxation to three dimensions by discussing tax-state transition under market transition and understanding taxation as the cause of political change (or regime resilience). Thus, this book answers Schumpeter's previously unheeded call to social science researchers to consider taxation as causes for these changes (Martin, Mehrotra, and Prasad 2009). I also engage in the institutional turn of comparative authoritarianism studies by examining an important state institution rather than a democratic-looking institution to provide an endogenous institutional explanation of authoritarian resilience with causal mechanisms. By approaching state capacity through the lens of taxation, the book also sheds some light on state-society relationships.

This chapter first summarizes the empirical findings that show how China's taxation system contributes to authoritarian resilience and discusses the theoretical implications of these findings. It builds an endogenous institutional explanation of authoritarian resilience, which political scientists consider a major theoretical challenge to the institutional turn of comparative authoritarianism. Then it compares contemporary China to ancient China and other countries, as well as discusses recent changes to the institution of taxation. These comparative studies reveal the underpinnings of my theoretical argument and provide general theoretical leverage.

Taxation as a Causal Variable

Scholarship recognizes taxation as an important state institution but rarely examines its effect on politics.[1] While scholars have extensively discussed fiscal decentralization and its impact on economic growth in China, most of these studies do not discuss its impact on bureaucratization, market formation, and governance quality.[2] Further, they do not examine tax structures and taxation administration as causal variables.[3] This book discusses the neglected issues by examining China's institutions of taxation and tax-state transition and their impact on the three governance problems under authoritarian rule.

Taxation, Market Formation, and Economic Growth

Isaac Martin and Monica Prasad note that while the economic literature does not support firm conclusions about the levels and structures of taxation that support economic growth, myriad studies with mixed conclusions make "a strong case that taxation is a central issue in development" (2014, 337). New institutionalism has demonstrated that taxation, as a core state institution, shapes the economic-development trajectories of different countries (North 1990; North and Thomas 1973; Acemoglu, Johnson, and Robinson 2002, 2005).

The political challenge is that many developing countries cannot achieve the simultaneously capable but constrained state that new institutionalism calls for: they have either weak states or predatory states. I use the term "agent-discipline problem" to refer to the problem of preventing government predation. China has achieved almost four decades of rapid economic growth, notwithstanding some slowdown since 2008. How might it build a strong and less predatory state without either a constitutional government or market-preserving federalism, two institutions that are vital to economic growth (North and Weingast 1989; Weingast 1995)? A comprehensive review of literature is beyond the scope of this book, but many scholars agree that China's economic reform began with (fiscal) decentralization. The fiscal relationship between the central and local governments had changed significantly, shifting from absolute centralization to a high level of decentralization (some scholars call this "fiscal federalism") since the early 1980s. Since the 1994 TSR, China continues to have a highly decentralized fiscal system. However, fiscal decentralization does not necessarily lead to market-preserving federalism (Treisman 2007; Cai and Treisman 2006), which operates under very strict conditions,[4] most of which were and are not met in China. For example, China lacked a common market, which implies high asset mobility and labor mobility, during the 1980s and early 1990s. Moreover, China's governments have not had strong budget constraints until today and have accumulated a great amount of government debt. The 1994 TSR has institutionalized both central-local fiscal relationships and taxation administration to some degree and therefore provides the institutional foundation for a market and bureaucracy.

Other theories, such as local state corporatism (Oi 1992) and the local developmental state (Blecher and Shue 1996), understand government at every level as development oriented and do not discuss the agent-discipline problem. As this book shows in various ways, fiscal decentralization does in fact motivate local governments, but its disciplinary effects vary across regions. The CCP needs to further institutionalize the fiscal system to get out of the circle of "centralization leads to demotivation; decentralization leads to chaos" (一收就死, 一放就乱) (F. Zhou 2006, 115), and refeudalization and the bureaucracy had many characteristics of patrimonialism.

China is experiencing dual transitions, a market transition associated with a tax-state transition. So it needs to (re)build both the market and bureaucracy to promote economic growth. Based on process tracing and comparative case studies, I developed a revised coevolution theory of market and bureaucratization and argue that fiscal decentralization and tax-base change both play an important role in this mutual transformation process. The historical dimension or process tracing refers to the last forty years of economic and (limited) political reform. The fiscal decentralization of the 1980s destroyed the bureaucracy system and drove local governments and their bureaus to act both predatorily and developmentally. As chapters 3 and 4 demonstrate, local governments have rationalized their bureaucratic systems and disciplined agents to some degree since the mid-1990s as they started to rely more on private enterprises for revenue under regional competition. Private enterprises emerged and became more mobile. Economic reform has led to changes in asset mobility and the tax base for the Chinese government and its local branches, thus improving the bureaucratization process and the performance of formal institutions (governance quality). The market and bureaucracy mutually transformed each other and coevolved. Private entrepreneurs also have increased opportunities to express their point of view to government through formal and informal channels. The co-optation of private entrepreneurs resolves the cooperation problem to some degree, elicits investment, and is more likely to improve local government's responsiveness.

Rapid economic growth and improved governance quality helped the CCP achieve legitimacy and sustain power. However, the current taxation system has also had negative consequences. The half-tax state has generated great inequality and is highly inefficient. Further, the soft budget constraints associated with the half-tax state have caused the accumulation of a great amount of local government debt. The under-institutionalized taxation system is biased toward well-connected enterprises and individuals, generating collusive government-business relationships. Thus, the current taxation system worsens the growth dilemma while resolving the representation dilemma.

Taxation and State Capacity

State capacity has reemerged as a hot topic of debate in recent years, and this book engages with this debate and reminds us that we should not take an oversimplified view of state capacity. Tax, which can be measured as a share of GDP, reflects the state's extractive capacity. It has strong spillover effects on other capacities: abundant tax revenue can rationalize bureaucracy and support other government functions. China's market and tax-state transitions have not weakened the authoritarian state's strength. Unlike Russia's government, the CCP has not lost control over government revenue (Solnick 1996).[5] Abundant tax revenues enable the authoritarian government to modernize its military force, fund many government functions, expand social-welfare programs, acquire support, and reduce protests. Thus, the CCP has incentive and made investments to improve its extractive capacity under the double transition. There are three reasons for improved taxation capacity.[6] First, a rapidly growing economy enlarges the tax base; at the same time the development of market and financial sectors reduces transaction costs for taxation.

Second, a large taxation system is the institutional foundation of high taxation capacity. China had a taxation bureau under the Ministry/Bureau of Finance at different levels of government until the 1994 TSR. Two independent and vertically managed taxation bureaus, the SAT and LTB, replaced it; between them they have about one million employees.[7] The SAT and LTB are more professional than their predecessor and have up-to-date information technology and equipment,[8] a rationalized management system, and an improved taxation capacity.

Third, a strong and repressive party-state backs the taxation bureaus. On the one hand, the CCP has the political power and clout to reform the current institution of taxation to improve its infrastructural power to better face various fiscal crises (such as those in the early 1990s).[9] Under the tax-state transition, the CCP's centralized political power, especially its effective nomenklatura system,[10] is crucial to instigating reform of the taxation system.[11] This power has allowed it to rationalize the tax administration (within defined limits), set "hard" tax targets for different levels of taxation bureaus, and recentralize taxation power since 1994. The CCP further centralized taxation power by merging the SAT and LTB in June 2018. Powerful coercive organs, including the police and military police, courts, and procuratorate, have backed the taxation bureaus to repress tax resistance and (selectively) punish illegal taxation behavior.

The CCP has obtained two of the infrastructural state power mechanisms Dan Slater and Sofia Fenner (2011) describe. First, it extracts revenue to support other government functions, including coercive power and public-service provision, as well as co-opting supporters.[12] Second, it registers information on businesses and individuals, which requires a coherent and capable bureaucracy and helps build state capacity to penetrate society.[13] However, the Chinese state still suffers some weaknesses in its infrastructural power. As Lou Jiwei, former minister of finance (March 2013–December 2016), admitted publicly, the central government faces challenges to reforming direct taxes, especially in the areas of real estate tax and individual income tax. The first weakness is that the state's capacity to register business and individual income or wealth information is still very limited. There are far too many government bureaus in charge of registering different properties with limited coordination and communication between them. This is both a result and a cause of historically relying on nontax revenue instead of direct taxes.

The second weakness is that China's de facto fiscal federalism is unbounded. After two decades of fiscal reform, unfunded local governments still have soft budgetary constraints. In other words, the central government continues to suffer weak agent-discipline capacity. While it can still *motivate* local governments to promote economic growth and revenue increase via incentives, it has limited capacity to *regulate* their development strategies and various predatory behaviors. On the one hand, local governments have more expenditure obligations than their taxation power, and they are able to take out almost unlimited bank loans from local government-owned banks, where these debts are usually collateralized by land. On the other hand, local residents and their representative institutions (LPCs) have minimal power to constrain government's expenditure. According to Roy Bahl (1998), without some degree of effective political decentralization and local autonomy (i.e., local legislature's budgetary power and ability to make local political leaders accountable), fiscal federalism cannot function.

Third, the tax-target system is a modern version of the tax-farming system with the impact of the legacy of the planned economy.[14] While it can extract fiscal revenue effectively (though not efficiently), this rigid system is not an effective policy instrument for macroeconomic management because it does not automatically rise and decline with the economy. While the central government emphasizes tax reduction to stimulate economic growth, it also sets a high tax growth rate and therefore makes tax reduction hard to implement. In some cases, when tax revenue is reduced, local governments and taxation bureaus collected more fees and fines to meet the target. Therefore, several recent rounds of structural tax reduction have not substantially reduced the overall tax and nontax burden of enterprises.

State capacity, or more precisely, state capacities, includes more than just extractive capacity. Miguel Centeno, Atul Kohli, and Deborah Yashar provide a definition of state capacity: "the organizational and bureaucratic ability to implement governing projects" or "whether state agencies can fulfill their commonly accepted mission and mandate in terms of organizational design, training, cohesion, and reach" (2017, 4). While we recognize that taxation provides needed government revenue to build a modern bureaucracy,[15] as well as provide better public services and stronger repressive power, therefore helping maintain authoritarian rule, the tendency of increased taxation capacity leads to increased representation, and its complicated relationship with growth can ultimately threaten authoritarian resilience. The current tax state also allows the CCP to coerce potential rivals, cultivate dependence among capitalists, and register citizens (Slater and Fenner 2011). Therefore, tax revenue alone does not reveal how tax administration empowers the ruler; we need to go beyond an oversimplified definition of state capacity.

Beyond Extractive Capacity

Does the state's increased extractive capacity lead to decreased despotic power? Rapid economic growth, significantly increased taxation capacity, and governance quality help the CCP maintain legitimacy and purchase loyalty. However, the representation dilemma remains. Economic growth has generated a large middle class and an emerging capitalist class. Modernization theory predicts that the middle class will have an increasing consciousness of their rights, and new institutionalism predicts that entrepreneurs will demand rule of law and increased representation (see, e.g., Dickson 2016). The tax-state transition also challenges China's authoritarian rulers because becoming a tax state requires deep engagement with society to tax while maintaining the despotic power that communism conferred.

I argue that there are three instruments that the CCP has used to resolve the representation dilemma: "democratic-looking" institutions, the half-tax state, and an under-institutionalized tax administration. Chapter 5 examines the democratic-looking institutions—local legislature and its direct elections—which are important tools for sustaining authoritarian rule by carrying out the following functions: co-opting resource-rich private entrepreneurs and providing credible commitment, which therefore resolves the cooperation problem to some degree (see also Hou 2019). Evidence also suggests that existing wisdom about democratic-looking institutions may be inaccurate or inapplicable in China. The weak and degenerated electoral connection weakens the LPC's representation and co-optation functions. Explaining authoritarian resilience in light of institutions without encountering the exogenous or epiphenomena problem requires examining why private entrepreneurs participate in local legislatures. Specifically, if LPC and LPPCC positions are carrots, taxation becomes the stick.

I argue that China's tax-state transition is still partial, even after more than three decades of marketization. Relying heavily on nontax revenues and indirect taxes weakens taxpayers' bargaining power, reduces the perception of their tax burden, and bolsters the state's autonomy. Tables 2.1 and 2.3 show the stages of tax-state transition: China has transitioned from type V (communist state) to IV (adversarial tax state), enabling it to resolve or alleviate both the growth and representation dilemmas in the short term, although in the long term it may face challenges to sustaining economic growth, thus worsening the growth dilemma.

Authoritarian regimes often practice coercive taxation. However, coercion damages economic growth and social stability, as the agricultural tax did (Bernstein and Lü 2003), which becomes undesirable as the market transition proceeds. Therefore, the CCP has legal and legitimate ways of selectively punishing those who try to challenge its authority rather than having to resort to coercion. By setting high and untenable nominal tax rates but allowing rampant tax evasion, the under-institutionalized taxation system helps the CCP generate both forbearance and fear among private entrepreneurs, therefore resolving the representation dilemma, at least in the short term. Tamir Moustafa and Tom Ginsburg (2008) argue that authoritarian states use their judicial branches to establish social control and sideline political opponents and to bolster their claim to legitimacy.[16] I find that since 2007 China's tax-administration regime has served similar functions. As an effective tool for legal repression, tax administration provides a solid foundation for social control.

The under-institutionalized tax administration empowers the CCP for social control, but at the cost of worsening the other two governance problems. On the one hand, private entrepreneurs seek patron-client ties and citizens have low tax consciousness; therefore, they do not demand representation, which could help CCP leadership improve agent-discipline capacity. On the other hand, while under-institutionalized tax administration reduced real tax burdens and promoted economic growth during the 1980s to 2010s, in recent years we have seen that it generates more suspicion and worries about tax burdens and even security about private property rights among private entrepreneurs, who become more reluctant to make further investments; and the central government's structural tax-reduction program seems too late to stimulate investment. Therefore, the cooperation problem is worsened. In other words, the under-institutionalized tax administration is a fundamental cause of limited-access order, which we discuss in detail later.

State-Society Relations through the Lens of Taxation

Improving infrastructural state power without weakening the state's despotic power can also shed some light on the theory of state-society relations. I elaborate on this by engaging with a Tocquevillian perspective of state. Along with the earlier examination of market-bureaucracy coevolution as a mutual transformation between state and society, this book investigates some important aspects of state-society relationships through the lens of taxation.

In her classic piece on state theory, Theda Skocpol distinguishes Weberian and Tocquevillian perspectives of the state. The Weberian perspective proceeds "from an understanding of states as organizations with varying capacities to deal with challenges of control and direction," based on level of bureaucratization and fiscal revenue; the Tocquevillian perspective "focuses on the *indirect* effects of state structures and actions on patterns of politics" (1985, 21). As Skocpol points out, Tocqueville developed this perspective in *The Old Regime and the Revolution*. She describes a perspective that, in addition to affecting states' autonomous and intentional behaviors, other factors also matter

> because their organizational configurations, along with their overall patterns of activity, affect political culture, encourage some kinds of group formation and collective political actions (but not others),

and make possible the raising of certain political issues (but not others).... The investigator looks more macroscopically at the ways in which the structures and activities of states unintentionally influence the formation of groups and the political capacities, ideas, and demands of various sectors of society. (Skocpol 1985, 21)[17]

In line with Skocpol's description, Tocqueville (1998) considers taxation to be a key state activity.[18] On this basis he develops two lines of inquiry regarding fiscal sociology: how taxation serves as a tool of divide and rule (both between classes and within class) for the state by setting different types of tax, amount of tax, and ways of tax collection for different classes; and what kinds of habits of submission and dependence are generated through the state's deep participation in the economy, what Tocqueville called "industry policies" (Swedberg 2009, 252).[19]

This book contributes to both lines of inquiry by studying how the Chinese state configuration and overall patterns of activity, especially the three dimensions of the institution of taxation, associated with other institutions, influence formation of the most resource-rich group, the private entrepreneurs, and their political capacities, ideas, and demands. Chapters 2, 3, and 4 discuss in depth how the institution of taxation as a state configuration (as de facto fiscal federalism and a half-tax state) affects private entrepreneurs, and chapters 5 and 6 discuss the overall patterns of activity of the under-institutionalized taxation administration and its impact on the capitalists' political capacities, ideas and demands. I elaborate further here to develop the theory.

Decades of economic growth and transitions have changed the power balance between the state and society in China. As Victor Nee and Rebecca Matthews wrote two decades ago: "Power—control over resources—shifts progressively from political disposition to market institution" (1996, 910). It has also brought many changes to patterns of domination, making violence unappealing and ideological indoctrination ineffective (Lee and Zhang 2013). But the nature of domination has not changed. The state still directly controls many material resources, including revenue resources, land, and access to loans. It still monopolizes legal, coercive, and ritual resources. Tax collection has been legalized to some degree, even though there are substantial limitations. The institution of taxation has thus become the ideal instrument of legal repression, giving the CCP a tool of legal repression rather than using coercion. This co-optation through deterrence is what Andrew Nathan has recently called a very important characteristic of the Chinese authoritarian state, which has "learned . . . how to use the forms of law to support repression" (2015, 162), a growing practice among many authoritarian regimes. Or is it a set of "cheap strategies for controlling" citizens, as Lily Tsai (2017, 314) argues? As Jean Oi (1989) and Rachel Stern and Jonathan Hassid (2012) demonstrate in their studies of peasants' agricultural taxpaying and journalists' and lawyers' self-censorship, combining extreme punishment with ambiguous rules can be a very effective means of control.[20] At the same time, the institution of taxation plays the role of co-optation via patronage (offering privileges) and is an effective legal repression instrument that co-opts by both deterrence and patronage. Thus, unlike democratic-looking institutions and coercive institutions, it could achieve both compliance and cooperation at the same time. Therefore, this book also responds to Milan Svolik's (2012) critique that most studies have not acknowledged that coercion and co-optation functions/institutions complement each other.

Forbearance (as a general form of co-optation via patronage) and legal repression (as co-optation via deterrence) are two sides of a single coin. Forbearance has three distinct features: above-minimum institutional capacity, political intention of nonenforcement, and revocability (Holland 2016, 233–234). The laws and regulations set very high standards while allowing noncompliance, but the state reserves the power of revocability, and in the taxation case, revocability means different degrees of punishment and could serve as legal repression. However, to have an advantage of forbearance and legal repression also generates many externalities, and the ruler will face a hard choice about whether to institutionalize tax administration and transform forbearance to effective enforcement while setting reasonable tax rates.

Mary Gallagher (2017) also finds similar logic in China's labor laws. She argues that the party-state sets high standards that the employers are unable to meet but leaves implementation to unorganized workers without any support network (see also D. Fu 2017). Gallagher also reveals that "the state's incomplete adoption of legality feeds workers' disenchantment and radicalization" (2017, 194), generating a vicious circle of legislation, mobilization, and state intervention. This requires further reform of the current legal system, but further reform may hurt authoritarian rule as well.

A comparison between taxation on business and taxation on agriculture, and the methods the government uses to collect both, would provide some theoretical leverage of the state-society relationship. Given the low asset mobility of agricultural production, rural taxation can be very coercive and predatory (M. Moore 2008). When the central government failed to discipline predatory behaviors by revenue-eager local governments, tax and nontax burdens became very high; rural taxation generated tax riots, as it has regularly in Chinese history, most recently in the 1990s and early 2000s (Bernstein and Lü 2003). The central government responded to the legitimacy and governance crisis by putting forth moral and ideological doctrines, making laws, policies, and regulations to discipline local agents from predatory taxation. While these efforts had only limited direct effects, they gave the peasants political opportunity to frame their resistance as "rightful" and local governments' behavior as "illegal" based on central government policies or law (O'Brien 1996). Kevin O'Brien explained that

> rightful resistance is a form of popular contention that (1) operates near the boundary of an authorized channel, (2) employs the rhetoric and commitments of the powerful to curb political or economic power, and (3) hinges on locating and exploiting divisions among the powerful. In particular, rightful resistance entails the innovative use of laws, policies, and other officially promoted values to defy "disloyal" political and economic elites; it is a kind of partially sanctioned resistance that uses influential advocates and recognized principles to apply pressure on those in power who have failed to live up to some professed ideal or who have not implemented some beneficial measure. (1996, 33)

However, rightful resistance against rural taxes (as well as some nontax burdens) did not stop local governments from predatory taxation despite some mild successes until 2006, when the central government abolished agricultural taxes nationwide.[21] Table 7.1 compares the agricultural tax and business tax's roles and mechanisms in sustaining authoritarian rule.

Private entrepreneurs find it difficult to use "rightful resistance," at least in the Chinese context. The under-institutionalized taxation system, especially its high nominal tax rates, along with the official socialist ideology,[22] leaves limited space for entrepreneurs to frame their tax burdens as illegal or wrong.[23] Thus, legal repression and patron-clientelism successfully demobilized most efforts by private entrepreneurs to act collectively to resist tax collection.

Table 7.2 compares rightful resistance, legal repression, and forbearance as three informal institutions and their functions for three gover-

Table 7.1. Comparison of agricultural and business taxation

Institution	Agricultural taxation (broadly defined)	Business taxation (broadly defined)
State actors	Grassroots government officers	Tax officer, local government leaders
Social actors	Peasants	Private entrepreneurs (as winners of reform)
Mechanisms of sustaining/weakening authoritarian regime	Weakens the party-state by generating wide grievances and riots	Infrastructural state power
Social actors' strategies	Popular resistance and "rightful resistance"	Patron-clientelism (sometimes via legislature co-optation)
Micro-foundations of maintaining authoritarian rule	Abolition of taxes and provision of public services	Forbearance with legal repression, tax reduction during economic crisis

nance problems. To summarize, both forbearance and legal repression are informal taxation practices that deviate from legal rational domination as Weber defines it. Legal repression, as Richard Swedberg notes, "is indispensable to rational capitalism through its predictability and hostile to political capitalism" (1998, 69). Therefore, while informal taxation practices help the CCP improve its infrastructural power without substantially weakening its despotic power, they also set limitations for sustainable development because of the limited-access order they reflect and help generate. Before elaborating on this point by looking forward, we need to look back to explain how we got here.

Toward an Endogenous Institutional Explanation of Authoritarian Resilience

Democratization theories focus on either structural-level or individual-level (elite) variables but tend to neglect institutional variables. With the institutional turn of comparative authoritarian studies, scholars have begun to take institutions seriously. Specifically, the governance problems of social control, cooperation, power sharing, and agent discipline are good starting points to examine an institution's functions or institutional mechanisms of maintaining or weakening authoritarian rule.

Table 7.2. Comparison of three informal practices/institutions

	Rightful resistance	Legal repression	Forbearance
Defining characteristics	Set high moral and legal standards for local agents, empowering social actors to resist agents' abuse of power	Set high moral and legal standards for social actors, generating risk and uncertainty	Set high moral and legal standards for social actors, but intentionally not strictly implemented
Social control	Negative effects, rising rights consciousness may weaken the party-state	Positive effects, generating fear, cheap strategy for control	Negative effects, may loosen social control, should be used with legal repression to strengthen social control
Cooperation	—	Negative effects, incredible commitment	Positive, more investment
Agent discipline	Positive effects, as mutual control between state and society, reduce despotic power	Negative effects, improving government's despotic power	Negative effects, agents have more opportunity for rent seeking
State-society relationship	Mutual empowerment of central government and social actors in short term but threatening authoritarian rule in long term	Asymmetric mutual dependence between state and capitalists*	

* See C. Zhang 2019.

However, institutional explanations of authoritarian resilience have many shortcomings. Notably, they lack grounding in institutional theory and tend to be exogenous. Thus, Thomas Pepinsky argues that political institutions could have only "epiphenomenal" rather than "more fundamental" effects on authoritarian resilience (2014, 631). As illustrated in figure 7.1, a political institution's effect on authoritarian rule (path B) is epiphenomenal if political elites can easily manipulate it, if structural variables determine it (path A), or if institutional origins (from structure or

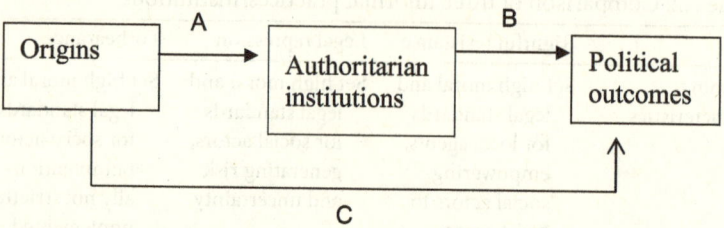

Figure 7.1. From institutional origins to political outcomes. Source: Pepinsky 2014, 632.

more fundamental institutions) directly impact the outcomes (path C). Pepinsky proposes that identifying a specific institution's causal effect on political outcome (e.g., authoritarian resilience) requires a research design that traces origins and changes of the specific institution under examination. I seek to do that here, showing that taxation contributes to CCP stability by resolving, alleviating, or deteriorating the governance problems.

As Pepinsky warned, using a specific institution as a causal variable carries the risk of oversimplification and may neglect the endogeneity problem. This book both engages with and contributes to the scholarly effort to build an endogenous institutional explanation for authoritarian resilience by embedding the institution of taxation with other institutions and discussing the interaction between institution and structure.[24] Schumpeter (1991) argues that taxation can both cause and reflect political and social changes. Recently, Timothy Besley and Torsten Persson (2014) have posited that state capacity (fiscal and legal capacity) and economic development have complementarity (two-way feedback). In other words, authoritarian rule and taxation politics feed each other, which makes the fiscal-sociological explanation of authoritarian resilience an endogenous institutional explanation. This book thoroughly lays out how the institution of taxation increases the CCP's resilience, but I have not explained how the single-party rule affects the institution. I elaborate on this reverse causality here and acknowledge the complementarity between taxation and one-party rule. Before examining taxation and authoritarian resilience, I briefly review and introduce the institutional complex and endogenous institutional change theories to provide a solid theoretical foundation.

Institutional Complex and Endogenous Institutional Change

Without an institutionalism theory, especially institutional change theory, any institutional explanation of authoritarian resilience could be misleading.[25] However, explaining institutional change is still a core challenge to institutionalism; therefore, it is worthwhile to discuss it in more detail. First-generation institutionalism theorists generally have focused on exogenous institutional change theories that employ comparative statistics. They attributed institutional changes to exogenous factors such as international war, colonization, economic crises, and natural disasters.[26] Second-generation institutionalism theorists were more interested in why and how institutions change (Boone 2003; Campbell 2010; Thelen 2001). Some scholars attempted to endogenize institutional change. For example, Avner Greif and David Laitin (2004) use the concept of "quasi-parameter" (2004, 633), and Paul Pierson (2004) uses feedback effects. These approaches do reveal institutional-change mechanisms. However, efforts to distinguish between endogenous change and external shock, locate turning points, and address negative feedback remain in their infancy.[27]

Another school of the second-generation institutional change theory embeds the principal institution (or the operational rules) under study into a broader institutional context. Researchers in this school, such as George Tsebelis (1990), posit that institutions do not work alone but are linked to other institutions and that understanding change requires examining this web of institutions. Elinor Ostrom (2005) argues that there are two types of linkages among institutions in an institutional complex (or institutional cluster). One is the link with organizations at the same level (institutional complementarity),[28] and the other, and more fundamental form, is the link with organizations at different levels (institutional hierarchy). She notes that examining these linkages shifts "levels of analysis from one situation to a deeper rule-changing situation" (Ostrom 2005, 64). Institutional change theories based on the horizontal linkage include institutional layering, conversion, and friction (Thelen 2004; Orren and Skowronek 2004); institutional amphibiousness (Ding 1994);[29] and institutional complementarities, institutional contradictions and tensions (Orren and Skowronek 2002, 2004), and institutional diversity.[30] While well developed, these particular theories tend to be efficient arguments that neglect conflict and power (Knight 1992; Moe 2005).[31]

Institutional change theory based on institutional hierarchy is critically underexplored, but institutional hierarchy is not. Douglass North (1990) discusses institutional hierarchy in relation to organizations and suggests that the principal-agent theory is a suitable method to study institutional hierarchy. Following this hierarchical complex logic implicitly, George Tsebelis and colleagues used the veto player in a political system to explain reform processes and policy making (Tsebelis 2002; König, Tsebelis, and Debus 2011). James Mahoney and Kathleen Thelen (2010) build on this to create a theory and typology of gradual institutional change based on veto possibilities and level of discretion in interpretation and enforcement. However, these are still explicitly exogenous institutional change theories since the political context is exogenous and causes a unidirectional change of the institution under analysis. Though it has many implicit elements of endogenous institutional change, they are not explicitly illustrated.

While it is beyond the scope of this book to completely build and formulate an endogenous institutional change theory, figure 7.2 provides an outline, considering institutional complex, quasi-parameters, and feedback. In China, the "higher-level institution" is the party institution that has some degree of power to manipulate the "principal institutions"—in this analysis, the institution of taxation and the democratic-looking institutions. These institutions in turn generate structural effects, including economic growth, inequality, fiscal capacity, and social demand for more political participation. These structural effects are "quasi-parameters" because they are not exogenously determined. The party leaders respond to these quasi-parameters in the form of an iterative feedback mechanism to adjust the institution of taxation with both structural and institutional constraints.

Various institutions that might function beneath the party institution change through this hierarchical institutional-change mechanism, which has important implications for political development. In ceding to this mechanism, the authoritarian state shows its institutional flexibility, adaptability, and resilience (Shambaugh 2008), but with some limitations. The next section applies this hierarchical institutional change theory to taxation and authoritarian resilience.

Endogenous Institutional Explanation of Authoritarian Resilience

This section traces the origins and changes in the institution of taxation. Based on the endogenous institutional change theory discussed earlier and

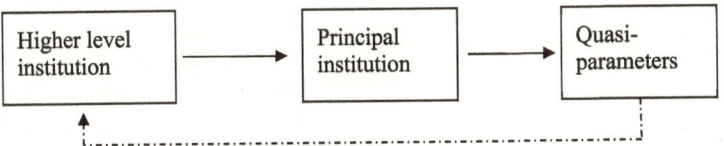

Figure 7.2. A model of endogenous institutional change.
Note: Dashed arrows refer to feedback effects.

Pepinsky's framework, I develop an endogenous explanation illustrated in figure 7.3. In earlier chapters, I discuss both path B (the three mechanisms that resolve the growth and representation dilemmas) and path C (how two dilemmas are related to the three governance problems). Path A uses the institution of taxation as the "symptom" of political change. Thus, I trace the recursive causal relationship that reflects the origin and change of the institution to build an endogenous institutional explanation of authoritarian resilience.

The CCP is an adaptive and powerful single party, whose centralized political power has played a key role in reforming the institution of taxation. Typically, recentralization of fiscal power is politically difficult because subnational governments resist. The 1994 TSR recentralized taxation power by building two independent and vertically managed taxation bureaus and assigning different taxes to different levels of government. It also rationalized tax administration to some extent and made it top down, significantly improving the government's taxation capacity. In addition, the CCP still wishes to develop SOEs for both ideological and instrumental reasons, such as maintaining socialism, which is principally characterized as single-party rule.[32] SOEs maintain China as a half-tax state. The CCP also hesitates to enact a real estate tax in China because it might increase direct taxes; thus, the CCP emphasizes indirect taxes, such as its recent major reform to have the VAT replace the enterprise income tax.

The fact that the CCP could substantially reform the TSR taxation system does not mean an authoritarian ruler can manipulate the institution of taxation. The institution has a degree of institutional stickiness. Even the CCP top political leaders benefit from a modicum of consensus about tax reform among the ruling coalition (i.e., the Politburo and its Standing Committee, as well as the powerful revolutionary elders). Similarly, there is a need to compensate the provinces to elicit their cooperation. Under factional politics, consensus is hard to achieve (e.g., C. Li 2012). Reciprocal accountability in which national leaders and provincial lead-

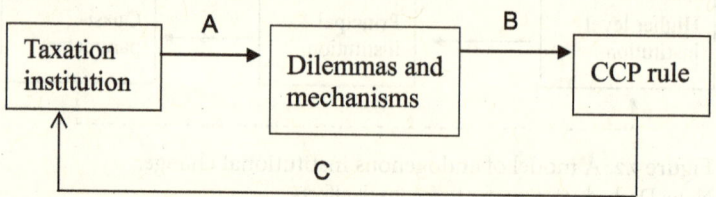

Figure 7.3. Endogenous causality between taxation and CCP resilience.

ers are interdependent (Shirk 1993) and fragmented authority under which ministries and provinces need long negotiation times to even formulate a policy (Lieberthal 1992) also create stickiness. Taxation reform also requires leadership, even political entrepreneurship. To ensure that reforms were made, Premier Zhu Rongji served as the economic tsar in the 1990s and used a divide-and-rule strategy when he bargained with provincial leaders.[33]

Taxation reform has had many unintended consequences. Before TSR, fiscal decentralization led to the blossoming of TVEs and the decline of "two ratios" (tax/GDP and central government's share of national tax revenue); after TSR, rapid economic growth generated much more tax revenue for the central than the local governments in the form of large amounts of land revenue, while local governments acquired debt backed up by land revenue. These unintended consequences are quasi-parameters (Greif and Laitin 2004) that cause top leaders to have to recalibrate their calculations. They are also difficult to change. I adopt Besley and Persson's (2011) methodology, addressing the epiphenomena problem by dividing institutional development into two stages: initially, the ruler chooses whether to invest in building taxation capacity; then, having decided to invest, institutions of taxation become important because of their inertia, which sets institutional constraints on the ruler.

Another limitation on the central government is that local governments comply with tax reform only if they have guaranteed increasing revenue. So the central government can touch only the increased tax revenue. Providing benefits to tax officers who implemented policy also enables TSR. They benefited from rapidly increased tax revenue by receiving increased bonuses (because of their performance) and more discretionary power (and therefore more personal benefits). The self-serving bureaucracy also benefited from the reform. While the central government might have been able to implement TSR without concern for these stakeholders—it did punish leaders in developed provinces that hesitated to implement reform (Cai and Treisman 2006)—the carrot proved far more effective. Reform has thus far reached only partial equilibrium.[34] Thus, the impetus to provide carrots limits the CCP's reform measures.

The coevolution of the market and bureaucracy could also be regarded as endogenous institutional change based on an adaptive informal institution.[35] Kellee Tsai (2006) describes this informal institution to explain the rise of private enterprises in China. I diverge from Tsai's theory in two critical aspects. First, I emphasize the mutual transformation of the state (bureaucratization and LPC) and the market, rather than just the emergence of the market; Tsai studies the rise of the private sector only. Second, I emphasize the power asymmetry between local government and private enterprises. Asset mobility and an under-institutionalized taxation system shape the bargaining power of private enterprises.

The institution of taxation is also horizontally embedded in an institutional complex. The institutions reviewed in chapter 1, especially coercive institutions, strengthen the tax bureaus' taxation capacity in many ways. On the one hand, the military and police deter tax riots, while the judicial branch makes tax evasion illegal and weakens taxpayers' bargaining power. On the other hand, increased revenue pushes the bureaucratization process and improves coercive capacity. In other words, these institutions are complementary.

Therefore, I build a recursive causal relationship between authoritarian party resilience and the institution of taxation. However, this complementarity between single party and the institution of taxation is far from a virtuous circle, as the "development cluster" (Besley and Persson 2011, 6) and "effective state" suggest,[36] so representation is crucial for the virtuous circle to be completed. Without effective political participation, it is hard to resolve the agent-discipline problem and to constrain state power. This leads to a further question: What will happen in the future? As Besley and Persson (2011) observe, the state needs to invest to build taxation capacity; the Chinese government built two separate and independent tax administrations (merged in 2018) that have one million employees. Besley and Persson (2011, 2014) argue that taxation and legality are complementary in developed countries. Thus, there is no growth dilemma, even when the tax portion of GDP is high. However, in a developing country such as China, legality and fiscal capacity have not necessarily complemented each other. Given that representative legislatures at different levels have very limited budgetary power (Ma and Lin 2015), the highly unmatched fiscal system and soft budget constraints drove local government leaders to overspend. This led to the accumulation of huge local government debt. Along with the other problems the tax state faces, the current taxation system threatens sustainable economic growth and therefore may threaten authoritarian rule in the future.

Comparative Relevance

A comparative perspective could give the China case more theoretical leverage in terms of both authoritarian resilience and regime transition. Comparative study refers to comparing contemporary China with ancient China and China with other countries.

Historical Comparison

Historians have found a "dynastic cycle" throughout Chinese history: most Chinese dynasties experienced a period of economic growth, expanded government, and improved but predatory extractive capacity and rampant corruption, leading to economic stagnation and fiscal crisis, sometimes hastened by natural disasters. Fiscal crisis led to overextraction from the poor, and this in turn triggered rebellion. Rebellion led to further predation and therefore a breakdown of dynasties, with or without invasion by nomads (Kuhn 2002).[37]

Indoctrinated with the Confucian ideas of "low taxes and levy" (轻徭薄赋) and "love the people" (爱民) and deeply influenced by their experiences of the failed old dynasties, most founding emperors of newly established dynasties set low tax rates (usually 10 percent or lower) to encourage production and recovery from wartime destruction. Keeping state administration small avoided the costs of a larger bureaucracy and supported low taxes (S. Mann 1987, 4). Thus, the growth dilemma posed few challenges when a dynasty first took power. Some dynasties even stipulated that they would "never increase the tax rate" (*Yongbu jiafu* 永不加赋) and set this as an ironclad rule to warn their successors to discipline themselves and their officials to implement benevolent governance (*Renzheng* 仁政). Iwai Shigeki describes such rules as implementing a "quota system" (原额主义) (2004, 3), and Ping He (2004) calls it an "incomplete fiscal system" (*bu wanquan caizheng*).

These ideas and policies, along with political stability, led to economic recovery and growth in the early years of each of China's dynasties, which were associated with rapid population growth. This triggered expansion of government, so more fiscal revenue was required to deal with both the necessary public-goods provision and corruption. While the quota system prevented tax increases and new taxes, extra-budgetary revenue, including illegal taxes and fees, rose and became hard to control. Some emperors, with assistance from their prime ministers, tried to prevent predation via an institutionalized taxation system, under the logic of "tax-for-fee" reforms.[38] Some of these reforms had some success, but new fees arose as time passed, and new reform was required. Chinese historian Hui Qin (1994) describes the vicious cycle in which dynasties collapsed under economic pressure as the Huang Zongxi Law, referencing the famous thinker of the Late Ming and Early Qing dynasties who first described the cycle.

According to Weber, the Qin Empire (221–207 BC) developed a bureaucratic system very early on, but it did not develop into a modern bureaucracy (1968, 1049). Because of the very limited surplus that the agricultural economy could generate, Chinese dynasties were able to build only a small government with limited functional differentiation and limited penetration into rural society to govern a large society.[39] Melinda Zelin summarizes the challenges of the Qing dynasty: "weak agricultural fiscal base, poorly articulated distinctions between public and private revenues, and intense competition, both within and without the bureaucracy, for the limited surplus product of the realm" (1984, xii). Local governments were very small; the emperor, with the assistance of his ministries, appointed county heads with three to five assistants who were on the official payroll list. Governing a county required employing additional staff (吏), but the central government did not provide salaries for them. Thus, county heads had little choice but to collect illegal taxes and fees to pay staff and meet unfunded mandates. These extra-budgetary revenues were outside the remit of higher-level government monitoring and audit purview and easily degenerated into a system of outright corruption. Bribes also supported local and central supervisors, who would not retain a county head who did not pay bribes (Ch'u 1988). Thus, corruption led to more corruption and destroyed society and economy (P. He 2010).

Emperor Yongzheng of the Qing dynasty (1722–1735) significantly increased local government heads' salaries through setting Yanglianyin (养廉银),[40] which covered both higher salaries and necessary public expenditures, when he reformed the taxation system, as well as legalized some once-illegal taxes (火耗归公, return of the meltage fee to the public coffers). While Yongzheng's reform was a significant success in rationalizing the fiscal system and bureaucracy system, its impact gradually faded after his death, and institutionalized corruption and tax evasion reemerged (Zelin 1984).[41] A series of wars and rebellions intensified the need for revenue after the mid-nineteenth century, and officials and Li worked with local gentry to tax farmers far more than they could afford. As a result, the dynasty's fiscal revenue did increase, but not proportional to the total extraction from society. The tax farmers took a large share of this extraction, which Prasenjit Duara has called "state involution" (1988, 73–74; see also S. Mann 1987, chap. 9). Debin Ma and Jared Rubin theorize this paradox of power by developing a "principal-agent model which reveals that absolutists, unconstrained by rule of law and unable to commit to not predating on their tax-collecting agents (and the masses) may find it optimal to settle for a low wage-low tax equilibrium, while permitting agents to keep extra, unmonitored taxes." They argue that "low investment in administrative capacity is a conscious *choice* for an absolutist since it substitutes for credible commitment to refrain from confiscation from its agents" (2019, i).[42]

In terms of composition of fiscal revenue, Chinese dynasties were half-tax states. While the government monopolized the iron, salt, wine, and tea trades to extract a huge amount of rent, the direct taxes based on land and labor were usually the major tax sources until the state introduced an indirect tax (*Lijin* 厘金) in 1850 during the Taiping Rebellion, and it quickly became an important part of state revenue. Earlier Chinese state policies toward trade "tended to cycle between periods of benign neglect, or even nurturant support, and periods of confiscatory taxation" (S. Mann 1987, 9). The royal family also owned land, but it was an insignificant source of income in most dynasties.[43] In response to both internal and external wars, the Qing government started to collect more indirect taxes after the mid-nineteenth century. Yeh-Chien Wang (1974) calculates that in 1908, total indirect taxes (salt tax, customs, *Lijin*, and domestic tariffs) exceeded land tax. Heavy indirect taxes and the practice of tax farming, along with other institutional limits and political instability, blocked industrialization in nineteenth- and early twentieth-century China.

Dynasties also faced the representation dilemma, even though taxation based on agriculture tends to be coercive rather than consensual because of the immobility of land. Tax bargaining occurred between local government and the gentry, who served as brokers between government and peasants. While in some cases the gentry acted as representatives of their communities to protect peasants from being overtaxed, they generally supported overtaxation (of the poor) in exchange for tolerance of their illegal tax evasion. Thus, they served as tax farmers rather than representatives, which led to state involution and, ultimately, economic stagnation. Philip Kuhn finds that brokers were strongly connected with county heads, who relied on them to meet their revenue targets. He describes the brokers and defective taxation system as two serious problems for local government, calling it the "commercialization of county government" (Kuhn 2002, 98).

Evidence also suggests that dynasty survival and taxation had a recursive causal relationship. While centralized political power was a precondition for successful fiscal reform, fiscal revenue surplus further strengthened dynastic rule (S. Mann 1987). Few successful fiscal reforms (especially Zhang Juzheng's reform in the Ming dynasty and Emperor Yongzheng's reform in the Qing dynasty) raised fiscal revenue, constrained corruption, improved governance quality, and extended regime longevity.

If we use Weber's fiscal sociology theory (Swedberg 1998; Weber 1951, 1968) to reexamine the relationships among state, society, and market in imperial China (Weber 1951), we find several factors that tended to encourage political capitalism but not market capitalism. First, a traditional taxation system, including some elements of tax farming, monopolistic profit-making enterprises for salt and mining, and liturgical obligations attached to political status, was negative to market capitalism but positive to political capitalism. It also included some elements of deliveries in kind and compulsory services, which discouraged all types of capitalism. Second, the system fell between traditional domination (patrimonialism) and feudalism, which was also negative to market capitalism but weakly positive to political capitalism.[44]

Contemporary China has clearly broken the vicious cycle of dynasty change, and the tax system is one important reason. It has eliminated the tax brokers of precommunism through agriculture collectivization (Kuhn 2002) and investment in building taxation capacity by building a taxation bureaucracy (S. Mann 1987). But state monopolization still plays an important role in providing fiscal revenue, the taxation system is still under-institutionalized,[45] and centralized fiscal power leads the local government to collect a large amount of extra-budgetary revenue. Rural taxation in the 1980s and early 2000s before agricultural taxes were abolished was very similar to the system of a hundred years ago.[46] However, fiscal decentralization, implemented as tax farming in the 1980s,[47] was different from tax farming in imperial China because it promoted rapid industrialization. Industrialization makes modern economic growth possible and provides an enlarged and reliable tax base to build a modern bureaucracy burdened with various responsibilities. A substantially improved taxation system has improved state capacity in many ways, leading to the emergence of a modern state. Nonetheless, it has many defects.

Comparative Implications with Other Countries

This book engages the emerging literature on developing countries' taxation and provides a different trajectory of taxation and state rebuilding without war, threat of war, or domestic civil conflict (e.g., Tilly 1990; Ertman 1997; Lieberman 2003; Slater 2010). The TSR occurred in a time of peace. However, the Anti-Japanese War (1932–1945), the Civil War (1945–1949), and the Korean War (1950–1953) played important roles in building a strong totalitarian state in China,[48] and they have an important historical legacy that shapes tax-state transition and state rebuilding in the reform era. Comparing China to other countries shows that different events lead to different outcomes. As Barrington Moore's (1966) seminal work on the origins of democracy and dictatorship suggests (see also Smith 2007), the sequences of revolution and commercialization shape development trajectories in modern times (illustrated in Table 7.3).

Western Europe's classic state building from the seventeenth to nineteenth century involved weak state authorities trying to claim power resources from strong societal actors through tax bargaining. However, China's post-totalitarian (or authoritarian) state faced different situations. The CCP faced a weak market that had recently emerged from the state and a weak society that decades of war, land reform, and the Cultural Revolution had completely transformed.[49] Endowed with a strong post-totalitarian state, the China case differs from other developing countries where the states fail to improve taxation capacities even though there is neither international war (or the threat of war) nor domestic conflict (Herbst 2000; Piracha and Moore 2016).

Comparison with other postcommunist states could be more fruit-

Table 7.3. Revised development trajectories of Barrington Moore

Sequence		Commercialization/industrialization		
		First	Later	No
Revolution	First	—	Transitional economy: Post-Maoist China	Communism: Soviet Union and Maoist China
	Later	Democracy: Britain and United States; Germany and Japan after 1945*	—	
	No	Fascism: Germany and Japan before 1945		India before 1970

* The Axis Powers' treaties after World War II were not technically revolutions, but the social-structure changes imposed by the United States were functionally equivalent.

ful, since all postcommunist states experienced tax-state transition under similar international contexts.[50] Gerald Easter (2008) describes tax collection in these contexts as a process of state (re)building that involves redistribution of abundant power resources (coercive, economic, and bureaucratic-legal), a legacy of the old regime, between state and society as well as within the state itself. Comparing Poland and Russia, Easter finds that these two countries, representing eastern Central European and former Soviet Union countries, experienced different trajectories of state rebuilding. These differ from each other in three important ways. First, while Poland experienced tax bargaining between the state and organized labor, Russia had limited tax bargaining.[51] Second, Poland achieved higher tax compliance than Russia and enhanced its state capacity and legitimacy; Russia had windfall revenue from natural resources and radical tax reform. Third, Poland has developed legal mechanisms to resolve revenue disputes, with respect to private property rights and civil society's monitoring; Russia has few checks on state power, and the distinction between state and society remains indistinct.[52] Marc Berenson (2018) adds to this debate by giving a detailed analysis of the institution of taxation in Russia, Poland, and Ukraine. In Besley and Persson's (2011) terminology, Poland belongs to the "development cluster" while Russia does not.

Russia is transitioning from a full communist to a rentier state while

China is transitioning from a communist to a half-tax state. Thus, China's current tax state is more like Russia than Poland but has elements of Poland's system. On the one hand, China differs from the development cluster in several ways: no rule of law, no democracy, and a very limited and regressive social-welfare program (Gao 2010). On the other hand, because of its gradualism strategy of economic reform, China does a better job of improving both fiscal capacity and legal capacity than Russia.[53] In other words, China is able to resolve the growth dilemma and representation dilemma, while Russia can resolve only its representation dilemma through building a rentier state.

With the legacy of a strong state, China also differs from other developing countries where states failed to improve taxation capacities (see Piracha and Moore 2016 for South Asian countries; Bernardi, Fraschini, and Shome 2006 for South and East Asia). Most developing countries suffer the "failure of centralized bureaucratic administration," which is "predictable in the context of poor communications, transportation, and information processing," and this "has led many African states to partially privatize administrative systems; these are usually called semi-autonomous revenue authorities" (Kiser and Karceski 2017, 12).[54]

What will happen in the future? While most eastern Central European countries have moved from A to C, shown in table 7.4, will China and Russia stay in A, move to B, or to C or D under certain circumstances? To answer this question, we need to investigate elite politics to examine how the power-sharing problem can be resolved, but this is beyond the scope of this research. However, an examination of the limitations of the three taxation mechanisms could shed light on this question.

Table 7.4. Typologies of states

		Despotic power	
		Strong	Weak
Infrastructural power	Strong	A: Totalitarianism/post-totalitarianism/strong authoritarianism	C: Established democracy/development cluster
	Weak	B: Weak authoritarianism	D: Anarchy/failed democracy

Conclusion and Theoretical Implications   237

Looking Forward: Limitations of Taxation Mechanisms for
Authoritarian Resilience

The three taxation mechanisms have worked well in resolving the two dilemmas in the last decades, helping the CCP achieve both rapid economic growth and regime stability. China has become a middle-income country along with regime stability. This book mainly discusses how these mechanisms have worked up to this time. However, we also need to be aware that these institutions of taxation suffer several weaknesses, including lack of capacity to collect information; under-institutionalized, unfair tax burdens, regressive in nature; unbounded fiscal federalism; and modern tax farming. Therefore, the current taxation system is self-subversion since both the growth and representation dilemmas are changing as China becomes a middle-income country. The CCP's major economic challenge now becomes getting out of the middle-income trap rather than the poverty trap; thus, the old governing tools need to be updated. The challenges of moving out of the middle-income trap could be very different from moving out of the poverty trap, and the requirement for government quality could be much higher than at the early industrialization stage.

To get out of the middle-income trap and achieve sustainable economic growth, first and most important, China should be able to upgrade its industrial structure, moving upward in the global value chain to reap more profits. It should shift its comparative advantage from low-value-added manufacturing and assembling, in which China cannot compete with South and Southeast Asian countries, to technological innovation, designing, and marketing. Peter Evans has strongly argued that upgrading industry requires collaborative government-business relationships that combine state autonomy and embeddedness. A labor-repressive bureaucratic authoritarian regime could be very successful in promoting the early stage of industrialization, as in the cases of Argentina and Brazil (O'Donnell, 1979), South Korea (Evans 1995), and China demonstrate. However, embedded autonomy demands much higher government quality; it also requires more coherent bureaucracy aims in promoting upgrades of industry and collaborative relationships with businesses. Both of these are still weak in China;[55] further efforts to reform the system of bureaucracy is required. To reform the under-institutionalized taxation administration is among these efforts. Without an institutionalized taxation system, both bureaucracy coherence and government-business embeddedness are hard to build. Institutionalizing tax administration will also change the regional tax competition, leaving local governments with limited space to create tax breaks. This is the first new challenge.

Second, getting out of the middle-income trap requires the Chinese government to reduce high-level income and wealth inequality to build a large domestic market and reduce international dependence.[56] It in turn requires building a tax system that relies more on direct taxes; that is more progressive, further reducing the size of SOEs (World Bank 2013); and that cuts off local governments' reliance on land revenue. The paradox is, if all these reforms are taken, then the half-tax state will transform into a full-tax state, and the representation dilemma will emerge.[57]

Third, the current de facto fiscal federalism also needs to be reformed to motivate local governments to carry out industrial upgrading and reduce local government debt. As the third generation of fiscal federalism suggests (Rodden 2006; Treisman 2007), Chinese-style fiscal federalism is successful. Local governments lack taxation autonomy but have high autonomy in raising nontax revenue, especially land-related income, while LPCs have very limited budgetary power. As a result, local governments still have a severe soft-budget-constraint problem and have accumulate a great amount of debt. This generates negative consequences that may harm economic growth and social stability, therefore weakening authoritarian rule. Furthermore, under a performance-pressure system, the under-institutionalized taxation system has created a race to the bottom rather than a race to the top in regional competition for investment. Instead of improving public services, disciplining predatory government apparatus, and pushing for industrial upgrading, many local governments use tax breaks, pollution havens, and cheap land to attract investment. The CCP merged the SAT and LTB in June 2018, which makes tax administration vertically managed. This may improve the Taxation Bureau's independence from local government in the long run, but it is too early to study its effects. The other recent adjustments, including reducing tax and fee burdens and reassigning VAT share between central and local governments, may help alleviate two dilemmas in the short term, but they are policy responses rather than institutional reforms and may have only limited effects.

Besides these new challenges, as demonstrated in figure 7.4, there is an old challenge that tax burdens have become higher and higher since the mid-1990s (only in 2016 and 2019 have rates of tax growth been lower), as seen when we compare the growth rate of nominal GDP and tax revenue.

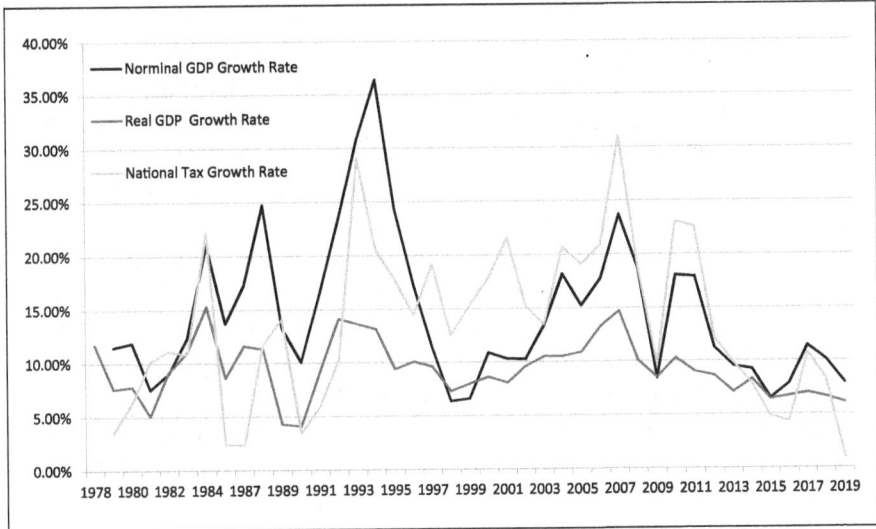

Figure 7.4. Comparison of nominal GDP, real GDP, and national tax growth rates, 1978–2019. Data from 1985 are omitted to make the numbers comparable. In 1985, the national tax growth rate was 115% due to implementation of the new corporate income tax. Source: Ministry of Finance of the People's Republic of China 2020.

Facing the sustainable-economic-growth challenge, old institutions,[58] including the institution of taxation, should be reformed and changed to adapt to new realities, which Jiang Zemin calls "advances with time" (与时俱进) (2006, 282). As Wu Jinglian, a prominent economist who participated intensively in policy making, writes, Deng Xiaoping talked about pushing political reform ahead to support economic reform when he heard a report by the party's Central Leading Group on Financial and Economic Affairs in September 1986 on a comprehensive reform program that aims to simultaneously reform the price, tax, and public finance systems (价税财配套改革) (Wu 2018, 110–111).[59] This reflects the mutual dependence of political reform and economic reform, though the former was narrowly defined as separation of party from government, decentralization, and reduction of government size (Deng 1993, 177). The comprehensive reform program was suddenly abandoned by Premier Zhao Ziyang for unknown reasons, and economic reform has "drawn back" to the old reform program: a combination of SOEs contracting and expansive microeconomic policies (Wu 2018, 111; see also Lou 2013, 67). This drawback from comprehensive reform in 1986 reflects partial-reform equilibrium, which means that those who gained an advantage in earlier reform have become vested interest groups trying to block further reform (Hellman 1998); there could also be serious path-dependence effects that exclude some reform options.[60] As China moves into a middle-income economy, it seems clearer that the two taxation dilemmas are turning into a single dilemma.[61] That is, the tension between growth and representation increases. Moving to a full-tax state and institutionalized tax administration will change the nature of tax compliance. On the one hand, citizens will have greater consciousness of their rights and may demand more political participation. On the other hand, legal repression will not be a good tool for social control. As a result, quasi-voluntary compliance will be required to elicit compliance, and the more independent capitalists will demand more representation.

I find that unlike democratic states, authoritarian states such as China can build taxation capacity only by forgoing development of a not-rule-of-law taxation system and relying more on indirect taxes and nontax revenue, which help resolve the representation dilemma (at least over the short term). At the same time, to push the government toward more redistributive policies and more spending on social-welfare programs requires a more representative government that responds to citizens' demands in a more socially moral and responsible way, as fiscal constitutionalism theories would suggest. Therefore, to achieve sustainable economic growth, China may have to build a more rules-based taxation system and some mechanism of political accountability, including empowered PCs at different levels through which a rule-based system could be implemented and administered,[62] in addition to its recent readjustment of the central-local fiscal relationships.

Discussion

It is hard to predict what will happen in the future in the case of China, but there are several implications. As Daron Acemoglu and James Robinson (2012) argue, an extractive institution may lead to economic growth but is unsustainable. This raises other questions: What further steps will the CCP take, and what are the political implications? Should China abolish its extractive institution and develop an inclusive institution to achieve further economic growth? To answer these questions, I engage with the debate of duration and transition from limited-access order to open-access order and the theory of the double balance developed by Douglas North, John Wallis, and Barry R. Weingast (2006, 2009).[63] Widely spread patron-clientelism suggests limited-access order (the natural state) defined by North, Wallis, and Weingast: "Personal relationships, who one is and who one knows, form the basis for social organization and constitute the arena for individual interaction, particularly personal relationships among powerful individuals" (2009, 2). Open-access social order is characterized by impersonal and universal rules and is associated with rule of law and democracy. Open-access social order is hard to achieve in developing countries.[64] The theory of the double balance suggests that economic and political systems both tend to be open access or to be limited access. It "implies that sustaining fundamental changes in either the economic or political system cannot occur without fundamental changes in the other" (North, Wallis, and Weingast 2006, 6). Or as Deng Xiaoping said, further economic reform may demand further political reform. North, Wallis, and Weingast (2006) argue that there are three important mechanisms that contribute to a transition from limited- to open-access order: a fiscal mechanism, institutions of representation, and (economic and political) international competition. This book engages with the fiscal mechanism and institution of representation and therefore contributes to the double balance theory.

Regarding the fiscal mechanism, North, Wallis, and Weingast argue that "if changes of access generate a significant fiscal return to the state, and the fiscal benefits of more open access can be shared throughout the dominant coalition, it is possible for a small change to survive" (2006, 64).[65] This is true for the CCP's initiation of a market transition; however, the CCP also realized that a partial transition (as state capitalism) serves its interest better than a full market transition for generating easy fiscal revenue,[66] as well as generating dependence and fear among capitalists, therefore eliciting their compliance.[67] But now that the CCP is facing increasing negative consequences of the current institution of taxation, will this provide a new opportunity for further fiscal and political reform, which may lead to an open-access order?[68] On the one hand, the CCP merged the SAT and LTB to reduce tax breaks provided by local governments, which shows its willingness to institutionalize the taxation system.

On the other hand, the CCP hesitates to decrease indirect taxes and nominal tax rates or reduce the state sector. These suggest that CCP leaders are not determined to push reform ahead to build a rule-of-law system when it may conflict with other important goals, including economic growth and the party's durability.

For the institution of representation, the second mechanism suggested by North, Wallis, and Weingast (2006) and other studies of China's "representative institution" (Sun, Zhu, and Wu 2014, 2) suggest, the powerless PCs at different levels strengthen patron-clientelism, co-opting resource-rich capitalists, rather than generate representation and accountability.[69] Though the CCP proposed to give PCs budgetary power in its reform program (CCP Central Committee 2013), nothing significant has been implemented after seven years.

To summarize, the two most important mechanisms that may lead to open-access order have failed to work in China so far. If we look at it from a comparative perspective, the fiscal and representation mechanisms worked together as "representation through taxation" in Western Europe under some circumstances (M. Mann 1993; Stasavage 2011; Tilly 1990). While many developing countries are unable to build extractive capacity (see, e.g., Piracha and Moore 2016), the postcommunism cases differ from classic state building in which weak state authorities try to claim power resources from strong societal actors (Easter 2008).[70] For those countries that have developed extractive capacity (as China), like North, Wallis, and Weingast (2009), Acemoglu and Robinson (2012) argue that the extractive institution is persistent and its transition toward an inclusive institution depends on critical juncture and even contingency, therefore is hard to predict; whereas Dan Slater and Joseph Wong (2013) find cases of transition through concession, especially in East Asia. This could apply to the China case only if the CCP initiates reform to build a rule-of-law institution of taxation when confronting crisis (Lou 2013; Jia and Liu 2015, 115),[71] under which the capitalists will have more courage to demand representation and the ruler will have strong incentive to adopt a representative institution to elicit quasi-voluntary compliance, as the fiscal constitution theory suggests.[72]

However, the CCP has responded to economic slowdown since 2017 by structural tax reduction (结构性减税) rather than reform of the institution of taxation,[73] and the merger of the SAT and LTB led to private-sector-wide worries of centralized and improved taxation capacity.[74] The CCP has responded to the economic crisis caused by COVID-19 with further structural tax reduction and market reform, again without reform of the institution of taxation toward rule of law. Therefore, examining the institution of taxation's three mechanisms under the perspective of limited- and open-access orders can shed light on the comparative study of authoritarianism, either its durability or democratic transition. But so far we have no good reason to be optimistic for such a transition.

Notes

Introduction

1. The CPPCC, a consultative organization that co-opts social-economic elites, is under the leadership and control of the CCP Central Committee's United Front Work Department. The chairman of the CPPCC serves as a member of the CCP Politburo's Standing Committee.
2. The CNDCA is one of eight satellite parties in China, composed of intellectuals and businessmen.
3. The ACFIC is a ministry-level official mass organization that represents private enterprise. Its president is a vice chairman of the National Committee of CPPCC.
4. There is a great amount of literature on this topic. Some examples are Diamond 1997; Diamond and Plattner 1996, 2001; Huntington 1991; Linz and Stepan 1978, 1996; O'Donnell and Schmitter 1986; O'Donnell, Schmitter, and Whitehead 1986; and Przeworski 1995, 2000.
5. There is no standardized definition of these terms; for example, "authoritarian survival" here is close to "authoritarian durability" defined by Steven Levitsky and Lucan Way as "the capacity to survive crises" (2012, 870). However, this book tries to take degree of stability as a continuous/ordinal variable.
6. Anna Grzymala-Busse (2011) provides a theoretical and methodological discussion on temporality and duration.
7. Structural theories include both modernization theory (e.g., Lipset 1959; Przeworski and Limongi 1997) and class theory (B. Moore 1966; Huntington 1991; Rueschemeyer, Stephens, and Stephens 1992).
8. These include coercive institutions, stability maintenance, and democratic-looking institutions, which I give a comprehensive critical review in chapter 1.
9. Tocqueville is another pioneer in fiscal sociology for his study *The Old Regime and the Revolution* on how taxation influenced the class structure and tends to influence nearly all aspects of a country: "The right of taxation . . . to some extent contains all other rights." And he states in a note, "Generalization: taxation source of everything." The French state used taxation as a tool to divide and rule by assigning different types of taxes to different classes and thereby alienating them from each other (Swedberg 2009, 252–253).

10. Schumpeter (1991) develops a typology of state based on its revenue sources: In a feudal-domain state the rulers do not fund the state by tax but by the rulers' own land, with dues paid by their peasant serfs and customs. A tax state uses tax as the major fiscal revenue source. He defines tax-state transition as the transition from a feudal-domain state to a tax state. Evan Lieberman expands on these categories, identifying five ideal types: skeletal, rentier, communist, and tax state, which includes two subtypes: adversarial and cooperative tax state (2003, 54–60). Chapters 1 and 2 elaborate on the typologies of the tax state.

11. Isaac Martin, Ajay K. Mehrotra, and Monica Prasad write in a review article: "We think that the field may be poised to rewrite conventional accounts of modernity itself by placing the social relations of taxation at the center of any historical or comparative account of social change" (2009, 2). For another important edited volume concerning taxation politics, see Brautigam, Fjeldstad, and Moore 2008.

12. I do not discuss this mechanism in detail in this book but briefly discuss it in chapters 1 and 2 because the half-tax state works through citizens rather than private entrepreneurs, which are the focus of this book. With Bruce Dickson I am conducting quantitative studies on how the half-tax state (working with official media) influences Chinese urban residents' perception of the fairness of their tax burden and therefore their support for the regime.

13. For government-business relationships, see Evans 1995; Maxfield and Schneider 1997; and Van de Walle 2001.

14. For an argument that case studies reveal causal mechanisms, see George and Bennett 2005.

15. While Cheng Li (2012) argues that the regime has been weakened during recent developments in Chinese politics, what happened after 2012, however, suggests that Xi Jinping is becoming a strong and powerful personal leader as factional politics have changed and the CCP has initiated a comprehensive reform plan, but Li may have underestimated the CCP's adaptive capacity.

Chapter 1

1. Sima (2008, 1366). *Shiji* is a monumental history of ancient China and the world completed around 94 BC by the Han dynasty official Sima Qian after having been started by his father, Sima Tan, grand astrologer to the imperial court. The work covers world history as it was then known to the Chinese as well as a twenty-five-hundred-year period from the age of the legendary Yellow Emperor to the reign of Emperor Wu of Han (汉武帝) in the author's own time.

2. As the most powerful political institution in China, the CCP Central Committee's Politburo meets twice each year to specifically discuss the CCP's economic policies.

3. Although the CCP Central Committee and State Council issued some adminis-

trative and financial policies to control the asset bubble, property tax was not proposed to the NPC until April 2021.

4. China replaced its business tax with a national VAT (营改增) in 2016.

5. For a summary of that report, see *Caixin* 2015.

6. This chapter and chapter 2 discuss the half-tax state in detail. Here I note that on November 1, 2018, Xi Jinping remarked in a meeting with entrepreneurs, to give them confidence, that private enterprises contribute greatly to the country, including contributing 50 percent of total national tax revenue in the last decade.

7. In these works, Swedberg summarizes and rebuilds their fiscal sociology theories based on his reading and interpretation of their works, with which I try to engage and further develop based on the China case. Fiscal sociology did not develop as Schumpeter predicted with enthusiasm in 1918, and even Schumpeter himself turned to other topics afterward. It became an almost neglected topic until the late 1980s when James Curtis complained that "taxation is probably the most significant political phenomenon that political scientists have left relatively unexplored. There are extensive literatures on the economics and law of taxation, but few efforts have been made to understand the role of taxation in state development and behavior or even to begin the formulation of political theories of taxation" (1989, 1424).

8. Milan Svolik argues that to sustain power or achieve authoritarian survival, authoritarian rulers face two political problems: authoritarian control of the ruled and authoritarian power sharing within the ruling coalition (2012, 2). Jennifer Gandhi (2008) proposes compliance and cooperation as two challenges for authoritarian rulers. Tamir Moustafa and Tom Ginsburg (2008) provide a comprehensive summary of authoritarian rulers' governance problems through the perspective of judiciary politics, arguing that independent courts in authoritarian regimes serve five basic functions. First, courts allow the state to establish and exercise social control (thus addressing the social-control problem). Second, courts can give the regime a veneer of democratic legitimacy. Propagating laws—and empowering courts to enforce them—allows the state to claim that it is bound by the law. Third, courts are a tool of administrative control (thus addressing the agent-discipline problem). By empowering courts to accept administrative lawsuits, the central government can use the courts as a fire alarm to warn the central government about deviation of state agents from national laws. Fourth, courts can help provide a credible commitment to businesses. A court that is empowered to resolve property-rights disputes independently of the state may help authoritarian rulers build confidence in the quality of the business environment, thereby spurring economic activity (i.e., the cooperation problem). Fifth, courts can be used to depoliticize policy making.

9. For a comprehensive discussion of the mutual dependence between state and capitalists, see Przeworski 1990 and Winters 1996.

10. For a theoretical discussion of these impetuses for cooperation, see Migdal, Kohli, and Shu 1994 on mutual empowerment; Evans 1995 on state-society synergy; and Xu Wang 1999 for a comprehensive review.

11. The grabbing hand/helping hand debate in the political economy of development indicates the ways in which this influence might work, but both sides agree the influence exists.

12. Central-local government relationships are very complicated, as the third-generation federalism literature suggests. These relationships have political, administrative, fiscal, and judiciary dimensions (Treisman 2007). This book focuses on the fiscal dimension, which I measure in relation to the soft versus hard budget constraint. I also discuss the political dimension.

13. Christian Lessmann and Gunther Markwardt (2010) find that a free press is a necessary precondition for a successful decentralization program.

14. For a study of agent discipline in Chinese history, see Thornton 2007.

15. Jean Oi (1992) provides a good argument for how fiscal decentralization motivates local officials to be the spear of reform.

16. This is a core idea for state-society synergy in state-society relation theories; the best example is Peter Evans's (1995) "embedded autonomy."

17. In a comparative study of Russia, Poland, and Ukraine, Marc Berenson (2018) also uses the institution of taxation to discuss agent discipline (as bureaucratization) and social control (as tax compliance).

18. Peter Lorentzen (2013), Daniela Stockmann (2013), and Gary King, Jennifer Pan, and Margaret Roberts (2013), among many others, find that the CCP has developed a sophisticated control and censorship strategy, which plays an important role in sustaining authoritarian rule in the era of the information revolution and market economy. For example, Lorentzen argues that the CCP adopts a sophisticated media-control strategy, "permitting journalists to report aggressively on low-level malfeasance in order to improve governance, but constantly adjusting the amount of reporting in order to avoid giving discontented citizens enough information to be certain about whether a revolt would receive sufficient support to be worthwhile" (2013, 412). Internet censorship, again, is very expensive because the government needs to establish new agencies at all levels of government and pay high salaries to attract well-trained computer scientists.

19. For example, Zhengxu Wang and Ern Ser Tan (2013) find that traditional culture plays an important role in explaining citizens' support of regimes in Asian countries, including China. Jessica Weiss (2014) argues that nationalism could be dangerous to the regime because it is hard to demobilize once established.

20. Linz lays out ten characteristics of coercion under totalitarian systems (1975, 217–218) and ten characteristics of using coercion in totalitarianism, which include its unprecedented scale and the size and complexity of state and/or party organizations for coercion (2000, 102).

21. I owe this point to Mary Gallagher.

22. A powerful party organization that exists at all five levels of party government, the CPL typically draws its membership from the court, procuratorate, police department, Justice Bureau, and State Security Department. Central CPL reached its peak during 2002–2012, when its head was one of nine members of the CCP Politburo's Standing Committee.

23. For a contingent argument, see Boudreau 2004.

24. Xi Jinping's anticorruption campaign revealed many hidden stories of military control and factional struggle in Beijing. For example, in 2015 *Jiefangjun bao*, the official newspaper of the People's Liberation Army, revealed in the Xu Caihou and Guo Boxiong cases that President Hu Jintao had limited control over the military. The Zhou Yongkang case reveals that Zhou, then a member of the CCP Politburo's Standing Committee and head of the CPL, tried to use the police force to serve his personal political goals and stage a coup (which international media reported, but Chinese outlets mentioned it only in metaphors, never directly).

25. According to Kai Zhou and Xiaojun Yan (2014, 4) and Yongshun Cai (2008, 431), the number of reported "mass [protest] incidents" (*quntixing shijian*, a term encompassing protests, demonstrations, petitions, rallies, large-scale riots, and other assorted collective actions) skyrocketed from 8,700 in 1993 to 87,000 in 2015 and more than 180,000 in 2010.

26. Targeting grassroots government should complement the broader institution—that is, the intergovernmental relationships that localize and compartmentalize protests (Cai 2008).

27. The stability-maintenance system can also backfire directly by leading to factional struggle within the party. This occurred when the head of the central CPL, Zhou Yongkang, significantly improved his power within the Politburo's Standing Committee during 2007 to 2012 by empowering the mechanisms of the stability-maintenance system that were under his personal control. Then Zhou used this powerful organization for political struggle. Also see Dali Yang 2017.

28. Joel Migdal (1988) finds a similar dilemma between building state capacity and maintaining personal power. Barbara Geddes (1994) also finds a similar paradox and argues that politicians' answer to this paradox is to maximize power even at the cost of state capacity and economic growth.

29. Gandhi (2008) admits this and argues that the costs of sustaining a coalition could be high and becomes higher when the economy becomes more complex. Abel Escribà-Folch calls the support coalition for authoritarianism a "rent-delivery strategy" (2012, 686). Joseph Wright (2008) finds that the legislature's impact on economic growth is contingent on the nature of the legislature, whether it is binding or nonbinding. Also see Gallagher and Hanson (2009).

30. Thomas Pepinsky argues that "because institutions are political creations," they are "epiphenomena" rather than causes of resilience and have no independent impact (2014, 649). He says that scholars err in attributing resilience to democratic institutions because they fail to make this distinction. Carl Knutsen and Håvard Nygård make related critiques and refute the democratic-looking institutions' explanation of regime durability by identifying an association between democratic-looking institutions and short-lived authoritarian regimes. They propose that other "regime characteristics are highly consequential for regime-survival prospects" (2015, 657). For a theoretical discussion of rational choice institutionalism' weaknesses, including functionalism and tautology, see Elster 2000.

31. Organizational power is the power to stay in power, "to resist opposition challenges," "to control civil society, co-opt or divide oppositions, repress protest, and/or steal elections" (Levitsky and Way 2010, 54).

32. Nomenklatura is regarded as "the most systematic form of administrative formalization of benefits to party membership and service" (Svolik 2012, 170), but Svolik does not publicly state its criteria for promotion. As I discuss later, the CCP has publicly stated its criteria for promotion of cadres, although top leaders may have different priorities.

33. Susan Shirk (1993) finds that political centralization and factionalism explain economic and political reform in China; Hongbin Cai and Daniel Treisman (2004) argue that political centralization plays an important role in promoting economic growth. Study of the nomenklatura system is the most productive field concerning Chinese politics in the last decade. A number of scholars have pointed out that this system works to motivate local government officials to promote economic growth and revenue extraction (Whiting 2001, 2004; Shih, Adolph, and Liu 2012; Landry, Lü, and Duan 2018; Lü and Landry 2014; C. Xu 2010).

34. Cheng Li advances a different view of the institutionalization of the CCP, arguing that "three paralleled developments, namely, 1) weak leaders, strong factions; 2) weak government, strong interest groups; and 3) weak Party, strong country" reflect the weakness of the CCP (2012, 595). But a 2015 interview by *People's Forum* (*Renmin luntan*) suggests that Li has changed his point of view since 2014 when Xi Jinping had consolidated power. More recently, Shirk (2018) finds that institutionalization has been weakened under the Xi era, with a focus on power sharing.

35. While Xi Jinping's high-profile anticorruption campaign could be considered to have improved agent discipline, scholars also find strong evidence of factional struggles (power sharing) at different party-state levels. See Shirk 2018 for anticorruption as personalistic power concentration; and Zhu and Zhang 2017, at the province level.

36. As chapter 3 lays out, like government organizations, China's People's Liberation Army (PLA) established many enterprises to raise funds in the 1980s and 1990s, just as local governments did. The military's involvement in the economy at that time generated many serious problems, including rampant smuggling and military corruption. Jiang Zemin made great effort to pull the military back to the barracks and cut off their enterprises in 1998. He openly described this effort as crucial to the regime's survival. See Jiang 2006. Xi Jinping also made significant effort to cut off the military from running businesses.

37. For data on this spending, see Lee and Zhang 2013, 1485; and Zhou and Yan 2014.

38. For example, see Bernstein and Lü 2003; Perry 2001; Whiting 2011; and Zhang and Heurlin 2014.

39. Slater (2010b) describes domestic conflict as the source of state building in Southeast Asia but also addresses taxation.

40. Infrastructural power is a concept developed by Michael Mann (1984). A similar concept, state capacity, was developed by Theda Skocpol (1985) and Joel Migdal (1988),

who listed four types of state capacity: penetration, regulation, extraction, and appropriation (of resources in determined ways). Infrastructural power is also similar to Levitsky and Way's organizational state power (2010).

41. Taxes and other revenue could be used for both institution building and coalition building (Slater 2010b).

42. In Central China, local governments overtaxed the peasants through various types of fees, fines, and surtaxes in the 1990s and generated serious tax riots (Bernstein and Lü 2003; Kennedy 2007; Thornton 2004).

43. Daron Acemoglu, Simon Johnson, and James Robinson find that in Latin American colonies where the colonizers built "extractive institutions" (i.e., predatory taxation institutions), the economies tended to stagnate or grow slowly. Even when these regions were much better developed at the beginning of colonization, they started lagging in growth because the colonizers built "institutions of private property" in poor colonies (2002, 1235).

44. For descriptions of state financial crises as the main cause of revolutions worldwide, see Kuhn 2002; Skocpol 1979; and Goldstone 1991.

45. For empirical tests of this fiscal constitutional theory, see Timmons 2005, 2010. Acemoglu proposes the accountability paradox of the strong tax state, but he leaves the question of why concomitancy exists unanswered (2010; Acemoglu, Johnson, and Robinson 2002).

46. In Migdal's (1988) terminology, the state's efforts to achieve social control transforms mainly the society/market without transforming the state itself in the direction of being penetrated or controlled by the society.

47. This book does not address the role of abundant revenue resources in regard to the power-sharing problem, but other scholars have done so, as a challenge to both authoritarian-party regimes (Acemoglu 2010; Wintrobe 1998) and hegemonic-party regimes (Magaloni 2006).

48. Slater (2003, 2010a) focuses on the ruler's personal despotic power and how it contributes to strong infrastructural power. He argues that autocrats can manipulate institutions (including the democratic-looking ones) to strengthen their power (Slater 2010a), thus implying that institutions are epiphenomenal rather than causal. Svolik (2012) argues that structure and agencies in authoritarian regimes determine institutional choices. Building convincing endogenous institutional change theory has been challenging for scholars who favor institutional explanations for resilience.

49. Lieberman provides an analytical framework for studying tax institutions. He defines the tax state as "the aggregate of a set of relationships between the state executive and state bureaucracy on the one hand, and citizens or taxpayers on the other, manifest in a set of national tax policies and administrative practices." He writes that "taxation involves two main sets of tasks: the establishment of a set of tax policies that codify what the state is entitled to collect, and the implementation of those policies in the form of administration" (Lieberman 2003, 43–45). For a discussion of informal institutions, see Helmke and Levitsky 2004.

50. An exception is Susan Whiting's (2001) study of private-enterprise taxation, which she used as a dependent variable influenced by local governments' dependence on the private sector for revenue.

51. For a discussion of how agricultural taxation led to tax resistance and weakened authoritarian resilience in China, see Bernstein and Lü 2003; for how the CCP dealt with tax resistance in rural China, see Takeuchi 2014.

52. Leakage is the gap between potential and actual tax revenues, partially explained as tax evasion.

53. Weber (1968) considers state bureaucracy, which is separated from the means of administration and paid a fixed salary funded by tax revenue, as indispensable for the smooth working of rational capitalism. For a systematic illustration of Weber's fiscal sociology, see Swedberg 1998.

54. Some quantitative studies show that fiscal decentralization before 1994 did not contribute to economic growth in China when other factors are controlled. For example, see Jin and Zou 2005.

55. In Cai and Treisman's (2004) framework of four types of decentralization, nomenklatura and the cadre evaluation and promotion system are based on political centralization. Political centralization accompanies fiscal and administrative decentralization, which shapes the local government officials' incentives and development strategies (also see C. Xu 2010).

56. The CCP used the term "commodity economy" (商品经济) instead of "market economy" (市场经济). A commodity economy allows only limited mobility for products but not for production factors (especially capital and labor). While the CCP's Fourteenth National Congress proposed the use of the term to build a market economy in 1992, it had not received ideological legitimacy.

57. Whiting (2001) finds that local governments in the south of Jiangsu Province tended to tax private enterprises heavily. Similarly, Edward Steinfeld (1998) finds that SOEs in Northeast China were heavily taxed and local governments had no hard budgetary constraint.

58. An adversarial tax state has a regressive tax system that taxes rich people lightly, while a cooperative tax state has a progressive tax system. In Lieberman's typology of the tax state, the Chinese state before 1978 was communist (2003, 5).

59. National Bureau of Statistics (NBS) data show that China's Gini coefficient fell to 0.474 in 2012 after rising to 0.491 in 2008 (the low was 0.3706 in 1997). The Gini coefficient is a measure of the inequality of income among households and can vary between zero (absolutely equal) and one (absolutely unequal).

60. Whether high-level inequality blocks long-term economic growth is still under debate; however, Chinese policy makers believe that high inequality in China decreases domestic demand and makes the economy highly dependent on foreign trade and investment.

61. Legal scholar Wei Cui of the University of British Columbia Law School calls China's tax administration "non-rule-based" (2015, 190). Cui argues that China's admin-

istrative decentralization leads to a system in which taxpayers lack complete information about the tax law and thus heed the preferences of local tax administrators. However, they live in fear of being caught cheating and know that they are very likely underpaying according to the law. In this book, I provide more detail on the under-institutionalization of China's taxation system. Using a political economy perspective, I focus on the power asymmetry between government and business rather than the transactional costs. Drawing on this research, in this chapter I discuss elements Cui does not address in his (albeit valuable) research, based on in-depth interviews with tax administrators and entrepreneurs and archives research. I also embed tax administration in the broader political institution, especially the "pressure-based system," to explain the persistence of the under-institutionalized taxation system and non-rule-based tax collection. Under-institutionalization also differs from "structured uncertainty," "one of the most important institutional features of the Chinese political economy," which is defined as "an agreement to disagree about the goals and methods of policy, a condition leading to intrinsic unpredictability and, hence, to inherent ambiguity in implementation. This ambiguity leads to some tolerance of multiple interpretations and implementations of the same policy. Therefore, structured uncertainty is an institutional condition that cements multiplicity of action without legitimizing a specific course or form of behavior as the proper one" (Breznitz and Murphree 2011, 12).

62. Privately owned businesses in China contribute to state revenue through fees, fines, and coerced "donations" as well as formal taxes. All of these could be regarded as part of their tax burden, and the mechanism that applies to these payments is also under-institutionalized.

63. Legal repression is "the discretionary use of legal instruments—such as tax, libel, or defamation laws—to punish opponents. Although such repression may involve the technically correct application of the law, its use is selective and partisan rather than universal" (Levitsky and Way 2010, 9).

64. For a theoretical discussion of an effective taxation system, see Kiser and Schneider 1994.

65. A senior tax law professor suggests that at that time, given the limited capacity of tax collection and a narrow tax base, the NTA intentionally set the nominal tax rates high. Interview by the author, Beijing, June 11, 2015.

66. Rong et al. (1998) and Xuedong Yang (2012) coined the term to describe the nomenklatura, defining it as a system in which "in order to achieve the economic 'catch-up' plan and meet the targets set by the supervisors, the county- and township-level political organizations assign targets, which can be measured quantitatively, to lower-level organizations and individuals who must reach their assigned targets in a given time. Cadres' ability to meet these targets will be awarded or punished both economically and politically."

67. I agree with Morrison about the importance of nontax revenue, but I consider institutionalization far more significant than Morrison does.

68. Therefore, this book goes beyond the infrastructural state-power mechanism

to sustain the authoritarian regime and reveals the limitations of existing explanations related to the capacity of the state to penetrate civil society and to use this penetration to enforce policy throughout its entire territory.

69. For an argument using quasi-parameters to explain endogenous institutional change, see Greif and Laitin 2004.

70. China has only two types of direct election: village committee election and township- and county-level LPC deputy election. While the first has attracted extensive academic attention and its impact on good governance and democratization is still under debate, the second has received very limited attention.

Chapter 2

1. The *Great Learning*, written by Confucius and his students about twenty-four hundred years ago, is one of four classic readings that records Confucius's thoughts. It includes many discussions on how to be a perfect person and how to rule a country.

2. Anne-Robert-Jacques Turgot (1727–1781) was a famous French economist and statesman who served as intendant of Limoges (1761–1772), minister of the navy, and then minister of finance under Louis XVI, a position he was forced to resign in 1776 when the public failed to accept his reforms, the factor that made court intrigue against him successful. This quote is from a letter to David Hume in the appendix of the book.

3. The draft law to implement a vehicle and ship tax also received more than one hundred thousand comments in October 2010.

4. Ironically, when the SAT asked landlords to provide lease contracts as evidence for a tax exemption, many if not most refused to provide them for fear that the SAT might tax their rents. The SAT responded by promising to collect no taxes on rents.

5. Xianglin Xu (2020) has developed a theory on social-transformation crisis (driven primarily by marketization reform) and state governance challenges. This book follows a similar line of inquiry but has a narrow focus.

6. There are many books on the fiscal history of the PRC, especially concerning the TSR, some written by former ministers and officers of the Ministry of Finance and SAT; for example, see Zuo Liu 2000, 2014; Liu and Fu 2018; Jia and Zhao 2008; Jin 2008; Xie 2009; and B. Wang 2009.

7. It is beyond the scope of this book to discuss taxation and state building before the reform era. Susan Mann (1987) provides an excellent study on this issue, especially on commerce taxation and bureaucratization, with some theoretical discussion.

8. "M-form" and "U-form" are two ways of organizing a planned economy. In the M-form economy, "the Chinese hierarchy has been of a multi-layer–multi-regional form based on a geographic principle which emerged in 1958." It facilitated "sustained entry and expansion of the non-state sector." In contrast, "the organization structures of both Eastern Europe and the former USSR were of a unitary form based on the functional and specialization principles (the 'U-form' economy)" (Qian and Xu 1993, 542).

9. All-China Federation of Industry and Commerce (2007a, 2014). On November 1, 2018, President Xi Jinping presided over a high-profile symposium on private enterprise at the Great Hall of the People in Beijing, where the NPC annual conference is held every year. "Over the past 40 years, the private sector of the economy has become an indispensable force behind China's development," Xi said. He noted that the private sector has become the main contributor to job creation (over 80 percent of new urban employment), technological innovation (over 70 percent), GDP (over 60 percent) and an important source of tax revenue (over 50 percent), adding that the sector has played an important role in developing the socialist market economy, transforming government functions, transferring surplus rural labor, and exploring the international market. Xi said, "The private sector's contributions are undeniable for the country to be able to make miraculous achievements in economic development." He emphasized that the party's viewpoint on adhering to the basic economic system is "clear and consistent," and there has never been any irresolution. See *Xinhua* 2018.

10. Christopher McNally uses the term "Sino-capitalism": "Sinocapitalism relies on informal business networks rather than on legal codes and transparent rules. It also assigns the Chinese state a leading role in fostering and guiding capitalist accumulation. China, ultimately, is a large developing economy with a distinct socialist and imperial legacy. Central to Sino-capitalism's institutional structure is a unique duality that combines top-down state-led development with bottom-up entrepreneurial private capital accumulation" (2012, 744).

11. Kellee Tsai (2005) calls them "capitalists without a class" because they lack a common basis for identity, reliance on the state, profit rate margins, and so on.

12. Xi Jinping's high-profile speech was made after a wave of wide suspicions of the CCP's policy shift toward the private sector during 2018. He tries to make a credible commitment to assure private entrepreneurs' confidence: "Any word or action that denies, doubts, or wavers over the country's basic economic system is not in line with the principles and policies of the party and the country.... All private companies and private entrepreneurs should feel totally reassured and devote themselves to seeking development.... Private enterprises and private entrepreneurs belong to our own family." For the official English-language report, see *Xinhua* 2018; for the full text in Chinese, see http://www.gov.cn/xinwen/2018-11/01/content_5336616.htm.

13. According to Richard Swedberg, Weber cautiously builds causal linkages between types of taxation systems (modern taxation system, tax farming, and benefices) and types of capitalism (rational market capitalism and political capitalism) (1998, 59–61). Benefices endow individuals with a right to an income for life in exchange for services (59).

14. The communist state is one of Lieberman's five types of tax state, under which "the state's role in the economy is so large that it virtually eliminates the private sphere of the economy. There is effectively no taxation in such cases as the state controls the means of production and need not gain cooperation from non-state actors in order to obtain resources" (2003, 55).

15. It mainly includes turnover taxes (VAT, business tax, and consumption tax), behavior taxes, and customs duties.

16. The CCP's policy makers regard the tax-state transition as part of the market transition (CCP Central Committee 2014).

17. Most sociologists who study market transition neglect taxation. Sometimes it is mentioned but not studied; for example, "Power is not zero sum in the relationship between redistributor and producer, as evidenced by the rapid increase in both state revenues and household savings in China" (Nee and Mathews 1996, 915).

18. Two articles and four books provide the information in this section: The Party Team, SAT Headquarters 2008; Wong and Bird 2008; Jia and Zhao 2008; Jia and Liu 2015; Landry 2008; and Zuo Liu 2014.

19. In the early 1950s, the left and right wings of the party debated which approach to taxing private and state-owned enterprises would best support the development of a socialist economy. Bo Yibo's taxation policy treated SOEs and private enterprises equally. Mao and his supporters attacked it as a policy to help the capitalist class. For details, see Dai and Zhao 2011 and Lin 2011. After the defeat of the right, which supported limited private economy and equal tax rates for capitalists (高饶集团, Gao Gang and Rao Shushi, two CCP Politburo members charged with conspiracy to take power from Mao Zedong in the 1950s), privately owned enterprises were highly taxed until their elimination in the late 1950s. During the Cultural Revolution, taxation was regarded as a means of class exploitation to be abandoned, the taxation system was destroyed, and tax officers were dismissed. Taxation was used to curb speculation and development of capitalism; help the planned economy work properly; adjust distribution within the state and collective and among individuals; and tighten the budget constraint so SOEs could improve their efficiency.

20. For a discussion about how the FCS (interacting with the cadre evaluation system) promotes economic development, see Oi 1992 and Whiting 2001. For the negative effects (lack of development) in SOE-dominated regions that counteract these effects, see Steinfeld 1998.

21. This taxation reform is part of the nationwide SOE reform in the mid-1980s meant to strengthen the autonomy of SOEs and make them responsible for their profits or losses (*zifu yingkui* 自负盈亏).

22. The SOE bonus was introduced during the early stage of SOE reform (profit for tax) as a means to give the SOE managers and workers incentive to work harder and make profits. When the bonus is high, the government taxes the bonus to reduce unequal income distribution. The SOE adjustment tax was added to absorb "unreasonably high" SOE profits, which reflected the limitations of the nascent market economy (monopolization, fluctuating prices of supply and demand) (Zuo Liu 2014). Later on the SOE bonus tax was converted into a personal income tax, and the SOE adjustment tax was canceled and reintroduced as SOE profit remittance until 2007.

23. Another reason for tax reform was that the FCS failed to separate the enterprise

from the government, which was another important goal for economic reform (F. Zhou 2012).

24. The fragmented authoritarianism model studies three dimensions, with a focus on the last two: value integration, structural distribution of resources and authority, and processes of decision-making and policy implementation (Lieberthal 1992, 6). This book focuses mainly on the structural distribution of fiscal resources.

25. State Administration of Taxation, "Key Points of Implementing Tax Sharing System Reform," 1993, cited in Zuo Liu 2000, 281.

26. In 1950, tariffs produced 0.356 billion yuan, and agricultural taxes, 1.910 billion. See Ministry of Finance of People's Republic of China 2012, 450.

27. However, at that time, the CCP took over private ownership via coercion or threat of coercion.

28. "Price scissors" refers to a situation in which the price of food fell and the price of manufactured goods rose; see Knight 1995.

29. At the same time, because SOEs' profit rate decreased rapidly, some SOEs suffered increasing deficits. The net contribution of their profit remittances to fiscal revenue decreased and has been negative since 1985 because of government subsidies for SOEs. In 1994, government reduced the subsidies and abolished SOE profit remittances. In 2006, the subsidy was −0.5 percent of national tax revenue. See Ma 2011.

30. Other enterprises (including foreign enterprises) paid the remaining 8.6 percent in 1993.

31. In 1994, categories included SOEs; collective enterprises; private enterprises (民营企业); the individual sector (个体经济); joint ventures; stockholding enterprises; foreign-invested enterprises; and Hong Kong–, Macau-, and Taiwan-invested enterprises.

32. This reflects the CCP's ideological concern.

33. This section relies on secondhand sources to give an overall picture of SOE evolution and its contribution to fiscal and tax revenues. It does not discuss ongoing SOE reform. For an in-depth exploration of literature in English of these issues from 1928 to 2008, see Bian 2015 and Li and Putterman 2008.

34. State Administration of Taxation 1993; National Bureau of Statistics, People's Republic of China 1992.

35. Factional politics is a major area of study for Chinese politics; for example, see Nathan 1973; Fewsmith 2001; and Shih, Adolph, and Liu 2012.

36. The Zhou Yongkang case suggests that his faction controlled both Sino-Pec and Petro China, two major SOEs and the top two-taxpayers, who paid 661.1 trillion yuan in 2015 (the national total tax was 11,060.4 trillion yuan). Zhou Yongkang, a member of the CCP Politburo's Standing Committee and in charge of the powerful Commission of Politics and Law, built a faction and allied with other Politburo members, including Bo Xilai. He tried to take power in 2012 through illegal means.

37. Chinese SOEs are also good places for patronage, as noted in reports by major

central government–owned SOEs to the CCP's CCDI. For example, the Industrial and Commercial Bank of China (ICBC), China's largest bank and, according to *Forbes*, the most profitable company in the world in 2014, reported that among 691 cadres (middle-level managers and staff) at its headquarters, 240 were family members of these managers and staff. This is just one among many other ICBC problematic issues.

38. Forty high-level SOE managers and chairmen were charged with corruption during November 2012 to May 4, 2014. See *People's Daily Online* 2014.

39. For a discussion of the evolution of the extra-budgetary fund and land-transfer fees as a major source of local government, see Whiting 2011 and Ong 2014.

40. Additional fees related to land are not accounted for in this figure because data were unavailable.

41. For more detail on institutional background and evolution, see Chen and Chen 2012, chap. 3.

42. The May 1989 policy required local government to submit 40 percent to the central government; the September 1989 policy required 32 percent, and the 1992 regulation reduced the amount to 5 percent (Chen and Chen 2012, 43).

43. Because the CCP relinquished local governments' control of the banks in the late 1990s, banks began to demand stable backing to make loans to local governments, which led local governments to use land to ensure their loans. Since local governments were not allowed to borrow, they established government-owned enterprises called "financial platforms" to take out loans (F. Zhou 2012).

44. Increased reliance of local governments on land-transfer fees increased land costs for enterprises. The resulting housing bubble added to the labor cost.

45. China's stimulus of 4 trillion yuan was crucial to maintaining the GDP in 2008.

46. Though land-transfer fees provide a term of use of forty, fifty, and seventy years, respectively, for land for commercial use, industrial use, and residential use, a number of scholars have argued that charging new fees at the end of these terms will be politically dangerous because the media will be very critical. The expiration of some of these terms in April 2016 led the *People's Daily* to argue that charging new fees would be a grave error. See *People's Daily* 2016.

47. This is not unique to County Warm River. The year 2014 witnessed the rapid decline of land revenue in many regions. See Z. Zhang 2015; see also *Economic Information Daily* 2015.

48. For a study of how the land-transfer fee and agricultural tax lead to social grievance and disputes and how these disputes are resolved or not resolved without hurting the authoritarian regime, see Whiting 2011 and Zhang and Heurlin 2014.

49. For information on rural taxation and riots, see Bernstein and Lü 2003 and Thorton 2004.

50. For example, see Y. Guo 2012 and *Sina* 2015.

51. The importance of steamed bread for people in North China is similar to that of bread for Americans.

52. A less rigorous approach, used in an online survey in February 2009, also showed

that more than half of respondents do not know where the tax revenues go. Forty-five percent said they did not know what kind of taxes they paid, a smaller portion than reported in the Research Center for Contemporary China of Peking University study, but the selection process, which would naturally attract people with a keen interest in taxes, may have skewed results. See *China News Weekly* 2011.

53. Greater reliance on individual income tax and effectively zero tax on investments—a product of the under-institutionalization of the taxation system—also heightens inequality, as the middle and poorer income classes rely on salary while wealthy people have investments.

54. Wang Xiaolu and Wing Tang Woo (2011) point out that the NBS uses the Gini coefficient based on household income in the NBS Household Survey, which conflicts with the level reported in the NBS Economic Census, both of which are lower than their own rigorous survey of a large, nationwide sample. They determine the Gini coefficient to be 0.47 to 0.50 because of "hidden household income." Data released by the China Family Financial Investigation and Research Center determined the Gini coefficient to be 0.61 for 2010, when NBS reported it at 0.481. See *Sina* 2012.

55. There used to be peasant tax riots before abolition of agricultural taxes. For a discussion about how the CCP seeks to control peasants who have lost their land, see Whiting 2011 and Lee and Zhang 2013.

56. Under Jiang Zemin and Hu Jintao, this system was highly functional. However, while Xi Jinping's anticorruption campaign has removed many corrupt SOE leaders, most of them are regarded as belonging to the Zhou Yongkang faction, and the recent investigation of chairmen and CEOs of some financial SOEs is regarded as CCP leadership's determination to regulate the financial market.

57. In China, land is owned by the state, and citizens have the right to use it for only seventy years; also, the housing price includes a very high land-transfer fee. The property tax is duplicate taxation of property that taxpayers do not own.

58. There is much Chinese literature on the nature and consequences of a property tax. In this discussion I rely mainly on Li et al. 2018 and S. Zhang 2012.

59. Findings in this chapter reflect dozens of interviews with tax officers in different regions. For example, I spent two weeks in County Cool Mountain's LTB in Shanxi, talking to tax officers and private entrepreneurs and reading their archives and journals. I also interviewed experts and scholars on tax law, including Professor Xiong Wei at Wuhan University and Yao Xuan'ge, a senior tax officer who now works as the vice president of the Tax Study Association of Xi'an city's SAT and as deputy editor of the *Journal of Grassroots Taxation Studies*.

60. With 175 members and bimonthly meetings, the NPC Standing Committee of the Eleventh NPC is the most active of the permanent NPC, which has 2,987 deputies and meets once a year. The CCP Central Committee's Standing Committee was the sole body that approved China's 1994 tax reform; neither the NPC Standing Committee nor the NPC approved the law. The NPC and its Standing Committee approved only three of the eighteen types of tax included in the law. In March 2015, the NPC passed a revised

Legislature Law that gave tax-legislation power back to the NPC and its Standing Committee over the course of three years.

61. Mao Zedong, in the early stage of the "antiright" movement, called taxes a symbol of "class struggle within the party." Tax policy making was a highly politicized issue in the 1950s (Lin 2011, 241–243).

62. Since tax evasion is a sensitive topic, some informants did not want to admit it explicitly. When I asked them indirectly, for example, whether other enterprises evade taxes, all of them said yes, and some even explained why it is necessary to evade taxes.

63. US businessperson, interview by the author, Beijing, May 7, 2015.

64. Entrepreneur, interview by the author, Beijing, May 27, 2010.

65. Senior tax officer, interview by the author, Hunan, July 13, 2010.

66. For details, see Lou 1995, pt. 2.

67. The 2008 reform reduced the corporate income tax rate from 33 percent to 25 percent and 20 percent for low-profit small enterprises.

68. Xiong Wei and Yao Xuan'ge, interview by the author, Jiangxi, June 15, 2015. Yao acknowledged that since tax-collection capacity has been improved significantly, tax rates set two decades ago have become too high.

69. For an excellent analysis of tax administration before the TSR, see Whiting 2001, chap. 5.

70. The SAT is a ministry-level bureau under the central government and has branches nationwide. The provincial LTBs were the highest authorities for administration of each province's local taxation and had branches throughout the provinces. The taxation bureaus' budget and personal management are independent from the local government.

71. Senior tax officer, interview by the author, Hunan, July 13, 2010.

72. For discussion of the fiscal crisis (or extraction capacity crisis) of the central government and policy proposals, see Wang and Hu 2001. Ching Kwan Lee (1998) argues that the 1994 tax reform has failed because it could not raise the tax/GNP ratio and the central government's share of tax in the following years. But he is incorrect because the long-term trend is that both indicators started to increase in the next few years and continued to increase after that.

73. Tax officer, interview by the author, County Cold Mountain, Shanxi, June 6, 2010.

74. Jin Xin (2008), then head of the SAT who participated in the TSR, disagrees with separation of the two administrations but does not provide reasons, following the party discipline to not divulge information. Some counties, such as Wuhai in Inner Mongolia, tried to make the county SAT and LTB work together to reduce collection costs, but it is illegal to merge these two institutions.

75. However, banks (most of which are state owned) do not share information with tax bureaus.

76. The PRC's overtaxation played a key role in stimulating the revolution, but the system in place until 1993 was based on its predecessor, tax farming. Both systems had

one collector in charge of a given jurisdiction who had targets to meet, but the PRC abandoned the practice of allowing tax collectors to keep anything collected above their targets and made them government officials. See Duara 1988.

77. Much Chinese literature discusses the one-person-in-charge-of-all system. See H. Yu 2007.

78. For many enterprises, the degree of predatory behavior is still a function of their closeness with government.

79. Susan Whiting (2001) also describes the excessive burden on tax collectors in the 1980s.

80. See County Warm River People's Congress Standing Committee 1992.

81. For full text of the law, see http://www.gov.cn/banshi/2005-08/31/content_146791.htm.

82. In Machel Lipsky's terminology, these tax officers are "street-level bureaucrats" (1980).

83. Given the rapid rise in housing prices since 2009, government officers in many regions cannot afford an apartment on their salary; this also applies to my other cases.

84. Senior tax officer, interview by the author, Shanxi, June 22, 2010. Gray income is a kind of illegal income though not technically a bribe.

85. For a comprehensive introduction to GTP, see C. Wang 2015 and Winn and Zhang 2013.

86. For discussion of the cadre evaluation system, see Y. Huang 1996 and Whiting 2001, 2004. For discussion of the importance of taxation for the top CCP cadres, see Shih, Adolph, and Liu 2012. Social stability has become more important since Hu Jintao came to power and proposed the harmonious society ideology. As some local government officials say, "Economic development is the first task [*diyi yaowu*]; social stability is the first obligation [*diyi zeren*]." See *People's Daily* 2012a.

87. I observed this in my fieldwork, but see also Tan and Zhou 2009.

88. See Tan and Zhou 2009. Minjun Tan and Shuangling Zhou work in the Audit Office of Hunan Province; therefore, they have insiders' information on how the taxation system works on the ground.

89. Senior tax officer, interview by the author, Hunan, July 13, 2010. If the higher-level LTB sets the target at an 8 percent growth rate, then the county government may set it at 12 percent. Depending on its bargaining power, the county LTB can get some of its overage back as part of its budget.

90. LTB director, interview by the author, Shanxi, June 20, 2010.

91. Tax officer, interview by the author, Shanxi, June 11, 2010.

92. The Tax-Inspection Bureau is a subunit of the LTB and SAT office; the director of the bureau is second in power in the county LTB or SAT office. Senior tax officer, interview by the author, Hunan, July 13, 2010.

93. Senior tax officer, interview by the author, Hunan, July 13, 2010; senior tax officer, interview by the author, Zhejiang, August 25, 2010.

94. For discussion of the local government intentionally setting low tax rates to

encourage development of private enterprises in Wenzhou Prefecture, South Zhejiang Province, see Whiting 2001.

95. There are also other tactics, and even the *People's Daily* reported such misconduct. In January 2017, the governor of Liaoning Province, Chen Qiufa, acknowledged in a government report concerning the province PC that prefectures and counties reported faked fiscal data from 2011 to 2014; see L. Li 2017. For tax purchase and borrowing money to pay tax at the township level, see Tian and Zhao 2008.

96. LPC officer, interview by the author, Zhejiang, April 23, 2010.

97. Tax officer, interview by the author, Shanxi, June 22, 2010.

98. Tax officer, interview by the author, Shanxi, June 22, 2010.

99. LTB director, interview by the author, Shanxi, June 23, 2010.

100. Tax officer, interview by the author, Zhejiang, April 17, 2016.

101. Tax officer from Jiangsu Province, interview by the author, Beijing, December 7, 2014. See also Sun and Yu 1999.

102. The local party committee and government still maintain influence over the SAT office because it provides a significant part of its budget, and the social and political embeddedness discussed in the previous section still exists.

103. My interviews with tax officers in Beijing and Zhejiang confirm that the new SAT has improved the performance of many tax officers but with substantial regional variations. Some of them still have problems with personnel issues, mostly because the leadership positions have been reduced and thus the opportunity for promotion. One informant said, "The effectiveness of reform depends on the SAT officer leaders' capability." Tax officer, interview by the author, Zhejiang, July 21, 2019; tax officer, interview by the author, Beijing, November 21, 2019.

104. Yu Bin, spokesman for the Development Research Center of the State Council, a ministry-level official think tank, acknowledged in 2017 that to stabilize economic growth, the Chinese government will rely on not only investment but also reduction of enterprises' tax and fee burden to stimulate their "vitality." See Xiaoxiao Zhou 2017.

105. Data on media conferences are provided by the Ministry of Finance. See *People's Daily Online* 2018 and Yang Z. 2019.

Chapter 3

1. County Warm River PC document, 1996. (Note: In chapters 3–6, many sources are from government documents that are not publicly available. I do not furnish website sources in some cases to protect the anonymity of counties or people.)

2. County Warm River government website, 2015.

3. The 2004 constitution emendation protects private property rights.

4. For information on bureaucratic resistance to SOE reform in the 1980s, see Shirk 1993. Barry Naughton (1995) also notes that market reform "grew out of the plan."

5. Non-budgetary funds are sources of income that do not depend on the state

budget, including renting out offices to Western corporations, selling the profitable part of a public enterprise's output of goods on the open market, or selling weapons to other countries, such as the sales of ballistic-missile gyroscopes to Iran.

6. "Benefices" means that an individual (an official) is endowed with a right to an income for life in exchange for services. As Nicolas Van de Walle described it, "Office-holders almost systematically appropriate public resources for their own uses and political authority is largely based on clientelist practices, including patronage, various forms of rent-seeking and prebendalism" (2001, 51–52).

7. According to Weber, a modern bureaucracy involves recruitment based on technical competence, dominance of a spirit of formalistic impersonality, and elimination of "the office-holder who rules by virtue of status privileges and the appropriation of the means and powers of administration" (1968, 225–226). Only a large, functionally differentiated commodity economy, based on industrialization, will generate enough surplus to fund a modern bureaucracy. For a summary and elaboration, see Swedberg 1998.

8. However, some rural and black markets did exist. For a discussion of bureaucracy in the Mao era, see Schurmann 1968 and Harding 1981.

9. For a comprehensive discussion of asset mobility, see Winters 1996.

10. For the state's role in building a national market, see Polanyi 1957 and Vries 2015.

11. The emergence of a market economy was a recursive process: the government of County Warm River played a role with many other county-level governments in generating a free-market economy, which the central government endorsed and promoted. For similar research on how the central local governments interacted with each other in bringing about fiscal-system reform in China, see Whiting 2001.

12. Unfunded obligations are those the central government does not pay or assign revenues.

13. The county government's bureaus either managed these enterprises for the county or owned them directly. Literature on TVEs focuses on county-owned enterprises but neglects bureau ownership.

14. Jean Oi uses the term "local state corporatism" to describe the TVEs and argues that the fiscal contract system empowered local governments with the fiscal incentives and necessary capital (1992, 100). For discussion of the regional diversity of TVEs, see Whiting 2001. For a discussion of TVEs that includes collectively and privately owned enterprises, see Y. Huang 2008. For a comprehensive review of regional development models, see C. Zhang 2020.

15. Even today, the Chinese economy relies heavily on government investment rather than consumption, which is a major structural weakness. In macroeconomic theory, the term "multiplier effect" refers to an increase in spending (or investment) that produces an increase in national income and consumption greater than the initial amount spent.

16. Some of the collective TVEs had competitive advantages over the SOEs.

17. This weakens Scott Gehlbach's argument that taxation has produced representation in Russia and elsewhere in Eastern Europe. He correctly points out that tax-hungry

local governments can create a new industry to make revenue and provide "good industry policies" to keep revenue growing (Gehlbach 2008, 10), but he fails to point out that this mechanism depends on local governments helping the industries monopolize the local market. Therefore, I describe these industry revenues as rent rather than tax revenue.

18. Chinese tobacco offices still monopolize tobacco sales today, but they allow cigarettes to be sold outside the area where they are produced, which has weakened the government's monopoly.

19. The dual-track price system is the intermediate stage between the state-controlled and the free-market price systems. In 1981, the central government allowed some enterprises that had fulfilled their planned production quotas to sell their surplus output at market prices, while their planned quota production was sold at state-set prices.

20. Records, second discussion workshop, eighteenth meeting of the seventh county PC Standing Committee, 1991.

21. Records, second discussion workshop, eighteenth meeting of the seventh county PC Standing Committee, 1991.

22. In other regions, such as Anhui Province, the AIC maintained strict inspection of cigarette sales even into the early 2000s.

23. China's gradualist economic reform of SOEs started with the double-track price system, in which there was a low in-system price (within the planned economy and SOEs) and high out-system price (in the market). Therefore, China avoided the hyperinflation of other postcommunist countries. Allowing powerful people to make a lot of profit by taking the in-system material and selling it on the out-system market had reduced officials' resistance to reform.

24. Records, eighteenth meeting of the seventh county PC Standing Committee, 1991.

25. Another two industries are handcrafted glass and LED technologies.

26. Records, Zhang X, speaking at the eighteenth meeting of the seventh county PC Standing Committee, 1991.

27. In the 1980s, only private enterprises that had fewer than eight workers were legal and thus were not regarded as engaging in class exploitation.

28. Peng Fan, Weihua Wang, and Shaoguang Wang (2009) used the police department as a case study and argued that this FCS helped improve state capacity where there were severe budgetary constraints. While they were right to point out that increased police capacity was a positive consequence, they ignored the fact that the police may have been selectively providing service to people who could "afford" the service, spending most of their resources and efforts on collecting fines and fees, and aligning with organized crime to earn extra income.

29. Records, eighteenth meeting of the seventh county PC Standing Committee, 1991.

30. Zhejiang Province initiated a provincewide examination of law enforcement conducted by PCs at different levels during 1994 to 1998.

31. Lianfangdui is a semiofficial organization that organizes young people in the township to assist the police in maintaining social order. Members could be part-time or full-time, but both positions are underpaid; therefore, the organization can recruit only unqualified people who are willing to charge fines and fees.

32. County Warm River's PC document, January 1997.

33. As a powerful party organization, the party's CDI is responsible for dealing with the party and government officials' corruption. The committee investigates and punishes a corrupt party member before the individual is sent to the prosecutor and court.

34. The party discipline cadre also said that County Warm River's Association of Protecting Private Enterprises was the first such official organization in China, since Zhejiang Province had (and still has) the most active private economy in the country.

35. Records, second discussion workshop, eighteenth meeting of the seventh county PC Standing Committee, 1991.

36. As formally addressed in official documents, the county government found it difficult to meet the obligation of payroll finance, meaning that total fiscal revenue was not enough to pay salaries of public employees.

37. A county PC executive deputy complained that all government bureaus had their own independent bank account (*xiao jinku*), including the Bureau of Finance, which was in charge of canceling *xiao jinku*. He also criticized the Bureau of Audit for not examining *xiao jinku* effectively. County Warm River PC meeting record, July 15, 1997.

38. The central government, with the leadership of Vice Premier Zhu Rongji, enacted a series of economic reforms, including TSR.

39. Marketization reform under Premier Zhu Rongji in the mid-1990s included reforms of different types of markets: capital and ownership (privatization), loan (bank system), and labor. The stated objective was to prevent the government from intervening in many microeconomic activities so it could focus on macroeconomic regulation.

40. Jeffrey Winters calls similar government strategies "zonal capitalism" (1996, 199).

41. To maintain the anonymity of County Warm River, I do not provide the source here.

42. The option existed to simply build factories illegally, but this would incur fines, the amount of which varied depending on how well one knew the officials.

43. A county PC deputy proposed disciplining township tax officers who went to the industry zone to collect taxes, and the county government stopped them from doing so again.

44. County Warm River's PC document, December 1999.

45. Many reforms initiated by the central government after the late 1990s were important, particularly government restructuring and separating income from expenditure (*shouzhi liangtiaoxian*). For a discussion of the central government's efforts to "rebuild the leviathan," see D. Yang 2004. Local governments may have no incentive to implement higher-level governments' policies if these policies hurt their interests. See Migdal 1988 and O'Brien and Li 1999.

46. The county government found and canceled 1,120 bank accounts for government

bureaus in the years leading up to 2007. These bank accounts were used for nontax revenues (fees, surtaxes, fines, etc.) for different government bureaus. Some accounts held revenue from only one specific fee.

47. County government report, 2014.

48. Four private entrepreneurs, interviews by the author, Zhejiang, May 16, 2016.

49. County Warm River's PC document, March 2005.

50. Government bureaus get back a small portion of collected fees and fines, which gives them incentives to collect and enforce rules.

51. The 1994 document is available at http://www.gov.cn/zhuanti/2015-06/13/content_2878960.htm; and the 1998 document is available at http://www.gd.gov.cn/zwgk/wjk/zcfgk/content/post_2722921.html.

52. For a comprehensive analysis of land revenue and land finance, see F. Zhou 2012.

53. For the dynamic of the protest against taking land and increased compensation in China, see Heurlin 2016.

54. Various informants, interviews by the author, County Warm River, 2012–2016.

55. "County Warm River's Audit Report on Budgetary Implementation and Other Fiscal Income and Expenditure (Year 2006)," County Warm River's PC document, March 2006.

56. The Bureau of Land Resources, which is in charge of land acquisition and urban planning, and the Bureau of Construction, which is in charge of real estate market regulation, have the greatest influence. As an informant (a party cadre) told me, "If the CDI ever investigates the Bureau of Construction, I am pretty sure that many of its staff members are deeply involved in corruption. Most of its middle-level officials drive BMWs." Interviews by the author, Zhejiang, May 14, 2016.

57. Various informants, interviews by the author, County Warm River, 2012–2016.

58. I do not provide links to this media report to protect the identity of County Warm River.

59. According to World Bank scholars, governance quality comprises "the traditions and institutions by which authority in a country is exercised. This includes (1) the process by which governments are selected, monitored and replaced, (2) the capacity of the government to effectively formulate and implement sound policies, and (3) the respect of citizens and the state for the institutions that govern economic and social interactions among them" (Kaufmann, Kraay, and Zoido-Lobaton 1999, 1). But this definition focuses on the national level.

60. The theory of the growth machine describes the city as the product of the pursuit of growth by political and economic alliances. Land and real estate development is the core of local economic growth, and common interests in land mobilize a wide range of local elites into a governing coalition (Logan and Molotch 1987; Molotch 1976).

61. *Fenquan* also means "decentralization," of which de facto fiscal federalism is the best example. *Jiquan* (集权) refers to centralization and concentration.

62. In the terminology of this book, the old socialist ideology–oriented local agent discipline was weakened. The adaptive informal institutional change theory overem-

phasizes local initiatives and underestimates the activeness and initiation of the central government. The central government's decision to decentralize empowered local government and grassroots actors with the freedom to run businesses in the early 1980s, which initiated the private sector. The central government also does not simply endorse an adaptive informal institution after it has generated a legitimacy crisis. The central government's signals, for example, Deng Xiaoping's southern tour, played an important role in encouraging private-sector development.

63. This differs from Ang's (2017) argument that "preexisting 'weak' institutions" allow the formation of a market economy.

64. Given the research focus, I consider the central government's TSR and proposal for building a socialist market economy as exogenous in this chapter. I discuss the endogeneity of fiscal reform in chapter 7.

Chapter 4

1. The resignation of provincial governors is very rare in China; the only other case was the resignation of Beijing's governor, Meng Xuenong, during the 2003 SARS crisis. Coincidently, Meng was also forced to resign in Shanxi, only seven months after being appointed governor there. When he left Shanxi, he said, "It is hard to be an official in Shanxi [jinguan nandang]." Later on Meng denied saying it, but his successors (the current party secretary and governor) were asked similar questions when they took office in Shanxi.

2. Coal-mine manager, interview by the author, Shanxi, May 26, 2010.

3. Senior researcher, a colleague of the party secretary of a coal-mining county in Hebei Province (located at the border of Shanxi Province, and thus similar to my Shanxi cases), interview by the author, Shanxi, June 3, 2010.

4. The party secretary of Shanxi Province, Wang Rulin, admitted the serious corruption in Shanxi Province in March 2015 during the national Two Sessions (*lianghui*). See J. Yang 2015.

5. There are some serious cases of government-business collusion and corruption in Zhejiang, but overall, governance in Zhejiang is better than in the other two provinces.

6. Business environment (营商环境) became a hot topic for the CCP in the last few years, and the State Council enacted the "Regulation of Improving Business Environment" in October 2019. The CCP uses the World Bank's definition of business environment: "doing Business measures the processes for business incorporation, getting a building permit, obtaining an electricity connection, transferring property, getting access to credit, protecting minority investors, paying taxes, engaging in international trade, enforcing contracts, and resolving insolvency" (World Bank 2020, 2).

7. For details of the performance-driven cadre evaluation system, see Rong et al. 1998 and Whiting 2001, 2004.

8. For a theoretical discussion based on a country-level study, see Shafer 1994.

9. Chapter 1 describes the resignations of two Shanxi Province governors after mine disasters occurred shortly after their appointments. These disasters also led to the merging of small coal mines.

10. In some counties in Shanxi, the remaining coal resources can be extracted for another ten to thirty years.

11. Until recently, Chinese coal miners worked using only lamps, shovels, and baskets. Some used mules or horses to carry the coal out of the mine. The equipment and working conditions in the 1990s and even the early 2000s were like those in eighteenth-century Britain and just as dangerous.

12. Because of the high discount rate and low technology, they also mined in a wasteful way by extracting only the easy-to-mine coal. The extraction rate of County Cold Mountain's mine was 30 percent in the early 1990s. By 1998 it had improved to 60 percent, but even today it lags behind the rates in modern mines. For a similar coal-mining county, see L. Zhang 2010.

13. Local people call the coal mines "underground enterprises" while terming other enterprises "on the ground." These coal mines were the collectively owned TVEs in these regions.

14. For regional variations in the privatization of collectively owned TVEs, see J. Zhang 2009. Zhang argues that in southern Jiangsu Province, because of the strong government, elites manipulated privatization. But in southern Zhejiang Province's Wenzhou, privatization was more transparent and democratic because of a weaker government.

15. Government officials could obtain only "dry stock" (*gangu* 干股), which does not require money for purchase and cannot be exchanged for other assets. Holders of dry stock receive profit dividends, which has the benefit of incentivizing government officials to protect a particular manager from Mafia attacks as well as interference by the government.

16. Informants did not generally tell me about their own experiences of corruption, but some did tell me that such corruption is real. When I asked them about a media-reported case in Yangquan Prefecture in which a policeman illegally and violently seized a large coal mine from a private owner and then sold it to another investor at a very high price, they said such incidents were common in Shanxi Province.

17. The regulatory government bureaus sell certificates and permits to coal mines that do not meet safety standards. The mine bosses spend a lot of money to "buy" these certificates and permits to facilitate the process and reduce investment in safety equipment.

18. The largest group of investors came from Wenzhou, Zhejiang. After more than a decade of capital accumulation through running private enterprises, people in Wenzhou had large amounts of mobile capital with which to make nationwide investments. Because the government set very severe limitations for investment of private capital in many SOE-monopolized industries, a large share of this capital flowed into real estate

and coal mining, as speculation, which made mobile capital immobile. One informant told me that there were also many investors from Beijing, but they kept a low profile to avoid media attention. Coal-mine manager, interview by the author, County Cold Mountain, Shanxi, June 6, 2010. I also heard that there were many investors from Fujian Province and some from Beijing, but they are less visible.

19. This was higher than a rural resident's average annual income in County Cold Mountain at the time and equal to more than 70 percent of average income in the county in 2010.

20. *New Beijing News* 2004. The coal-mining industry was a sensitive topic when I conducted fieldwork in Shanxi in May and June 2010. The provincewide movement to close and merge coal mines was in progress, and few mine bosses would talk with me. My informants in the county government validated this and other in-depth news reports.

21. Senior official, interview by the author, Shanxi, June 8, 2010.

22. County official, interview by the author, Shanxi, June 14, 2010.

23. Coal transportation was and is an important source of local government's fiscal revenue. It is easy to tax the coal-transportation company, which has always been state owned, and is also easy to calculate and collect coal tax on the trucks and trains by setting up toll stations. However, even these stations were a major source of corruption: government officials' relatives staff them and collect bribes in lieu of fees; railway company (an SOE) employees also collect bribes. All of these practices promote tax evasion by the collectors. Even the *People's Daily* published an article criticizing this issue in Shanxi (Ji 2010).

24. There are a number of reports on this famous case, including X. Hu 2001.

25. This case has also been reported widely and in-depth; for example, see *China Youth Daily* 2011.

26. This term has no equivalent in English, but the closest translation is "institutional corruption."

27. I do not cite the media reports here to maintain the confidentiality of my informants.

28. Informant, interview by the author, Shanxi, May 26, 2010.

29. For example, the county government tried to reach an agreement with a large SOE to take over a bankrupt SOE in the county, but it focused on providing low-interest bank loans instead of improving the investment environment.

30. Zhang moved to Shanxi from Beijing in 2001 to serve as deputy governor of Shanxi Province. He was appointed provincial governor in January 2004 and promoted to party secretary in July 2005.

31. Chief financial officer and coal-mine manager, interview by the author, Shanxi, June 13, 2010.

32. Tax officer, interview by the author, Shanxi, June 13, 2010.

33. Coal-mine owner, interview by the author, Shanxi, June 8, 2010.

34. Mr. Yu, private entrepreneur, interview by the author, Zhejiang, March 15, 2010.

35. I based this narrative on Bao and Wang 2002; Lu 1999: Lu and Wang 2008; and The Comprehensive Department of State Council 2014. My informants also referenced the government's decision to promote market development in the 1980s. To attract businessmen and investment, the county government set very low tax rates compared to those in neighboring counties, including the one in which my informant was a township and, later, county leader (interview by the author, Zhejiang, July 26, 2006). But government-business relationships also had a negative side: enterprise owners gave government officials shares in private enterprises in exchange for permits and protection from unreasonable fines and fees and harassment from hooligans (informant, interview by the author, Zhejiang, March 12, 2011).

36. Trade association presidents, interview by the author, Zhejiang, February 2002; for details, see Wang and Zhang 2014.

37. This innovation won the Award for Local Government Innovation in China in 2005.

38. The county government gives the Bureau of Investment Promotion the power to "lead and coordinate with" other related bureaus, including the SAT office, LTB, AIC, People's Bank (the central bank's local branch), Committee of Economic Affairs, Bureau of Environment Protection, and Bureau of Land Resources, to help investors complete all administrative registrations with one phone call. An informant told me that these measures had improved County Z's investment environment and that service at government bureaus had improved significantly. The principle is called "wash your face before you can invite any investment" (*xilian zhaoshang*) (interview by the author, Chongqing, August 13, 2009).

39. Officials of Investment Promotion Bureau, interview by the author, Chongqing, August 9, 2009.

40. My informant told me that the other mechanism to make the government commitment credible is for government to build its reputation to attract further investment, thus making economic development sustainable. However, this individual-to-individual contact system is personalized rather than institutionalized, which creates opportunities for corruption. The mechanism for SOEs to make investments in other regions is different from that of private enterprises since SOE managers have formal party or government titles to make their voices heard within the party-state.

41. Informant, interview by the author, Chongqing, August 12, 2009.

42. County Yiwu empowers the official labor union (*gonghui*) to protect migrant labors and also has representatives from the migrant-labor township PC.

43. An informant, who works in the party's organizational department at the provincial level, told me that local governments in some western provinces set very high targets that are impossible to meet for attracting investment (interview by the author, Hunan, August 13, 2008). This is one reason that County X's party secretary focused intently on one enterprise that could help him meet the target.

44. Another motivation is the land-transfer fee, which made up about 30 percent of local revenue in 2012 (informant, interview by the author, Hunan, July 8, 2013).

45. Senior officer, interview by the author, Hunan, July 19, 2008. Since 2000, local government debt has been a serious problem; an informant working in county government told me that County X's is more serious than the 2008 financial crisis in China. Media reports of local debt include News.163.com, n.d.; and Xinhua 2011.

46. Senior government official, interview by the author, Hunan, September 26, 2009.

47. For a critical review, see Putnam, Leonardi, and Nanetti 1993; and Holmberg, Rothstein, and Nasiritousi 2009.

48. Predatory government bureaus can collect large amounts of extra-budgetary revenue (which composes a high percentage of GDP), but government tax revenue (budgetary revenue) and long-term fiscal income both decline.

49. For a theoretical discussion of business and other types of industry, see Maxfield and Schneider 1997.

50. This finding also resonates with Yuhua Wang's (2015) findings on foreign direct investment's (FDI) impact on rule of law in China.

Chapter 5

1. Liu explained that the 2008 international economic crisis, which reduced exports significantly, had lowered his rank as a taxpayer in the year 2009.

2. "Model Worker" used to be an honorable title for workers who made great contributions to society, but in a reversal of the party's former view of entrepreneurs as exploitative capitalists, most of China's current model workers are entrepreneurs. Having the title "Model Worker" is more competitive than having a title such as "LPC deputy," and it confers both political privileges and socioeconomic benefits such as a high standard of medical care and social welfare.

3. In some counties, vehicle license numbers signify political status: for example, 0001 is for the party secretary, 0002 is for the county head, and 0003 is for the deputy party secretary.

4. No statistics reveal how many LPC deputies are private entrepreneurs. Thus, it is hard to decipher accurate numbers and percentages. Private entrepreneurs have no specific category and are categorized into other "social groups," such as workers, peasants, intellectuals, and cadres, which obscures them in statistics. The LPPCC has a category called "economical group" (*Jingji jie*), but many private entrepreneurs are classified in other groups (such as technology or cadre).

5. In my fieldwork I found that around 30 percent of LPC deputies were private entrepreneurs in my four case counties and in one district of Taiyuan city, the capital of Shanxi Province (various informants, interviews by the author, Zhejiang, April 14, 2010, and July 3, 2010; Shanxi, May 26, 2010, and June 15, 2010). The in-depth media report in *Oriental Outlook Weekly* (2011), a Xinhua News Agent weekly journal, also finds that around 30 percent of the deputies of county and prefecture LPCs in Hengyang Prefecture are private entrepreneurs (Z. Huang 2008). Young Nam Cho (2008) finds that dur-

ing 1993–1997, the cadre deputies were the largest group in the NPC (28.3 percent), but the worker and peasant group was the largest in the lower-level PCs in Tianjin Municipality (29.1 percent) and Nankai District in Tianjin (46 percent; cadre deputies were 17.4 percent). There is no special category of private entrepreneurs in Cho's statistics; in fact, they are "hidden" in other categories. If you are a peasant entrepreneur (which means you were/are a peasant and you run a company) and an LPC deputy, then you are a peasant deputy; if you are an entrepreneur and have an urban residence, then you will be a worker deputy; and if you run a high-tech enterprise, then you will be an intellectual deputy.

6. As the last several party's National Congress meetings report, the CCP's political reforms are very limited. In the party's meeting report of the Eighteenth National Congress, LPC reform and rule of law are two major components of political reform. However, very limited actions have been taken in the last six years.

7. For a recent application of modernization theory to China's democratization future, see Liu and Chen 2012.

8. For a comprehensive review of Barrington's theory, see Mahoney 2003. A number of theorists have criticized Moore's theory for neglecting the role of the working class in promoting democratic transition; see, for example, Rueschemeyer, Stephens, and Stephens 1992; and Collier and Collier 1991.

9. For details, see A. Chen 1999 and Cho 2008. The LPC Standing Committees' annual reports in different regions also reflect these changes.

10. The structural-functional analytical framework originates from David Easton's political system theory and was developed by Gabriel Almond in the 1960s. See Almond and Powell 1966. Critiques of structural functionalism include Western concepts traveling to developing countries: structural functionalism tries to find functionally equivalent organizations in the developing countries, though they may not exist or have very different functions. For example, see March and Olsen 1989. For a review of the use of the structural-functional analytical framework of PCs in China, see Cho 2008, chap. 1.

11. However, Guo does not conduct fieldwork on direct election in his case county; instead, he turns to a big city such as Shenzhen to study the election and independent candidates.

12. The polity that combines legislative and executive powers differs from the parliamentary system because there is no independent court system. Like the executive branch, the courts are also responsible and accountable to the legislative branch

13. For details, see Cho 2010.

14. The LPPCC thus resembles the House of Commons in Britain more than the Senate in the United States, but the LPPCC is not a branch of legislature but a consulting organ.

15. There are eight so-called democratic parties (*Minzhu dangpai*) besides the CPC in China: China Revolutionary Committee of the Kuomintang, China Democratic League, China Democratic National Construction Association, China Association for the Promotion of Democracy, Chinese Peasants' and Workers' Democratic Party, China

Zhi Gong Dang, Jiusan Society, and Taiwan Democratic Self-Government League. But they cooperate with rather than work against the CPC. And their memberships are very limited; the largest has fewer than two hundred thousand members. For details, see *People's Daily Online*, n.d.

16. Some vertically led bureaus, such as the two tax bureaus, have independent power to appoint and remove personnel.

17. For example, the Political-Legal Committee (zhengfawei) leads the Bureau of Public Security, the prosecutors, the court, and the Bureau of Justice. The Agriculture Committee (nongwei) coordinates the agriculture-related bureaus.

18. The central government tries to strengthen the control of local government by not having the main leaders (party and government) from the jurisdiction they govern, a practice with a long history in China.

19. Wenling city PC Standing Committee director, interview by the author, Zhejiang, March 21, 2010.

20. When there were more than two deputy party secretaries, only the government head and the executive deputy government head were members of the LPSC. Since 2005, the CCP Central Committee has permitted the LPSCs to have only two deputy party secretaries. Therefore, most LPSCs have one or more Standing Committee member deputy government heads (*changwei fuxianzhang*), an additional member from the government

21. In Chinese, 党委动口，政府动手，人大举手，政协拍手. Warm River County PC deputy, interview by the author, Zhejiang, March 5, 2010.

22. Deng Xiaoping, the former leader and "designer of the reform," gave a famous talk on how to reform the party-state leadership system in 1980. He called for deconcentrating power from the party, the Party Standing Committee, and the party secretary and redistributing the power and functions to the government, social, and economic organs. A "separation of party and government" reform followed in the 1980s. However, this reform stagnated in the 1990s and was reversed in the late 1990s and 2000s.

23. Director Huang, speech at the seventh meeting of the ninth LPC Standing Committee of County Warm River, February 23, 1992.

24. District government officer, interview by the author, Beijing, July 21, 2010.

25. The evaluation for the AIC was particularly poor, with the deputies heavily criticizing its officials

26. Based on the LPC meeting records of County Warm River, 1993.

27. Two county PC directors, interview by the author, Zhejiang, March 21, 2010.

28. Young Nam Cho (2010) also finds that LPC leaders' willingness is the key to a powerful LPC.

29. Don Slater (2003) also finds that authoritarian rulers in Southeast Asia can intentionally manipulate the legislature by empowering or weakening it to serve their interests and sustain power.

30. Cho (2010) calls it a process of marketization and legalization.

31. Some journalists argue that the 1980s were the golden age of NPC reform, under the leadership of Peng Zhen and Wan Li. See Shu 2010.

32. For details, see A. Chen 1999 and Cho 2010. We can also see these developments when reading the LPC Standing Committees' annual reports from different regions. For example, the 2004 annual report of County D described the county PC Standing Committee's work in 2004 as follows: (1) to serve the people's interests as the starting point and goal of all their work; (2) to promote rule by law as the most important goal, which means promoting governance by law and ensuring justice; (3) to improve supervision (of the government, court, and prosecutor) as an important task, which has achieved significant results; (4) to institutionalize the personal appointment and removal procedure; (5) to train the deputies to improve their work performance. The report also acknowledges the importance of the party leadership and government's cooperation, the deputies' hard work, and the support of all social groups. In some annual reports in other counties, they put being "under the party's leadership and working around the party and government's important projects" at the beginning.

33. Meeting records of County Warm River's PC Standing Committee, May 1992. Perhaps this is also the reason that Cho thinks that private-entrepreneur deputies in the LPC play exemplary roles.

34. For an excellent discussion of elections that are not free and competitive in the "competitive authoritarian" countries, see Levitsky and Way 2010.

35. These are government-run social organizations, they have full-time employees salaried by the government, and their leaders have formal administrative powers and are under the management of the party's Organization Department. The mass organizations differ from other social organizations because they do not need to register every year.

36. See J. He 2010. My fieldwork, however, produced some different findings.

37. Like other decision-making processes in Chinese politics, this process also follows the principle of "democratic centralism," which gives the party and party secretary the final decision-making power without any institutional checks.

38. This is the nomenklatura system: the Communist Party committee selects and manages officials of any importance, including elected leaders. It is called "the party manages the cadres" (*dang guan ganbu*) and was expanded to a broader category later: "the party manages the person with ability" (*dang guan rencai*).

39. As an important institution for the party's united-front strategy, which aims to co-opt social economic elites from different social classes and groups, the LPPCC has quotas for members from different social classes and groups: the economic group, commerce and industry, science, technology, education and medical, religious, and so on.

40. The 2010 Election Law has a discriminal rule that the rural vote is weighted only as one-fifth to one-eighth of an urban vote, but the rural voters will get equal voting rights in 2011 according to the new election law.

41. To give an example at the NPC, Hu Jintao is the party's general secretary and the president, as well as a deputy of the NPC. Since there is no electoral district for the central government (and party), he is elected from Tibet, where he served as party secretary for years in the late 1980s, though he is neither a resident nor a voter of Tibet.

42. Township government head, interview by the author, Zhejiang, March 17, 2010.

43. Deputy county LPC director, interview by the author, Zhejiang, July 3, 2010.

44. Senior tax officer, interview by the author, Shanxi, June 13, 2010.

45. The party secretary successfully made both of them deputies in the provincial PC and NPC. In return, in addition to benefits such as low land prices, he got investments and personal benefits from each of them (each gave him 60,000 to 80,000 yuan). See *China's Youth Daily* 2010.

46. Senior LPC official, interview by the author, Zhejiang, July 3, 2010.

47. Township government head, interview by the author, Zhejiang, March 17, 2010.

48. See W. Huang 2004 and Guo 2007. For discussion of cases concerning how competitive elections in urban areas and community pressure make the deputies representative and accountable, see Guo 2007. However, his analysis is descriptive and the cases are not systematically collected in his field regions.

49. My fieldwork in Shanxi Province suggests that even the richest counties there do not have commercialization in LPC deputy elections. But news reports suggest that buying votes in LPC elections is also common in Hunan. See Z. Huang 2010. Given the sensitivity of this issue and the barriers to reporting, it seems likely this is a wider phenomenon.

50. Informant, interview by the author, Zhejiang, March 1, 2010.

51. Informant, interview by the author, Zhejiang, April, 3, 2010.

52. Mr. Wang, private entrepreneur and senior county PPCC member, interview by the author, Zhejiang, March 11, 2010.

53. Informant, interview by the author, Zhejiang, March 10, 2010.

54. The police cannot detain or arrest an LPC or LPPCC deputy without the permission of the Standing Committee of the LPC and LPPCC.

55. Two senior LPC officers, interviews by the author, Zhejiang, August 11, 2009, and April 15, 2010.

56. See, for example, Ao 2005 and Xiaoyan Wang 2007. Wang finds another possible incentive is to promote institution reform, which means that private entrepreneurs are interested in changing the government's policy and some administrative rules. However, Wang argues that private entrepreneurs do not have the vision and interest to promote political change, which is much beyond their ability and too risky.

57. Private entrepreneur, interview by the author, Zhejiang, March 2, 2010.

58. Private entrepreneur, interview by the author, Zhejiang, March 12, 2010.

59. Driver for County Warm River's PPCC, interview by the author, Zhejiang, March 16, 2010.

60. LPC deputy, interview by the author, Zhejiang, April 11, 2010.

61. Informant, interview by the author, Zhejiang, December 29, 2013.

62. Informant, interview by the author, Zhejiang, June 11, 2014.

63. Local businessman, interview by the author, Zhejiang, March 12, 2010.

64. LPC official, interview by the author, Zhejiang, March 15, 2010. His complaint is true because I also found other sources of information that cross-validate his argument, including meeting many LPC and LPPCC leaders with LPC deputies and LPPCC mem-

bers in an expensive KTV (a karaoke bar or club) during their annual meeting when I was invited there by a friend who knows some of them. One of my informants, a senior LPPCC member, LPC deputy, and Democratic Party member, complained to me that "these entrepreneur deputies are political whores! They spent money to buy votes, and when they get elected, others should pay them for their votes" (interview by the author, Zhejiang, May 13, 2010).

65. Very few counties have offices for many deputies, but Wenling city in Zhejiang Province had more than forty such offices in 2010; see *Zaobao* 2010. The NPC Standing Committee forbade deputies to have offices in August 2010; see *China Business News* 2010. For an official explanation (or justification) for canceling PC deputy offices, see B. Li 2010. However, Hu Jintao's report on the recent Eighteenth National Party Congress suggests that building a PC deputy contact office (*zai renda sheli daibiao lianluo jigou*) is an important part of political reform.

66. However, the most active LPC's role in local politics is still very limited.

67. In China, most monopolized industries are run by SOEs.

68. The township government is busy only when there are important tasks (such as maintaining social stability during the NPC and NPPCC meetings in March, family planning, and collecting the agricultural tax before it was abolished); during other times the township government officials have a lot of time for leisure. But the county government bureaus are different, as there are more daily tasks to fulfill and more severe monitoring. The LPC office is like a county government bureau in County Warm River.

69. Informant, interview by the author, Zhejiang, March 15, 2010; informant, interview by the author, Zhejiang, April 10, 2010.

70. A government official complains that the deputy proposals are of low quality, hard to implement, self-interested, and so on. But he also admits that they have real pressures from the LPC now (interview by the author, Zhejiang, April 10, 2010). Also, the Party Committee requires that the satisfaction rate should be no lower than 95 percent as a target that the government must meet; therefore, government bureaus have a strong incentive to meet the LPC deputies' demand.

71. The so-called sunshine salary (*yangguang gongzi*) is a nationwide policy but is implemented with various degrees of success in different regions. It aims to have all types of government officials' income monitored and to reduce or even eliminate income gaps between different government bureaus. County Warm River and Wenling have much better implementation of this policy, while County Cold Mountain has achieved only limited success.

72. According to an LPC officer in County W, "Vote purchasing means the private-entrepreneur candidate values the title 'LPC deputy'; it is not necessarily a bad thing" (interview by the author, Zhejiang, July 6, 2010).

73. Mr. Shu, senior county PC deputy, interview by the author, Shanxi, May 22, 2010.

74. Shu, interview.

75. County PPCC official, interview by the author, Shanxi, June 7, 2010.

76. County Cold Mountain *Yearbook*, 2009.

77. For a comprehensive discussion of LPC and representation through taxation in Wenling, see Ye 2018.

78. He also served as the county government deputy head before he became deputy party secretary. He was promoted director of the county PC Standing Committee in 2009. Given his working experience, he is a powerful figure in local politics because both the party secretary and county head are from other regions.

79. The total budget was 50 billion yuan in 2010.

80. This includes a 35 million yuan construction project to conserve water.

81. I was invited to attend this conference and observe the participatory budgeting in Zeguo township in March 2010.

82. This point was also confirmed by my other interviews in Hunan on July 26, 2009, and Shanxi on May 25, 2010. A Shanxi government official explained, "A wrong [achievement] project may costs tens of millions or even billions, and no one benefits from it. It is much more serious than corruption [which can hardly exceed one million]." During a conference on participatory budgeting organized by the China Development Research Foundation in May 2006, a deputy prefecture government head in Gansu Province commented that the party secretary openly announced that only he and the government head can discuss the personnel and fiscal issues; others are not allowed to touch these two "high-voltage wires."

83. Zhang Xueming, interview by the author, Zhejiang, July 7, 2010.

84. Scientific and democratic decision-making was an important goal of political reform for Deng Xiaoping in the 1980s.

85. Author's conference notes (government official speech) at Wenling, July 7, 2010.

86. Zeguo is a "central town" with some independent budgetary power (most towns do not have this budgetary power); the township's administrative level is also higher at a semi-county level. Another township, Xinhe, also started democratic deliberation meetings in the early 2000s.

87. The Central Compilation and Translation Bureau is a semi-ministry-level party organ and an official think tank. China's Local Government Innovation Award was founded in 2003 to encourage local governments (at the county and township levels) to pursue innovative experiments in local governance.

88. Street office is an administrative level below the city level; it equals a township but has no PC or PPCC.

89. Wenling is ranked the twelfth best-developed county of China's twenty-eight hundred counties.

90. Zhang Xueming, interview by the author, Zhejiang, July 7, 2010.

91. Author's conference notes from a speech by Mr. Ziang, township head of Zeguo, at Wenling, 2010.

92. Mr. Jiang, township head of Zeguo, interview by the author, Zhejiang, July 8, 2010.

93. Juan Tang describes this change as one from "confirmative election" (确认性选举) to "competitive election" (竞争性选举) (2004, 11).

94. Truex (2016) finds that the NPC has a system of "representation within bounds," encouraging deputies to reflect the needs of their constituents, but only for nonsensitive issues. This allows the regime to address citizen grievances while avoiding incendiary political activism.

95. To some degree, Gandhi assumes that the authoritarian state is a unitary actor; she also does not specify the preferences of different actors that she discusses (2008, 182).

96. I disagree with Hou's (2019) theory that the LPC provides protection for property rights and therefore for economic growth because a county PC could have only dozens of private entrepreneurs as deputies, while there may be thousands of private entrepreneurs in a county who are left unprotected by the LPC (and LPPCC) and therefore might be unable to promote economic growth. So there are other mechanisms that work to protect private property rights.

97. For two excellent review articles, see Roniger 2004 and Hicken 2011.

98. The CCP Central Committee regarded vote purchasing in the LPC election as a severe violation of party discipline.

99. Scholars who study village elections find vote buying; see, for example, Takeuchi 2014.

100. One reason is that these candidates are not organized by competitive parties, so it is hard for them to make policy promises.

101. According to the World Bank scholars, governance quality consists of "the traditions and institutions by which authority in a country is exercised. This includes (1) the process by which governments are selected, monitored and replaced, (2) the capacity of the government to effectively formulate and implement sound policies, and (3) the respect of citizens and the state for the institutions that govern economic and social interactions among them" (Kaufmann, Kraay, and Zoido-Lobaton 1999, 1). On its website, the World Bank lists twelve indicators of good governance: corruption, nepotism, collusion, effectiveness, responsiveness, political stability, regulatory framework, rule of law, poverty reduction, public awareness, staff development, and (economic) restructuring, plus three indicators for decentralization: local autonomy, voice and accountability, and transparency. This list is comprehensive, but it mixes institutional characteristics with institutional outcomes and therefore provides limited analytical leverage.

Chapter 6

1. Elections of prefecture and higher levels of PC deputy are indirect. These deputies are elected by lower-level PC deputies.

2. However, there is no requirement for the class/group compositions of deputies because they are supposed to be elected by the voters; in practice there are quotas for different social groups, including doctors and nurses.

3. Staff member of county PPCC, interview by the author, Zhejiang, March 11, 2011.

4. Though Moore (1966) takes a strong bourgeoisie as a prerequisite for democracy, he also argues that its role in promoting democracy depends on other factors, such as the ruler's repressive capacity and the strength of the landed class. In other words, the bourgeoisie's strength is defined relative to state power and the power of other classes. Unfortunately, many of his followers often neglect this point.

5. State dependence "refers to the degree to which private sector profitability is subject to the discretionary support of the state," typically "delivered in the form of subsidized inputs, protected market position, close collaboration in the definition of economic policy, and state containment of labor and the capital poor" (Bellin 2000, 180). As I discuss later, capital's demand for democracy shown at the top right could be opportunism rather than leaning democratic.

6. Carles Boix (2003) argues that while inequality leads to elites' resistance to democracy, high asset mobility protects the rich from being excluded from redistribution policies and therefore contributes to democracy consolidation. Dan Slater, Benjamin Smith, and Gautam Nair (2014) revise this argument by pointing out that the lack of infrastructural power (taxation administrative capacity) is manifested in a general incapacity among postcolonial states to impose significant direct taxes on their wealthiest citizens.

7. Bruce Dickson (2008) argues that the party co-opts private entrepreneurs because they are important for promoting economic growth, creating job opportunities, and increasing fiscal revenue, all of which are important for the party's legitimacy.

8. For example, Kellee Tsai argues that *assertive* private entrepreneurs may promote democracy in China because they are willing and able to challenge the state. But she also finds that these assertive people need to ally with state actors when other state organizations challenge them, which does not seem to support her broader argument regarding democratization. This argument is close to Joel Migdal's "state-in-society" approach: neither the state nor society is a unitary actor. Some parts of society may ally with some part of the state to challenge another state organ (or its alliance with some other social groups; Migdal 2001). Therefore, instead of promoting democracy as a unified social class, some privileged capitalists ally with government organs to get specific privileges rather than push for institutional reform (K. Tsai 2007).

9. Some companies in large cities have more reasons for tax compliance, because the taxation administration is more institutionalized and the state has reduced the tax burden for some companies, especially foreign companies. But tax evasion remains rampant (senior tax officer, interview by the author, Hunan, July 13, 2010).

10. Private entrepreneur, interview by the author, Beijing, June 2, 2010.

11. Forbearance explains the situation since the late 1990s, when the taxation bureaus had significantly improved their taxation capacity through infrastructural investments (increased staff members, better education and training, up-to-date IT equipment). Before that, enforcement was weak.

12. Tax evasion lower than 30 percent of the total required taxes can be punished with a fine that is one to five times the amount of unpaid tax and up to three years

imprisonment, and tax evasion exceeding 30 percent of the total required taxes can be punished by three to seven years of imprisonment and a fine of up to five times the amount of unpaid tax. The previous law specified the amount to be 0.1 million yuan; in 2008 it was revised and no specific amount was listed.

13. Mr. Zheng told me that if he pays enough bribe to the LTB officers, the charge could be dismissed. But he considered this a last resort since it could be very expensive.

14. Mr. Zheng, entrepreneur, interview by the author, Zhejiang, July 21, 2009, and August 3, 2010.

15. Informant in SAT office, County Z, interview by the author, Hunan, July 13, 2010.

16. A senior tax officer in County Warm River admits this is true (interview by the author, Zhejiang, October 9, 2018).

17. Private entrepreneur, interview by the author, Zhejiang, April 27, 2010.

18. Various informants, interview by the author, Shanxi, May 28, 2010.

19. Senior tax officer, interview by the author, Shanxi, May 27, 2010.

20. The CCP used the same tactics in the early 1950s to deter private entrepreneurs and threatened them to "voluntarily" allow the government to nationalize their enterprises. See M. Huang 2010, chaps. 10–14.

21. There is a time-lag effect because the annual tax target is set up based on the previous year's economic performance and prediction of the coming year's economic performance. The tax target will affect the tax administration and other government bureaus' efforts to collect taxes and nontax revenue.

22. Of course, it would be fruitful to study the more recent survey data and to make comparisons, but this is beyond the scope of this book.

23. The research team built a random sampling framework nationwide, but it is very difficult to conduct a survey for private entrepreneurs in China (and other countries). The research team trained the interviewers, who work in the local Federation of Industry and Commerce and the local AIC, and asked them to do the sampling and interview. These nonprofessional interviewers did not conduct the interviews strictly according to the requirements.

24. Level of government refers to an administrative level that includes the Party Committee, government, the LPC, and the LPPCC. In the three municipalities, the lowest level, street (*jiedao*), has the same administrative level as a county but no LPC or LPPCC.

25. The PES data set includes some questions related to local government and trade associations, but the questions are not very specific on the evaluation of local governance quality and, therefore, have serious validity problems. Therefore, I drop these questions as measurements of governance quality.

26. According to the "Bylaw on Forbidden Apportions for Enterprises" issued by the State Council in 1988, apportion includes "behaviors that ask enterprises to provide money, material, and human service by any means that are not allowed by laws and regulations" of "government organs, social organizations, the military, enterprises, and

public institutions." The bylaw is available in Chinese at http://www.law-lib.com/law/law_view1.asp?id=52275.

27. In China, donation could be voluntary or involuntary. In many cases, the government would ask the enterprises to "donate" to something specific, which could be constructing a primary school, a bridge, or a government building.

28. A private entrepreneur being a Party Committee member is illegal according to law and the party's regulations, but some private entrepreneurs are government officials or Party Committee members. Since most private entrepreneurs who are government officials (seventy out of ninety) also have other political titles, I do not include it as an indicator for political status.

29. To simplify the analysis, I use only the "membership" indicator but not membership in the standing committees.

30. Tax administration is still not institutionalized. But it is hard to reflect this in the data set, which is self-reported by the respondent; therefore, the obvious illegal practices are underreported. For example, a coal-mining enterprise may exceed its production limit but would not report it.

31. It is difficult to say whether the CCP intentionally generates such a system and situation, but once they are in place, the CCP has little incentive to change them. Taxation is only one source of private entrepreneurs' vulnerability; powerful organs such as the police, courts, and procuratorates can also use legal repression against private entrepreneurs when rule of law is absent. For example, after Xi Jinping's November 1, 2018, speech to private entrepreneurs in which he promised to improve the environment for development, the Supreme Court of the People, the Supreme Procuratorate of the People, and the Ministry of Public Security each announced that they should "not to apply criminal law to civil and economic disputes." See *Legal Weekly* 2021.

Chapter 7

1. There are three comprehensive reviews of fiscal sociology. John Campbell (1993) shows that most studies focus on taxation as the consequence of political and social economic changes. Isaac Martin and Monica Prasad (2014) later show that research focuses on how taxation affects inequality and economic development. More recently, Edgar Kiser and Steven Karceski (2017) consider the institution of taxation (tax revenue, tax structure, and tax administration) as the cause of political and social economic changes and discuss three issues: the interaction between structure and institution, a contractual view of taxation, and a focus on state capacity. This book also discusses these three issues (I had finalized most of this book manuscript independently when the Kiser and Karceski paper was available online).

2. Max Weber (1950) discusses market formation and the process of bureaucratization in Europe.

3. There is, however, a great amount of rentier-state literature that studies windfall revenue from natural resources.

4. The conditions of market-preserving federalism include hierarchy within government and sharp distinctions between areas of responsibility and power; primary authority over the economy within jurisdictions among subnational governments; policing of the common market at the national level; hard budget constraints for all governments; and institutionalized authority and allocation of responsibility among different levels of government (Montinola, Qian, and Weingast 199, 55).

5. Tax revenue declined before 1994 in terms of tax revenue's portion of GDP and the central government's portion of national revenue.

6. Marc Berenson's (2018) theoretical framework of state capacity in postcommunist countries uses state capacity, mainly taxation capacity, as a dependent variable.

7. The official statistic is half a million (Ministry of Finance of the People's Republic of China 2013, 703). However, this includes only civil servants (*gongwuyuan*) and excludes public-service-unit employees (*shiyebian*). Various media, including a public document by the SAT headquarters, have reported that there are one million tax officers (State Administration of Taxation 2018).

8. The improvement of IT technology (Golden Tax Project, or *Jinshui gongchen* I, II, and III) helps the Taxation Bureau improve its information-collection and monitoring capacities substantially.

9. In the early 1990s, the CCP faced a fiscal crisis when the tax/GDP ratio and the central tax/national tax ratio were decreasing rapidly. At that time the central government could not raise necessary tax revenue to cover its expenditures (Wang and Hu 2001).

10. The CCP is a classic case of Milan Svolik's ideal type of resilient single party (2012, 167–168). As Svolik describes, such parties have three common organizational features that sustain authoritarian rule: hierarchical assignment of service and benefits, political control over appointments, and selective recruitment and repression. As discussed in the "pressure-based system" or cadre evaluation system in which the taxation system is embedded, the CCP's institutional capacity was crucial to recentralizing its taxation system and improving its effectiveness. See also Cai and Treisman 2006; D. Yang 2006; and Zhan 2009.

11. In a comparative study of the Soviet Union (1985–1991) and China (1979–1994), Steven Solnick (1996) argues that the CCP maintained its hierarchical authority while the Soviet Union did not. For a discussion of recentralization of taxation power, see Whiting 2001 and Zhan 2009.

12. Benjamin Smith and Dan Slater do not explicitly address this last point, but it is crucial for authoritarian resilience.

13. This infrastructural power resonates with the organizational strength that Steven Levitsky and Lucan Way (2010) consider to be the most important domestic factor for authoritarian resilience.

14. The tax-target system is a tax-farming system; it is modern because it eliminates the nongovernmental tax farmers or brokers.

15. Theda Skocpol notes, what Max Weber defines as the core elements of the modern state, that a "state's territorial integrity, financial means, and staffing" determine its capacity, and she therefore advises that investigation of state capacities to realize goals should start from these elements (1985, 17).

16. Tamir Moustafa (2007) identifies three additional functions of the courts: strengthening administrative compliance within the state's own bureaucratic machinery and solving coordination problems among competing factions within the regime; facilitating trade and investment; and implementing controversial policies to allow core elements of a regime to distance themselves politically. China's tax institution does not perform these functions.

17. This resonates with the concept of organizational power (Levitsky and Way 2010).

18. According to Richard Swedberg, Tocqueville argues that the state in the old regime influenced (with "a devastating effect") the social and economic structure of the country in three important ways: through taxation, the sale of offices (could be regarded a specific form of taxation), and industrial policy (2009, 252). Joseph Schumpeter (1991) also holds a similar view, as demonstrated in the epigraph.

19. Two lines of inquiry are summarized and elaborated by Swedberg (2009, 252–258). Table 6.1 is a revision of Eva Bellin's (2000) typology based on dependence generated by industry policies and fear generated by taxation.

20. Stern and Hassid also discuss "control parables" as a strategy of ruling, which "harden limits on activism by illustrating a set of prescriptions designed to prevent future clashes with authority" (2012, 1230).

21. For discussion on land seizure and demolitions, see Heurlin 2016.

22. Taxation was regarded as a means of class struggle until the 1980s. It is of course possible for "unreasonable" tax assessment to be regarded as predatory or illegal. For example, a tax riot occurred in October 2011 in the Zhili town of Huzhou, Zhejiang, which targeted mainly the suddenly raised tax rate (from 343 yuan per machine to 620) rather than taxation itself, which had been in place for several years.

23. The "death-tax rate" slogan in late 2016 attracted wide attention and responses from scholars and businesses, but the government censored such discussion in the media and on the internet.

24. Kiser and Karceski (2017) emphasize structure.

25. David Art (2012) and Thomas Pepinsky (2014) criticize the "institutional turn of authoritarianism" because it suffers two weaknesses: it takes a simplified version of rational choice institutionalism, and it tends to be functionalism. Art argues that "these works adopt an overly simplistic view of how institutions and organizations matter. To varying degrees, the authors all use institutions and organizations as convenient placeholders for a variety of different causal mechanisms that are left underspecified" (2010, 363).

26. Vernon Ruttan and Yujiro Hayami (1984) propose a demand-and-supply model of institutional change, which integrates resource endowment, technical change, and culture endowment. Daniel Bromley presents a critical review of institutional change theories of the 1980s, which he argues are based on the concept of efficiency and, therefore tautology (1989, chap. 2).

27. For a critical review of these theories, see L. Chen 2008. For a comprehensive and critical review of institutional change theories, see J. Campbell 2010.

28. Examining institutions at the same level, some scholars emphasize the mechanism of institutional complementarities, and some emphasize institutional friction. According to Peter Hall and David Soskice (2001), two institutions can be said to be complementary if the presence (or efficiency) of one increases the returns from (or efficiency of) the other. See also Streeck and Thelen 2005 and Crouch 2010.

29. Also termed "institutional conversion," institutional amphibiousness means the use of existing institutions for new or alternative purposes (Thelen 2004).

30. Institutional diversity focuses on institutional resilience in times of crisis. For a comprehensive review of literature on capitalism, see Hall and Soskice 2001 and Thelen 2001.

31. On the contrary, institutional change based on hierarchical linkage can better deal with conflict and power.

32. The CCP emphasizes "four basic principles" (*sixiang jiben yuanze* 四项基本原则) for reform: the socialist road, the people's democratic dictatorship, Marxism-Leninism and Mao Zedong Thought, and the leadership of the Communist Party of China. But the first three are ambiguous and easy to manipulate; only CCP leadership is not.

33. Zhu Rongji describes the meetings in which he discussed TSR with ministries and provincial leaders as well as a report that summarizes the negotiation between the provinces and Jiang Zemin (Zhu 2011, vol. 1). All of these provide evidence of institutional stickiness.

34. For a description of partial-reform equilibrium, see Hellman 1998.

35. In regard to an adaptive informal institution, Kellee Tsai argues that "formal institutions comprise a myriad of constraints and opportunities that may motivate everyday actors to devise novel operating arrangements that are not officially sanctioned. With repetition and diffusion, these informal coping strategies may take on an institutional reality of their own. In contrast to deep-rooted, 'primordial' informal institutions, which tend to resist change, the resulting norms and practices can be called adaptive informal institutions because they represent creative responses to formal institutional environments that actors find too constraining" (2006, 117–118).

36. "Development cluster" is a combination of a high level of economic development, rule of law, democracy, and social welfare. Mark Dincecco also finds that long-term economic growth depends on evolution from the old regime, characterized by fiscal fragmentation and absolutist spending control, to the effective state, characterized by fiscal centralization and spending oversight by parliament (2015, 904).

37. Given the great amount of literature on taxation in Chinese history, this section provides only a limited survey of the literature relevant to this book. For a recent comprehensive review with international comparison, see Vries (2015). See also Brandt, Ma, and Rawski 2014.

38. Famous examples include Wang Anshi of the Song dynasty, Zhang Juzheng of the Ming dynasty, and Emperor Yongzheng of the Qing dynasty.

39. County government's two major functions were tax collection and maintenance of social stability. It was also supposed to support education and charity and provide necessary infrastructure. Given the limited fiscal revenue it could obtain, county government used to work with the local gentry to carry out all these functions.

40. Yanglian literally means "money [silver] for clean officers."

41. The traditions of the dynasties dictate that when a man in power dies, all the political measures he instituted no longer hold (*Renwang zhengxi* 人亡政息).

42. For a similar but more comprehensive analysis of how the interaction of imperial political and economic institutions blocked long-term economic growth, with in-depth analysis of the institution of taxation, see Brandt, Ma, and Rawski 2014.

43. Shigeki (2004) notes that royal land played a very limited role in financing the state, and gradually the royal family ceded it to rich people, who agreed to pay higher tax rates on these lands than applied to other lands.

44. There was a hot debate over Weber's explanation on the undevelopment of market capitalism in imperial China. While it is beyond this book's scope to furnish a comprehensive review of this debate (fortunately, Von Glahn 2016 provides one), I provide a selective review to highlight the fiscal dimension of the debate: William Skinner (1965, 1977) and William Rowe (1984) both disputed Weber based on their studies of regional markets in rural and urban China, guilds, and businessmen's self-governance. However, a close examination would suggest that the evidence they presented did not convincingly undermine Weber's fiscal sociology theory. Rowe, for example, recognizes the importance of government's fiscal incentives and bureaucracy predation or protection in determining business's development. He also endorses the Taiping Rebellion's destruction of the government's monopolistic power over the salt, tea, and wood trades that provided opportunity for the emergence of private businesses and guilds. Rowe also limits his study to the traditional trades, ignoring industrialization.

For a different understanding of the state-business relationship in the salt industry during the Qing dynasty, see Kwan 2001 and G. Huang 2019. Many studies show that in the Late Qing dynasty the state discouraged industrialization (such as China's mercantilism), which supports Weber's theory (Chan 1977; Feuerwerker 1958). Timothy Brook (1999) provides a comprehensive and critical review of the debate on sprouts of capitalism in Chinese, English, and Japanese literature, engaging or not engaging with Marx and Weber's theories. Some Chinese scholars in different periods also make similar arguments without referring to Weber (e.g., Fu 2008; Zhiwei Liu 2019). To make a counterargument for the Great Divergence, Peer Vries (2015) studies centralization, rationalization of bureaucracy, and most important, state capacity based on the size of its fiscal system.

45. A major difference is that ancient Chinese governments set nominal tax rates low, while the CCP sets them high. Although both lead to official discretionary power, asset mobility constrains government power in contemporary China.

46. See Bernstein and Lü 2003.

47. Susan Mann suggested (and correctly predicted) that for the problem of government predation of enterprise in the early 1980s, "a return to some form of liturgical governance in the marketplace may offer a solution" (1987, 213).

48. There was also a threat of war with the Soviet Union during the 1960s and 1970s.

49. Barry Naughton (1995) describes emerging from the state as "growing out of the plan." While David Stasavage (2016) tends to emphasize contingency and chance for the rising of "representation and consent" in Europe, he still uses size (small size reduces transaction costs for maintaining assemblies) and weak rulers (tax bargaining is necessary) as two structural variables.

50. Or as Skocpol (1979) puts it, world historical time.

51. According to Gerald Easter (2008), Russia experienced two stages of taxation. First, it used the elite-bargaining revenue strategy in which tax policy was manipulated in discrete deals made between agents of the central state and postcommunist elites. Later, it used purely coercive taxation.

52. Scott Gehlbach (2008) provides a different logic of representation through taxation. He argues that when the government is eager for fiscal revenue, local government will represent the economic sectors or enterprises that are easy to tax and neglect hard-to-tax sectors. The governments, in turn, formulate policies to promote these easy-to-tax sectors.

53. This differs from the view held by Besley and Persson (2011).

54. For a comprehensive discussion of why a revolutionary legacy empowers a party and promotes economic growth, see Bizzarro et al. 2018.

55. For a discussion of regional variations of government- and foreign-enterprise relationship in China, see L. Chen 2018.

56. The CCP's very recent strategy of "dual circulation" well reflects this challenge. Dual circulation is defined as a policy that "takes the domestic market as the mainstay while letting internal and external markets boost each other." Analysts have viewed the model as a viable solution for China to build up resilience against external shocks and share its opportunities for development with the rest of the world (*Xinhua* 2020).

57. Bruce Gilley claims that "the CCP will rationally continue to rely on inefficient and inequitable taxation because of the political costs of pursuing a modern taxation system" (2017, 452).

58. For a comprehensive discussion on labor law and industry upgrading, see Gallagher 2017.

59. According to Lou Jiwei, this comprehensive reform program includes the basic ideas of tax-sharing reform implemented in 1994 (cited in Jia and Zhao 2008, 334).

Donglian Xiao (2019) argues that the reasons for aborted reform include lack of consensus among national political leaders and interest conflicts among ministries.

60. There are many definitions of path dependence. An influential definition is provided by James Mahoney: "Path dependence characterizes specifically those historical sequences in which contingent events set into motion institutional patterns or event chains that have deterministic properties" (2000, 507).

61. Bruce Dickson discusses many possible types of "dictator's dilemma." He finds that "each element of the Party's survival strategy presents a dilemma," lists examples of such dilemmas, and acknowledges that "each of these steps presents a dilemma common to authoritarian regimes: rather than solidifying its hold on power, it may instead create greater challenges" (2016, 3). This logic also applies in analysis of the institution of taxation.

62. Minister of Finance Lou Jiwei (2013) admits that in the long run, rule of law and civil society are necessary for improving the fiscal and taxation systems.

63. The double balance theory integrates "a theory of economic behavior with a theory of political behavior by demonstrating how political systems manipulate the economy in order to sustain political stability, limit violence, and provide social order" (North, Wallis, and Weingast 2006, 4). Acemoglu and Robinson (2012) discuss extractive and inclusive institutions, two slightly different concepts of limited- and open-access orders. Besley and Persson (2011) define a similar concept of open-access order, "development clusters," as a strong correlation between types of government institutions, political repression or violence, and a country's level of income. They argue that there are three pillars necessary to achieve a development cluster: fiscal capacity, legal capacity, and lack of violence.

64. Weber's fiscal sociology's "most exciting and innovative part" is "his interpretation of the relationship between financing and type of domination" (Swedberg 1998, 61). Legal-rational domination is the only type of domination that is "indispensable to rational capitalism through its predictability and hostile to political capitalism" (69). A close comparison of Weber's typologies of domination and two social orders of North and colleagues will find that legal-rational domination is close to open-access order, while the other three types of domination (charismatic, traditional, and their combination as reflected in feudalism) are close to limited-access order.

65. This fiscal mechanism is also recognized by Lou Jiwei, who argues that "fiscal system reform is in a crucial position which connects economic reform, political reform and transition toward a civilized society" (2013, 320–321).

66. Jun Ma (2011) provides a good study of how relying on SOEs and "hidden taxes" has limited political change in China. For a theoretical debate on how a dominant party's access to public finance, especially from SOEs, strengthens its power, see Greene 2010.

67. For a discussion on how institutional uncertainty influences tax compliance in developed democratic countries, see Alm, Jackson, and McKee 1992.

68. This resonates with Besley and Persson (2011) on the ruler's need to invest in legal capacity to improve fiscal capacity.

69. Roy Bahl (1998) argues that to make fiscal decentralization work, a precondition is local autonomy (including but not limited to direct election of the local legislature and political leaders, the legislature's budgeting power and rights to borrow, and transparency).

70. Therefore, we can make a timing and sequence (Pierson 2004) argument by comparing transitional countries and the other two types.

71. We now introduce the term "(modern) fiscal state," another important term along with "tax state," which is characterized as having a consistent legal system and a consolidated monetary and fiscal regime under independent sovereignty; effective power centralization, professional taxation bureaucracy, and minimal tax farming; a broad tax base; and, more important, a credit-based fiscal system with sustainable credit tools (Dincecco 2011; W. He 2013; Stasavage 2011). There are some gaps between China's current tax state and the fiscal state, especially the rule of law and broad tax base. Given that the state directly owns and controls the bank system, credit tools are not very important for this book's analysis; therefore, the concept of fiscal state does not add much analytical leverage here.

72. Fiscal constitution theory is based on consensual taxation rather than coercive taxation (M. Moore 2008). Margaret Levi (1988) builds a theory of quasi-voluntary compliance. Some Chinese officers also agree with this. For example, Lou Jiwei, former minister of finance (March 2013–November 2016), argued that to further reform the taxation and fiscal system, China should empower the LPC with effective budgetary power and develop a civil society and democracy to monitor local government's taxation and expenditure (2013, 136–138).

73. The State Council responded by structural tax reduction, which slowed the rate of growth of national tax revenue in 2018 (8.3 percent) and 2019 (1 percent).

74. The merger of the SAT and LTB in June 2018 and assigning collection of social-insurance funding to the new SAT caused widespread concern about higher tax and nontax burdens for the private sector. To relieve private entrepreneurs' concerns (of both rising burdens and the rumor of nationalization of the private sector), Xi Jinping met many private entrepreneurs at the Great Hall of the People to signal credible commitment for developing the private sector. But this commitment is based on personal reputation rather than institutional arrangements.

References

Acemoglu, Daron. 2010. "Institutions, Factor Prices, and Taxation: Virtues of Strong States?" *American Economic Review* 100: 115–119.

Acemoglu, Daron, Simon Johnson, and James A. Robinson. 2002. "Reversal of Fortune: Geography and Institutions in the Making of the Modern World Income Distribution." *Quarterly Journal of Economics* 117: 1231–1294.

Acemoglu, Daron, Simon Johnson, and James A. Robinson. 2005. "Institutions as the Fundamental Cause of Long-Run Growth." In *Handbook of Economic Growth*, vol. 1A, edited by Philippe Aghion and Stephen Durlauf, 385–472. Amsterdam: Elsevier.

Acemoglu, Daron, and James A. Robinson. 2006. *Economic Origins of Dictatorship and Democracy*. New York: Cambridge University Press.

Acemoglu, Daron, and James A. Robinson. 2012. *Why Nations Fail: The Origins of Power, Prosperity, and Poverty*. New York: Crown Business.

Albertus, Michael, and Victor Menaldo. 2012. "Coercive Capacity and the Prospects for Democratization." *Comparative Politics* 44 (2): 151–169.

All-China Federation of Industry and Commerce. 2007a. *Bluebook of Non-state-owned Economy: 2005–2006* [Zhongguo minying qiye fazhan baogao]. [In Chinese.] Beijing: Sheke wenxian chubanshe.

All-China Federation of Industry and Commerce. 2007b. *The Large-Scale Survey on Private Enterprises in China: 1993–2006* [Zhongguo minying qiye fazhan baogao]. [In Chinese.] Beijing: China Industry and Commerce Association Press.

All-China Federation of Industry and Commerce. 2014. *Bluebook of Non-state-owned Economy: 2012–2013*. [In Chinese.] Beijing: Sheke wenxian chubanshe.

Alm, James, Betty Jackson, and Michael McKee. 1992. "Institutional Uncertainty and Taxpayer Compliance." *American Economic Review* 82 (1): 1018–1026.

Almond, Gabriel A., and G. Bingham Powell. 1966. *Comparative Politics: A Developmental Approach*. Boston: Little, Brown.

Ang, Yuen Yuen. 2016. *How China Escaped the Poverty Trap*. Ithaca, NY: Cornell University Press.

Ang, Yuen Yuen. 2017. "Do Weberian Bureaucracies Lead to Markets or Vice Versa? A Coevolutionary Approach to Development." In *States in the Developing World*, edited by Miguel Centeno, Atul Kohli, Deborah J. Yashar, and Dinsha Mistree, 280–306. Cambridge: Cambridge University Press.

Ansell, Ben W., and David Samuels. 2014. *Inequality and Democratization: An Elite-Competition Approach*. Cambridge: Cambridge University Press.

Ao, Daiya. 2005. *Siying Qiyezhu jieceng de Zhengzhi Canyu* [The private entrepreneur strata's political participation]. Guangzhou: Sun Yat-sen University Press.

Ardanaz, Martin, and Carlos Scartascini. 2013. "Inequality and Personal Income Taxation: The Origins and Effects of Legislative Malapportionment." *Comparative Political Studies* 46:1636–1663.

Art, David. 2012. "What Do We Know about Authoritarianism after Ten Years?" *Comparative Politics* 44:351–373.

Associated Press. 2012. "Ai Weiwei Loses Appeal against $2.4M Tax Fine." *The Guardian*, September 27. https://www.theguardian.com/world/2012/sep/27/ai-weiwei-loses-appeal-tax-fine.

Bahl, Roy. 1998. "Implementation Rules for Fiscal Decentralization." Paper presented at the International Seminar on Land Policy and Economic Development, Land Reform Training Institute, Taiwan, November 17.

Bao, Weimin and Yisheng Wang. 2002. "Yiwu Model: A Historical Analysis from Township Economy to Market Economy," [In Chinese] *Zhejiang Social Science*. 5: 147–151.

Beck, Hermann. 1995. *The Origins of the Authoritarian Welfare State in Prussia: Conservatives, Bureaucracy, and the Social Question, 1815–70*. Ann Arbor: University of Michigan Press.

Bellin, Eva. 2000. "Contingent Democrats: Industrialists, Labor, and the State in Late-Developing Countries." *World Politics* 52 (2): 175–205.

Bellin, Eva. 2003. "Reconsidering the Robustness of Authoritarianism in the Middle East: Lessons from the Arab Spring." *Comparative Politics* 44: 127–149.

Benjamin, Dwayne, Loren Brandt, John Giles, and Sangui Wang. 2008. "Income Inequality during China's Economic Transition." In *China's Great Economic Transformation*, edited by Loren Brandt and Thomas G. Rawski, 729–795. Cambridge: Cambridge University Press.

Berenson, Marc. 2018. *Taxes and Trust: From Coercion to Compliance in Poland, Russia and Ukraine*. Cambridge: Cambridge University Press.

Bernardi, Luigi, Angela Fraschini, and Parthasarathi Shome, eds. 2006. *Tax Systems and Tax Reforms in South and East Asia*. New York: Routledge.

Bernstein, Thomas P., and Xiaobo Lü. 2003. *Taxation without Representation in Contemporary Rural China*. Cambridge: Cambridge University Press.

Besley, Timothy, and Torsten Persson. 2011. *Pillars of Prosperity: The Political Economics of Development Clusters*. Princeton, NJ: Princeton University Press.

Besley, Timothy, and Torsten Persson. 2014. "The Causes and Consequences of Development Clusters: State Capacity, Peace and Income." *Annual Reviews of Economics* 6: 927–949.

Best China News. 2016. "Death Tax Advocates Li Weiguang No Longer Speak, the Death Tax Rate Does Not Exist?" *Best China News*, December 24. http://www.bestchinanews.com/Finance/7261.html.

Bian, Morris. 2015. "Explaining the Dynamics of Change: Transformation and Evolution of China's Public Economy through War, Revolution, and Peace, 1928–2008." In *State Capitalism, Institutional Adaptation, and the Chinese Miracle*, edited by Barry Naughton and Kellee S. Tsai, 201–222. New York: Cambridge University Press.

Bird, Richard M. 2015. "Improving Tax Administration in Developing Countries." *Journal of Tax Administration* 1 (1): 23–45.

Bizzarro, Fernando, John Gerring, Carl Henrik Knutsen, Allen Hicken, Michael Bernhard, Svend-Erik Skaaning, Michael Coppedge, and Staffan I. Lindberg. 2018. "Party Strength and Economic Growth." *World Politics* 70 (2): 275–320.

Blecher, Marc J., and Vivienne Shue. 1996. *Tethered Deer: Government and Economy in a Chinese County*. Stanford, CA: Stanford University Press.

Block, Fred. 1981. "The Fiscal Crisis of the Capitalist State." *Annual Reviews of Sociology* 7:1–21.

Boix, Carles. 2003. *Democracy and Redistribution*. Cambridge: Cambridge University Press.

Boone, Catherine. 2003. *Political Topographies of the African State: Territorial Authority and Institutional Choice*. New York: Cambridge University Press.

Boudreau, Vince. 2004. *Resisting Dictatorship: Repression and Protest in Southeast Asia*. Cambridge: Cambridge University Press.

Brancati, Dawn. 2014. "Democratic Authoritarianism: Origins and Effects." *Annual Review of Political Science* 17:1–14.

Brandt, Loren, Debin Ma, and Thomas G. Rawski. 2014. "From Divergence to Convergence: Reevaluating the History behind China's Economic Boom." *Journal of Economic Literature* 52 (1): 45–123.

Brandt, Loren, and Thomas G. Rawski, eds. 2008. *China's Great Economic Transformation*. New York: Cambridge University Press.

Brandt, Loren, and Eric Thun. 2015. "Competition and Upgrading in Chinese Industry." In *State Capitalism, Institutional Adaptation, and the Chinese Miracle*, edited by Barry Naughton and Kellee S. Tsai, 154–198. New York: Cambridge University Press.

Brautigam, Deborah, Odd-Helge Fjeldstad, and Mick Moore. 2008. *Taxation and State-Building in Developing Countries: Capacity and Consent*. New York: Cambridge University Press.

Breznitz, Dan, and Michael Murphree. 2011. *Run of the Red Queen: Government, Innovation, Globalization, and Economic Growth in China*. New Haven, CT: Yale University Press.

Bromley, Daniel W. 1989. *Economic Interests and Institutions: The Conceptual Foundations of Public Policy*. New York: Basil Blackwell.

Brook, Timothy. 1999. "Capitalism and the Writing of Modern History in China." In *China and Historical Capitalism: Genealogies of Sinological Knowledge*, edited by Timothy Brook and Gregory Blue, 110–157. New York: Cambridge University Press.

Brownlee, Jason. 2002. "Low Tide after the Third Wave: Exploring Politics under Authoritarianism." *Comparative Politics* 34 (4): 477–498.

Brownlee, Jason. 2007. *Authoritarianism in an Age of Democratization*. New York: Cambridge University Press.

Bueno de Mesquita, Bruce, Alastair Smith, and Randolph M. Siverson. 2003. *The Logic of Political Survival*. Cambridge, MA: MIT Press.

Cai, Hongbin, and Daniel Treisman. 2005. "Does Competition for Capital Discipline Governments? Decentralization, Globalization, and Public Policy." *American Economic Review* 95 (3): 817–830.

Cai, Hongbin, and Daniel Treisman. 2006. "Did Government Decentralization Cause China's Economic Miracle?" *World Politics* 58 (4): 505–535.

Cai, Yongshun. 2008. "Power Structure and Regime Resilience: Contentious Politics in China." *British Journal of Political Science* 38: 411–432.

Cai, Yongshun. 2015. *State and Agents in China: Disciplining Government Officials*. Stanford, CA: Stanford University Press.

Caixin. 2015. "Chinese Academy of Fiscal Sciences: The Growth Rate of Grassroots Government Revenue Is Declining." [In Chinese.] *Caixin*, December 22. http://finance.caixin.com/2015-12-22/100891201.html.

Caixin. 2016. "Records of Finance Minister Lou Jiwei's Replies to Journalists on 'Finance Work and Fiscal Reform.'" [In Chinese.] *Caixin*, March 7. https://topics.caixin.com/2016-03-07/100916895.html.

Campbell, Andrea. 2012. "Policy Makes Mass Politics." *Annual Review of Political Science* 15 (1): 333–351.

Campbell, John. 1993. "The State and Fiscal Sociology." *Annual Review of Sociology* 19: 163–185.

Campbell, John. 2010. "Institutional Reproduction and Change." In *The Oxford Handbook of Comparative Institutional Analysis*, edited by Glenn Morgan, John Campbell, Colin Crouch, Ove Kaj Pedersen, and Richard Whitley, 87–117. New York: Oxford University Press.

Cao, Zhenghan, and Jinchuan Shi. 2009. "Seizing the Initiative in Economic Growth: A Theoretical Hypothesis and Case Study of Chinese Local Government Strategies Responding to the Reformation of the Market Economy." [In Chinese.] *Chinese Sociology Review* 4:1–27.

CCP Central Committee. 2006. "Decision of the CCP Central Committee on Some Major Issues concerning Building Socialist Harmonious Society." [In Chinese.] http://www.gov.cn/govweb/gongbao/content/2006/content_453176.htm.

CCP Central Committee. 2014. "Decision of the Central Committee of the Communist Party of China on Some Major Issues concerning Comprehensively Deepening the Reform." China.org.cn, January 16. http://www.china.org.cn/china/third_plenary_session/2014-01/16/content_31212602.htm.

Centeno, Miguel Angel. 1994. "Between Rocky Democracies and Hard Markets: Dilemmas of the Double Transition." *Annual Review of Sociology* 20: 125–147.

Centeno, Miguel Angel, Atul Kohli, and Deborah Yashar. 2017. "Unpacking States in the Developing World: Capacity, Performance, and Politics." In *States in the Developing*

World, edited by Miguel Angel Centeno, Atul Kohli, and Deborah Yashar, 1–34. New York: Cambridge University Press.

Chan, Wellington K. K. 1977. *Merchants, Mandarins, and Modern Enterprise in Late Ch'ing China*. Cambridge, MA: Harvard University East Asian Research Center.

Chen, An. 1999. *Restructuring Political Power in China: Alliances and Opposition, 1978–1998*. Boulder, CO: Lynne Rienner.

Chen, Jie, and Bruce Dickson. 2008. "Allies of the State: Democratic Support and Regime Support among China's Private Entrepreneurs." *China Quarterly* 196: 780–804.

Chen, Ling. 2008. "Preferences, Institutions and Politics: Re-interrogating the Theoretical Lessons of Developmental Economies." *Review of International Political Economy* 15: 460–479.

Chen, Ling. 2018. *Manipulating Globalization: The Influence of Bureaucrats on Business in China*. Stanford, CA: Stanford University Press.

Chen, Xi. 2013. *Social Protest and Contentious Authoritarianism in China*. New York: Cambridge University Press.

Chen, Yongjie. 2016. "How Much Does the Private Sector Contribute to National Tax." [In Chinese.] *China Private Business [Zhongguo Minshang]* 2: 48–50.

Chen, Zhiyong, and Lili Chen. 2012. *A Study of the "Land Finance" Problems and Its Governance*. [In Chinese.] Beijing: Jingji Kexue Chubanshe.

Chen, Zhouxi. 2009. "Tax Inspection in Wenzhou." [In Chinese.] *Jingji Guanchabao*, September 14, p. 9.

China Business News. 2010. "The First LPC Deputy's Working Office Was Canceled (by the NPC Standing Committee)." *China Business News (diyi caijing ribao)*, August 31.

China Coal Mine Annals Editorial Team. 1999. *China Coal Mine Annals. [Zhongguo Meitan Zhi]*. Beijing: Meitan gongye chubanshe.

China Daily Online. 2011. "China's NPC to Reconsider Individual Income Tax Law." [In Chinese.] *People's Daily Online*, April 24. http://www.chinadaily.com.cn/china/2011-04/25/content_12386980.htm.

China Land Surveying and Planning Institute. 2006. "Local Governments' Land Use Strategy." [In Chinese.] *China Land [Zhongguo Tudi]* 7: 8–10.

China News Weekly. 2011. "An Era of 'Tax Burden Perception': The Waking of Taxpayers." [In Chinese.] *China News Weekly*, January 7. http://news.ifeng.com/c/7fZFVeLVwxy.

China Times. 2015. "Macro-tax Burden Reaches 37% in China, SMEs Are Overburdened." [In Chinese.] *Sina*, August 22. http://finance.sina.com.cn/china/20150822/034323035817.shtml.

China Youth Daily. 2010. "Two Peasant Entrepreneurs Became People's Congress Deputies by Bribing the Prefecture Party Secretary in Caohu, Anhui." [In Chinese.] January 8. https://xian.qq.com/a/20100108/000022.htm.

China Youth Daily. 2011. "The Former Party Secretary of Chenzhou Prefecture's Road to Prison: Being an Official Benefits You for a Short Term, Having Enough Money Benefits You Lifelong." [In Chinese.] http://www.zznews.gov.cn/news/2011/0114/43472.shtml [site no longer available].

Cho, Young Nam. 2002. "From 'Rubber Stamps' to 'Iron Stamps': The Emergence of Chinese Local People's Congresses as Supervisory Powerhouses." *China Quarterly* 171 (3): 724–740.

Cho, Young Nam. 2010. *Local People's Congresses in China: Development and Transition.* Cambridge: Cambridge University Press.

Ch'u, Tung-tsu. 1988. *Local Government in China under the Ch'ing.* Cambridge, MA: Council on East Asian Studies, Harvard University.

Chu, Ren. 2009. "Rethinking Legal Regulation of Coal Mine Disasters." Working paper, Shanxi Academy of Social Science.

Collier, Ruth Berins, and David Collier. 1991. *Shaping the Political Arena: Critical Junctures, the Labor Movement, and Regime Dynamics in Latin America.* Princeton, NJ: Princeton University Press.

Confucius. 1971. *Confucian Analects, "The Great Learning" and "The Doctrine of the Mean."* Translated by James Legge. New York: Dover.

Cook, Steven. 2007. *Ruling but Not Governing: The Military and Political Development in Egypt, Algeria, and Turkey.* Baltimore: Johns Hopkins University Press.

County Warm River Committee of Finance and Economics. 2007. "Improve Nontax Revenue Management, Promote Regional Economic Development." December. County Government Archive.

County Warm River People's Congress Standing Committee. 1992. Records of the Eighth Meeting. County Government Archive.

Crouch, Colin. 2010. "Complementarity." In *The Oxford Handbook of Comparative Institutional Analysis*, edited by Glenn Morgan, John Campbell, Colin Crouch, Ove Kaj Pedersen, and Richard Whitley, 117–138. New York: Oxford University Press.

Cui, Wei. 2015. "Administrative Decentralization and Tax Compliance." *University of Toronto Law Journal* 65 (3): 186–238.

Curtis, James L. 1989. "Review of *Of Rule and Revenue*." *American Political Science Review* 83 (4): 1424–1426.

Dahl, Robert Alan. 1998. *On Democracy.* New Haven, CT: Yale University Press.

Dai, Maolin, and Xiaoguang Zhao. 2011. *Biography of Gao Gang.* [In Chinese.] Xi'an: Shanxi Renmin Press.

Deng, Xiaoping. 1993. *Selected Works of Deng Xiaoping.* Vol. 3. [In Chinese.] Beijing: Renmin Press.

Deng, Yanhua, and Kevin J. O'Brien. 2013. "Relational Repression in China: Using Social Ties to Demobilize Protesters." *China Quarterly* 215: 533–552.

Diamond, Larry Jay. 1997. *Consolidating the Third Wave Democracies.* Baltimore: Johns Hopkins University Press.

Diamond, Larry Jay, and Marc F. Plattner. 1996. *The Global Resurgence of Democracy.* Baltimore: Johns Hopkins University Press.

Diamond, Larry Jay, and Marc F. Plattner, eds. 2001. *The Global Divergence of Democracies.* Baltimore: Johns Hopkins University Press.

Dickson, Bruce J. 2008. *Wealth into Power: The Communist Party's Embrace of China's Private Sector*. New York: Cambridge University Press.

Dickson, Bruce J. 2016. *Dictator's Dilemma: The Chinese Communist Party's Strategy for Survival*. Oxford: Oxford University Press.

Dimitrov, Martin K. 2013. *Why Communism Did Not Collapse: Understanding Authoritarian Regime Resilience in Asia and Europe*. New York: Cambridge University Press.

Dincecco, Mark. 2011. *Political Transformations and Public Finances: Europe, 1650–1913*. New York: Cambridge University Press.

Dincecco, Mark. 2015. "The Rise of Effective States in Europe." *Journal of Economic History* 75 (3): 910–918.

Ding, Xueliang. 1994. "Institutional Amphibiousness and the Transition from Communism." *British Journal of Political Science* 24 (3): 293–318.

Duara, Prasenjit. 1988. *Culture, Power, and the State: Rural North China, 1900–1942*. Stanford, CA: Stanford University Press.

Easter, Gerald. 2008. "Capacity, Consent and Tax Collection in Post-communist States." In *Taxation and State-Building in Developing Countries*, edited by Deborah Brautigam, Odd-Helge Fjeldstad, and Mick Moore, 64–88. Cambridge: Cambridge University Press.

Economic Daily. 2020. "Big Tigers Hunted: Ministry and Province-Level Officials Investigated since the 18th Party Congress." [In Chinese.] *Economic Daily*, November 3. http://district.ce.cn/newarea/sddy/201403/03/t20140303_2403198.shtml.

Economic Daily. 2021. "After the 18th and 19th National Congress of the Communist Party of China, the List of Senior Officials at the Provincial and Ministerial Level and above Is the Most in Shanxi." [In Chinese.] *Economic Daily*, January 26. http://district.ce.cn/newarea/sddy/201410/03/t20141003_3638299.shtml.

Economic Information Daily. 2015. "Housing Downturn Led to Local Governments' Fiscal Deficit: A Few Prefectures and Counties Fail to Pay Salaries." [In Chinese.] *Sina*, December 24. http://news.sina.com.cn/c/nd/2015-12-24/doc-ifxmxxst0371678.shtml.

Elias, Norbert. 1982. *The Civilizing Process*. Oxford: Blackwell.

Elster, Jon. 2000. "Rational Choice History: A Case of Excessive Ambition." *American Political Science Review* 94 (3): 685–695.

Ertman, Thomas. 1997. *Birth of the Leviathan: Building States and Regimes in Medieval and Early Modern Europe*. New York: Cambridge University Press.

Escribà-Folch, Abel. 2012. "Authoritarian Responses to Foreign Pressure: Spending, Repression, and Sanctions." *Comparative Political Studies* 45 (6): 683–713.

Evans, Peter B. 1995. *Embedded Autonomy: States and Industrial Transformation*. Princeton, NJ: Princeton University Press.

Evans, Peter B., and James Rauch. 1999. "Bureaucracy and Growth: A Cross-national Analysis of the Effects of 'Weberian' State Structures on Economic Growth." *American Sociological Review* 64 (5): 748–765.

Evans, Peter B., Dietrich Rueschemeyer, and Theda Skocpol, eds. 1985. *Bringing the State Back In*. New York: Cambridge University Press.

Fairbanks, Charles H., Jr. 1999. "The Feudalization of the State." *Journal of Democracy* 10 (2): 47–53.

Fan, Peng, Weihua Wang, and Shaoguang Wang. 2009. "The Trajectory and Logic of State Coercive Capacity Building." [In Chinese.] *Jingji Shehui Tizhi Bijiao* 5: 33–43.

Feuerwerker, Albert. 1958. *China's Early Industrialization: Sheng Hsuan-huai (1844–1916) and Mandarin Enterprise*. Cambridge, MA: Harvard University Press.

Fewsmith, Joseph. 2001. *Elite Politics in Contemporary China*. Armonk, NY: M. E. Sharpe.

Flora, Peter, and Jens Alber. 1981. "Modernization, Democratization, and the Development of Welfare States in Western Europe." In *The Development of Welfare States in Europe and America*, edited by Peter Flora and Arnold Heidenheimer, 37–80. London: Routledge.

Forrat, Natalia. 2012. "The Authoritarian Welfare State: A Marginalized Concept." Buffett Center Comparative-Historical Social Science Working Paper No. 12-005. https://arch.library.northwestern.edu/downloads/mp48sd02h?locale=en.

Fu, Diana. 2017. *Mobilizing without the Masses: Control and Contention in China*. New York: University Printing House.

Fu, Yiling. 2008. *Collections of Papers on Social Economic History of Ming and Qing Dynasties*. [In Chinese.] Beijing: Zhonghua shuju.

Gallagher, Mary E. 2017. *Authoritarian Legality in China: Law, Workers, and the State*. New York: Cambridge University Press.

Gallagher, Mary, and Jonathan K. Hanson. 2009. "Coalitions, Carrots, and Sticks: Economic Inequality and Authoritarian States." *PS: Political Science and Politics* 42: 667–672.

Gallagher, Mary, and Jonathan K. Hanson. 2013. "Authoritarian Survival, Resilience, and the Selectorate Theory." In *Why Communism Did Not Collapse*, edited by Martin K. Dimitrov, 185–204. Cambridge: Cambridge University Press.

Gandhi, Jennifer. 2008. *Political Institutions under Dictatorship*. New York: Cambridge University Press.

Gandhi, Jennifer, and Ellen Lust-Okar. 2009. "Elections under Authoritarianism." *Annual Review of Political Science* 12: 403–522.

Gandhi, Jennifer, and Adam Przeworski. 2007. "Authoritarian Institutions and the Survival of Autocrats." *Comparative Political Studies* 40 (11): 1279–1301.

Gao, Qin. 2010. "Redistributive Nature of the Chinese Social Benefit System: Progressive or Regressive?" *China Quarterly* 201:1–19.

Geddes, Barbara. 1994. *Politician's Dilemma: Building State Capacity in Latin America*. Berkeley: University of California Press.

Geddes, Barbara. 1999. "What Do We Know about Democratization after Twenty Years?" *Annual Review of Political Science* 2: 115–144.

Gehlbach, Scott. 2008. *Representation through Taxation: Revenue, Politics, and Development in Postcommunist States*. New York: Cambridge University Press.

George, Alexander L., and Andrew Bennett. 2005. "Comparative Methods: Controlled Comparison and Within-Case Analysis." In *Case Studies and Theory Development in the Social Sciences*, edited by Alexander L. George and Andrew Bennett, 67–124. Cambridge, MA: MIT Press.

Gerschenkron, Alexander. 1962. *Economic Backwardness in Historical Perspective: A Book of Essays*. Cambridge, MA: Belknap Press of Harvard University Press.

Gilley, Bruce. 2017. "Taxation and Authoritarian Resilience." *Journal of Contemporary China* 26:452–464.

Ginsburg, Tom, and Tamir Moustafa. 2008. *Rule by Law: The Politics of Courts in Authoritarian Regimes*. New York: Cambridge University Press.

Goldscheid, Rudolf. 1994. "A Sociological Approach to Problems of Public Finance." In *Classics in the Theory of Public Finance*, edited by Richard Musgrave and Alan Peacock, 202–213. New York: St. Martin's.

Goldstone, Jack A. 1991. *Revolution and Rebellion in the Early Modern World*. Berkeley: University of California Press.

Gould, Andrew, and Peter J. Baker. 2002. "Democracy and Taxation." *Annual Review of Political Science* 5: 87–110.

Greene, Kenneth F. 2007. *Why Dominant Parties Lose: Mexico's Democratization in Comparative Perspective*. Cambridge: Cambridge University Press.

Greene, Kenneth F. 2010. "The Political Economy of Authoritarian Single-Party Dominance." *Comparative Political Studies* 43: 807–834.

Greif, Avner. 2006. "The Birth of Impersonal Exchange." *Journal of Economic Perspectives* 20 (2): 221–236.

Greif, Avner, and David Laitin. 2004. "A Theory of Endogenous Institutional Change." *American Political Science Review* 98: 633–652.

Greitens, Sheena Chestnut. 2016. *Dictators and Their Secret Police: Coercive Institutions and State Violence*. New York: Cambridge University Press.

Guan, Zhong. 1998. *Guanzi: Political, Economic, and Philosophical Essays from Early China*. Translated by Rickett Allyn. Princeton, NJ: Princeton University Press.

Guo, Jigang. 2007. "A Study of Deputies in Local People's Congress in China." PhD diss., National University of Singapore.

Guo, Xuezhi. 2012. *China's Security State: Philosophy, Evolution, and Politics*. New York: Cambridge University Press.

Guo, Yixin. 2012. "Disaggregating the Middle Class's Tax Burdens." [In Chinese.] *21st Century Economic Report*, March 3, p. T03.

Grzymala-Busse, Anna. 2011. "Time Will Tell? Temporality and the Analysis of Causal Mechanisms." *Comparative Political Studies* 44 (9): 1267–1297.

Haggard, Stephan, and Robert R. Kaufman. 1995. *The Political Economy of Democratic Transitions*. Princeton, NJ: Princeton University Press.

Haggard, Stephan, and Robert R. Kaufman. 2012. "Inequality and Regime Change: Democratic Transitions and the Stability of Democratic Rule." *American Political Science Review* 106 (3): 495–516.

Hall, Peter A., and David W. Soskice. 2001. *Varieties of Capitalism: The Institutional Foundations of Comparative Advantage*. New York: Oxford University Press.

Hamilton, Gary, and Nicole Woolsey Biggart. 1988. "Market, Culture, and Authority: A Comparative Analysis of Management and Organization in the Far East." In "Organizations and Institutions: Sociological and Economic Approaches to the Analysis of Social Structure," supplement to *American Journal of Sociology* 94: S52–S94.

Harding, Harry. 1981. *Organizing China: The Problem of Bureaucracy, 1949–1976*. Stanford, CA: Stanford University Press.

He, Junzhi. 2010. "Independent Candidates in China's Local People's Congresses: A Typology." *Journal of Contemporary China* 19 (64): 311–333.

He, Ping. 2004. "The Mechanisms of How the Incomplete Fiscal System Destroys Society in the Qing Dynasty." [In Chinese.] *Xueshu Yanjiu* [*Academic Research*] 6: 89–94.

He, Wenkai. 2013. *Paths toward the Modern Fiscal State: England, Japan, and China*. Cambridge, MA: Harvard University Press.

Heilmann, Sebastian, and Elizabeth J. Perry, eds. 2011. *Mao's Invisible Hand: The Political Foundations of Adaptive Governance in China*. Cambridge, MA: Harvard University Asia Center.

Hellman, Joel. 1998. "Winners Take All: The Politics of Partial Reform in Postcommunist Transitions." *World Politics* 50 (2): 203–234.

Helmke, Gretchen, and Steven Levitsky. 2004. "Informal Institutions and Comparative Politics: A Research Agenda." *Perspectives on Politics* 2 (4): 725–740.

Herbst, Jeffrey Ira. 2000. *States and Power in Africa: Comparative Lessons in Authority and Control*. Princeton, NJ: Princeton University Press.

Hess, Steve. 2013. *Authoritarian Landscapes: Popular Mobilization and the Institutional Sources of Resilience in Nondemocracies*. New York: Springer.

Heurlin, Christopher. 2016. *Responsive Authoritarianism in China: Land, Protests, and Policy Making*. Cambridge: Cambridge University Press.

Hicken, Allen. 2011. "Clientelism." *Annual Review of Political Science* 14: 289–310.

Holland, Alisha. 2016. "Forbearance." *American Political Science Review* 110 (2): 232–246.

Holland, Alisha. 2017. *Forbearance as Redistribution: The Politics of Informal Welfare in Latin America*. New York: Cambridge University Press.

Holmberg, Soren, Bo Rothstein, and Naghmeh Nasiritousi. 2009. "Quality of Government: What You Get." *Annual Review of Political Science* 12: 135–161.

Hou, Yue. 2019. *The Private Sector in Public Office: Selective Property Rights in China*. New York: Cambridge University Press.

Hsiao, Kung-chüan. 1967. *Rural China: Imperial Control in the Nineteenth Century*. Seattle: University of Washington Press.

Hu, Jingguo. 2011. "The Property List of a Patrol Police Captain: 27 Apartments and 20 Gambling Houses." [In Chinese.] *Banyuetan* 2. http://news.sohu.com/20110223/n2 79489691.shtml.

Hu, Xiaoguang. 2001. "The Collapse of 'Empire Black Pig.'" [In Chinese.] *Modern Wave* [*Shidaichao*] 10: 45–48.

Huang, Guoxin. 2019. *State and Market: Salt Trade under Ming and Qing Dynasties.* [In Chinese.] Beijing: Zhonghua shuju.

Huang, Mengfu, ed. 2010. *A History of Chinese Private Economy: A Record.* [In Chinese.] Beijing: Zhonghua gongshang lianhe chubanshe.

Huang, Weiping, ed. 2004. *Research Report on Contemporary Chinese Politics* [*Dangdai zhongguo zhengzhi yanjiu baogao*]. Beijing: Shehui kexue chubanshe.

Huang, Xian. 2015. "Four Worlds of Welfare: Understanding Subnational Variation in Chinese Social Health Insurance." *China Quarterly* 222:449–474.

Huang, Yasheng. 1996. *Inflation and Investment Controls in China: The Political Economy of Central-Local Relations during the Reform Era.* New York: Cambridge University Press.

Huang, Yasheng. 2008. *Capitalism with Chinese Characteristics: Entrepreneurship and the State.* New York: Cambridge University Press.

Huang, Zhijie. 2008. "The Private Entrepreneurs Buy Off Votes in the Prefecture PC Election." *Oriental Outlook Weekly* [*Liaowang Dongfang Zhoukan*]. http://hn.cnr.cn/xwzx/gngj/200802/t20080218_504706959.html.

Huang, Zhijie. 2010. "Two Bribed the Prefecture Party Secretary and Became People's Congress Deputies." *China Youth Daily*, January 8. https://xian.qq.com/a/20100108/000022.htm.

Huaxia. 2016. "Ma Yun Talks on Four Principles of Government Business Relationships." [In Chinese.] *Huaxia*, May 9. http://www.huaxia.com/tslj/rdrw/2016/05/4834113_2.html.

Huntington, Samuel. 1968. *Political Order in Changing Societies.* New Haven, CT: Yale University Press.

Huntington, Samuel. 1991. *The Third Wave: Democratization in the Late Twentieth Century.* Norman: University of Oklahoma Press.

Huntington, Samuel, and Clement Moore. 1970. *Authoritarian Politics in Modern Society: The Dynamics of Established One-Party Systems.* New York: Basic Books.

Ji, Ye. 2010. "Separating Power to Chop off the Black 'Benefit Chain' [*Quanli fenli, zhanduan heise liyilian*]." *People's Daily*, November 18, p. 11.

Jia, Kang, and Wei Liu. 2015. *Transformation of Fiscal and Taxation System.* [In Chinese.] Hangzhou: Zhejiang University Press.

Jia, Kang, and Quanhou Zhao, eds. 2008. *China's Fiscal System from 1978 to 2008: Retrospection and Prospect* [*Zhongguo caishui tizhi gaige 30 nian: Huigu yu zhanwang*]. [In Chinese.] Beijing: Renmin Press.

Jiang, Yuliang. 2012. "Reflection of Democratic Legislature Practices in China: The 'Open-Door Legislation' in Individual Income Tax as an Opportunity." [In Chinese.] *Knowledge Economy* [*Zhishi jingji*] 23:5 3–54.

Jiang, Zemin. 2006. *Selected Works of Jiang Zemin.* Vol. 3. [In Chinese.] Beijing: Renmin Press.

Jiefangjun bao. 2016. "What Is Real Loyalty?" [In Chinese.] *Jiefangjun bao*, December 22, p. 1.

Jin, Jing, and Heng-fu Zou. 2005. "Fiscal Decentralization, Revenue and Expenditure Assignments, and Growth in China." *Journal of Asian Economics* 16 (6): 1047–1064.

Jin, Xin. 2008. *Selective Works of Jinxin on Taxation [Jinxin shuishou wenxuan]*. [In Chinese.] Beijing: China Taxation Press.

Kaufmann Daniel, Aart Kraay, and Pablo Zoido-Lobaton. 1999. "Governance Matters." World Bank Policy Research Working Paper 2196. http://documents1.worldbank.org/curated/en/665731468739470954/pdf/multi-page.pdf.

Kennedy, John. 2007. "From the Fee-for-Tax Reform to the Abolition of Agricultural Taxes: The Impact on Township Governments in Northwest China." *The China Quarterly* 189: 43–59.

King, Gary, Jennifer Pan, and Margaret E. Roberts. 2013. "How Censorship in China Allows Government Criticism but Silences Collective Expression." *American Political Science Review* 107 (2): 1–18.

Kiser, Edgar, and Joshua Kane. 2001. "Revolution and State Structure: The Bureaucratization of Tax Administration in Early Modern England and France." *American Journal of Sociology* 107: 183–223.

Kiser, Edgar, and Steven Karceski. 2017. "Political Economy of Taxation." *Annual Review of Political Science* 20: 6.1–6.18.

Kiser, Edgar, and Joachim Schneider. 1994. "Bureaucracy and Efficiency: An Analysis of Taxation in Early Modern Prussia." *American Sociological Review* 59: 187–204.

Knight, Jack. 1992. *Institutions and Social Conflict*. New York: Cambridge University Press.

Knight, John. 1995. "Price Scissors and Intersectional Resource Transfers: Who Paid for Industrialization in China?" *Oxford Economic Papers* 47 (1): 117–152.

Knutsen, Carl Henrik, and Håvard Mokleiv Nygård. 2015. "Institutional Characteristics and Regime Survival: Why Are Semi-democracies Less Durable than Autocracies and Democracies?" *American Journal of Political Science* 59 (3): 656–670.

Kohli, Atul. 2004. *State-Directed Development: Political Power and Industrialization in the Global Periphery*. Cambridge: Cambridge University Press.

König, Thomas, George Tsebelis, and Marc Debus. 2011. *Reform Processes and Policy Change: Veto Players and Decision-Making in Modern Democracies*. New York: Springer.

Kornai, János. 1992. *The Socialist System: The Political Economy of Communism*. Princeton, NJ: Princeton University Press.

Kuhn, Philip A. 2002. *Origins of the Modern Chinese State*. Stanford, CA: Stanford University Press.

Kwan, Man Bun. 2001. *The Salt Merchants of Tianjin: State-Making and Civil Society in Late Imperial China*. Honolulu: University of Hawai'i Press.

Lai, Alexis. 2012. "Chinese Dissident Artist Ai Weiwei Loses Tax Evasion Appeal." *CNN*, September 27. https://edition.cnn.com/2012/09/27/world/asia/china-ai-weiwei-tax-evasion-appeal.

Landry, Pierre F. 2008. *Decentralized Authoritarianism in China: The Communist Party's Control of Local Elites in the Post-Mao Era*. Cambridge: Cambridge University Press.

Landry, Pierre, Xiaobo Lü, and Haiyan Duan. 2018. "Does Performance Matter? Evaluating Political Selection along the Chinese Administrative Ladder." *Comparative Political Studies* 51 (8): 1074–1105.

Lee, Ching Kwan. 1998. *Gender and the South China Miracle: Two Worlds of Factory Women*. Berkeley: University of California Press.

Lee, Ching Kwan. 2007. *Against the Law: Labor Protests in China's Rustbelt and Sunbelt*. Berkeley: University of California Press.

Lee, Ching Kwan, and Yonghong Zhang. 2013. "The Power of Instability: Unraveling the Microfoundations of Bargained Authoritarianism in China." *American Journal of Sociology* 118 (6): 1475–1508.

Legal Weekly. 2021. "Cases Issued by the Judicial Organs Strictly Prohibit Criminal Means to Intervene in Civil Economic Disputes." [In Chinese.] January 14. http://m.legalweekly.cn/qyyf/2021-01/14/content_8406687.html.

Lessmann, Christian, and Gunther Markwardt. 2010. "One Size Fits All? Decentralization, Corruption, and the Monitoring of Bureaucrats." *World Development* 38 (4): 631–646.

Levi, Margaret. 1988. *Of Rule and Revenue*. Berkeley: University of California Press.

Levitsky, Steven, and Lucan A. Way. 2010. *Competitive Authoritarianism: Hybrid Regimes after the Cold War*. New York: Cambridge University Press.

Levitsky, Steven R., and Lucan A. Way. 2012. "Beyond Patronage: Violent Struggle, Ruling Party Cohesion, and Authoritarian Durability." *Perspectives on Politics* 10: 869–889.

Li, Bojun. 2010. "PC Deputies Don't Need Deputy Office Is Determined by Our National Conditions [Renda Daibiao Bu She Gongzuoshi shi you Woguo Guoqing Jueding de]." [In Chinese.] *Xinhua*, September 28. http://news.xinhuanet.com/legal/2010-09/28/c_12615229.htm [site no longer available].

Li, Cheng. 2012. "The End of the CCP's Resilient Authoritarianism? A Tripartite Assessment of Shifting Power in China." *China Quarterly* 211: 595–623.

Li, Hongbin, and Li'an Zhou. 2005. "Political Turnover and Economic Performance: The Incentive Role of Personnel Control in China." *Journal of Public Economics* 89: 1743–1762.

Li, Lihui. 2017. "Ministry of Finance Staff Reveals Four Tactics of Fiscal Data Fraud." *People's Daily*, January 22. https://www.sohu.com/a/124948272_611346.

Li, Qiang. 2001. "State Re-building in a Post-totalitarian State." [In Chinese.] *Strategy and Management [Zhanlue yu Guanli]* 6: 83–86.

Li, Weiguang, 2011. "The Wakening of Taxpayer Consciousness." [In Chinese.] *Southern Weekend*, November 5. http://www.infzm.com/content/64472.

Li, Weiguang, Lingzhen Yao, Shuguang Zhang, Tianyong Zhou, Zhengwen Shi, and Changdong Zhang. 2018. "Real Estate Tax: The New Departure Tax Reform in

China: China's Tax Transformation and Local Governance Innovation." [In Chinese.] *Exploration and Free Views* 3: 4–15, 17–27, 109.

Li, Weiye, and Louis Putterman. 2008. "Reforming China's SOEs: An Overview." *Comparative Economic Studies* 50: 353–380.

Liao, Haiqing. 2009. "Office of Weiwen Comes to Front." [In Chinese.] *Nanfengchuang* 8: 44–46.

Lieberman, Evan S. 2003. *Race and Regionalism in the Politics of Taxation in Brazil and South Africa*. New York: Cambridge University Press.

Lieberthal, Kenneth. 1992. "Introduction: The 'Fragmented Authority' Model and Its Limitations." In *Bureaucracy, Politics, and Decision Making in Post-Mao China*, edited by Kenneth Lieberthal and David M. Lampton, 1–32. Berkeley: University of California Press.

Lin, Yunhui. 2011. *Moving toward Socialism: The Transformation of China's Economy and Society (1953–1955)*. [In Chinese.] Hong Kong: Chinese University of Hong Kong Press.

Linz, Juan J. 1975. "Totalitarian and Authoritarian Regimes." In *Handbook of Political Science: Macropolitical Theory*, vol. 3, edited by Fred Greenstein and Nelson W. Polsby, 175–412. Boston: Addison-Wesley Educational Publishers.

Linz, Juan J. 2000. *Totalitarian and Authoritarian Regimes*. Boulder, CO: Lynne Rienner.

Linz, Juan J., and Alfred C. Stepan. 1978. *The Breakdown of Democratic Regimes*. Baltimore: Johns Hopkins University Press.

Linz, Juan J., and Alfred C. Stepan. 1996. *Problems of Democratic Transition and Consolidation: Southern Europe, South America, and Post-communist Europe*. Baltimore: Johns Hopkins University Press.

Lipset, Seymour Martin. 1959. "Some Social Requisites of Democracy: Economic Development and Political Legitimacy." *American Political Science Review* 53: 69–105.

Lipsky, Michael. 1980. *Street-Level Bureaucracy: Dilemmas of the Individual in Public Services*. New York: Russell Sage Foundation.

Liu, Jiayi. 2008. "Audit Report on the Central Government Budget Implementation and Other Fiscal Income and Expenditure of Year 2007." [In Chinese.] August 27. http://www.gov.cn/gzdt/2008-08/28/content_1081292.htm.

Liu, Jianwen, and Ying Geng. 2015. "Exercise the Delegated Taxation Legislature Power according to Law: Reflections and Constructions." [In Chinese.] *Guojia Xingzheng Xueyuan Xuebao* 5: 31–35.

Liu, Shangxi, and Zhihua Fu. 2018. *The Fiscal Code of China's Development (1978–2018)*. [In Chinese.] Beijing: Renmin Press.

Liu, Shouying, Zhifeng Wang, Weifan Zhang, and Xuefeng Xiong. 2020. "The Exhaustion of China's 'Land-Driven Development' Mode: An Analysis Based on Threshold Regression." [In Chinese.] *Management World* 36 (6): 80–92, 119, 246.

Liu, Yu, and Dingding Chen. 2012. "Why China Will Democratize." *Washington Quarterly* 35 (1): 41–63.

Liu, Zhiwei. 2019. *Tribute-Levy System and Market: Collections of Papers on Social Eco-*

nomic History of Ming and Qing Dynasties. [In Chinese.] Beijing: Chinese Book Company.

Liu, Zuo. 2000. *China's Tax System from 1949 to 1999*. [In Chinese.] Beijing: China Taxation Press.

Liu, Zuo. 2014. *China's Tax System Reform under Socialist Market Economy (from 1992 to 2013)*. [In Chinese.] Beijing: China Taxation Press.

Logan, John R., and Harvey L. Molotch. 1987. *Urban Fortunes: The Political Economy of Place*. Berkeley: University of California Press.

Lorentzen, Peter. 2013. "China's Strategic Censorship." *American Journal of Political Science* 58: 402–414.

Lou, Jiwei, ed. 1995. *Macro-economic Reform: Background, Vision, Plan, and Practice*. [In Chinese.] Beijing: Yiye Guanli Press.

Lou, Jiwei. 2008. *A Collection of Lou Jiwei's Works on Economic Reform*. [In Chinese.] Beijing: Zhongguo fazhan chubanshe.

Lou, Jiwei. 2011. "China Needs to Further Reform Six Systems." [In Chinese.] *Bijiao* [*Comparison*] 6:1–8.

Lou, Jiwei. 2013. *Rethinking China's Intergovernmental Fiscal Relationships*. [In Chinese.] Beijing: Zhongguo caizheng jingji chubanshe.

Lu, Lijun. 1999. "The Rise of 'China Commodity Market' and the Yiwu Model of Rural Market Economy Development," [In Chinese] *Jingji Shehui Tizhi Bijiao* 1: 71–79.

Lu, Lijun and Zuqiang Wang. 2008. *Professional Market: The Evolution of Regional Market* [Zhuanye Shichang: Difangxing Shichang de Yanjin]. Shanghai: Gezhi Chubanshe. Lü, Xiaobo, and Pierre Landry. 2014. "Show Me the Money: Inter-jurisdiction Political Competition and Fiscal Extraction in China." *American Political Science Review* 108 (3): 706–722.

Lü, Xiaobo. 2014. "Social Policy and Regime Legitimacy: The Effects of Education Reform in China." *American Political Science Review* 108 (2): 423–437.

Luong, Pauline Jones, and Erika Weinthal. 2006. "Rethinking the Resource Curse: Ownership Structure, Institutional Capacity, and Domestic Constraints." *Annual Review of Political Science* 9: 241–263.

Ma, Debin, and Jared Rubin. 2019. "The Paradox of Power: Principal-Agent Problems and Administrative Capacity in Imperial China (and Other Absolutist Regimes)." *Journal of Comparative Economics* 47 (2): 277–294.

Ma, Jun. 2011. "Toward a Tax State: A Study of Fiscal State Transition in China." [In Chinese.] *Jilin University Journal* 1: 18–30.

Ma, Jun. 2013. "Debt Risks in Local China." *Australia Journal of Public Administration* 72 (3): 278–292.

Ma, Jun, and Muhua Lin. 2015. "The Power of the Purse of Local People's Congresses in China: Controllable Contestation under Bureaucratic Negotiation." *China Quarterly* 223: 680–701.

Machiavelli, Niccolò. 2005. *The Prince*. Translated by Peter Bondanella. Oxford: Oxford University Press.

Magaloni, Beatriz. 2006. *Voting for Autocracy: Hegemonic Party Survival and Its Demise in Mexico.* New York: Cambridge University Press.

Magaloni, Beatriz, and Ruth Kricheli. 2010. "Political Order and One-Party Rule." *Annual Review of Political Science* 13: 123–143.

Mahoney, James. 2000. "Path Dependence in Historical Sociology." *Theory and Society* 29 (4): 507–548.

Mahoney, James. 2003. "Knowledge Accumulation in Comparative Historical Analysis: The Case of Democracy and Authoritarianism." In *Comparative Historical Analysis in the Social Sciences,* edited by James Mahoney and Dietrich Rueschemeyer, 131–174. Cambridge: Cambridge University Press.

Mahoney, James, and Kathleen Ann Thelen. 2010. *Explaining Institutional Change: Ambiguity, Agency, and Power.* New York: Cambridge University Press.

Manion, Melanie. 2009. "Chinese Congressional Representation as an Institution." Paper presented at the 2009 annual meeting of the American Political Science Association, Toronto, Canada, September 2–5.

Manion, Melanie. 2014. "Authoritarian Parochialism: Local Congressional Representation in China." *China Quarterly* 218: 311–338.

Manion, Melanie. 2016. *Information for Autocrats: Representation in Chinese Local Congresses.* New York: Cambridge University Press.

Manion, Melanie. 2017. "'Good Types' in Authoritarian Elections: The Selectoral Connection in Chinese Local Congresses." *Comparative Political Studies* 50 (3): 362–394.

Mann, Michael. 1986. *The Sources of Social Power.* Vol. 1. Cambridge: Cambridge University Press.

Mann, Michael. 1993. *The Sources of Social Power.* Vol. 2. Cambridge: Cambridge University Press.

Mann, Susan. 1987. *Local Merchants and the Chinese Bureaucracy, 1750–1950.* Stanford, CA: Stanford University Press.

Mao, Shoulong, and Xiaozhong Lu, eds. 2009. *Government Governance Innovation Model: The Exploration of "Two Operation Demonstration" of Shanxi's LTB* [*Zhengfu zhili moshi chuangxin yanjiu: Shanxi dishui "liangge caozuo shifan" gaige tansuo*]. [In Chinese.] Beijing: Zhongguo shuiwu chubanshe.

March, James G., and Johan P. Olsen. 1989. *Rediscovering Institutions: The Organizational Basis of Politics.* New York: Free Press.

Martin, Isaac William, Ajay K. Mehrotra, and Monica Prasad. 2009. *The New Fiscal Sociology: Taxation in Comparative and Historical Perspective.* New York: Cambridge University Press.

Martin, Isaac, and Monica Prasad. 2014. "Taxes and Fiscal Sociology." *Annual Review of Sociology* 40 (1): 331–345.

Maxfield, Sylvia, and Ben Ross Schneider. 1997. *Business and the State in Developing Countries.* Ithaca, NY: Cornell University Press.

McCubbins, Mathew, and Thomas Schwartz. 1984. "Congressional Oversight Overlooked: Police Patrols versus Fire Alarms." *American Journal of Political Science* 28 (1): 165–179.

McNally, Christopher A. 2012. "Sino Capitalism: China's Reemergence and the International Political Economy." *World Politics* 64 (4): 741–776.

Migdal, Joel S. 1988. *Strong Societies and Weak States: State-Society Relations and State Capabilities in the Third World*. Princeton, NJ: Princeton University Press.

Migdal, Joel S. 2001. *State in Society: Studying How States and Societies Transform and Constitute One Another*. New York: Cambridge University Press.

Migdal, Joel S., Atul Kohli, and Vivienne Shue. 1994. *State Power and Social Forces: Domination and Transformation in the Third World*. Cambridge: Cambridge University Press.

Ministry of Finance of the People's Republic of China. 1992–2020. *Finance Yearbook of China*. [In Chinese.] Beijing: Zhongguo caizheng chubanshe.

Ministry of Finance of the People's Republic of China. 2010. *Nationwide Fiscal Statistics of Prefectures, Cities, and Counties 2007* [*Quanguo dishixian caizheng tongji ziliao*]. [In Chinese.] Beijing: Zhongguo caizheng jingji chubanshe.

Ministry of Finance of the People's Republic of China. 2013. "Lou Jiwei Interprets the Key Points of Deepening Fiscal and Taxation Reform at the Third Plenary Session." [In Chinese.] November 21. http://www.mof.gov.cn/zhuantihuigu/cztz/mtbdljw/201311/t20131121_1014343.html.

Ministry of Finance of the People's Republic of China. 2016. "Report on 2015 National Land Transfer Income and Expenditure." http://www.gov.cn/xinwen/2016-04/05/content_5061328.htm.

Ministry of Land Resource of People's Republic of China. 1999–2017a. *China Land Resource Statistic Yearbook* [*Zhongguo Guotu Ziyuan Tongji Nianjian*]. Beijing: Dizhi chubanshe.

Ministry of Land Resource of People's Republic of China. 1999–2017b. *Ministry of Land Resource Annual Report* [*Zhongguo Guotu Ziyuan Gongbao*]. http://www.mnr.gov.cn/sj/tjgb/ [site no longer available].

Moe, Terry. 2005. "Power and Political Institutions." *Perspectives on Politics* 3:215–233.

Molotch, Harvey. 1976. "The City as a Growth Machine: Toward a Political Economy of Place." *American Journal of Sociology* 82 (2): 309–332.

Montinola, Gabriella, Yingyi Qian, and Barry R. Weingast. 1995. "Federalism, Chinese Style: The Political Basis for Economic Success in China." *World Politics* 48: 50–81.

Moore, Barrington. 1966. *Social Origins of Dictatorship and Democracy: Lord and Peasant in the Making of the Modern World*. Boston: Beacon Press.

Moore, Mick. 2008. "Between Coercion and Contract: Competing Narratives on Taxation and Governance." In *Taxation and State-Building in Developing Countries: Capacity and Consent*, edited by Deborah Brautigam, Odd-Helge Fjeldstad, and Mick Moore, 34–63. New York: Cambridge University Press.

Morrison, Kevin. 2009. "Oil, Nontax Revenue, and the Redistributional Foundations of Regime Stability." *International Organization* 63: 107–138.

Morrison, Kevin. 2014. *Nontaxation and Representation: The Fiscal Foundations of Political Stability*. New York: Cambridge University Press.

Morse, Yonatan. 2012. "The Era of Electoral Authoritarianism." *World Politics* 64 (1): 161–198.
Moustafa, Tamir. 2007. *The Struggle for Constitutional Power: Law, Politics, and Economic Development in Egypt*. Cambridge: Cambridge University Press.
Moustafa, Tamir, and Tom Ginsburg. 2008. "Introduction: The Functions of Courts in Authoritarian Politics." In *Rule by Law: The Politics of Courts in Authoritarian Regimes*, edited by Tom Ginsburg and Tamir Moustafa, 1–22. New York: Cambridge University Press.
Nathan, Andrew J. 1973. "A Factionalism Model for CCP Politics." *China Quarterly* 53:34–66.
Nathan, Andrew. 2003. "Authoritarian Resilience." *Journal of Democracy* 14 (1): 6–17.
Nathan, Andrew. 2015. "China's Challenge." *Journal of Democracy* 26 (1): 156–170.
National Bureau of Statistics, People's Republic of China. Various years. *Zhongguo tongji nianjian* [China statistical yearbook]. Beijing: Zhongguo tongji chubanshe.
Naughton, Barry. 1995. *Growing out of the Plan: Chinese Economic Reform, 1978–1993*. New York: Cambridge University Press.
Naughton, Barry. 2007. *The Chinese Economy: Transitions and Growth*. Cambridge, MA: MIT Press.
Naughton, Barry, and Kellee Tsai, eds. 2015. *State Capitalism, Institutional Adaptation, and the Chinese Miracle*. New York: Cambridge University Press.
Nee, Victor, and Rebecca Matthews. 1996. "Market Transition and Societal Transformation in Reforming State Socialism." *Annual Review of Sociology* 22: 401–436.
New Beijing News. 2004. "From a Peasant to Millionaire: The Story of a Coal Mine Boss in County A of Shanxi Province." *New Beijing News* [*Xin jingbao*], November 16.
News.163.com. n.d. "Chinese Local Governments' Debt Has Increased from 4 Billion to 7 Billion Yuan in Several Months." Accessed April 28, 2011. http://news.163.com/10/0603/07/68845UL7000146BD.html [site no longer available].
North, Douglass C. 1981. *Structure and Change in Economic History*. New York: Norton.
North, Douglass C. 1990. *Institutions, Institutional Change, and Economic Performance*. New York: Cambridge University Press.
North, Douglass C., and Robert Thomas. 1973. *The Rise of the Western World: A New Economic History*. Cambridge: Cambridge University Press.
North, Douglass C., John Wallis, and Barry R. Weingast. 2006. "A Conceptual Framework for Interpreting Recorded Human History." *NBER Working Paper* 12795. http://www.nber.org/papers/w12795.
North, Douglass C., John Wallis, and Barry R. Weingast. 2009. *Violence and Social Orders: A Conceptual Framework for Interpreting Recorded Human History*. Cambridge: Cambridge University Press.
North, Douglass C., and Barry. R. Weingast. 1989. "Constitutions and Commitment: The Evolution of Institutions Governing Public Choice in 17th-Century England." *Journal of Economic History* 49 (4): 803–832.
O'Brien, Kevin J. 1994a. "Agents and Remonstrators: Role Accumulation by Chinese People's Congress Deputies." *China Quarterly* 138: 359–380.

O'Brien, Kevin J. 1994b. "Chinese People's Congresses and Legislative Embeddedness: Understanding Early Organizational Development." *Comparative Political Studies* 27 (1): 80–107.
O'Brien, Kevin J. 1996. "Rightful Resistance." *World Politics* 49 (1): 31–55.
O'Brien, Kevin J. 2009. "Local People's Congresses and Governing China." *China Journal* 61: 131–141.
O'Brien, Kevin J., and Lianjiang Li. 1999. "Selective Policy Implementation in Rural China." *Comparative Politics* 31: 167–186.
O'Brien, Kevin J., and Lianjiang Li. 2006. *Rightful Resistance in Rural China*. New York: Cambridge University Press.
O'Connor, James. 1973. *The Fiscal Crisis of the State*. New York: St. Martin's Press.
O'Donnell, Guillermo A. 1979. *Modernization and Bureaucratic-Authoritarianism: Studies in South American Politics*. Berkeley: Institute of International Studies, University of California.
O'Donnell, Guillermo A., and Philippe C. Schmitter. 1986. *Transitions from Authoritarian Rule: Tentative Conclusions about Uncertain Democracies*. Baltimore: Johns Hopkins University Press.
O'Donnell, Guillermo A., Philippe C. Schmitter, and Laurence Whitehead. 1986. *Transitions from Authoritarian Rule: Comparative Perspectives*. Baltimore: Johns Hopkins University Press.
Oi, Jean C. 1989. *State and Peasant in Contemporary China: The Political Economy of Village Government*. Berkeley: University of California Press.
Oi, Jean C. 1992. "Fiscal Reform and the Economic Foundations of Local State Corporatism in China." *World Politics* 45: 99–126.
Oi, Jean C. 1999. *Rural China Takes Off: Institutional Foundations of Economic Reform*. Berkeley: University of California Press.
Olson, Mancur. 1982. *The Rise and Decline of Nations: Economic Growth, Stagflation, and Social Rigidities*. New Haven, CT: Yale University Press.
Olson, Mancur. 1993. "Dictatorship, Democracy, and Development." *American Political Science Review* 87 (3): 567–576.
Ong, Lynnette. 2012. "Between Developmental and Clientelist States: Local State-Business Relationships in China." *Comparative Politics* 44 (2): 191–209.
Ong, Lynnette. 2014 "State-Led Urbanization in China: Land Revenue and 'Concentrated Villagers.'" *China Quarterly* 47 (3): 162–179.
Oriental Outlook Weekly. 2011. "The Rectification of Government Officials in Shanxi Makes a Great Shock: The Cadres Are the Key for Reform." [In Chinese.] *Sina*, January 31. http://news.sina.com.cn/c/sd/2011-01-31/091321903917.shtml.
Orren, Karen, and Stephen Skowronek. 2002. "The Study of American Political Development." In *Political Science: The State of the Discipline*, edited by Ira Katznelson and Helen Milner. New York: Norton.
Orren, Karen, and Stephen Skowronek. 2004. *The Search for American Political Development*. Cambridge: Cambridge University Press.
Ostrom, Elinor. 2005. *Understanding Institutional Diversity*. Princeton, NJ: Princeton University Press.

Pan, Jennifer. 2020. *Welfare for Autocrats: How Social Assistance in China Cares for Its Rulers*. New York: Oxford University Press.

Party Team, SAT Headquarters. 2008. "Thirty Years of Keeping the Pace with Time: China's Tax System Keeps Reform and Developing in the Reform and Opening Up Period." [In Chinese.] *Jingji ribao* [*Economy Daily*] December 17, p. 10.

Pearson, Margaret M. 1997. *China's New Business Elite: The Political Consequences of Economic Reform*. Berkeley: University of California Press.

Pei, Minxin. 2006. *China's Trapped Transition: The Limits of Developmental Autocracy*. Cambridge, MA: Harvard University Press.

People's Daily. 2012a. "Economic Development Is the First Task [*diyi yaowu*]; Social Stability Is the First Obligation [*diyi zeren*]." *People's Daily*, September 28. http://star.news.sohu.com/20120928/n354153288.shtml.

People's Daily. 2012b. "Lou Jiwei Interprets Key Points of the Third Session of Eighteenth CCP Central Committee on Fiscal Reform." [In Chinese.] *People's Daily*, November 21. http://www.mof.gov.cn/zhuantihuigu/cztz/mtbdljw/201311/t20131121_1014343.html.

People's Daily. 2016. "What's after the End of Housing Land Tenure?" [In Chinese.] *People's Daily*, April 18. http://house.people.com.cn/n1/2016/0418/c164220-28283411.html.

People's Daily Online. 2014. "Chart: 40 SOE Executives 'Lost' over Anticorruption." [In Chinese.] *People's Daily Online*, May 4. http://ccnews.people.com.cn/n/2014/0504/c141677-24970350.html.

People's Daily Online. 2015. "Xi Jinping Reiterated Mao Zedong's 'Knife Handle' Theory with Profound Significance." [In Chinese.] *China.com*, January 20. http://news.china.com/domestic/945/20150120/19228040.html.

People's Daily Online. 2018. "Ministry of Finance: Tax Cuts and Fee Reductions Exceeded 1 Trillion Yuan in 2017." [In Chinese.] *People's Daily Online*, January 25. http://finance.people.com.cn/n1/2018/0125/c1004-29787655.html.

People's Daily Online. n.d. "Democratic Parties." Accessed March 18, 2021. http://english.people.com.cn/data/China_in_brief/Political_Parties/Democratic%20Parties.html.

Pepinsky, Thomas B. 2009. *Economic Crises and the Breakdown of Authoritarian Regimes: Indonesia and Malaysia in Comparative Perspective*. New York: Cambridge University Press.

Pepinsky, Thomas. 2014. "The Institutional Turn in Comparative Authoritarianism." *British Journal of Political Science* 44 (3): 631–653.

Perry, Elizabeth. 2001. "Challenging the Mandate of Heaven: Popular Protest in Modern China." *Critical Asian Studies* 33 (2): 163–180.

Pierson, Paul. 2004. *Politics in Time: History, Institutions, and Social Analysis*. Princeton, NJ: Princeton University Press.

Piracha, Mujtaba, and Mick Moore. 2016. "Revenue-Maximising or Revenue-Sacrificing Government? Property Tax in Pakistan." *Journal of Development Studies* 52 (12): 1776–1790.

Polanyi, Karl. 1957. *The Great Transformation*. Boston: Beacon Press.
PRC Constitution. 2003. [In Chinese.] Beijing: Falü Chubanshe.
Przeworski, Adam. 1990. *The State and the Economy under Capitalism*. Chur, Switzerland: Harwood Academic Publishers.
Przeworski, Adam. 1995. *Sustainable Democracy*. Cambridge: Cambridge University Press.
Przeworski, Adam. 2000. *Democracy and Development: Political Institutions and Well-Being in the World, 1950–1990*. Cambridge: Cambridge University Press.
Przeworski, Adam, and Fernando Limongi. 1997. "Modernization: Theories and Facts." *World Politics* 49 (2): 155–183.
Putnam, Robert D., Robert Leonardi, and Raffaella Nanetti. 1993. *Making Democracy Work: Civic Traditions in Modern Italy*. Princeton, NJ: Princeton University Press.
Qian, Kai. 2010. "A Literature Review of 'the Advance of the Public Sector and the Retreat of the Private Sector.'" [In Chinese.] *Jingji yanjiu cankao* 60: 37–43, 45.
Qian, Yingyi, and Barry R. Weingast. 1997. "Federalism as a Commitment to Preserving Market Incentives." *Journal of Economic Perspectives* 11: 83–92.
Qian, Yingyi, and Chenggang Xu. 1993. "M-Form Hierarchy and China's Economic Reform." *European Economic Review: Papers and Proceedings* 37: 541–548.
Qin, Hui. 1997. "The Development Trend of Peasants' Burdens: A Report of Tsinghua University Students' Village Survey (4)." [In Chinese.] *Gaige* 2:56–61, 86.
Qiushi Magazine. 2015. "The Purpose of All Kinds of SOE Reform Is to Strengthen SOEs' Role." *Qiushi Magazine*, June 3.
Reuter, Ora John, and David Szakonyi. 2019. "Elite Defection under Autocracy: Evidence from Russia." *American Political Science Review* 113 (2): 552–568.
Rithmire, Meg E. 2014. "China's 'New Regionalism': Subnational Analysis in Chinese Political Economy." *World Politics* 66 (1): 165–194.
Robinson, James A., Ragnar Torvik, and Thierry Verdier. 2014. "Political Foundations of the Resource Curse: A Simplification and a Comment." *Journal of Development Economics* 106 (1): 194–198.
Rodden, Jonathan. 2006. *Hamilton's Paradox: The Promise and Peril of Fiscal Federalism*. Cambridge: Cambridge University Press.
Rong, Jingben, Zhiyuan Cui, Shuanzheng Wang, Xinjun Gao, Zengke He, and Xuedong Yang. 1998. *From the Pressure-Based System to Democratic Cooperative System: Political Reform at the County and Township Level*. [In Chinese.] Beijing: Zhongyang Bianyi Press.
Roniger, Luis. 2004. "Political Clientelism, Democracy, and Market Economy." *Comparative Politics* 36 (3): 353–375.
Rowe, William T. 1984. *Hankow: Commerce and Society in a Chinese City, 1796–1889*. Stanford, CA: Stanford University Press.
Rueschemeyer, Dietrich, Evelyne Huber Stephens, and John D. Stephens. 1992. *Capitalist Development and Democracy*. Chicago: University of Chicago Press.
Ruttan, Vernon, and Yujiro Hayami. 1984. "Toward a Theory of Induced Institutional Innovation." *Journal of Development Studies* 20: 203–257.

Saxonberg, Steven. 2001. *The Fall: A Comparative Study of the End of Communism in Czechoslovakia, East Germany, Hungary, and Poland*. Amsterdam: Harwood Academic Publishers.

Saxonberg, Steven. 2013. *Transitions and Non-transitions from Communism: Regime Survival in China, Cuba, North Korea and Vietnam*. Cambridge: Cambridge University Press.

Schumpeter, Joseph. 1991. "The Crisis of the Tax State." In *The Economics and Sociology of Capitalism*, edited by Richard Swedberg, 99–140. Princeton, NJ: Princeton University Press.

Schurmann, Franz. 1968. *Ideology and Organization in Communist China*. Berkeley: University of California Press.

Shafer, D. Michael. 1994. *Winners and Losers: How Sectors Shape the Developmental Prospects of States*. Ithaca, NY: Cornell University Press.

Shambaugh, David L. 2008. *China's Communist Party: Atrophy and Adaptation*. Berkeley: University of California Press.

Sheng, Feng. 2004. "Shining Industry Zone of County Warm River." [In Chinese]. *Zhejiang Daily*, January 16.

Sheng, Hong, and Nong Zhao. 2013. *China's State-Owned Enterprises: Nature, Performance and Reform*. Singapore: World Scientific.

Shi, Jinchuan, and Chen Qian. 2008. *Space Transformed: The Urbanization Process in Zhejiang Province*. [In Chinese.] Hangzhou: Zhejiang University Press.

Shigeki, Iwai. 2004. *A Study of the Fiscal System in Late Imperial China*. [In Japanese, translated into Chinese by Yong Fu 2011.] Beijing: Social Science Academic Press.

Shih, Victor, Christopher Adolph, and Mingxing Liu. 2012. "Getting Ahead in the Communist Party: Explaining the Advancement of Central Committee Members in China." *American Political Science Review* 106 (1): 166–187.

Shirk, Susan L. 1993. *The Political Logic of Economic Reform in China*. Berkeley: University of California Press.

Shirk, Susan L. 2018. "China in Xi's 'New Era': The Return to Personalistic Rule." *Journal of Democracy* 29 (2): 22–36.

Shleifer, Andrei, and Robert W. Vishny. 1998. *The Grabbing Hand: Government Pathologies and Their Cures*. Cambridge, MA, Harvard University Press.

Shu, Lin. 2010. "The Golden Age of Legislation." [In Chinese.]. *China News Week*, November. https://news.qq.com/a/20101126/000802_1.htm.

Shue, Vivienne, and Christine Wong. 2007. *Paying for Progress in China: Public Finance, Human Welfare and Changing Patterns of Inequality*. New York: Routledge.

Sima, Qian. 2008. *Shiji: Records of Grand Historian*. [In Chinese.] Changsha: Yuelu Shushe.

Sina. 2012. "In 2010, the Gini Coefficient of Chinese Households." *Sina*, December 10. http://finance.sina.com.cn/china/20121210/100213952992.shtml.

Sina. 2013. "Liu Chuanzhi Responds to 'Businessmen Only Talk Business' Critiques." [In Chinese.] *Sina*, December 31. http://finance.sina.com.cn/hy/20131231/100417806826.

Sina. 2015. "Who Touched Taxpayer Xiaoming's Wallet?" [In Chinese.] *Sina*, February 27. http://www.rmzxb.com.cn/zt/2015qglh/lhyw/452257.shtml.

Skinner, G. William. 1965. *Marketing and Social Structure in Rural China*. Tucson: University of Arizona Press.

Skinner, William. 1977. *The City in Late Imperial China*. Edited by G. William Skinner and Hugh D. R. Baker. Stanford, CA: Stanford University Press.

Skocpol, Theda. 1979. *States and Social Revolutions: A Comparative Analysis of France, Russia, and China*. New York: Cambridge University Press.

Skocpol, Theda. 1985. "Bringing the State Back In: Strategies of Analysis in Current Research." In *Bringing the State Back In*, edited by Peter Evans, Dietrich Rueschemeyer, and Theda Skocpol, 1–38. New York: Cambridge University Press.

Slater, Dan. 2003. "Iron Cage in an Iron Fist: Authoritarian Institutions and the Personalization of Power in Malaysia." *Comparative Politics* 36: 81–101.

Slater, Dan. 2010a. "Altering Authoritarianism: Institutional Complexity and Autocratic Agency in Indonesia." In *Explaining Institutional Change: Ambiguity, Agency, and Power*, edited by James Mahoney and Kathleen Ann Thelen, 132–167. New York: Cambridge University Press.

Slater, Dan. 2010b. *Ordering Power: Contentious Politics and Authoritarian Leviathans in Southeast Asia*. New York: Cambridge University Press.

Slater, Dan, and Sofia Fenner. 2011. "State Power and Staying Power: Infrastructural Mechanisms and Authoritarian Durability." *Journal of International Affairs* 65: 15–29.

Slater, Dan, Benjamin Smith, and Gautam Nair. 2014. "Economic Origins of Democratic Breakdown? The Redistributive Model and the Postcolonial State." *Perspectives on Politics* 12 (2): 353–374.

Slater, Dan, and Joseph Wong. 2013. "The Strength to Concede: Ruling Parties and Democratization in Developmental Asia." *Perspectives on Politics* 11 (3): 717–733.

Slemrod, Joel, and Shlomo Yitzhaki. 2002. "Tax Avoidance, Evasion and Administration." In *Handbook of Public Economics*, edited by Alan J. Auerbach and Martin S. Feldstein, 1423–1442. Amsterdam: Elsevier.

Smith, Benjamin. 2005. "Life of the Party: The Origins of Regime Breakdown and Persistence under Single-Party Rule." *World Politics* 57 (3): 421–451.

Smith, Benjamin. 2007. *Hard Times in the Lands of Plenty: Oil Politics in Iran and Indonesia*. Ithaca, NY: Cornell University Press.

Solnick, Steven. 1996. "The Breakdown of Hierarchies in the Soviet Union and China." *World Politics* 48 (2): 209–238.

Solnick, Steven. 1998. *Stealing the State: Control and Collapse in Soviet Institutions*. Cambridge, MA: Harvard University Press.

Stasavage, David. 2011. *States of Credit: Size, Power, and the Development of European Polities*. Princeton, NJ: Princeton University Press.

Stasavage, David. 2016. "Representation and Consent: Why They Arose in Europe and Not Elsewhere." *Annual Review of Political Science* 19: 145–162.

State Administration of Taxation. 1990–2019. *China Taxation Yearbook*. [In Chinese.] Beijing: China Tax Press.

State Administration of Taxation. 2009. "Announcement of the Taxpayer's Rights and Obligations." November 6. http://hainan.chinatax.gov.cn/sxpd_19_4/28122411.html.

State Administration of Taxation. 2018. "SAT and LTB Administration System Reform" [Guoshui dishui zhengguan tizhi gaige, women yiqi zouguo]. December 18. http://www.chinatax.gov.cn/n810219/n810724/c3987667/content.html.

Steinfeld, Edward S. 1998. *Forging Reform in China: The Fate of State-Owned Industry.* New York: Cambridge University Press.

Steinmo, Sven. 1993. *Taxation and Democracy: Swedish, British, and American Approaches to Financing the Modern State.* New Haven, CT: Yale University Press.

Stern, Rachel, and Jonathan Hassid. 2012. "Amplifying Silence: Uncertainty and Control Parables in Contemporary China." *Comparative Political Studies* 45 (10): 1230–1254.

Stockmann, Daniela. 2013. *Media Commercialization and Authoritarian Rule in China.* New York: Cambridge University Press.

Streeck, Wolfgang, and Kathleen Ann Thelen. 2005. *Beyond Continuity: Institutional Change in Advanced Political Economies.* New York: Oxford University Press.

Sun, Xiaoyi, and Ronggui Huang. 2016. "Extension of State-Led Growth Coalition and Grassroots Management: A Case Study of Shanghai." *Urban Affairs Review* 52 (6): 917–943.

Sun, Xin, Jiangnan Zhu, and Yiping Wu. 2014. "Organizational Clientelism: An Analysis of Private Entrepreneurs in Chinese Local Legislatures." *Journal of East Asian Studies* 14 (1): 1–29.

Sun, Xuliang, and Huiling Yu. 1999. "Local Fiscal Budgetary Receipts Fulfilled by Fabricated Taxes Is Undesirable." [In Chinese.] *Journal of Shandong Taxation* 8: 62–63.

Sun, Ying. 2014. "Municipal People's Congress Elections in the PRC: A Process of Co-option." *Journal of Contemporary China* 23 (85): 183–195.

Svolik, Milan. 2012. *The Politics of Authoritarian Rule.* New York: Cambridge University Press.

Swedberg, Richard. 1998. *Max Weber and the Idea of Economic Sociology.* Princeton, NJ: Princeton University Press.

Swedberg, Richard. 2009. *Tocqueville's Political Economy.* Princeton, NJ: Princeton University Press.

Takeuchi, Hiroki. 2014. *Tax Reform in Rural China: Revenue, Resistance, and Authoritarian Rule.* Cambridge: Cambridge University Press.

Tan, Minjun, and Shuangling Zhou. 2009. "Research on the Causes and Countermeasures of Local Fiscal Budgetary Receipts Fulfilled by Fabricated Taxes." [In Chinese.] *Finance and Banking* [*Caiwu yu jinrong*] 120: 73–77.

Tang, Juan. 2004. "From Confirmative Election to Competitive Election: Based on Case Study of 2003 Shenzhen District Level Elections," [In Chinese] *Nanjing Social Science* 03: 39–43.

Taylor, Brian. 2013. *State Building in Putin's Russia: Policing and Coercion after Communism.* New York: Cambridge University Press.

The Comprehensive Department of State Council. 2014. *Yiwu Report Yiwu Road: A Model of China's Market in Reform and Open Up*. [In Chinese] Beijing: Zhongguo Jingji Chubanshe.

Thelen, Kathleen. 2001. "Varieties of Capitalism: Trajectories of Liberalization and the New Politics of Social Solidarity." *Annual Review of Political Science* 15: 137–159.

Thelen, Kathleen. 2004. *How Institutions Evolve: The Political Economy of Skills in Germany, Britain, the United States, and Japan*. New York: Cambridge University Press.

Thornton, Patricia. 2004. "Comrades and Collectives in Arms: Tax Resistance, Evasion and Avoidance Strategies in Post-Mao China." In *State and Society in 21st-Century China: Crisis, Contention, and Legitimation*, edited by Peter Hays Gries and Stanley Rosen, 87–104. New York: Routledge Curzon.

Thornton, Patricia. 2007. *Disciplining the State: Virtue, Violence, and State-Making in Modern China*. Cambridge, MA: Harvard University Asia Center.

Tian, Xianghua. 2008. "The Yiwu Model of Government Innovation: Everything Is for the Market." [In Chinese.] *China Business News* [*Diyi caijing ribao*], April 31, p. A5.

Tian, Yi, and Rui Zhao. 2008. *Taxiang Zhi Shui* [The taxes from another county]. Beijing: Zhongxin chubanshe [China CITIC Press].

Tiebout, Charles. 1956. "A Pure Theory of Local Expenditures." *Journal of Political Economy* 64: 416–424.

Tilly, Charles. 1990. *Coercion, Capital, and European States, AD 990–1990*. Cambridge, MA: B. Blackwell.

Timmons, Jeffrey F. 2005. "The Fiscal Contract: States, Taxes, and Public Services." *World Politics* 57: 530–567.

Timmons, Jeffrey F. 2010. "Taxation and Representation in Recent History." *Journal of Politics* 72:191–208.

Tocqueville, Alexis de. 1998. *The Old Regime and the Revolution*. Chicago: University of Chicago Press.

Treisman, Daniel. 2007. *The Architecture of Government: Rethinking Political Decentralization*. New York: Cambridge University Press.

Treisman, Daniel. 2020. "Democracy by Mistake: How the Errors of Autocrats Trigger Transitions to Freer Government." *American Political Science Review* 114 (3): 792–810.

Truex, Rory. 2016. *Making Autocracy Work: Representation and Responsiveness in Modern China*. New York: Cambridge University Press.

Tsai, Kellee S. 2002. *Back-Alley Banking: Private Entrepreneurs in China*. Ithaca, NY: Cornell University Press.

Tsai, Kellee S. 2005. "Capitalists without a Class: Political Diversity among Private Entrepreneurs in China." *Comparative Political Studies* 38 (9). https://doi.org/10.1177/0010414005277021.

Tsai, Kellee S. 2006. "Adaptive Informal Institutions and Endogenous Institutional Change in China." *World Politics* 59: 116–141.

Tsai, Kellee S. 2007. *Capitalism without Democracy: The Private Sector in Contemporary China*. Ithaca, NY: Cornell University Press.

Tsai, Lily L. 2017. "Bringing in China: Insights for Building Comparative Political Theory." *Comparative Political Studies* 50 (3): 295–328.

Tsebelis, George. 1990. *Nested Games: Rational Choice in Comparative Politics*. Berkeley: University of California Press.

Tsebelis, George. 2002. *Veto Players: How Political Institutions Work*. Princeton, NJ: Princeton University Press.

Turgot, Anne-Robert-Jacques. 1971. *Reflections on the Formation and the Distribution of Riches*. Reprints of Economic Classics. Originally published in 1770. New York: A. M. Kelley.

Turley, Gerald. 2006. *Transition, Taxation and the State*. Aldershot, UK: Ashgate.

Van de Walle, Nicolas. 2001. *African Economies and the Politics of Permanent Crisis, 1979–1999*. New York: Cambridge University Press.

Von Glahn, Richard. 2016. *The Economic History of China: From Antiquity to the Nineteenth Century*. New York: Cambridge University Press.

Vries, Peer. 2015. *State, Economy and the Great Divergence: Great Britain and China, 1680s–1850s*. London: Bloomsbury Academic.

Walder, Andrew G. 1986. *Communist Neo-traditionalism: Work and Authority in Chinese Industry*. Berkeley: University of California Press.

Walder, Andrew. 1996. "Introduction." In *China's Transitional Economy*, edited by Andrew Walder, 1–17. Oxford: Oxford University Press.

Wallace, Jeremy. 2014. *Cities and Stability: Urbanization, Redistribution, and Regime Survival in China*. Oxford: Oxford University Press.

Wang, Bingqian. 2009. *China's Fiscal System from 1949 to 2009: Retrospection and Reflection* [*Zhongguo caizheng 60 nian: Huigu yu sikao*]. Beijing: China Fiscal and Economics Press.

Wang, Changlin. 2015. "Twenty Years of Golden Tax Project: Practices, Influences, and Implications." [In Chinese.] *Dianzi zhengfu* 6: 104–110.

Wang Haiping. 2016. "A Case of Fiscal Revenue Decline." [In Chinese.] *21st Century Business Herald*, July 22. http://epaper.21jingji.com/html/2016-07/22/content_43838.htm.

Wang, Jianlin. 2015. "Wang Jianlin: It Is Nonsense to Say That [Business Should] Keep Distance from the Government in China." [In Chinese.] https://www.sohu.com/a/14811874_115048.

Wang, Jinjun, and Changdong Zhang. 2014. "The Interactional Mechanisms between NGO and Government in the Horizontal and Vertical Networks: A Comparative Case Study of Trade Associations' Strategies." [In Chinese.] *Journal of Public Administration* 5: 88–108.

Wang, Shaoguang, and Angang Hu. 2001. *The Chinese Economy in Crisis: State Capacity and Tax Reform*. Armonk, NY: M. E. Sharpe.

Wang, Shifeng. 2012. "Where Do the 28 Billion Electricity Extra Fees Go?" *Tencent Finance*, May 21. https://finance.qq.com/a/20120521/000883.htm.

Wang, Xiaolu, and Wing Tai Woo. 2011. "The Size and Distribution of Hidden Household Income in China." *Asian Economic Papers* 10 (1): 1–26.

Wang, Xiaolu. 2013. *Strategic Thinking on National Income Distribution.* [In Chinese] Beijing: Xuexi Chubanshe.

Wang, Xiaoyan. 2007. *The Private Entrepreneurs' Political Participation* [Siying qiyezhu de zhengzhi canyu]. Beijing: Shehui kexue wenxian chubanshe.

Wang, Xu. 1999. "Mutual Empowerment of State and Society: Its Nature, Conditions, Mechanism, and Limits." *Comparative Politics* 31 (2): 231–249.

Wang, Yanfei, and Jing Shuiyu. 2016. "Minister Says Property Tax Is 'Next Task.'" *China Daily*, July 26. http://www.chinadaily.com.cn/business/2016-07/26/content_26219239.htm.

Wang, Yeh-Chien. 1974. *Land Taxation in Imperial China, 1750–1911.* Cambridge, MA: Harvard University Press.

Wang, Yingyao. 2017. "Why Tax Policy Is Not Politics in China: Public Finance and China's Changing State-Society Relations." *Politics and Policy* 45 (2): 194–223.

Wang, Yuhua. 2015. *Tying the Autocrat's Hands: The Rise of the Rule of Law in China.* New York: Cambridge University Press.

Wang, Yuhua, and Carl Minzner. 2015. "The Rise of the Chinese Security State." *China Quarterly* 222: 339–359.

Wang, Zhengxu, and Ern Ser Tan. 2013. "The Conundrum of Authoritarian Resiliency: Hybrid Regimes and Non-democratic Regimes in East Asia." *Taiwan Journal of Democracy* 9 (1): 199–219.

Wank, David L. 1999. *Commodifying Communism: Business, Trust, and Politics in a Chinese City.* Cambridge: Cambridge University Press.

Waterbury, John. 1997. "Fortuitous By-Products," *Comparative Politics* 29 (3): 383–402.

Weber, Max. 1950. *General Economic History.* Glencoe, IL: Free Press.

Weber, Max. 1951. *The Religion of China: Confucianism and Taoism.* Glencoe, IL: Free Press.

Weber, Max. 1968. *Economy and Society: An Outline of Interpretive Sociology.* New York: Bedminster Press.

Wedeman, Andrew. 2003. *From Mao to Market: Rent Seeking, Local Protectionism, and Marketization in China.* Cambridge: Cambridge University Press.

Weingast, Barry. 1995. "The Economic Role of Political Institutions: Market-Preserving Federalism and Economic Development." *Journal of Law, Economics, and Organization* 11: 1–31.

Weiss, Jessica Chen. 2014. *Powerful Patriots: Nationalist Protest in China's Foreign Relations.* Oxford: Oxford University Press.

White, Gordon, and Jack Gray. 1988. *Developmental States in East Asia.* New York: St. Martin's Press.

White, Stephen. 1993. "Economic Performance and Communist Legitimacy." *World Politics* 38 (3): 462–482.

Whiting, Susan H. 2001. *Power and Wealth in Rural China: The Political Economy of Institutional Change*. New York: Cambridge University Press.

Whiting, Susan H. 2004. "The Cadre Evaluation System at the Grassroots: The Paradox of Party Rule." In *Holding China Together*, edited by Barry Naughton and Dali Yang, 101–119. New York: Cambridge University Press.

Whiting, Susan H. 2011. "Values in Land: Fiscal Pressures, Land Disputes, and Justice Claims in Rural and Peri-Urban China." *Urban Studies* 48 (3): 569–587.

Winn, Jane K., and Angela Zhang. 2013. "China's Golden Tax Project: A Technological Strategy for Reducing VAT Fraud." *Peking University Journal of Legal Studies* 4: 1–33.

Winters, Jeffrey A. 1996. *Power in Motion: Capital Mobility and the Indonesian State*. Ithaca, NY: Cornell University Press.

Wintrobe, Ronald. 1998. *The Political Economy of Dictatorship*. New York: Cambridge University Press.

Wong, Christine. 2009. "Rebuilding Government for the 21st Century: Can China Incrementally Reform the Public Sector?" *China Quarterly* 200: 929–952.

Wong, Christine, and Richard Bird. 2008. "Fiscal System in China: A Work in Progress." In *China's Great Economic Transformation*, edited by Loren Brandt, 429–466. Cambridge: Cambridge University Press.

Worker's Daily. 2006. "The Shanxi Province Governor Requires Government Officials to Change 'Office Idea' to Improve the Government's Reputation/Trustworthiness." [In Chinese.] *Worker's Daily* [*Gongren Ribao*], July 6. http://gov.people.com.cn/GB/48377/4564537.html [site no longer available].

World Bank. 2013. *China 2030: Building a Modern, Harmonious, and Creative Society*. Washington, DC: World Bank.

World Bank. 2020. *Doing Business 2020: Comparing Business Regulation in 190 Economies*. Washington, DC: World Bank.

Wright, Joseph. 2008. "Do Authoritarian Political Institutions Constrain? How Legislatures Affect Economic Growth and Investment." *American Journal of Political Science* 52 (2): 322–343.

Wu, Jinglian. 2018. *China's Economic Reform in Progress* [*Zhongguo jingji gaige jincheng*]. Beijing: Zhongguo Dabaike Quanshu Press.

Xi, Jinping. 2015. "Xi Jinping's Speech When Meeting Outstanding County Party Secretaries of the Country's Outstanding County." *Xinhuanent*, June 30. http://www.xinhuanet.com//politics/2015-09/01/c_1116430730.htm.

Xia, Ming. 2008. *The People's Congresses and Governance in China toward a Network Mode of Governance*. New York: Routledge.

Xiao, Donglian. 2019. *Road of Exploration: China's Economic Reform during 1978–1992* [*Tanyi zhilu: 1978–1992 nian de zhongguo jingji gaige*]. Beijing: Shehui kexue chubanshe.

Xiao, Jie. 2017. "Facilitating the Establishment of Modern Fiscal System." *People's Daily*, December 20.

Xie, Xuren, ed. 2009. *China's Fiscal System from 1949 to 2009* [*Zhongguo caizheng 60 nian*]. Beijing: Economic Science Press.

Xinhua. 2006. "Li Yizhong: There Are Serious Government Business Collusion and Dereliction of Duty and Malpractice behind Industry Accidents." [In Chinese.] *News of CCP*, December 21. http://cpc.people.com.cn/GB/64093/64371/5197614.html.

Xinhua. 2011. "The Chinese Government Monitors Local Government Debt Comprehensively to Reduce Risk." *Xinhua News Agency*, http://news.xinhuanet.com/politics/2011-03/07/c_121159080.htm [site no longer available].

Xinhua. 2016. "Xi Jinping: Stick to China's Basic Economic System Steadily." [In Chinese.] *Sohu*, March 9. http://news.sohu.com/20160309/n439812068.shtml.

Xinhua. 2018. "Xi Stresses Unswerving Support for Development of Private Enterprises." *Qiushi*, November 2. http://english.qstheory.cn/2018-11/02/c_1123651044.htm.

Xinhua. 2020. "China Focus: Understanding 'Dual Circulation' and What It Means for World." *Xinhua*, September 5. http://www.xinhuanet.com/english/2020-09/05/c_139345700.htm.

Xinmin wanbao. 2013. "National Bureau of Statistics Releases China's GINI Coefficient for 2003–2012 for the First Time." [In Chinese.] *Xinmin wanbao*, January 19. http://shanghai.xinmin.cn/msrx/2013/01/19/18245564.html.

Xu, Chenggang. 2010. "The Fundamental Institutions of China's Reforms and Development." *Journal of Economic Literature* 49 (4): 1076–1151.

Xu, Shanda. 2003. "Golden Tax Project: A Practice of Political System Reform." [In Chinese.] *China Taxation* 4: 4–10.

Xu, Xianglin. 2020. *Social Transformation and State Governance in China: Theory, Path, and Policy Process*. Beijing: Foreign Language Teaching and Research.

Yan, Xiaojun. 2011. "Regime Inclusion and the Resilience of Authoritarianism: Local People's Political Consultative Conference in Post-Mao Chinese Politics." *China Journal* 66: 53–75.

Yan, Yingzhuan. 2016. "Wang Min Is under Investigation for Seriously Violated Party Rules." [In Chinese.] *Sina*, March 4. http://news.sina.com.cn/c/2016-03-04/doc-ifxpzzhk2164160.shtml.

Yang, Dali L. 2004. *Remaking the Chinese Leviathan: Market Transition and the Politics of Governance in China*. Stanford, CA: Stanford University Press.

Yang, Dali L. 2006. "Economic Transformation and Its Political Discontents in China: Authoritarianism, Unequal Growth, and the Dilemmas of Political Development." *Annual Review of Political Science* 9: 143–164.

Yang, Dali L. 2017. "China's Troubled Quest for Order: Leadership, Organization and the Contradictions of the Stability Maintenance Regime." *Journal of Contemporary China* 26: 35–53.

Yang, Jia. 2015. "Wang Rulin Tells You How Serious Is the Corruption in Shanxi." *China*

Net, March 7. http://photo.china.com.cn/2015lh/2015-03/07/content_34979961.htm.

Yang, Xuedong, 2012. "A Pressure System: A Brief History of a Concept." [In Chinese.] *Shehui kexue* 11: 4–12.

Yang, Zhiyong. 2019. "The Scale of Tax and Fee Reduction in 2018 Is about 1.3 Trillion Yuan: How Can Tax Reduction Be Better?" [In Chinese.] *Baidu*, January 19. https://baijiahao.baidu.com/s?id=1623080897165990709&wfr=spider&for=pc.

Ye, Jing, 2018. "No Money, No Representation." *Politics and Society* 46 (1): 81–99.

You, Yu. 2012. "Is It a Sustainable Economic Great Leap? A Fiscal Analysis of Chongqing's Rapid Economic Growth." [In Chinese.] *Chinese Public Administration Review* 4: 27–51.

Yu, Hong. 2007. "From Zhuanguanyuan to Shuiguanyuan: The Evolution of China's Tax Administration." [In Chinese.] *China Taxation* [*Zhongguo shuiwui*] 4: 15–16.

Yu, Long. 2018. "Merging SAT and LTB and Deepening Fiscal System Reform." *Modern Management Science* [*Xiandai guanli kexue*] 9: 28–30.

Yuan, Huaming. 2005. "Renda Daibiao Gonbgzuoshi Shengwen" [The rise of the PC deputy's office]. *Guancha yu Sikao* [*Observation and Deliberation*] 2. http://www.cnki.com.cn/Journal/H-H1-GCYS-2005-02.htm.

Zaobao. 2010. "The First Full Time PC Deputy Is Canceled on Mainland [Neidi Shouge Zhuanzhi Renda Daibiao Gongzuoshi bei Jiaoting]." [In Chinese.] *Zaobao.com*, August. http://www.zaobao.com/wencui/2010/08/ifeng100831.shtml [site no longer available].

Zelin, Melinda. 1984. *The Magistrate's Tael: Rationalizing Fiscal Reform in Eighteenth-Century Ch'ing China*. Berkeley: University of California Press.

Zhan, Jing. 2009. "Decentralizing China: Analysis of Central Strategies in China's Fiscal Reforms." *Journal of Contemporary China* 19 (60): 445–462.

Zhang, Changdong. 2017a. "A Fiscal Sociological Theory of Authoritarian Resilience." *Sociological Theory* 35 (1): 39–63.

Zhang, Changdong. 2017b. "Reexamining Election Connection for Authoritarian China: The Local People's Congress and Its Private Entrepreneur Deputies." *China Review* 17 (1): 1–27.

Zhang, Changdong. 2019. "Asymmetric Mutual Dependence between the State and Capitalists in China." *Politics and Society* 47 (2): 149–176.

Zhang, Changdong. 2020. "Reexamine Regional Models of China's Economic Growth: Toward an Integrated Analytical Framework." *Sociology Compass* 14 (5). https://doi.org/10.1111/soc4.12781.

Zhang, Changdong, and Christopher Heurlin. 2014. "Power and Rule by Law in Rural China." In *Resolving Land Disputes in East Asia*, edited by Hualing Fu and John Gillespie, 248–272. New York: Cambridge University Press.

Zhang, Fan. 2010. "306 Government Officials Were Punished and Publicized during the Government Rectification in Shanxi." [In Chinese.] *Xiaokang Magazine*, October 4. http://www.dzwww.com/special/ts/jdf/201010/t20101004_5878998.htm.

Zhang, Jianjun. 2009. *Marketization and Democracy in China*. London: Routledge.

Zhang, Lihua. 2010. "Hongdong County: The Transition of a Coal Mine County." *Diyi caijing ribao*, December 2, p. A4.

Zhang, Shouwen. 2012. "Three Fundamental Issues in the Legislation of Property Tax." [In Chinese.] *Taxation Studies* 330: 48–53.

Zhang, Song. 1996. "A Discussion on Legislation for Basic Law of Tax in China." [In Chinese.] *Shuiwu yu Jingji* [*Taxation and Economy*] 6: 5–9, 69.

Zhang, Yueran. 2020. "Political Competition and Two Modes of Taxing Private Homeownership: A Bourdieusian Analysis of the Contemporary Chinese State." *Theory and Society* 49: 669–707.

Zhang, Zhiwei. 2015. "Cases of Fiscal Revenue Decline." [In Chinese.] *Caijing*, February 2. http://magazine.caijing.com.cn/20150202/3813217.shtml.

Zhao, Dingxin. 2001. *The Power of Tiananmen: State-Society Relations and the 1989 Beijing Student Movement*. Chicago: University of Chicago Press.

Zheng, Minghuai. 2006. "The Political Economy of Township Government Debt." [In Chinese.] *Hubei jingji xueyuan xuebao* 2: 99–100.

Zhou, Feizhou. 2006. "Ten Years after Tax Sharing Reform: Institution and Its Implications." [In Chinese.] *Zhongguo shehui kexue* 6: 100–115, 205.

Zhou, Feizhou. 2012. *Take Interest as Interest: Fiscal Relationship and Local Government Behavior* [*Yili weili*]. Shanghai: Sanlian Press.

Zhou, Kai, and Xiaojun Yan. 2014. "The Quest for Stability: Policing Popular Protest in the People's Republic of China." *Problems of Post-communism* 61 (3): 3–17.

Zhou, Li'an. 2007. "Governing China's Local Officials: An Analysis of Promotion Tournament Model." [In Chinese.] *Economic Research* [*Jingji yanjiu*] 7: 36–50.

Zhou, Xiaoxiao. 2017. "Stable Growth in 2017 Is More Dependent on Tax Cuts, Local Governments Have More than Enough Financial Resources." [In Chinese.] *21Jingji*, January 10. http://epaper.21jingji.com/html/2017-01/10/content_54410.htm.

Zhu, Jiangnan, and Dong Zhang. 2017. "Weapons of the Powerful: Authoritarian Elite Competition and Politicized Anticorruption in China." *Comparative Political Studies* 50 (9): 1186–1220.

Zhu, Rongji. 2011. *Zhu Rongji on the Record* [*Zhu Rongji jianghua shilu*]. Beijing: Renmin Press.

Index

Page numbers in italics refer to figures and tables.

Acemoglu, Daron, 240, 242, 251n43, 251n45, 287n63
agent discipline: identified as one of the three governance problems, 5; incentives provided for its resolution by de facto fiscal federalism, 33–36, 146–48, 192, 204–5; and the need for free media in authoritarian regimes, 19–20; power-sharing problems related to, 18–20, 228–29; and reliance on nontax revenue, 54
Ai Weiwei, 190
Alber, Jens, 24
All China Federation of Industry and Commerce (ACFIC), 1–2, 245n3, 255n9
Ang, Yuen Yuen, 34, 96–97, 120, 267n63
Ansell, Ben W., 184
anticorruption campaigns. See national anticorruption campaign
Art, David, 4, 33, 283n25; institutional explanations of authoritarian resilience critiqued by, 24, 283n25
authoritarian regimes: economic growth as crucial to performance legitimacy and popular support, 18, 30–31, 121, 146, 213, 216; free media needed in, 19–20, 248n13; resilience during market transition of, 3, 5; strategies of repression, 18; taxation dilemma of growth, 6, 30; taxation dilemma of representation, 6, 30–31. *See also* agent discipline; cooperation; social control
authoritarian resilience: and censorship, 20, 29, 248n18; coercive institutions proposed by scholars, 20–22, *21*, 248n20; endogenous institutional explanation of, 10, 211, 222–24; the half-tax state as a double-edged sword for, 32, 73–74, *74*; impact of tax resistance stimulated by agricultural taxation on, 29, 50, 53, 69, 76, 221, 252, 258n48; institutional explanations proposed by scholars, 20, 247n8, 251n48; and institutionalized single-party regimes, 4, 26, 282n10; private entrepreneurs' reluctance to challenge authoritarian rule, 191–92; and tax-state transition in the PRC, 5; and under-institutionalized taxation administration, 7, 32, 40–42, 185–92, 238; and welfare state authoritarianism, 24–26

Bahl, Roy, 215, 288n69
Bellin, Eva, 184
Berenson, Marc, 235n76, 248n76, 282n6
Bernstein, Thomas P., 201
Besley, Timothy, 42, 224, 228; concept of "development clusters," 229, 235–36, 284n36, 287n63
Bird, Richard M., 38–39, 73

321

322   INDEX

bureaucratization of the PRC: and the agent-discipline problem, 19–20; asset mobility associated with the level of bureaucratization, 139; stage one (before 1980) (command administration), 95–96; stage two (1980–1993) (refeudalization), 95–96; stage three (mid-1990s–present); and taxation, 192–93, *193*. *See also* modern bureaucracy in the PRC (mid-1990s–present)

Cai, Hongbin, 250n33, 252n55
Cai, Yongshun, 21, 23, 248n26, 249n25
Campbell, John, 281n1
Centeno, Miguel Angel, 216
Central Commission of Discipline and Investigation (CCDI), investigation of Wang Min, 2–3
Chen, Ling, 284n27, 286n55
Chen, Yongjie, 55, 60–61
China's National Democratic Construction Association (CNDCA), 1, 2, 245n2
Chinese Academy of Social Sciences, 11, 194
Chinese Communist Party (CCP): aspects of its institutionalization that drive its resilience (according to Nathan), 26–27; censorship strategy of, 20, 29, 248n18, 283n23; coercive institutions utilized for social control, 21; crises faced control of its military and armed police force, 22; "four basic principles" (*sixiang jiben yuanze*), 284n32; ideology to serve the people, 25; institutionalization of, 250n34; Organization Department of, 86, 162, 274n35, 274n38; performance legitimacy and popular support achieved by, 146, 213, 216; taxation as a tool of legal repression for the CCP, 219–20; and the Zhou Yongkang corruption case, 191, 249n24, 249n27, 257n36, 259n56. *See also* Cultural Revolution; Deng Xiaoping
CCP Central Committee, 273n20,
278n98; tax reform of 1994 approved by, 259n60
Chinese People's Political Consultative Conference (CPPCC), 44; about, 245n1; and the president of the ACFIC, 245n2; twelfth annual session (2016), 1–2. *See also* Wang Jianlin
Cho, Young Nam, 153, 170, 273n28, 273n30, 274n33
Chongqing: ineffective relations between government and business in, 124; land finance as unsustainable and risky in, 68; as a pilot city for property tax collection, 75. *See also* County Z (Chongqing)
coevolution of market and bureaucracy, 94–97, *98*; Ang's coevolutionary model distinguished from the author's, 34, 96–97, 120, 267n63; County Warm River as a model of, 97, 99–100; incentives provided by de facto federalism under certain conditions, 6, 34, 146
Commission of Politics and Law (CPL), 21, 22, 248n22; and the Zhou Yongkang corruption case, 191, 249n24, 249n27, 257n56
Confucius and Confucian ideas, 43, 230, 254n1
cooperation: identified as one of the three governance problems, 5; impetuses for, 18, 101, 237; and the power-sharing problem, 20
co-optation via deterrence, 7, 40, 220
County C (Zhejiang), 162
County Cold Mountain (Shanxi): coal mine regulation in, *134*; coal mines in, *129*; coal-resource related taxes, *199*; County D compared with, 139, 141; County Warm River compared with, 9, 126–27, *127*, 131; economic decline affecting LTB tax targets in, 89; favoritism available to tax bureau officials in, 87; the LPC's institutional arrangements in, 173–74; selection as a primary county case, 9, *10*; tax revenue structure of its LTB, *198*

Index 323

County D (Shanxi): access to favoritism available to tax bureau officials in, 87; annual report of the PC Standing Committee of, 274n32; coal mining industry in, 139–40; County Cold Mountain compared with, 139, 141; economic decline affecting LTB tax targets in, 89–90; selection as a complementary case for implicit bargaining, 9, *10*

County Warm River (Zhejiang): as a coevolutionary model of bureaucracy and market, 97, 99–100; County Cold Mountain compared with, 9, 126–27, *127*, 131; economic decline affecting LTB tax targets in, 90; fiscal income (2014), *58*; free-market economy generated by, 263n11; government fund revenue breakdown (2014), *59*; lack of targets set by the Tax-Inspection Bureau of, 87–88; land-transfer fees relied on, 62, 64, 66, 115–16; LPC elections in, 165, 167–69, 181; the LPC's institutional arrangements in, 172–73, 276n68, 276nn70–71; rampant tax evasion in, 90; revenue breakdown for, *58*, *64*, *69*; selection as a primary county case, 9; sizes and value of land in, 117–19, *117*; stage one of its coevolution, 100–109; stage three of its coevolution, 114–19; stage two of its coevolution, 109–14; tax administration prior to reform, 82–83, 89; taxes paid by enterprises raised to meet tax targets in, 89; tax revenue breakdown (2014), *58*

County Wenling (Zhejiang): "democratic deliberation meeting" held in, 123–24, 174–78; development in, 176, 277n89; the LPC's institutional arrangements in, 163, 171, 276n65; selection as a secondary county case for comparing LPCs, 9, *10*

County X (Hunan): autonomy of tax bureaus illustrated by a story from, 78–79; compared with other selected counties, 139; effort to attract business investment in, 145–46; local government debt in, 271n45; selection as a complementary case for implicit bargaining, 9, *10*; story about the Tax Bureau in, 188–89

County Yiwu (Zhejiang): commerce in, 141–42; compared with other selected counties, 139; institutional innovations made in, 143; selection as a complementary case for implicit bargaining, 9, *10*

County Z (Chongqing): compared with other selected counties, 139; measures taken to improve investment in, 145, 270n38; selection as a complementary case for implicit bargaining, 9, *10*

Cultural Revolution (1966–1976): destruction of the taxation system during, 49, 51, 76, 256n19; its political chaos as a driving force for reform, 47; private entrepreneurs treated as enemies during, 93

Curtis, James L., 247

de facto fiscal federalism: authoritarian resilience associated with negative consequences of, 32; conditions that incentivize coevolution of market and bureaucracy, 6, 34, 146; cooperation and economic growth promoted by, 6, 7, 33–36, 120–21, 210; and incentives for solving the agent-discipline problem, 34–36, 215; role in resolving the three governance problems, 7; and the term *Fenquan* ("decentralization"), 120, 266n61; and the three stages of the fiscal system in the PRC, 51–52, 238; under-institutionalized taxation embedded in, 186–92. *See also* pressure-based systems (*yalixing tizhi*)

democracy and democratization: authoritarian control distinguished from social control under democracy, 18; class theory of democratization proposed by Moore (Barrington),

democracy and democratization (*continued*)
150, 183, 272n8, 279n4; co-optation of democratic institutions by autocratic rulers, 18, 23–24, 179; the LPC as democratic looking institution, 178–80, 182; and the need for free media, 19–20, 248n13; open-access social order associated with, 241; and private entrepreneurs' fear of redistribution oriented policies, 184, 191; private-sector capital's low demand for, *184*, 184–85; and typologies of states, *236*. See also elections

Deng, Yanhua, 22–23
Deng Xiaoping, 43, 93, 157, 239, 241, 267n62, 277n84
Dickson, Bruce, 25, 30, 185, 246n12; types of "dictator's dilemma" discussed by, 287n61
Dincecco, Mark, 284n36
Duara, Prasenjit, 232

Easter, Gerald, 235, 286n51
elections: commercialization of, 164–66, 180, 275n49, 276n64; direct elections in China, 8, 254n70; of LPC deputy candidates, 153, 154, 162, 164, 167–68; and patron-clientelism, 179; and rural electoral districts, 162–63
endogenous institutional change, 254n69; and the coevolution of the market and bureaucracy, 229; explanation of authoritarian resilience, 10, 211, 222–24, 227–30; and institutional change theory, 225–26; institutional explanations of authoritarian resilience, 251n48; and problems of endogeneity, 10, 180, 224; and quasi-parameters, 42, 225, 226, 227, 228
Evans, Peter B., 20; on embedded autonomy, 237, 248n16

Fairbanks, Charles, on the feudalization of the Russian government, 93
Fan, Peng, 264n28

Fenner, Sofia, infrastructural power mechanisms of taxation proposed by, 28, 206
fiscal constitution theory, 242, 251n45, 288n72
fiscal contracting system (FCS), 12; local state governments empowered by, 34; and Oi's (Jean) local state corporatism theory, 34, 212, 263n14
fiscal decentralization:and the agent-discipline problem, 34–35, 212–13; and Oi's (Jean) local state corporatism theory, 34, 212, 248n15, 263n14
fiscal sociological theory of authoritarian resilience: chapter one, 14–42passim; as an endogenous institutional explanation, 211, 224; the need for such a theory, 16
fiscal sociology: defined, 16; and the literature on taxation, 16–17, 281n1; Tocqueville's lines of inquiry, 5, 219, 245n9, 283n18
fiscal system in the PRC: pilot program for property tax in, 75; stages of, 51
Flora, Peter, 24
forbearance, 40, 181, 182, 187, 206

Gallagher, Mary E., 220, 248n21
Gandhi, Jennifer, 5, 247n8; on authoritarian control, 18, 23–24, 249n29, 278n95
Geddes, Barbara, 4, 26, 249n28
Gehlbach, Scott, 31, 263–64n17, 286n52
Gilley, Bruce, 286n57
Ginsburg, Tom, 23, 217, 247n8
Golden Tax Project (GTP), 85, 282n8
Goldscheid, Rudolf, 209
Greene, Kenneth, 37, 61–62, 74
Greif, Avner Laitin, David, 225
growth dilemma: the current taxation system in China as a threat to sustainable economic growth, 229–30; and the middle-income trap, 237–38, 286n56; and the performance legitimacy of authoritarian governments,

6, 30–31; relationship to the three governance problems, 32, 32
Guo, Jigang, 153, 275n48
Guo, Xuezhi, 21

half-tax states: authoritarian resilience associated with negative consequences of, 32, 73–74, 74; Chinese dynasties viewed as, 232; citizens' perception of their tax burden reduced by, 6, 36, 69, 217, 246n12; contemporary China as, 49–50, 235; role in resolving the three governance problems, 6–7, 237; SOEs maintenance of China as a half-tax state, 27, 36, 227
Hassid, Jonathan, 220, 283n20
He, Ping, 231
Holland, Alisha, 19, 40, 187, 220
Hou, Yue, 170
Hsiao, Kung-chüan, 5
Hu, Angang, 52–53
Hu, Jintao, 259n56; controlling the "knife" of the CPL emphasized by, 21; creation of "harmonious society" called for, 22, 24–25, 261n86
Huang, Ronggui, 119
Huang Zongxi Law, 231
Hunan Province: LPC elections in, 167, 275n49; rampant tax evasion in, 77. *See also* County X (Hunan)
Huntington, Samuel: on the challenges of social-economic change, 29, 47, 48; on the degree of government as the most important political distinction among countries, 3; on the role of parties in improving government capability, 26

Industrial and Commercial Bank of China (ICBC), problematic issues of, 258n37

Jiang, Zemin, 239, 239n36, 259n56, 284n33; controlling the "knife" of the CPL emphasized by, 21
Johnson, Simon, 251n43

Karceski, Steven, 218n1
Kiser, Edgar, 218n1
Knutsen, Carl Henrik, 4, 249n30
Kohli, Atul, 216
Kuhn, Philip A., 233

Laitin, David, 225
land finance: agricultural taxes, 29, 50, 53, 69, 76, 221, 252; and local governments' revenue, 115–19; and the short-term economic growth of the CCP, 66. *See also* land-transfer fees
land-transfer fees: and the CCP's transition from a communist to a tax state, 55; and compensation for loss of taxation power, 12, 38, 64–65; decreasing local government's reliance on, 38; management of, 65–66, 68; terms of, 66, 258n46
Lee, Ching Kwan, 260n72
Lessmann, Christian, 248n13
Levi, Margaret, 35, 92; quasi-voluntary theory of, 31–32, 288n72
Levitsky, Steven: authoritarian durability defined by, 245n5; on legal repression, 253n63; on organizational power and authoritarian stability, 26, 250n31, 251n40, 282n13
Li, Cheng, 246, 250n34
Li, Hongbin, 35
liberal market economic systems: authoritarian regimes toppled by, 3; impact on TVEs in County Warm River, 103–4
Lieberman, Evan: five ideal states defined by, 246n10, 255n14; the tax state defined by, 251n49
Lieberthal, Kenneth, 53
limited-access social order: and the concept of extractive institutions, 287n63; and patron-clientelism, 241; transition to open-access order, 241–43; Weber's typologies of domination compared with, 287n64
Linz, Juan J., 21, 248n20
Liu, Chuanzhi, 182

326 INDEX

Local People's Congress (LPC), 2; as a democratic-looking institution that affects private entrepreneurs, 178–80, 182; as an inclusive regime institution, 160, 166–70, 178–79

Local People's Congress (LPC)—rationalization aspect, scholarship on, 152

Local People's Congress (LPC)—representation dilemma: and the commercialization of LPC deputy elections, 164–66, 275n49; incentives to encourage private entrepreneurs to run in elections, 167–70, 189–90, 275n56; representation-through-taxation mechanism as a problem, 13, 166; scholarship on, 152–54

Local People's Political Consultative Conference (LPPCC), 2; as a democratic-looking institution that affects private entrepreneurs, 182; deputy party secretaries limited to two, 273n20; inclusiveness of, 153–54

Local Tax Bureaus (LTB), and pressure-based tax administration (tax targeting), 87–90

Lorentzen, Peter, 248n18

Lou, Jiwei, 215, 287n65, 287n65, 288n72; on Individual Income Tax (IIT), 44; property-tax promised by, 14

LTBs, and the provincial administration, 260n70

Lü, Xiaobo, 201

Luong, Pauline Jones, 123, 147

Ma, Debin: "principle-agent model" of, 232

Ma, Jack: on four principles of government business relationships, 182

Ma, Jun: on how relying on SOEs and "hidden taxes" has limited political change in China, 60, 287n66

Machiavelli, Niccolò, 5, 25, 183

Mahoney, James, 226; on path dependence, 287n60

Manion, Melanie, 152, 153

Mann, Michael, 28, 31, 250n40
Mann, Susan, 254n7, 286n47
Mao Zedong: embrace of "power from the gun," 21; and the "four basic principles" (*sixiang jiben yuanze*) emphasized by the CCP, 284n32
market transition in the PRC: and the need for state-society synergy, 101, 237; stage one (before 1980), 46–47; stages of, 46–47
Markwardt, Gunther, 248n13
Martin, Isaac William, 212, 246n11, 281n1
Matthews, Rebecca, 219
McNally, Christopher A., 255n10
Mehrotra, Ajay K., 246n11
Migdal, Joel S., 249n28, 250n40; state-in-society "mutual transformation" approach of, 19, 31, 97, 251n46, 279n8
modern bureaucracy in the PRC (mid-1990s–present): and de facto fiscal federalism, 34; as the third stage of bureaucratization of the PRC, 95–96
Moore, Barrington, 151, 183, 234, 235, 272n8, 279n4
Morrison, Kevin: on the destabilizing effect of increased taxation, 29, 30, 31–32, 36; on the importance of nontax revenue for authoritarian resilience, 37, 74, 253n67; on spending and regime stability, 25, 41, 74, 253n67
Morse, Yonatan, 4, 8
Moustafa, Tamir, 23, 217, 247n8, 283n16

Nair, Gautam, 279n6
Nathan, Andrew J.: on aspects of the CCP's institutionalization that drive its resilience, 26–27
national anticorruption campaign, 250n35; CCDI's investigation of ministers and officials, 2–3; collusion of capitalists with the party-state revealed by, 191; stories of military control and factional struggle revealed by, 249n24
National People's Congress (NPC), 2; and the amendment to the Indi-

vidual Income Tax (IIT) Law, 43–45; and citizens' awareness of taxation, 70; responsiveness of its deputies to constituents, 278n94; tax legislation power delegated to the State Council by the NPC Standing Committee, 75; tax reform of 1994 not approved by, 259n60

Naughton, Barry, 45, 47, 262n4, 286n49

Nee, Victor, 219

nomenklatura system of the CCP: and the CCP's Organization Department, 86, 155, 162, 274n38; and performance-based cadre evaluation, 26, 250n32, 253n66; and the reform of the taxation system, 214, 250n33, 282

nontax revenue, 33; the agent-discipline problem worsened by, 54, 118; inequality in China related to, 53–54, 73. *See also* land finance; state-owned enterprises (SOE)

North, Douglass, 45; institutional hierarchy discussed by, 226; theory of double balance developed by, 241–42, 287n63

Nygård, Håvard Mokleiv, 4, 249n30

O'Brien, Kevin J., 22–23, 152, 153, 161, 164, 170, 221

Oi, Jean C., 220; local state corporatism theory of, 34, 212–13, 248n15, 263n14

Olson, Mancur, 24, 35

open-access social order: the CCP's transition to, 241–43; and the concept of inclusive institutions, 287n63; "development clusters" concept of Besley and Persson compared with, 287n63; rule of law and democracy associated with, 241; Weber's legal-rational domination compared with, 287n64

Ostrom, Elinor, 225

Pan, Jennifer, 25, 248n18

Pepinsky, Thomas B., 4, 33, 159, 206, 223, 224, 249n30; institutional explanations of authoritarian resilience criticized by, 223–24, 224, 283n25

Persson, Torsten, 42, 224, 228; concept of "development clusters," 229, 235–36, 284n36, 287n63

Pierson, Paul, 225

Poland, 235–36, 248n17

Prasad, Monica, 212, 246n11, 281n1

pressure-based systems (*yalixing tizhi*): description of, 86; governance dilemmas in the CCP addressed by, 32; tax administration as, 39–40, 86, 253n61. *See also* tax-target systems

private-enterprise survey (PES): and the ACFIC, 11, 194; governance quality measured by four indicators based on PES data, 195–96; limitations of its data set, 195, 280n25; tax burden indicators on, 195–96, *196*

Putnam, Robert D., question concerning quality of governance, 13, 123, 146, 180

rationalization of bureaucracy: effectiveness in reducing corruption, 27; regional variation of LPC rationalization and representation, 159; and the Taxation Bureau, 85

rentier state, 37, 46, 49, 147, 235, 236, 282n3

representation dilemma: increased taxation capacity as a means to increase representation, 216, 240; as one of two taxation dilemmas for authoritarian governments, 6, 31–32; rational choice institutional explanations of, 31–32; relationship to the three governance problems, 32, *32*; social control related to, 32; and tax bargaining in imperial China, 232–33

Robinson, James, 240, 242, 251n43, 287n63; on the impact of resources on economic and political consequences, 37

Rowe, William T., 285n44

Rubin, Jared, "principle-agent model" of, 232

328   INDEX

Russia: China's current tax state compared with, 235–36; taxation and state building in, 235, 263–64n17, 286n51

Schumpeter, Joseph, 92, 209, 210; on fiscal sociology, 1, 5, 16, 31, 247n7, 283n18; on taxation as a cause for social and political change, 33, 224; typology of state based on it revenue sources developed by, 246n10

Shanxi Province: coal resources in, 268; "landslide corruption" in, 124, 135. *See also* County Cold Mountain (Shanxi); County D (Shanxi)

Shigeki, Iwai, 230–31

Shirk, Susan L., 250n33, 250n34

Sima, Qian: *Shiji*, 14, 246n1

single-party regimes: and authoritarian resilience, 4, 26, 282n10; and the institution of taxation, 227–30; SOE's as the backbone of, 62, 227

Skocpol, Theda, 250–51n40

Slater, Dan, 242; on the infrastructural power mechanisms of taxation, 28, 184, 206, 215; on the lack of infrastructural power mechanisms of taxation among postcolonial states, 279n6; ruler's despotic power and its contribution to infrastructural power as a focus of, 251n48

Smith, Benjamin: infrastructural power mechanisms of taxation proposed by, 28, 206; on the lack of infrastructural power mechanisms of taxation among postcolonial states, 279n6

social control: authoritarian control distinguished from social control under democracy, 18; identified as one of the three governance problems, 5; and the power-sharing problem, 20; the representation dilemma related to, 32; and under-institutionalized taxation embedded in de facto fiscal federalism, 186–92

Solnick, Steven, 19, 282n11

Stasavage, David, 286n49

State Administration of Taxation (SAT), 246; and the central government bureaucracy, 260n70; merging with the LTB into the new SAT, 15, 91, 242, 288n74; and the organizational structure of tax administration in China before 2018, 78–80, 79

state capacity: and the agent-discipline problem, 19–20; and bureaucratization, 28, 215; definition of, 216; and the paradox of building state capacity and maintaining personal power, 22, 249n28, 250n40; the role of parties in improving government capability, 26. *See also* taxation capacity

state-owned enterprises (SOE): as the backbone of single-party rule, 62, 227; as the basis of the socialist economic system of the PRC, 55–62, 56, 57, 58; bonuses offered to managers and workers, 62, 256n22; city investment corporations (*Chengshi touzi gongsi*) established in County Warm River, 116–17; corruption associated with, 62, 74, 258n38, 259n56; gradualist economic reform of, 264n23; party and government titles of SOE managers, 270n40

Stern, Rachel, and Jonathan Hassid, 220, 283n20

Stockmann, Daniela, 248n18

Sun, Xiaoyi, 119

Sun, Xin, 153–54

Svolik, Milan, 5, 25; authoritarian control defined by, 18; on regime resilience through co-option and direct political control, 26, 220, 247n8, 251n48, 252n32, 282n10

Swedberg, Richard, 16, 222, 247n7, 255n13, 283n18, 287n64

Tan, Ern Ser, 248n19

tax administration: defined by Lieberman (Evan), 33, 76; and the Golden Tax Project (GTP), 85, 282n8; historical China compared with contemporary China, 230–34; as "non-rule-based" according to Wei Cui, 252–53n61; organizational structure of tax administration in China before 2018, 78–81, 79; as a pressure-based system (*yalixing tizhi*), 39–40, 86, 253n61, 282n10. See also State Administration of Taxation (SAT); Tax-Sharing Reform (TSR); tax-state transition in the PRC

taxation: and authoritarian welfare expenditure, 25–26; and CCP's resilience, 224; as complementary with legality in developed countries according to Besley and Persson, 224, 229; destabilizing effect of increased taxation (according to Morrison), 29, 30, 31–32, 36; fiscal sociology of, 16; infrastructural power of, 6, 12, 28–29, 184, 206; as a means of class struggle during the Cultural Revolution, 49, 51, 76, 256n19, 256n19; representation-through-taxation mechanism as a problem, 13, 31, 166; as a tool of legal repression for the CCP, 219–20; VAT for business (*yinggaizeng*), 53. See also half-tax states; Tax-Sharing Reform (TSR)

taxation capacity: authoritarian states' building of, 214, 240; increased taxation capacity as a means to increase representation, 216, 240; and private entrepreneurs' concerns about tax and nontax burdens with the merger of the SAT and LTB, 242, 288n74; and state capacity in postcommunist countries, 282n6; of taxation bureaus since the late 1990s, 279n11. See also under-institutionalized taxation

taxation reform: centralization of taxation by the CCP, 53, 214, 227; focus of in China before, 52, 1984; merging of SAT and LBT into a new SAT, 15; and VAT for business tax (*yinggaizeng*), 14, 52, 227. See also Tax-Sharing Reform (TSR)

tax breaks: and corruption, 108; and the discretional power of tax bureaus, 90; as an incentive for private entrepreneurs to run in an election, 167, 189–90; and market development, 112, 115, 142, 145–46; and under-institutionalized taxation, 186, 237–38, 238

tax burdens: citizens' tax burden, 6, 36, 44, 69–70, 71, 72, 217, 246n12; indicators on the PES questionnaire, 195–96, 196; and private entrepreneurs' concerns about tax and nontax burdens with the merger of the SAT and LTB, 242, 288n74; rampant tax evasion resulting from, 186–87; reference to the "death-tax rate," 91, 283n23; structural and institutional causes of tax and nontax burdens, 192–93; Zhou Dewen on the tax burden for SMEs, 186

tax evasion: as an adaptive informal institution, 187; and the deinstitutionalization of tax regime, 186–90, 269n23; the discretionary power of tax bureaus as a cause of, 90, 168, 182, 189; in imperial China, 232, 233; punishment set by China's Criminal Law, 187, 279–80n12; rampant tax evasion in Hunan Province, 77; TSR's curtailing of, 82–84; by TVEs, 104; and the under-institutionalized taxation system, 210, 217

tax farming, 237; and the fiscal decentralization of the 1980s, 234; in the imperial China, 232–33; the tax-target system as a modern version of, 215–16

Tax-Sharing Reform (TSR): institutional foundation for a market a bureaucracy provided by, 212; land-transfer fees increased in compensation for loss of taxation power resulting from, 64–65; negative consequences of, 53–54, 64; negative impact on central-local fiscal relationships of, 68, 80; recentralization and rationalization of tax administration by, 39, 53, 81–82, 227; Zhu Rongji's promotion of, 284n33

tax-state transition in the PRC: and authoritarian resilience, 5; impact on the three governance problems, 210–11; implications for tax administration, 75–76, 214; implications for taxation dilemmas, 49–50, *49*, 210–11; and M-form and U-form economies, 46, 254n8; and stages of, *46*
tax-target systems, 283n14; as a modern version of the tax-farming system, 215–16, 283n14; pressure-based administration of LTBs facilitated by, 87–90; rule of law of taxation violated by, 40, 86
Thelen, Kathleen, 226, 284n29
three governance problems: the CCP's efforts to address them, 15, 210–11; relationship to the two dilemmas, 32, *32*; taxation's complementary role in their resolution, 5; and tax-state transition in the PRC, 210–11; the three types of tax states related to, 48–50. *See also* agent discipline; growth dilemma; representation dilemma; cooperation; social control
Tiebout, Charles, 36
Tilly, Charles, 31
Tocqueville, Alexis de, 210; fiscal sociology of, 5, 219, 245n9, 283n18; perspective on state structures, 218–19
Torvik, Ragnar, on the impact of resources on economic and political consequences, 37
Treisman, Daniel, 250n33, 252n55
Truex, Rory, 153, 278n94
Tsai, Kellee S.: on adaptive informal institutions, 34, 120–21, 187, 284n35; on the promotion of democracy by assertive private entrepreneurs, 279n8
Tsai, Lily L., 220
Tsebelis, George, 225, 226
Turgot, Anne-Robert-Jacques, 43, 73, 254n2

under-institutionalized taxation administration: and authoritarian resilience, 7, 32, 40–42, 185–92, 238; economic growth harmed by, 238; forbearance and fear generated by, 182, 185, 210; limited-access order associated with, 217–18, 221–22, 242–43; reformation via the institutionalization of the taxation system, 237–38, 241–42; role in resolving the three governance problems, 6–7, 205; and tax collection in China, 38–40, 75–76, 233–34

Verdier, Thierry, on the impact of resources on economic and political consequences, 37

Wallis, John, 45, 241–42, 287n63
Wang, Jianlin, on running a company in China, 190
Wang, Min, CCDI's investigation of, 2
Wang, Shaoguang, 52–53, 264n28
Wang, Wiaolu, 62, 259n54
Wang, Xiaoyan, 275n56
Wang, Yeh-Chien, 232
Wang, Yuhua, 207
Waterbury, John, 37
Way, Lucan A.: authoritarian durability defined by, 245n5; on legal repression, 253n63; on organizational power and authoritarian stability, 26, 250n31, 282n13
Weber, Max, 92; fiscal sociology of, 5, 16, 233, 252n53, 255n13, 285n44; legal rational domination defined by, 222; perspective on state structures, 218; on tax administration and its implications for bureaucratization, 210; typologies of domination, 287n64
Weingast, Barry, 45, 241–42, 287n63
Weinthal, Erika, 123, 147
Whiting, Susan, 35, 50, 66, 250n33, 250n38, 252n50, 252n57
Weiss, Jessica Chen, 248n19
Wong, Christine, 73, 242
World Bank, on good governance, 278n101
Wright, Joseph, 249n29
Wu, Yiping, 153–54

Xi Jinping, 239n36; controlling the "knife" of the CPL emphasized by, 21; private entrepreneurs addressed by, 47, 247n6, 255n9, 255n12, 288n74; sincerity and honesty in relationships between government and business called for, 1–2, 182; Zhejiang Province regarded as leading reform in China, 124
Xiao, Donglian, 287n59
Xu Chenggang, 94–95
Xu Xianglin, 45, 254n5

Yan, Xiaojun, 153–54, 249n25
Yashar, Deborah, 216
You, Yu, 68

Zelin, Melinda, 231
Zhang, Jianjun, 268n14
Zhejiang Province: Association for Protecting Private Enterprises in, 107; public participation and transparency in its local government, 124; regarded as leading reform in China by Xi Jinping, 124; tax riot in Zhili town of Huzhou, 283n22. *See also* County C; County Warm River; County Wenling; County Yiwu
Zhou Dewen, on the tax burden for SMEs, 186
Zhou, Kai, 249n25
Zhou, Li'an, 35
Zhu, Jiangnan, 153–54
Zhu, Rongji: divide-and-rule strategy of, 228; market-oriented reforms of, 68, 265nn38–39. *See also* Tax-Sharing Reform (TSR)

NEW TIMES

GLOBAL STUDIES IN EDUCATION

A.C. (Tina) Besley, Michael A. Peters,
Cameron McCarthy, Fazal Rizvi
General Editors

Vol. 5

PETER LANG
New York • Washington, D.C./Baltimore • Bern
Frankfurt • Berlin • Brussels • Vienna • Oxford

NEW TIMES

Making Sense of Critical/ Cultural Theory in a Digital Age

EDITED BY Cameron McCarthy,
Heather Greenhalgh-Spencer, and Robert Mejia

PETER LANG
New York • Washington, D.C./Baltimore • Bern
Frankfurt • Berlin • Brussels • Vienna • Oxford

Library of Congress Cataloging-in-Publication Data

New times: making sense of critical/cultural theory in a digital age /
edited by Cameron McCarthy, Heather Greenhalgh-Spencer, Robert Mejia.
p. cm. — (Global studies in education; v. 5)
Includes bibliographical references and index.
1. Social sciences—Philosophy. 2. Social sciences—Study and teaching.
3. Critical theory. 4. Internet--Social aspects. I. McCarthy, Cameron.
II. Greenhalgh-Spencer, Heather. III. Mejia, Robert.
H61.15.N39   300.1—dc22   2010053220
ISBN 978-1-4331-1278-2 (hardcover)
ISBN 978-1-4331-1277-5 (paperback)
ISSN 2153-330X

Bibliographic information published by **Die Deutsche Nationalbibliothek**.
Die Deutsche Nationalbibliothek lists this publication in the "Deutsche
Nationalbibliografie"; detailed bibliographic data is available
on the Internet at http://dnb.d-nb.de/.

Cover design by Steven Doran

The paper in this book meets the guidelines for permanence and durability
of the Committee on Production Guidelines for Book Longevity
of the Council of Library Resources.

© 2011 Peter Lang Publishing, Inc., New York
29 Broadway, 18th floor, New York, NY 10006
www.peterlang.com

All rights reserved.
Reprint or reproduction, even partially, in all forms such as microfilm,
xerography, microfiche, microcard, and offset strictly prohibited.

Printed in the United States of America

CONTENTS

Foreword   ix
DOUGLAS M. KELLNER

Acknowledgements xiii

Introduction: Mapping the New Terrain. 1
CAMERON MCCARTHY, HEATHER GREENHALGH-SPENDER, & ROBERT MEJIA

Section I—New Times

1. Theory through Practice: A History of Cultural Studies   23
   ROBERT MEJIA

2. Labor and Totality in "Participatory" Digital Capitalism   51
   ERGIN BULUT

3. Seeing Red: Ruptured Identity and the Representation of Black American Women Living with HIV and AIDS   70
   CAROLYN RANDOLPH

4. Reconstructing Race and Education in the Class Conquest of the City and the University in the Era of Neoliberalism and Globalization 86
CAMERON MCCARTHY

Section II—Reconfigurations of Governance/Technologies of Subjectivity

5. The Cultural Logic of Search and the Myth of Disintermediation 107
MATTHEW CRAIN

6. Freedom Devices: Neoliberalism, Mobile Technologies, and Governance 129
STEVEN DORAN

7. Glocal Transgender: Transgender Longing and Belonging in the Shadow of 9/11 148
STEPHEN HOCKER

8. Re-imagining Harvey Milk: Queering Identity Politics 171
ALICE LIAO

Section III—Reterritorializing Bodies

9. From Masculinity to Cybermasculinity: Marginalizing the Other in "DCinside" 195
JUNGMIN KWON

10. Displaced Bodies and Governmentality: Lessons from the CHA Website 229
CRYSTAL THOMAS

11. Body/Flesh of the Teacher in the Digital Age 254
HEATHER GREENHALGH-SPENCER

Section IV—Global Regimes and Local Transformations

12. Understanding Neoliberalism and Its Implications for Contemporary Educational Policies 277
VIVIANA PITTON

13. Traveling Policies: Mobility, Transformations and Continuities in
    Higher Education Public Policy   303
    RODRIGO BRITEZ

14. M: A Critical Analysis of a Cultural Artifact   329
    JAMES GEARY

    Afterword: Manifesto for Education in the Age
    of Cognitive Capitalism   349
    MICHAEL A. PETERS

    Contributors   365

    Index   373

Foreword

DOUGLAS M. KELLNER

Over the past several decades contemporary societies and the global (dis)order have been undergoing significant social and technological transformation with the continuous emergence of new media and new forms of culture and communication. With dramatic proliferations of computer and digital technologies in the 1980s, dramatic shifts emerged in the economy, society, and culture with critical theories adopting discourses of the new and the postmodern to describe the dramatic mutations taking place in every sphere from the economy to everyday life.

With this explosion of new media and emergent forms of digital culture and communication from the 1990s through the present, critical theories have faced the challenge of engaging the new and emergent, both in terms of new objects of theory and new types of critical theory. Following British cultural studies, the editors of *New Times: Making Sense of Critical/Cultural Theory in a Digital Age* adopt the rubric "New Times" for the shifting constellations of the contemporary moment. Attempting to map a shifting global terrain, the studies collected here reflect on new media that are transforming our lives, thoughts, modes of communication and interaction, and very identities—and have developed new theories to engage these constellations.

In this force-field of the new, theories co-evolve with new media and new forms of culture and society, requiring vigilance, self-reflexivity, and a critical spirit to make connections, see the novelties and challenges, and resist the hype. The contemporary moment is still one in which all that is solid continues to melt into air (Marx and Engels), and (post)modernities and identities are described as flexible, fluid, and liquid, with transformation and mutation dominant tropes in contemporary critical theory. Yet despite the vertigo of the new, the editors and authors attempt to map this shifting terrain and a panorama of new media and forms of economy, society, the polity, culture and identity. Sections of the text engage "New Times," "Reconfigurations of Governance/Technologies of Subjectivity," "Reterritorializing Bodies," and "Global Regimes and Local Transformations." Individual authors take on specific configurations of culture and theory to grasp changes and novelties in the force-field of the new and to highlight as well old boundaries, continuities, and continuing forms of inequality and oppression.

The authors and readers of these studies face the challenge of avoiding one-sided theories that would grasp dramatic changes in the economy, polity, and society in reductive fashion, yet they seek to confront the rigidities as well as fluidities of capital, the state, institutions like the family, schools, and the media, and the continuation of hierarchies and oppressions of class, gender, race, and sexuality. Certainly capitalism is today flexible, liquid, and fast, but differences between the rich and the poor continue to grow, and inequalities and the power of capital often seem to intensify. Yes, many live on-line and digital culture becomes for some increasingly virtual, but materialities continue to starve, impoverish, and oppress individuals who cannot afford the luxury of either the virtual good life or the good life itself.

New media destabilize this terrain and the old boundaries of hierarchy, inequality, and oppression but also allow dominant and nimble social actors and institutions to increase their power and control. New media can generate a new politics of resistance and solidarities but also provide the old ruling classes and powers new forms of wealth, power, and domination. Identities are indeed more hybrid, fluid, and flexible, and yet racism, sexism, classism, and homophobia continue to exist, often in virulent new forms, like cyberbullying.

What, then, are the emergent forms of critical and cultural theory that attempt to engage the shifting and obdurate modes of the contemporary? Different authors in *New Times* necessarily and beneficially adopt various and diverse strategies of presentation and critique, and my conclusion, after reading through these studies, is that new critical/cultural studies need to be inter-

or trans-disciplinary in a terrain in which boundaries between the economic, political, social, and psychological often overlap and even implode, yet old forces of domination continue to control many spheres of existence. This trans-disciplinary theory should be historical, grasping the novelties of new media, forms of culture and communication, and everyday life, but grasping continuities with old forms of oppression and domination that continue to exist. Indeed, new critical/cultural theories confront novel configurations of immateriality and the virtual, but also new forms of the material and of domination across axes of class, gender, race, sexuality, and other domains of lived experience. We are increasingly affected by multiplying forms of the global and expanding global world, yet at the same time the national and local continue to play key roles in our lives, leading theorists to engage dialectics of the local, national, and global to address problems and challenges of the contemporary moment.

Since the old and the new co-exist and evolve in new ways, and new media and forms of virtual culture produce constant changes and transformation, theory too must evolve and engage the challenges of the contemporary. The project of critical/cultural theory in this complex and sometime vertiginous flux is thus to engage forms of the new, see continuities and discontinuities with the old, and combine critique and negation with hope and possibilities. The studies that follow contribute, in their own ways, to this project and provide critical/cultural theory with new tools to map the terrain of contemporary culture and society and weapons of critique to analyze, criticize, and transform. The varying texts in the following collection thus attempt to both analyze and critique society and culture in the new millennium, helping us to understand the novelties and continuities of the present age, and to reflect on what theories and practices we need for engaging the challenges of the emergent forms of the virtual.

LOS ANGELES, OCTOBER 8, 2010

Acknowledgments

New Times: Making Sense of Critical/Cultural Theory in a Digital Age is first and foremost the product of an open, student-centered pedagogical process continuing the distinctive tradition of Cultural Studies initiated at the University of Illinois by James Carey, Lawrence Grossberg, Cary Nelson and Paula Treichler among others. It took the form of a series of elaborated conversations on the future of Cultural Studies, particularly in light of the transforming meanings of technology, history, governance, identity and the body in the new millennium—the Digital Age.

The fellow travelers in these discussions are the participants of the University of Illinois' Institute of Communication Research Student/Faculty Research and Writing Collaborative—a long-standing collective that has been in continuous operation since the 1990s. The authors come from several colleges across campus, consist of various nationalities, ethnic affiliations, class backgrounds, and sexual orientations, emphasizing the centrality of diversity to the realization not only of this project but the experience of the Writing Collaborative in general.

Members of the Writing Collaborative were, and continue to be, actively involved in other intellectual groups, and they brought those "external" conversations back with them when we met at our regular Friday meetings. These communities outside of the Writing Collaborative were fruitful spaces in which members shared early versions of their chapters and received the additional intellectual and emotional support necessary to see this project to fruition. Due to the importance these groups have served, we wish to thank the Center for East Asian and Pacific Studies' Korea Workshop, the InfoStructure: Intersections Between Social and Technological Systems "Focal Point" project, the Institute of Communications Research's Women of the Black Atlantic collective, and the Unit for Criticism and Critical Theory.

In addition, we especially would like to thank the Institute's former director, Cliff Christians, and the current director and head of the University of Illinois' Department of Media and Cinema Studies, Angharad Valdivia, for their unwavering support and provision of research assistance. We were fortunate that the University's College of Media provided the Collaborative with the now famous room, 336 Greg Hall, as the working space for our operations and regular deliberations. For this, we wish to express sincerest gratitude to the Deans Walt Harrington and Janet Slater. The Senior Editors of the Global Studies in Education Series for Peter Lang, Tina Belsey, Michael Peters, Fazal Rizvi and our colleague, Cameron McCarthy must also be thanked. They have been keen supporters of this project from its inception. We are grateful to Christopher Myers, the Managing Editor at Peter Lang-New York, and his colleagues in acquisitions, production and marketing—Patricia Mulrane Clayton, Bernadette Shade and Catherine Tung.

Finally, the editors wish to express our sincerest thanks to the members of this Friday meeting group who transformed themselves into the most earnest of contributors to this volume. Speaking particularly for the two graduate student editors, Heather and Robert, we are particularly grateful and honored to have worked so intimately with the authors whose work is found within these pages. We became editors almost inadvertently, and it is our hope that this "happy accident" will have granted us the opportunity to illustrate how much we respect you all—not just as fellow intellectuals, but amazingly wonderful people. Thank you.

Introduction

CAMERON MCCARTHY, HEATHER GREENHALGH-SPENCER, & ROBERT MEJIA

> Social science categories are becoming zombie categories, empty terms in the Kantian meaning. Zombie categories are living dead categories, which blind the social sciences to the rapidly changing realities inside the nation-state containers and outside as well.
> —BECK, 2002, P. 24

> Today the most popular title in our literature takes the form "The End" [. . .]. This is the "structure of feeling," to use Raymond Williams' felicitous phrase, of our time, mingling apocalyptic and redemptive endings.
> —CAREY, 2002, P. 197

In grappling with Dewey's enigmatic comments regarding the relationship between society, culture, and communication, James Carey (2009) invoked the anti-intellectualist spirit of the day and remarked, "if you need sociologists to inform you whether or not you have a ruling class, you surely don't" (p. 12). In a similar vein, one could say that if you need a media studies scholar to tell you that you are living in the new times of a digital age, well, then you probably aren't. But, perhaps this claim is too simplistic: in spite of his skepticism, Carey retained hope in the intellectual endeavor of exploring new commitments and new practices. It was Carey's wrestlings with Dewey that brought about a radical reconfiguration of communication; communication was recognized as a constitutive cultural ritual. Because Carey was willing to engage the seemingly obvious, the human-centered notion of *ritual* has allowed for contemporary media scholars to analyze the formal characteristics of a given communicative act. Using the concept of "ritual," it becomes possible to explore the new times of this digital age without risk of falling into the trap of technological determinism as advanced by some strands of media ecology (e.g., Postman, 1986).[1]

Today, we face a similar challenge: how does one speak of the new? The question has become so mundane and the answer so obvious that to not respond properly seems to evoke outrage, even amongst those who ironically disagree on the appropriate response! (e.g., Curran, 2006; Frasca, 2003; Juul, 2001; McChesney, 2004; Postman, 1986). Those operating under (or against) the broad rubric of new media studies are adamant that a radical structural break marks the difference between old and new communications technologies (Frasca, 2003; Juul, 2001; Postman, 1986). The evidence for such a perspective is abundant. In only the last twenty years, we have witnessed the massive integration of the personal computer, the Internet, mobile communications, social networking, and other new media technologies. The communications landscape has so transformed that new media "start-ups" are now able to politically and economically challenge old media companies: Amazon versus Barnes & Noble; Google versus the Baby Bells; Nintendo versus Sony; et cetera. Culturally, new media technologies have so saturated the social (see Doran, in this volume) that the idea of using an old media technology, such as a boom box, has faded away along with the popularity of *Saved by the Bell*, *A Flock of Seagulls*, *The Karate Kid*, and other cultural relics of the 80s. Even when these cultural artifacts persist, through the nostalgia of their remembrance, the tendency seems to be to reconstruct, rather than re-live, the contents of the past in the form of the present: remastering the *Star Wars* series (1997); remaking *The Karate Kid* (2010); and, even recycling the past as a vehicle for parody, e.g., *The Wedding Singer* (1998). These are not flippant new media developments but rather represent significant cultural transformations that have already had dramatic effects on contemporary society; even if scholars cannot agree if that is a positive or negative development (e.g., Benkler, 2009; Starr, 2009).

In contrast to new media scholars, more guarded media theorists tend to see the structural continuity of contemporary media as evidence that technological developments, in and of themselves, do not constitute social transformations. In this regard, the focus on technology, as a thing in itself, functions as a red herring that takes the critical gaze away from the more important political economic structures of society (Curran, 2006; McChesney, 2004). Scholars operating in this tradition present equally compelling counter-evidence as those engaged with the new media rubric. Yes, new communications technologies have been developed, but their deployment has frequently been within the service of capital and not democracy. One only needs to reference the popular *Palm Centro* commercials to learn, quite blatantly, that these new devices are not intended to expand the public sphere but rather to amplify the political and economic (see Crain, in this volume). The commercial announces:

> Life is busy; but, some people seem to get more done than others. *Multitaskers.* They found a way to do several things all at once; and when the *Palm Centro was designed, Sprint thought of these people.* Then we gave it Sprint Speed. You can email, text, chat, go online, so fast, people may wonder how many of you there really are. ([italics added], Sprint, 2007)

During this advertisement, the above quote is read pleasantly, all while images of people are shown doing everyday and mundane activities (i.e., waiting for a train) as they struggle to balance the increasing encroachment of work upon leisure. Throughout the commercial, the cell phone is advertised explicitly as a technology that will immerse you further in this world of capital. This is not a case of reading too deeply into one commercial (as other examples are prevalent), but rather an acknowledgment that advertisements are powerful sources of interpellation: *they tell us how to use a product properly.* In this regard, the governmentality of media discourse has a longer history than that which new media theorists would typically acknowledge; old-school capitalists have been making a profit from the intersections of media, news, products, and placement, long before the Internet represented a viable platform (McChesney, 1999; Nichols & McChesney, 2009).

As noted, both old and new media theorists have made compelling arguments in support of their historical claims: structural continuity or radical break. The problem, as Vincent Mosco (1989) notes, is that the new media perspective is naïve in its understanding of historical processes; or, as Carolyn Marvin (1988) puts it, "*New Technologies* is a historically relative term" (p. 3). Yet, too much emphasis on the long duration of historical development represents an equally untenable ethical dilemma (Mosco, 1989); this is because, as Jacques Ellul (1964) argued:

> The ideal Man is an escapism which eases every kind of enormity with tranquilizing abstractions. [. . .] What is important is not the adaptability of Man [sic], but the adaptability of men [sic]. We shall find the answer, not in the immortal soul of the Species, but in the preservation of our own souls, which are, perhaps, not immortal. (pp. 397–398)

In essence, those operating under the rubric of old media studies have a tendency to downplay the significance of the lived experience of those who currently occupy the historical space. As E.P. Thompson (1998) famously wrote, to write poorly of those who did the best they could (e.g., as in those who today buy a cell phone because they believe it a necessity), is to write with "the enormous condescension of posterity" and to ignore that "they lived through these times of acute social disturbance, and we did not" (p. 60). And in the same vein, new media theorists do the working class no favors when they advocate the adoption of new technologies as the panacea for their social ills—especially when those very technologies are both the product of cheap labor and designed to extract even more labor from the bodies of its users. Hence, both the old and new media traditions remain unsatisfactory in their construction of historical change, as an all or nothing reality.

The interventions by Mosco and others into this debate of the old versus the new have resulted in significant theoretical contributions. For instance, new "old" media studies have persuasively argued that new communications technologies have continued to transform the phenomenological experience of engaging old media artifacts themselves (Gitelman, 2008); in essence, old media artifacts are not structurally sound repositories of content, but rather, since these media contents exist within a network of other media systems, changes or additions to one node transform the experience in another. In essence, old media are "always already new" (Gitelman, 2008). Likewise, others, like Jonathan Sterne (2006), have illustrated how new media developments are not just about the internal relationship between a yet-to-be-captured content and its formal container, but also the cultural flow and manipulation of those contents via the medium—in essence, new media practices. These scholarly interventions are necessary as they help to combat the debilitating tendency for old media theorists to look longingly towards the past and ignore the "cultural gaps" that are to be found in all media technologies, which are necessary for the production and maintenance of alternative cultures, such as hiphop (Franzen & McLeod, 2008; Sterne, 2006). These new "old" media studies theorists have also avoided the pitfalls that seem to plague some strands of new media studies by taking heed that technologies are not ahistorical developments but rather emerge out of particular social conditions and transform due to ongoing cultural engagement (Sterne, 2005).

As a critical collective of contributors to *New Times: Making Sense of Critical/Cultural Theory in a Digital Age*, we have sought to navigate this path of the "new" in light of the tensions and theoretical contributions addressed above. This is necessary if we are to better understand the direction of the pivotal social dynamics in the new century; for in spite of all the insights provided, much of the intellectual contributions cited above remain constrained to the particular histories of their technological apparatuses: sound reproduction (Sterne, 2005); telephony (Marvin, 1988); broadcasting (McChesney, 1999); et cetera. For critical scholars looking to understand the broader socio-cultural field, there is the feeling that these isolated micro-histories have contributed to the disjuncture between the theoretical and methodological efforts of proponents of a radically transformed reality. As powerful as the contributions of media studies have been, the absolute emphasis on the omnipresence and omnipotence of the media has contributed to a theoretical reductionism whereby either "all history becomes media history" or "all of history is prehistory until network television" (Nerone, 2003, p. 100). These monocausal approaches have never been adequate, but they appear all the more easily dismissed (sometimes too hastily) at this particular juncture of history in which it seems that the "teeth gritting harmony" of contemporary society is becoming increasingly untenable (Goss, 1999). Hence, while it may be useful to emphasize the harmonic convergence of various institutional state apparatuses, for the sake of political intervention, this must always be done with an eye to messy and contested space of lived experience (Goss, 1999; Hall, 2001); failure to do so means to develop theoretically vapid "god" and "devil" terms which lack the structural integrity upon which to establish a politically sound social movement (Brown, 2006).

Likewise, though it is not the project of this edited volume to revisit this ground in any systematic way, there is the sense that the critical macro-theoretical traditions, such as that of Marxism, have been pushed too far beyond their intellectually productive comfort zones: past the self-contained parameters of the nation state; past the pivotal relevance of the soldiering white working class as the subject/object of history; and past the clean divide of production and consumption, work and leisure. Of course, critical scholars have become increasingly cognizant of this problem; particularly, cultural studies has in recent years taken up the task of a persistent and reflexive Marxist revisionism. Stuart Hall, for example, has constantly pointed to the need to raise a new horizon of analysis in these new times of the "free market written on the body politic" (Hall cited in Roman, 2005, p. 78). Paul Willis (2005) has written about the impact of what he calls a "third wave" of technological modernity bearing down on a disorganized working class and the arrival of the new post-Fordist order of chronic unemployment and outsourcing of jobs. Anoop Nayak

(2003) has pointed to a new spatiality and cultural geography in urban centers in which globalization keeps throwing immigrants up against native white working class actors now torn from even their most secure enclaves. Each of these scholars has issued notice of the declining theoretical purchase of critical theory; James Curran (2006), in particular, goes farther by brilliantly pointing to the way in which the new values of possessive individualism, neoliberalism, and the collapse of Eastern Communism have worked reflexively back onto the theoretical peregrinations of cultural studies scholars themselves. Yet, while each of these scholars has convincingly demonstrated the declining theoretical purchase of contemporary critical theory, they nevertheless seem to evince a kind of nostalgia for a remorselessly vanishing past (McCarthy and Logue, 2009).

The Logic of the Book

In *New Times: Making Sense of Critical/Cultural Theory in a Digital Age*, we seek to get beyond nostalgia and chest beating for critical theory in order to map some of the main currents and pivotal problems spawned in the new millennium. This is a new era that some have called neoliberalism or neoliberal globalization. We see critical theory, particularly in its cultural studies incarnation, as still viable but only as one theoretical lens on the complex contemporary reality that keeps changing and evolving (Kellner, 1995, 2005). We are, after all, now firmly living in a postindustrial order where the processes of technological change, the transnational dispersal of cultural and economic capital, the rapidity of movement and migration of populations, the proliferation and amplification of images through computerization, the ubiquity of smart technologies and small-handheld mobile devices such as the mobile phone, GPS systems, digital gaming, and indeed our very bodies participate in the elaboration of a new order. There is a new infrastructuralism (see Doran, in this volume) that is defined by a saturating convergence and overlapping of all of the long-standing distinctions deployed in neo-Marxist cultural analysis. Quite literally the cultural analysis flowing out of the neo-Marxist paradigm is now overtaken by these events.

Like the rest of the social sciences, against which it has previously revolted, it now seems fair to say that critical theory's analysis of the social formation is now overtaken by the dawning of a new set of dynamics. It seems the perceptual/conceptual/linguistic apparatus of socio-cultural analysis on the whole is now unable to diagnose the global predicament we are in, seemingly reinforcing the very structures we seek to subvert. Our entire perceptual, conceptual, and linguistic apparatus is in need of overhaul as we come to recognize the rise of networked societies in which traditions, affiliations, and "cultures" (subcultures or not), are now disembedded from the moorings of the final property of any group (Tomlinson, 2007). There has been a flattening out of cultures and traditions integrated into the global expansion of markets and flexible models of production of capital pursuing new sites of value in increasingly alienated contexts (Bauman, 2010; Sennett, 2008). We have reached a stage in this new millennium where the old "conflict" versus "consensus" metaphors, "your traditions versus mine" do not seem to apply. Instead of models based on conflict and resistance, increasingly social groups are being defined by overwhelming patterns of transnational hybridities, new forms of association, affiliation and feeling that seem to flash on the surface of life rather than to plunge deeper down into some kind of neo-Marxist substructure. These are the hybridities, dialogisms, and performativities spoken of by Shirley Anne Tate (2005). As Tate (2005) notes, identity becomes multiple, contextual, and not necessarily rooted in place, race, or nation. Identity loses its grounding and becomes liquid: liquid asset. This new order is held together by a new model of power which we could call "convergence," as Henry Jenkins (2006) and Mark Deuze (2007) have chosen to name it. It does not have a negative pole. It is what Foucault has described as a "productive" not "repressive" model of power. It articulates difference into ever-more extensive systems of association, flat-lining the edges of culture into a pastiche of marketable identities, tastes, neuroses and needs processed through the universalization of the enterprise ethic (Comaroff & Comaroff, 2009; Klein, 2000, 2007). It lays traditions down side by side, layering them in ever-new ephemeral patterns and intensities—whole elements and associations given in one place can now be instantaneously found in another. If Paul Willis's nationally and geographically inscribed "lads" were the poster children of the old industrial order of yesteryear guarding the territory of their known world on the shop floor, today, it is Jenny Kelly's Afro-Canadian youth, cell-phone in hand, patching together their identities from the surfeit of signs and symbols crossing the border in the electronic relays of US television, popular music, digital game and cyber culture who now stand in as the subject/object of the new, post-industrial era (Kelly, 2003). It is the post-apartheid youth of South Africa, as Nadine Dolby tells us, who now assign more value to markers of taste—Levis and Gap jeans, Nikes or Adidas, rap or rave—than ancestry and place in their elaboration of the new criteria of ethnic affiliation

(Dolby, 2001). It is also the world (noted by Cameron McCarthy, in this volume) of the "White Highlands" of Tyneside, Newcastle in the Northeast of England in which white working class youth without work collide with black immigrant youth from the colonies—from Pakistan, India and the Caribbean. It is, finally, the world of Shane Meadow's provocative film, *This Is England* (2007), about a group of skinheads roaming the English Midlands who are trying to make sense of the postindustrial world of immigrants, chronic unemployment and constrained futures (McCarthy, in this volume). It is a world of people without place, workers without work, identity without ancestry—a world of liquid signifiers.

All these developments reveal a fragmentation of the world of working class youth and the infusion of the populations of urban centers, throughout the metropolitan world, with new identities linked directly to transnational movement of cultural and economic capital as well as intensified patterns of hyper-consumption. All these developments are turning the old materialism versus idealism debate on its head. It is the frenetic application of forms of existence, forms of life, the dynamic circulation and strategic deployment of style, and the application of social aesthetics that now govern political rationalities and corporate mobilization in our times. The new representational technologies are the new centers of public instruction and legitimation, providing the venue for the work of the imagination of the great masses of the people. The new representational technologies provide the forum for the ordering and categorization of people's pasts and presents, and the stage upon which they will plot their futures. They are creating instant traditions and nostalgias of the present in which our pasts are disembedded, separated out as abstract value, and then integrated into new semiotics systems and techniques of persuasions, new forms of costuming/clothing that quote Che, Mao, Fidel and Marx, and "revolution" in the banality of commodified life. The publicity of one brand of dish-washing liquid as having "revolutionary" effects is just one good example of the brazen re-articulation of the terms and traditions in the brave new world in which we live. Who now owns the terms that define the authentic traditions of radicalism that have informed our works all these years? Who now has final purchase on the terms "resistance," "revolution," "democracy," "participation," and "empowerment?" The massive work of textual production is blooming in a crucible of opposites—socially extended projects producing the cultural citizen in the new international division of labor, in which the state may not be a first or the final referent.

But the matter goes further. The new driving logics of globalization and transnationalism are articulated most profoundly in the workings of "flexible capitalism" in the constitution of a new information or digital age (Bauman, 2000, 2009, 2010; Schiller, 2003, 2010; Sennett, 1998, 2006, 2008). These logics have unsettled the process of social integration of modern subjects into late-modern institutions. All late-modern forms of association and affiliation are therefore coming under the banner of new identities. The dynamics associated with global capitalism (the rapid and constant dispersal of cultural and economic capital across national boundaries, the intensification and rapidity of movement and migration of people across borders, the amplification of electronic mediation and the work of the imagination of the great masses of the people) reveal themselves in what Zygmunt Bauman (2010) and Richard Sennett (2008) describe as a general lightness of being or liquidity of all social relations and social arrangements of late modernity. This liquidity and lightness are evidenced by the strategic disposition of multinational corporations such as Adidas, Nike, Reebok, Microsoft and others towards what Naomi Klein (2002, 2007) calls "immateriality," where advertising, branding and R&D displace the emphasis on inventories of products as the primary organizational focus of these juggernaut commercial institutions. We live in a time and space where new international divisions of labor, as well as the production, distribution and circulation of goods and services, are being coordinated over enormous distances, numerous nations and markets. There is a new level of instability and immateriality linked in with the new synchronicities of culture; the disembedding of forms of life and meaning of style from one setting and their transplantation in another. This move into the more ephemeral realm of digital and transnational capitalist culture is what Richard Sennett (2008) sees as marking our decline in theodicy, meaning, and the control over craft in all forms of late-modern labor processes, including intellectual and bureaucratic labor and the organization of knowledge. There is a relentless recasting of the key frameworks of living in the modern world—and it is proceeding and accelerating at a blinding pace.

These contemporary transitions have taken place in a context where the relations between government, society, the individual and the market have undergone profound transformations. This neoliberal shift has resulted in new discursive relations and practices that emphasize a capitalist-infused version of individual freedoms, autonomy and "choice" (Bansel, 2007; Brown, 2006). These new discursive practices can be understood as a response to both the shortcomings of what many critics have considered as an overprotective Welfare State (or "nanny state") and the persuasive and widespread claims about the inevitability of globalization and of workplace changes (Davies & Bansel, 2007). In this context, characterized by what John Clarke (2007) refers to as the subjugation of the social, post-welfare state subjects are expected (and constructed) to willingly be responsible for their own well-being. As envisioned in government policy documents and practices, academic texts, labor-market rhetoric, and education and training materials, subjects become international citizens of a global economy—which requires citizens themselves to be up to date and to take advantage of the numerous possibilities at their disposal. The post welfare-state subject is positioned as socially and economically mobile. As Bansel (2007) argues:

> This mobility is lived at the site of subjectivity, social location and work. Discourses of stable personalities with suitability for specific types of employment and of jobs or careers for life are displaced by the discourse of the mobile portfolio worker. Mobile portfolio workers are constituted as likely to have multiple careers for which they will need to be reeducated or retrained. As portfolio workers they accumulate skills, knowledges and experiences that ensure not only their mobility, but also their flexibility, as they shift through multiple careers in the knowledge economy, supported through often self-funded lifelong learning. Flexible workers not only shift careers and the subjectivities that accrue to them but are also adapted to working conditions that demand increasing flexibility in terms of contracts, hours of work, rates of pay, casualization, levels of responsibility and so on. (p. 288)

Furthermore, as Nairn & Higgins (2007) have argued, the flexible, or better yet, the entrepreneurial subjects of twenty-first century capitalism are expected not only to adapt to but also to create the incessant and constant changes in education and work (they must create productive activity, not just participate in it!). In this way, as Susan Robertson and Roger Dale (2002) maintain, the risk of precariousness and failure implicated in any entrepreneurial work resides now on the individual rather than on an external institution or organization. As some authors have pointed out, the construction of the "entrepreneurial self" privileges some subjects as they feel a sense of social belonging and stability in identity.[2] Still, one cannot overlook the tensions between those discourses emphasizing the freedom to choose, endless opportunities, improved lifestyle and social mobility and the realities of a job market where choices are limited, opportunities are constrained and social mobility promises remain unfulfilled for many. These discourses position individuals as the locus of success or failure; based on their self-discipline, hard work, ambition, personality and efforts, they will either fail or succeed in procuring for their well-being. Success (or failure) is conceived in their narratives as individual driven, not as socially constructed (Sennett, 1998). Missing in these discourses is any consideration of the differential and inequitable positions of subjects in terms of economic, social and cultural capital, age, gender, class, race, ethnicity, ability, and sexual orientation. These discourses are based on the assumption that all subjects are equally positioned to identify, mobilize, and create productive or successful choices.

Although this type of neoliberal discourse is imbued with unquestioned presuppositions regarding "freedom" and "self-determination," one cannot fail to notice its normative nature. In relation to this, it is being argued that, under global capitalism, neoliberal technologies and practices work by shaping docile subjects who are closely governed, but who conceive themselves as inherently free (Rose, 1999). Similarly, Griffin (2007) claims that neoliberal discourse "structures and communicates appropriate types of and limits to human behavior and acceptable social aspirations" (p. 223). As Davies and Bansel (2007) put it, this type of discourse contributes to the shaping of a new ethics of the subject: "Individuals are linked into society through acts of socially sanctioned consumption and responsible choice in the shaping of something called a 'lifestyle'" (Davies & Bansel, 2007, p. 252). In this narrative, the subject is unambiguously middle class, a wholehearted consumer of goods and investments (material and symbolic). Furthermore, Griffin (2007) argues, this dominant discourse relates "successful" behavior "almost exclusively with a gender identity embodied in dominant forms of heterosexual masculinity" (p. 220). She illustrates this by reference to World Bank discourses, which in her view, foster development policies and practices designed in accordance with gendered hierarchies of meaning, representation and identity. The normative and "neutral" language of whiteness is also invoked as part of the shaping of this neoliberal subject. Although the mainstream discourse of global capitalism presents itself as color-blind under the guise of racial justice, authors like Duggan (2003) claim just the opposite: it is "saturated with race" (p. xvi). Dominant neoliberal discourses rely on race-neutral language to support the argument that race is no longer a factor in life opportunities and achievement (especially in the U.S.). As Davis (2007) argues:

> By rejecting race, formerly racialized "others" can be fully incorporated as consumptive citizens with no racial barriers to their participation in the economy. Neoliberalism, then, willfully misconstrues and dismisses the reality of racism as a powerful explanatory factor in analyzing persistent racial inequities. (p. 350)

How are these inequalities concealed? According to Davis (2007), neoliberal discourses operate by "relocating racially coded economic disadvantage and reassigning identity-based biases to the private and personal spheres" (p. 349).

By privatizing the discourse on race (i.e. defining racial problems as private ones), a color-blind logic allows people to maintain individualistic interpretations of racial inequalities (Quiroz, 2007) and, thus, reinforces the invisibility of white privilege. These scenarios of race, gender, sexuality and nation now broaden the sphere of what is relevant for critical attention as we seek to grasp the key dynamics operating in the new century.

As contributors, we maintain throughout this volume that global capitalism under neoliberalism "cannot be abstracted from race and gender relations, or other cultural aspects of the body politic. Its legitimating discourse, social relations, and ideology are saturated with race, with gender, with sex, with religion, with ethnicity, and nationality" (Duggan, 2003, xvi). It is our contention that mainstream neoliberal discourses tend to obscure how rich and complex multilayered racial, ethnic, class, youth and gender contemporary identities are. In *New Times: Making Sense of Critical/Cultural Theory in a Digital Age*, contributors offer a much-needed critique of global-neoliberal transparency—a type of representational social technology that we maintain forestalls an understanding of current global capitalism as a system which now vaunts individual entrepreneurism as the panacea for not only all economic woes but all social problems as well. Contributors to this volume variously explore how—ideologically and culturally—did we get here? What is the role of the plurality of changing histories, technologies, identities, bodies, and governance in the prosecution of the new order? Our purpose here is to "write into the history of [late] modernity the ambivalences, contradictions, and the tragedies and ironies that attend it" (Chakrabarty, 2000, p. 43).

Key Themes

New Times: Making Sense of Critical/Cultural Theory in a Digital Age is divided into four sections. The first section of the book, "New Times," scrutinizes the ways that late modern actors are increasingly positioned in fragmented space and time (Nayak, 2003). For the social observer, there is no simple or single place to stand outside this sweeping sense of the reordering of society and the general tumult in social relations. These are the terms of "flexible" capital, as Larry Grossberg (2005) and Richard Sennett (2006, 2008) have told us: the ripping up of social bonds, the disorder of relations of manual and bureaucratic labor, the wrecking of key pillars of North Atlantic modernity (the caring state, the engaged citizen subject, and the availability of work) all illustrate these radical developments. In this "New Times" section, contributors all try to make sense of these developments as they bear down on the institutional space of critical/cultural theory. Our special focus here is on the discipline of Cultural Studies. Here, contributors specifically aim to address the question regarding the current relevance of contemporary cultural studies. Employing a broad array of critical methodologies, contributors to this section engage the contemporary critique of cultural studies. Calling upon a tradition of critical historiography, Robert Mejia ("Theory through Practice: A History of Cultural Studies") argues that cultural studies must remember the sign of the body, as a signifier of the experience of struggle, if it is to retain any claim to materiality. Ergin Bulut ("Labor and Totality in 'Participatory' Digital Capitalism"), with his commitment to historical materialism and new digitality, suggests that cultural studies retains its materiality to the extent that it takes ideological structures and centrality of commodity production to global capitalism seriously. Fusing these two perspectives, Carolyn Randolph ("Seeing Red: Ruptured Identity and the Representation of Black American Women Living with HIV and AIDS") argues that communication matters precisely because it is an ideological and identifying structure that acts upon bodies. Cameron McCarthy ("Reconstructing Race and Education in the Class Conquest of the City and the University in the Era of Neoliberalism and Globalization") concludes by taking up issues of race and class in a time and place where those concepts are unstable, shifting, multifaceted and masking identifiers.

Four essays make up Section Two: "Reconfigurations of Governance/ Technologies of Subjectivity." The four contributors to this section—Stephen Hocker ("Glocal Transgender: Transgender Longing and Belonging in the Shadow of 9/11"), Alice Liao ("Re-Imagining Harvey Milk: Queering Identity Politics") Steven Doran ("Freedom Devices: Neoliberalism, Mobile Technologies, and Governance") and Matthew Crain ("The Cultural Logic of Search and the Myth of Disintermediation")—collectively seek to reconfigure notions of governance, technology and subjectivity. Government has been decentered. It no longer has an origin. It has become fluid: it moves, it condenses, it diffuses. This is all to say that modern populations are increasingly governed not through state action but by power distributed throughout the social body. Institutions and cultural practices, "new media" notwithstanding, have become sites at which individuals are transformed into the subjects necessary for such governance, and it is through the production of proper subjects that late capitalism/advanced liberalism/the postmodern is able to function. The chapters in Section Two investigate the ways that subjects are produced under the conditions of advanced liberalism and how certain subjectivities are strategically deployed in the service of the expansion and regeneration of liberal democracy and capitalist accumulation. Starting from the premise that the subject is the means by which power operates, the chapters in this section look at subjectivity as a technology through which governance is possible. Focusing on questions of identity, independence, and citizenship, these papers collectively trouble the myth of the coherent subject and bring to light the contradictions of the neoliberal subject.

Section Three, "Reterritorializing Bodies," directs attention to the reterritorialization of bodies, flesh, and identity in the digital age. The turn of the twenty-first century has produced new bodily experiences and technological interactions that flatten the boundary between cyberspace and physical reality in a way that renders subjectivity more plastic. Even while space is thickened by a multiplication of identity possibilities within the container of the Internet, old stratifications—class, race, gender—still shape our attempts to negotiate present-day relationships. The chapters in this section interrogate and deconstruct the erasure and vulnerability of the body within the paradoxes of virtual interactions and governmentality (that is, modes of discipline). Directing our attention to the reconstitution of the urban subject and re-narration of place in the new logics of gentrification, Crystal Thomas ("Displaced Bodies and Governmentality: Lessons from the CHA Website") presents an analysis of the Chicago Housing Authority's website. In this chapter, she seeks to account for the increasing number of strategies used to discipline public housing residents within the neoliberal conception of good citizenship. In her chapter ("From Masculinity to Cybermasculinity: Marginalizing the Other in DCinside"), Jungmin Kwon illustrates the reconfiguration of the sexist gaze enabled by the freedom of image manipulation in Korea's male-centered cyberspace. Heather Greenhalgh-Spencer ("Body/Flesh of the Teacher in the Digital Age") traces the kinesis of the teacher's "flesh," made vivid by the movement between the built and online classroom in which teacher-student interactions presume a fluid yet steady and knowable identity. Greenhalgh-Spencer seeks to investigate the performances, rituals, knowledges, and silences of the classroom; how the body figures into these moments in both material and on-line classrooms. What each of these contributors is mapping is how power/knowledge works to stabilize a range of identities projected onto the digitized body—a body that is presumed to be "lost in space." These assemblages, pressured as they are by the millennium, create new territories, new paradigms, new projects, and new categories that ask for our attention. The current time has ushered in different representations and relationships to bodies; the impacts of this difference beckon.

Contributors to the final section, "Global Regimes and Local Transformations," speak back to the volume taken as a whole. They take up issues of body, governance, communication, and technology and situate it within this age of neoliberalism. The first two contributors—Viviana Pitton ("Understanding Neoliberalism and Its Implications for Contemporary Educational Policies"), Rodrigo Britez ("Traveling Policies: Mobility, Transformations, and Continuities in Higher Education Public Policy")—look at the new practices emerging from the changing social, political, economic and cultural relations brought about by global neoliberalism. The authors share a general understanding of neoliberalism as a set of political and economic ideas that place great emphasis on market logics and the extension of market relationships to all human action domains. However, they reject an understanding of neoliberalism as a uniform paradigm and rather focus on its unevenness, on the different neoliberalisms generating new policy practices and new forms of knowledge production and consumption, and on surveillance and practices of cultural and social resistance that seem almost incomprehensible outside the context of their own emergence. The last chapter in Section IV is written by James Geary ("M: A Critical Analysis of a Cultural Artifact"). In this chapter, Geary replies to his fellow contributors by pointing to the importance of language and the unwitting and under-analyzed way in which a single letter ("M") helps us to organize and render intelligible our needs and desires at the beginning of the twenty-first century. We are in fact positioned by the things that we consciously do and the things that we allow to escape our notice. The ultimate aim of contributors to this final section is to situate the understanding of "new times" in the contested and rambunctious environment of sweeping change taking place in the domains of education, culture and economy of emergent as well as metropolitan countries.

The edited volume concludes with an Afterword from Michael Peters in which he responds to the book as a whole, as well as maps out the new directions in politics and policy that the creative industries of media and informational production have begun to provoke. He marks out some of the new practices of this digital and neoliberal moment.

We live in a fraught present where history, resistance, identity, flesh and cultural practices are being re-made, re-narrated, and re-deployed. We live in a moment of constant kinesis. There is no settling of dust, only shifting sands. We want new ways of making meaning in a world of constant rumble/rupture/digital spin. But, how does one take up, gather in, or penetrate an era in which so much dissipates? How does one intervene in the era of liquid modernity—as Zygmunt Bauman aptly sums up the age? *New Times: Making Sense of Critical/Cultural Theory in a Digital Age* emerges from this moment of felt historic uncertainty and attempts to explore some of the issues of the age.

Contributors to this collection remain committed to tracing the contours of this moment in order to provide useful theoretical analysis and methodological and practical interventions.

Notes

1. Carey's emphasis on ritual as a humanistic enterprise did not prevent some of his critics from charging him with technological determinism. Yet, to do so was to ignore that "technology is thoroughly cultural from the outset (Carey, qtd. in Nord, 2006, p. 124). Hence, in this regard, Carey saw technology as the political crystallization of a particular cultural practice; as such, was both infused with and subject to power.
2. Although some authors have rightly pointed out that at a time when the "entrepreneur" has been elevated in the public sphere to the status of a dominant and privileged subject (Du Gay, 1996;), becoming an entrepreneurial self may contribute to constructing a recognizable identity and a sense of social belonging (Nairn & Higgins, 2007).

References

Bansel, P. (2007). Subjects of choice and lifelong learning. *International Journal of Qualitative Studies in Education, 20*(3), 283–300.

Bauman, Z. (2000). *Liquid modernity*. Cambridge, UK: Polity.

Bauman, Z. (2009) *Does ethics have a chance in a world of consumers?* Cambridge, MA: Harvard University Press.

Bauman, Z. (2010) *Living on borrowed time: Conversations with citlali Rovirosa-Madrazo*. Cambridge, UK: Polity.

Beck, U. (2002). The cosmopolitan society and its enemies. *Theory, Culture & Society, 19*(1–2), 17–44.

Benkler, Y. (2009). Correspondence: A new era of corruption. *The New Republic*. Retrieved from http://www.law.harvard.edu/news/2009/03/04_benkler.html

Brown, W. (2006). American nightmare: Neoliberalism, neoconservatism, and de-democratization. *Political Theory, 34*(6), 690–714.

Carey, J. W. (2002). The sense of an ending: On nations, communications, and culture. In C. A. Warren & M. D. Vavrus (Eds.), *American Cultural Studies* (pp. 196–237). Urbana, IL: University of Illinois Press.

Carey, J. W. (2009). *Communication as culture: Essays on media and society*. New York: Routledge.

Chakrabarty, D. (2000). *Provincializing Europe: Postcolonial thought and historical difference*. Princeton, NJ: Princeton University Press.

Clarke, J. (2007). Subordinating the social? Neo-liberalism and the remaking of welfare capitalism. *Cultural Studies, 21*(6), 974–987.

Comaroff, J., & Comaroff, J. L. (2009). *Ethnicity Inc.* Chicago: University of Chicago Press.

Curran, J. (2006). Media and cultural theory in the age of market liberalism. In J. Curran & D. Morley (Eds.), *Media and Cultural Theory* (pp. 129–148). London: Routledge.

Davies, B., & Bansel, P. (2007). Neoliberalism and education. *International Journal of Qualitative Studies in Education, 20*(3), 247–259.

Davis, D. A. (2007). Narrating the mute: Racializing and racism in a neoliberal moment. *Souls: A Critical Journal of Black Politics, Culture and Society, 9*(4), 346–360.

Deuze, M. (2007). *Media work*. Cambridge: Polity.

Dolby, N. (2001). *Constructing race: Youth, identity, and popular culture in South Africa.* Albany, NY: State University of New York Press.

Duggan, L. (2003). *The twilight of equality? Neoliberalism, cultural politics, and the attack on democracy.* Boston, MA: Beacon.

Du Gay, P. (1996). Organizing identity: Entrepreneurial governance and public management. In: S. Hall & P. du Gay (Eds.), *Questions of cultural identity* (pp. 151–169). London: Sage Publications.

Ellul, J. (1964). *The technological society* (J. Wilkinson, Trans.). New York: Vintage.

Franzen, B., & McLeod, K. (Writer) (2008). *Copyright criminals* [Film]. USA.

Frasca, G. (2003). Simulation versus narrative: Introduction to ludology. In M. J. P. Wolf & B. Perron (Eds.), *The video game theory reader* (pp. 221–235). New York: Routledge.

Gitelman, L. (2008). *Always already new: Media, history, and the data of culture*. Cambridge, MA: MIT Press.

Goss, B. M. (1999). *Teeth gritting harmony: The ideology of neo-liberalism*. University of Illinois, Urbana-Champaign, IL.

Griffin, P. (2007). Sexing the economy in a neo-liberal world order: Neo-liberal discourse and the (re)production of heteronormative heterosexuality. *British Journal of Politics & International Relations, 9*(2), 220–238.

Grossberg, L. (2005). *Caught in the crossfire: kids, politics, and America's future*. Boulder, CO: Paradigm.

Hall, S. (2001). Cultural studies and its theoretical legacies. In V. B. Leitch, W. E. Cain, L. A. Finke, B. E. Johnson, J. P. McGowan, & J. L. Williams (Eds.), *The Norton anthology of theory and criticism* (pp. 1898–1910). New York: W. W. Norton.

Jenkins, H. (2006). *Convergence culture: Where old and new media collide.* New York: New York University Press.

Juul, J. (2001). Games telling stories? A brief note on games and narratives. *Game Studies, 1*(1).

Kellner, D. (1995). *Media culture: Identity and politics between the modern and the postmodern.* New York: Routledge.

Kellner, D. (2005). *Media spectacle and the crisis of democracy: Terrorism, war, and election battles (Cultural politics & the promise of democracy)*. Boulder, CO: Paradigm.

Kelly, J. (2003). *Borrowed identities*. New York: Peter Lang.

Klein, N. (2000). *No logo*. New York: Picador.

Klein, N. (2007). *The shock doctrine: The rise and fall of disaster capitalism*. Toronto: Knopf.

Marvin, C. (1988). *When old technologies were new*. New York: Oxford University Press.

McCarthy, C., & Logue, J. (2009) Reading against the grain: Examining the status of the categories of class and tradition in the scholarship of British cultural studies in light of contemporary popular culture and literature. *Policy Futures in Education, 7*(2), 145–160.

McChesney, R. W. (1999). *Rich media, poor democracy: Communication politics in dubious times.* New York: New Press.

McChesney, R. W. (2004). U.S. media at the dawn of the twenty-first century. In R. W. McChesney & B. Scott (Eds.), *Our unfree press: 100 years of radical media criticism* (p. 400). New York: New Press.

Mosco, V. (1989). *The pay-per society: Computers and communication in the information age (Essays in critical theory and public policy).* Toronto: Garamond.

Nairn, K., & Higgins, J. (2007). New Zealand's neoliberal generation: Tracing discourses of economic (ir)rationality. *International Journal of Qualitative Studies in Education, 20*(3), 261–281.

Nayak, A. (2003). *Race, place and globalization: Youth cultures in a changing world.* New York: Berg.

Nerone, J. (2003). Approaches to media history. In A. N. Valdivia (Ed.), *A companion to media* (pp. 93–114). Malden, MA: Blackwell.

Nichols, J., & McChesney, R. W. (2009). The death and life of great American newspapers. *The nation.* Retrieved from http://www.thenation.com/doc/20090406/nichols_mcchesney/single

Nord, D. P. (2006). James Carey and journalism history. *Journalism History, 32*(3), 122–127.

Postman, N. (1986). *Amusing ourselves to death: Public discourse in the age of show business.* New York: Penguin.

Quiroz, P. A. (2007). *Adoption in a color-blind society.* Lanham, MD: Rowman & Littlefield.

Robertson, S., & Dale, R. (2002). Local states of emergency: The contradictions of neo-liberal governance in education in New Zealand. *British Journal of Sociology of Education, 23*(3), 463–482.

Roman, L. (2005). States of insecurity: Cold war memory, "global citizenship" and its discontents. In C. McCarthy, W. Crichlow, G. Dimitriadis, & N. Dolby (Eds.), *Race, identity and representation in education* (pp. 73–94). New York: Routledge.

Rose, N. (1999). *Powers of freedom.* Cambridge: Cambridge University Press.

Schiller, D. (2003). Digital capitalism: A status report on the corporate commonwealth of information. In A. Valdivia (Ed.), *A companion to media studies* (pp. 137–156). Oxford, U.K.: Blackwell.

Schiller, D. (2010). *How to think about information.* Urbana, IL: University of Illinois Press.

Sennett, R. (1998). *The corrosion of character.* New York: Norton.

Sennett, R. (2006). *The culture of new capitalism.* New Haven, CT: Yale University Press.

Sennett, R. (2008). *The craftsman.* New Haven, CT: Yale University Press.

Sprint. (2007). *Palm centro: Sprint speed.* Retrieved from http://www.youtube.com/watch?v=NHhgJxmJ7XU

Starr, P. (2009). Goodbye to the Age of Newspapers (Hello to a New Era of Corruption). *The New Republic.* Retrieved from http://www.tnr.com/story_print.html?id=a4e2aafc-cc92-4e79-90d1-db3946a6d119

Sterne, J. (2005). *The audible past: Cultural origins of sound reproduction.* Durham, NC: Duke University Press.

Sterne, J. (2006). The death and life of digital audio. *Interdisciplinary Science Reviews, 31*(4), 338–348.

Tate, S. (2005). *Black skins, black masks: Hybridity, dialogism, performaitivity.* Hants, UK: Ashgate.

Thompson, E. P. (1998). Preface from the making of the English working class. In J. Storey (Ed.), *Cultural theory and popular culture: A reader* (pp. 57–60). Englewood Cliffs, NJ: Prentice Hall.

Tomlinson, J. (2007). Globalization and cultural analysis. In D. Held & A. McGrew (Eds.), *Globalization theory: Approaches and controversies* (pp. 148–170). New York: Polity Press.

Willis, P. (2005). Afterword: Foot soldiers of modernity—the dialectics of cultural consumption and the 21st century school. In C. McCarthy, W. Crichlow, G. Dimitriadis, & N. Dolby (Eds.), *Race, identity and representation in education* (pp. 461–480). New York: Routledge.

SECTION I

New Times

· 1 ·

Theory Through Practice

A History of Cultural Studies

ROBERT MEJIA

Of Disciplines and History for Life

The politics of disciplinary legitimacy are often fraught with tensions surrounding questions of authenticity. As the rhetorician Lloyd Bitzer (1968) argues, the worth of a particular field of inquiry is understood to be contingent upon (1) its proper articulation of a relevant problematic and (2) its continued representational status as capable of meeting that very exigency. This articulation of exigency as centered on a problematic (i.e., a constellation of concerns) rather than mere problem is central to the continued sustenance of disciplinary legitimacy.[1] Were a discipline to be founded on a mere problem (however large it may be), then its relevance would extend only so far: should the discipline actually resolve the situation, then its attachment to a single concern marks it as necessarily obsolete; or, more realistically, should the discipline proclaim that the solution is, and always will be, an incomplete project, then its failure to successfully grapple with a single, isolated incident marks it as an impotent discipline of study—why bother? Developing a proper constellation of concerns (i.e., a problematic) however, (re)presents the world as a complex whole of which the discipline is merely one element (but an important element nevertheless) of a contested space called history; history becomes the field of legitimation that warrants the emergence of certain exigencies, while at the same time obscuring the necessity of others (Doxtader, 2008; Steinberg, 1996; Weber, 1958a). Whereas some may see this deployment of history as a moment of mere rhetoric (in its most dubious connotation), as an invocation of a false exigency, the formation of a constellation of historically situated concerns, myth or otherwise, carries with it an explanatory force that *has historical effects* (Lowenthal, 1998). Hence, new disciplinary practices, as Stuart Hall (1994) argues, emerge that function as more than just academic concerns and matter a great deal politically to the extent that changes in a particular problematic "do significantly transform the nature of the questions asked, the forms in which they are proposed, and the manner in which they are adequately answered" (p. 520). In this regard, the articulation of a "new" problematic is always a political intervention because in formulating an exigency the new discipline seeks to grab hold of the reins of history.

Controlling history matters, for the field is the terrain of social change; history is the space whereby various actors engage in conflict over access to its power of legitimation (Weber, 1958b). In this world as such, the historian (as *historically* conceived) takes on the function of a witness of legitimation (Ginzburg, 1992): which party controlled (however incompletely) the mechanisms of history at which moment in time? And were these moments of power enacted justly? Yet, this articulation of the historian as witness in effect obscures the nature of the historical enterprise: at the very moment in which the present is conceived as an effect of history, those same mechanisms of its historical production (i.e., the official history) are concealed as an act of objectivity (Jay, 1992). All the world is historical, except the historian. It is in this moment that speaking of history autobiographically becomes an effective means by which to destabilize, and thereby expose, the *camera obscura* that is the historical enterprise (Dening, 1992; Fraser, 1997; Hall, 2001). While the autobiography is typically thought of as a means of "seizing the authority of authenticity," its emphasis on the personal becomes a means by which to reinsert the political in relation to the grand narrative of conventional history (Hall, 2001, pp. 1898–1899). Such an autobiographical intervention is hence necessary, not as a means of recentering history, and setting the record straight but rather as a method for rearticulating the very politics of a particular problematic.

This chapter is one such attempt to rearticulate the problematic that is cultural studies. The reason for this intervention is not to be found in the exigency of a grand disciplinary crisis, as the field is currently experiencing a moment of calm: the great debate of the nineties between political economy and cultural studies appears to have worn itself out (Curran & Morley, 2006). Nor is such an intervention warranted due to any presumed authority on my part: I am merely a graduate student. Yet, it is precisely due to the acquiescence of disciplinary crisis and my relatively unprivileged status in the field that such a rearticulation of the problematic is necessary. Without granting a hierarchy to the justification of the project, let me further articulate my intervention as follows. First, the absence of disciplinary tension ought to be understood as a moment of profound political danger (Hall, 2001). Those moments of disciplinary calm (whether elective or otherwise) are instances whereby the notion of the politics of intellectual work is vulnerable to substitution by the displacement of intellectual work for politics; this is the moment when we forget the messiness of life, its existence as struggle (Hall, 2001). With the increased privatization of academia, however, we can no longer afford to keep separate intellectual work (theory) from intellectual labor (life)[2]: neoliberalism is no longer something that is happening "out there," but is something that is also undergoing permutations "in here" as well (Brown, 2006; Wilson, 2010). Second, as relatively new (but not completely new) participants to the disciplinary conversation, it is time that members of my intellectual cohort begin to take a stand within the problematic; for it is we, as graduate students and adjunct faculty members, that are most vulnerable to shifts in disciplinary legitimacy—which are frequently initiated and subsequently settled without our consent. Contemporary shifts in state and federal budget priorities may have introduced the notion of a "furlough" to the tenured faculty of California and Illinois, and elsewhere, but as Robin Wilson (2010) notes, the proportion of tenured or tenure track instructors has fallen from 57 percent in 1975 to 31 percent in 2007. In essence, the crisis is not new, but has a history, and we, graduate students and adjunct faculty members, are its consequences. As a final note, this evocation of the collective is not meant to obscure the fact that I alone stand as the author of this chapter but rather to situate the collective memory of this intellectual history in relation to the theoretical legacies of the discipline; I may be the sole author of this chapter, but all acts of writing emerge from the specific socio-historic moment of its production (Foucault, 2003b; Williams, 1985, 2001), so let not my name become a stumbling block for the politics of this piece.

Interventions such as this chapter must exist, for the continuation of any political project is contingent upon its ability to be reformulated by those newcomers who would practice it (Burke, 1974; Carey, 2006; Lowenthal,

1998); and, when the politics of the project seem to have gone awry, an eye towards history is needed as a means of searching for what Walter Benjamin (2006) calls, "the sign of a messianic zero-hour of events, or put differently, a revolutionary chance in the struggle for the suppressed past" (Sec. XVII). This means, ironically, that to place history in the service of new life, we must first desecrate it by keeping nothing sacred (Nietzsche, 1980, 2003); only then, will we have avoided the "dogmatic traps, premature closures, formulaic formulations or rigid conclusions" (West, 1999, p. 133) of the "nostalgia for what never was'" (Jansen, 2009, p. 223). Thus, in the effort to keep this political project that we call cultural studies going, I conduct my historical enterprise as follows: first, I provide a retelling of the emergence of British cultural studies; second, I trace the historical positioning of U.S. cultural studies within the field of communications; third, I revisit the debates of the 1990s between cultural studies and political economy; and fourth, I take my stand in relation to what I believe needs to be done to sustain the critical edge of contemporary cultural studies. The history of cultural studies could be, and has been, written differently; however, this history is my attempt to rearticulate the problematic in such a way as to allow for the continued relevance of cultural studies in the particular exigencies of these new times.

British Cultural Studies

As a U.S. intellectual seeking to theorize the problematic of cultural studies through the lens of autobiography, beginning this narrative with the history of British cultural studies would appear to undermine such a project—as my lived experiences have been limited to the North American context. If my autobiographical approach rearticulates the same history as that of the grand narrative of the field, then perhaps the autonomy of my autobiography is also written within the very structure of the discipline. Perhaps, however, it is not a matter of any presumed authenticity that lies submerged within my body; disavowed through the process of my education. Instead of a return to authenticity (or a mourning of its absence), we can understand this moment of rearticulation as an instance by which the very history of the grand narrative takes a "necessary detour" through the body (Hall, 2001, p. 1906). This "necessary detour" through the body affords the individual the opportunity to wrestle with history, and it is only through such struggles that one finds what appears to be a purely intellectual exercise matters a great deal politically (Dening, 1992; Foucault,

2003a). It is for this reason, to explore the political implications of such wrestling with history, that I begin with British cultural studies. As Larry Grossberg (1997) argues, even if the history of British cultural studies has achieved the status of an origin myth, its narrative remains relevant for its impact on the contemporary imagination of cultural studies practitioners. To understand the emergence of British cultural studies, two historical trajectories warrant our attention: the legacy of British literary theory and the struggle over Marxism amongst the Communist Party Historians' Group. While these two genealogies intersect at various points throughout their history, it is useful to disentangle them for the sake of historical analysis—while always keeping an eye attuned to the reality of their simultaneity. To illuminate the point, let us begin our discussion of the intellectual structure of British cultural studies by means of comparison with that of German cultural theory.

As with any intellectual intervention, the theoretical field is populated prior to one's arrival. Hence, within Germany, the cultural Marxism of the Frankfurt School was shaped not only by "the withering away of the revolutionary working class," but also the intellectual legacy of German philosophy (Jay, 1996, pp. 41–44). This influence can be read within Adorno and Horkheimer's analysis of the rise of fascism in the West, *The Dialectic of Enlightenment: Philosophical Fragments*. Written in 1944 at the height of Nazism, Adorno and Horkheimer's (1997) critique of the cultural industry was dependent upon Kant's (1998) configuration of the subject as divided into three parts: animality, humanity, and personality. Within this formulation, the morality of a subject is contingent upon her ability to lay claim to some notion of universality, which meant subjugating the specificity of lived experience (animality and humanity) to the transcendent rule of pure reason (which was found within the realm of personality) (Kant, 1998). This interpretation of morality allowed for the Frankfurt School to understand the weakening of the proletariat as due to the cultural industry's manipulation of the consumer's personality: the cultural industry tricks the individual into believing that one's animality (e.g., sex) and humanity (e.g., popularity) are to be held above the moral law of pure reason (e.g., freedom). The philosophically inclined cultural theory of the Frankfurt School provides a relevant point of contrast for understanding the significance of the English context to British cultural studies: not philosophy, but literary theory.[3]

In contrast to the philosophically infused Frankfurt School, British cultural theory was built around the two intellectual traditions: English literary theory and Marxist historiography (Dworkin, 1997; Johnson, 1986–1987). Like the

Frankfurt School, cultural theorists associated with the Centre for Contemporary Cultural Studies sought to understand why a socialist revolution had failed to manifest. Yet, whereas the Frankfurt School conceived of the cultural industry (and by extension the bourgeoisie) as stifling the ability of the proletariat to construct a revolutionary mass society, British cultural studies sought to understand why the proletariat seemed to resist class analysis in the first instance (Hoggart, 1998; Thompson, 1966; Williams, 1983). This British emphasis on delineating the category from the content can be traced to the intellectual legacy of the "culture and society" tradition of British literary theory and the historical materialism of the Communist Party Historians' Group (Dworkin, 1997). Hence, it is necessary to discuss the contributions of both groups: first, British literary theory, and second, the Communist Party Historians' Group.

Matthew Arnold, F. R. Leavis, T. S. Eliot, and other English literary theorists associated with the "culture and society" tradition, were concerned with the decline of aristocratic virtues in the wake of industrialism and modern capitalism (Dworkin, 1997). For these thinkers, capitalism represented a radical transformation in the material base of society: the aristocracy was losing its privileged status as the producer of cultural goods, and in its place, mass society was emerging without the historical foundations to produce an adequate culture of its own (Leavis, 1998). Culture, as such, referred not to a "whole way of life" (Williams, 1983, p. 282), but rather "the best which has been thought and said in the world" (Arnold, 1998, p. 7). Arnold's formulation of culture as a thing (e.g., a piece of art) rather than a practice (e.g., a whole way of life) would ultimately obscure the very historical contingency of all cultural forms. This would later be rectified by T. S. Eliot (1976), with his emphasis on the "practice" of culture, but so too would he uncritically accept the cultural superiority of the social elite. In essence, the cultural theory of the "culture and society" group understood culture as an ahistorical thing, in spite of its historical production: a work of art once produced would always be a work of art.[4] As such, the "culture and society" thinkers evaluated a given civilization based on the timelessness of its cultural contributions; and given their propensity to associate culture with the elite, it is difficult to imagine how alternative class strata (or other social formations) could produce viable new cultural forms: "The minority [educated elite] is being cut off as never before from the powers that rule the world. [. . .] The prospects of culture, then, are very dark" (Leavis, 1998, p. 18). In spite of the cultural conservatism of the "culture and society" group, early practitioners of British cultural studies were greatly influenced by the centrality these thinkers placed on the significance of culture for the functioning of a healthy society (Dworkin, 1997).

Educated as they were in the "culture and society" tradition, early cultural studies practitioners construed their disciplinary problematic around two interlocking problems: the problem of the masses (i.e., the working class) and the problem of culture (i.e., popular culture). These two theoretical poles would constitute the source of much productive intellectual friction throughout the early years of cultural studies. As Arnold, Eliot, and Leavis had already suggested, the notions of culture and society were not synonymous: culture constituted a thing and/or a "whole way of life," whereas society referred to social categories, such as family and institutionalized religion (Arnold, 1998; Eliot, 1976; Leavis, 1998). Ostensibly the difference is not pure, as the very notion of family and religion is not merely a social category but also a cultural construction; nevertheless, the distinction provided an analytic whereby the critic could explore the heterogeneity of a social formation.

This tension between theoretical category and cultural practice was central to the work of cultural studies pioneer Raymond Williams. Williams (1983) was highly critical of orthodox Marxists for failing to understand the nuances between category (of analysis) and culture (of experience):

> If you get into the habit of thinking that a bourgeois society produces, in a simple and direct way, a bourgeois culture, then you are likely to think that a socialist society will produce, also simply and directly, a socialist culture, and you may think it incumbent on you to say what it will be like. [. . . .] But if we are to agree with Marx that 'existence determines consciousness,' we shall not find it easy to prescribe any particular consciousness in advance. (pp. 282–283)

Due to their conflating society with culture, Williams (1983) was arguing that the culture produced by the Russian communist party was as equally illusionary as the false consciousness produced by capitalism. As it relates to scholarship outside of the politically conspicuous realm of socialism, Williams would continue to argue for the distinction between culture and society—as he believed their manipulation functioned as a political act. For instance, in his study on television, Williams (1993) critiqued the misapplication of the term "mass" in "mass communication." For Williams (1993), the term "mass" represented a misidentification of the social audience as intrinsic within the cultural element; in essence, television may be targeted towards a particular social formation (i.e., the public), but its mode of production (elite) and means of consumption (typically in isolation or small groups) marked it as anything but mass culture. By tracing the contemporary etymology of the word "mass," Williams (1993) argued that its application can be, ironically, understood as both illustrating a contempt for popular culture (as opposed to high culture) and a desire to politically control the masses. Hence, in contrast to Arnold, Leavis, and Eliot, this delineation between culture and society allowed for Williams as well as cultural studies other key founders, Richard Hoggart and E. P. Thompson, to recuperate the viability of the social formation of the working class as a political entity in opposition to arguments of cultural decay (Hoggart, 1957; Thompson, 1966; Williams, 1983). For Hoggart and Williams, this inversion of the cultural theory stemmed from their class position as members of the working class (Dworkin, 1997). For Thompson, this critical perspective stemmed from his affiliation with the Communist Party Historians' Group (Dworkin, 1997).

The formation of the Communist Party Historians' Group (CPHG) in 1946 served as a pivotal moment in the development of Marxism within the British context (Dworkin, 1997; Johnson, 1986–1987). The group's political formation functioned as an embodied synthesis of the Marxist problematic: structure and agency. As a group positioned within a larger communist orthodoxy, the CPHG understood Marxism to be a science guaranteeing the triumph of a socialist revolution (Dworkin, 1997). In this regard, the method of historical materialism, as practiced by Marx in *Capital* and *A Contribution to the Critique of Political Economy*, become the proper means of conducting historical analysis. From this perspective, it is the class struggle and not the individual struggle that is worthy of analysis: "individuals are [to be] dealt with here only in so far as they are the personifications of economic categories, the bearers [Träger] of particular class-relations and interests" (Marx, 1990, p. 92). Yet, in the same instance, many members of the CPHG were heavily influenced by their political involvement in the British Popular Front movement of the 1930s and 1940s (Dworkin, 1997).[5] And, as had the Frankfurt school, members of the CPHG were confronted with the historical failure for a socialist revolution to emerge. Yet, whereas the Frankfurt School's response called for a political intervention within the realm of aesthetics (Adorno & Horkheimer, 1997; Benjamin, 2006), the CPHG responded with a politics of collective volition (Dworkin, 1997).[6] The CPHG's involvement with Popular Front politics held that "faith in historical inevitability was no substitution for political minded action" (Dworkin, 1997, p. 26). This emphasis on collective action, even if somewhat constrained, allowed for the CPHG to hold two contradictory, but productive, positions: the structural determinism that placed its faith in historical materialism; and, the voluntarism that satisfied the group's humanistic desires. That Marx articulated both positions, with his emphasis on the inevitability of history (i.e., theory; Marx, 1990) *and* the importance of class struggle (i.e., practice; Marx, 1913), allowed for the CPHG and other Marxists at the time to co-exist in spite of the conflict and debate that arose from these contradictions (Dworkin, 1997).

The CPHG's theoretical tension between structure and agency proved to be a fruitful, if not conflict-ridden, period in the development of British Cultural Marxism in the 1940s and 1950s. It afforded the CPHG an opportunity to engage the British Popular Front politics within a broader theoretical framework of historical materialism. The telos of a postponed and still theoretically inevitable socialist revolution became the criterion for evaluating the efficacy of political action (Dworkin, 1997). Moreover, like the division between culture and society, the fracturing of political practice into concerns of structure and agency created a means by which members of the CPHG could think through the problem of the masses. This influence on cultural studies can be seen in Thompson's classic work, *The Making of the English Working Class*. Written in 1963, Thompson, like Williams before, sought to correct the dehumanizing effect of seeing a social category (i.e., class) as intrinsic within the cultural formation (i.e., the community). As it existed in orthodox Marxism, as well as conventional historical and sociological analysis, the category of the structure had come to superimpose a theoretical ideology onto the object of analysis. However, while a class analysis may be targeted towards a particular social formation (i.e., the working class), its mode of application (i.e., a theoretical exercise) differs from its mode of production (i.e., a lived experience). This is not to suggest that class formations do not exist, but that they can only exist within the specificity of the historical struggle (Thompson, 1966). Understanding class consciousness to emerge within the moment, and not a priori, functions to vindicate the presumed false consciousness of the working class:

> Their [the working-class] communitarian ideals may have been fantasies. Their insurrectionary conspiracies may have been foolhardy. But they lived through these times of acute social disturbance, and we did not. Their aspirations were valid in terms of their own experience; and, if they were casualties of history, they remain, condemned in their own lives, as casualties. (Thompson, 1966, p. 13)

As had Williams, Thompson's intervention sought to recuperate the legitimacy of lived experience from the overdetermination of structure. Yet, the significance of Thompson's argument, and its point of departure from that of

Williams, lies within the centrality of the concept of struggle. Williams, Thompson (1961a, 1961b) felt, had eviscerated the experience of struggle from the essence of class formation. Thompson was not arguing for a return to the Marxist conflation between culture and society but rather the recognition that the relationship between these two terms is one of conflict. Such an intervention was necessary in order to procure a space whereby critical political action could manifest: politics was re-theorized as the instance whereby humanity struggles with a sociohistorical formation not of its own making.

The formative years of British cultural studies resulted in several theoretical legacies. The inversion of the cultural hierarchy, as advanced by Hoggart, Williams, and Thompson, would set the foundation for the later works in cultural studies, such as Dick Hebdige's *Subculture: The Meaning of Style*. First published in 1979, Hebdige's analysis of British working class subcultures, and subsequent argument that their style was a means of culture resistance, is contingent upon the rearticulation of culture as a whole way of life—or in Thompson's case, a whole way of struggle. As a whole way of life, rather than the best of all that has been said, alternative cultural practices could be analyzed as a means of uncovering "the concealed fundamentals of history" (Hebdige, 2006, p. 7); by infusing early cultural studies with semiotics, Hebdige sought to learn how the space of the body (sign) functions as a means (signifier) of historical practice (signification). Additionally, Thompson's struggle against crude Marxist theoreticism would provide the disciplinary platform for future studies of conceptual becoming: the idea that identity is a perpetual historical formation rooted in struggle (Gilroy, 2006). Yet, if the genealogy of British cultural studies has thus far been presented as a pleasant frolic through the history of ideas, it is important to echo Stuart Hall's (2001) observation that the Birmingham Centre for Contemporary Cultural Studies could more appropriately be understand as a space of "theoretical noise": "It was accompanied by a great deal of bad feeling, argument, unstable anxieties, and angry silence" (Hall, 2001, p. 1899). The productive tension between culture and society, agency and structure, led to the development of significant theoretical work that transcended the disciplinary boundaries; however, the "theoretical noise" of the Centre was not mere hyperbole, as several public separations would later occur, of which Thompson's own disengagement in 1979 is perhaps most famous.[7] Yet, while "theoretical noise" may lead to a "great deal of bad feeling," and result in intellectual casualties, as with Thompson's departure, the emphasis on theoretical struggle remains perhaps the greatest legacy of British cultural studies—even if such a notion has fallen to the wayside of contemporary practice (Hall,

2001).

To better understand the contemporary disavowal of theory as struggle, it is necessary now to visit the American trajectory of cultural studies and its rise to dominance. Like the British context of the 1970s, so too would the American intellectual milieu undergo a series of growing pains in the 1990s; however, while American cultural studies has historically held a critical position, the outcome of the theoretical struggle of the 1990s would result in the intellectual acquiescence of rendering politics academic, in contrast to politicizing the academy in the first instance.[8]

American Cultural Studies

The roots for contemporary cultural studies research in the United States began in Ann Arbor, Michigan, during the late 1880s (Carey, 2009). There, at the University of Michigan, interactions between John Dewey, Herbert Mead, Robert Park, Charles Cooley, and Franklin Ford, would set the intellectual foundations for what would come to be known as the search for the great community: a unified monocultural nation-state (Carey, 2009). This search for a great community was neither new nor unique for U.S. history; from its inception, U.S. cultural politics can be understood as operating within this tension of a need for community versus the desire for expansion. If on one hand, national expansion was seen as a part of the nation's destiny, on the other, that very expansion was seen as a threat to the fragile political communities that currently existed, particularly in the Northeastern states (Saxton, 2003). Concern for the state of the union led some to believe that the emergence of the telegraph, in 1844, offered one possible solution to the nation's pending dissolution (Carey, 2009; Czitrom, 1982). While it failed to avert the war, the telegraph led to major structural transformations in print journalism and U.S. cultural politics in general. As the media historian Daniel Czitrom (1982) notes: at the beginning of the 1800s there were approximately 235 newspapers, or one for every 22,500 people; by 1899, there were 16,000 newspapers, or one for every 4,750 people (p. 18). Hence, it is not surprising that John Dewey and his colleagues believed that "the only possible social science" should be the study and development of such media (Dewey qtd. in Carey, 2009, p. 110)[9]; as only communications technologies could successfully mediate the tensions between expansion and community.

For John Dewey and his colleagues, the search for the great community began with the democratic possibilities of new communications technologies.

While this optimism was not new, its philosophical exposition was significant for the future development of American cultural studies. In his 1927 book, *The Public and Its Problems*, John Dewey (1927) would write:

> We have the physical tools of communication as never before. The thoughts and aspirations congruous with them are not communicated, and hence are not common. Without such communication the public will remain shadowy and formless, seeking spasmodically for itself, but seizing and holding its shadow rather than its substance. Till the Great Society is converted into a Great Community, the Public will remain in eclipse. Communication can alone create a great community. (p. 142)

Like the general public, Dewey believed that the telegraph and other new communication technologies represented a significant break in communications history. However, where Dewey and his colleagues differed, and hence were revolutionary, was in their emphasis in their theorizing of communications processes. The Chicago School theorists, as Dewey and his colleagues would later be called, thought that the expansion of the Great Society, as brought about by the industrial revolution, was lacking an equally significant counterpart of a communications revolution (Rogers, 1997)[10]; the rapid expansion of society had broken the traditional bonds of community, as conventional communications technologies (e.g., the pre-telegram press) were unable to properly adapt: old media moved too slowly. Yet, even this formulation is not quite accurate, as members of the Chicago School also believed the community was transformed through communicative practices: "society not only continues to exist *by* transmission, *by* communication, but it may fairly be said to exist *in* transmission, *in* communication" (Dewey, 1955, p. 5). Hence, technologies such as the telegram were believed to not just bring people closer but also fundamentally transformed those very relationships. With communication processes at the heart of their cultural analyses, John Dewey and the other members of the Chicago School would set the intellectual foundations for the critical-democratic tradition of American cultural studies.

During this same period, in the early 1920s, political pressure had worked to professionalize the journalism industry in the effort to curb corporate corruption (McChesney, 2007). Journalism schools were established; and while they lay intellectually dormant for much of the 1920s, they would gain political significance in the 1930s (McChesney, 2007). At the same time, with societal unrest developing from the effects of the Great Depression and political tension growing in Europe, propaganda studies began to attract scholarly attention (McChesney, 2007).[11] At first, the emergence of propaganda studies was not necessarily subversive to the critical-democratic agenda of the Chicago School

(Jansen, 2009). Indeed, the work of Walter Lippmann could be interpreted to resonate with the critical tradition of the Frankfurt School: "in a world falsely conceived, our own characters are falsely conceived, and we misbehave" (Lippmann, 1949, pp. 115–116). However, as U.S. involvement in World War II became more immanent, the critical edge of propaganda studies was disavowed in favor of an uncritical formulation of the good nation versus foreign evil (McChesney, 2007); and along with it, so too was the critical-democratic tradition of early American communication studies fractured off into its own, barely subsistent subfield of American cultural studies—prior to this moment, they (American culture studies and American communication studies) shared the same genealogy.

The advent of U.S. involvement in World War II significantly altered the intellectual trajectory of communication studies. The government considered communications research to be of central importance to the war effort (Czitrom, 1982; Rogers, 1997). Relatively benign, but important messages of public information regarding food and gas rationing required improved methods of communication. But, in addition, the prior studies in propaganda were co-opted as a means for the U.S. government to produce its own (McChesney, 2007). When contrasted with the horrific reports coming out of Europe, these governmental attempts at "misinforming" its own public were seen as necessary for the greater good, and many social scientists lent their support to the wartime efforts (Rogers, 1997). As it concerns the trajectory of communications research, on December 15, 1941 Wilbur Schramm, an English professor from Iowa, would write Archibald MacLeish, the Director of the Office of Facts and Figures (OFF): "Perhaps more than any previous war this is likely to be a war of communication" (qtd. in Rogers, 1997, pp. 13–14).[12] Two weeks later, Schramm was appointed as OFF's educational director (Rogers, 1997). With an operating budget of $1.5 million, the department's responsibility consisted of developing what was called "white propaganda," propaganda aimed at domestic audiences (Rogers, 1997). After his service, Schramm would go on to establish several major communications research programs: Iowa (1943), Illinois (1947), and Stanford (1955). As Robert McChesney (2007) notes, this military influence, by way of Schramm and other "administrative" scholars, had the effect of eviscerating critical research from the discipline of communications studies.[13]

Yet, while lacking an institutional base, critical cultural research was able to persist within the margins of communication studies (McChesney, 2007). This was particularly challenging as the cultural context of the U.S. post-

World War II made it politically difficult to operate within a critical vein (Melody, 1993). Anti-communist sentiment, such as that of McCarthyism, meant that scholars operating within a Marxist tradition had to think carefully, lest they find themselves blacklisted like critical scholars such as W. E. B. Du Bois. In spite of these challenges, scholars, such as Dallas Smythe and Herbert Schiller were able to find spaces, such as the International Association of Media and Communication Research (IAMCR), for the sustenance of critical cultural theory (Meehan, 2004).[14] These venues, however, were not merely enclaves for critical theorists to find solace and enter into hibernation while they awaited a more receptive cultural milieu. Rather, important critical scholarship was able to thrive in these spaces in spite of the cultural challenges (Meehan, 2004). Important work, such as Smythe's *Communications: Blindspot of Western Marxism* (1977) and "On the Audience Commodity and Its Work" (1981/2006) took to task critical scholars for failing to account for how audiences are produced as a result of media consumption for the purpose of being sold to advertisers. Scholars associated with this tradition, which has come to be called the Political Economy of Communication, made valuable contributions to U.S. cultural theory in that they sustained, and developed the critical edge of early propaganda research. Additionally, these scholars remained (and have continued to remain) active in policy making decisions, thereby maintaining the critical-democratic tradition of American cultural studies (Bodroghkozy, 2005; Meehan, 2004).

The work of political economists represented a small but vibrant enclave for critical cultural theory in an era when such work was not just unpopular but politically dangerous (Meehan, 2004; Melody, 1993). When, however, James Carey emerged on the scene, that tradition was all but rejected. While Carey shared with the political economists a common appreciation for the work of C. Wright Mills, he (Carey) disdained any intellectual project that moved the impetus of cultural theory from the analysis of human agents to that of structural apparatuses (Carey, 1995). As such, Carey bypassed much of the gains in critical cultural theory developed by the political economists in favor of tracing an intellectual lineage to the Chicago School by way of Harold Innis and Clifford Geertz.[15] Carey's appreciation for Mills, however, while not significantly important to his work, did serve as a pragmatic means for him to acknowledge the work of political economy, while simultaneously dismissing it. This was possible due to Carey's understanding of the Dewey and Lippmann debate. Carey (2009) understood Dewey and Lippmann as sharing a common concern for the state of modern democracy. The difference, however, was that Dewey's democratic vision believed in the capacity for an intelligent public (humanist), whereas Lippmann's version required a system of experts to guide the easily manipulated masses (anti-humanist) (Carey, 2009). As such, Carey (1995, 2009) had placed most political economists within the Lippmann tradition of cultural theory, since he believed their work shared a similar anti-humanist bent. However, with Mills, Carey could appreciate his advocacy for an "authentic democratic community and [struggle] against the manipulation of political economics, *and academic elites*" ([italics added] Carey, 2009, p. 29). His embrace of Mills, hence, allowed for Carey to claim appreciation for the work of *some* political economists, while simultaneously dismissing the tradition—Mills included—as possessing a "relatively crude conception of culture" (Carey, 2009, p. 31).

Seeking a revival of the humanist tradition of cultural theory, Carey updated the work of Dewey by infusing his (Dewey's) search for the great community with the work of Innis and Geertz. Carey (2009) translated Dewey's differentiation between "by" and "in" transmission to advocate for a ritual approach to communication. Carey's (2009) approach suggested that communication processes mattered just as much as communication contents. Carey (2009) intended this ritual approach to communication as an analytic for disentangling the "symbolic processes whereby reality is produced, maintained, repaired, and transformed" (p. 19). This may sound remarkably structuralist, however, Carey's (2009) rearticulation of this paradigm in ritualistic terms was heavily influenced by Geertz's notion that "man is an animal suspended in webs of significance he himself has spun" (Geertz, 1973, p. 5).[16] In essence, a ritual approach to communication sought to understand how human-centered communication processes transformed the experience of community. Carey's call for a cultural approach to communication has been critiqued for failing to offer a workable model (Nord, 2006), yet it nevertheless remains a valuable contribution to the contemporary understanding of cultural theory. Moreover, Carey's (2009) emphasis on the importance of communication forms has helped to sustain the tradition of the Canadian School within contemporary cultural studies. This has led to charges of technological determinism (Nord, 2006), yet it has helped (or ought to help) contemporary practitioners of cultural studies to remember that technology is not a neutral carrier of communication content but rather carrirs its own biases of communication (Carey, 2009; Innis, 2008). For Carey (2009), a careful analysis of these cultural forms would be necessary were one to ever realize the noble dream of cultural theory: the realization of a critical-democratic society.

While significant contributions were made by Carey's "recovery" of the Chicago and Canadian Schools for cultural theory, his intervention was somewhat nostalgic (i.e., utopian) and glossed over any sustained treatment of power (Grossberg, 1997; Nord, 2006). In many respects, this criticism of Carey is reminiscent of that of tension between E. P. Thompson's (1961a, 1961b, 1981) formulation of culture as a "whole way of struggle" and Raymond Williams's "structure of feeling" (Williams, 1977, 1983, 2001). This should not be surprising, for if in my effort to trace what is distinctly American (and British) about cultural studies, I have given the impression of two isolated, self-sustaining traditions, let me offer the following as a brief addendum.

As James Curran (2006) is quick to point out, intellectual developments cannot be divorced from the material conditions of their production. Hence, it is not surprising that both American and British cultural studies emerged from the ashes of unrealized utopianisms at roughly the same moment in global history. Significant global transformations were underway within the West during the formative pre-history (1880s to 1960s) of American and British cultural studies (Grossberg, 1997).[17] This was a period of shifting global hegemony, catastrophic world wars, transformations in time and space (due to new communications technologies), the women's suffrage movement, the civil rights movement, and the dream (or fear) of a socialist revolution, not to mention other global and national changes; in a word, social upheaval (and its potential) would have seemed to be a regular state of affairs. The emergence of scholars concerned with maximizing the utopian possibilities of the moment should not be surprising, and that is in fact just what American and British cultural theorists hoped to accomplish (Carey, 2009; Grossberg, 1997). In addition, transnational cross-fertilization occurred as disciplinary figures were well aware of each other, at least as early as the 1960s (Adam, 2009), and prominent cultural theorist Larry Grossberg was disciplined in both American and British cultural studies during the 1960s and 1970s. Yet, in spite of this common global exigency and the existence of intellectual exchange, the cultural situatedness of these two different spaces matters. American cultural theory was built on a search for the great community, which was believed to be found within the procuring of institutional support for journalism and educational reform (Carey, 1979; Dewey, 1927; McChesney, 2007).[18] British cultural theory, however, was seeking to understand why a socialist revolution had not yet occurred (Hoggart, 1957; Thompson, 1961a, 1961b; Williams, 1983, 2001), and this called for the development of an organic intellectual (Hall, 2001).

These were important political projects in their own right; and, as

Thompson (1966) was apt to note about the English working class, the same applies here, who am I to judge the success or failure of those who have come before me, and whose sacrifices now make my critique possible? "They lived through these times of acute social disturbance, and we did not" (Thompson, 1966, p. 13). This is true, so I come not to evaluate their lived experiences, but my own; they made their lives worth living, now I seek to do the same. To do this requires that I, as Sue Jansen (2009) suggests, acknowledge that "the successes of the original progressives, not just their defeats, helped shape the problematic present" (p. 223). What may have made sense in their time, may no longer make sense now, hence, we critique.

Political Economic Amnesia

This period that I now step into evokes feelings of intellectual malaise. Prior to the mid-1980s, much of the critical work in American cultural theory consisted of reading groups (Rosaldo, 1994), supplemental subject matter (Adam, 2009), or presentations at non-mainstream conferences (Meehan, 2004), as its practitioners had not yet succeeded in gaining wide-spread institutional support. Yet, in the 1980s, with the rise of Thatcherism in Britain and Reaganomics in the U.S., contemporary cultural politics were in disarray. Groups based on previous forms of nationalist and/or Marxist politics found their political purchase lacking in the face of a post-civil rights, post-feminism, and in essence, post-identity society. Having already placed an emphasis on the cultural aspects of communication, and hence necessitating what can be seen as a "history from below," both American and British cultural studies were in a prime position to emerge as intellectual leaders in this newly postmodern world. With books and articles such as Hall et al.'s (1978) *Policing the Crisis: Mugging, the State and Law and Order*, Hebdige's (1979/2006) *Subculture: The Meaning of Style*, Carey's (1974) *The Problem of Journalism History* and (1975) *A Cultural Approach to Communication*, amongst others, leading the way, cultural studies began to achieve political and intellectual purchase amongst a key segment of the academy, graduate students (Nord, 2006; Rosaldo, 1994). As graduate students began to gravitate towards the field, and prominent "old school" critical theorists, such as Fredric Jameson and Étienne Balibar, began to join them, a series of massive conferences were held that signaled the advent of institutional support for cultural studies (McChesney, 2007; Nelson, 1991; Newton, Kaiser, & Ono, 1998; Rosaldo, 1994).

For all the institutional support, however, cultural studies experienced significant growing pains that resulted in a de-emphasis of its political economic tradition. Some would openly embrace this development (Carey, 1995); some would seek reconciliation (Murdock, 1995), but nearly everyone involved would leave with a bad taste in their mouth (Garnham, 1995a, 1995b; Grossberg, 1995). While it is true that for some life went on as usual, and these scholars continued to operate *as if nothing had happened* (McChesney, 2007; Meehan et al., 2010), for young scholars, such as Aniko Bodroghkozy (2005), these debates mattered:

> For a young scholar like me this [debate between political economy and cultural studies] was far more than an academic battle among competing intellectual paradigms. If you were a grad student in the Telecommunication section of the Department of Communication Arts at the University of Wisconsin-Madison in the 1990s, this was about you.

What Bodroghkozy cannot say, but needs mentioning, is that this was about jobs. This acknowledgment in no way denigrates the seriousness of the debate that occurred in the 1990s. Some lines were drawn for very good reasons, as both sides had legitimate claims; but jobs matter too. Jobs matter, because on one hand, they grant the academic the institutional support to conduct research that might otherwise go unexplored—such as due to a lack of financial resources, or the absence of an intellectual community. Yet, jobs also matter because institutional support carries with it certain expectations of what constitutes good research and thus can function to discourage the undertaking of other important political projects. This is what Hall (2001) meant when he spoke of "institutionalization as a moment of profound danger" (p. 1908).

Revisiting this era may seem like old bones to some, as indeed the tension does seem to occupy less prominence (Curran & Morley, 2006); however, just because a debate no longer occupies the center, this does not mean it is not rupturing in the periphery. Moreover, if we understand graduate students and adjunct faculty to be those who most readily occupy the margins of academia, then it is particularly insidious that we are left to deal with the residue of a conflict not of our own making.[19] If I sound bitter, well, I just might be. That said, the point of what follows is not to retell the history of the debate between political economy and cultural studies and take out any intellectual angst on one side or the other. That history can be found elsewhere, and my treatment of it will not serve the purpose of what I hope to accomplish here.[20] Rather, what I set out to do in the following section is to provide a series of observations regarding what I believe is ailing contemporary cultural studies and what we (particularly graduate students) might do about it.

Cultural Studies: Work in Progress

From the moment of cultural studies institutional inception, prominent cultural theorists were apprehensive of what it would mean (Hall, 2001; Nelson, 1991; Rosaldo, 1994). Cultural theorists from already established departments, such as anthropology, were anxious as to how this new disciplinary kid on the block would interfere with its traditional object of study (Rosaldo, 1994). Those who had been left behind, institutionally, if not necessarily theoretically, such as political economists, were critical of what they saw as support for questionable research in the first place (Garnham, 1995a; McChesney, 2002). These external critiques were, and continue to be, questions of legitimacy. If anything, I hope that the above history helps to calm and/or reject those critiques out of hand. What I am interested in is not whether cultural studies should exist but rather how it might continue to do so. Since my concern is how it is that those on the margins (graduate students and adjunct faculty) might sustain this critical project, my focus will be on that danger which I believe to be particularly pertinent for this community: the fetishism of the concept.[21]

As intellectual movements shift from the periphery to the center, institutional forces encourage the development of particular concept fetishisms. Specific theoretical paradigms emerge as carrying with them a particular amount of intellectual capital that can then proceed to be deployed for the procurement of jobs, grants, and other institutional resources (Hall, 2001; McChesney, 2002). Theoretical sophistication is valuable as it offers the means by which to think otherwise; and this ability to think otherwise is a necessary component for the production of an alternative political movement (Cabral, 1966; MacCabe, 2008). Yet, the moment when theoretical sophistication becomes the end in and of itself, and becomes something of a religious orthodoxy, is when we have succumbed to the fetishism of the concept (Downing, 2005). Concept-fetishism is an intellectual, and hence political, danger because it collapses the productive tension between the conceptual (theoretical) framework and the object of analysis onto itself (MacCabe, 2008). What is left after the collapse is not a political synthesis but the elision of the referent itself. Now it is true that the referent is effaced in the first instance due to the semiotic sign-system that pervades all cultural experience; but, so too do objects of analysis (i.e., the referents) carry with them competing systems of signification. In other words, cultural theory is a necessarily messy intellectual enterprise because we must test our critical frameworks against the embodied experiences of those we claim to re-present (Bérubé, 2009; Hall, 2001; MacCabe, 2008). When we succumb to concept-fetishism, the messiness of analysis disappears, and in its place, the theoretical ends become an explanation in the first and last instance. Neoliberalism, does anyone know what it means? Nope, but we sure as hell know it's the problem. Parroting the popular intellectual language of the time may carry with it a certain amount of social capital, but it amounts to theoretical naivety and equally indefensible cultural analysis (Downing, 2005). The sad fact is, however, that these concepts are useful, but indiscriminate usage has robbed them of their political power.

To salvage what is useful about theory, we as young scholars must remember that theoretical sophistication necessitates struggle (Hall, 2001). From experience, I know this to be particularly difficult, as the last thing anyone wants is to look uninformed; but if we are to take theory seriously, and value the political contributions it can make, we must treat it seriously and push back. Two practical solutions for doing so, I believe, are as follows: (1) read the original source material when possible; (2) allow for concepts to intellectually gestate. The first (reading) may seem obvious, and an elementary principle of what it means to be an academic. However, academics are human, and I find that many of us take shortcuts, just like everyone else.[22] This means that source material, especially that of the archaic or "incomprehensible" kind, is typically ignored in favor of more contemporary or "accessible" interpretations. Lest readers believe this is merely symptomatic of contemporary graduate students, Jansen (2009) points out that for roughly the last 30 years, most cultural theorists took John Dewey and Walter Lippmann to be theoretical adversaries, when in fact their own writings and correspondences suggest they held much in agreement. This miscasting of the relationship, Jansen (2009) argues, stems from the ascension of Carey's 1982 characterization of the Dewey-Lippmann exchange in adversarial terms. Carey (2009) did this to advance a particular political agenda which was incompatible with what he saw as the anti-humanist implications of Lippmann's cultural analysis. This matters for us, however, because in constructing Dewey as an angelic figure of the progressive era, it "substitutes 'nostalgia for what never was' for the critical realism we urgently need" to address the problems of today (Jansen, 2009, p. 223).

The second practical thing we can do to salvage the political efficacy of theory is to give concepts time to gestate. This is necessary, for one's first encounter with theory is likely to leave one either disappointed by its disarming simplicity or aggravated by its impenetrable complexity. Allowing for a theory to settle (which itself is a form of struggle) may allow for one to see the particular nuances of a seemingly mundane claim. For instance, Carey (2009) may have mangled the Dewey-Lippmann debate, but he did have the insight to see the beauty of Dewey's (1955) statement on the duality of communication. Additionally, Gayatri Spivak's (1988) command of language and theoretical sophistication will always leave me searching for a dictionary, thesaurus, and phone call to a more senior scholar, but perhaps these actions must be undertaken as a part of the process of making meaning. Yes, I can now understand why the subaltern cannot speak—it is because the referent is obscured at the moment of representation—but I perhaps would have never come to this conclusion had I not struggled through her writing. As one final comment regarding this proposal (that we allow for theory to gestate), I'd like to suggest that we also allow a space for others to do the same. We do our peers no favors when we act as if the theoretical framework which took us enormous amounts of time to comprehend is common sense. As Stuart Hall (2006, 2008) is apt to remind us, that which appears to be common sense is in fact the most ideological. In other words, when we speak as if theory is obvious, then it has entered the realm of concept-fetishism; and, by extension, our evocation of these theoretical frameworks do not contribute to the possibility of thinking otherwise, but rather pressure others to submit to the hegemony of that particular intellectual paradigm.

Conclusion

An embodied cultural practice is the only means by which the struggle of politics can take place. Life exists in this struggle. These struggles are not always pleasant, and often lead to "theoretical noise" and institutional rupture. Yet, these conflicts are necessary if we are to move beyond the politics of deference (concept-fetishism) that we currently see in contemporary academia: these are the moments whereby one's lived experiences are uncritically deferred in place of the expertise of the critical authority (e.g., Foucault). This means that we ought to live autobiographically in relation to our disciplinary histories and its theoretical legacies. We must reinsert the personal, not as a means for solipsism, but as a path to the political. This is what Carey (2006) meant when he spoke of life as a perpetual autobiography, the last instance of which, the biography becomes another's "auto." In line of a pure conclusion, a desire to circumvent and obscure the openness of this call for intellectual struggle, I offer these final thoughts (and only in the first instance, for there is never a last). I still believe the field of cultural studies has much to offer the academic and political world.

That it continues to speak to graduate students and undergraduates alike is perhaps a testament to its ongoing political relevance. Yet, we must be hesitant and question whether this resonance stems from an uncritical endorsement of those very politics or its counter-hegemonic engagement (MacCabe, 2008). Struggling with theory does not mean leaving the clean air of meaning only to suffocate in the messiness of the reality below. It means doing both, grappling with that middle space where theory and practice meet, that moment where everything makes sense as soon as it fades away. We realize that just like those who came before us we must live pragmatically and take hold of the reins of history in order to make our own lives livable—and in turn trust those who come after us to understand that we lived through these times of acute social disturbance, and they did not.

Notes

1. Building upon the work of Althusser, Stuart Hall (1994) deploys the term "problematic" to emphasize the historical particularity of any given political enterprise, including critical theory: "What is important are the significant *breaks*—where old lines of thought are disrupted, older constellations displaced, and elements, old and new, are regrouped around a different set of premises and themes. Changes in a problematic do significantly transform the nature of the questions asked, the forms in which they are proposed, and the manner in which they can be adequately answered" (p. 520). For Althusser's formulation of the problematic refer to Louis Althusser, *For Marx*, trans. Ben Brewster (London: Allen Lane, 1969), 32–34.
2. I use the term "intellectual labor" to underscore the physical and mental exertion that goes into the production of academic knowledge. This differs from "intellectual work" insofar as work has come to be synonymous with occupation, which functions to obscure the embodied element of a given job; work, hence, comes to mean the task, and not the one who undertakes the task. In contrast, by using the term "intellectual labor," we are emphasizing that something is extracted from the intellectual during the moment of academic production.
3. This point is not to create a false binary between philosophy and literary theory but rather to foreshadow the difference between the impact of German philosophy on the Frankfurt School and English literary theory on the Centre for Contemporary Cultural Studies.
4. Here it is important to note that for the "culture and society" group, art and culture were relatively exclusive terms. These terms were not synonymous with paintings, music, literary production, or other modes of what we would conceive of as cultural production. Rather, art and culture were reserved for those things that were deemed to appeal to the tastes of the aristocratic society.
5. The British Popular Front belonged to a larger global coalition. This movement consisted of predominantly left-leaning activists concerned with preventing the rise of fascism (Dworkin, 1997).

6. This claim is not meant to disparage the theoretical contributions of the Frankfurt School. Rather, it is meant to highlight the pessimism embodied within the work of its two most prominent scholars, Adorno and Horkheimer. As my analysis of their Kantian influence suggested, the inverting of the Kantian hierarchy by capitalism left the proletariat in a state of inhumanity. The logical solution to such a predicament is not a further empowering of the individual per say, as to do so would merely stimulate the consumptive drive; rather, the critical intellectual project hinged on the ability to reset the logical structure of the masses: the revolution could not come from below.
7. See Dennis Dworkin (1997) for a more engaged treatment of Thompson's departure (pp. 235–45). In addition, it is important to note that Thompson never held a teaching position at the Centre. Rather, Thompson's contributions to the development of cultural studies functioned as that of an intellectual participant in the Centre's larger theoretical debates, as well as with the personal correspondence he maintained with such figures as Stuart Hall. However, after the irreconcilable differences that emerged from the 1979 History Workshop debate, Thompson's correspondence with Hall and other members of the Centre would end.
8. I am indebted to my readings of both Stuart Hall's (2001) *Cultural Studies and Its Theoretical Legacies*, and Walter Benjamin's (2006) "The Work of Art in the Age of Mechanical Reproduction," in coming to this formulation. That being said, this indictment is not meant to disparage the work of my seniors, such as Dana Cloud, Kent Ono, Marc Rich, Cameron McCarthy, and others, who are doing relevant political work in a multitude of ways: political organizing (Cloud), sexual assault intervention programming (Rich), establishing institutional support (Ono), and the mentoring of young critical scholars (McCarthy), amongst other important activities.
9. This quote of John Dewey comes from lecture notes taken by Charles Cooley.
10. John Dewey, Herbert Mead, and Robert Park would later become involved with the Chicago School of Sociology (Rogers, 1997).
11. Everett Rogers (1997) argues that propaganda studies never functioned as a major branch of early communications research. While that may be so, on pages 14 and 15, during his discussion of World War II, Rogers documents that propaganda research was conducted on behalf of the U.S. government. While it is true that this research existed outside of communication departments technically, as they did not yet exist, it is a bit disingenuous to minimize the significance of propaganda research to the procurement of governmental funding for communications research; which again, Rogers's own history shows.
12. Rogers (1997) notes that this letter was written 8 days after the Japanese attack on Pearl Harbor.
13. When Wilbur Schramm left the University of Illinois in 1957, Charles Osgood was promoted to director of the Institute of Communications Research (ICR). In a personal conversation with communications historian John Nerone, he noted that having been a strong critic of U.S. militarism, Osgood was shocked and disheartened to learn of the significant amount of funding the ICR had been receiving from the CIA.
14. It should be noted that the International Association of Media and Communication Research (IAMCR) was not founded until 1957, whereas Dallas Smythe began teaching in 1948.

15. It is important to note that Carey utilized the term "Chicago School" to encapsulate those thinkers explicitly concerned with the relationship between communication processes and the (im)possibility of a great community. Hence, the term "Chicago School" speaks more to a loose intellectual tradition rather than a specific intellectual community (Carey, 2009).
16. Carey (2009) is aware that Geertz (1973) is taking this notion from his (Geertz) interpretation of Max Weber, but it still remains that Carey cited Geertz, and not Weber when developing his notion of ritual.
17. To this history we could also include the Frankfurt School as evidence of the significance of this era in the rise of critical cultural theory, as these three different schools of thought all seem to emerge during the same period.
18. Some, perhaps even Bob himself, will question my inclusion of McChesney as a figure of American cultural studies. However, I justify his inclusion much in the same way that E. P. Thompson is considered a key figure in the development of British cultural studies. In fact, I believe the tension between McChesney, as a political economist, and contemporary cultural studies has much to do with the events of the 1990s, just as Thompson's experience in the late 1970s resulted in a similar parting of ways.
19. This claim warrants clarification. I am in no way suggesting that graduate students and adjunct faculty are the subaltern members of the university. We are not. Janitors, Food Service workers, and the other relatively invisible, and poorly paid members of the university are. However, what I do mean to suggest by this debate, is that when it comes to matters of intellectual labor, graduate students and adjunct faculty, as well as undergraduate students, operate at the margins—even if those margins are unfortunately supported by the physical labor of various subaltern groups.
20. If you are interested in that history, however, you can turn to the original sites of those debates. To start, I recommend seeking out *Critical Studies in Mass Communication* (1995). Additionally, the debates that occurred regarding structuralism within British cultural studies may also prove to be a useful frame of reference. For information on that, I recommend Raphael Samuel's *People's History and Socialist Theory*.
21. This is not to suggest that these comments will not be relevant to full and/or tenure track professors, but rather that I believe the notion of concept-fetishism is that which graduate students and adjunct faculty are perhaps most vulnerable to, and ironically, best equipped to resist. Additionally, there are other items that are worth discussing, such as the allure of substituting of intellectual work for politics (Hall, 2001) and object-fatalism (Bulut, this volume), but for the sake of my reader's patience, and my own treatment of the subject, I dedicate this section solely to the notion of concept-fetishism.
22. For a fascinating account of the transforming nature of information processes and the challenges this represents, see Crain in this volume.

References

Adam, G. . S. (2009). Foreword. In *Communication as culture: Essays on Media and Society* (pp. ix–xxiv). New York: Routledge.

Adorno, T. W., & Horkheimer, M. (1997). The *dialectic of enlightenment*. London: Verso.
Althusser, L. (1969). *For Marx* (B. Brewster, Trans.). London: Allen Lane.
Arnold, M. (1998). Culture and anarchy. In J. Storey (Ed.), *Cultural theory and popular culture: A reader* (pp. 7–12). Englewood Cliffs, NJ: Prentice Hall.
Benjamin, W. (2006). The work of art in the age of mechanical reproduction. In M. G. Durham & D. M. Kellner (Eds.), *Media and cultural studies: Keyworks* (pp. 18–40). Malden, MA: Blackwell.
Bérubé, M. (2009, September 14). What's the matter with cultural studies? *The Chronicle of Higher Education*. Retrieved from http://chronicle.com/article/Whats-the-Matter-With/48334/,
Bitzer, L. F. (1968). The rhetorical situation. *Philosophy and Rhetoric*, (1), 1–14.
Bodroghkozy, A. (2005). Media studies for the hell of it? Second thoughts on McChesney and Fiske. *FlowTV*.
Brown, W. (2006). American nightmare: Neoliberalism, neoconservatism, and de-democratization. *Political Theory*, 34(6), 690–714.
Burke, K. (1974). *The philosophy of literary form*. Berkeley, CA: University of California Press.
Cabral, A. (1966). *The weapon of theory*. Paper presented at the Tricontinental Conference of the Peoples of Asia, Africa and Latin America. Retrieved from http://www.marxists.org/subject/africa/cabral/1966/weapon-theory.htm
Carey, J. W. (1974). The problem of journalism history. *Journalism History*, 1, 3–5, 27.
Carey, J. W. (1975). A cultural approach to communication. *Communication*, 2(1), 1–22.
Carey, J. W. (1979). A plea for the university tradition. *Journalism Studies*, 55, 483–488.
Carey, J. W. (1995). Abolishing the old spirit world. *Critical Studies in Mass Communication*, 12(1), 82–88.
Carey, J. W. (2006). In remembrance of Jim Carey. Library Director David Shedden talks to Jim Carey in this 1991 Interview. Retrieved from http://www.poynter.org/media/mediacast/pub/1019/podcast.asp?id=1019
Carey, J. W. (2009). *Communication as culture: Essays on media and society*. New York: Routledge.
Curran, J. (2006). Media and cultural theory in the age of market liberalism. In J. Curran & D. Morley (Eds.), *Media and cultural theory* (pp. 129–148). London: Routledge.
Curran, J., & Morley, D. (2006). Editor's introduction. In J. Curran & D. Morley (Eds.), *Media and cultural theory* (pp. 1–13). London: Routledge.
Czitrom, D. J. (1982). *Media and the American mind: From Morse to McLuhan*. Chapel Hill, NC: University of North Carolina Press.
Dening, G. (1992). *Mr. Bligh's bad language: Passion, power and theatre on* The Bounty. New York: Cambridge University Press.
Dewey, J. (1927). *The public and its problems*. Denver, CO: Alan Swallow.
Dewey, J. (1955). *Democracy and education: An introduction to the philosophy of education*. New York: Macmillan.
Downing, J. D. H. (2005). Where we should go next and why we probably won't: An entirely idiosyncratic, utopian, and unashamedly peppery map for the future. In A. N. Valdivia (Ed.), *A companion to media studies* (pp. 495–512). Malden, MA: Blackwell.
Doxtader, E. (2008). The [rhetorical] question of exception, for now. *Communication and critical/cultural studies*, 5(2), 212–217.
Dworkin, D. (1997). *Cultural marxism in postwar Britain: History, the new left, and the origins of cultural studies*. Durham, NC: Duke University Press.

Eliot, T. S. (1976). *Christianity and culture: The idea of a Christian society and notes towards the definition of culture*. San Diego, CA: Harcourt Brace.

Foucault, M. (2003a). Nietzsche, genealogy, history (D. F. Brouchard & S. Simon, Trans.). In P. Rabinow & N. Rose (Eds.), *The essential Foucault* (pp. 351–369). New York: New Press.

Foucault, M. (2003b). What is an author? In P. Rabinow & N. Rose (Eds.), *The essential Foucault* (pp. 377–391). New York: New Press.

Fraser, N. (1997). Rethinking the public sphere: A contribution to the critique of actually existing democracy. In N. Fraser (Ed.), *Justice interruptus: Critical reflections on the 'postsocialist' condition* (pp. 69–98). London: Routledge.

Garnham, N. (1995a). Political economy and cultural studies: Reconciliation or divorce? *Critical studies in mass communication*, *12*(1), 62–71.

Garnham, N. (1995b). Reply to Grossberg and Carey. *Critical studies in mass communication*, *12*(1), 95–100.

Geertz, C. (1973). *The interpretation of cultures*. New York: Basic.

Gilroy, P. (2006). British cultural studies and the pitfalls of identity. In M. G. Durham & D. M. Kellner (Eds.), *Media and cultural studies: KeyWorks* (pp. 381–395). Malden, MA: Blackwell.

Ginzburg, C. (1992). Just one witness. In S. Friedlander (Ed.), *Probing the limits of representation: Nazism and the 'final solution'* (pp. 82–96). Cambridge, MA: Harvard University Press.

Grossberg, L. (1995). Cultural studies vs. political economy: Is anybody else bored with this debate? *Critical Studies in Mass Communication*, *12*(1), 72–81.

Grossberg, L. (1997). Cultural studies: What's in a name? (one more time). In L. Grossberg (Ed.), *Bringing it all back home: Essays on cultural studies* (pp. 245–271). Durham, NC: Duke University Press.

Hall, S. (1994). Cultural studies: Two paradigms. In N. B. Dirks, G. Eley, & S. B. Ortner (Eds.), *Media, culture & society: A critical reader* (pp. 520–538). Princeton, NJ: Princeton University Press.

Hall, S. (2001). Cultural studies and its theoretical legacies. In V. B. Leitch, W. E. Cain, L. A. Finke, B. E. Johnson, J. P. McGowan, & J. L. Williams (Eds.), *The Norton anthology of theory and criticism* (pp. 1898–1910). New York: W. W. Norton.

Hall, S. (2006). Encoding/decoding. In M. G. Durham & D. M. Kellner (Eds.), *Media and cultural studies: Keyworks* (pp. 163–173). Malden, MA: Blackwell.

Hall, S. (2008). The narrative construction of reality. *Context*, 6.

Hall, S., Critcher, C., Jefferson, T., Clarke, J., & Roberts, B. (1978). *Policing the crisis: Mugging, the state and law and order*. New York: Holmes and Meir.

Hebdige, D. (1979/2006). *Subculture: The meaning of style*. London: Routledge.

Hoggart, R. (1957). *The uses of literacy: Aspects of working-class life, with special references to publications and entertainments*. London: Chatto & Windus.

Hoggart, R. (1998). The full rich life and the newer mass art: Sex in shiny pockets. In J. Storey (Ed.), *Cultural theory and popular culture: A reader* (pp. 42–47). Englewood Cliffs, NJ: Prentice Hall.

Innis, H. A. (2008). *The bias of communication*. Toronto: University of Toronto Press.

Jansen, S. C. (2009). Phantom conflict: Lippmann, Dewey, and the fate of the public in modern society. *Communication and critical/cultural studies*, *6*(3), 221–245.

Jay, M. (1992). Of plots, witnesses, and judgments. In S. Friedlander (Ed.), *Probing the limits of representation: Nazism and the 'final solution'* (pp. 97–107). Cambridge, MA: Harvard University Press.

Jay, M. (1996). *The dialectical imagination: A history of the Frankfurt School and the Institute of Social Research, 1923–1950*. Berkeley, CA: University of California Press.

Johnson, R. (1986–1987). What is cultural studies anyway? *Social text, 16*, 38–80.

Kant, I. (1998). Religion within the boundaries of mere reason. In A. Wood & G. di Giovanni (Eds.), *Religion within the boundaries of mere reason and other writings* (pp. 31–191). Cambridge: Cambridge University Press.

Leavis, F. R. (1998). Mass civilization and minority culture. In J. Storey (Ed.), *Cultural theory and popular culture: A reader* (pp. 13–21). Englewood Cliffs, NJ: Prentice Hall.

Lippmann, W. (1949). *Public opinion*. New York: Macmillan.

Lowenthal, D. (1998). Fabricating heritage. *History and Memory, 10*(1).

MacCabe, C. (2008). An interview with Stuart Hall, December 2007. *Critical Quarterly, 50*(1–2), 12–42.

Marx, K. (1913). *The eighteenth brumaire of Louis Bonaparte* (D. De Leon, Trans.). Chicago: Charles H. Kerr.

Marx, K. (1990). *Capital: Volume I* (B. Fowkes, Trans.). London: Penguin.

McChesney, R. W. (2002). Whatever happened to cultural studies? In C. A. Warren & M. D. Vavrus (Eds.), *American cultural studies* (pp. 76–93). Urbana, IL: University of Illinois Press.

McChesney, R. W. (2007). *Communication revolution: Critical junctures and the future of media*. New York: New Press.

Meehan, E. (2004). Moving forward on the left: Some observations on critical communications research in the United States. *The Public, 11*(3), 19–30.

Meehan, E., Anderson, J., McAllister, M., Bae, C. G., Davis, I., Han, D., et al. (2010). *Institutional approaches*. Paper presented at the Institute of Communications Research: Reunion.

Melody, W. (1993). Dallas Smythe: A lifetime at the frontier of communications. *Media, Culture and Society, 15*, 295–297.

Murdock, G. (1995). Across the great divide: Cultural analysis and the condition of democracy. *Critical Studies in Mass Communication, 12*(1), 89–95.

Nelson, C. (1991). Always already cultural studies: Two conferences and a manifesto. *The Journal of Midwest Modern Language Association, 24*(1), 24–38.

Newton, J., Kaiser, S., & Ono, K. A. (1998). Proposal for an MA and Ph.D. programme in cultural studies at UC Davis. *Cultural Studies, 12*(4), 546–570.

Nietzsche, F. (1980). *On the advantage and disadvantage of history for life* (P. Preuss, Trans.). Indianapolis, IN: Hackett.

Nietzsche, F. (2003). *Thus spoke Zarathustra* (R. J. Hollingdale, Trans.). London: Penguin.

Nord, D. P. (2006). James Carey and journalism history. *Journalism History, 32*(3), 122–127.

Rogers, E. M. (1997). *A history of communication study*. New York: Free Press.

Rosaldo, R. (1994). Whose cultural studies? *American anthropologist, 96*(3), 524–529.

Saxton, A. (2003). *The rise and fall of the white republic: Class politics and mass culture in nineteenth-century America*. London: Verso.

Smythe, D. W. (1977). Communications: Blindspot of Western Marxism. *Canadian Journal of Political and Social Theory, 1*(3), 1–27.

Smythe, D. W. (1981/2006). On the audience commodity and its work. In M. G. Durham & D. M. Kellner (Eds.), *Media and cultural studies: KeyWorks* (pp. 230–253). Malden, MA: Blackwell.

Spivak, G. . C. (1988). Can the subaltern speak? In C. Nelson & L. Grossberg (Eds.), *Marxism and the interpretation of culture* (pp. 271–313). Urbana, IL: University of Illinois Press.

Steinberg, M. (1996). Cultural history and cultural studies. In C. Nelson & D. P. Gaonkar (Eds.), *Disciplinarity and dissent in cultural studies* (pp. 103–129). New York: Routledge.

Thompson, E. P. (1961a). The long revolution (Part I). *New Left Review*, (9), 24–33.

Thompson, E. P. (1961b). The long revolution (Part II). *New Left Review*, (10), 34–39.

Thompson, E. P. (1966). *The making of the English working class*. New York: Vintage.

Thompson, E. P. (1981). The politics of theory. In R. Samuel (Ed.), *People's history and socialist theory* (pp. 396–409). London: Routledge & Kegan Paul.

Weber, M. (1958a). Politics as vocation (H. H. Gerth & C. W. Mills, Trans.). In H. H. Gerth & C. W. Mills (Eds.), *From Max Weber: Essays in Sociology* (pp. 77–128). New York: Oxford University Press.

Weber, M. (1958b). The social psychology of the world religions (H. H. Gerth & C. W. Mills, Trans.). In H. H. Gerth & C. W. Mills (Eds.), *From Max Weber: Essays in Sociology* (pp. 267–301). New York: Oxford University Press.

West, C. (1999). The new cultural politics of difference. In C. West (Ed.), *The Cornel West reader* (pp. 119–139). New York: Basic Civitas.

Williams, R. (1977). Structures of feeling. In *Marxism and literature* (pp. 128–135). Oxford: Oxford University Press.

Williams, R. (1983). *Culture and society*. New York: Columbia University Press.

Williams, R. (1985). *Keywords: A vocabulary of culture and society*. New York: Oxford University Press.

Williams, R. (1993). *Television: Technology and cultural form*. London: University Press of New England.

Williams, R. (2001). *The long revolution*. Ontario: Broadview.

Wilson, R. (2010). Tenure, RIP: What the vanishing status means for the future of education. *The Chronicle of Higher Education*. Retrieved on July 4, 2010 from http://chronicle.com/article/Tenure-RIP/66114/

· 2 ·
Labor and Totality in "Participatory" Digital Capitalism

ERGIN BULUT

The Representation of Youth

The topic of youth has been an issue of great importance and interest to every historical social formation. It has drawn considerable attention both in academic writings and the political realm. Youth have been thought of either as a troublesome, problematic category (socially defined population) and/or the vanguard of social progress (Mungham & Pearson, 1976). In a similar way, other scholars have come up with different paradigms to explain the youth phenomenon: youth as a biological category, a distinctive social group, and/or a cultural construct (McCulloch, Stewart, & Lovegreen, 2006). When we trace the emergence of the discourse surrounding youth and adolescence, we inevitably come across the name G. Stanley Hall, who described youth as a transitional period and labeled it as a storm and stress era, characterized by changes in the body (Hall, 1916).[1] In time, this mainstream model has been attacked by various scholars who have emphasized youth as a constructed and invented category of modernity (Griffin, 1993; Ben-Amos, 1995). Furthermore, the traditional school of thought and its more recent manifestations have been criticized because they construct a narrative of a classless, raceless, and genderless, namely homogenous, body of youth—which is ultimately described as a Coca-Cola generation who are at war with the world of the adults (Mungham & Pearson, 1976, pp. 2–3).

Yet, it was not actually until the 1960s that we witnessed the emergence of academic works which aimed to overcome the lack of theoretical and political categories such as class in mainstream youth studies (Downes, 1966; Hargreaves, 1967). In particular, it was the Birmingham School that really made working class youth studies and analyses of subcultures flourish. Factors contributing to Birmingham's academically productive environment included the overall rebellious atmosphere of 1960s, and the interaction between the famous British Marxist Historian E.P. Thompson's journal *The Reasoner* and the student-led *Universities and Left Review*.[2] That said, the major impetus behind the emergence of research that focused on the working class youth experience can be tied to the encounters the "center" had with Western Marxism—a period that can be called "after Marx" (Sparks, 1996, p. 84). Among all the fascinating cultural studies works of the period, Paul Willis' *Learning to Labor* (1981) can be regarded as a prominent precursor to subsequent working class youth studies. Engaging in a philosophical debate regarding structure and agency, Willis forced his readers to think about the process of social reproduction in a then-industrialized Britain. He argued that it was the very agency and resistance of the working class youth (represented as white and male), against schooling authority and the ideology of meritocracy, that informed their employment in the area of manual labor. His classical ethnography demonstrated that working class 'lads' preferred manual labor, since it represented masculine values, as opposed to mental labor, which they referred to as effeminate and thus attributed to their peers whom they called ear'oles.[3] In sum, *Learning to Labor* represented the introduction of human subjects into the texture of the social totality by providing a humanistic element to structural analyses, taking seriously the very agency of marginalized youth.[4]

Similar notions of resistance, agency, or creative consumption as used by Willis were employed by other scholars from the same tradition who focused on subcultures and consumption. One such work looked at the symbolic resistance of young people to the culture which dominated them (Hall & Jefferson, 1976). In a similar vein, the stability of meaning-making processes was questioned and signifiers were argued to be floating; subcultures were defined as subversive and active (Hebdige, 1988; McRobbie, 1990). Others argued that the audience has the power to resist the meanings within the dominant culture (Fiske, 1987). As it can be discerned, the overarching feature of these works—while acknowledging their differences—is the rejection of the high-low culture distinction, the emphasis on consumers as active agents, consumption as resistance, and an understanding of the realm of culture as autonomous, almost deprived of its intricate relationship with the economy.

These trends within cultural studies have been criticized with reference to the context within which they took place (Curran, 2006). In his provocative essay, Curran criticized what I prefer to call "a turn to agency" in media and cultural studies. He linked this shift in the research agenda of cultural studies to four major developments: the end of real socialism; the cultural revolt of the 1960s; the rise of the feminist movement and influx of women entering the workforce as low-wage service workers; and, globalization. He further attacked the rising influence of postmodernism and the celebration of market and cultural populism in cultural studies. This populism, directly tied to such political processes as the "phenomenon of postmodernism, the eclipse of radical critique and politics, the rise of aesthetic populism and accentuated consumerism, the technological renewal of capital, the call for an aesthetic of cognitive mapping, and so forth" (McGuigan, 1992), was also made possible through the politically attractive move to Gramsci (Harris, 1992). In other words, once a scholar celebrated consumption with reference to Gramsci and his notion of hegemony, it would be easy to guarantee a location on the left-hand side of the political scale.[5]

The emphasis on agency and consumption was also addressed by Paul Willis (2003), who provided a periodization of three different waves of modernization, the third of which he called "commodity and electric culture" (p. 402). Echoing his earlier arguments from *Common Culture*, in "Foot Soldiers of Modernity," Willis (2003) underlines the contemporary blurring of forms of consumption and production and asks the crucial question:

> While the continuing educational question for first wave modernization concerns whether state education is a means of liberation or ideological confinement for the unprivileged majority, the late modernist question for the same social group concerns whether the commodification and electrification of culture constitute *a new form of domination or a means of opening up new fields of semiotic possibility*. Are the young becoming culturally literate and expressive in new ways, or are they merely victims of every turn in cultural marketing and mass media manipulation? ([emphasis added], p. 405).

His answer is neither domination nor the opening up of new possibilities, but rather a cautious remark to contemporary educators that they need to find ways "to separate the predatory from the creative and entertain a practical hope for practical action" (Willis, 2003, p. 412). In other words, Willis is definitely critical of the processes of commodification that sweep through youth culture, but at the same time he tries to point to those liminal spaces within which educators can engage the more creative and subversive, and possibly political, patterns of youth consumption.

As it concerns Willis' (2003) notion of the "commodification and electrification of culture" (p. 405), the first thing that comes to one's mind is the Internet. Indeed, the immersion of youth with technology and their participation on the Internet are enormous. As Kahn and Kellner (Global Youth Culture) argue, youth "generally comprise the most media and technologically literate societies and multinational corporations that trade in global media commodities actively target [these] young people as a consumer class, now believed to be worth more than $2 trillion in potential sales."[6] Given these figures, it is almost impossible not to scrutinize the nature and meaning of youth participation in relation to the political economy of Internet platforms. These figures themselves are important but need to be dealt with more specifically with reference to the web 2.0 applications of participatory new media. How do youth engage with these platforms? What is attractive in these sites? To answer these questions, I focus on web 2.0 applications (e.g., Facebook, MySpace, Linkedin, and YouTube) since these platforms are actively and intensely used by young people and therefore need to be understood in relation to global capitalism. To achieve that goal, I now move on to delineate some of the features of contemporary capitalism.

Capitalism in Transition 1: Prosumption, Craft Consumer, Participation and Convergence

That capitalism has radically been transformed is undeniable. It is not the same capitalism for which Karl Marx wrote his analyses.[7] So, then, what are the general shifts in the global economy and the way capitalism operates?

In attempting to underline certain trends, George Liagouras (2005) maintains that there has been a transition towards an information-intensive technical system which is characterized by the concept of the weightless economy; the proliferation and the amelioration of symbolic and relational systems (pp. 21–23). He argues that investment in intangible capital (e.g., R&D, training, software, and long-term marketing investment) has become more important than the mechanization of labor processes (Liagouras, 2005, p. 23). Along these lines, various terms have been used to define this phase of capitalism including digital capitalism (Schiller, 1999), cognitive capitalism (Dyer-

Witheford & de Peuter, 2009), informational capitalism (Castells, 2000) or prosumer capitalism (Ritzer & Jurgenson, 2010). Among these different terms, I will focus on understanding the term "prosumer" and the blurring between production and consumption in relation to Web 2.0 applications.

According to Ritzer and Jurgenson (2010), there is a trend towards unpaid labor and the offering of products at no cost in contemporary capitalism. They argue that prosumption (the term acquired by combining production and consumption) has actually always been central to capitalism.[8] They further maintain that this blurring, which includes putting consumers to work, actually accelerated after the birth of fast food. For instance, since that time, the public has come to be accustomed to pumping one's own gasoline, using ATMs, and checking in at hotels and airports via electronic kiosks. In that case, what is new? First, they argue that in the age of web 2.0 consumption, capitalists are less capable of controlling contemporary prosumers, and the nature of exploitation has changed in that "prosumers seem to enjoy, even love, what they are doing and are willing to devote long hours to it for no pay" (Ritzer & Jurgenson, 2010, p. 22). Additionally, they claim that prosumer capitalism is one of abundance and prosumers do not pay fees for the services they receive from websites like Facebook. Overall, these authors disagree with arguments that foreground exploitation and claim that we might be witnessing the emergence of a new form of capitalism. This argument resonates well with Campbell's (2005) notion of the "craft consumer." This concept of the consumer is such that s/he is neither a rational actor (economic), a "dupe" (Frankfurt School), nor a postmodern, self-conscious symbol manipulator.[9] For Campbell (2005), the craft consumer is one who already has identity and aims to "transform commodities into personalized objects" the action of which allows "creativity and self expression" (p. 28).

These two examples clarify the kind of argument that pertains to web 2.0 applications in general. While Ritzer and Jurgenson (2010) provide some useful descriptions of the trends in contemporary capitalism, I argue that the fact that prosumers enjoy and are willing to use the services provided by web 2.0 does not necessarily exclude the possibility of exploitation. In this respect, are we defining exploitation based on one's willingness to participate, or simply the expropriation of one's labor and leisure, or the blurring and combination of both? Also, what is the historical totality in which Campbell's "craft consumer" is put to work—if not global capitalism which is highly compatible with consumer choice as long as there is no organized collective political action that targets the repressive and exploitative structures? While, admittedly, Campbell provides a delicate analysis regarding the class character of his craft consumer, we still need to be cautious about the new patterns of consumption in contemporary capitalism since the extent to which it provides room for alternative political possibilities is questionable in terms of the expansionary character of commodification and the exclusive character (in terms of race, gender, class, ability, etc.) of craft consumption. For instance, as it has been maintained with reference to social networking sites and mobile devices, what is happening in our contemporary age can also be interpreted in such ways that "teenagers equipped with portable electronic confessionals are simply apprentices training and trained in the art of living in a confessional society" (Bauman, 2007, p. 3). In other words, young people—or whoever participates in electronically mediated life—are learning to become adjusted to a precarious life; trying to remain constantly online and connected to various sorts of capital, without losing sight of their social background.

And yet, even critical scholars with a refined analysis of web 2.0 applications have a tendency to equate participation with freedom. For instance, danah boyd (2008) states that social network sites—especially MySpace—are the key to becoming cool in school and constitute the mechanisms through which young people experience identity formation, status negotiation and peer-to-peer sociality (p. 119). Despite her later (forthcoming) focus on race and class, and their role in terms of how youth differentiate their identity on MySpace and Facebook, boyd (2008) still cannot avoid creating a false binary between prohibiting *or* allowing access to youth in these platforms—as if the effects of contemporary capitalism can be quarantined to a particular space. Moreover, her use of the term "impression management" is ironic in its failure to give an account of the commodification one must undergo when "managing" one's identity—whether online or offline.[10] She further argues that "MySpace is the civil society of teenage culture" (boyd, 2008, p. 121) and hence seems to overestimate the possibilities offered by network sites. The problem, I argue, is twofold. First, as she herself addresses in her forthcoming work, civil society, whether 'real' or 'virtual,' is not devoid of conflict. Second, the problem is beyond morality; as she succinctly addresses in her discussion of the contradictory anxiety felt by adults towards online youth activity. Hence, the issue is not whether agency on the web is good or bad; rather, it is an extremely political issue that requires a perspective focusing on property relations based on power. Who owns MySpace and sets the rules of participation? Does participation in web 2.0 applications reflect a radical change in social property relations? In this respect, she seems to fall short of addressing the issue of how the labor and leisure time of young people are being turned into profit by corporations such as News Corp., the parent company of MySpace.

Henry Jenkins is another scholar who overestimates the significance of participation and subsequently constructs a smooth picture of consumption/production. Despite his reservations about what he calls "convergence culture," Jenkins (2006) cannot refrain from producing a liberatory rhetoric which almost implies that corporate structures are there to empower the fans and the consumers. When focusing on the visibility, agency and "empowerment" of fans, Jenkins (2006) actually fails to grasp the historical reasons as to why corporations are willing to provide the consumer with a higher level of "participation." To address these historical reasons, and provide a more theoretically sound stance, it is necessary that I now discuss as to why convergence or fan participation is even desired from the perspective of producers.

Capitalism in Transition 2: Web 2.0 and Connecting Ourselves to Death

Capitalism is a globalised system of crises and innovation. Even though we have been told that it represents the end of history and will bring peace and prosperity to the world (Fukuyama, 1993), we have just witnessed a catastrophic global economic crisis that actually encompasses the whole social system. In order to overcome its cyclical crises, capitalism uses technology as a central tool for innovation (Kellner, 1989; Mandel, 1975). As it has been aptly argued in relation to technology and the Internet, contemporary capitalism is increasingly moving towards a situation where the sole aim is "to try to squeeze every last drop of value out of the system by increasing the rate of innovation and invention through the acceleration of connective mutation" (Thrift, 2006, p. 281).[12] The configuration of contemporary capitalism is now such that there is a desire "to rework consumption so as to draw consumers much more fully into the process" and to actively reengineer "the space of innovation" (Thrift, 2006, pp. 281–282). In this environment, marketing gurus are celebrating the power of the consumers. Indeed, "a specter is haunting contemporary marketers" (Zwick, Bonsu, & Darmody, 2008, p. 164), and this specter is the consumer, who is hailed as the omnipotent person whose ideas and suggestions are fervently embraced by the corporations. This co-creation economy is "driven by the need of capital to set up processes that enable the liberation and capture of large repositories of technical, social, and cultural competence in places previously considered outside the production of monetary value" (Zwick et al., 2008, p. 166). As it can be discerned, co-creation does not exclude the question of exploitation and actually "represents an effort to re-rationalize key drivers of economic growth, innovation and new product development by bringing within the confines of the company walls an autonomous, unpaid, and creative consumer workforce" (Zwick et al., 2008, p. 168).

Nevertheless, participation by consumers and fans in the production process reveals an ambivalent, if not celebratory, response from academics (Tapscott & Williams, 2006).[13] No matter how critical they are, such analyses entail a risk in considering consumption to be liberatory—as if production no longer exists. As it is brilliantly argued, "if production does not seem to occupy a major place in our consciousness presently, it may be because, it has been moved elsewhere" (Dirlik, 1997, p. 209). Moreover, what is happening is exactly the ultimate expansion of capitalism and processes of value creation beyond the workplace and towards our private lives in a "fun" and "participatory" way. Through constant communication and interactivity, the imagination, desire and capacity of every consumer is incorporated into the process of production and logics of accumulation. The playful experience of consumers is co-opted and this potential has been realized by corporations. Despite the charming and hopeful discourse of not only corporations and management gurus but also optimistic academics, other scholars have called for a re-thinking of the promises of the Internet and participatory media (Fuchs, 2008).[14]

So, then, what is happening on the ground as far as participatory media is concerned? To offer an example, YouTube, for instance, presents itself as a democratic broadcast platform.[15] Nevertheless, there are techniques in place that prioritize some videos for the sake of enhancing advertisement, which constitutes one aspect of Google's efforts to monetize the site (Wasko & Erickson, 2009; Miller, 2009). Apart from financial figures, what is at stake is the subjectivity of the consumer in that connectivity means interaction "outside" of the corporeal. Hence, capitalism is actually preparing the pedagogic infrastructure for a new century that will increasingly transform lives into digital liquidity. Therefore, I argue that, the appealing sides of constant connectivity need to be thought through in relation to global capital, whose present objective is "to increase the economic efficiency of networks by allowing them to be shared more thoroughly and effectively among many users" (Schiller, 1999, p. xv). In that regard, I echo Andrejevic's (2009) concern: what is the potential for interactive exploitation, and what does YouTube, as an interactive platform, present to advertisers? Even though Andrejevic raises questions as to whether it is appropriate to use the word exploitation in the Marxian sense, the concept has taken hold beyond wage relations and has brought user-generated fun culture into modern capitalism.[16]

LinkedIn, a profit-making social networking site for professionals, offers another example. With 42 million members, the website operates in four languages. In order to reach more people, the managers of the website asked its users (or prosumers) in a mid-2009 survey whether they would be willing to translate the site into other languages. As Ritzer and Jurgenson (2010) note, "they were asked to do the work for no pay" (p. 24). LinkedIn is not unique in this regard: Google requested that its users provide free art for its browser Chrome; and, Facebook asked its users to translate the explanatory page on the site into more than 20 languages (Ritzer & Jurgenson, 2010). Ritzer and Jurgenson maintain that the Facebook translators were also asked to offer suggestions for preferred wording.

Think about MySpace. It is undeniable that MySpace provides music bands with a space to promote themselves. From a critical perspective, however, it is also undeniable that MySpace, as a web 2.0 platform, paves the way for the realization of free labor. That is, "in addition to the corporate mining and selling of user-generated content" the labor performed on web 2.0 like MySpace would include "tastes, preferences and general cultural content constructed therein" (Cote & Pybus, 2007, p. 90). In other words, the contradictory nature of technology and commodities—with both their potentials and destructive nature—as it has been documented brilliantly by Walter Benjamin (2006), manifests itself clearly in these websites[17]. While MySpace provides a platform for users to appear in a virtual space, the construction of online identities turns the work of those same users into a form of volunteer labor. This website—as it has been argued with reference to the notion of immaterial labor and its inclusion of communicative, emotional and linguistic features—"explicitly situates this subjective turn within the active and ongoing construction of virtual subjectivities across social networks" (Cote & Pybus, 2007, p. 90).[18] As Cote and Pybus brilliantly posit, many of the users of this website are young people and "one of the most fundamental tasks they *learn* is a kind of online personal brand management in a network comprised by multiple lines of valorization—both social and capitalist" (Cote & Pybus, 2007, p. 95). This definitely evokes boyd's (2008) notion of "impression management" and raises questions as to how some online platforms act as market within which actors try to negotiate and realize their value virtually. To put it in extreme words, the commodification of human body and soul has gone online. One's value now comes to depend on online connections, profile picture or how one constructs his/her taste on a networking site.

From these accounts of the incorporation of the consumer into the value creation process, it becomes obvious that life itself has become a social factory (Hardt & Negri, 2000), within which exploitation becomes almost ubiquitous; especially with the advent of more mobile devices that boost connectivity and interactivity. Emotions, movements and participation of consumers on the web are increasingly pumping blood into digital capitalism. Against this background, what follows is an attempt to theorize these developments based on an attempt to productively incorporate Marx's notion of "general intellect."

The notion of "general intellect" refers to that point in the development of capital when "the creation of real wealth will come to depend [on] technological expertise [and] organization [i.e., social management]" (Dyer-Witheford, 1999, p. 219). To put it in other words, "the organization of increasingly complex production systems around technology and machinery mediates social interaction in such a way that the workers' cognitive, social, and affective competences become integral to the labor process" (Zwick et al., 2008, p. 178). As Zwick et al. further argue, this process is not necessarily limited to wage labor. Work can be free and unpaid (Terranova, 2000), as opposed to what previous scholars have called, "prosumers" (Ritzer & Jurgenson, 2010), "craft consumers" (Campbell, 2005), or "convergence culture" (Jenkins, 2006). Web 2.0 applications are perfect locations for this free labor to take place. In this respect,

> General intellect then refers to a set of competencies (increasingly centered around cognitive, cultural, linguistic, and affective capabilities) [and] contemporary [. . .] capitalism posits any interaction and all communicative action as, potentially, a form of labor, and therefore inserts social cooperation squarely into the sphere of material production of life. (Zwick et al., 2008, p. 178)

Through this process, surplus value extraction is realized and this, according to Zwick et al., takes place in two forms. First, one pertains to the condition that consumers are not compensated in the value co-creation, *except for the joy and recognition* they get. Second, the consumer, as the value co-creator, actually "ends up increasing the price she has to pay for her creation" (2008, p. 180).

One can disagree with the picture portrayed here. I can hear the assertions that I am demeaning the meaning-making processes of consumers and neglecting their resistant possibilities. Yet, the story of corporate domination and the subsumption of subjectivity are far more telling than stories of resistance or participation. We are living in such times that "innovation and creativity are generated neither by docile workers nor docile customers but increasingly by what scholars have called 'consumer proletariat'" (Arvidsson, 2006, p. 73). The "natural state of alienation and defiance" for these consumer proletariat "fuels a constant desire to create oppositional forms of consumption relative to the aesthetic and functional norms of standardized and mass-marketed symbols of consumer culture" (Zwick et al., 2008, p. 183). As it is aptly emphasized, "it is *precisely* the non-identification with commodities available in the market that brings about the kind of creative labor power of consumers that companies value" ([emphasis added] Zwick et al., 2008, p. 183). In other words, the subversive and creative potential of customer dissidence is the very lubricant that fuels the crisis-prone capitalism (Frank, 1999). Under these historical conditions, one wonders: to what extent can we claim that digital participation is inherently empowering? What about the persistence of racial and gender inequalities within the web as has been addressed by scholars (Nakamura, 2008; Cassell & Jenkins, 1998)? If it is indeed the case that even looking and seeing are sources of value (Beller, 2006), what are the political implications of new media and cultural studies scholarship that tends to focus on the text in and of itself; thereby, isolating the text from the structures of power, and thus perceiving of web 2.0 as inherently open to participation—as if it is independent of the social totality? Again, and finally, under these historical conditions, ought we not to be suspicious that there exist philanthropic initiatives with the sole purpose of connecting the world to the web?

Remembering Labor, Totality and Critical Theory

Cultural studies and media studies did a great service by incorporating youth cultural consumption into academic scholarship. Yet, the extent to which this youth scholarship offers any workable pedagogy is questionable. As we all know, pedagogy was central to the Birmingham School, and the school's whole project was more about the political possibilities of transformation, rather than just celebrating consumer participation just because it exists. In this respect, I want to argue for a cultural analysis that remembers the centrality and inevitability of labor and totality in our social existence. In line with Dirlik (1997), I want to point to the urgency to "remember" production and labor. Just because there are no industrial factories around the campuses in the First

World—which are also now facing a deep crisis especially in the social sciences and humanities for obvious reasons—does not necessarily mean that labor has lost its importance.

While emphasizing the centrality of labor, I do not aim to reproduce the binary categories of production and consumption or adhere to hybrid categories. Rather, I call for a historical understanding of global capitalism in relation to political economy, labor, aesthetics, and representation within a totality. Whereas the notion of totality is a highly contested and historically charged term, I rather want to focus on this very concept in a Jamesonian sense, in that our everyday life existence (part) is mediated through the globally interconnected market forces (whole).[19] In other words, the whole is a combination of all the mediated parts. Following this way of thinking, I want to underline the interrelated nature of cultural production and consumption within the First World to the rest of the world (and to Third World within the First World), which happens to assemble or recycle—in racialized and gendered forms—many technological artifacts that are hailed as magical connectivity tools or platforms. I argue that while representation and the nature of participation are extremely important, one also needs to situate these technological artifacts and platforms as the ideal commodities of late capitalism, which not only connects people but also constitutes relations of commodity fetishism that creates amnesia regarding the exploitative relationships making those artifacts materially possible.

The notion of totality is significant in another sense. It is clear that "there has been a general move away from the totalistic emphasis that marked the earlier Anglo-American reception of continental Marxism" (Jay, 1984, p. 513). Nevertheless, Fredric Jameson has defended the concept against proponents of postmodern thought including Francois Lyotard. As opposed to the claims that totality is totalitarian and is about control, Jameson followed another path through Sartre, Lukács and Adorno (Miklaucic, 2004, p. 66). The importance of the notion, for our case, comes from the very fact that the totality proposed here, and in Jameson, is not one that is closed. It acts as a reminder of the expansionary logic of capitalism. It rather symbolizes the center which acknowledges contingency but also always reminds the structural characteristics of capitalism and therefore tries to understand the relationship between the part and the whole in a dialectical and historical manner. This is why Jameson (2006) calls postmodernism the cultural dominant of late capitalism, within which there are dominant trends of consumption and aesthetics, but this, as Jameson rightly argues, does not necessarily produce a closed totality:

> What happens is that the more powerful the vision of some increasingly total system or logic—the Foucault of the prisons book is the obvious example—the more powerless the reader comes to feel. Insofar as the theorist wins, therefore, by constructing an increasingly closed and terrifying machine, to that very degree he loses, since the critical capacity of his work is thereby paralysed, and the impulses of negation and revolt, not to speak of those of social transformation, are increasingly perceived as vain and trivial in the face of the model itself. (Jameson, 2006, p. 486)

Then, this totality has more to do with understanding the social with its dominants, while not closing the door to any possibilities since Jameson's understanding of history is completely materialist. In other words:

> Jameson's totality is not a monolithic, seamless and self-replicating web of undifferentiated and unified forces [...] Nothing new can arise in a closed totality and there can be no exception; instead, everything flows unerringly toward the final unity. An open totality, in contrast, is defined by the free play of differences that are not recuperable within any unity. (Hardt & Weeks, 2000, p. 21)

Therefore, the contradictory nature of technology and commodities once again becomes central to our argument.

What we are witnessing, to evoke the words of Stuart Hall (1996), are "Internet platforms and technology without guarantees." In this context, I call for caution against the celebratory accounts of technology and new media. Interestingly, new media applications are hailed as platforms that foster participation, meeting different cultures and establishing a multicultural society. Nevertheless, we need to think of the emergence of these technologies within a larger historical totality; the very totality within which discourses of multiculturalism emerge and are supported by global institutions and markets (Zizek, 1997). Also, I strongly argue that we need to remember that there is a whole tradition of critical theory with which cultural studies once fervently engaged and can benefit from continuing to do so. This is especially important in that the fascination with new media and technology risks affirming the discourse of trade journals like *Wired* and promoting a cyber-libertarianism attitude that works well with contemporary liberalism, since what matters is the choice of the consumer, who is thought to be independent of market forces.[20] Ultimately, I urge scholars to remember labor, the notion of totality, and the usefulness of critical theory in terms of understanding contemporary changes in our society. Otherwise, any analysis that fails to look at property relations and situate "participation" in new media within global capitalist totality will bear the risk of celebrating the market. And even worse, if we refrain from understanding the social as a totality then we risk becoming immersed in analyses that fetishize connectivity (which also implies disconnectivity) and end up affirming the barbaric to "civil" nature of capitalist progress (Benjamin, 1969).[21]

Notes

1. For a contextualization and historicizing of how this body of knowledge constructs and governs youth in relation to modernity, see Lesko, 1996. Lesko in this comprehensive piece draws on a Foucauldian perspective and elaborates on how knowledge defines the terrain of scientific knowledge and creates subjects. Additionally, she links how the discourse on adolescence is directly linked to modernist ideals such as progress, patriarchy and colonialism.
2. These two journals would then give birth to *New Left Review*. For a historical account of British Cultural Studies, see Dworkin (1997) and Mejia (this volume).
3. Ear'oles refers to the students more invested in schooling than the lads. Thus, they are mocked by the lads who think that schooling and mental work are effeminate. We need to note that Willis's work was both welcomed and criticized. On the one hand, it was received positively for paving the way for incorporating the subjective experience and agency of the actors into class analysis. On the other hand, it was criticized for not taking seriously the impact of the masculine-feminine relationship on working class women (McRobbie, 1980). Willis was also attacked for celebrating the lads' actions and ultimately presenting them in a romantic manner (Walker, 1985). For a useful volume on Willis's work within the framework of globalization, see (Dolby & Dimitriadis, 2004).
4. Willis's later works *Common Culture* (1990) and *The Ethnographic Imagination* (2000) followed a similar path of argumentation. Written within a conjuncture within which more than four million jobs were lost in the UK, *Common Culture* focused on the agency and creativity of human subjects in relation to consumption. *The Ethnographic Imagination*, on the other hand, invites the reader to rethink the contradictory nature of cultural commodities since they can be used by young people in meaning-making and subversive processes.
5. Here, it is absolutely crucial to remember the historical context within which Gramsci wrote about hegemony and the more contemporary context (and manner) within which he has been appropriated within the discipline of cultural studies. To begin with:

    The discipline of writing in the *Notebooks* is political rather than academic. Despite great intellectual breadth, there is a concentration on political strategy and the 'effective reality' of the time. In the dire circumstances of incarceration in a fascist prison, Gramsci is doing politics by proxy. He seeks a route to social transformation and popular agency that takes account of historical and contemporary realities. (Johnson, 2007, p. 97)

    As Johnson further brilliantly argues, one's reading and understanding of Gramsci also has to be contextualized. In this respect, one needs to take the 1970s and 1980s as moments of *transitions* into account. In other words, these were the times that marked the first phase of the neoliberal order, a time of crisis that precipitated new strategies of capital accumulation, dismantling of Social Democracy and the deflection of the desire for a fairer world first into the appetite for household consumption, then into individualized consumerism. For me, the appropriation of Gramsci by some of the cultural studies scholars were also quite problematic in a more theoretical sense in that:

> Gramsci's notes on "Americanism and Fordism" make particularly clear that hegemony is about the *relation of superstructures to structure*, including the relation of social and cultural organization to economy, or "the necessities of production" [. . .] Hegemony is not about cultural politics only. There can be no rule by cultural means alone. Yet culture enters into every move of the powerful or those who seek emancipation. Hegemony involves the force of economic relations—including the offer of higher wages for instance, a key, but not permanent, feature of the Fordist adaptation ([emphasis added, Johnson, 2007, p. 99)

6. With reference to UN figures, Kahn and Kellner (Global Youth Culture) maintain that 1.1 billion young people are considered to be the major source of growth for global media culture.
7. Having said that, I argue that claims that Marx's analysis of capitalism was rigid and is now outdated are extremely unsubstantiated. If it is hard to read *Capital* (Marx, 1990), one may want to have a look at *Communist Manifesto* (Marx & Engels, 2001) to see the vivid and fluid description of capitalism which constantly needs to renew and reinvent itself to avoid crises or to maximize its competitive edge and profits. For a brilliant analysis of the text and innovative and the self-destructive nature of capitalism, see Berman (1982).
8. It is interesting that Ritzer and Jurgenson (2010) refer to Marx, who is always criticized for ignoring the realm of consumption, and argue that he "fully understood that production always involved consumption" (Ritzer & Jurgenson, 2010, p. 14). At some level, this makes sense since producing, as Marx once argued, involves consuming one's body and consuming is a necessity step so that the worker can produce the next day.
9. I strongly disagree with the simple equation of critical theory with consumers as dupes, since such arguments tend to approach the valuable insights of this tradition from an ahistorical fashion.
10. Her employment of the term "impression management" raises questions as to how this indeed becomes something to be managed through the use of various resources and capital.
11. This subheading obviously has been inspired by Neil Postman's (1986) *Amusing Ourselves to Death*.
12. This is not to say that capitalism had not already been working to "squeeze every last drop of value out of the system" and that we are now confronting a completely new phase. Rather, I want to emphasize the acceleration of this process; and, as Thrift (2006) also argues, primitive accumulation, or accumulation by dispossession (Harvey, 2003), still goes on all around the world, as the contemporary U.S. presence in the Middle East demonstrates.
13. Ritzer and Jurgenson (2010) and boyd's (2008) analyses are definitely not celebratory but seem to fall short of understanding capitalism as a totality, which has become something of a sin word to use in today's academic environment. On the other hand, Jenkins' (2006) and Tapscott and Williams' (2006) analyses can be regarded as celebratory of the consumption as agency and viewing the Internet as signaling a new "liberatory" economy.

14. Here is some striking information: "the total GDP of all 53 African states was US$ 1,000,913 billion in 2007. The total assets of the top six knowledge corporations (AT&T, Vodafone, Verizon, Deutsche Telekom, Nippon, Telefonica) were US$1,132,41 billion in 2007 and hence larger than the total African GDP" (Fuchs, 2009, p. 78).
15. For an excellent critique of platforms, their promises, failures and politics, see (Gillespie, 2010).
16. Andrejevic makes a distinction between user-generated content and user-generated data and claims that it is the latter that is more appropriate to be taken away from the interactive worker. He also strives to locate the word exploitation not to *Capital* but to Marx's *1844 Manuscripts* and in a sense evokes an implied relationship of alienation, rather than pure exploitation. One interesting remark of his is that it is not the critical theorists but rather the marketing people who understood Marx's *1844 Manuscripts* to incorporate the users into the production (Andrejevic, 2009, pp. 418–419).
17. For an excellent discussion and reconstruction of Benjamin's *Arcades Project* and his discussion of technology as revolutionary potential and risks of commodification and repression, see (Buck-Morss, 1991).
18. The notion of "immaterial labor" has been critiqued on various aspects. As it has been rightly argued, these "new circuits of capital look a lot less immaterial and intellectual to the female and Southern workers who do so much of the grueling physical toil demanded by a capitalist general intellect whose metropolitan headquarters remain preponderantly male and Northern" (Dyer-Witheford, 1999, p. 71). Also, to what extent this immaterial labor is not material is questionable (Dowling, 2007).
19. For a detailed and eloquent analysis of the term "totality," see Martin Jay (1984). In his book, Jay not only provides a wonderfully written intellectual history but also contemporary debates about the concept as far as the rise of poststructural critique is concerned.
20. Any criticism that talks about domination or is inspired from critical theory meets frowning eyes, most probably implying, "you don't understand the youth, you elitist!" Nevertheless, I assume the remarks by Esther Leslie (n. d.) regarding contemporary reception of critical theory is worth quoting at length in that she brilliantly demonstrates the politics of how critical theory is taught in universities:

    A widespread campaign to cauterize Adorno's thought entails university teachers handing out to their classes a photocopy of the chapter on the mass culture industry from *Dialectic of Enlightenment*, followed by a discussion which ends up emphasizing the positive role television and magazines can play in entertaining the young and in improving race relations. The gap between students' experience and Adorno's accusations is so wide that he is easily cast as a blinkered reactionary. Teachers ally themselves with existing society, damning reflection and critique as an elitist pursuit, unprofitable and unproductive. [. . . .] In this game, Adorno has become a cipher for Marxist thought in general. Middleclass commonsense cannot imagine criticism of class society in its totality, and so interprets any charge against commodification and commercial manipulation as mere snobbery.

21. Here, I have in mind Benjamin's critique of progress. In his *Theses on the Philosophy of History*, Benjamin (1969) says: "There is no document of civilization which is not at the same time a document of barbarism" (p. 256).

References

Andrejevic, M. (2009). Exploiting YouTube: Contradictions of user-generated labor. In *The YouTube reader* (pp. 406–424). Stockholm: National Library of Sweden.

Arvidsson, A. (2006). *Brands meaning and value in media culture*. London: Routledge.

Bauman, Z. (2007). *Consuming Life*. Cambridge: Polity.

Beller, J. (2006). *The cinematic mode of production: Attention economy and the society of the spectacle*. Interfaces, studies in visual culture. Hanover, NH: Dartmouth College.

Ben-Amos, I. (1995). Adolescence as a cultural invention: Philippe Ariès and the sociology of youth. *History of the Human Sciences*, 8(2), 69–89.

Benjamin, W. (1969). *Illuminations*. New York: Schocken.

Benjamin, W. (2006). The work of art in the age of mechanical reproduction. In M. G. Durham & D. M. Kellner (Eds.), *Media and cultural studies: Keyworks* (pp. 18–40). Malden, MA: Blackwell.

Berman, M. (1982). *All that is solid melts into air: The experience of modernity*. New York: Simon & Schuster.

boyd, d. (2008). Why youth love social network sites: The role of networked publics in teenage social life. In D. Buckingham (Ed.), *Youth, identity, and digital media* (pp. 119–142). Cambridge, MA: MIT.

boyd, d. (forthcoming). White flight in networked publics? How race and class shaped American teen engagement with MySpace and Facebook. In L. Nakamura & P. Chow-White (Eds.), *Digital race anthology*. New York: Routledge.

Buck-Morss, S. (1991). *The dialectics of seeing*. Cambridge, MA: MIT.

Campbell, C. (2005). The craft consumer: Culture, craft and consumption in a postmodern society. *Journal of Consumer*, 5(1), 23–42.

Cassell, J., & Jenkins, H. (1998). *From Barbie to Mortal Kombat: Gender and computer games* (illustrated edition.). MIT.

Castells, M. (2000). *The rise of the network society* (2nd ed.). Oxford: Blackwell.

Cote, M., & Pybus, J. (2007). Learning to immaterial labour 2.0: MySpace and social networks. *ephemera*, 7(1), 88–106.

Curran, J. (2006). Media and cultural theory in the age of market liberalism. In J. Curran & D. Morle (Eds.), *Media and cultural theory* (pp. 129–149). New York: Routledge.

Dirlik, A. (1997). The postmodernization of production and its organization: Flexible production, work and culture. In *The postcolonial aura: Third world criticism in the age of global capitalism* (pp. 186–220). Colorado: Westview.

Dolby, N., & Dimitriadis, G. (2004). *Learning to labor in New Times*. London: RoutledgeFalmer.

Dowling, E. (2007). Producing the dining experience: Measure, subjectivity and the affective worker. *ephemera*, 7(1), 117–132.

Downes, D. (1966). *The delinquent solution*. London: Routledge & Kegan Paul.

Dworkin, D. (1997). *Cultural Marxism in postwar Britain*. London: Duke University Press.

Dyer-Witheford, N. (1999). *Cyber-Marx: Cycles and circuits of struggle in high-technology capitalism*. Urbana, IL: University of Illinois Press.

Dyer-Witheford, N., & de Peuter, G. (2009). *Games of empire: Global capitalism and video games*. Minneapolis, MN: University of Minnesota Press.

Fiske, J. (1987). *Television culture*. London: Methuen.

Frank, T. (1999). *The conquest of cool*. Chicago: University of Chicago Press.
Fuchs, C. (2008). Book review: *Wikinomics*. *International Journal of Communication, 2*, 1–11.
Fuchs, C. (2009). Information and communication technologies and society: A contribution to the critique of the political economy of the Internet. *European Journal of Communication, 24*(1), 69–87.
Fukuyama, F. (1993). *The end of history and the last man*. New York: Avon.
Gillespie, T. (2010). The politics of platforms. *New Media and Society, 12*(3), 347–364.
Griffin, C. (1993). Starting titles and reservations: A century of adolescence: From 1880 to 1980. In *Representations of Youth: The Study of Youth and Adolescence in Britain and America* (pp. 1–26). Cambridge, MA: Polity.
Hall, G. S. (1916). *Adolescence*. New York: Appleton.
Hall, S., & Jefferson, T. (Eds.). (1976). *Resistance through rituals: Youth subcultures in post-war Britain*. London: Hutchinson.
Hall, S. (1996). The problem of ideology: Marxism without guarantees. In D. Morley & K. Chen (Eds.), *Stuart Hall: Critical dialogues in cultural studies* (pp. 25–47). London: Routledge.
Hardt, M., & Negri, A. (2000). *Empire*. Cambridge, MA: Harvard University Press.
Hardt, M., & Weeks, K. (Eds.). (2000). *The Jameson reader*. Oxford, UK: Blackwell.
Hargreaves, D. (1967). *Social relations in a secondary school*. London: Routledge & Kegan Paul.
Harris, D. (1992). *From class struggle to the politics of pleasure: The effects of Gramscianism on cultural studies*. London: Routledge.
Harvey, D. (2003). *The new imperialism*. Oxford, UK: Oxford University Press.
Hebdige, D. (1988). *Subculture: The meaning of style*. New accents. London: Routledge.
Jameson, F. (2006). Postmodernism, or the cultural logic of late capitalism. In D. Kellner & M. G. Durham (Eds.), *Media and cultural studies: KeyWorks* (pp. 482–520). Oxford: Blackwell.
Jay, M. (1984). *Marxism and totality: The adventures of a concept from Lukács to Habermas*. Berkeley, CA: University of California Press.
Jenkins, H. (2006). *Convergence culture*. New York, London: NYU Press.
Johnson, R. (2007). Post-hegemony: I don't think so. *Theory, Culture and Society, 24*(3), 95–110.
Kahn, R. & Kellner, D. *Global youth culture*. Retrieved 27 September 2010, from http://richardkahn.org/writings/culturalstudies/globalyouthculture.pdf
Kellner, D. (1989). *Critical theory, Marxism and modernity*. Baltimore, MD: Johns Hopkins University Press.
Leslie, E. *Adornoism—a ME mmanifesto*. Retrieved 27 September 2010, from http://www.militantesthetix.co.uk/adorno/twamani.htm
Lesko, N. (1996). Denaturalizing adolescence: The politics of contemporary representations. *Youth and Society, 28*(2), 139–161.
Liagouras, G. (2005). The political economy of post-industrial capitalism. *Thesis eleven, 81*, 20–35.
Mandel, E. (1975). *Late capitalism* (Rev. ed.). London: NLB.
Marx, K. (1990). *Capital: Volume 1: A critique of political economy*. London: Penguin.
Marx, K., & Engels, F. (2001). The communist manifesto. In W. E. Cain, L. A. Finke, B. E. Johnson, J. McGowan, & J. J. Williams (Eds.), *The Norton anthology of theory and criticism* (pp. 769–773). New York: Norton.
McCulloch, K., Stewart, A., & Lovegreen, N. (2006). We just hang out together: Youth cultures and social class. *Journal of Youth Studies, 9*(5), 539–556.

McGuigan, J. (1992). *Cultural populism*. London: Routledge.
McRobbie, A. (1980). Settling accounts with sub-culture. *Screen Education*, (34), 37–50.
McRobbie, A. (1990). *Feminism and youth culture*. Basingstoke: Macmillan.
Miklaucic, S. (2004). *Playful labors: Narrative, work and digital games* (PhD). UIUC, Champaign.
Miller, T. (2009). Cybertarians of the world unite: You have nothing to lose but your tubes! In P. Snickars & P. Vondereau (Eds.), *The YouTube reader* (pp. 424–441). Stockholm: National Library of Sweden.
Mungham, G., & Pearson, G. (1976). Introduction: Troubled youth, troubling world. In *Working class youth culture* (pp. 1–10). London: Routledge.
Nakamura, L. (2008). *Digitizing race: Visual cultures of the Internet*. Minneapolis, MN: University of Minnesota Press.
Postman, N. (1986). *Amusing ourselves to death: Public discourse in the age of show business*. New York: Penguin.
Ritzer, G., & Jurgenson, N. (2010). The nature of capitalism in the age of the digital 'prosumer.' *Journal of Consumer Culture*, 10(13), 13–36.
Schiller, D. (1999). *Digital capitalism: Networking the global market system*. Cambridge, MA: MIT Press.
Sparks, C. (1996). Stuart Hall, cultural studies and Marxism. In *Stuart Hall: Critical dialogues in cultural studies* (pp. 71–102). London, New York: Routledge.
Tapscott, D., & Williams, A. D. (2006). *Wikinomics: How mass collaboration changes everything*. New York: Portfolio.
Terranova, T. (2000). Free labor: Producing culture for the digital economy. *Social text*, 18(2), 33–58.
Thrift, N. (2006). Re-inventing invention: New tendencies in capitalist commodification. *Economy and Society*, 35(2), 279–306.
Walker, J. (1985). Rebels with our applause? A critique of resistance theory in Paul Willis's ethnography of schooling. *Journal of Education*, 167(2), 63–83.
Wasko, J., & Erickson, M. (2009). The political economy of YouTube. In P. Snickars & P. Vondereau (Eds.), *The YouTube reader* (pp. 372–387). Stockholm: National Library of Sweden.
Willis, P. (1981). *Learning to labor: How working class kids get working class jobs*. New York: Columbia University Press.
Willis, P. (1990). *Common culture*. Bristol, PA: Open University Press.
Willis, P. (2000). *The ethnographic imagination*. Cambridge: Polity.
Willis, P. (2003). Foot soldiers of modernity: The dialectics of cultural consumption and the 21st-century school. *Harvard Educational Review*, 73(3), 390–415.
Zizek, S. (1997). Multiculturalism, or, the cultural logic of multinational capitalism. *New Left Review*, 225(September–October), 28–51.
Zwick, D., Bonsu, S., & Darmody, A. (2008). Putting consumers to work: Co-creation and new marketing govern-mentality. *Journal of Consumer Culture*, 8(2), 163–196.

· 3 ·
Seeing Red

Ruptured Identity and the Representation of Black American Women Living with HIV and AIDS

CAROLYN RANDOLPH

Window of Opportunity

The field of communications research faces a critical moment in which it must rethink its treatment of race, ethnicity, and identity in relation to globalization under neoliberalism. Changes to the way the Centers for Disease Control and Prevention report sub-populations living with HIV and AIDS as well as the recent anti-immigration legislation passed in Arizona bear witness to questions over the role of diversity in American life. Displaced workers, refugees, and naturalized citizens rupture traditional categories of identity as they search for ways to be counted in the midst of tremendous shifts in the broader social and cultural landscape. Communications research—as the study of human interaction—is uniquely positioned to not only account for, but intervene in these complex cultural processes, especially those that criminalize racial and ethnic groups in need of State protections. However, this inter-discipline remains reluctant to adopt alternative paradigms and research approaches that emphasize race and ethnicity as innovative lines of academic inquiry. Instead, much of the scholarship divests itself of any interest in these areas. As such, this chapter calls for the field of communication to adopt an intersectional approach as a way to contest existing ways of analyzing race and ethnicity. An intersectional approach represents race and ethnicity as contested sites of meaning (cultural constructions) that already always intersect gender, class, and sexuality. By deploying an intersectional analysis, this chapter describes how Black American women, living with HIV and AIDS, formulate and articulate a situated identity that ruptures traditional categories of race, ethnicity, gender, class, and sexuality. Overall, this chapter contributes to the development of a more productive framework for theorizing emerging identity formations or how social actors—acting within various institutions—define and redefine social reality.

Ruptured Identity

Individual and group identity is complex. Informed by the combination of race, ethnicity, gender, class, sexuality, physical ability, religion, and nationality, in a social world that privileges certain categorizations over others, identity represents a contested site of struggle over meaning "constituted within, not outside representation" (Hall, 1996a, p. 4). Therefore, identity signs in as a key moment in the cultural circuit where the relationship between culture (routinely regarded as the production and circulation of meaning) and power is articulated and observable.

The study of identity, then, explores the interaction between text (symbolic) and body (material) to describe how social actors navigate various institutions (i.e., media, medicine, government, religion, and education). In the contemporary social world, ordinary, everyday people more readily encounter popular media images and formulate personal narratives (subjectivity and identity) in direct relation to the discourses of race, ethnicity, gender, class, and sexuality offered up by these cultural texts. Mainstream media tend to reproduce essentialist notions of culture, race, and ethnicity "inevitably grounded in the impossible assumption of origin, unity and racial purity" (Brah, 1992, pp. 126–145). Thus, identity is routinely categorized as biological or historical; race as Black or White; gender as masculine or feminine; sexuality as heterosexual or homosexual; and, class as rich or poor. Yet, essentialist binarism is academically and politically untenable, increasingly under contestation, and difficult to sustain. "These conceptual binarisms foreclose nonwhite interethnic relationships and put on hold those who do not fit easily into preexisting binarisms" (Shohat & Stam, 2003, p. 4).

However, categories of identity are constantly ruptured and sutured back together in ways that are unexpected, potentially productive, and generative of new opportunities for academic inquiry. Within this theoretical framework, representations of identity—namely race and ethnicity—put forth by mainstream media function as a form of discursive normalization; as an instrument of state power that disciplines multiplicity through homogenization (Foucault, 1995; hooks, 1994). The normalization of these identity categories occurs through their production and reproduction in a variety of institutions, among them political, legal, medical, and academic. Although normalization potentially curtails the productive formation of new embodied practices, alternative corporealities, and ruptured identities, racial and ethnic identity normalization is never complete because it is inherently embedded in multiple positionalities through its persistent intersections with class, gender, and sexuality. Consequently, within traditional U.S. race and ethnic social structures, select groups vex governmentality through their unclassifiable nature such as undocumented immigrants (Lugones, 2003; Valdivia, 2004). Racial and ethnic identification is equally fraught with tensions over rigid classifications and the foregrounding of social, cultural, and nationalistic markers of difference within the group (Smith, 1992; Staff, 2001).

Demographic changes and the unstable history of racial and ethnic categorization ultimately point to a critical moment of destabilization or "discursive rupture" between historical norms and lived contemporary practices. Discourse is as a set of social, cultural, political, and legal practices that support particular forms of knowledge or ways of knowing (see also, Foucault, 1981). As such, categories of U.S. racial and ethnic identity is codified through discourse, as a set of social, cultural, political, and legal practices that support and are reified through the production of academic knowledge (Haney-Lopez, 2006; Ladson-Billings, 2000). Therefore, emerging identity formations serve as "discursive ruptures," pointing to moments of failure and conflict within a set of practices. Rupturing identity or emerging identity formations are embedded with notions of resistance that "storm the discourse of dominant structures" (Halberstam, 2006). In the end, they exploit the ways dominant ideology and practices are not always internally consistent. Foucault (1984) summarizes:

> Through the themes of health, progeny, race, the future of the species, the vitality of the social body, power spoke *of* sexuality and *to* sexuality; the latter was not a mark or a symbol, it was an object and a target. Moreover, its importance was due less to its rarity or its precariousness that to its insistence, its insidious presence, the fact that it was everywhere an object of excitement and fear at the same time. Power delineated it, aroused it, and employed it as the proliferating meaning that had always to be taken control of again lest it escape; it was an *effect with a meaning value* ([emphasis in original], p. 269).

Therefore, the discourse about sexuality, like the discourse about race and ethnicity, is always internally contradictory and productive of new fields of power. As an "object and a target," the discourse about sexuality simultaneously resulted in repression by the State and produced emergent social formations (ruptured identities) that celebrated the sexualization of the body. Similarly, racial and ethnic identity categories are always contained through dominant societal structures, such as the U.S. Department of Public Health, while simultaneously generating oppositional embodied practices. Postcolonial feminist scholarship has documented the ways in which the normalization of categories of racial and ethnic identity always fails to account for the ideological ambivalences, shifting identity practices, and liminal positions of subjectivity that produce politically and culturally oppositional moments (Moraga, 1981; Stoler, 1995).

In addition, postcolonial feminist scholars have moved beyond Foucault's preoccupation with whiteness and maleness to recuperate subjugated bodies of knowledge that reconfigure power and identity at the intersection of multiple forms of difference. . For instance, Spivak (1998) rescues from the historical periphery the discourse of nationalist women involved in India's fight for independence that had been written out of Britain's colonial narrative, thereby drawing into question the gendered and racialized power relations embedded in the categories of colonizer/center and colonized/periphery. Postcolonial queer and/or feminist scholars who deploy an intersectional analysis are increasingly claiming the periphery and margins as productive sites for theorization, including: Harewood's (2005) discussion of peripheral cultural spaces as sites of oppositional empowerment for racialized, sexualized, and classed citizens; Clayton's (1996) work on the closet as a sanctuary where queers of color can nurture collectivity and develop alternative identities; and, Collins' (2000) discussion of African American women as "outsider-insiders," who develop an oppositional form of consciousness, all point to a window of opportunity for new areas of academic inquiry.

Furthermore, in the United States, the dominant Black and White racial binary increasingly fails to account for those who do not identify as either—such as the nearly 8 percent of U.S. citizens (Hispanic and non-Hispanic) who identify as "two or more races" or "some other race" (U.S. Census, 2000). The dominant gender binary, that divides the world into a masculinity and femininity encoded through white normativity, erases those bodies who transgress these boundaries or whose gendered and racialized bodies have never been fully articulated into the national gender discourse—transgendered bodies, intersexed bodies, Asian bodies, Black bodies, Latina/o bodies, and HIV/AIDS bodies. Dominant categories of identity contribute to the production of critical gaps and erasures in the U.S. media, such as the mainstream news coverage of the alleged Duke University lacrosse team gang rape of a Black woman which proved ill equipped to narrate the convergence of race, ethnicity, gender, class, and sexual differences surrounding both the victim and the defendants. As Moorti (2002) suggests media narratives of rape ultimately reify race and gender stereotypes that erase the act of sexual violence itself. Like mainstream media, communications research does not, but must, account for ruptured identity formations that expose new forms of agency, power, and control in the contemporary social world.

Race and Ethnicity in Communications Research

Race, ethnicity, and feminist scholars argue that disciplinary territorialization often produces its own set of binary logics (Dyson, 2005; hooks, 1994; Ladson-Billings, 2000; Valdivia, 2000). By asking how select bodies get represented and how various research approaches position these bodies, we can better understand the evolution of communications as a type of disciplining technology and a productive, dynamic, and multiperspectival field of inquiry.

Journals serve as the benchmark of intellectual inquiry. As it regards communications, the *Journal of Communication*—a major communication journal—readily avoids complex discussions of race, ethnicity, identity, and communication, despite almost twenty years of cutting-edge work in this area. The disciplinary areas represented in the *Journal of Communication* often pay little attention to how race and ethnicity intersect dimensions of interpersonal, feminist, intercultural, international, or gay, lesbian, bisexual and transgender communication. Instead, the *Journal of Communication* reproduces dominant discourses of race and ethnicity as innate biological and/or historical characteristics rather than sites for deeper analysis. In relation, the broader field of communications research engages in racist, ethnocentric, sexist, elitist, and homophobic disciplinary practices—several of which are institutionalized—that marginalize and/or altogether exclude theoretical traditions and methodological frameworks that decenter elite heteronormative white male knowledge production. Specifically, communications research uses distinguished graduate programs, recruitment and retention, scholarly publications in major peer-reviewed communications journals, and the tenure process to produce and reproduce a historical narrative of the field's foundation and future. This epic story of an intellectual odyssey parallels the *Illiad*. More importantly, it privileges white males as "founding fathers" of the field without consideration that several were European Jews in exile from Nazi Germany writing through their lived experience as racialized others in the context of a U.S. black/white racial binary. . As such, this whitewashed historical narrative legitimates a preoccupation with whiteness and maleness in communications research.

When categories of race and ethnicity are emphasized in communications research, they are often not examined in terms of the multipositionality or the intersections of race, ethnicity, gender, class, and sexuality (Valdivia, 2000). Studies on race, ethnicity, and the media do not readily account for gender, class, nationality, religion, and sexuality that cut across the very categories of race and ethnicity this body of work seeks to address. For analytical purposes, people are classified with a single racial and/or ethnic term that does not represent the greater diversity that appears within these groups. This is not to suggest that this type of strategic essentialism is ineffective. To the contrary, the structural success of Civil Rights, Women's Rights, the LBGT movement, and more recently Hip Hop would not be possible without shared expressions of group identification. As Hip Hop signs in for transnational and diasporic identity formations (Lipsitz, 1997), so too must the inter-discipline of communications adopt alternative paradigms and research approaches—often marginalized within the field—that theorize ruptured identity formations.

A burgeoning body of scholarship that prescribes an intersectional approach to public discourses of how class, ethnicity, race, gender, and sexuality circulate through pop culture is informative of how social actors negotiate difficult, intimate, and complex conversations about the function of diversity in democratic life and the status of multicultural bodies within the fabric of national identity (Dill & Zambrana, 2009). This work represents an innovative line of academic inquiry. Considering that the study of race and ethnicity in media and communication is consumed with representation, an intersectional approach that extends beyond a discussion of negative and positive images to address the ways select bodies, distinct spaces, and methodological and theoretical approaches influence and contribute to our understanding of communications as an interdisciplinary field fills a gap that literally begs for more research. Consequently, the aim is to move the study of communication out of the transmission model into a more complex understanding of human interaction as a vehicle for creating meaning (Boateng, 2003; Moorti, 2002). Thus, an intersectional approach provides a productive intervention in the dominant paradigms of communication research.

Increasing transnational flows expose dynamic reformations of traditional categories of identity; communication scholars working across the fields of postcolonial, cultural studies, and critical race theory have recuperated these fragmented and hybrid multicultural bodies (Durham, 2004; Gilroy, 1996; hooks, 2000; Ladson-Billings, 2000; Lubiano, 1992; Min-ha, 1989; Molina-Guzmán, 2005; Moorti, 2002; Obler, 1995, 2005; Ono & Sloop, 2002; Parameswaren; 2002; Sandoval, 2000; Santa Ana, 2002; Shohat & Stam, 2003). Multicultural bodies that embody the intersection of difference—i.e., race, ethnicity, gender, class, sexuality, physical ability, and national origin— signal ways of knowing and making sense of day-to-day life and everyday lived experiences that never fold neatly into essentialized and hiearchical categories of whiteness or blackness. Because, as Ladson-Billings (2000) argues, White Western intellectual thought is an entire system of knowing or viewing the world, to understand contemporary communication processes it is necessary to decenter whiteness and maleness and dominant constructions of racial and ethnic identity by reclaiming multi-perspectival "systems of knowing," or what Cherrie Moraga (1981) refers to as "bodies of knowledge."

Feminist scholars contribute some of the most significant interventions in the study of race and ethnicity in communication research. By asserting that teen girls are active in creating and disseminating their own messages about body and beauty, McRobbie (1997) suggests individuals are active participants making sense of complex cultural processes and producing alternative knowledge in opposition to dominant ways of knowing. In a sense, McRobbie describes what Bobo (1995), Bui (2006), Rojas (2004), and Durham (2004) outline as interpretive communities from distinct racial and ethnic groups with historically shared experiences. These scholars deploy an intersectional approach—a critical analytic interdisciplinary tool—to interrogate the convergence of race, ethnicity, sexuality, gender, and class, in the context of communication research in order to recuperate subjugated knowledge and subordinated groups. Exemplifying the productivity of intersectional analysis is the work of Durham and Baéz (2007), Hernandez and Rehman (2002), and Molina-Guzmán and Valdivia (2004) which all conceive of a Black and Latina symbolic physicality that narrates racial and ethnic identity as fluid, changing, and always in dynamic and comparative relation to other racialized, gendered and sexualized bodies. Within this paradigm, the interaction between text (symbolic) and body (material) is an active negotiation with traditional categories of identity, where race and ethnicity always appear "historically in articulation, in a formation, with other categories and divisions" (Hall, 1996b, p. 444). Together, these scholars provide a much-needed intervention to the study of multicultural bodies and emerging identity formations in communications research.

An Intersectional Analysis of Ruptured Identities

HIV/AIDS remains a crisis of representation for Black American women.[1] According to the Centers for Disease Control and Prevention (2006), Black American women account for more than 70% of all newly reported cases of HIV and AIDS infection, morbidity, and mortality among U.S. women.[2] Yet, many of the available popular media images serve as a cautionary tale that render mute the emerging identity formation articulated by Black American women living with HIV and AIDS. In contrast, the stories by Black American women living with HIV and AIDS raise culturally relevant questions regarding agency, control, and new relations of power in a contemporary social world, being done and undone by processes of neoliberal globalization. Writing early in the HIV/AIDS epidemic, Stuart Hall posits, HIV/AIDS is "a question of who gets represented and who does not [. . .] it is a site at which people will die, but desire will also die if certain metaphors do not survive or survive in the wrong way" (as cited in Proctor, 2004, p. 3). More importantly, it is a question of *how* select HIV/AIDS bodies get represented that requires scholars to operate in these moments of tension or discursive rupture to fully realize the potential of what communication studies can do. For Black American women living with HIV and AIDS, an intersectional analysis of their contemporary representation is indeed a matter of life and death. Therefore, it is imperative that we critically engage popular culture as it informs the psychological and material conditions faced by this distinct socially-defined population.

Black American women more readily identify as HIV positive than they did more than two decades ago. It is important to note that this is not entirely about acknowledging one's status but identifying as a distinct community within broader U.S. race and ethnic formations—namely, Black American and African American—that historically and systematically homogenize intergroup dynamics. The author and international HIV/AIDS activist, Marvelyn Brown, declares that she is a "young, beautiful, and (HIV) positive" Black woman, signals a shift in the social and cultural landscape wherein publicly identifying as a Black American woman living with HIV/AIDS bespeaks a "new" identity formation at the intersection of race, gender, class, sexuality, and AIDS stigma (see Brown & Martin, 2008); an identity that is potentially profitable for industries looking to develop and/or capitalize upon new forms of labor, commodity, and consumption (see Collins, 2006). Rae Lewis-Thornton, the first openly HIV positive African American woman to be featured on the cover of *Essence* magazine, articulates some of the distinct experiences of Black American women who are vulnerable to sexual assault, partners who refuse to practice safer sex, rejection from traditional and non-traditional institutions, and poverty. In her blog, "Rae Lewis-Thornton: Diva Living with AIDS",[3] Lewis-Thornton (2010) navigates multiple and simultaneous forms of oppression that work in concert to thwart self-representation. Together, Brown and Lewis-Thornton lay claim to a distinct interpretive community that constitutes the very racial and ethnic formations their bodies inherently disrupt. Therefore, Black American women living with HIV and AIDS represent a ruptured identity formation. They articulate this collectively situated identity loosely developed out of their lived experience, including their interaction with popular media images that contest and/or affirm their social reality. Specifically, they confront traditional categories of race, ethnicity, gender, class, and sexuality made "commonsense" in popular culture that mischaracterize Black American women—namely, the black female body and/or black female sexuality—as abnormal in comparative relation to White women (see Gilman, 1992).

Traditionally, feminist scholars examining popular media images of women and HIV/AIDS offer up several narratives to which women can subscribe (Juhasz, 1990; Triechler, 1999). However, as self-identified queer black feminist scholar Evelynn Hammonds (1997) posits, these cultural texts carve up two categories of women: those deserving of protection and those undeserving of protection. Within traditional U.S. racial [and ethnic] social structures, Black American women are relegated to the ranks of those unworthy of State protections. Specifically, early media images of Black women living with HIV/AIDS were constrained to the dehumanizing representation of Black women and men as 'at-risk' solely based on their biological and physiological make-up or what is commonly referred to as "race" and "ethnicity" in biomedicine (i.e., skin color, skeletal structure, hair type, genetic composition, DNA, reproductive function, and metabolic rate). Today, the familiar trope of victim/villain is presented as both entertainment and education regarding HIV/AIDS among Black Americans. Since 1998, *Black Entertainment Television* (BET)—a subsidiary of Viacom—has partnered with the Kaiser Family Foundation and

Centers for Disease Control and Prevention to develop culturally relevant public service announcements and new media and social network campaigns to target young Black Americans and Latina/os. This multi-faceted campaign includes a special programming that often uses the familiar victim/villain trope. It is important to note that the trope of victim/villain is not exclusive to the representation of Black American women and men living with HIV/AIDS, as it is emerged from the broader context of HIV/AIDS in which infected gay white men, hemophiliacs, heroin users, and Haitians traditionally represented "vectors of disease" that were (and continue to be) vilified as routes of potential infection that victimize an otherwise health public (see also Treichler, 1999). However, what is specific to the trope of victim/villain in the context of HIV/AIDS among Black Americans (routinely regarded as Black AIDS) is that Black American women, regardless of income and education, represent both victims and villains. Specifically, Black American women are represented as victims of Black American men—particularly men who "secretly" sleep with other men, but do not identify as gay (routinely regarded as men on the down low or DL)—who are assumed to be the cause of HIV and AIDS infection among heterosexual Black American women. Simultaneously, Black American women—whether HIV positive or negative—are vilified as a [potential] threat to themselves and the general public to which they come in frequent contact, although it is never discussed how they could potentially infect the general (read: white and/or male) public.

Consequently, it is individual irresponsibility—risky lifestyle choices and illicit sexual practices—always already tied to biological and/or physiological notions of race and ethnicity that represent the "problem" of Black AIDS, rather than systemic structures of racism and ethnocentrism, including poverty and access to quality affordable healthcare, that are contributors to the overall poor health outcomes of Black people everywhere. In turn, the bodies of Black American women living with HIV/AIDS are targets for new forms of policing and containment developed after 9/11 (see also Carby, 1992). Specifically, the representation of Black American women living with HIV/AIDS as villains performs a new type of labor for emerging industries such as public health security and bioterrorism preparedness that depend on racialized ethnic bodies, specifically the black and brown bodies of women as well as men, to secure billions in government funding each year. In addition, the representation of Black American men as sexual predators produces and reproduces racist and ultimately homophobic stereotypes of Black men as a hypersexual, aggressive, and criminal, validating their overrepresentation in the prison industrial complex (Dixon & Linz, 2000; Entman & Rojecki, 2000; Mastro & Stern, 2003; Neuendorf, Jeffres, & Atkins, 2000; Oliver, 2003). Combined, this generates moral panics and greatly strains efforts to redirect funding for research, treatment, and care into Black American communities. However, in spite of this, self-identified Black American women living with HIV and AIDS are able to confront popular media images and the material conditions that thwart self-definition.

Individual interviews and reflexive participant observation conducted from May 2005–August 2008 with a group of self-identified Black American women living with HIV and AIDS in Chicago reveal that they actively negotiate a racial and ethnic identity that accounts for the intersections of gender, class, and sexuality while rupturing the very same categories that seek to discipline them. Each woman confronts violent encounters with the State; moments of extreme poverty, drug addiction, and employment in "illegal" sex work; instances of molestation, rape, and domestic violence; and systematic exclusion from the agendas of grassroots social organizations including Civil Rights, Human Rights, Hip Hop, Feminist, and LGBTIQ movements. In addition, they turn the trope of victim/villain on its head to recuperate victimhood—a narrative traditionally reserved for white women who adhere to a normative heterosexual middle-class white femininity—to increase their visibility and secure government resources for treatment and care. Whether implicitly or explicitly, they collectively redefine Black American women living with HIV and AIDS as social actors who clarify the boundaries of complex social and cultural processes that render them "victim" to HIV/AIDS and other structural forms of social inequality—ideological, interpersonal, and institutional—that adversely affect their health.

Self-identified Black American women living with HIV/AIDS not only articulate a ruptured identity that helps them navigate various institutions as acts of daily survival but frequently mobilize their ruptured identity to face HIV/AIDS. For instance, Ida W. Byther-Smith—a self-identified Black American woman living with HIV and AIDS—is the founder and CEO of the Jo-Ray House, an organization located in the predominately African American neighborhood on the south side of Chicago (IL). The Jo-Ray House offers housing, case management, community education, and family support to people and communities impacted by HIV/AIDS. Although her organization serves mostly HIV-infected men, Ida W. Byther-Smith uses her personal story to empower others living with HIV/AIDS while confronting systemic structures of racism, sexism, poverty, homophobia, and HIV/AIDS stigma.

Conclusion

More scholarship regarding Black American women living with HIV and AIDS is needed, especially as we move towards a national HIV/AIDS strategy that will set the course for how we treat U.S. racial and ethnic communities impacted by HIV/AIDS. This case study demonstrates that Black American women living with HIV and AIDS clearly articulate their distinct needs and answers relevant questions as to the role of the State in the lives of its most vulnerable populations. Black American women living with HIV and AIDS also represent a ruptured identity formation and growing cross-section of the U.S. population that must be invited and central to conversations regarding a domestic HIV/AIDS policy.

In addition, this chapter demonstrates that an intersectional approach to the study of race, ethnicity, and identity in communications research unveils new relations of power in the contemporary social world and foments academically rich scholarship. It challenges existing ways of analyzing race and ethnicity that reproduce patterned relations of social inequality in dominant paradigms, research approaches, and institutionalized practices of the discipline that are legitimated by a "canon" that privileges whiteness and/or maleness. Finally, that so many ordinary, everyday people reformulate established categories of race and ethnicity or rupture traditional identity categories in relation to the very discourses of race, ethinicity, gender, class, and sexuality that seek to discipline multicultural bodies—is a testament to the intellectual-cultural production of subordinated people and the potential for collective social action that is ethical, democratic, and realizes the productive potential of human diversity.

Notes

1. In "Seeing AIDS: Race, Gender, and Representation" (1997), Evelynn Hammonds refers to HIV/AIDS a "crisis of representation" for Black women. Therefore, this chapter is an extension of her work and an attempt to answer her call for cultural critics who are fully invested in addressing the social and political implications of the cultural representation of U.S. Black women living with HIV and AIDS.
2. Black American refers to people of the African Diaspora living in the United States. African American refers to a distinct racialized ethnic community within the United States who often descend from African slaves. While these terms are not always interchangeable, the majority of women who participated in this study used them in this way.

Therefore, for the purpose of this article, I use Black American.
3. "Diva" is commonly used among self-identified Black American women to represent a woman who is ambitious and discriminating in her tastes. See also, Beyoncé, "Diva."

References

Boateng, B. (CTA). Intellectual property, cultural production, and the location of Africa. In Valdivia, A.N. (Ed.), *A companion to media studies* (565–577). Malden, MA. Blackwell Publishing.

Bobo, J. (1995). *Black women as cultural readers*. New York, NY: Columbia University Press.

Brah, A. (1992). Difference, diversity and differentiation. In Donald, J. & Rattansi, A. (Eds.), *'Race,' culture and difference*. (pp. 126–145). Printed by The Open University, London: Sage.

Brown, M., & Martin, C. (2008). *The naked truth: Young, beautiful, and (HIV) positive*. New York: HarperCollins.

Bui, Diem-My. (2006, May). *Bodies of experiences: Dialogues with Vietnamese American artists*. Paper presented at the meeting of the 2nd International Congress of Qualitative Inquiry, Urbana-Champaign, IL.

Carby, H. (1992). Policing the black woman's body in the urban context. *Critical Inquiry, 18*(4), 738–755.

Centers for Disease Control and Prevention (2006). "Morbidity and Mortality Weekly Report."

Clayton, J. (1996). Closet ain't nothin' but a dark and quiet place for . . . ? *Art Journal 55*(4), 51–54.

Collins, P. (2000). *Black feminist thought: Knowledge, consciousness, and the politics of empowerment* (2nd ed.). New York: Routledge.

Collins, P. (2001). *Black sexual politics: African Americans, gender and the new racism*. New York: Taylor & Francis.

Collins, P. (2006). New commodities. New consumers: Selling blackness in the global marketplace. *Ethnicities, 6*(3), 297–317.

Dill, B. T., & Zambrana, R. E. (2009). *Emerging intersections: Race, class, and gender in theory, policy, and practice*. New Brunswick, NJ: Rutgers University Press.

Dixon, T., & Linz, D. (2000). Overrepresentation and underrepresentation of African Americans and Latinos as lawbreakers on television news. *Journal of Communication, 50*(2), 131–154.

Durham, M. G. (2004). Constructing the "new ethnicities": Media, sexuality and diaspora identity in the lives of South Asian immigrant girls. *Critical Studies in Media Communications, 21*(2), 140–161.

Durham, A., & Báez, J. M. (2007). A tail of two women: Exploring the contours of difference in popular culture. In S. Springgay & D. Freeman (Eds.), *Curriculum and the cultural body* (pp. 130–145). New York: Peter Lang.

Dyson, M. (2005). *Why I hate Abercombie & Fitch*. New York: New York University Press.

Entman, R., & Rojecki, A. (2000). *The black image in the white mind: Media and race in America*. Chicago: University of Chicago Press.

Foucault, M. (1981). *The history of sexuality: An introduction*. London: Penguin.

Foucault, M. (1984). Right of death and power over life. In P. Rabinow (Ed.), *The Foucault reader* (pp. 258–272). New York: Pantheon.
Foucault, M. (1995). *Discipline and punish: The birth of the prison.* New York: Vintage.
Gilman, S. (1992). Black bodies, white bodies: Towards an iconography of female sexuality in late nineteenth-century art, medicine, and literature. (pp. 171–197). In Donald, J. & Rattansi, A. (Eds.), *'Race,' culture, and difference.* Printed by the Open University, London, Sage.
Gilroy, P. (1996). British cultural studies and the pitfalls of identity. In J. Curran, D. Morley, & V. Walkerdine (Eds.), *Cultural studies and communications.* (pp. 35–49). London: Edward Arnold.
Halberstam, J. (2006). *Notes on the productive nature of failure.* Presented at the Illinois Program for the Humanities Lecture Series, Urbana-Champaign, IL.
Hall, S. (1996a). Introduction: Who needs 'identity'? In Hall, S. and duGay, P. (Eds.), *Questions of cultural identity* (pp. 4). Thousand Oaks, CA: Sage.
Hall, S. (1996b). What do we mean when we talk about the body and sexuality? Introduction. In Hall, S.; Held, D.; Hubert, D.; and Thompson, K. (Eds.), *Modernity: An introduction to modern societies.* (pp. 364–394). Malden: MA. Blackwell.
Hammonds, E. M. (1997). Seeing AIDS: Race, gender, and representation. In N. Goldstein & J. Manlowe (Eds.), *The gender politics of HIV/AIDS in women* (pp. 113–126). New York: New York University Press.
Haney-López, I. (2006). *White by law: The legal construction of race.* New York: New York University Press.
Harewood, S. (2005). *Calypso, masquerade performance and post national identities.* Dissertation. Institute of Communications Research: University of Illinois Urbana-Champaign, IL.
Hernandez, D., & Rehman, B. (Eds). (2002). *Colonize this! On today's feminism.* New York: Seal.
hooks, b. (1994). *Teaching to transgress: Education as the practice of freedom.* New York: Routledge.
hooks, b. (2000). *Feminist theory from margin to center.* Cambridge, MA: South End.
Juhasz, A. (1990). The contained threat: Women in mainstream AIDS documentary. *Journal of Sex Research* 29(1), 25–46.
Ladson-Billings, G. (2000). Racialized discourse and ethnic epistemologies. In N. Denzin et al. (Eds.), *Handbook to Qualitative Research.* (pp. 257–277). Thousand Oaks, CA: Sage.
Lewis-Thornton, R. (2010). *Rae Lewis-Thornton: Diva living with AIDS.* Retrieved from http://www.raelewisthornton.com
Lipsitz, G. (1997). *Dangerous crossroads: Popular music, postmodernism and the politics of place.* New York: Verso.
Lubiano, W. (1992). Black ladies, welfare queens, and state minstrels: Ideological war by narrative means. In T. Morrison (Ed.), *Rac-ing justice, engendering power: Essays on Anita Hill, Clarence Thomas, and the construction of social reality.* (pp. 323–363). New York: Pantheon.
Lugones, M. (2003). *Pilgrimages/peregrinajes: Theorizing coalition against multiple oppressions.* New York, NY: Rowman & Littlefield.
Mastro, D. E., & Stern S. R. (2003). Representations of race in television commercials: A content analysis of prime-time advertising, *Journal of Broadcasting and Electronic Media, 47*(4), 638–647.

McRobbie, A. (1997). The e's and anti-e's. In M. Ferguson & P. Golding (Eds.), *Cultural Studies in Question* (pp. 170–186). Thousand Oaks, CA: Sage.

Min-ha, T. (1989). *Woman, native, other. Writing postcoloniality and feminism*. Bloomington, IN: Indiana University Press.

Molina-Guzmán, I. (2005). Gendering Latinidad in the Elián news discourse about Cuban women, *Latino Studies, 3*, 179–204.

Molina-Guzman, I., & Valdivia, A. N. (2004). Brain, brow, and booty: Latina iconicity in U.S. popular culture, *Communication Review, 7*(2), 205–221.

Moraga, C. (1981). Theory in the flesh. In C. Moraga & G. Anzaldúa (Eds.), *This bridge called my back: Writings by radical women of color*. San Francisco, CA: Aunt Lute.

Moorti, S. (2002). *The color of rape: Gender and race in television's public spheres*. Albany, NY: SUNY Press.

Neuendorf, K. A., Jeffres, L. W., & Atkins, D. (2000). Explorations of the Simpson trial "racial divide," *Howard Journal of Communications, 11*(4), 247–266.

Oboler, S. (1995). *Ethnic labels/Latino lives: Identity and the politics of (re)presentations in the United States*. Minneapolis, MN: University of Minnesota.

Oboler, S. (2005). *Keynote Address*. Presented at the meeting of the 2nd Latina/o Graduate Student Conference, Urbana-Champaign, IL.

Oliver, M. B. (2003). Race and crime in the media: Research from a media effects perspective. In A. N. Valdivia (Ed.), *A Companion to Media Studies* (pp. 421–436). London: Blackwell.

Ono, K., & Sloop, J. (2002). *Shifting borders: Rhetoric, immigration and California's Proposition 187*. Philadelphia, PA: Temple University Press.

Parameswaran, R. (2002). Local culture in global media: Excavating colonial and material discourses in National Geographic, *Communication Theory, 12*(3), 287–315.

Proctor, J. (2004). *Stuart Hall*. London: Routledge.

Rojas, V. (2004). The gender of Latinidad: Latinas speak about Hispanic television. *Communication Review, 7*(2), 125–153.

Sandoval, C. (2000). *Methodology of the oppressed*. Minneapolis, MN: University of Minnesota Press.

Santa Ana, O. (2002). *Brown tide rising: Metaphors of Latinos in contemporary American public discourse*. Austin, TX: University of Texas Press.

Shohat, E., & Stam, R. (Eds.). (2003). *Multiculturalism, postcoloniality, and transnational media*. New Brunswick, NJ: Rutgers University Press.

Smith, T. (1992). Changing racial labels: From 'Colored' to 'Negro' to 'Black' to 'African American. *The Public Opinion Quarterly, 56*(4), 496–514.

Spivak, G. (1998). Can the subaltern speak? In C. Nelson & L. Grossberg, (Eds.), *Marxism and the interpretation of culture.* (pp. 271–313) Chicago, IL: University of Illinois Press.

Staff, L. (2001, March 31). Blacks split on disclosing multiracial roots. *The New York Times*. Retrieved from http://web.lexis-nexis.com/universe/printdoc

Stoler, A. (1995). *Race and the education of desire: Foucault's history of sexuality and the colonial order of things*. Durham, NC: Duke University Press.

Treichler, P. A. (1999). *How to have theory in an epidemic: Cultural chronicles of AIDS*. Durham, NC: Duke University Press.

U.S. Census Reports. (2000). "American factfinder: Demographic/ethnicity/race." Retrieved from http://factfinder.census.gov/servlet/QTTable?_bm=y&-geo_id=01000US&-qr_name=DEC_2000_SF1_U_QTP4&-ds_name=DEC_2000_SF1_U

Valdivia, A. (2000). *A Latina in the land of Hollywood*. Phoenix, AZ: University of Arizona Press.

Valdivia, A. (2004). Latinas as radical hybrids: Transnationally gendered traces in the mainstream media. *Global Media Journal*, 3(4), 1–21.

· 4 ·

Reconstructing Race and Education in the Class Conquest of the City and the University in the Era of Neoliberalism and Globalization

CAMERON MCCARTHY

On June 24, 2004, Mayor Daley announced a dramatic new plan to revitalize Chicago Public Schools (CPS). Called Renaissance 2010 (Ren2010), the plan called for closing 60 to 70 public schools and opening 100 new schools, two thirds of which would be run by private organizations and staffed by teachers and school employees who are not members of CPS unions. It is not surprising that the plan was announced at an event hosted by the Commercial Club of Chicago (hereafter Commercial Club), an organization of the city's top financial, corporate, and political elites. A year earlier, the club's Civic Committee had issued "Left Behind," a report that called for the "creation of at least 100 public charter schools that increase parental choice and put meaningful competitive pressure on chronically failing neighborhood schools" (Civic Committee of the Commercial Club of Chicago, 2004). On July 16, 2004, the mayor presided over the opening of Millennium Park, a new 24.5 acre, $500 million public-private venture to create a world-class park, sculpture garden, and performance space on Chicago's lakeshore. Millennium Park is the crowning jewel in a refurbished downtown landscape of parks, museums, tourist attractions, upscale shops, residential spaces, and cultural venues.

Seemingly unrelated, these two events capture the intersection of school policy and neoliberal urban development in the United States. (Lipman & Haines, 2007, pp. 471–472)

Race and the Struggle over the Iconography of the City

In what follows in this chapter, I look at the city as a site of a great struggle over the iconography of the present and the future; a struggle with a powerful material neoliberal dimension consequential to the new terms of race and education in the twenty-first century, an era of globalization. I look at the city not as a fixed and bounded geographical location but as a powerful discursive field and mobilizing project of will formation, integrating and disintegrating new resources, populations and identities in the contradictory and radically volatile environment of flexible and predatory capital (Bauman, 2007; Sennett, 2006, 2008). In this dynamic environment, race is deployed as a strategic multiculture for managing the rough edges of the transformation of the city from a localized, industrialized and administrative complex to a global formation foregrounding finance capital, tourism, gentrified construction and commercialized residential development.[1] A new global sign has, thus, been hung out from the walls of the city, beckoning all to see its new edifices, parks, restaurants and enclaved districts. I argue, further, that this mobilization of the city as a rejuvenated and revivified complex of desires and will formation—appropriating multiculture as a strategy of negotiating the powerful contradictions of its globalizing economies—is not only articulated to the bounded settlement of the city but is applied to the context of education in the reorganization of knowledge and the institutional restructuring of the university as it transforms itself into the new international "knowledge city." The new knowledge city has its birthing in a time of fiscal woes and the rise of a narrow-minded, administrative instrumentalism that champions the universalization of the enterprise ethic as the salve to financial woes precipitated by state disinvestment in public education.

But I begin here by first making a necessary detour to a more reflexive and thoughtful alternative vision of the city consecrated in the painterly photography of Roy DeCarava. It is DeCarava's vision that serves as a prod to my critique of the visible world of the neoliberal remaking of the city on the backs of displaced minorities. I begin this essay with a detour through this tangential but quite relevant terrain related to the discussion of race and education and the class conquest of the city. Roy DeCarava was an extraordinarily reflective humanist photographer who painted the city (Harlem, New York City) in light, as a vital landscape peopled by the black working class subject pursuing the meaningful life, even in constraint (See DeCarava & Hughes, *The Sweet Flypaper of Life*, 1984; NPR, 2009). DeCarava, who died last November at the age of 89, was born and raised by a single parent (a Jamaican immigrant to the United States) and grew up during the time of the Harlem Renaissance. After the Second World War, he not only helped to pioneer a transformation of the journalistic use of the camera from simple mimesis to an art akin to the subtleties and nuances of painting in light but also captured a rich plurality of the tonalities and ranges of black life in the city (DeCarava & Hughes, 1984; Kennedy, 2009). He sought to foreground the humanity and the dignity of black people at a time when dominant institutions sought to degrade and repress black identities in the generation of invented pathologies. I believe it is this kind of humanism, this commitment to a social phenomenology, this kind of informed advocacy that is a deep abiding intuition in the work of artists like DeCarava that must inform our work as scholars of cultural studies operating in the curriculum field in the brave new world of hyper-capitalism that races into the twenty-first century. It is work like this that elevates to a vital, indispensable level of importance the intervention of the critical scholar as a social observer and as a model of thoughtfulness in a context in which acquisitive, predatory instincts and the universalization of the enterprise ethic now seek a class conquest of the city. This is the neoliberal dominant of which I will say more a little later. It is precisely DeCarava's black subjects whom the new vision of the global city now discards as an old iconography, an unusable marker and reminder of its industrial failure and the segregationist models of stratification still etched in a spatial organization of a city like Chicago. Following DeCarava's humanist framing of city life, I offer a critique of these largely unchecked developments in which I seek to interdict a certain transaction of neoliberalism and globalization in the context of a city that has brought the educational enterprise under the grip of a new identity linked to these graven instincts of late capital.

These neoliberal developments set particular institutional configurations in place that serve to materially exacerbate the circumstances of social and educational provision for minorities while, paradoxically, utilizing multiculture as a strategic mobilizing force for privatization and utilitarian goals (McCarthy, 1998; McCarthy, Giardina, Harewood, & Park, 2003; McCarthy, Rezai-Rashti, & Teasley, 2009). Within this framework, new authorizations of the use of race and marginalized culture have been assumed that require no necessary warrant from minority groups who might otherwise have regarded race and cultural heritage as a final property.

Above all, this chapter, as an intervention in current debates over race, proceeds on one central working assumption: the study of racial logics in the new century is not to be methodologically separated from a keen assessment of the entailment and imbrication of race in the new, powerful dynamics associated with flexible capitalism, globalization and the neoliberal policy environment. This approach effectively connects race to class in the understanding of the particular mobilization of the discourse of multiculture that has as its subject an ecumenical, cross-ethnic, cross-dressing (domestic and foreign) professional middle-class agent—the beneficiary of gentrification in the city and narrowed, utilitarian goals in the university. The variable of race cannot be separated from the broad features of postindustrialization and the remaking of social relations and the re-narration of social identities which this implies (Nayak, 2003; Wallace, 1990). Further, racial dynamics cannot be specifically sliced off from the new policy environment that these new-century developments have proffered—an environment defined by the predatory pursuit of new sources of immaterial value in culture and education and in the landscape of the popular.

Neoliberalism and Education in the Globalizing City

Neoliberalism, for me, is not simply, as others such as John and Jean Comaroff (2009) have defined it: the universalization of "an ethic of enterprise" (p. 22). Instead, I consider neoliberalism, through its real-existing modes of implantation and effects of displacement, as the great unmooring of things—of long-held social relations; the disembedding or ripping up of social bonds and social categories that we have used to apprehend modern life and modern institutions. Categories such as "work," "class" and "race" are now having their old contents emptied out and are being assigned new meanings that can evoke and call up contradictory moral resources and political purposes (Bauman, 2007; Beck, 1992).

I believe we are at a point in the new developments associated with capitalism, flexible capitalism, hyper-capitalism that could be described as a new primitive or predatory stage, a time of the relentless search for new sources of value in ever-new quarters of everyday life and immaterial reality. As Paul Willis (2005) notes in his essay "The Foot Soldiers of Modernity," late capitalism is not simply appropriating from nature but is engaged in the excavation of human nature or the fomenting and raiding of desires, anxieties, fears and needs for identity and affiliation in a world in which movement, restlessness, and ephemerality define existence and experience. Naomi Klein has noted this in her book, *No Logo* (2000), in which she talks about capitalism's investment in immateriality—that is, in research and design and branding and its divestment of the factory and the inventory of products, devolving this task to EPZs (Export Production Zones in the Third World) and the relentless race to the bottom. As Naomi Klein noted in her book *The Shock Doctrine* (2007):

> During the 1990s, many companies that had traditionally manufactured their own products and maintained large, stable, work forces became known as the Nike model: don't own any factories, produce your products through an intricate web of contractors and subcontractors, and pour your resources into design and marketing. Other companies opted for the alternative, Microsoft model: maintain a tight control center of share holder/employees who perform the company's 'core competency' and outsource everything else to temps, from running the mailroom to writing code. Some called the companies that underwent these radical restructurings 'hollow corporations' because they were mostly form with little tangible content left over. (p. 341)

Cities and states compete globally to house these "hollow shells." New York City alone houses the headquarters of 43 of the top revenue earners on the 2009 Fortune 500 list.

Capitalism's relentless accumulation process—this foraging for new value, for new areas of the life world to absorb within its grip—is articulated across a wide swath of postindustrial societies as knowledge, creative energies, and cultural archives come under the grip of new identities generated in the wake of capitalization and commodification (Schiller, 1999, 2003, 2006). The logics of new capitalism are articulated to a broad range of developments linked to the state and social institutional dynamics of class, race and gender in which educational institutions (even as they become less of a guarantor of a tight nexus between schooling and work) are crucial sites for the playing out of expanded and predatory programs of new capital. Education stands squarely in the cross-hairs of this "turn" in acquisitive capital towards the conquest of immaterial resources.

Pauline Lipman and David Hursh (2007) point to these developments occurring in the city of Chicago where, in policy initiatives articulated in documents such as *Chicago Metropolis 2020* (2002), *Left Behind* (2003), and *Renaissance 2010* (2004), business leaders associated with the Chicago Commercial Club lay out models of reform that re-imagine Chicago as a global city in which a multicultural, multinational middle class are the cultural brokers and consumers of new city spaces and services.² Education becomes a critical transactional resource in these new developments.

> As indicated above, Renaissance 2010 includes not only remaking the public schools but the city itself. Renaissance 2010 is part of a larger project to raze low-income African American communities, with the goal of gentrifying areas with new condominiums, luxury apartments, and retail services. Renaissance 2010 reveals the increasing ability of corporations to reshape both the city and schools in their own interests, using neoliberal education and economic policies to recreate Chicago as a global city central to financial, real estate and service industries. (Lipman and Hursh, 2007, p. 161)

Scholars have tended to characterize neoliberalism and globalization as a dramatic set of processes that explode out of the center of metropolitan countries re-ensnaring world peripheries into new forms of twenty-first century incorporation that follow the tracks of cultural and economic imperialism (Comaroff & Comaroff, 2009; Klein, 2007; Miyoshi, 1998; Wallerstein, 2008). I believe, following Lipman and Hursh (2007), we now also need to look more closely at how the universalization of the enterprise ethic is working back within the metropolitan societies themselves. How are these developments impacting groups differentially located in metropolitan centers? How is globalization, in an uneven manner, throwing ethnic groups up against each other in real-existing contexts and in the context of the imaginary universe of simulation produced in the processes of electronic mediation and consumption?

This is the world, for example, of the "White Highlands" of Tyneside, Newcastle in the Northeast of England in which white working class youth without work—as Anoop Nayak (2003) notes—collide with black immigrant youth from the colonies, from Pakistan, India and the Caribbean. This is the world of Shane Meadows' provocative film, *This Is England* (2007), about a group of skinheads roaming the English Midlands who are trying to make sense of the postindustrial world of immigrants, chronic unemployment and constrained futures. It is also the world of Southside, Chicago—the property of the Robert Taylor Homes (once the largest housing project in the United States) razed and transformed into the new mixed-income housing development called "Legends South."³ "Legends South" appropriates the historical past of South Side Chicago where late nineteenth/early twentieth century immigrant African Americans from the U.S. South—facing a hostile refusal of services and other blatant forms of discrimination—created their own "city within a city:" Bronzeville. It is in Bronzeville that world famous performers such as Louis Armstrong, Mahalia Jackson, and Nat "King" Cole performed and blossomed. These days, you can get your own condominium in the Mahalia Jackson or the Coleman Hawkins wing of this pastiche of vernacular new millennial buildings—a multipurpose development complex of luxury apartments and mixed-income residences blossoming forth from the old markers of Bronzeville into the new iconography of Legends South. You can fill out your application in English, Japanese, Spanish, French, German or Italian. Michael's Development Corporation and the Chicago Housing Authority will translate your every request. This razing and scouring of the earth for mix-use property is also true in the Caribbean, in Latin America and many other cities in the United States as they reposition themselves towards neoliberal globalization. These developments often mean forcible deracination and relocation of poor, minority low-income dwellers to "stressed suburbs" or "suburbs at risk"—an outward pressure to satellite towns and communities (Anyon, 2005, p. 77). It is this process which the venerable cultural geographer and Marxist historian, David Harvey (2005) calls, appropriately, "accumulation by dispossession" (p. 154).

The city, then, is a most pivotal place to capture these dynamics. The royal battle over youth, schools and the future is taking place within the remaking of the city as cities such as Chicago, Buenos Aires, New York, Nottingham, Manchester transform themselves from administrative and industrial centers to brand spanking new global metropolises. But there is more. The city has become the catchment area of the play of the new energies in the late modern world (Harvey, 1989, 2005). Its central role, according to social observers such as Saskia Sassen (2006) and Richard Sennett (2006), is more and more that of a beachhead for finance capital and tourism and for the resettlement of multinational and multiethnic professional classes who must be courted with evergreen parks, magnet schools, high-end shopping and five-star restaurants. Here, for example, is how the Chicago Department of Cultural Affairs (2010) describes the city in a recent press release:

> From its delectable dining to its family-friendly attractions, Chicago has received numerous awards praising the city as a great travel destination. Since 2003, Chicago has received such titles and awards as:
> - City of the Year—*GQ Magazine* (2008)
> - One of the Top 10 Cities in the World—*Lonely Planet's Best in Travel 2009* (2008)

- Ranked the number one US destination for LGBT business travel (and number five for leisure travel) by Community Marketing, Inc.'s "13th Annual LGBT Tourism Study" (2008)
- Out of three U.S. cities surveyed, Chicago residents were the 'most satisfied overall,' reported that Chicago is an 'easy place to live' and were 'most confident about the future of their city'—*Veolia Observatory Survey of Urban Lifestyles*, conducted by Veolia Environment (2008)
- Voted North America's "City of the Future" by the Financial Times publication *Foreign Direct Investment Magazine* (2007–08)
- Voted #2 top art destination in the 'Big Cities category' of *AmericanStyle* magazine's list of Top 25 Arts Destinations for 2008 (2008)
- Best Skyline—America's Favorite Cities poll, Travel + Leisure [sic] (2007)
- Best Food/Dining & Best Pizza—America's Favorite Cities poll, *Travel + Leisure* (2007)
- Best Business Trip (that's secretly fun)—America's Favorite Cities poll, *Travel + Leisure* (2007)
- Best Sports Fan's Vacation—America's Favorite Cities poll, *Travel + Leisure* (2007)
- Chicago's Green City Market rated as one of the top ten great farmers markets in the US by chef and author Alice Waters (2007)
- More five diamond restaurants than any other city in the nation (Alinea, Arun's, Avenues, Charlie Trotter's, Everest, Seasons and Tru)—AAA (2007)
- Best Restaurant City in America—GQ (2006)
- Top 50 Destinations for Summer 2006: Millennium Park #1, North Michigan Avenue #2—Priceline.com
- 2006 American Institute of Architects (AIA) Honor Award for Regional and Urban Design—Millennium Park
- Top 2006 U.S. Destination—as ranked by Orbitz.com (2006)
- Among the top three cities most traveled by adults with disabilities—Open Doors Organization (2006)
- "Bicycle Friendly Community" designation by The League of American Bicyclists (2005)
- #1 most dog-friendly city to visit in North America—DogFriendly.com (2005)

As with Chicago, the late modern city has become the site of powerful migratory flows of immigrants—the "tourist" and the "vagabond"—seeking new fortunes and new narrations on life histories (Bauman, 1998, p. 77).[4] But I believe the city, as an organizing and orienting principle, both derives from and sets off tremendous discursive, moral and political force and will formation. The city is therefore not only a protected and fortified space ("a human settlement where strangers are likely to meet" as Richard Sennett famously defines it in *The Fall of Public Man* [1976, p. 39]) but also operates as a productive political trope or metaphor, or vector—a heuristic and workable platform through which the volatile economic, cultural, and social currents let loose in globalization can be negotiated and the rich teeming spoils of globalization can be harnessed. The city, then, is also a space of the political imaginary in which late-modern subjects—much like the citizens of modernizing nineteenth-century Paris of Honoré Balzac's *Human Comedy* (1803/2006) or Honoré Daumier's cartoons and caricatures describing the human foibles of the deracinated peasants and teeming middle classes entering the Second Empire of Paris of Louis Napoleon III—can hitch a ride to the rollicking and rambunctious future (Harvey, 2003).

The New Terms of Race, Education and the City

If the first part of this chapter is about the city's appropriation and incorporation of culture and education within its acquisitive economic purposes, the second part is about education's appropriation of the city as a workable metaphor for resource mobilization and the narration of its distinctiveness to the world. This idea of the city usurps the state as a workable trope in the struggle over the iconography of modern life taken on by institutions and units such as the school and the university. In this sense, educational institutions are both sites of management and modulation critical to riding the hurly-burly futures of the new, gentrifying global city. But they are also sites engaged in identity makeovers as "cities" or "citadels" in their own right. It is from this discursive vector of the city that these institutions re-imagine themselves as players in the global arena. The University of Illinois at Chicago (UIC) makes this plain in its *Strategic Plan Version 1.3: "Access to Excellence"* (June 30, 2006):

> America is becoming much more global and diverse [...] The world may not be quite as flat as Thomas Friedman suggests in his recent book, but one of the de facto measures of "globalization" is the almost universal "internationalization" of the world's research universities as they work not only to retain their own countries' students and researchers, but also to attract students and research from around the world. The competitive edge American universities once held over other higher education institutions is no longer a given, and universities like UIC will have to work harder than ever to attract and retain the best and the brightest. (p. 10)

Indeed some estimates, such as that of Alan Ruby's in a recent *University World News Report* (2009) article titled "GLOBAL: International Students: a $100 Billion Business?," put the international student industry—that the University of Illinois at Chicago is directing its attention towards—at over a hundred billion dollars worldwide, with the U.S. accounting for about sixteen billion dollars of it. The goal here is to liberate and tap new revenue streams in the vast reserve army of international students and to harness their intellectual labor. This strategic play for the world in the city or the university takes on a frenetic urgency as these educational institutions struggle to respond to futures that are constantly being stirred up, dirempted and unsettled. It is a framework that neuters race and redirects it to multiculture and new purposes. The University of Illinois at Chicago's Strategic Plan is again illuminating here.

> The United States is expected to be the major net receiver of international migrants, with projections estimating 1.1 million immigrants annually from 2005 to 2050. It is also projected that the Caucasian population will drop to around 50 percent by 2050 in the United States. America is becoming much more global and diverse. Given this trend and the increasingly global nature of markets, employers will require greater knowledge of other countries and cultures, as well as increased language capabilities. (p. 10)

Of course, it must be noted that the university's deployment of multiculture is not the only model of the lifting up of diversity out of the self-correcting context of immigrant plurality or minority cultural assertion. The project of multiculture follows a profoundly disturbing path as well, serving to unstitch as well as to paste over the contradictions of modern life. It is in this context in which all forms of modern institutional identities are being stirred up—a context in which a great struggle over the iconography of the present and the future is taking place—that racial logics are achieving, paradoxically, a lightness of being. Identities become lifted out of the old forms of structuration and grids linked to particular group ancestry and geography and get put into new volatile, cultural, political/economic and semiotic asymmetries—put to new work. For some time now, one of the most powerful illustrations of the post civil rights world in which we live has been the fact that "race," "racialness," even "racism" as a critical moral resource and property has been put to new work by unbenevolent authors of revanchism[5]—vitriolic forms of resentment and moral evaluation in which the white middle classes blame the minority poor for their problems (McCarthy, 2003; Wilson, 2007). Whether it is Arizona's largely white legislators passing a law that bans ethnic studies in schools because they maintain it teaches racial hatred against whites, or Fox Channel's Glenn Beck, calling President Barack Obama racist, or British cricket spectators charging their Australian counterparts of racism for calling them "pommes" or "wops," or Portuguese detectives in the case of a missing girl, taking righteous offense of what they saw as the British characterization of them as "slow,"[6] racial discourses are coming under new forms of authorization and racial identities are being dirempted from place, ancestry, geography and language by forces of late modernity linked to the amplification of images and processes of cutting and mixing of commodified culture and consumerism (Dolby, 2001, 2006; Comaroff & Comaroff, 2009). This liquid modernity is being played out in the class conquest of the city, as I discussed earlier, as well as deeply informing the reorganization of knowledge in the educational setting such as the university. Race enters into the programmatics of the university as useable multiculture, fully absorbable into the agendas of neoliberal globalization.

The Neoliberal Context of Race and Education

The university and schooling are not inured from these dynamic material practices associated with neoliberalism. As Nancy Cantor and Paul Courant (2003) have pointed out, there are three dimensions of neo-liberalism or the universalization of the enterprise ethic that are transforming the racialized context and life world of schools and universities for the optimization of the public good: molding culture, economy and politics, and ideology into a template of the new educational order. These three neoliberal tendencies have an alienating or disorganizing impact on minority access to the knowledge city and the status of racially subjugated institutional knowledge building taken as a whole. These developments can be identified as follows.

First, there is *virtualization*: the process of managing the university as an online community and a paperless world. Our preoccupation with craving information, speed, and efficiency suppresses the very idea of communication as the ritual of community-making via face to face collectivities. It also undermines the fostering of the crucial value of empathy in human relations. Virtualization within the university now normalizes one-way edicts from administration downwards to the plebs, rather than the two-way street of the superhighway to openness proffered in the early prophecies of the workings of online communities (Deuze, 2007). Ubiquity serves the purpose of administrative inoculation from the difficult issues that diversity presents to curriculum reform and the organization of knowledge. We are to trade in quotas and representative numbers of groups rather than in an intellectual culture of diversity, which, I am arguing, virtualization should and must be used to enhance.

Second, there is the logic of *vocationalization*: the insistence on consistently derived and derivable returns on education. The goal is to maximize returns on investment as in the market. "Our students' course-taking preferences often focus on areas likely to maximize future returns (pre-professional, technology-intensive-globalization)" (Cantor & Courant, 2003, p. 5). This investment in the enterprise ethic within the university has meant that, on many campuses, there has been an eroding of support for the humanities and humanistic social sciences generally and minority curricular enhancements in particular. For example, as Cantor and Courant have pointed out, "representation [i.e., student enrollment] in superior humanities programs at public universities has dramatically declined between 1982 [and the present]" (p. 5). And yet, it is precisely these courses that provide the best preparation for democratic citizenship and critical thinking. Vocationalization of school knowledge also has the effect of both marginalizing and re-narrating subjugated knowledges such as African American Studies, Asian American Studies or Latina/o Studies as professional competencies; expertise useful largely for managing the tensions between competing groups over the scarce resources in the university setting and beyond.

The third tendency in the process of educational neoliberalization is the practice of *fiscalization:* bottom-line budgeting as the ruling measure of viability for all departments and units of educational institutions. We live in a context of expanding budgetary crisis within the economy generally and within education particularly. There are increasing demands for accountability and fiscalization—the application of bottom-line rationality to all education decision making. These pervasive measuring, accountability, and feasibility pressures have forced the humanistic disciplines and alternative postcolonial and indigenous minority knowledges on the defensive. The pressure of rationalization has placed humanistic programs in doubt, forcing them to establish new codes and rules of the game (i.e., cutting programs, not replacing retiring faculty, etc). Even programs such as literature, art history, philosophy, and so forth that are unlikely ever to be profit-making enterprises are feeling the pressure of the bottom line. We are trapped in the market place logic of student credit hours and sponsored research objectives. The immediate casualties are ethnic and area studies programs, interdisciplinary research, collaborative research, and writing projects. Ultimately, education as a public good is being compromised to privatization. Our greatest challenge, then, is to preserve the autonomy of the teaching-learning process, the autonomy of intellectual production, and the reproduction of critical minority and majority scholars.

Nancy Cantor and Paul Courant (2003) understand these trends as fiscal and budgetary dilemmas; I see them here as deeply cultural in the sense that they set off particular configurations of interests, needs, desires, beliefs and system-wide behavioral practices in the life world of universities and schools with respect to ethos and milieu and the organization of knowledge, the regulation of individual and group relations in these institutions, and the sorting and sifting of social and cultural capital of different class and ethnicity-based groups.

The long and short end of these developments is that of a double logic in the university's educational direction toward greater privatization of its creative and cultural resources. On the one hand, the deployment of the discourse of multiculture is oriented towards enhancing revenues from fee-paying international students, while on the other, the commitment to minority programming in the university is being undercut. The new work of multiculture underscores the great struggle over the identity and representation of the university to itself and to the world. The university echoes the city in its search for a new self and control over the narration of its present and future. And in the contemporary circumstances, competitive and acquisitive principles more clearly mark out the mission of the university for these desperately acquisitive times—far away from the starting principles that defined many of these educational institutions as organizations for the public good and in the public's interest.[7]

Conclusion: Thinking into the Future in Education

I believe—taking on board the import of Roy Decarava's photographic humanism with which I began this chapter—the critical pedagogue and critical educational researcher must push back against this known world of educating based on imperatives that are so narrowly defined by the universalization of the enterprise ethic now guiding the city. This means working beyond the success/failure couplet which often closes off larger questions of context, change, and transformation occurring in the lives of young people. It means conceiving of research and pedagogical action that integrates humanistic imperatives of verstehen or understanding into the educational enterprise; recognizing, like Wilhelm Dilthey, Hans-Georg Gadamer, Cornel West, and Roy DeCarava, that human actors act back on their conditions of life. We must have a commitment to seeing the world through the eyes of youth, their parents and their teachers in the school setting. I believe we are living in a time of profound change as education comes under the grip of a new identity defined by globalization and neoliberalism. Our research practices must take us into the eye of the storm of these hurly-burly transformations taking place in the city, suburban and rural-suburban towns, and the university and school contexts where the orientation to global and local multiculture represents quite literally a "line of flight" (Deleuze, 1987, p. 14).

What I have tried to underscore in this chapter, then, are all the ways these tensions around race, culture, space, neoliberal economics and public policy now play out *vis-à-vis* education. As scholars such as Zygmunt Bauman (2000, 2007) and Richard Sennett (1998, 2006) have alluded to, we live in an age of fundamental insecurity and vulnerability—the precarious age of flexible capitalism. All of this has profound implications for education as it transacts multiculture. More and more, young people must be prepared to live in a world that offers little recourse to personal, social, or economic stability. Smaller and smaller groups of elites are competing and thriving in the emerging information and knowledge economy, leaving the vast majority of youth and young adults with few prospects outside of poorly paying service sector jobs with limited benefits. Moreover, these young people cannot fall back on ready-made and stable notions of self and community as did previous generations (Grossberg, 2005; Willis, 2005). As noted above, these too have been de-stabilized by global forces and trajectories.

Ultimately, the enormous social, cultural, and material dislocations of the last decade have destabilized any certainty around the traditional twin roles of schools: preparing young people for work and for citizenship. This new landscape, I argue, demands a different set of understandings as to what constitutes what some call "the research imaginary" in education today (Dimitriadis & Weis, 2007). How we contextualize and understand what we envision as education and how we think about students, particularly (minority youth) has implications for who gets what type of educational experience and who gets what type of access to schooling. This seems at the heart of any discussion of youth culture today—the idea that we no longer can claim fullness of knowledge over young people's lives and that we need to renegotiate, in a very fundamental way, what counts as "meaningful" education for youth. Always we must read these educational developments back into the historical context of radical dynamics overtaking everyday life; connecting education to the material fortunes and political complexes in flash points such as the city—one of the key sites of the orchestration and coordination of the privatizing enclosure of the social commons and the handing over of education to instrumentalism and refeudalization. Under these circumstances, race and education are articulated to each other in new terms—wholly absorbed into the logics of neoliberal globalization.

Ultimately, I have sought to focus on these new terms of race by showing the ways in which the logics of neoliberalism and globalization are defining the contemporary frameworks and relations between education and society. In many ways society has imploded into education, and education has expanded deep into society—arguably, film, television, the Internet, popular culture and popular music may be the ascendant centers for educating the young about each other and the foreigner in their midst and in the world. It is a context in which old ways of thinking about race are untenable and new methodologies and theories are in short supply.

Notes

1. By "multiculture," I am referring to the strategic, institutional and mobilized use of the discourse of cultural diversity or cultural representativeness as a form of orchestrated assimilationism and inclusivity that blunts the pain of resource scarcity derived from brutal competition over scarce resources. This aggressive competition for resources increasingly defines modern institutional and social life. The aim is to distribute minority culture in visible inoculating amounts in otherwise dominant culture domains in order to blunt minority protest and to enhance access to material social rewards for professional middle class elites of all ethnic affiliations. This is, in other words, the deployment of ethnic heritage as a project of social and political legitimation.
2. The Commercial Club of Chicago is a powerful commercial interest group whose origins go back to the late 1870s. Consisting of an elite group of prominent Chicago businessmen, the Commercial Club directs concentrated attention to civic affairs, public policy and the economic development and to the spatial planning of the city. Of special note is the fact that the club has exercised a strong hand in the city's recent efforts to transition into a global city. This is reflected in its high profile social and economic planning agenda which it lays out in its report entitled *Chicago Metropolis 2020: Preparing Metropolitan Chicago for the 21st Century* (2002) as well as its education for the future policy perspectives detailed in *Left Behind* (2003). The club has been a prominent pressure group in directing educational reform such as those represented in the Renaissance 2010 program of the Chicago Public Schools.
3. You can see the razing of the Robert Taylor Homes Housing Project on YouTube (http://youtube.com/watch?v=k—Gs1veNYE&feature=related).
4. The "tourist," for Bauman (1998), represents the elite flaneur or jetsetter who travels unconstrained, sampling multicultural fare and environments across the well-heeled settings of the world. The "vagabond" travels in different circles as part of the reserve army of labor—domestics, porters, taxi drivers, dishwashers, the perpetually subordinate under classes of the peripheries of metropolitan countries.
5. Revanchism refers to the strong retributive thoughts and actions of members of dominant white groups that are expressed against immigrants and minorities, often in the form of

resentment-filled violence (See David Wilson's *Cities and Race: America's New Black Ghetto* [2007]).
6. A four-year-old British girl who went missing from the Praia da Luz Hotel in Portugal in May 2007. Her well-to-do professional middle class British parents had chosen to leave their daughter and another infant in a hotel room while they went out to dinner. The child has not been found and is now presumed dead or captured. The subsequent police investigation by the Portuguese officials has led to heady charges and counter charges of discrimination in the news media of these two countries (Burnett, 2007).
7. I speak particularly of the land grant institutions, which are the subject of Cantor and Courant's (2003) analysis mentioned at the beginning of this section of the chapter.

References

Anyon, J. (2005). *Radical possibilities*. New York: Routledge.
Balzac, H. (1803/2006). *The human comedy*. Charleston, SC: BiblioBazaar.
Bauman, Z. (1998). *Globalization: The human consequences*. New York: Columbia University Press.
Bauman, Z. (2000). *Liquid modernity*. Cambridge, UK: Polity.
Bauman, Z. (2007). *Consuming life*. Cambridge: Polity.
Beck, U. (1992). *Risk society: Towards a new modernity*. New Delhi: Sage.
Burnett, V. (2007, September 8). Parents of girl lost in Portugal are suspected. *New York Times*, 1. Retrieved from http://www.nytimes.com/2007/09/08/world/europe/08portugal.html?_r=3
Cantor, N., & Courant, P. (2003). Scrounging for resources: Reflections on the whys and wherefores of higher education finance. In *New Directions for Institutional Research, 119*, 3–12.
Chicago Department of Cultural Affairs. (2010). Chicago's Accolades. Retrieved from http://www.explorechicago.org/city/en/about_the_city/press_room/press_kit_template/Chicago_s_Accolades.html
Comaroff, J., & Comaroff, J. L. (2009). *Ethnicity Inc*. Chicago: University of Chicago Press.
Commercial Club of Chicago. (2002). *Chicago metropolis 2020: The metropolis index, 2002*. Chicago: Commercial Club of Chicago.
Commercial Club of Chicago. (2003). *Left behind: A report of the education committee of the civic committee*. Chicago: Commercial Club of Chicago.
Commercial Club of Chicago. (2004, June 24). Chicago business leaders applaud Renaissance 2010—Pledge financial and technical support. Retrieved from http://www.lqe.org/News%20&%20Events/100NEWSchools-PressRelease.pdf
DeCarava, R., & Hughes, L. (1984). *The sweet flypaper of life*. Washington DC: Howard University Press.
Deleuze, G. (1987). *A thousand plateaus*. Minneapolis, MN: University of Minnesota Press.
Deuze, M. (2007). *Media work*. Cambridge, UK: Polity.
Dimitriadis, G., & Weis, L. (2007). Globalization and multicited ethnographic approaches. In C. McCarthy, A. S. Durham, L. C. Engel, A. A. Filmer, M. D. Giardina, & M. A. Malagreca (Eds.), *Globalizing cultural studies: Ethnographic interventions in theory, method, and policy* (pp. 323–342). New York: Peter Lang.
Dolby, N. (2001). *Constructing race: Youth, identity, and popular culture in South Africa*. Albany, NY: State University of New York Press.

Dolby, N. (2006). Popular culture and public space in Africa: The possibilities of cultural citizenship. *African Studies Review*, 49(3), 31–47.
Fortune. (2009). Cities with 5 or more FORTUNE 500 headquarters. Retrieved from http://money.cnn.com/magazines/fortune/fortune500/2009/cities/
Grossberg, L. (2005). Cultural studies, the war against kids, and the re-becoming of America. In C. McCarthy W. Crichlow, G. Dimitriadis, & N. Dolby (Eds.), *Race, Identity and Representation in Education* (pp. 349–368). New York: Routledge.
Harvey, D. (1989). *The condition of postmodernity*. Cambridge, MA: Blackwell.
Harvey, D. (2003). *Paris: Capital of modernity*. New York: Routledge.
Harvey, D. (2005). *A brief history of neoliberalism*. Oxford: Oxford University Press
Kennedy, R. (2009). Roy DeCarava, Harlem insider who photographed ordinary life, dies at 89, *New York Times*. (October 29, B 19).
Klein, N. (2000). *No logo*. New York: Picador.
Klein, N. (2007). *The shock doctrine: The rise and fall of disaster capitalism*. Toronto: Knopf.
Lipman, P., & Haines, N. (2007). From education accountability to privatization and African American exclusion—the case of Chicago Public Schools, *Educational Policy*, 21(3), 471–502.
Lipman, P., & Hursh, D. (2007). Renaissance 2010: The reassertion of ruling-class power through neoliberal policies in Chicago. *Policy Futures in Education*, 5(2), 160–178.
McCarthy, C. (1998). *The uses of culture: Education and the limits of ethnic affiliation*. New York: Routledge.
McCarthy, C. (2003). All consuming identities: Race, class, mass media, and the pedagogy of resentment in the age of difference. In A. Valdivia (Ed.), *A Companion to Media Studies* (pp. 513–528). Oxford, UK: Blackwell.
McCarthy, C., Giardina, M., Harewood, S., & Park, J.-K. (2003). Contesting culture: Identity and curriculum dilemmas in the age of globalization, postcolonialism and multiplicity. *Harvard Educational Review* 73(3), 449–465.
McCarthy, C., Rezai-Rashti, G., Teasley, C. (2009). Race, diversity, and curriculum in the era of globalization. *Curriculum Inquiry*, 39(1), 75–94.
Meadows, S. (2007). *This is England*. London: FilmFour.
Miyoshi, M. (1998). "Globalization," culture and the university. In F. Jameson & M. Miyoshi (Eds.), *The cultures of globalization* (pp. 247–270). Durham, NC: Duke University Press.
Nayak, A. (2003). *Race, place and globalization: Youth cultures in a changing world*. New York: Berg.
NPR. (2009, October 30). Remembering Roy DeCarava's 60 years of photos. Retrieved from http://www.npr.org/templates/story/story.php?storyId=114287231
Ruby, A. (2009, September 27). Global: International studies: A $100 billion business? *University World News*. Retrieved from http://www.universityworldnews.com/article.php?story=20090925022811395
Sassen, S. (2006). *Cities in a world economy*. London: Sage.
Schiller, D. (1999). *Digital capitalism*. Cambridge: MIT Press.
Schiller, D. (2003). Digital capitalism: A status report on the corporate commonwealth of information. In A. Valdvia (Ed.), *A Companion to Media Studies* (pp. 137–156). Oxford, U.K.: Blackwell.
Schiller, D. (2006). *How to think about information*. Urbana, IL: University of Illinois Press.

Sennett, R. (1976). *The fall of public man*. New York: Knopf.
Sennett, R. (1998). *The corrosion of character*. New York: Norton.
Sennett, R. (2006). *The culture of the new capitalism*. New Haven, CT: Yale University Press.
Sennett, R. (2008). *The craftsman*. New Haven, CT: Yale University Press.
UIC. (2006. June 30). Access to excellence. Retrieved from http://www.uillinois.edu/strategic-plan/plans/UIC_Strategic_Plan_v1.3_6.30.06.pdf
Wallace, M. (1990). *Invisibility blues: From pop to theory*. New York: Verso.
Wallerstein, I. (2008). The modern world-system as a capitalist world-economy. In F. Lechner & J. Boli (Eds.), *The globalization reader* (2nd ed. pp. 55–61). London: Blackwell.
Willis, P. (2005). Afterword: Foot soldiers of modernity: The dialectics of cultural consumption and the 21st-century school. In C. McCarthy, W. Crichlow, G. Dimitriadis, N. Dolby (Eds.), *Race, identity and representation in education*. (pp. 461–480).
Wilson, D. (2007). *Cities and race: America's New Black Ghetto*. New York: Routledge.

SECTION II

Reconfigurations of Governance/Technologies of Subjectivity

· 5 ·

The Cultural Logic of Search and the Myth of Disintermediation

MATTHEW CRAIN

A review of World Wide Web traffic statistics over the last decade leaves no doubt that search engines have emerged as an indispensable point of access to networked digital media. Search engines are consistently among the most heavily visited online spaces. In essence, using search engines to seek out information online has become a new form of popular media engagement. For those privileged with access and means, Web search has attained such normalcy as an everyday practice that we have arguably become a "search engine society" (Halavais, 2009).

Building on research that addresses search technologies primarily as tools of information gathering, this chapter interrogates the cultural stakes of a digital media landscape in which search engines have emerged as a new center of gravity. It attempts to push the boundaries of a behavioral framing of search into a broader terrain in which search affords a cultural logic consequential to modern subjectivities situated in relation to information saturation, global communications networks, and dynamic processes of informationalized capitalism. The cultural logic of search engines is primarily addressed in three capacities. First, the development of search technologies is examined in relation to information surfeit: the modern experience of content overload. Second, the marketing discourses and technical affordances of search engines are shown to be implicated in coordinating a relation to knowledge as a neutral, modular, and instantly accessible totality. Crucially, this relation is predicated on a myth of disintermediation, in which search engine firms seek to efface their role as information brokers. Third, the function of search engines in advancing information and user commodification is discussed in terms of market imperatives and the trend to rebrand as "decision engines."

The earliest literature on Web search technologies focused largely on practical problems of evaluating and improving the technical mechanics of search engine functionality.[1] In the last decade, researchers from various disciplines have produced a growing body of non-technical scholarly literature that examines search engines and digital information gathering more generally (for overviews of this work, see Bar-Ilan, 2003; Hargittai, 2007; Jansen & Pooch, 2001; Spink & Zimmer, 2008). On balance, much existing research has investigated search engines in terms of the composition and presentation of search results or as determinate locations to isolate and study information-seeking practices (see Jansen, Booth & Spink, 2008; Rieger, 2009).[2] Surveys, participant observation, statistical analyses of transaction logs, and mixed methods studies have been employed to determine "indicators" of search engine usage along a range of socioeconomic variables.

Without discounting the value of existing research, such focused examinations often do not address larger questions regarding the macro-level social and cultural work of search as a pervasive mode of media engagement. Every day millions of people enter text strings into search engine interfaces that return automated and seemingly objective lists of results in fractions of a second. Have expectations about knowledge and information changed in relation to search practices? What of the corporate wealth that has been generated by the popularization of search? Ultimately, what does the practice of searching signify in the 21st century? Addressing these questions cannot be limited to the task of outlining the methods employed by users to track down this or that bit of information. Crucially, it must also entail sustained analysis of the ways in which we are compelled to seek information, the manners in which search practices frame approaches to knowledge formation, and the means and objectives embedded in the production of search engines themselves.

This chapter surveys these issues by attempting to articulate a broad cultural logic implicated by the search form. The primary area of concern is not how people employ search technologies to acquire information, a behavioral question, but rather how search orients people to information in relation to modern conditions of information surfeit and a globalized neoliberal political economy. The technological affordances of search engines and the material conditions of their production and use enact a cultural logic that increasingly intercedes in the daily experiences of millions of Web users globally. This technocratic cultural logic produces a veneer of objective utility while it effaces an array of "epistemological biases" (Postman, 1985, p. 78) that reproduce the capitalist social relations in which search engines are embedded. Importantly, producers of Web search engines are working to expand their operational domain into more and more realms of lived experience, a process that further commodifies practices of knowledge formation.

As the editors of a recent volume on Web search point out, the "scholarly study of Web searching spans a multidisciplinary collection of researchers" (Spink & Zimmer, 2008, p. 3); yet, there is no articulation of a theoretical foundation for studying search within a critical communications framework. This is a missed opportunity given that for over half a century critical communications scholars have developed a robust approach to social theory in which communications media play an essential role in the constant production and reproduction of the social and cultural fabric. This general perspective is summarized by James Carey (2009), who demonstrated throughout his work the ways in which modes of communication have "drastically altered the ordinary terms of experience and consciousness, the ordinary structures of interest and feeling, the normal sense of being alive, of having a social relation" (p. 1). Here, media are conceptualized not simply as mechanisms of information dissemination but as technological assemblages deeply implicated in producing orienting frameworks to the social world.

This framework is heavily indebted to Harold Innis who advanced the notion that, as media forms become dominant within given social formations, they create "biases" which strongly influence the cultural orientations and value systems of a given society (Innis, 1999). Implicit in Innis' work and famously articulated in Marshall McLuhan's aphorism "the medium is the message" is a rejection of any conceptual separation of form and content. Just as "information" does not somehow exist abstractly outside of contingent social relations and subjectivities, modes of communication transmission are not merely such. Despite its particular grandiosity, McLuhan's work remains significant because of his insistence that the formal structures and properties of media technologies must be taken seriously and that the "message" of any particular media artifact can never be fully abstracted from its technological manifestation. In other words, the cultural work of making meaning cannot be adequately theorized as transmission alone. Media that are said to "transmit" messages exert their own force upon generated meanings, search engines notwithstanding.

Interrogations of media and technology perpetually run the risk of slipping into the intellectual desert of technological determinism. Rather than unveil determination in a strict sense, the present task is to investigate historical processes of "setting limits and exerting pressures" (Williams, 1977). This necessitates taking the cultural and political, economic work of technology seriously, which means considering how technology reproduces and is produced by dynamic social relations. This perspective allows for an interrogation of search engines beyond what Carey (2009) termed the "transmission model" of communication. More than mere reflections of culture, media are "templates for social relations" that function not by virtue of their determination but via their "intelligibility" (Adam, 2009, p. xx). The critical communications vantage point provides an opportunity to sketch out insights to be gained from viewing search engines in terms of culture, instead of strictly within the confines of behavior or cognition. It also helps to avoid the pitfalls that accompany a quasi-utopian postmodern reading of search engines that focuses intently on digital media's emancipatory potential via radical breaks from past forms of information organization.

Information Saturation

Search engines must be situated in relation to information saturation, a social condition becoming increasingly normalized for millions of people. Information saturation is the result of the swiftly expanding universe of content and communicative capacity that has been engendered by the technical convergence of analog media into computerized forms, the emergence of new types of "born digital" media, and dramatic increases in the scale and scope of networked communication systems. Perhaps the most visible expression and central motive force of the info-laden "network society" (Castells, 1996) is the global Internet. Forged out of the Cold War-era U.S. military-industrial-academic complex (Abbate, 2000), the Internet took shape as individual computer scientists, engineers, and hobbyists implemented and repurposed directives from the Department of Defense and the National Science Foundation to produce an evolving set of infrastructures and protocols for distributed electronic communications. Literally a network of networks, the Internet relies on rather formalized software and hardware standards to paradoxically enable wide flexibility of purpose and massive potential for growth.

Indeed, the "size" of the Internet has expanded by orders of magnitude since its early construction among selected laboratories at military bases, private contractors, and engineering programs at elite universities. Such exponential growth has been realized in part due to the proliferation of networking and computing hardware stemming from decades of state and private investment in the information technology sector and from increasingly globalized chains of production and finance (Schiller, 1999). In the 1990s, the nexus of personal computing, the World Wide Web protocols, graphical browsers, and network investment by telecommunications firms set the conditions to popularize Internet use and spurred an exponential growth in networked digital content and communication. In 1993, the entire public Web reportedly consisted of 130 sites (Battelle, 2005, p. 40). By 1998, the Google search engine index alone cataloged 26 million Web pages while a recent estimate put the total number of unique Web addresses at over one trillion (Alpert & Hajaj, 2008).

Notwithstanding so-called "legacy" media systems, the proliferation of networked gaming, digital television services, and mobile content add further to the enormity of the networked information-scape, even beyond the expanses of the Web. While information surfeit of this scale is a condition of experience for a privileged global minority, it is nevertheless a minority of many millions (ITU, 2008). This social context characterized by ubiquitous information has compelled Deuze, Blank, and Speers (2009) to argue for a reformulated ontological theorization of lives "lived not *with* media, but *in* media" (p. 1, emphasis in original). The *media life* perspective begins with the premise that "the whole of the world and our lived experience in it can be seen as framed by, mitigated by, and made immediate by immersive, integrated, ubiquitous and pervasive media" (p. 1).

As the volume of networked digital information has grown, so too have systems of information classification, indexing, retrieval, and presentation.[3] On the Web, many early systems for organizing content took shape as informal lists and directories; modern search giant Yahoo began as a "guide to the Web" published by the firm's founders (Battelle, 2005, p. 58). Still in the early 1990s, content portal sites maintained by human labor were common starting points for many users. Yet, as the Web expanded, it became impossible to index without automation. From this usability and software engineering quandary the modern Web search engine evolved through a variety of Darwinian incarnations—spiders, crawlers, and robots—each premised on the automated archival indexing of Web content into databases made searchable for end users.

Modern search engines are paragon information systems, now the second most popular Internet application, surpassed only by e-mail. A series of studies by the Pew Internet and American Life Project found that by 2009 some 88 percent of adult Internet users in the United States had used a search engine (Pew Internet, 2009). More importantly, nearly half of those who utilize search engines do so on a daily basis, a proportion that has steadily increased from just one-third of all users in 2002 (Fallows, 2008). Market analysts have estimated that in March 2009, approximately 14.3 billion Web searches were performed in the U.S. alone, amounting to roughly half a billion searches per day (Zeman, 2009).

The Myth of Disintermediation

Approaching the mundane problems encountered in everyday mediated experiences, one is hard pressed to deny that search engines are expedient and often precise tools for "tracking down" information from the routine to the arcane. Search engines mitigate the experience of information saturation, making the vastness of the Web manageable by providing convenient access to requested information. Undoubtedly, this basic level of utility has been integral to their popularization. Likewise, the highly interactive access to customized information provided by search engines evades limitations related to scarcity and control inherent in many "old media" forms. Unlike the newspaper, broadcast television, or even the library card catalog, search engines are not as acutely limited by material, temporal, or editorial constraints. Yet, the practical day-to-day solutions offered by Web searching obscure the broader cultural work of the search operation and the ways in which the search engine discursively and technologically masks the conditions under which results are actually produced and displayed.

Reanimating the bankrupt promise of the Internet to eliminate unnecessary and obstructive intermediaries between people and pure information, search engine producers construct a myth of disintermediation. The pursuit of disintermediation requires rendering search technology itself invisible, whereby it achieves perceived neutrality. Discursively, this move toward self-effacement grew out of a developmental period in which search technology, as such, was much more conspicuous. Modeling early Internet portals, the first large-scale search engines marketed themselves as curated gateways to the Web. In 1998, the popular Lycos search engine commissioned a national televised advertising campaign likening its service to the personalized assistance of a

Himalayan Sherpa. In one television spot a Sherpa speaking in the fragmented English of the exotic other warns viewers "when you don't know where you going, you need help from guide or you get lost [sic]."[4] Other early search leaders such as Yahoo and Excite constructed similar marketing narratives premised on the basic idea of guidance.

Throughout this period the landscape of Web search was undergoing rapid transformation. As noted, the size and popularity of the Web grew exponentially in the late 1990s and new engines such as Google began to improve upon the range, accuracy, and speed of existing search technologies. A second generation of search engines transitioned away from self-construction as "portals" and "guides" to a more pronounced pursuit of disintermediation. Attempting to stay ahead of this shift, Lycos in a subsequent advertising campaign swapped out the wise Sherpa for a perky canine, yet this was no guide dog. The new face of Lycos was instead a blindly obedient and blisteringly fast Labrador Retriever that instantly fetched whatever was asked of him. Instead of drawing attention to its role as a guide to the Web personified in the image of a Sherpa, Lycos began to erase its function as a mediator by simplifying its role to that of the loyal retriever, a non-persona existing only to connect users to requested information.

The technological affordances of search engine interfaces and the attending user experiences materially anchor the discursively constructed myth of disintermediation in design and practice. Google's utilitarian page layout is a key example whereby users encounter a simple logo and query input interface situated on a blank white page. Regardless of design particularities, the basic mediated experience afforded by all search engines is premised on interaction. Users access a website, key a query into the search interface, and are rapidly presented with a list of browsable results ranked according to "relevance." Massive lists of results—much too long for a single person to sift through in any reasonable amount of time—appear to be exhaustive in scope, objective by nature, and neutral in display. Formatted into lists, information appears modular and decontextualized as search results from disparate origins are compiled into a uniform layout. Results give the impression of neutrality because they are organized according to ranking systems rationalized by the scientific logic of computation.

The myth of disintermediation is hardly new. As the notion of "professional journalism" was constructed in the early 20th century, "neutral and unbiased" (McChesney, 2004, p. 64) reporting became the gold standard of a model of news production that aimed to provide "just the facts." But unlike reading a newspaper, the interactive features of search engines materially engage users in the production of the myth of disintermediation. The act of searching presents the opportunity to subjectively participate in ostensibly unalloyed interaction with content. Direct and inescapably biased human editorial intervention is seemingly replaced by the neutral information stewardship of the computational machine, which like the Lycos Labrador Retriever, responds unwaveringly to user requests. Push media become pull media; broadcast replaced by narrowcast. With intermediaries purged, the search engine remains as an instrumental technology of information retrieval, but beyond the immediate usefulness of search, beyond appearances of comprehensiveness and objectivity, search results are perpetually incomplete and far from neutral.

The partiality of search results is manifested at the functional level of retrieval and display where certain information sources can be easily skipped over or buried within massive lists of results. More fundamentally, actually indexing the entirety of the Web is a technical impossibility. Current research estimates that the mass of Web content not indexed by search engines—the "dark Web"—is larger than the portion of the Web made accessible by search engines by orders of magnitude (He, Patel, Zhang & Chen-Chuan Chang, 2007). Despite this limitation, any indication of the incompleteness of search results is absent from most search engine interfaces. Rather, the search engine interface design insinuates comprehensiveness by listing page after page of results and displaying their aggregate number, often amounting to multiple millions. The problem of the "harvest and the display" method is that users are denied access to "precise information about the limits of the search or the representativeness of the corpus in which it is carried out" (Jeanneney, 2007, p. 68).

Even within the relatively modest sample of the Web cataloged by search engines, indexing algorithms and ranking systems are far from objective technical measures of relevance. Many ranking systems such as Google's PageRank algorithm use hyperlink connections to calculate Web page rankings and thus favor established content sources. Though popularity is not the only factor in determining rank, "success breeds success at the expense of newcomers, minorities, and marginals" (Jeanneney, 2007, p. 45). Contrary to utopian narratives of radical democratization of information on the Internet, search engines ultimately represent a "conservative force, increasing the attention paid to those people, institutions, and ideas that have traditionally held sway" (Halavais, 2009, p. 85). Moreover, the computational indexing methods employed to determine relevance are largely masked in their roles as intermediaries. Search engine algorithms are fiercely protected trade secrets, compounding their function as black boxes.

Understood in these terms, search is as much a technology of "ignoring as it is presenting" (Halavais, 2009, p. 57). A telling example involves Google's censorship of search results in China. In 2006 Google transplanted elements of its material business infrastructure into the People's Republic of China in order to increase its market-share within China's rapidly expanding economy. As a condition for operating within China's borders, Google complied with governmental mandates concerning the political censorship of Internet content and digital communication services. Specifically, Google actively removed what were deemed politically sensitive websites from the results lists of certain search queries, essentially filtering Web content according to the demands of the ruling Chinese Communist Party. In practice, Google.cn blocked thousands of Web addresses and keywords from its search results, effectively becoming a silent partner in state censorship (Human Rights Watch, 2006, p. 55).[5]

Additionally, automated indexing systems are subject to manipulation, hacking, and fraud. Search engine optimization (SEO) is an emerging branch of Internet marketing with the sole purpose of influencing search result rankings for clients. As e-commerce continues to grow in significance throughout many sectors of the economy, businesses, especially retailers, can live or die by the visibility afforded to them by search result rankings (Greenberg, 2007). After the devastating oil spill in the Gulf of Mexico in April 2010, BP (formerly British Petroleum), the firm responsible for the disaster, purchased key phrases such as "oil spill" on popular search engines so that the top sponsored results directed users to the company's official website (Friedman, 2010). Google auctions off premium-placed search results to the highest bidder, and BP capitalized on this market-based system in an attempt to frame public information about the spill.

Likewise, the term "Google bombing" came into common parlance in 2003 when bloggers and other amateur Web content producers coordinated a campaign to create numerous hyperlinks pointing the phrase "miserable failure" to the official biography of President George W. Bush on the White House website. Enough such links were created that Bush's biography became the top result for a query of "miserable failure" on most popular search engines (McNichol, 2004).

In 2007 Google users reported that when using the search engine to query the phrase "she invented," they received automated responses from the site's spellchecking system that prompted, "did you mean *he* invented" (Kane, 2007).

Similarly gendered suggestions were made for searches such as "she discovered" and "she saved," but not for "she followed" or "she failed." Meanwhile, searches for "he invented" did not elicit any suggested rewordings from the site. Google has since reluctantly adjusted this outcome, assuring users that its automated system merely offers query suggestions based on aggregated previous searches and the extant content of the Web. In other words, the firm invoked the myth of disintermediation to argue that its suggestion system simply represents the Web as it naturally exists and that it reflects the normal searching behaviors of its users. While this particular incident should probably not be taken as a demonstration of calculated sexism on the part of Google programmers, it does confirm that regardless of intent, purportedly neutral search technologies produce artifacts that reproduce strong cultural biases.

The Cultural Logic of Search

While search engines were developed to mitigate information saturation by providing a means for users to self-navigate the vastness of the Web, they clearly do more than merely compile relevant responses to user queries. Through largely invisible processes of hierarchical selection and representation, they produce lists of results that serve to assemble *particular* ways of knowing. In other words, search engines act as "coordinates of thought" (Carey, 2009, p. 162) that facilitate certain orientations not only to information per se but to the social world at large. As Neil Postman (1985) argued, "the media and communication available to a culture are a dominant influence on the formation of the culture's intellectual and social preoccupations" (p. 9).

As gateways to a vast global information-scape, search engines engender a cultural logic that registers the modern experience of globalization, the locally situated but geographically unencumbered experience of a "culture of immediacy" (Tomlinson, 2007). Read against the backdrop of older broadcast media forms, the practice of Web searching announces a more active encounter in which the complex multidirectional trajectories of globalization are enacted and sustained. In many respects, the experience of search tames the enormity of the Web, molding the digital mediascape into patterns that mimic the informational desires of users. Yet, this interactivity conditions a dynamic subjectivity whereby the searcher is positioned over and against the World Wide Web as a reified informational space. Search engines help to assemble a default setting in which Knowledge is a pre-existing monolith comprised of discrete bits, all of which are immediately accessible to individuals through the search interface.

Ask the right question to receive the correct response. A social relation is thus constructed in which global culture "yields to the dance of fingertips on the terminal keys" (Birkerts, 1994, p. 127). The Web is rendered complete and completely accessible; yet, as any spider knows, webs are equally defined by the negative spaces between strands.

A rationalized and instrumental view of knowledge as the assembly of factoids implicitly deemphasizes knowledges and knowledge practices that may require more sustained intellectual effort or time commitment.[6] As Naomi Baron (2008) notes, "much as automobiles discourage walking, with undeniable consequences for our health and girth, textual snippets-on-demand threaten our need for the larger works from which they are extracted" (p. 205). Indeed, increasing numbers of online news consumers indicate that they only read the headlines, bylines, and leads of the stories they encounter on search engines and news aggregators, rather than click through to read entire articles (Pew Project for Excellence in Journalism, 2010). The presumption to sort and rank all the world's information denies the simultaneously wondrous and horrific complexity of the social formation, what Cornel West (2009) has called the incontestable "funk" of human existence. The field of knowledge is thus rendered as a "lateral and synchronic enterprise susceptible to collage," rather than as a "depth phenomenon" (Birkerts, 1994, p. 127). It is constructed as something that can be unproblematically and objectively harvested, ranked, and, crucially, brought into the system of exchange value.

Again, the Lycos advertising campaigns of the late 1990s are instructive. Examined in succession, they illustrate more than the pursuit of disintermediation; they also draw attention to the changing construction of the Web from an esoteric and inaccessible informational space to a user-friendly repository for all knowledge. In the earlier Lycos ads, the assistance of the Sherpa was necessary to successfully traverse the mountainous terrain of the Web. The digital landscape was shown to be a harsh and confusing place where the ordinary user must seek assistance or risk "getting lost." The later ad campaign imagined the informational domain of the Web quite differently. Instead of the rugged Himalayas, the Lycos Labrador Retriever sprints around an inviting expanse of green pasture framed by blue skies. "Get Lycos or get lost" is replaced by a simple but catalytic new slogan that foregrounds user empowerment: "go get it."

The search engine Ask.com's one-time catchphrase, "instant getification," echoes this discourse, as do the major themes of Google's self-constructed company narrative. Throughout its rapid ascension to leadership in the global search market, Google has touted its commitment to openness and transparency, vowing to connect users to information better and faster than its competitors and with an absolute minimum of interference. Indeed, the firm's much-publicized corporate mission is to "organize the world's information and make it universally accessible and useful." This mantra not only advances the notion of search engines as neutral media technologies but also constructs an aura of benevolence around the firm's role as a leading broker of digital information. User empowerment is the constant refrain. What remains unmarked is what might be called the neoliberal trade-off whereby privacy is exchanged for convenience, knowledge seeking for consumption, information for commodity.[7]

Some commentators locate emancipatory potential within the ostensibly radical decontextualization of information engendered by the search operation. This perspective is prefigured by McLuhan (1995), who was incessantly optimistic regarding the "decentralizing, pluralistic force" (p. 306) of new electronic media to extend human consciousness and empower the dispersed masses to become citizens of a new global village. Allan Hanson (2004) and Michael Zimmer (2009) argue that greater opportunities for creativity and juxtaposition are fostered as the rhizomic index replaces the hierarchical classification scheme as the predominate mode of organizing digital information. It is claimed that indexing, because it is not beholden to inherited schemes of classification, provides new combinatory possibilities whereby the searcher may construct subversive readings of presented information.

This view highlights a process whereby search engines deconstruct the "original" or situated contexts and classifications of discrete bits of information by expropriating and sorting them according to new contexts determined by the searcher. Information is combined nonlinearly via associations, endlessly referencing outward. Yet this is only a partial description of the cultural work of the search operation. The "user-determined" contexts of search results are actually better conceptualized as negotiations between the goals, skills, and mindset of the searcher on the one hand and the affordances built in to a particular search engine technology on the other.

Considering the real diversity of content made accessible by search engines, it is easy to overestimate the extent to which the decontextualization of information is realized. While it is true that indexed search engines operate according to different logics than the established analog classification systems of traditional libraries and that they therefore produce different results and may even provide opportunities for liberating experiences of postmodern information assemblage, it is a mistake to assume that all of the "constraints" stemming from "culture's categories of classification" (Hanson, 2004, p. 353) are lost in translation to the digital form. Even within the jarring information harvest of search retrieval, there can never be total decontextualization; no last gasping breath of oppressive social master narratives. Rather, as search engines expropriate and sort lists of results, degrees of separation are placed between informational links and "original" environments, allowing for their enrollment into new contexts.

Search engines recontextualize information as immediate, modular, and discrete. Individual results may be divorced from their origins, but in the ordered result list they enter into new contexts that are the outcome of the interplay of user determination and the search interface, itself predominantly driven by market imperatives. Serendipitous discovery is valuable, but it cannot be held up absent historically grounded analysis of social and material relations. Yes, digital search introduces discontinuity from earlier forms of knowledge brokering, but there is no radical break because there is no substantial political economic reorganization.[8] Indeed, closer inspection of the cultural logic of search reveals a historical continuation of the enlargement of the sphere of capital accumulation.

The Business of Search: User Commodification

From its humble beginnings, search has grown into big business. Embedded in a historical context that saw the content of the Web grow beyond practical quantification for any single user, search engines were functionally designed to ease the frustration of information saturation, a technical response to an informational need. But the evolution of search engines has also been pushed forward by a transformation of the intentions of producers along a trajectory of "informationalized capitalism" (Schiller, 2006). In other words, the historical development of search engines is decidedly about much more than just a convenient solution to an intractable software engineering problem. Following Raymond Williams (2003), the "key question about a technological response to a need is less a question about the need itself than about its place in an existing social situation" (p. 12).

Clearly, the "existing social situation" in which Web search has come of age has been characterized by rapid technological, cultural, and political economic change. What developed originally as a response to the technical indexing challenges brought on by the popularization of the Web was quickly seized upon as a business opportunity by Silicon Valley investors.[9] While search engines were initially developed as a means to connect Web users to "relevant" content, they were subsequently refined in order to secure and monetize their positions as essential information brokers in the context of emerging digital content saturation. Perhaps the starkest evidence for this transformation is found in an early academic paper authored by Google cofounders Sergey Brin and Lawrence Page (1998) in which they outline in clear terms the undesirable outcomes of an advertising supported business model for search engines. Brin and Page explain how "advertising income often provides an incentive to provide poor quality search results" and predict that "advertising funded search engines will be inherently biased towards the advertisers and away from the needs of the consumers" (pp. 18–19). As Alexander Halavais (2009) has noted, "what a difference a decade makes" (p. 77).

Today Web search is an expanding sector of online commerce within the globally networked informationalized economy at large. The economic figures of Google, the global search leader, are revealing. In May 2009, in the midst of severe macroeconomic recession, Google's market capitalization, or the public estimation of the firm's net worth, stood at nearly $130 billion, making Google more valuable than the *combined* capitalizations of its closest search rival Yahoo ($22b) plus that of Dell Computers ($22b), a leading hardware manufacturer, Time Warner ($29b), the world's largest media conglomerate, and Nokia ($53b), a top manufacturer of mobile technologies (Google, 2009). In terms of market capitalization, Google is roughly on par with the over a century older global telecommunications giant AT&T ($150b). In 2007, Google recorded revenues of almost $17 billion and a net profit of nearly $4.2 billion. If revenue is compared directly to the gross domestic product of world nations, Google stands as a close equivalent to the national economies of Bolivia and Iceland (IMF, 2009). Crucially, 98.9 percent of Google's total revenues were generated by the firm's advertising operations (Datamonitor, 2008).

Currently there is no non-profit or state-supported search engine of major consequence. All of the market leaders in search are private firms and thus ultimately dedicated to the task of capital accumulation. Corporations such as Google, Yahoo, Microsoft, and InterActiveCorp dominate U.S. and Western European markets, each developing proprietary systems for indexing, storing, retrieving, displaying, and monetizing search results. Google is far and away the current market leader in the U.S., by most estimates facilitating over two-thirds of all Web searches (Experian Hitwise, 2009).

Decades before the existence of search engines, Dallas Smythe (1977) pioneered an analysis of the mass media business model as the production of "audience commodities."[10] Processes of commodification are central to a Marxist critique of capitalism in which the basic premise of the capitalist social relation is that workers are compelled to turn their labor power into commodities to be sold to capitalist owners of the means of production. The exploitative dynamic of this labor/capital relation is that workers create a surplus of value that is expropriated by capital and characteristically reinvested into the system, thus facilitating its expansion. Smythe's central insight was that the mass media system had become integral to capitalist accumulation and that its principal product was not content as such but rather the audience commodity. This particular commodity form is produced through audience attendance to media fare and then sold to advertisers for profit: "The work which the audience members perform for the advertiser to whom they have been sold is learning to buy goods and to spend their income accordingly" (Smythe, 1977, p. 243). In other words, audience commodities perpetuate the capitalist mode of production at large by creating both demand for advertised goods and consuming publics to purchase them.

Despite their apparent novelty as digital media, search engines in many ways reproduce the audience commodity business model of their forebearers in commercial print and broadcast sectors. The goal is to direct as much traffic as possible to search engine websites, to cultivate relationships with users in order to keep them coming back again and again, and to capture as much information as possible about user demographics and desires in order to leverage this data to create revenue streams. Again mirroring print and broadcast media, the most successful method of converting search engine traffic into revenue is targeted advertising, and search engines account for the majority of advertising expenditures online (Pew Project for Excellence in Journalism, 2010).

Search engines optimize the production of audience commodities in online space. While audience attention has been scarce since the inception of mass media, it is even more so in the context of information surfeit. As indispensable gateways to the Web, search engines have become immensely profitable virtual "trading floors" in an emerging online "attention economy" (Halavais, 2009, p. 71). Archiving more than just Web pages, search engines excel at compiling vast "databases of intentions" (Battelle, 2005) in order to match advertisers with their desired audience demographics. Search engine firms have engineered various strategies for integrating advertising into search results. Options range from variously placed display advertisements to paid inclusion of unmarked sponsored results, although the later is no longer widely practiced among leading firms.

Innovators in online advertising, search engines have pioneered the transition from contextual advertising, in which search terms trigger related ad content, to more advanced systems that take into consideration archived online behavior patterns and demographic information tied to specific users (Chester, 2007). By offering additional online services such as email, blogging, and personalized user interfaces, firms such as Google collect data from multiple sources in order to compile the detailed user profiles increasingly valued by advertisers looking to sell to "niche markets" (Turow, 2006). Through this monetized surveillance, search engine firms produce not audience commodities but, more precisely, user commodities. The surplus-generating activity of search engine users is not the "work of watching," but the work of seeking information online.

In a Marxist framework, the surplus generated by collective human activity, whether labor power or audience power, is appropriated by elites (a capitalist "ruling class") and the nature of this relation is exploitative. Through the production of user commodities, search engines reproduce the essential nature of the labor/capital relation online. The surplus generated by collective human activity, the "database of intentions," is again appropriated by a select few, in this case search engine firms, which harness this activity to improve the functionality of their products and, crucially, transform it into user commodities to be sold to advertisers.[11]

Remarkably, nearly two thirds of search engine users are unaware of even the basic tenets of search advertising practices, making no distinction between advertisements and "organic" search results, while only about one in six searchers is able to correctly identify sponsored content (Fallows, 2005). More telling is that a "vast majority" of search engine users find them to be "a fair and unbiased source of information" (Fallows, 2005).

Looking ahead, search engine firms are seeking out methods to quite literally further capitalize the trust of their users. Producers of search platforms are positioning search engines not only as the paramount information providers of the digital age but as trusted brokers of the knowledge required for the maintenance and reproduction of daily life. This is evidenced by the ongoing ambitious rebranding of certain search engines into "decision engines." Microsoft is leading the charge to construct their services in terms of decision-making rather than information-seeking in order to compete for market share and increase revenue streams. The debut advertising campaign for Microsoft's Bing decision engine rationalizes that users "want more than just information" and aims to provide more action-oriented search results:

We took a new approach to go beyond search to build what we call a decision engine. With a powerful set of intuitive tools on top of a world class search service, Bing will help you make smarter, faster decisions. (Microsoft, 2009)

Google frames a portion of its future business opportunities in terms of decision-making as well.[12] In 2008, the firm's Chairman and CEO Eric Schmidt (2008) argued that the goal of providing "perfect information access" is to "fundamentally change" the way Google users think about the way they spend their time and to increase influence over the formation of their desires. He described a vision in which Google would serve a much wider scope of informational needs beyond search queries, notably endeavoring to answer questions such as "what should I do this weekend?"

A majority of search engine users report that about half the information they search for is inconsequential, while the remainder is of substantial importance in their lives (Fallows, 2005). If search engines are to become decision engines, we must consider the implications for a searching populace that looks to search engines to answer a range of trivial as well as significant questions. For many Web users, a new verb has been assimilated into the lingua franca in the last decade. A new action has become the appropriate response to a dizzying array of questions in contemporary life. Where is the nearest hardware store? What are some uses for old coffee grounds? The solution is as simple as it is consistent: Google it. These search queries and the results they elicit may well be innocuous. But how should we spend our free moments? Which political party deserves support in an upcoming election? How should we educate our children? As engines of decision-making, Google and others will have answers for these too.

Conclusion

The present material reality is that search engines are increasingly dominant information gateways, a thousand uprooted Libraries of Alexandria centralized within a few search engine interfaces, now nearly ubiquitously accessible via mobile computing devices. Yet the remarkable access to information provided by search engines lies in constant tension with their calculated roles as information bottlenecks, effective arbiters of the Web's "winners" and "losers." The cultural logic of search is such that users are not inclined to become aware, much less question, this apparent authority. The myth of disintermediation perpetuates a false boundary between search engine technologies and the material relations of their production and use.

Progressive potential exists in the use of search engines as it does in many forms of networked information and communication, but we cannot make the fundamental error of abstracting technology from social and material contexts. There are no mere technologies and uses, only social technologies and social uses. While information and communication technologies like search engines do have determining effects on the contours of global capitalism, the reverse is equally true. Search engines did not simply arrive fully formed on any societal *tabula rasa*. Instead, a proper understanding of the cultural logic of search engines must firmly situate their growth within larger processes of capitalist development. In the continued age of corporate media, the cultural cannot be separated from the economic. To participate in one is to participate in the other.

The modern search engine industry anchored firmly in an advertising profit model, the willingness of search engine firms to rationalize clear violations of human freedoms of information, and the broadened scope of decision engine services on the horizon indicate some of the ways in which search engine producers both contribute to and are shaped by the dynamic reconfiguration of informationalized capitalism. As Dan Schiller (2006) argues, the long history of capitalism has been "sustained by ceaseless enlargement of markets for commodities and this trend continues today in information and culture" (p. 23). Since the latest persistent period of macroeconomic stagnation that began in the 1970s, political and economic decision-makers have recognized the need to seek out new realms of capital accumulation. The commodification of information and users advanced by search engines in the often-concealed ways outlined in this chapter is one mechanism whereby capitalist social relations are reproduced anew. Search engines not only provide a contemporary example of capital's dynamism in bringing formerly unproductive activity into the sphere of capitalist accumulation but also present an opportunity to reinvigorate a Marxist critique of capitalism in the digital era.

A paradox of studying media technologies is that, when they are new and not widely used, they can easily escape sustained attention; yet, as they grow pervasive, they become more ritualized and less strange and therefore threaten to recede from a critical vantage point. There can be no doubt that search engines are now an essential access point to networked digital media and culture. This chapter represents a preliminary attempt to begin to identify salient issues for social and cultural theory regarding search engines not only as a new form of popular media engagement, but also as a media technology that reproduces a particular cultural logic embedded in and enacting global informationalized capitalism.

Notes

1. A seminal paper by Brin and Page (1998), written prior to their creation of Google as a private firm, exemplifies this strand of research. In "The Anatomy of a Large-Scale Hypertextual Web Search Engine," the authors address technical problems related to the "quality and scalability" (p. 2) of online search engines, endeavoring to "bring order to the Web" by automating the task of "objectively" (p. 3) measuring the comparative importance of search results.
2. Notable exceptions include: Hargittai (2004); Hinman (2008); Introna and Nissenbaum (2000); and, Van Couvering (2007, 2008).
3. It is worth noting that information searching is neither "new" nor an area of practice confined to digitality. Systems of classification, storage, and retrieval implicated in the operation of information searching might be traced back to the emergence of writing itself. In the 1890s, vertical filing systems emerged as a major breakthrough in the storage and retrieval of large volumes of paper documents (Yates, 2000). Automated searching predates digital search engines by at least 70 years; as early as the 1920s, Herman Hollerith's analog punch-card tabulating machines were capable of recording, sorting, retrieving, and performing calculations upon large data sets.
4. For a focused analysis of the use of difference to market information and communication technologies, see Nakamura (2000).
5. At the time of writing, Google has withdrawn its operations from mainland China, citing security breaches and cyber-attacks as the rationale for leaving. In March 2010 Google began to redirect Chinese users to its unfiltered Hong Kong-hosted services (Helft & Barboza, 2010), but the situation remains tentative.
6. Remarks from Charles Ess on the Association of Internet Researchers email list helped to frame my thinking about this topic.
7. For an extended discussion of neoliberalism, see Pitton's chapter in this volume.
8. For an extended discussion regarding the importance of political economy for "new media" criticism, see Bulut's chapter in this volume.
9. The well-developed relationship between Stanford University and Silicon Valley investors served as an integral catalyst for the initial rounds of funding that enabled Google and other technology start-ups in the area to grow and prosper. For a historical analysis of this relationship see Leslie (1993).
10. Smythe's formulation has been criticized (see Murdoch, 1978), but it remains a provocative mode of analysis in the context of search engines.
11. Although beyond the scope of this chapter, it is worth noting that search engines' commodification of users compels a rethinking of the Marxist categories of productive and unproductive labor and forces a reconceptualization of class beyond the waged labor relation. The labor of search engine users, like the labor of audience members, is both immaterial and unpaid. Following Harry Braverman (1998), class does not depend on various concrete forms of labor; rather, it is a social relation between labor and capital and "as this relation is generalized throughout the productive processes it creates social classes. Therefore, the transformation of unproductive labor into labor which is, for the capitalist's purpose of extracting surplus value, productive, is the very process of the creation of capitalist society" (p. 286).

12. In recent years, Google has pursued a diversification of revenue streams, investing in energy provision, healthcare records, and mobile phone sectors among others.

References

Abbate, J. (2000). *Inventing the Internet*. Cambridge, MA: MIT Press.
Adam, G. S. (2009). Foreword. In J. Carey (Ed.), *Communication as culture* (Rev. ed., pp. ix–xxiv). New York: Routledge.
Alpert, J., & Hajaj, N. (2008, July 25). We knew the Web was big. *The official Google blog*. Retrieved from http://googleblog.blogspot.com/2008/07/we-knew-web-was-big.html
Bar-Ilan, J. (2003). The use of Web search engines in information science research. *Annual Review of Information Science and Technology, 38*, 231–288.
Baron, N. S. (2008). *Always on: Language in an online and mobile world*. Oxford: Oxford University Press.
Battelle, J. (2005). *Search: The inside story of how Google and its rivals changed everything*. New York: Portfolio.
Birkerts, S. (1994). *Gutenberg elegies*. New York: Fawcett Columbine.
Braverman, H. (1998). *Labor and monopoly capital*. New York: Monthly Review Press.
Brin, S., & Page, L. (1998). The anatomy of a large-scale hypertextual Web search engine. *WWW7/Computer Networks, 30*, 107–117.
Carey, J. (2009). *Communication as culture* (Rev. ed.). New York: Routledge.
Castells, M. (1996). *The rise of the network society. The information age: Economy, society and culture (Vol.1)*. Oxford: Blackwell.
Chester, J. (2007). *Digital destiny: New media and the future of democracy*. New York: New Press.
Datamonitor. (2008, August 22). *Google, Inc. company profile*. New York.
Deuze, M., Blank, P., & Speers, L. (2009). Media life working paper (version 1.2). Unpublished manuscript. Retrieved from https://scholarworks.iu.edu/dspace/handle/2022/3764
Experian Hitwise. (2009, October 6). *Google receives 71 percent of searches in September 2009*. Retrieved from http://www.hitwise.com/us/press-center/press-releases/google-searches-sept-09
Fallows, D. (2005, January 23). Search engine users. *Pew Internet & American life project*. Retrieved from http://www.pewInternet.org/Reports/2005/Search-Engine-Users.aspx
Fallows, D. (2008, August 6). Search engine use. *Pew Internet and American life project*. Retrieved from http://www.pewInternet.org/Reports/2008/Search-Engine-Use.aspx
Friedman, E. (2010, June 5). BP buys 'oil' search terms to redirect users to official company website. *ABC News*. Retrieved from http://abcnews.go.com/Technology/Broadcast/bp-buys-search-engine-phrases-redirecting-users/story?id=10835618
Google Finance. (2009, May 11). Retrieved from http://www.google.com/finance?q=goog
Greenberg, A. (2007, April 30). Condemned to Google Hell. *Forbes.com*. Retrieved from http://www.forbes.com/2007/04/29/sanar-google-skyfacet-tech-cx_ag_0430googhell.html
Halavais, A. (2009). *Search engine society*. Cambridge, UK: Polity.
Hanson, A. F. (2004). From classification to indexing: How automation transforms the way we think. *Social Epistemology, 18*(4), 333–356.

Hargittai, E. (2004). The changing online landscape: From free-for-all to commercial gatekeeping. In P. Day & D. Schuler (Eds.), *Community practice in the network society: Local actions/global interaction* (pp. 66–76). New York: Routledge.

Hargittai, E. (2007). The social, political, economic, and cultural dimensions of search engines: An introduction. *Journal of Computer-Mediated Communication, 12*(3), Article 1. Retrieved from http://jcmc.indiana.edu/vol12/issue3/hargittai.html

He, B., Patel, M, Zhang, Z., & Chen-Chuan Chang, K. (2007). Accessing the deep Web. *Communications of the ACM, 50*(5), 94–101. Retrieved from http://doi.acm.org/10.1145/1230819.1241670

Helft, M., & Barboza, D. (2010, March 23). Google shuts China site in dispute over censorship. *New York Times*. Retrieved from http://www.nytimes.com/2010/03/23/technology/23google.html

Hinman, L. M. (2008). Searching ethics: The role of search engines in the construction and distribution of knowledge. In Spink, A. & Zimmer, M. (Eds.), *Web search* (pp. 67–76). Berlin: Springer-Verlag.

Human Rights Watch. (2006). *Race to the bottom: Corporate complicity in Chinese Internet censorship*. New York.

Innis, H. (1999). *The bias of communication*. Toronto: University of Toronto Press.

International Monetary Fund. (2009, October). *World economic outlook database, October 2009: Nominal GDP list of countries*. Washington, DC. Retrieved from http://imf.org/external/data.htm

International Telecommunication Union. (2008). *Internet indicators: Subscribers, users, and broadband subscribers*. Geneva. Retrieved from http://www.itu.int/ITU-D/ICTEYE/Reports.aspx

Introna, L., & Nissenbaum, H. (2000). Shaping the Web: Why the politics of search engines matter. *The Information Society, 16*(3), 1–17.

Jansen, B. J., Booth, D. L., & Spink, A. (2008). Determining the informational, navigational, and transactional intent of Web queries. *Information Processing & Management, 44*(3), 1251–1266.

Jansen, B. J., & Pooch, U. (2001). A review of Web searching studies and a framework for future research. *Journal of the American Society for Information Science and Technology, 52*, 235–246.

Jeanneney, J. (2007). *Google and the myth of universal knowledge* (Teresa Lavender Fagan, Trans). Chicago: University of Chicago Press.

Kane, M. (2007, May 7). What's 'she' doing in Google search? *CNet News Blog*. Retrieved from http://news.cnet.com/8301-10784_3-9716528-7.html?tag=mncol

Leslie, S. W. (1993). *The cold war and American science*. New York: Columbia University Press.

McChesney, R. W. (2004). *The problem of the media*. New York: Monthly Review.

McLuhan, M. (1995). *Understanding media*. Cambridge, MA: MIT Press.

McNichol, T. (2004, January 22). Engineering Google results to make a point. *The New York Times*. Retrieved from http://www.nytimes.com/2004/01/22/technology/circuits/22goog.html?8hpib

Microsoft Corporation. (2009). *Introducing bing*. Retrieved from http://www.decisionengine.com/Letter.html

Murdoch, G. (1978). Blindspots about Western Marxism: A reply to Dallas Smythe. *Canadian Journal of Political and Social Theory, 2*(2), 109–119.

Nakamura, L. (2000). Where do you want to go today? In B. E. Kolko, L.Nakamura, & G. B. Rodman (Eds.), *Race in cyberspace* (pp. 15–26). New York: Routledge.

Pew Internet and American Life Project. (2009, April). *Trend data: Online activities, total.* Retrieved from http://www.pewInternet.org/Trend-Data/Online-Activites-Total.aspx

Pew Project for Excellence in Journalism. (2010). *Online: Summary essay.* Retrieved from http://www.stateofthemedia.org/2010/online_summary_essay.php

Postman, N. (1985). *Amusing ourselves to death.* New York: Penguin.

Rieger, O. Y. (2009). Search engine use behavior of students and faculty: User perceptions and implications for future research. *First Monday, 14*(12). Retrieved from http://firstmonday.org/htbin/cgiwrap/bin/ojs/index.php/fm/article/viewArticle/2716/2385

Schiller, D. (1999). *Digital capitalism.* Cambridge, MA: MIT Press.

Schiller, D. (2006). *How to think about information.* Urbana, IL: University of Illinois Press.

Schmidt, E. (2008, October 20). *Presentation on the future of technology.* Speech presented at Bloomberg Headquarters, New York. Retrieved from http://www.youtube.com/watch?v=rD_x9LW5QRg&feature=PlayList&p=8DA4469A806827DA&index=0

Smythe, D. (1977). Communications: Blindspot of Western Marxism. *Canadian Journal of Political and Social Theory, 1*(3), 1–27.

Spink, A., & Zimmer, M. (2008). Introduction. In A. Spink & M. Zimmer (Eds.), *Web search* (pp. 3–8). Berlin: Springer-Verlag.

Tomlinson, J. (2007). Globalization and cultural analysis. In D. Held & A. McGrew (Eds.), *Globalization theory: Approaches and controversies* (pp. 148–170). New York: Polity.

Turow, J. (2006). *Niche envy.* Cambridge: MIT Press.

Van Couvering, E. (2007). Is relevance relevant? Market, science, and war: Discourses of search engine quality. *Journal of Computer-Mediated Communication, 12*(3), Article 6. Retrieved from http://jcmc.indiana.edu/vol12/issue3/vancouvering.html

Van Couvering, E. (2008). The history of the Internet search engine: Navigational media and the traffic commodity. In Spink, A. & Zimmer, M. (Eds.), *Web search* (pp. 177–206). Berlin: Springer-Verlag.

West, C. (2009, April 2). *Has the dream been realized?* Speech presented at University of Illinois, Urbana-Champaign.

Williams, R. (1977). *Marxism and literature.* Oxford: Oxford University Press.

Williams, R. (2003). *Television.* London: Routledge.

Yates, J. (2000). Business use of information and technology during the industrial age. In A. D. Chandler & J. Cortada (Eds.), *A nation transformed by information* (pp. 107–136). Oxford: Oxford University Press.

Zeman, E. (2009, April 16). Google's gain is Yahoo's pain. *Information Week.* Retrieved from http://www.informationweek.com/blog/main/archives/2009/04/googles_gain_is.html

Zimmer, M. (2009). Renvois of the past, present and future: Hyperlinks and the structuring of knowledge from the Encyclopedie to Web 2.0. *New media & society, 11*, 95–113.

· 6 ·

Freedom Devices

Neoliberalism, Mobile Technologies, and Governance

STEVEN DORAN

As I sit here writing this, I'm listening to "Ceremony" by New Order as it plays on my *iPhone*. At various points during the afternoon, I will pick up this device and undertake any number of what are now routine actions: I will check my email and my text messages; I will look up the bus schedule and the weather and a colleague's email address; I will get turn-by-turn directions to some obscure Midwestern locale; I will hold it up to the speakers of my computer so that I might identify an unknown song posted on a friend's blog. As I work, it will intermittently beep and vibrate, notifying me of incoming communications: reminders of tomorrow's appointments; alerts that someone has commented on a picture I've posted on Facebook; gentle notifications that my AT&T and Visa bills are both due this week. Were it another afternoon, one in which I were perhaps going for a walk in some picturesque and idyllic landscape, I might take a picture, and then I might run that picture through the image editing software on my iPhone that allows me to artificially age it or crop it or adjust its color saturation so that it will impress my Web 2.0 peers when I post it on Flickr (something which I might also do during my walk). I might play one of the many games I've installed on the phone but have yet to finish, or I might test my hearing with an interesting little application that plays a series of diminishing beeps into my ears through my headphones. Oh, and I might even make a phone call. Impressive as it was in 2007 when it was released, the iPhone fails to dazzle anyone anymore. What is central to recognize is the extent to which this little device has become imbricated in the quotidian goings-on of a typical graduate student.

The iPhone and its ilk—the *Palm Pre*, the *BlackBerry Storm*, the *Motorola Android* and other smartphones—are frequently pointed to as radically altering the nature and experience of everyday life (Garcia-Montes, Caballero-Munoz, & Perez-Alvarez, 2006; Geser, 2006; Ling, 2004; Plant, 2002; Wellman, 2001; Wilken, 2006). These technologies are consequential to the extent that they represent the convergence of communication, information, media, and space, and in doing so represent the technological edge of a series of ongoing social, cultural, and political economic transformations that mark this new millennium. A brief consideration of an object like the iPhone makes clear the ways in which it is implicated with multiple facets of life including media, surveillance, consumption, space, citizenship, labor, commerce, identity, migration, interpersonal relationships, and governance. These objects represent the sites where these forces intersect and collide and are becoming central to our experience of modern life.

As mobile information and communication technologies—or ICTs—continue to grow in their seeming ubiquity and centrality in everyday life, wireless devices have emerged as important technologies through which the proper citizens of neoliberalism are constructed and governed. Technology, mobility, and communication have become central to modern citizenship, and the new social and cultural configurations that form around these emergent subjects are of growing significance. Further, in light of the growing importance of these technologies in the operations of everyday life, the cell phone has become a site of contested signification. This state of affairs demands interrogation: to what extent is mobile technology implicated in these new networks of power, information, and capital? How can we most clearly and productively capture the ways that citizenship and governance are constructed and deployed in contemporary society? And by what guiding logics has the citizen-user of mobile technology emerged as a discursive site where the multiple and contradictory forces of politics, governance, commerce, and identity converge and intersect?

This chapter focuses on the multiple significations that swarm around mobile phones, the way in which their users are configured as mobile citizens within neoliberal democracies, and the contradictions that are inherent in such a figure. What emerges is that, while these objects are culturally produced as "freedom devices"—objects that enable users to become agents within contemporary neoliberalism—they also foreground the contradictory ways that "freedom" is deployed by transforming those same agents into objects of neoliberal rule. A tangle of liberty and surveillance, coupled with the conceptual flexibility of freedom under neoliberalism, has emerged as the marker of an increasingly technologically mediated contemporary life. Further, the growing reliance on information technologies such as the mobile phone reflects a shift towards a type of infrastructuralism in which networks of technology, information, and communication constitute the ideological and material scaffolding of modern societies.

But while they hold the promise of freedom for their users, mobile phones serve contradictory purposes in neoliberal societies. A number of nations have begun to police the virtual space of mobile communication; enacting legislation that places entire populations under potential surveillance by state entities, service providers, and application developers. Through these legislative maneuvers, the contradictions of neoliberal citizenship and governance come to the fore. Mobile ICTs are not only sites where these contradictions become evident but have become, more importantly, a tool in their very production and maintenance. Ultimately, the notion of "freedom" emerges around these technological artifacts as a discursive strategy that embodies multiple, often contradictory, impulses and purposes within a framework of neoliberal governmentality; at once encouraging individual autonomy, while also justifying increasing levels of surveillance.

Neoliberal Governmentality

This chapter takes as its starting point the premise that contemporary modes of social and political organization, of national and international economic policies, of managing the routines of everyday life, and of state governance, can be best described by the concept of neoliberalism. Neoliberalism is a term that has been deployed to describe phenomena as disparate as NAFTA and self-esteem, and few accounts of the concept have proven to be as capable in addressing its breadth as has Foucault's analytic of governmentality (Foucault, 1988, 2003). Foucault used governmentality—or art of government—to capture how power is deployed to shape the "conduct of conduct" in contemporary societies and illustrated how different historical epochs possessed different governmentalities that allowed for the construction of proper citizens and forms of rule. Situating neoliberalism within an analytic of governmentality avoids essentializing it to a set of economic tenets championing free trade, deregulation, and globalization and instead foregrounds the ways in which neoliberal governmentality encompasses a host of strategies and techniques by which multiple domains of life are regulated. In this sense, "governmentality explains homologies across neoliberal economic policies in the market and the everyday discipline and character-development programs used by teachers in public schools to foster a particular kind of calculative accountability" (Nadesan, 2008, p. 1).

Neoliberalism is not just a set of practices and beliefs advancing the merits of a free market economy and the liberties of the individual; it comprises the collection of strategies, calculations, and knowledges through which neoliberalism is able to come into being and operate. While often conceptually reduced to a set of economic and political policies and orientations that champion enterprise, trade, corporatization, decreased taxation, small government and competition, the functioning of a neoliberal order requires a set of enactable knowledges that extend beyond the political and the economic. Intense globalization and marketization have emerged as neoliberalism's signifiers, and frequently, intellectuals from the left rightly point to the disastrous effects these processes have had the world over. But the formulation of neoliberalism in narrowly economic ways constructs it as an ideology against which another—more egalitarian, more emancipatory, more ethical—ideology is to be advanced to achieve "real" liberation. The one-dimensional conception of neoliberalism as simply entailing economic policies encourages us to envision it as an abstract, external force to which people are passively subjected: the mistaken ideology of greedy businessmen and wrong-headed conservative politicians. In conceiving of neoliberalism in this way, we risk overlooking ways in which it constitutes other sets of knowledges and behaviors beyond the economic, carried out by individual subjects through which neoliberal governmentality emerges as a coherent social formation.

Focusing on neoliberalism as a set of knowledges and techniques that regulate multiple realms of life allows to us think about how it manifests as a coherent set of actions undertaken as much by normal citizens as by the corporate and government elite and reconstitutes the plane of possible intervention in such terms. In her astute analysis of neoliberalism's myriad conceptual and theoretical incarnations, Viviana Pitton (this volume) points to a body of contemporary scholarship that focuses on the self-regulatory nature of neoliberalism's governmental operations. This condition is made possible by the increasing repositioning of risk away from the state and onto the individual and the concomitant responsibilization of neoliberalism's citizens. It is from this position, one in which subjects think of themselves and behave as "proper citizens" of neoliberalism, that the macrostructures of neoliberalism can be articulated. The fiscally oriented policies and politics of neoliberalism achieve coherence only in a mutually constitutive relationship with particular ways of thinking about and organizing the citizen, the community, and the population as well as the economy and the nation. Thinking about neoliberalism in this sense does not diminish the role of the economic in its formulation; instead, it resituates it as one realm, among many, in which the subject of neoliberalism is produced and governed.

Given the maxim of minimal intervention, neoliberal governmentality is often pointed to as utilizing techniques "that seek to shape conduct by working through our desires, aspirations, interests and beliefs" (Dean, 1999, p. 11). From a Foucauldian perspective, neoliberal governmentality facilitates the production and government of citizens in part by following the postulate to "govern at a distance" (Nikolas Rose, as cited in King, 2006, p. xxix), and in this way the governmental operations of neoliberalism have become dispersed throughout the social body. Social institutions, cultural resources, economic policies, and even ways of thinking about the self (e.g. self-esteem) can be seen as strategies of government. In this way, citizens are shaped to be amenable with the interests and goals of neoliberalism with little direct intervention of the state in the lives of the individual.

Freedom and Neoliberal Citizenship

Freedom itself is the primary technique of neoliberalism in the production and governance of citizens. As Mitchell Dean (1999) writes:

> A useful way of thinking about liberalism as a regime of government [...] is to consider the multiple ways it works through and attempts to construct a world of autonomous individuals, of "free subjects" [....] This is a subject whose freedom is a condition of subjection. (p. 193).

Within a dominant paradigm of neoliberalism, free citizens are constructed through those discourses, techniques, and strategies that situate freedom within a system of regulation and control from a distance. But within this framework, attaining individual freedom often necessitates the willing submission to the governmental power of the state.

Freedom and domination have become two sides of the same coin. In a context where citizens are ruled, governed, and controlled via the deployment of personal freedom as a technology of power, enacting that freedom necessarily entails working in accordance with the power from which it emerged. Being free means being ruled. In this way, neoliberal citizenship can be characterized by both the continued pursuit of individual freedom as well as by systems of domination which are becoming increasingly material, invisible, and infrastructural. The neoliberal citizen is thus a paradoxical figure, at once "free"—that is, capable of self-management and autonomy—but at the same time subject to a governmental power that regulates and manages conduct through the strategic deployment of such freedom.

As the direct influence of the state is retracted from the life of the citizen, its governmental aims are achieved through the construction of strategic allegiances with private enterprise and by advancing a discourse of citizenship that focuses on the autonomy and self-determination of the individual in achieving his own freedom, happiness, and security. As a function of this maxim to govern from a distance, the citizen of neoliberalism becomes not only autonomous but is simultaneously tasked with the responsibility of managing this autonomy appropriately and effectively. Thus, neoliberal government is necessarily self-government, and the central strategy of the neoliberal state is the diffusion of this government throughout the social body. In turn, the government of citizens manifests in a variety of arenas: education, medicine, consumption, recreation, media and so on. The "free citizen" of neoliberalism is a strategic construction that permits for the smooth operation of neoliberal governmentality.

Properly configured "free citizens" are necessary for the governmental operations of neoliberalism to operate in a smooth and increasingly self-regulatory way. Under neoliberal systems of rule, freedom becomes the primary technical modality by which citizenship is articulated and the "free citizen" becomes the primary vehicle by which neoliberal governmental aims are achieved. As such, the availability of "autonomous" technology becomes a necessary prerequisite for the possibility of both accessing and managing this freedom. In this regard, wireless devices are embedded in an economy of signification in which they are conferred manifold and often contradictory meanings and figure into the production and governance of neoliberal citizens in a number of ways. By examining their cultural production via their representation in media as well as in policy documents, we can see how these devices are framed as embodying, promoting, and disseminating the ideological dictates of neoliberalism as they are reflected in the rhetoric of individual freedom, autonomy, self-enterprise, choice, and self-management that surround cell phones and other mobile information technologies.

Neoliberalism, Mobile Technology, and Liberty

As mobile ICTs adopt advanced computing, location awareness, and media capabilities, they become increasingly important sites for the mobilization of a cultural power at which the manifold and contradictory strategies of governmentality intersect and collide. In his research on the growth of communications infrastructure in the 19th century, Andrew Barry (1996) argues that "communications networks have come to provide the perfect material base for liberal government" (p. 123), enabling society to "come to know itself and to govern itself on the basis of its own knowledge" (p. 128). In a similar way, wireless devices provide the material and ideological scaffolding for neoliberalism and aid in the production of the self-determining, self-enterprising, and autonomous citizens required for neoliberal governmental operations to function.

By looking at the way these devices are represented in popular media, it becomes evident that they are constructed as increasingly important tools in the production of neoliberal citizenship. Whether a cell phone user is using her device to manage her blood-sugar levels, to avoid the inherent dangers of a dark, isolated laundry room in the basement, or to manage her ever-growing network of work associates, she is depicted as being increasingly able to be self-governed—that is, exercise her freedom—through her careful and strategic deployment of the mobile phone as a freedom device. Through techniques such as these, the optimally efficient, responsible, and free citizen emerges through the figure of the mobile phone. By using freedom as a strategic technical modality, neoliberalism is able to commandeer and utilize these practices in pursuit of its governmental aims by framing the individualization, responsibilization, and entrepreneurialization of the subject within the conceptual framework of liberty.

In any number of television and print commercials, cell phones are positioned as central to the creation and maintenance of the neoliberal citizen. In a spot from Telus Mobility, a Canadian mobile phone service provider, the neoliberal ideological investments in personal freedom and autonomy are explicitly mapped onto the body of the cellular phone. The spot opens with a close-up of a meerkat in an empty white space (see Figure 1). As the camera pulls back strings swell in the background. The shot cuts to a white frame with the words "We believe in liberty", before quickly cutting back to the shot of the meerkat, now accompanied by two companions. The music begins to crescendo and chanting voices are added to the mix. Another cut to a white frame with "We believe in community" across it before returning to the meerkats, now a veritable herd. As the camera continues to pull back and as the music intensifies, a dark shadow falls over the diminutive mammals as they look to the sky. A close up of a raindrop falling to the ground and the words "We believe in instant weather forecasts." The ad closes with the meerkats standing bewildered in the rain and the words "We believe in smartphones for all", before presenting in quick succession the array of smartphones Telus has on offer. The final image is of the Telus logo and their trademark slogan, "The future is friendly."

Figures 1. Smartphones as "Freedom Device," from Telus Mobility: Meerkat Commercial. ©Telus Mobility. (See Epic, 2008).

This commercial, not surprisingly titled "Epic" (Epic, 2008) given its score, is explicit in its mapping of neoliberalism's ideological commitment to liberty onto the body of the mobile phone. The smartphone becomes the physical incarnation of liberty, but further, the rhetorical linkage made between freedom and instant weather forecasts—notably phrased as a matter of "belief"—construes the practices made possible via the smartphone as the enactment of the individual liberty central to the neoliberal citizen. In the span of 15 seconds, the narrative of the commercial moves from the grand abstract notion of liberty to the ability of accessing weather forecasts on the go, making each the equivalent of the other. In these terms, the smartphone both contributes to and permits the individual to enact the freedom central to the neoliberal citizen. In another commercial, from E*Trade (Smuggler & Krallman, 2008), a company that provides Internet-based software for trading stock and managing one's portfolio, the emancipatory potential of personal investing is foregrounded. In a 2008 spot, a baby sits at his computer and tells the audience about a new service provided by E*Trade called "Mobile Pro" (see Figure 2); a service that allows subscribers to trade stocks and receive streaming quotes on their BlackBerry handheld device:

> [Baby speaking to the camera while holding a Blackberry]: Look at this. I'm a free man. I can go anywhere I want now and trade. E*Trade Mobile Pro. Right on my BlackBerry. (Phone vibrates) Wait, hang on, gettin' an email . . . (Gasps while looking at email) Oh, bad girl! Man! (Snickers) Anyway, you know, I can get streaming quotes on the—(Phone rings) God, relentless. Hang on one second. (Into handset) Hey girl, can I hit you back?

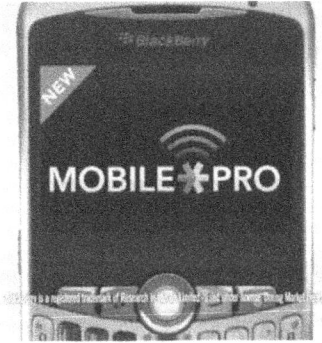 

Figures 2. Freedom so easy that a baby can do it, from E*Trade: Baby Commercial. ©E*Trade. (See Smuggler & Krallman, 2008).

[Announcer speaking over a graphic of the Mobile Pro software interface: New E-Trade Mobile Pro. Trade Stocks. Get streaming quotes. Anytime. Anywhere. There are a thousand new accounts a day. At E-Trade.

This commercial reflects the ways in which mobile phones have been constructed as technologies of the self, objects through which people are able to constantly reflect upon and evaluate the positioning of the self within the framework of appropriate neoliberal citizenship. It is clear in this commercial that the mobile phone is a technology by which the individual becomes a free subject. The opening statement of the commercial proclaims just this: as the baby holds up the BlackBerry for the viewer to see, he says, "Look at this, I'm a free man," presenting as self-evident the fact that the BlackBerry is the vehicle through which the baby achieves his freedom. This device allows him to manage his stock portfolio wherever and whenever he likes, making the perpetual management of the self a possibility for the mobile citizen. The obvious emancipatory potential of the control of one's personal finances is subsumed in this commercial by the heightened liberatory practices enabled by the smartphone. The baby is free not simply because he can invest his money as he sees fit, but because he can now do so wherever he might find himself and whenever it might be. True freedom is framed as the ability to manage the self remotely, unconstrained by geography. In this way, mobility becomes a powerful signifier of the freedom of the neoliberal citizen.

These commercials promote a type of cultural citizenship in which the individual is impelled to view himself as central to the establishment and maintenance of his own security, autonomy, and liberty. The mobile phone figures centrally in what is an instructional script for how to become a better citizen by deploying certain techniques and strategies. In this light, these commercials play an important role not only in the shaping of various meanings attached to wireless technologies, but in establishing a narrative of neoliberal citizenship that entails in viewers a logic of self-governance and individual freedom. The figure of the mobile phone embodies the responsibility, security, autonomy, and freedom that are central to the neoliberal citizen and has come to occupy a position of priority within neoliberal societies. The instant weather forecast, as with mobile stock-trading, is liberty manifest, and in this formulation, as a technology through which the free citizen of neoliberalism manifests, the smartphone becomes a freedom device.

For instance, in June of 2009, in response to what were widely seen as illegitimate presidential elections, Iranian citizens protested widely and were met with violent crackdown from the state. As traditional media outlets were closed down and foreign journalists forced out of the country, the Internet became the only venue for opposition views to be voiced. But access to the Internet was also extremely limited by the state, and so services such as Twitter, YouTube, and Facebook, online utilities that are extremely flexible in their modes of access and thus more difficult to block, become the primary venues where news of the protests could get out. Referred to by the popular press as "The Twitter Revolution," the events of June 2009 were seen by many as possible only because of the spread of mobile ICTs into Iran. Using their phone's photography, video, email, and text capabilities, protestors were able to distribute stories, images, and videos over these web applications.

In addition, Twitter has frequently been portrayed in the press as standing in opposition to totalitarian regimes and promoting freedom by allowing for the access and distribution of information:

> Last month an anticommunist uprising in Moldova was organized via Twitter. Twitter has become so widely used among political activists in China that the government recently blocked access to it, in an attempt to censor discussion of the 20th anniversary of the Tiananmen Square massacre. (Johnson, 2009)

And in response to the growing use of the term "Twitter Revolution" in the summer of 2009, Marc Ambinder (2009) wrote in *The Atlantic*:

> It's too easy to call the weekend's activities the first revolution that was Twittered, but when histories of the Iranian election are written, Twitter will doubtless be cast as a protagonal technology that enabled the powerless to survive a brutal crackdown and information blackout by the ruling authorities

In these accounts, mobile ICTs are framed as empowering individuals in opposition to oppressive political and military forces. The cell phone delivers to these people the possibility of liberation in the form of access to and the dissemination of information. Likewise, on the domestic front, cell phones are depicted as imbuing individuals with the power of the investigative journalist, uncovering truths kept secret by those in positions of authority and power. A 2008 story about a video of police misconduct taken by a citizen journalist goes as far as to say:

> The availability of cheap digital technology—video cameras, digital cameras, cellphone cameras—has ended a monopoly on the history of public gatherings that was limited to the official narratives, like the sworn documents created by police officers and prosecutors. The digital age has brought in free-range history. (Dwyer, 2008)

In this account, these technologies are imbued with the power to do nothing less than radically transform history. Handheld devices that bring together technologies ranging from photography to GPS to telephony are construed as delivering to their users the potential for increased democratic participation and the ability to speak truth to power, not to mention an enhanced degree of autonomy and self-reliance. By using these objects, individuals enhance their ability to be good citizens.

Surveillance, Power, and Governance

While the mobile phone is discursively framed as a freedom device, it also serves the inverse function of placing its users within a number of complex strategies and networks of power. The mobile phone embodies contradictory impulses, functioning to empower but also regulate the mobile citizen. In part this regulation is a function of neoliberalism's capability to govern from a distance with technologies such as cell phones contributing to the self-regulatory nature of neoliberal governmental operations. At the same time, a number of countries have begun to use these technologies for surveillance and have implemented data retention laws that require service providers to maintain records of users cellphone use including location information, duration of communication, and the identity of the individuals on both ends of the phone call. This information may be kept for the purposes of more easily policing and capturing criminals who use these technologies in their illegal activities but in the end functions to place entire populations within a system of state-sponsored surveillance and discipline.

In 2006, the European Union passed the Data Retention Directive, an agreement that required service providers of cellular telephony in the EU member states to retain user information for a period of no less than six months and no more than two years (Directive number 24 of 2006). Included in the data to be retained were: the originating and destination phone numbers; the name and address of subscribers on both ends; the date, time and duration of all calls; unique identification information for relevant hardware being used for both calling and called parties; and data that would identify the geographic location of the origin and destination of the phone calls. In short, this directive legislated the creation of a vast database of information, storing records of every phone call made within the EU Member States. Governments would be able to tell who was calling whom, when, where from, and using what type of equipment. This was to be done "in order to ensure that the data are available for the purpose of the investigation, prosecution, of serious crimes as defined by each Member State in its national law" (Directive number 24 of 2006, p. 56). These measures were taken in a global political climate that had been recently shaken by terrorist attacks in Madrid and London in 2004 and 2005, respectively, and the World Trade Center attacks of 2001. Each of these attacks had utilized mobile phones in their organization and deployment, and thus the passing of a directive that allowed for the monitoring of mobile phone users seemed an appropriate action to take in light of the perceived growth in the threat of terrorism.

In the U.S., the New York Police Department has started tracking the cell phones of people who are arrested by recording the device's IMEI number, a unique identifier attached to the handset that allows authorities to track the position of the device within a cellular network (Parascandola, 2009). In May 2010, legislation was introduced into the U.S. Senate that would require users of pre-paid cell phones to disclose their identities upon purchase and for service providers to keep records of users' identification information (Yahoo! News, 2010).

In 2009, the Spanish government implemented similar legislation requiring all purchasers and users of pre-paid mobile phones to present government-issued identification at the time of purchase or to register with their service providers if they were presently using one of these devices anonymously (Diaz, 2009). Undertaken under the ominous moniker of "¡Identifícate!" or "Identify Yourself," Spain implemented a nation-wide media campaign encouraging users of these devices to register lest their cell phone service get cut off.

As a consequence of the emerging problem of the mobile citizen, many states have become invested in specific notions of what constitutes proper and improper use of this cellular technology as can been seen in the legal maneuvers described above. Ostensibly, improper communication constitutes those exchanges that facilitate criminal or terrorist activity—the legislation described above was enacted under just this rubric—but the upshot of these laws is that the field of improper use is greatly expanded beyond that which is strictly criminal. While this legislation is intended to aid in apprehending terrorists and other criminals, this possibility is only brought about by placing the mobile phone using population at large under compulsory industry and state surveillance. In turn, these governmental tactics not only facilitate the apprehension of terrorists but also establish a new truth about the nature of mediated communication and citizenship: improper use of cellular technology is not just that which is undertaken with criminal intent but any activity conducted via this technology that is done anonymously. To put it another way, as contemporary governance becomes increasingly reliant on the networks of information, communication, and technology that increasingly functions as material and ideological scaffolding for neoliberal orders, visibility within these structures becomes a requirement of good citizenship.

The growth and popularity of these technologies pose a problem for the state that finds itself needing to invent strategies for regulating conduct on and through these devices. The panic and heavy-handedness with which these states have approached the regulation of cell phones and cell phone users reflect not only the very real threat new modes of technologically based terrorism pose to these countries but also the extent to which emerging ICTs fail to fit in with established modes of power and governance. While it is the conduct of terrorists and criminals that these measures are primarily and ostensibly meant to regulate, the conduct of the normal cellphone using population is equally and perhaps even more powerfully controlled and regulated.

For instance, in an article on the technology blog Gizmodo, writer Jesus Diaz (2009) suggests that the Spanish government's "¡Identifícate!" campaign is:

> Just like when Franco was dictator [and hence] does [sic] these irrational fears justify a campaign to control the communication of private citizens, specially [sic] when the bad guys can avoid the controls and use alternative methods to wreak havoc in society?

Similarly, in April 2008, the Open Rights Group, an organization that seeks to protect civil liberties from infringement by digital technologies, was part of a group of NGOs and professional organizations that jointly submitted a brief to the European Court of Justice asking "the court to annul an EU directive ordering the blanket registration of telecommunications and location data of 494 million Europeans" (Wintle, 2008). The directive in question was, of course, the Data Retention Directive passed by the EU in 2006. In the brief, the group made such claims about the directive as the following:

> While it threatens to inflict great damage on society, its potential benefit appears, overall, to be little. Data retention can support the protection of individual rights only in few and generally less important cases. A permanent, negative effect on crime levels is not to be expected [....] [With data retention in place] citizens constantly need to fear that their communications data may at some point lead to false incrimination or governmental or private abuse of the data. Because of this, traffic data retention endangers open communication in the whole of society. (Wintle, 2008)

That this surveillance is so objectionable is because the limits of neoliberal governance are ostensibly found in the freedoms of the citizen. This means that the government is "good" insofar as it does not infringe upon these freedoms. The surveillance of cell phone users and the collection of their information are seen, in this light, as encroachments upon the fundamental freedoms that are promised by and that provide the very conditions for neoliberalism. The heavy-handed control being enacted through these systems of surveillance seems to be in direct opposition to the defining traits of these governmental logics. But even though citizens' freedoms are seemingly trampled upon by this surveillance, the neoliberal state can account for this by appealing to the very liberty ICT devices promise to their users in the first instance: increased security through individual responsibility.

The governmental logics of neoliberalism demand that the responsibility for this securitization—of state and nation, but also, by implication, of individual, family and friends—falls, in part, on the shoulders of the self-governing citizen. The same political regime that distributes throughout the social body responsibilities that once fell within the purview of the state—health care, education, old age security, welfare—logically allocates the task of ensuring national security in part to a nation's citizens. Being vigilant against terrorist threats is everyone's responsibility. Equally, the survival of individual freedom is contingent on those measures that protect the society. The free citizens of neoliberalism are recruited into regimes of securitization that depend on the enacting of their "freedom" in order to operate properly.

Through a series of discursive maneuvers, neoliberalism allows for these systems of surveillance to be translated from strategies of discipline into a tactics of individual responsibilization and autonomy: given that, like many governmental operations, the onus for ensuring national security is diffused throughout society, to the extent that participation in these systems of surveillance can be discursively attached to the defense of the country against attack, part of being a good citizen is accepting, or even willingly subjecting oneself to, the surveillance of one's cell phone activities by the state. The equivalency constructed between surveillance and freedom in this discourse means that the power exercised through state surveillance is the very condition by which the free subject of neoliberalism can emerge. Autonomy and self-governance—the signifiers of this freedom—are achieved only by submitting to this power, in this case as it is exercised through surveillance. It is particular to neoliberalism that freedom and control are mutually constituted positions; one is possible only with the other.

Conclusion

The cell phone embodies the contradictions inherent in neoliberal citizenship. At once it is empowering, providing users with the tools necessary to become good citizens. At the same time it is used for state and industry surveillance, situating its users within systems of domination. People are now able to do things they were once unable to do for themselves or unable to do outside of specific geographies or locations, and the possibility of doing this is framed by neoliberalism as individual autonomy and freedom.

Emerging mobile ICTS serve neoliberalism by performing the dual functions of aiding in the construction of properly configured free citizens and by situating those citizens within systems of regulation and surveillance from a distance as a function of that very freedom. But while it would be convenient to paint this surveillance with the broad brush of domination, it is not easy to do so. As much as it might infringe upon their individual freedoms, citizens also have a stake in their own surveillance. This investment manifests in the gated communities of the suburbs, in the surveillance cameras of shopping malls, and even in the cameras embedded in modern cell phones.

As citizens, users of these devices are themselves invested in the technology as modes of lateral and upward surveillance. The events that occurred in Iran perfectly capture the extent to which surveillance is less an undesired outcome of mobile communications technology and is instead part of the promise the technology makes to us. As a technique of governmental power, surveillance is not proprietary to the state but can also be effectively used by the citizen against the state, as with the situation in Iran, as well as against other citizens. In light of the threat this lateral and upward surveillance poses to established forms of state power, a number of U.S. states have begun arresting individuals who film police officers with mobile or similar devices (McElroy, 2010). Charges against these citizen journalists have been brought only in those cases in which officers were captured partaking in illegal or compromising activities and not when filmed conducting normal police work. This reflects how these new technologies can frustrate traditional power and allow for the creation of spaces in which conflicting notions of citizenship and democracy can be inserted, making comprehensible the increasingly panicked attempt by the state to harness and regulate these devices and their users.

Equally, and more commonly, this type of citizen surveillance is evident in the emergence of citizen journalism. In these cases, mobile ICTs are seen as empowering and are again cast as tools of liberation, furnishing individuals with the power not only to be self-governing but as being able to resist oppression. In this way, it is evident that the governmental operations of neoliberalism have the potential to exceed the state because surveillance, like other articulations of power under the logics of neoliberal governmentality, is distributed to multiple points throughout society.

This paradoxical characteristic of neoliberal citizenship is made possible by a broader process of infrastructuralism that, in part, underscores the operations of neoliberal governance and power. Infrastructuralism refers to the extent to which the affordances allowed by the often unseen yet material systems that support and animate our social, political, cultural, and economic systems establish a framework that promotes certain actions, behaviors, and ways of thinking while limiting others. This tendency is easily overlooked under neoliberalism as these systems—communications, media, information, even the electrical grid and so on—have a built-in opt-out option. No one is forced to own a cell phone, for instance, and if an individual is put off by the surveillant potential of the device, then they can always just choose not to use it. This argument is effective in that it strategically employs the freedom of choice of the neoliberal consumer/citizen. The free citizen is, above all, free to choose.

But what this argument overlooks is the extent to which multiple technical apparatuses have infiltrated everyday life and the ways in which their owners are—knowingly or unknowingly—monitored by using them. As well, it fails to recognize the extent to which technological literacy and participation is increasingly a condition of cultural citizenship. To not have a cell phone or to not know how to use the Internet is not just to make a consumer choice to "opt-out" but is to actually not participate in a significant part of modern life. A technocultural logic of surveillance underscores the functioning and use of many emerging technologies and has come to saturate our popular understandings of these technologies and systems. In many ways, citizens are forced to (or even sometimes happily) accept that using the Internet, or TiVO, or our cell phones means that someone somewhere knows what we're doing, what we're watching, what we're reading, or where we're going. Further, this logic has been normalized to the extent to which this surveillance is framed as a convenient or helpful property of these technological systems. So, as mobile ICTs become increasingly ubiquitous and continue to contribute to this often unseen infrastructuralism, the logics by which they function, propagate and saturate our popular imagination about these devices and in turn legitimate the systems of surveillance they animate.

The mobile phone is culturally constructed as a freedom device, signifying the lightness, uniqueness, and untetheredness of contemporary life. But it is also implicated in a far more complex system of rule and power. The freedom of the neoliberal citizen as it is brought into being by artifacts such as smartphones and the practices they enable also functions as a form of disciplinary power to the extent that citizens are governed and monitored by and through the strategic deployment of freedom by the state and its partners. This contradiction of freedom and domination inherent in the neoliberal citizen is in part made possible by the technological infrastructuralism that has come to define the 21st century life. Mobile communications technology plays an increasingly central role on even a global scale in the fluid application of this type of governmental power. An examination of contemporary mobile ICTs illustrates the complicated ways in which governance and citizenship, freedom and domination, function in a constant state of tension in contemporary societies.

References

Ambinder, M. (2009, June 15). The revolution will be Twittered. *The Atlantic*. Retrieved from http://www.theatlantic.com/politics/archive/2009/06/the-revolution-will-be-twittered/19376/

Barry, A. (1996). Lines of communication and spaces of rule. In A. Barry, N. S. Rose, & T. Osborne (Eds.), *Foucault and political reason: Liberalism, neo-liberalism, and rationalities of government* (pp. 123–142). Chicago: University of Chicago Press.

Dean, M. (1999). *Governmentality: Power and rule in modern society*. London; Thousand Oaks, CA: Sage.

Diaz, J. (2009). *Spain disconnecting pre-paid phones in November unless users identify themselves*. Retrieved from http://i.gizmodo.com/5164100/spain-disconnecting-pre%20paid-phones-in-november-unless-users-identify-themselves

Directive number 24 of 2006. (2006). *Official Journal of the European Union*, 105, 54.

Dwyer, J. (2008, July 30). When official truth collides with cheap digital technology. *The New York Times*.

Epic. Taxi. (2008). [Video/DVD] Taxi.

Foucault, M. (1988). The political technology of individuals. In H. Gutman, P. H. Hutton, & L. H. Martin (Eds.), *Technologies of the self: A seminar with Michel Foucault* (pp. 145–162). Amherst, MA: University of Massachusetts Press.

Foucault, M. (2003). Governmentality. In P. Rabinow & N. S. Rose (Eds.), *The essential Foucault: Selections from essential works of Foucault, 1954–1984* (pp. 229–245). New York: New Press.

Garcia-Montes, J. M., Caballero-Munoz, D., & Perez-Alvarez, M. (2006). Changes in the self resulting from the use of mobile phones. *Media Culture Society*, 28(1), 67–82.

Geser, H. (2006). Is the cell phone undermining the social order?: Understanding mobile technology from a sociological perspective. *Knowledge, Technology & Policy*, 19(1), 8–18.

Johnson, S. (2009, June 5). How Twitter will change the way we live. *Time*.

King, S. (2006). *Pink ribbons, inc.: Breast cancer and the politics of philanthropy*. Minneapolis, MN: University of Minnesota Press.

Ling, R. S. (2004). *The mobile connection: The cell phone's impact on society*. San Francisco, CA: Morgan Kaufmann.

McElroy, W. (2010). *Are cameras the new guns?* Retrieved from http://gizmodo.com/5553765/are-cameras-the-new-guns

Nadesan, M. H. (2008). *Governmentality, biopower, and everyday life*. London: Routledge.

Parascandola, R. (2009, October 8). NYPD tracking cell phone owners, but foes aren't sure practice is legal. *New York Daily News*, Retrieved from http://www.nydailynews.com/news/ny_crime/2009/10/08/2009-10-08_number_please_nypd_tracking_cell_phone_owners_but_foes_arent_sure_practice_is_le.html

Plant, S. (2002). *On the mobile: The effects of mobile telephones on social and individual life*. Libertyville, IL: Motorola.

Smuggler (Producer), & Krallman, R. (Director). (2008). *E*Trade baby mobile*. [Video/DVD] Grey Group.

Wellman, B. (2001). Physical place and cyberplace: The rise of networked individualism. In L. Keeble & B. Loader (Eds.), *Community informatics: Shaping computer-mediated social relations* (pp. 17–42). London; New York: Routledge.

Wilken, R. (2006). From *stabilitas loci* to *mobilitas loci*: Networked mobility and the transformation of place. *Fibreculture* (6).

Wintle, G. (2008). *Fighting the data retention directive*. Retrieved from http://www.openrightsgroup.org/blog/2008/fighting-the-data-retention-directive/

Yahoo! News. (2010). *US lawmakers target pre-paid cellphone anonymity*. Retrieved from http://news.yahoo.com/s/afp/usattacksphonespolitics.

· 7 ·

Glocal Transgender

Transgender Longing and Belonging in the Shadow of 9/11

STEPHEN HOCKER

The current moment is witness to a rapid intensification of globalization as new media technologies increasingly make communication and flows of data across national borders possible (Shome & Hedge, 2002a). The rise of global capital and markets has created an increasingly interconnected and networked world (Castells, 2000; Mattelart, 2000; Deuze, 2007; Pitton in this volume), and like it or not, none can reasonably expect to disconnect from this leviathan. One of the discursive responses to this globalization has been an increased reliance on nativism, specifically regarding nationalism and citizenship. Against the backdrop of the threat of global terrorism or the global economic crisis, and the hysteria around both phenomena, it is easy to surmise that the problems of transgendered people are not a priority in relation to either national safety or economic security.[1] Perhaps, in times such as these, scholars might be tempted to turn their attention away from what some consider "minority" interests for those seen as "universal." Yet it is times such as these that sex and gender, as Gayle Rubin (1984/1993) reminds us, "acquire immense symbolic weight [...] become vehicles for displacing social anxieties, and discharging their attendant emotional intensity" (p. 277). Rather than ignoring or delaying a careful analysis of sex and gender in times of social stress, these become central sites for understanding culture.

It may seem, at first glance that the emergence of global terrorism and gender non-conformity have little to do with one another. This chapter attempts to critically interrogate the debates around gender non-conformity and understand them within the shifting borders between local and global contexts. This chapter briefly lays out the emergence of an expanding post-9/11 surveillance apparatus in the U.S., and analyzes its impact on transgendered people. In particular, I briefly examine the "Real ID Act," a law that standardizes requirements for identification documents, establishes the collection and maintenance of new national databases used to scrutinize, and limits the movement of bodies both within and across U.S. borders. It effectively inscribes which bodies are allowed to cross borders. The Real ID Act is a U.S. federal law (passed in 2005) that requires the implementation of specific security, verification, and issuance procedures for most state documents, including driver's licenses and identification (ID) cards, in order for them to be deemed acceptable by the federal government for boarding commercially operated airline flights and entering federal buildings and nuclear power plants. These new measures have implications beyond travel and entrance into secure sites, including access to employment as well as social services such as healthcare, depending on the direction that new healthcare reform measures take. The Real ID Act has far-reaching implications for immigrants and for asylum-seekers, placing the burden of proof on those who request asylum to provide corroborating documents that substantiate claims of persecution. The Real ID Act creates new categories of suspicion, not only for immigrants and asylum seekers, but also targets transgender populations. Transgendered people become ensnared in this surveillance apparatus when gender identification on state documents and ID cards do not match a person's gender presentation, or gender designations on different documents do not match each other. Given the various groups that are affected by the Real ID Act, how might advocacy organizations that have congealed around gender non-conformity respond?

In order to evaluate this response, I compare two major websites of mainstream transgender advocacy organizations—The National Center for Transgender Equality (NCTE) and the National Transgender Advocacy Coalition (NTAC)—with two websites from organizations that advocate for gender-variant people of color—the Audre Lorde Project (ALP) and the Sylvia Rivera Law Project (SRLP)—and their response to this new surveillance. This work arises out of a cultural studies tradition that attempts to question (following Foucault) the order of things—to consider how and why the social world has become reified as natural and self-evident. Specifically, I am concerned with how gender non-conforming bodies embedded in complex economic, social and cultural relations might be changed. To answer this, I attempt to locate gender non-conformity in a contemporary history and political economy of visibility. Visibility and concealment are not permanently attached to identities, and one of the central contentions of this chapter is that, because of shifts in economic conditions, movements of global capital, as well as political and cultural ruptures, the relations of visibility in circulation around gender non-conformity have shifted significantly.

Methodology

This chapter is a critical discourse analysis of transgender advocacy websites (following Mills, 2004), that is, a politically inflected form of analysis that attempts to understand both the construction of the transgender subject within wider social structures, in particular racial and class formations. I deploy a mixed method of analysis that combines critical discourse analysis with participant observation. I draw on extensive fieldwork in urban settings as well as national transgender gatherings and conventions; *in situ* interviews conducted in Northeastern Metropolitan Areas as well as various sites in the United States from 1995–2000. This is a particularly important period that witnessed the formation of transgender advocacy institutions. The ethnographic component, while not the focus of this analysis, is nevertheless crucial for several reasons. First and foremost, the ethnographic observations ground the findings in the quotidian world of everyday experience. Second, ethnographic insight is a useful tool that helps to highlight or make visible the "assumptions and pre-suppositions" implicit in the discourse of the websites (Fairclough, 2003, p. 40). Finally, fewer ethnographies could be complete without taking into account online resources, given their role in our everyday lives (Bealieu, (2005).

Theoretical Frame

The queer of color critique, probably first put forward by Gloria Anzaldúa (1987) uses "queer" as an analytic to describe "everything that does not fit" within standard categories or a social order (p. 7).[2] It is clear that Anzaldúa thought it productive to conceptualize difference across a range of social identifications, be they racial, sexual, gender, ethnic, class or ability. Anzaldúa also introduces the idea of borders to the discussion. Thus, for her, the nation-state, the airport, customs, and so forth are spaces where those who "belong" are demarcated from those who do not. Borders police a body's ability to signify belonging: either as a citizen, but more relevant, as human rather than not, as subject rather than object. At the border, one must not only produce the right papers or documents to establish belonging, one must also enact an orthodox presentation in order to look and act as if one could, should or would belong (Robertson, 2010). This identity work becomes most crucial when one's membership in a group is questionable.

In the current global political climate, border panics are everywhere. Whether at the macro level of the U.S./Mexican border or the micro level of gender variation, the permeability and indeterminacy of borders are deployed politically to raise anxiety and construct "everything that does not fit" as a threat rather than benign variation pure and simple. Undocumented workers and gender-variant people share what Garber (1992) calls a "category crisis." Butler's (1990) insight into gender trouble links the abjection of queer men's sexuality to the supposed permeability of the queer male body and penetration. Each of these disparate identities—trans, gay, or immigrant—can seem unrelated to one another, yet each is an example of border crossing. As Lugo (2008) astutely observes, borders are not just sites of crossing, but points of surveillance and inspection. As such, the border does not exist only on the periphery but in fact moves to the center. These inspection sites, where proof of belonging is demanded, are always shifting: in a public bathroom, the hospital or the airport. Increased border surveillance, scrutiny and inspection often enjoy popular support since such sanctions are oriented toward the Other, and it is seldom recognized that these new measures can be redeployed against anyone.

The "trans" prefix itself calls up both travel and the border. Generally, the prefix can mean to travel across, to move beyond a border. Hence, Jay Prosser (1998) articulates sex reassignment as a homecoming. Yet, as Judith Halberstam (2005) has pointed out, talking about borders and homes solely in a gender variant frame can work to erase and evade the important theoretical insights and contributions around borders that have developed within postcolonial and ethnic studies, including discussions of the differential transnational mobility of capital and bodies (Shome & Hedge, 2002a). Likewise, Shioban Somerville (2005) and Chandan Reddy (1988) explain how the legal histories of sexuality and race are intrinsically connected—specifically how anti-miscegenation laws normalize race through universalizing heterosexuality; yet these histories are narrated as disconnected, sequential, and progressive. For example: people of different colors can marry: next, marriage rights should be extended to monogamous gay and lesbian couples. Thus, a queer of color critique provides the analytic frame for this chapter. The mode of analysis is intersectional in that it explores the complexities of individual and group identity formations, and unveils the ways interconnected domains of power organize and structure inequality and oppression. Borrowing from Roderick Ferguson's (2004) model, I attempt to articulate "how intersecting racial, gender, and sexual practices antagonize and/or conspire with the normative investments of nation-states and capital" (p. 4). I focus on the effects of normative demands and how they influence transgender political resistance. By normative demands, I refer to the ways that organizations appeal to mainstream or dominant values of patriotism, heteronormativity, whiteness, and middle class values. I use Pierre Bourdieu's (1984) notion of symbolic capital to understand normativity and how it works. For Bourdieu, capital has four forms. First there is the economic or the traditional way we define capital as money or property. Second, there is cultural capital. This includes education, social and cultural knowledge. The third kind of capital is social capital, or the durable network of more or less institutionalized relationships of mutual acquaintance and recognition. Fourthly, there is symbolic capital. Like normativity, it is the embodiment of cultural values, and is used to describe resources available to people on the basis of social status or recognition (Calhoun, 2002). For Bourdieu, these forms of capital can be exchanged. And, they open up questions about what normativity or symbolic capital purchases groups and what it might cost.

Thus, I attempt to work against the bifurcation often seen in critical perspectives that force scholars to choose "culture" or "economy" as the operational center of their analysis. This, Valdivia (2006) astutely observes, is a malady in the Anglo-U.S. academy but unimaginable in Latin America or European contexts. Lisa Lowe and David Lloyd (1997) also reject this facile bifurcation, insisting that: "Rather than adopting the understanding of culture as one sphere in a set of differentiated spheres and practices, we discuss 'culture' as a terrain in which politics, culture and the economic form an inseparable dynamic" (p. 1).

While critical social theory has come to settle on the salience of the notion of "difference," at the same time, fragmentation of identity has become a hallmark of "modern" globalized industrialized, nation-states (Shome & Hedge, 2002b). Within the political arena, difference is either "accentuated, negotiated, bracketed or suppressed" (Fairclough, 2003, p. 40). Fairclough argues that through the workings of ideology, "particulars come to be represented as universals [or rather] particular identities, interests, and representations come under certain conditions to be claimed as universal" (p. 40). This dovetails elegantly with the ways in which I argue that "transgender" functions in many contexts as a "pseudo generic." At once it stands for a "generic" range of non-gender-normative identities or practices yet functions on another level to articulate a specific set of racial and class interests and perhaps a fairly narrow gender-variant orthodoxy. Aizura (2006) cogently argues that the ways in which 'transitioned' gender identity is performed are inflected by nation, race and class. In a similar vein, Valentine (2007) cautions against taking transgender as a self-evident category and demonstrates that not everyone uses transgender in the same way. Valentine (2007) maintains that, "transgender, or any other category, simultaneously carr[ies], enable[s], and restrict[s] meaning. [. . .] We need to be careful about what we mean by it, [. . .] what meanings it can bring with it and what the consequences of these might be" (p. 27). Rather than accept the term, as a transparent carrier of meaning, Valentine (2007) interrogates its history and its use, or maybe more correctly, its non-use within some gender variant populations: "how and to what effect is the concept deployed and what does it do?" (p. 27).

Ethnographic Insight

The ethnographic findings illuminate the structuration within transgender populations, specifically those sites that are defined as spaces of an official "transgender movement" are predominantly white and middle class. In contrast, most of the community sites in a large metropolitan area are predominantly African American and Latino/a and working class to poor. This bifurcation between the mostly white middle class movement and the more localized urban queer of color communities is an important structural hurdle that frames the way trans-activism is performed, and how activists view their constituency, and what trans-activism does. It is easy to see these two cultures simplistically as a division between the "haves" and "have-nots," but such an understanding based and focused on economic capital is flawed. While mainstream (white) trans-activists struggled for inclusion in gay community centers, gay bars and legislation, African American and Latino/a sex and gender dissidents carved out their own social spaces, organized in houses, wherein butches (masculine females), femme queens (feminine males) and butch queens hung out, often shared living spaces and wandered the city together.[3] While white GLBT people were more segregated along identity lines, African American and Latino/as knew each other more intimately across the range of identity formations.[4] African American and Latino/a femme queens did not have to struggle for inclusion in butch queen spaces.

This is a crucial point because it articulates a rationale, a particular logic if you will, as to why gender-non-conforming people of color might be reluctant to move from describing themselves as "gay," in favor of adopting the "transgender" identification. The reluctance of gender-non-conforming people of color to adopt "transgender" as a label is not only evident in the people I interacted with but also documented in other ethnographic works (Valentine, 2007; Manalansan, 1997). The very categorical distinction between "gay" and "transgender" creates a boundary between butch queens and femme queens that neither group can afford. By adopting a transgender identity as distinct from "gay," the gender-non-conforming queers of color give up social capital—that is, their shared affiliation. While white transgender people have little affiliation with white gays and lesbians, transgender as a category is seen as merely descriptive and more easily embraced. Yet few activists articulate or take seriously a logic for queer of color non-compliance with "transgender," many working off the logic of what Hoad (2007) calls a colonial model, that gender-non-conforming people are just earlier, less-developedversions of white counterparts. As one trans activist phrased it: "They (gender-non-conforming people of color) don't use 'transgender' because they don't have the language yet. Most of the work I do is education" (field notes, 1999). It never occurred to this activist to question the utility of "transgender" for gender-non-conforming people of color. The colonial discourse of development and progress still informs the way in which queer of color is seen as backward or underdeveloped, and whiteness seen as progressive. Resisting "transgender" as a label is often understood as the result of ignorance, rather than a reasonable response to a very different social context. Colonialism has far-reaching influence (Shome & Hedge, 2002b), as Parameswaran (2002) has demonstrated, media continue to reproduce colonial hierarchies of race, gender and nation, and "new media" and transgender advocacy websites are not necessarily different. Ferguson (2004) argues that we must "challenge the idea that (non-normative) social formations represent the pathologies of modern society" and instead situate them as produced as the constitutive Other to normative formations (p. 11).

When white trans people transitioned, they often sought interaction with psychologists or psychiatrists who recommended them for hormonal therapy and eventually surgeons in order to access body modifications. When African Americans and Latino/as accessed body modification, they procured hormones through extra-legal means, and found neighborhood practitioners who injected them with silicone, non-licensed non-professionals that set up neighborhood extralegal cottage industries. They did not access these transition technologies from medical personnel or institutions culturally charged with regulating gender or the body.[5] Often, the only "professional" the two groups would have in common would be the electrolysist for hair removal. These are strong patterns that ground the queer of color analysis that I attempt in what follows.[6]

To summarize, the ways in which gender nonconformity is performed are inflected by a range of other social identifications, such as race, ethnicity, national origin, ability, and social class, to name a few. Furthermore, what is commonly thought of within transgender populations as "transition"—that is, the surgical, hormonal, socio-gestural and sartorial practices that allow someone to move from one sexed category to another,—is not a "raceless" paradigm, or for that matter, independent of social class.[7] As I demonstrate here, the way in which gender-non-conforming people of color access body modification itself is very different than their white middle class counterparts.

The Websites

In this section I briefly describe the websites I examined for this chapter.

The National Center for Transgender Equality

The National Center for Transgender Equality (NCTE) calls itself a "national social justice organization." Located in Washington, DC, "devoted to ending discrimination and violence against transgender people through education and advocacy on national issues of importance to transgender people" (NCTE). Its stated goal is "empowering transgender people and our allies to educate and influence policymakers" (NCTE). Amid stock photographs of the capital building, NCTE says it "facilitates a strong and clear voice for transgender equality in our nation's capital and around the country."

The National Transgender Advocacy Coalition

The National Transgender Advocacy Coalition (NTAC) was formed from members of GenderPAC when GPAC dropped opposition to the "LGBT" lobbying group, the Human Rights Campaign (HRC). HRC came under attack by transgender groups, when it was learned that HRC was lobbying against the inclusion of transgender specific language in the Employment Non-Discrimination Act (ENDA), a bill that would offer protection from discrimination in employment for LGBT people. HRC staff believed the bill would not pass with language that specifically included protections for gender identity and gender presentation. NTAC is a small group without an office or much in the way of a discernable infrastructure. Their stated goal is to "provide a voice for transgendered individuals [and work towards] a time when no transgendered individual will have to hide in shame. When marriage, family, career, housing are no longer a privilege but a basic inalienable right" (NTAC).

The Sylvia Rivera Law Project

The Sylvia Rivera Law Project (SRLP) is a New York-based legal advocacy organization named for a transwoman of color, who was at the Stonewall riots, which are celebrated as the birth of the gay movement. The organization "works to guarantee that all people are free to self-determine their gender identity and expression, regardless of income or race, and without facing harassment, discrimination, or violence" (SRLP). SRLP was founded by trans attorney and activist Dean Spade (on the "understanding that gender self-determination is inextricably intertwined with racial, social and economic justice" (SRLP). Thus the project's aim is "to increase the political voice and visibility of low-income people and people of color who are transgender, intersex, or gender non-conforming" (SRLP). SRLP's stated goal is "to improve access to respectful and affirming social, health, and legal services for our communities. We believe that in order to create meaningful political participation and leadership, we must have access to basic means of survival and safety from violence" (SRLP).

The Audre Lorde Project

The Audre Lorde Project (ALP) is named for the African American poet and activist of the same name. Unlike the other sites that engage with lobbying and legal recourse, the Audre Lorde Project is a "Queer of Color" community center organization based in New York City. A "Lesbian, Gay, Bisexual, Two Spirit, Trans and Gender Non Conforming People of Color center for community organizing," the center's various projects include: "mobilization, education and capacity-building, we work for community wellness and progressive social and economic justice. Committed to struggling across differences, we seek to responsibly reflect, represent and serve our various communities" (ALP).

Fellow Travelers

I use the term "fellow traveler" to point to the ways in which NTAC and NCTE focus on transgender travel when discussing the implications of the Real ID Act.

It is also used to refer to the realm of the political, harkening back to the early days of the communist movement: it described people sympathetic to the goals of Marxism who never became official party members. This articulates for me the current ambivalence surrounding identity movements, specifically having an affinity for a movement, while being troubled by the exclusions and limitations of adopting an identity. The early homophile movement in the United States was influenced by and organized like the communist movement, and "fellow traveler" also became a queer codeword. In another ironic twist, "Fellow Traveler" is also the name of a website for gay travel, which at once recalls the early history of the gay movement as well as the neoliberal co-option of that history, not for a more substantive social change, but LGBT travel is offered instead: a libratory place one can, for the right price, visit.

In response to both the Advisory and the Real ID Act, the National Transgender Advocacy Coalition argued that trans populations would be mistreated and unfairly scrutinized. NTAC suggests that trans travelers bring their court-ordered name and gender change paperwork with them, noting that "while terrorists may make fake identifications, they won't carry name change documents signed and notarized by a court" (NTAC). This response both assumes and constructs an idealized transgender subject that has transitioned and transitioned through proper medical institutions. Trans people of color in urban settings who do not access body modification through medical or psychological authorities cannot obtain legal documents. They therefore lie outside the frame of NTAC's response. The idealized transgendered subjects, fully transitioned with proper paperwork, delegitimize other gender-variant people who are unwilling or unable to access transition through medicine and psychiatry and therefore cannot obtain the official paperwork through the courts. By ignoring these other intersecting identity markers, NTAC can advise trans subjects to be visible to security personnel in order to ensure safe passage through security check points. This suggests that these measures are a reasonable trade off to protect the public from the threat of terrorism. But NTAC, in this prescription, neglects the everyday ways that a variety of identities are produced and read as "non normative" and policed at these border sites where immigrants and ethnic or racialized others are often harassed and detained in the name of safety. This prescription legitimates the policing of non-normative bodies. By eliding a larger critique of state surveillance or policing, NTAC reifies a legitimate transgender citizen at the expense of others' gender-variant formations. It ultimately supports the State and its violence against people of color, especially Arabs, South Asians and Muslims, et cetera. It also relies upon *legality* which is, of course, racialized as Puar & Rai (2002), Reddy (1988) and Somerville (2005) argue. Legality is an always already racialized discourse (Ross, 2005). The use of legality, as the marker to differentiate trans people from terrorists, supports the state's categories of citizen and foreigner. The citizen is grudgingly "given" rights by the state, the non-citizen denied them. Furthermore, NTAC does not account for the ways in which identity documents have always been about the surveillance of the other (Robertson, 2010).

Likewise, regarding immigration, NCTE notes "United States law does not explicitly prohibit transgender people from visiting or immigrating to the U.S. Transgender people should face no significant or systemic difficulties in obtaining the vast majority of visas (i.e., tourists, students, employees of a company based in the U.S., etc.)" (NCTE). Transmigration is legitimated through the subject's relation to capital, they are either moneyed enough for leisure travel, or students garnering cultural capital, or labor. As Valdivia (2008) cautions, scholars should avoid romanticizing migration and recognize migration as a difficult choice people must make when their homes have been brutalized by state violence, or made economically unviable via dramatic shifts in global capital, or made unlivable through environmental degradation or other phenomena that have disrempted them.

An implicit assumption underlying the advice to expose oneself as trans by presenting proper work is that the trans traveler would receive a positive, or at least a non-violent, response—as if this kind of vulnerability is sure to be respected by unchecked agents of state power. Yet confidence in law enforcement, airport security, and the like points toward a confidence in one's other always already protected (normative) identities—for example, a reassurance that one retains the markers of symbolic capital, like whiteness, American citizenship, male privilege, class status, and so on. This allows a transgender subject within this configuration to feel entitled to state protection and immunity from state violence.

Jasbir Puar and Amit Rai (2002) cogently articulate how legitimacy is produced by othering in "Monster, Terrorist, Fag," arguing that the demand for patriotism in response to terrorist attacks produces "docile patriots," who normalize themselves precisely through distinguishing themselves from other marginalized groups. So the quest for symbolic capital is made through the deployment of symbolic violence, wherein one proves worth or value at the expense of another's value. NCTE makes the claim that one should be able to wear whatever one wants:

> Transgender people have as much right to travel as anyone else and we have a right to express any gender we want, any way we want while *traveling (with the exception of some head and face coverings)*. However, recent heightened airport security has meant increased scrutiny, harassment, and discrimination against trans people who fly. NCTE hopes this document will help make your air travel experience smoother. ([emphasis added], NCTE, "travel)

Thus, while NCTE makes the case that airport security unfairly targets trans people, who should be able to wear anything they want excepting some head and face coverings, there is an indirect reference to Islamic practices around hijab observances (which vary by culture and region and are not monolithic across Islam (Esposito, 2003)). As Sunera Thobani (2008) remarks, the veil or burqa is the central signifier of Islam in the West, and its use works to construct the Islamic woman as "unremediably other." NCTE's statement, while it places transgender interests more widely within U.S. rights discourse—i.e., the right to travel or the ability to make sartorial choices—leaves intact the prohibitions against traditional Muslim sartorial enactment and reifies the state's prohibitions. But more importantly, the statement serves to exclude Muslims from the category of "Transgender" and makes it impossible to "think" that transgender and "Muslim" might exist in the same body. What might an Islamic transgender person (within the male-to-female spectrum) wear if not the traditional head and face coverings from their region?

In many ways, Muslims and gender non-conformists share similar fates. Unable to fit within a binary gender system, somewhere between or outside of the linguistic categories of "he" or "she," trans bodies are often reduced to a dehumanizing "it." Likewise, orientalist understandings of Muslims locate them outside of western rationalism, outside of a moral order, prone to terrorism, and therefore, non-human, in the category of "animal." Both are seen as threats to national security, the moral or natural order and so forth. In what follows, I want to more closely examine the websites of those organizations that explicitly speak to the concerns of gender non-conformity among people of color from poor and working class backgrounds.

The Re-Order of Things

The primary strategies and responses offered by transgender advocacy organizations NTAC and NCTE tend to leave increased state intrusions intact and exclude protection for all but the most narrowly constituted of trans populations. The previous section, "Fellow Travelers," a play off of early gay and communist political organizing within the United States in the 1950's, laid out what identities were interpolated within transgender, and who was allowed to travel with the movement—i.e., who benefited from the gains of activism and who was excluded. Furthermore, it is important to note that whenever the Real ID Act was invoked within these sites, it was nearly always in relation to travel. NCTE, for example, mentioned travel 93 times. A focus on citizenship and travel necessarily orients these organizations to middle-upper classes that *can* travel, whether for work or pleasure. It also elides a discussion of asylum seekers and immigrants who are essentially forbidden to travel.

In contrast, when I first looked at sites like the Sylvia Rivera Law Project (SRLP) and the Audre Lourde Project (ALP), it was difficult to find any reference to the Real ID Act. It was only by using Google advanced search, as outlined by Kimberly Lawless and P. G. Schrader (2008), that I was able to find references to the Real ID Act. The two websites for these organizations (both located in New York) place the implications of the Real ID Act within a much broader context, and de-emphasize the relationship of the new regulations to travel. Instead, "travel" was displaced by a broader discussion of the impact of the Real ID Act on a range of issues. Even mainstream topics such as "Trans Marriage Recognition" are framed by a desire to have legal recognition for transnational marriages that include transgender asylum seekers (SRLP, "immigration"). What is at stake in such determinations is much more consequential in this context than the scenario outlined in NTAC's and NCTE's discussions of travel. In the quest for presenting the transgender subject as a "good citizen," NTAC and NCTE elide discussions of asylum and immigration in connection to the Real ID Act. This results in a failure to articulate the human suffering involved in state policies like the Real ID Act. Without a discussion of the context under which transgender migration occurs, readers are left to assume this is travel for leisure. It is disappointing to lose a vacation, heartbreaking to be unable to live with a long-term partner (in the case of immigration), or deadly if one is denied citizenship and sent back to a homeland where they will be injured or killed because of their gender presentation (in the case of asylum seekers). Likewise, the Audre Lourde Project works to articulate the human cost of prohibitions and interdictions at national borders as well as gender boundaries through various programming:

> On Tuesday, June 3rd, there will be a special panel discussion following the 8:10 PM screening of the documentary [. . .] on "Immigration & Asylum." Drawing from pan-

elists of a wide range of experiences who work with immigration and asylum, this discussion will seek to explore questions regarding immigration in the film, the fears of the Real ID Act and increasing state surveillance post 9/11, the emotional impact of immigration and asylum. (ALP, "214")

The implications of identification standards are wide ranging and often, in everyday ways, they are more fundamental than travel, and the queer of color websites better articulate a wider range of social problems that a lack of access to a recognized identification card presents. As the Sylvia Rivera Law Project points out, without access to recognized identification, trans subjects could be denied access to social services: "if an ID does not meet the [federal] standards, the holder of that ID may be turned away from federal benefit providers like Medicaid and Medicare, barred from getting on airplanes, and barred from entrance into federal buildings" (SRLP, "immigration").

Neither website discusses the impact of the Real ID Act without discussing the problems it presents to immigration and asylum seekers. For example, in a general statement about the REAL ID Act, the Audre Lorde Project offers this general statement:

> We oppose the guest worker program, the Real ID Act, enforcement provisions to build more walls and give greater powers to the Department of Homeland Security, increased barriers for asylum seekers, the HIV ban and other anti-immigrant policies that continue to divide our communities. (ALP, "173")

From this statement, it is clear that the Real ID Act is not separable from immigration policies and the needs of asylum seekers.

Likewise, the Sylvia Rivera Law Project more explicitly draws the connections between the Real ID Act and immigration, placing it within an anti-immigrant discourse, as part of: "The ongoing attack on immigrant rights [. . .] and it also further clarifies the dire need for our anti-oppression work" (SRLP, "newsletter"). SRLP views the Real ID Act as part of a larger historical project within the United States to maintain normative privileged status hierarchies: "The political agenda behind recent anti-immigrant bills, specifically H.R. 4437 and the REAL ID Act, is parallel to all historical agendas that sought to oppress people who are not the 'ideal majority': white, male, straight, non-trans, and wealthy" (SRLP, "newsletter"). In stark contrast to the NTAC and NCTE organizations that expend much of their ideological labor and invest much of their political capital constructing themselves as the legitimate transgender subject in opposition to the threatening foreigner/terrorist, SLRP unflinchingly asserts: "As an organization that serves transgender, gender non-conforming, and intersex people who are low income and/or of color, SRLP stands in solidarity against the anti-immigrant agenda that helps fuel the 'War on Terror'" (SRLP, "newsletter").

The representations of gender variant people of color that circulated before 9/11 already mapped well onto the figure of the terrorist. The most widely-circulating images of gender-variant people of color were on daytime talk shows like the *Jerry Springer Show*. Springer's producers, as Gamson (1998) discovers, adopted a dominant narrative for every show, a story of the "wild and wacky relationship"—a concept stolen from Riki Lake—in an effort to "young up" their audience, and increase ratings (pp. 60–61). Trans people of color appear not only with the most regularity in the talk show format but also on this particular version. The show's master narrative demanded an unconventional relationship and routinely featured trans people as sex and gender grifters, concealing their "true gender" (i.e., their "sex") to gain the trust of a heteronormative and normative-gendered person. The trans-gender grifters reveal their transgender status—or more correctly, their sex assignment at birth—to a jeering audience and a traumatized partner. The widespread circulation of this narrative locates treachery, deception, and victimization not in the institutional practices of television, medicine. or law or in the gender-normative behaviors and relationships they enforce, but instead in individual trans people's supposed artiface. The trans-as-gender-grifter robs his or her lover of symbolic capital, by taking from the lover or calling into question their heterosexual status. This narrative plays out in the legal arena in cases dealing with murder of gender-variant individuals that often revolves around the victim's responsibility to disclose their trans status or birth-assigned sex. Such cases imply or outright claim that the individual's dishonest concealment of their "true" sex was the root cause of the violent actions taken against them. This approach is clearly demonstrated in the narratives constructed around transgender teenager Gwen Araujo's murder (and sexual relationships) in 2002 (Beauchamp, 2009; Westbrook, 2008). Legal arguments, news articles and made-for-television movies converged to situate Araujo's murder in the context of a "trans panic" defense, centralizing the shock of discovery and frequently faulting Araujo for not revealing her assigned sex (Beauchamp, 2009; Westbrook, 2008).

Post-9/11 representations of gender non-conformity among people of color that currently circulate most widely in the U.S. include *RuPaul's Drag Races* (Logo TV) as well as appearances from Willy Ninja (from the House of Ninja) on *America's Next Top Model*.[8] Many would argue that this represents a radical break in representation for gender non-conforming people of color and progress. RuPaul and Ninja, after all, are *Jerry Springer's* children, those cross-dressing street kids who made good. Rather than practicing "craft" on the unsuspecting citizenry of New York, they both seem to have found legitimate employment in the fashion industry and, as the ultimate achievement, have become celebrities.[9] A more critical look would examine these images as part of the same visual political economy of neoliberal capitalism. Neoliberal capitalism no longer simplistically stigmatizes gender non-conformity, and in fact, celebrates it and relies on it. Neoliberal transnational capitalism denotes the stage of globalized capitalism characterized by David Harvey (2010) and others as the universal extension of a differentiated mode of production that relies on flexible accumulation and mixed production to incorporate all sectors of the global economy into its logic of commodification.

One could argue that the gender ambiguity of the metrosexual, for example serves the neoliberal interests by finding a new market for grooming and cosmetics. In the context of reality television, the talents for fraud and illusion—the naturalized traits of trans people of color—are re-purposed to serve neoliberal capitalism. If RuPaul and her minions can use their skills of illusion to fashion an outfit that makes viewers' waists appear slimmer than they actually are, so much the better. Thus the trope of the trans person of color as fraudulent is not challenged, just brought into the new economy. The narrative of "trans" success naturalizes competition and elides any serious attention to social structural constraints while it locates failure in individuals who did not work hard enough or believe enough. As Wendy Brown (2006) reminds us, one of the achievements of neoliberal citizenship is to produce economic, political, and social inequalities as personal failings, thus erasing socio-economic inequalities instituted by the state itself. RuPaul and Ninja can be pointed to as success stories, when in fact they represent an isolated island of exceptionalism in a sea of unemployed and under-employed gender non-conforming people of color.[10]

The Real ID Act creates new categories of suspicion around various types of people who must demonstrate "credibility" under the new provisions of real ID. An applicant's "credibility" is scrutinized along several axes. These categories include (but are not limited to) the following: (1) demeanor, candor, or responsiveness of the applicant or witness; (2) inherent plausibility of the applicant's or witness' account; (3) consistency between the applicant's or witness' written and oral statements; (4) internal consistency of each such statement; (5) consistency of such statements with other evidence of record (including the Department of State's reports on country conditions); and (6) any inaccuracies or falsehoods in such statements regardless of whether they go to the heart of the applicant's claim. Real ID removes the "presumption of credibility" for immigrants and asylum seekers. Given the current political economy of the image, how can a gender non-conforming person of color be seen as credible?

The answer, as evidenced by RuPaul's trajectory, would seem to be that of the trope of the male-to-female transgender beauty worker: the latest RuPaul project is Logo TV's *Drag U*, which is set up as a beauty university (run by RuPaul) in which "three biological tomboys enroll at Drag U to be the first draguating class in school history. Drag Professors Raven, Jujubee and Ongina transform these manly women into drag divas" on the series premiere (LOGO TV). That these "tomboys" could not be encouraged to present whatever gender permutation they wished—as one might reasonably expect from a fellow traveler like RuPaul, on a channel marketed to LGBT viewers—in fact functions much like a gender identity clinic, policing the women's gender presentation and coaching until they compete to become the most properly feminine, which is greeted by happy heteronormative families, who are elated at their rehabilitated wives and mothers.

The trope of the male-to-female transgender beauty worker has some currency outside the U.S. Anthropologist Mark Johnson (1997) documents the cultural belief that gender non-conforming queer males in the southern Philippines are imbued with an inborn talent for feminine aesthetic work in *Beauty and Power: Transgendering and Cultural Transformation in the Southern Philippines*. His work is relevant as he observes gender non-conformity in a world of contract labor and transnational consumers, ambivalent subjects celebrated as purveyors of beauty, yet vilified as "Americanized." This hybrid identity is negotiated between indigenous discourses of gender non-conformity within the southern Philippines, and the discourses of "gay identity and liberation" from western media (Johnson, 1997).

While RuPaul is the embodiment of the hyper visible, The Audre Lorde Project and the Sylvia Rivera Law Project do not advise gender variant people to come out, to reveal themselves. If we regard racial and ethnic identity as a *mostly* visible trait, the concept of "coming out" is required when one's identity is hidden or invisible. Perhaps, the ambivalence that queer people of color have to "coming out" as a political strategy is foregrounded by the experience of already being visible. Since some racial and ethnic markers are visible, bodies so marked have always been visible, yet this has not halted racism. SRLP notes these troubling times lead "to the polarization of communities that could otherwise work in coalition" as individuals attempt to divert surveillance onto other marginalized groups (SRLP, "brochure"). The Law Project suggests that assimilation—"going stealth" or claiming status as a good transgender citizen—has become a primary tactic for escaping state surveillance, targeting or persecution.

Since many of the new social movements view various identity formations as disconnected, sequential, and progressive, and this is a really powerful discursive formation, real structures of inequality are buttressed rather than challenges. For example, NCTE, on the other hand, linked to an *Advocate* article that specifically addressed Arizona's new anti-immigrant law, and asked LGBT people to join the fight (NCTE). As one respondent said on the Advocate Website: "I disagree that we should distract ourselves with [Arizona's Immigration Law] when we have so many other important things to worry about: DOMA, DADT, GENDA, bullying in schools, et cetera" (*Advocate*, "Lambda"). There is a hierarchy of what social issues need to be addressed and an order of those deserving "rights," and GLBT is next on the list—anything else is a distraction. According to this response, and these issues, defense of marriage, don't ask, don't tell, employment discrimination, and school violence only affect GLBT people who are citizens. This is not an isolated comment, others are directly hostile: "Oh fuck illegals. I'm not crying one bit for them. They have more rights in this country than gay Americans do. I will fight them getting any more rights before I get equal rights" (*Advocate*, "Arizona").

The queer of color websites re-order conceptual models, and decenter normative ideals that both NCTE and NTAC accept as self-evident. The least of which is the category of "transgender" itself, as with the case of the Audre Lorde Project, that lists an alphabet soup of identifications "LGBTSTCNC" rather than transgender; not to exclude transgender, after all, it is one of the 'T's, but to work against its ossification. Both queer of color websites work to decenter the citizen, as the subject deserving of rights, by bringing into view the noncitizen in extended discussions of immigration and asylum seekers. In their focus on the local, both websites decenter the national and are therefore more analytically capable of grasping the global.

Conclusion

Perhaps it is an ironic twist that SRLP and ALP, both limited to addressing the local, specifically New York City, are better equipped to address the global moment in which we find ourselves. While NTAC and NCTE both focused more widely on the "national," both organizations are imbricated within the nation and citizen and hence are too provincial to address the variety of gender non-conformity—and the draconian suppression of that expression globally. Furthermore, they are implicated in an orientalist,[11] Anglo-centric discourse that is ill equipped to address the radical shifts in global movement of people, capital and data. The queer of color websites, in contrast, "re-orient" the Real ID Act in connection with anti-immigration policies and global shifts in capital, and are much more capable of taking stock of the specifically neoliberal overtones of this policy. Neoliberalism, as David Harvey (2007) reminds us, "has pervasive effects on ways of thought to the point where it has become incorporated into the common-sense way many of us interpret, live in, and understand the world" (p. 3). The re-orientation that these sites perform, following Sara Ahmed (2006), wherein "orientation" is a direction, a pointing toward another object, is to point to a larger history, rather than simply one single day—"9/11"—to point to a larger history of militarism, zenophobia and colonialism that might make, ironically, better sense of that day.

It is a worthwhile project to analyze the ways that this new surveillance apparatus affects transgendered people. In fact, I appreciate the legal advice that NCTE and NTAC offer but believe it to be best understood as a tactic rather than a strategy. Following the distinction made by de Certeau (1984) between the tactics of the weak and the strategies of the powerful, I mean to argue that the legal "tactics" offered are often only useful to the most privileged of gender non-conforming populations. While it is useful information for gender non-conforming people to be able to navigate airports, and as advice for people who already have social privileges as to how to use the social advantages they already have, this is hardly a strategy in the context of the Real ID Act and the anti-immigrant moment we find ourselves. This chapter has been centrally concerned with borders, whether national or identity borders. Borders are places where those who do not belong are separated from those that do. Much of transgender discourse relies on borders between male and female and the travel between them. Following the insight of Lugo (2008) scholars should not just look at borders as boundary crossings but as sites of inspection and scrutiny. Both the Arizona Immigration Law and the Real ID Act work together to create a permanent class of "Alien-Citizens" or "questionable citizens," who must continually provide "evidence" of belonging, be they gender non-conforming, asylum seekers, or international laborers. It is also important to make note of the ways in which the discourse of terror serves to not only regulate national borders but to also police the boundaries of the normative within the state; and the borders, and the policing keeps moving further and further within the nation. It is tempting in times of stress and terror to be seduced by the calls for legitimacy and the normative. As Ferguson (2004) cautions, the entrapment of normativity is a "technique of discipline rather than a vehicle toward liberation." (p. 65) These "regulatory regimes" exclude people from legitimacy while "inspiring conformity." (Ferguson, 2004, p. 65).

Ostensibly, people support these laws because they are always oriented toward the other, yet the aim can always be re-oriented. It is tempting to give into the fear and align oneself with the dominant. At the same time, the primary strategies and responses offered by the national transgender advocacy organizations tend to leave increased state intrusions intact and exclude protection for all but the most narrow of trans populations. Thus in the pursuit of the symbolic capital of the normative, transgender activists squander social capital and alienate other racialized groups affected by state surveillance with whom they might otherwise form coalitions. Perhaps it is time to imagine a politics of coalition.

Notes

1. By "transgendered," I mean to designate people whose gender presentation transgresses socially assigned sex and gender roles and expectations—those who are unable or unwilling to conform to sex and gender norms. Transgender is an "umbrella" term used to describe a wide range of identities and experiences including, but not limited to transsexuals, FTMs, MTFs, cross-dressers, drag kings and queens, two-spirits, genderqueers and others. There is also a debate on the use of "transgender" vs. "transgendered people," and at this moment I am most comfortable using "transgendered people," mainly to continually re-inscribe gender non-conforming people within the human. Falling between or outside of the categories of "he" or "she," too often transpeople come to be understood as a dehumanized "it."
2. Anzaldúa was probably the first to demarcate "queer" as a critical tool to productively critique normative social formations and their exclusions.
3. A butch queen in the urban queer of color vernacular is a designation for what would be recognized elsewhere as a gay man. The "butch" designation has little to do with his gender presentation, and is only intelligible in relation to the femme queen.
4. This is not to argue that there was no racial conflict, but there seemed to be much more cohesion among a range of sex and gender non-conforming identities, perhaps because race was a more salient identity category than sexuality or gender.
5. I could cite numerous examples of how butches and femme queens resisted medical care and were suspicious of medicine, unlike their white, middle class counterparts who tend-

ed to be more trusting. I'm not certain that this only relates to class positions, either. The legacy of Tuskegee and historical accounts of enforced sterilization are other possibilities that might explain the wariness of people of color in utilizing medical services.
6. There were a few exceptions. I did encounter middle class African American gender-non-conformists who did not have the same nomenclature, or "transgender career paths" as their working class and poor counterparts (and didn't identify as femme queens). And I did meet a white middle-class transsexual who sought out silicone injections from the African American practitioners. The reader should not see these categories as totalizing but rather as a general tendency.
7. This critique that "transition" is not a "raceless" paradigm is informed by Johnson & Henderson's (2005) notion that "the closet," the central metaphor of gay oppression, is not a raceless paradigm.
8. He was featured in the Jenny Livingston documentary, *Paris Is Burning* (1987).
9. Craft is a word from Ball Culture that is a synonym for grifting, or conning people out of money.
10. For a similar argument of the ideological use of the "beauty contest" in the context of India, see Parameswaran (2004).
11. I am using Sara Ahmed's (2006) concept of orientation, as a particular pointing toward objects. Orientalism is a particular way in which the west is oriented toward the east

References

Aizura, A. Z. (2006). Of borders and homes: The imaginary community of (trans)sexual citzenship. *Inter-Asia Cultural Studies, 7*(2), 289–309.

Anzaldúa, G. E. (1987). *Borderlands/La Frontera: The New Mestiza*. San Francisco, CA: Aunt Lute.

Audre Lorde Project. (n.d.) Retrieved from http://www.alp.org

Bealieu, A. (2005). Sociable hyperlinks: An ethnographic approach to connectivity. In C. Hine (Ed.), *Virtual methods: Issues in social research on the Internet* (pp. 183–198). Oxford: Berg.

Beauchamp, T. (2009). Artful concealment and strategic visibility: Transgender bodies and U.S. State Surveillance after 9/11. *Surveillance and Society, 6*(4), 356–366.

Bourdieu, P. (1984). *Distinction: A social critique of the judgement of taste*. London: Routledge.

Brown, W. (2006). American nightmare: Neoliberalism, neoconservatism, and democratization. *Political Theory, 34*(6), 690–714.

Butler, J. (1990). *Gender trouble: Feminism and the subversion of identity*. New York: Routledge.

Calhoun, C. (2002). Symbolic capital. In C. Calhoun (Ed.), *Dictionary of the Social Sciences* (pp. 474–475). New York: Oxford University Press.

Castells, M. (2000). *The rise of the network society*. Oxford: Blackwell.

Charles, D., (2010, May 6). Reader Comments [Msg 8], "Lambda Legal: Arizona Law hurts us all." *Advocate*. Message posted to http://www.advocate.com/Politics/Commentary/Lambda_Legal_Arizona_Law_Hurts_Us_All/ Retrieved November 17, 2010.

de Certeau, M. (1984). *The practice of everyday life*. Berkeley, CA: University of California Press.

Deuze, M. (2007). *Media work*. Cambridge, UK: Polity.
Esposito, J. (2003). *The Oxford Dictionary of Islam*. Oxford, UK: Oxford University Press.
Fairclough, N. (2003). *Analysing discourse: Textual analysis for social research*. New York: Routledge.
Ferguson, R. (2004). *Aberrations in black: Toward a queer of color critique*. Minneapolis, (MN): University of Minnesota Press.
Flemming, R., (2010, May 6). Reader Comments [Msg 7], "Lambda Legal: Arizona Law hurts us all." *Advocate*. Message posted to http://www.advocate.com/Politics/Commentary/Lambda_Legal_Arizona_Law_Hurts_Us_All/ Retrieved November 17, 2010.
Gamson, J. (1998). *Freaks talk back: Tabloid talk shows and sexual nonconformity*. Chicago: University of Chicago Press.
Garber, M. (1992). *Vested interests: Cross-dressing and cultural anxiety*. New York: Routledge.
Halberstam, J. (2005). *In a queer time and place: Transgender bodies, subcultural lives (sexual cultures)*. New York: New York University Press.
Harvey, D. (2007). *A brief history of neoliberalism*. Oxford, UK: Oxford University Press.
Harvey, D. (2010). *The enigma of capital and the crisis of capitalism*. Oxford: Oxford University Press.
Hoad, N. (2007). *African intimacies: Race, homosexuality, and globalization*. Minneapolis, MN: University of Minnesota Press.
Johnson, M. (1997). *Beauty and power: Transgendering and cultural transformation in the Southern Phillippines*. Oxford, UK: Berg.
Johnson, P. E., & Henderson, M. (2005). The closet as raceless paradigm. In E. P. Johnson & M. G. Henderson (Eds.), *Black queer studies: A critical anthology*. Durham, NC: Duke University Press.
Lawless, K. A. & P. G. Schrader,(2008). Where do we go now? Understanding research on navigation in complex digital environments. In J. Coiro, M. Knobel, C. Lankshear, & D. J. Leu (Eds.), *Handbook of Research on New Literacies* (pp. 267–296). Mahwah, NJ: Lawrence Erlbaum.
Lowe, L. & Lloyd, D. (1997). "Introduction." In D. Lloyd &. L. Lowe (Eds.), *The politics of culture in the shadow of capital* (pp. 1–32). Durham, NC: Duke University Press.
Lugo, A. (2008). *Fragmented lives, assembled parts*. Austin: University of Texas Press.
Manalansan, M. (1997). "In the shadows of Stonewall: Examining gay transnational politics and the diasporic dilemma." In D. Lloyd & L. Lowe (Eds.), *The politics of culture in the shadow of capital* (pp. 485–505). Durham, NC: Routledge.
Mattelart, A. (2000). *Networking the world, 1794–2000*. Minneapolis, MN: Minneapolis University Press.
Mills, S. (2004). *Discourse: A new critical idiom*. London: Routledge.
Molina Guzmán, Isabel. 2005. Gendering Latinidad Through the Elián News Discourse About Cuban Women. *Latino Studies* 3(July): 179–204.
National Center for Transgender Equality. Retrieved from http://nctequality.org
The National Transgender Advocacy Center. Retrieved from http://www.ntac
Parameswaran, R. (2002). Local culture in global media: Excavating colonial and material discourses in the *National Geographic*. *Communication Theory*, *12*(3), 287–315.
Parameswaran, R. (2004). Spectacles of gender and globalization: Mapping Miss World's media event space in the news. *Critical Studies in Media Communication*, *22*(21:2), 346–370.
Prosser, J. (1998). *Second skins: The body narratives of transsexuality*. New York: Columbia University Press.

Puar, J. K. & Rai, A. S. (2002). "Monster, terrorist, fag: The war on terrorism and the production of docile patriots." *Social Text, 72*(20:3), 117–148.

Reddy, C. (1988). *Home, houses, non-identity: Paris is burning. Burning down the house: Recycling domesticity.* Boulder, CO: Westview Press.

Robertson, C. (2010). *The passport in America: The history of a document.* Oxford: Oxford University Press.

Ross, M. B. (2005). Beyond the closet as raceless paradigm. In E. P. Johnson & M. G. Henderson (Eds.), *Black queer studies: A critical anthology.* (pp. 161–189). Durham, NC: Duke University Press.

Rubin, G. (1984/1993). Thinking sex: Notes for a radical theory of the politics of sexuality. In C.S. Vance (Ed.), *Pleasure and Danger: Exploring Female Sexuality* (pp. 267–319). New York: Routledge.

Shome, R. & Hedge, R. S. (2002a). Culture, communication, and the challenge of globalization. *Critical Studies in Mass Communication, 19*(2), 172–189.

Shome, R. & Hegde, R. S. (2002b). Postcolonial approaches to communication: Charting the terrain, engaging the intersections. *Communication Theory, 12*(3), 249–270.

Somerville, S. (2005). Queer loving. *GLQ, 11*(3), 355–370.

Spade, D. (2008). Documenting gender. *Hastings Law Journal, 59*(4), 731–842.

Sylvia Rivera Law Project. Retrieved from http://www.srlp.org

Thobani, S. (2008). Gender and empire: Veilomentaries and the war on terror." In P. A. Chakravartty (Ed.), In *Global communications: Toward a transcultural political economy* (pp. 219–262). Lanham, MD: Bowman & Littlefield.

Valdivia, A. N. (2006) Introduction. In A. N. Valdivia (Ed), *A Companion to Media Studies* (pp. 1–18). Oxford: Blackwell.

Valdivia, A. N. (2008). Introduction. *Latina/o Communication Studies Today* (pp. 3–26). New York: Peter Lang.

Valentine, D. (2007). *Imagining transgender: An ethnography of a category.* Durham, NC: Duke University.

Westbrook, L. (2008). Vulnerable subjecthood: The risks and benefits of the struggle for hate crimes legislation. *Berkeley Journal of Sociology, 52*, 3–23.

· 8 ·

Re-imagining Harvey Milk

Queering Identity Politics

ALICE LIAO

2008 appeared to be the year of Harvey Milk: in January, Gus Van Sant's acclaimed *Milk* began shooting and was released by the end of the year (Winn, 2008); the California State Assembly passed a bill to permanently mark May 22nd (Milk's birthday) as Harvey Milk Day (Buchanan, 2008); on May 22nd, a memorial in Milk's honor was placed on permanent display in San Francisco's City Hall (Buchanan, 2008); on July 15, the first day that same-sex couples could obtain their marriage licenses in California, many paid homage to Milk's memorial as a way of thanking him for giving hope to Lesbian, Gay, Bi-Sexual, Transgender, and Questioning (LGBTQ) youth (Knight et al., 2008). With Milk's symbolic capital at, perhaps, an all-time high, it was not surprising that mainstream LGBTQ organizations deployed his iconography in the fight against Proposition 8 in California: legislation that forbade the state to legally recognize same-sex marriage. It is also perhaps not surprising that Milk, the first openly gay person elected to California office, would come to serve as an LGBTQ political icon. The question, hence, is not why did Harvey Milk suddenly reemerge as a social phenomenon in 2008, a full 30 years after having been assassinated, but rather what purpose did his resurrection serve?

To answer this question of deploying Milk as a rallying and disciplinary strategy (Foucault, 1995), an understanding of how queer identities have come to be discursively constructed is necessary. Since the Stonewall riots of 1969 and against the background of the New Social Movements (NSMs), sexuality-based identities have been constructed as new ethnicities (Gamson, 1995, p. 395). That is, LGBTQ movements have come to frequently model themselves after the women's suffrage and civil rights movements, calling for group solidarity and equal rights-oriented political activities. Unfortunately, these political strategies not only subject minority groups to a higher level of state surveillance and intervention but also presume essentialist, fixed group identities that then get imposed upon heterogeneous individuals. That is, civil rights strategies may be able to help new social movements obtain certain political goals, such as with the possibility of equality through the ever-tenuous mechanism of an identity-based affirmative action, but, these identity-based political gains function as highly-compromised set-pieces that frequently give off the air of progress, while simultaneously working to re-instate dominant hegemony—in spite of their paradoxical necessity (West, 2001). Moreover, in order to obtain these tenuous identity-based political gains, compromises must be made that frequently push subaltern groups aside for the sake of the "greater good" (Gamson, 1995); as a result, the coalition forces dissipate at the base level, until subset groups attempt to mobilize individuals for other political goals.[1] Therefore, for queer activism and politics to move beyond the short-term political gains of identity-based strategies, the subversion of contemporary notions of identity politics and the foregrounding of subjectivity/identity as a fluid, performative, and constantly reconstituted thing (Butler, 1990) may be required—necessary in order to deploy a subjectivity that is inclusive, multilayered, and multivalent.

It is within this context, I argue, that Harvey Milk reemerges as an organizing symbolic force. Hence, to understand Milk's political consequences, it is pertinent to continue upon this analysis of the historical and discursive constructions of LGBTQ identities within the U.S. From there, we may be able to trace the contours of what I contend are the subsequent assumptions of a proper queer political engagement which works to tactically mainstream as well as marginalize minority groups. To conduct this analysis, first, I look into the contemporary news coverage of Milk's political legacy in the LGBTQ-oriented newspaper, the *San Francisco Sentinel*.[2] Second, I look into the popular discourses that have come to surround Milk since his assassination: focusing primarily on representations of Milk's role in repealing California Proposition 6; his assassination; subsequent movements and activists that have come to self-identify as being inspired by Milk. Third, I conclude by tracing the "shadow of

Milk" in the media coverage of California Proposition 8.[3] Throughout this chapter, I argue that the contemporary remembrance of Milk disciplines queer subjects by producing a set of calculus (Foucault, 1990, 1995) that defines acceptable, or (re)presentable, queer behavior and political activities while subsuming a diversity of queer experiences and lives. This discourse on Milk reinforces mainstream and heteronormative rules for sexual, gender, racial, and political performance and thereby forecloses the emancipatory potential of alternative, non-assimilationist, non-marriage- or family-oriented political engagement. Hence, I propose that the resources from which we can re-imagine our subjectivities lie outside the purview of (hetero)normativity, and instead lie within the lived experiences and practices that resist conformity.

Civil Rights, the Left, Legalism

In order to identify what lies outside the purview of the dominant, I now turn to the historical conflation of the legal and the political in the United States that has shaped our strategies in advancing equality and liberation. This conflation has functioned to stifle the political potentiality of queer politics and activism; hence, it is necessary that we disentangle the two often intertwined but distinct notions of the legal and the political. In the introduction to *Left Legalism/Left Critique* (2002), Wendy Brown and Janet Halley trace the ways in which leftist political projects, post-civil rights, have historically come to be transformed into an alliance with liberal legalism. Since liberalism presumes the legitimacy of the state and individual freedom and equality before the law, it often equates rights with liberty and equal rights with equality. A leftist political position, on the other hand, critiques the liberal state and law as sites of subordination and inequality that "secures the interests of capital and class dominance," and are also "located in norms regulating a great variety of social relations, including class, gender, sexuality, and race" (Brown & Halley, 2002, pp. 5–7). Therefore, leftists understand the ambivalence in identity-based movements: while identities give subordinate minority groups voices and visibility to force the state to recognize their positions, in so doing, they also simultaneously request the state's regulation of non-majority (read: non-normative) activities and experiences.

However, in pursuing justice by means of civil rights, American leftists entered the liberal legalistic project. Brown and Halley (2002) call this project "classical American legalism": American liberalists, left- and right- wing, bind the complex movement politics to demands of state sanctioned rights (pp. 7–8).

If equality is thus to be measured by equal access to rights and opportunities, the "success" of African American movements has rendered the civil rights strategy *the model* in seeking justice for other increasingly stratified "minority" groups and/or identities.[4] In short, the rights discourses provide individuals of diverse groups and/or identities a legalistic gateway to their goals through an appeal to state regulations and protections.

My point here is not to deny the gains achieved by earning such rights, but rather to critique the presumption in the rights discourses that in a modern liberal state, law and legal reform not only promise but *will* ultimately guarantee equality and emancipation. This is incorrect for, as Brown and Halley (2002) contend, rights are the vehicle through which a range of ideological or disciplinary forces attain their materialization. Therefore, there is no natural relationship between legal rights and the leftist politics for equality and justice. Moreover, the entanglement of the legal and the political flattens complex and rich discussions of culture, society, economy, politics, and their co-formations of the lived experiences of social subjects to merely legal definitions.

New Ethnicity, Identity, Queer Politics

Having attempted to disentangle the political from the legal, equality from equal rights, I now aim to create a space whereby politics can take place outside, or at least in negotiation with, the law. To do this, it is necessary to reconfigure the notion of "new ethnicity" and "identity" in service of these new political contexts. This is because, according to social movement theories, the classical formation of an ethnic or racial identity is based on an interest-group model. Nagel (1994) notes, official ethnic categories provide "incentives for ethnic group formation and mobilization by designating particular ethnic subpopulations as targets for special treatment," which ensures that "politically controlled resources are distributed along ethnic lines" since "ethnic groups mean larger voting blocs and greater influence in electoral systems" (pp. 157–158). Gamson (1995) further suggests that "ethnic categories serve [. . .] as the basis for discrimination and repression [. . .] and thus as a logical basis for resistance" (pp. 393–394). In short, ethnic categories form a collective, essentialist identity to reference a unified and "authentic" experience of a particular oppressed group.[5] An ethnic identity, thus, is not only instrumental for political representation and resistance but presumes an already existing essence which is simply made visible through these movements (Gamson, 1992).

This essentialist conception of identity has long been deconstructed by social constructionist theorists since the 1970s and 1980s. Now, identities, or, in Roderick Ferguson's (n.d.) term, "modes of difference," are understood as products of social construction that can then be constantly contested and struggled over. Thus, understood within the history of social movements, this essentialist identity model persists in the discourses of boundary-making (the inclusion and exclusion logic of a community), rights-seeking (that equal access and opportunity can be obtained through assimilation), and representation politics (that power comes from positive *and* authentic images). Paradoxically, it is this essentialist model that enables deconstructionist movements; this is the transformative power that lies *within* the existing constraints and *through* the recognition of differences (Derrida, 1982) in the law, the state, class, gender, race, and other categories of inequality.

Then, what is "identity" in our contemporary culture, society, and politics? Stuart Hall (1989; 1996) and Du Gay (Hall & Du Gay, 1996) note that identity is a signifier for a discursive process of identification that is never complete. The fantasmatic unity of the term "identity" requires both a narrativization of the self and a constitutive outside that these narratives exclude. Therefore, the fictional nature of these processes not only interpellates the subject into its position through discursive practices but also (re)invents itself through articulation and re-articulation by using the sources of language, history, and culture. In this sense, identity functions as both the subject (through the process of subjection) and the object (through the process of subjectification) within a discourse; identity sutures the subject and discursive practices.

It is an impossible space that queer politics inhabits: queer politics must stand in stratifying and ramifying positions within, beyond, beneath, and in-between the normative discourses of identity politics and within the history of social movements in order to tease out the dissents and subvert the discursive formation of the dominant. These dissenting and subversive voices are the potential alternative sources for re-imagining identity. This positionality, in turn, is where queer subjects can coalesce; it sutures queer subjects into queer discourses. In the case study that follows, I trace an alternative narrative of Harvey Milk to enrich the repertoire of queer political imagination, because, as Hall (1989) notes, the presence of alternative stories helps to illuminate the gaps in dominant discourses.

"Harvey Milk": The Symbolic Engine

In this section, I aim to trace the lesser known stories of Harvey Milk by analyzing the news coverage of his political activities in the LGBTQ-oriented newspaper, the *San Francisco Sentinel*. I narrow my search by exploring the coverage from 1973, when Milk began running for the supervisorial office, to 1984, when Dan White (Milk's killer) was paroled. I chose the *San Francisco Sentinel* because, at the time of Milk's election, the *Sentinel* was the prominent newspaper for gay men and lesbians in the city of San Francisco. In addition, I delimit my examination primarily to reportage pertaining to Harvey Milk, not George Moscone or Dan White. I also deliberately do not choose only campaign-centered or rights-oriented coverage but rather focus on coverage of the more minute tactics that may provide the resources from which to re-imagine Milk. In particular, I am interested in looking into Milk's strategies of economic and political alliances for gay visibility and influence.

To begin, it is necessary to place Milk's views on economic issues within the context of his period's discourses on the economic power of the gay community. At this particular moment in San Francisco politics, the gay community was beginning to be recognized as a viable economic force; this is because, since gay people were believed to have a relatively high expendable income, they were deemed able to "help support restaurants, recreation, gardens, theaters, and music" (Gold, 1977, Nov. 6). As a result, Mayor Moscone openly added the gay community to the coalition of minorities necessary to run the city of San Francisco (Gold, 1977, Nov. 6). Moscone also reckoned that the problem for gay people was not economics (e.g., jobs) but rather harassment; he concluded, "[gay people] do respect property and property rights [. . . .] They're in business, as corporate managers, in creating jobs for others" (Gold, 1977, Nov. 6). As a contributing writer for the *San Francisco Sentinel* in 1974, Milk seems to have shared the same sentiment of this newly discovered gay economic power:

> There is a tremendous amount of economic power and strength in the San Francisco gay community. They will encompass not only retail business, restaurants, and bars, but also doctors, lawyers, realtor [. . . .] It will create a model that will be copied in other cities and other groups and will create a power that will be heard. It will have a positive economic force for all. (Milk, 1974, Feb. 28)

With this article and his later introduction of comprehensive gay rights legislation against the discrimination towards homosexuals in employment, Milk appeared to think that the only problem gay people had in employment was the experience of discrimination; and, that the high unemployment rate in the city at the time, as he wrote on February 1, 1974, had no effect on the gay community. As with Mayor Moscone's remark, Milk did not seem to think that poverty was a problem for the gay community as it was for the black community.

Milk believed his economic model would revitalize the economy on all three levels of governance (district, city, and national); in fact, however, it provokes a number of questions. First, the "upgraded," or gentrified, neighborhoods of the gay community had forced the local poor people to move elsewhere. In response, Moscone replied, "but you don't avoid cancer cures because it causes unemployment among X-ray technicians" (Gold, 1977, Nov. 6). Second, even if it were true that the gay community had not suffered from the economic oppression as had the black community, gays were in the minority of the Castro area; in fact, the majority of the population consisted of the poor, ethnic minorities, and the elderly (Davis, 1979, Jan. 12). Third, as reported in the *LA Times* on November 28, 1978, the Castro area became so expensive that even Milk himself was forced to move to upper Market Street (Zacchino, 1978, Nov. 28). It seems that plain oversight is an insufficient explanation as to why Milk did not take on poverty as a gay issue, or rather as a human issue, as well. An article on Milk's inauguration in the *San Francisco Sentinel* (1978, Jan. 12) reported that he discussed the "ways that San Francisco could create a more favorable climate for business in order to resurrect the economic health of this city, as well as across the nation." Hence, it is clear that, while the economy was a constant issue on his mind, Milk lacked specific economic solutions for all residents.

Politically—in the broader sense of both legalistic rights and representational governance—Milk was represented as apt to mobilize collective action within the gay community and build coalitions with minority groups. When the *Sentinel* first began, Milk served as a columnist representing the voice from the left within the gay community. From 1974 to the middle of 1977, there had been little coverage of Milk's campaigns, and the coverage that Mayor Moscone received consisted primarily of dissenting voices. As such, Milk's alliance with Moscone did little in helping him (Milk) win popularity amongst the gay community or the readership of the *Sentinel*.[6] On Milk's representation of Rev. Broshears as "a friend of the gay community" (Pickets Exorcize, 1974, Feb. 28)—even though the reverend backed the anti-gay politician Hayakaway—the *Sentinel* editorial wrote:

> Just because [Milk] is an upfront homosexual and has run for political office does NOT qualify him as a political expert [. . . .] Harvey Milk has lost all credibility with his insane endorsement of Rev. B[roshears] and should also retire from politics. (Editorial, 1976, Nov. 4)

On September 8, 1977, in an article criticizing Moscone's appointment of a Chief Administrative Officer who refused to provide any funding for gay cultural events, Paul Hardman (1977) wrote:

> The gay community must put its act together and get behind those [candidates] with a good track record in dealing with gay rights. There is always the problem dealing with unqualified gays who choose to run, or publicity seekers who merely crowded the ballot. They simply must be ignored.

With its vague tone, it is unclear whether Milk or his rival in district 5, Rick Stokes, was the unqualified gay candidate that should be ignored, but Milk clearly had not yet been received favorably by the gay community.

The fact that the *Sentinel* did not endorse Milk until October 6, 1977, after a mainstream newspaper, the *San Francisco Chronicle*, had already endorsed him, implies more of a bandwagon effect on the part of *Sentinel*. The endorsement read: "Of all the gay politicians seeking to represent District 5, we believe Harvey is more in contact with the gay movement and has better resources to bridge his gay and straight constituency" (*Sentinel* Endorses, 1977, Oct. 6). Milk was also noted for his ability to calm angry crowds after the anti-gay Orange Tuesday election in Florida (*Sentinel* Endorses, 1977, Oct. 6). In another endorsement of Milk, on November 3, 1977, the *Sentinel* wrote: "In many respects Harvey has been a pioneer, presenting himself to the population at large as a viable upfront gay candidate [. . . .] He's the first to be endorsed by a major newspaper, the *San Francisco Chronicle*" (*Sentinel* Endorses, 1977, Nov. 3). Here, the *Sentinel* seemed proud of being recognized by the mainstream. After Milk's election to the Board of Supervisors, the *Sentinel* reported:

> Harvey Milk has emerged from the recent election as the undoubted and unchallengeable leader of the gay movement in San Francisco. He not only represents gay citizens, and the fair minded people in the fifth district, he is the symbolic leader of gays everywhere. (Milk Sworn, 1978, Jan. 12)

In concordance, Milk's victory, as an upfront gay candidate, was construed as a great victory for the San Francisco Gay Democratic Club, which had these objectives: "gay rights and gay civil liberties and a respect for the human dignity of all people" (Hardman, 1978, Jan. 12. All of these examples illustrate that during the course of its coverage on Milk, the *Sentinel* had gradually consolidated its affirmative relationship to Milk, particularly with his central role as a leader out to defeat Proposition 6.

On December 1, 1978, just days after Milk's death, the *Sentinel* published a special issue with a full-page column and multiple short columns devoted to his legacy (Morris, 1978, Dec. 1; Mariana, 1978, Dec. 1). The newspaper wrote: since Milk's election, "the national media [has] latched on[to] the new gay phenomenon in San Francisco"; "Milk's become synonymous with the issue of gay rights"; Milk, "the gay leader, came to the forefront this year as a leading opponent of the oppressive Proposition 6"; and, that "Harvey Milk is survived by his brother, Robert, and gay men and women everywhere" (Smith, 1978, Dec. 1). Later, on December 29, 1978, the newspaper wrote, "political life in the gay community was dominated, though far from controlled, by the presence of one man: Harvey Milk, the first openly gay person elected to public office in the city" (1978—The Year, 1978, Dec. 29). While it is to be expected that critical language would be absent from the coverage of Milk's death, when placed within the longer history of coverage by the *Sentinel*, these eulogies point to the ways in which Milk's legacy has been reimagined—from the early days of distancing to the later days of championing.

Milk, Gay Liberation, and New Social Movements

Having discussed the coverage of Milk within the *San Francisco Sentinel*, it now may be instructive to locate the reimagining and recuperation of his legacy within the changing relationships of national leftist politics and the gay movement more broadly. As noted before, Brown and Halley (2002) analyze the gradual shift of leftist politics from radical critique to rights-oriented legalism in the 1970s and 1980s. Since then, the dominant discourses of leftist politics and the so-called new social movement have been framed, in terms of the gay movement, for example, as "gay rights, pro or con?" (Warner, 2002). Politicians have come to be expected to take a stance on either side of the dichotomy. This narrow framework thereby reduces complex social issues to a simplistic binarism. As, Steven Seidman (1993) notes, gay identity politics often "move back and forth between single-interest-group politics and a view of coalition politics as the sum of separate identity communities, each locked into its own sexual, gender, class, or racial politic" (Seidman, 1993, p. 105). This is a product of the larger phenomenon of the left turning towards legalism in the mid-1970s, which resulted in it becoming socially, ideologically, and politically decentered, and hence composed of "a plurality of movements, each focused on its own particular project of building an autonomous community, evolving its own language of social analysis, and forging an oppositional politic" (Seidman, 1993, p. 107).

Yet this ethnic/essentialist model has been challenged since its crystallization by "the struggles of individuals and groups who have been marginalized within these movements" (Seidman, 1993, p. 110). However, this dissent has been met with ridicule and scorn, thereby further marginalizing those subaltern voices. As with the other "natural" ethnic group movements, by the mid-1970s, the gay liberation movement came to an end: "the dominant agenda of the male-dominated gay culture became community-building and winning civil rights" and "gay men represented themselves as an ethnic group oriented toward assimilation (Seidman, 1993, p. 117)." It is within this context that we can conceive of alternative perceptions of Milk's role in the discursive gay movement.

New social movements including gay liberation are products of, or at least heavily influenced by, leftist politics (Seidman, 1993, p. 106). For instance, the *San Francisco Sentinel* was founded as a left-prone newspaper with only one column representing right-wing views in each issue. Harvey Milk also self-identified as a left-winger, and ran for office as an independent against partisan political party machines. This led the *Sentinel*, during the district electoral campaign of 1977, to denounce the Democratic Central Committee's involvement in the supposedly non-partisan elections on February 24 (Marina, 1977, Feb. 24). The *Sentinel* subsequently endorsed Milk on the criteria of his political and financial independence on October 6 (*Sentinel* Endorses, 1977, Oct. 6), and ultimately praised his election as a victory over "the Burton Machine" on November 17 (Milk Wins, 1977, Nov. 17). However, after Milk's inauguration, the paper would later call for solidarity among the gay community in order to secure gay political power (Shectman & Smith, 1978, Nov. 8). Tellingly, after the defeat of Proposition 6, the *Sentinel* celebrated it as a victory for the gay community rather than for civil or human rights (Shectman & Smith, 1978, Nov. 8; Comments, 1978, Dec, 1).

After Harvey Milk's death, news reportage, from both the left and the right, utilized his recently crystallized image as patron saint of the gay left to discipline Harry Britt, the appointed successor to Milk (Smith, 1979, Jan. 12). From the left, for example, Jack Davis (1979) criticized Britt as a fraud who "didn't feel bound by those agreements because he has only done it [setting up a process through which the people can articulate their needs] to make sure that Harvey's work was carried on" (Jan. 12). Davis continued "that [this] kind of unprincipled action was not the Harvey Milk I know." In effect, the columnist reinvested the "legacy of Harvey Milk" with certain uncompromising principles. On the contrary, however, prior evidence may have suggested otherwise.

One example, from a letter to the *Sentinel* on October 6, 1977, called Milk an opportunist who was "independent only when he has something to gain by being so. He can be far from being independent when it is otherwise to his advantage" (Kunig, 1977, Oct. 6.[7] In this sense, Milk does not seem to oppose undertaking strategic alliances and partaking in disingenuous behavior if it benefited what he considered to be "the big picture"—whatever that might have been.

From the right, articles appeared that sought to imbricate the coalition of the gay movement with the Democratic Party. The conservative columnist for the *Sentinel* wrote that since Harry Britt "will not be held out as a leader of the city's gay community," he would "have to move from his radical left base to a more moderate base in the tradition of the Democratic Party" (Morris, 1979, Jan. 12). On March 9, 1979, the Harvey Milk Gay Democratic Club (previously the San Francisco Gay Democratic Club), which was originally founded as a progressive alternative to the more moderate Alice B. Toklas Gay Democratic Club under the Democratic Party, endorsed Harry Britt only after the then-acting Democrat Mayor Feinstein had already appointed him. This shows that the Club consented to play the game of the machine, which in effect is reinvested in the legacy of Harvey Milk. This mainstream-Democrat-assimilating legacy became even more evident in 1984. On July 20, the annual dinners of both the Harvey Milk Club and the Alice B. Toklas Club attracted hundreds of "smart politicians." Given Alice B. Toklas' close association with the Democratic Party and this column's (Morris, 1979) embrace of an active member of the Harvey Milk Club, Democrat Harry Britt, both clubs had become in line with the agendas of the Democratic Party and were no longer independent.

The suturing of the LGBTQ community with that of the Democratic Party was symbolically completed when, on November 21, the *Sentinel* ran an article calling the "Rainbow Coalition" in California "the new patchwork politics of the Democratic Party" (Weizl, 1984, Nov. 21).[8] The *Sentinel*'s unproblematic acceptance of subsuming gays and lesbians to "Democratic" interests testifies to the need for self-regulation if the LGBTQ community is to operate within the institutionalized political parties of the state. Moreover, as reported in the *San Francisco Chronicle* on October 9, 2008, the Harvey Milk Lesbian Gay Transgender Democratic Club recently retained its endorsement for House Speaker Nancy Pelosi and rejected the anti-war activist, Cindy Sheehan (an independent candidate), even though, as the chair of the club's cannabis caucus Shona Gochenaur acknowledged, "this [anti-Pelosi vote] is what Harvey Milk would have done" (Wildermuth, 2008, Oct. 9). This progression of the new social movements, particularly the gay liberation movement, from a critical leftist stance to a mainstream, political party-alliance has had a significant impact on shaping the discourses of liberation and justice in the framework of a legalistic, rights-oriented rhetoric. And this framework has been reenacted and revitalized with the resurgence of the legacy of Harvey Milk through the release of the film, *Milk* (2008), the prominent LGBTQ issue of Proposition 8, and President Obama's stance of either pro- or anti-gay marriage.

If the power that oppresses, operating through the legalistic institution of the Democratic Party, has now been intertwined with gay rights, symbolized through the legacy of Milk, and, if gay rights to marriage, or gay rights in the form of legislation in general, have dominated the discourses and delimited our imagination of achieving liberation, where can we find the disruptive and productive power that can potentially re-articulate our imaginings of Harvey Milk and thereby reconstruct what it means to be a member of the queer community?

Milk, Obama, Proposition 8

I now turn to the contemporary news coverage of Harvey Milk, *Milk* (2008), Proposition 8, Obama's stance on gay marriage, and their inter-relations, in order to identify the dominant discourses surrounding these issues; to do this, I examine issues of the *San Francisco Chronicle*, the *LA Times*, and the *New York Times* from January 2008 to March 2009. As it turns out, not only was 1978 a year of Harvey Milk, so was 2008. In January 2008, Gus Van Sant's feature film *Milk* began shooting on-location in the Castro area. On February 22nd, the California State Assembly sought to permanently mark Milk's birthday (May 22nd) as Harvey Milk Day. On May 22nd, the Harvey Milk City Hall Memorial Committee unveiled Milk's bust at San Francisco City Hall. On July 15, many marked the first day that same-sex couples were eligible to receive marriage licenses in California by paying homage to Milk's memorial. Furthermore, Milk's iconography was deployed by mainstream LGBTQ organizations in the fight against California Proposition 8.

Indeed, news reports frequently emphasized the eerie similarities between Milk's fight against Proposition 6 in 1984 and the 2008, and ongoing, fight against Proposition 8. For instance, the optimistic tone of the *LA Times* suggested that Milk, as an icon reinvested with the current relevance of Proposition 8 and grassroots political campaigns among youth, gave hope to outraged California voters, even after the passage of Proposition 8, to keep on fighting

(Abramowitz, 2008, Nov. 21; LATWP News Service, 2008, Nov. 24).[9] Moreover, because ballot measures that discriminated against same-sex couples were approved in the states of Arkansas, Arizona, and Florida, as well as California, Proposition 8 went on to become a national phenomenon. On December 10th, The *New York Times* reported that "Proposition 8 may prove to be something of a perfect storm" that mobilizes a new generation of young gay people; they then proceeded to call this new wave "Stonewall 2.0" (McKinley, 2008, Dec. 10; Yes, Stonewall 2.0, 2008, Dec. 12), in which young gay activists use not only new technologies, such as Twitter and Facebook, for grassroots movements but also the old-school, more confrontational methods, like sit-ins and sickouts. In this sense, power appears to operate in two ways. On the one hand, an oppressive power works through the electoral democratic system that enables the majority to vote for discrimination against a minority group. On the other hand, even though the 2008 film *Milk* distills his life through the lens of the dominant paradigm—the glorification of representative office, the privileging of legalistic action as a means of governance, and the pragmatics of assimilationist politics—it nevertheless instilled disruptive tendencies within party-affiliated political traditions in the forms of grassroots movements, especially among young gay advocates. In this regard, Milk does seem to bring hope for a better future.

At the same time, the rights-seeking model of ethnic group identity politics also reigned prominent in the discourses surrounding Proposition 8. This was partly due to the fact that November 4, 2008, was not just a historically significant day due to the passage of Proposition 8, but also because it marked the election of Barack Obama. As the first African American president in the history of the United States, President Obama's election was hyped as signifying the end of an ugly racist chapter in U.S. history and the beginning of a post-racial American society. Some LGBTQ voters, because of their liberal tendency, voted in support of Obama in this presidential election and expressed disappointment to find that the majority of black and Latino voters who voted for Obama also voted for Proposition 8.[10] Letters from dissenting LGBTQ voters swarmed the *New York Times*:

> Even as we celebrate Barack Obama's historic election, it should be noted that according to exit polls in California, 70 percent of African American voters supported the gay-marriage ban. (Drescher, 2008, Nov. 7).
>
> On Election Day, we as a nation were able to exclaim a phrase uttered by the late, great Tim Russert: 'What a country!' The election of our nation's first African-American president was indeed historic. Yet while we helped close the book on one

ugly chapter of our nation's history, we left unfinished another. To see three states pass bans on gay marriage and one state bar gay people from becoming adoptive and foster parent was disheartening. (Hopkins, 2008, Nov. 7).

As Mr. Obama's victory showed, the path to change is arduous. Even as the nation shattered one barrier of intolerance, we were disappointed that voters in four states chose to reinforce another [. . .] that discriminates against couples of the same sex. (Editorial Desk, 2008, Nov. 6.)[11]

These sentiments resonated with the mainstreaming of leftist politics in the 1970s and 1980s; in essence, the desire for minority state representatives and for coalition building strategies amongst different interest-groups. The dissenting voices among LGBTQ voters grew even louder after President Obama chose Rev. Rick Warren, an outspoken opponent of abortion and same-sex marriage, to deliver the invocation at his inauguration. Tellingly, a letter to the *LA Times* commented that since Obama was now the president, *he swore allegiance to the U.S. Constitution, so his policies have to comply with the law*, not the Bible (LATWP News Service, 2008, Jan. 20); the rights-seeking model of ethnic group identity politics had come to saturate the political language of the LGBTQ community.

In the above letters, disappointed liberal LGBTQ voters seemed to suggest: first, that President Obama's election marked the end of racism; and second, that since LGBTQ voters *helped* to elect an African American to office, black voters should support gay rights in return; and third, since Obama was elected, he should represent the law and thereby the state. These responses illuminate, and ironically correspond with, the very shortcomings that exist within the three contemporary approaches to the goals of liberation and justice: representational democracy, rights-oriented coalition politics, and the legalistic state. First, representation in office does not end discrimination. To suggest that sexism would have no longer existed had Hillary Clinton been elected president is delusional. Similarly, elections of LGBTQ candidates to office have not automatically translated to the end of the homophobic sentiment in our society either. Second, rights-oriented coalition politics should not be the goal in and of itself. For example, even if Proposition 8 had been defeated and LGBTQ individuals were granted legal access to marriage, as a legal institution it would still remain a privileged space for those capable of subjecting themselves to state regulations. This would mean, subsequently, that to access the benefits of marriage—amicable taxation, visitation rights, social security privileges, and so on—one must grant the state the authority to intervene upon one's personal and intimate life; and those unwilling or unable—due to being single, living in a non-traditional-family lifestyle, et cetera—would be denied those same benefits. As such, coalition politics for rights that exclude and discriminate is not a promising path to ultimate emancipation.

As a final point, the above two propositions, representational democracy and rights-oriented coalition politics, are built upon the faulty foundation of the third, a legalistic state: representational democracy and rights-oriented coalition politics operate under the assumption that the law in and of itself is sacrosanct—even though the law yields uneven power and should not be taken in such light. If we learn one thing from the lightened verdict Dan White received for the killing of Moscone and Milk—as a result of his infamous "Twinkie Defense," which subsequently provoked the White Night Riots (Cole, 1979, Jun. 2)—the flaws in the criminal justice system are evident and exist to maintain the status quo. In the case of Proposition 8, once the popular vote was made to amend the constitution to ban same-sex marriage, even though the California Attorney General has openly opposed it as unconstitutional, the duty of Chief Justice Ron George is to uphold the discriminatory constitution, no matter how unjust.

Conclusion: Re-imagining Harvey Milk, Queering Identity Politics

In this chapter, I have traced the discourse on Harvey Milk in order to reinvest his legacy with a viable disruptive power that can potentially create a space whereby queer subjectivities and life politics can thrive. First, I have shown that subjectivities are fluid, porous, and constantly re-constituted through the course of life experiences. Such rich life experiences cannot be reduced to fixed, essentialist identity categories. Identity politics, which emerged from the civil rights movements in the 1950s and the new social movements of the 1970s and 1980s, has allowed for the creation of additional minority groups based on the ethnic formation model. At the same time, these identity politics have also presumed a pre-existent and coherent group identity and have maintained that this group solidarity is a necessary prerequisite for the pursuit of equality and legal rights. While suturing individual subjectivities within contemporary social contexts and practices, these "identities" in effect naturalize the discursive and strategic social formations of such categories; and hence, they exercise disciplinary power in defining the membership criteria of a given identity group and excluding those they deem incorrigible.

Second, I have argued that while the strategies of identity politics are effective in seeking special rights (in a narrow legalistic sense), equality and emancipation cannot be achieved through this mechanism. To operate within the realm of legalism, the identity politics of contemporary social movements must transform lived experiences and differences into a discourse of rights-seeking for multiple minority groups. Further, operating within the rhetoric of civil rights, contemporary identity politics flattens the complexity of the political into the legal. By mistakenly equating equality with equal rights, rights-oriented discourses delimit conflicting and contradictory, but ultimately productive and fertile, discussions to the framework of state-sanctioned legal definitions. Reducing the political to the legal through the vehicle of rights, the state consequently exercises power in the form of a law that simultaneously empowers/produces and discriminates/oppresses its subjects.

Third, if the law does not guarantee equality and emancipation, and if life politics is ultimately irreducible to legalism, then sites of conflict, marginality, and invisibility become the critical space whereby alternatives to dominant narratives and access to potentially disruptive power can be located. Investing and investigating on the edge—or from multiple, shifting and marginal positions—of the mainstream and the norms not only reinscribe the constitutiveness of the discursively constructed "outsides" (Derrida, 1982) but also change the dichotomous and hierarchical relationships of the center and the margin, of inclusion and exclusion, and of the normal and the deviant. And, it is in this place-less space of critical stances that queer politics and subjects can inhabit and coalesce. In other words, in order to liberate ourselves from an oppressive normativity, queer activistism must commit itself to a critical and reflexive engagement with incidents of injustice; injustice not based on a shared identity but on a common critique.

This analysis of the discourse of Harvey Milk provides ways in which we can better understand the current controversy of Proposition 8 and the other rights-seeking projects for specific minority groups. I have situated the political figure of Harvey Milk within the context of: a discursively essentialized gay identity; the assimilationist politics of the gay community; the legalistic rights-oriented politics of minority groups; the ongoing process of the mainstreaming of the left; the affiliation of leftist activism with that of the Democratic Party; and, of a coalition-based representative democracy. In this context, the legacy of Milk has often been reinvested with purposes that go along with those trends. His prominent "homosexuality" is thus politicized as a "trait" of his minority status and as a license for his representativeness of gay people; and, in effect, homosexuality becomes desexualized. In the case of Proposition 8, LGBTQ activists and the media alike have deployed the symbol of Milk as the hero who, legendarily, helped to defeat Proposition 6 and can therefore serve as an exemplary model and an inspirational figure in the fight for gay rights legislation. This legacy of Milk consequently entails not only continually fighting for gay rights, but also maintaining an alliance with the Democratic Party; an ongoing dedication to assimilation; and the building of political coalitions amongst presumably differently categorized groups. As such, in the wake of the passage of Proposition 8, Milk's legacy in the dominant discourse provides for politically strategic maneuvers and works to mobilize the younger generation. Milk has become the symbol for a contemporary gay rights movement that will fight for equality by any means necessary.

At the same time, however, his legacy also robs us of our critical stance and hinders us from finding alternative ways to fight for equality. We must keep in mind that equality does not mean "gay marriage, pro or con?" Instead, we need look into the problematics hidden from the dominant discourses of Proposition 8. For example, in "Beyond Gay Marriage," Michael Warner (2002) argues that because of the discriminatory nature of the institution of marriage, the pursuit of the right to same-sex marriage not only has dominated "the political imagination of the national gay movement" (p. 261) and thus placed the concept of "success" for LGBTQ political activism under the jurisdiction of the courts, it has also further impeded queer politics from resisting the state regulation of sexuality. With these unforeseen consequences:

> If the campaign for marriage requires such a massive repudiation of queer culture's best insights on intimate relations, sex, and the politics of stigma, then the campaign is doing more harm than marriage could ever be worth. (Warner, 2002, p. 266)

Implicitly, I infer, Warner's critique is that by employing the rhetoric of equality, civil rights, and subsequently legal benefits, same-sex marriage discourse: forecloses the legitimacy of other ways of intimate relationships; ignores the structural and discursive tactics in the law, economy, and culture that normalize and thus construct marriage as "desirable," and, more importantly, reduces "the world-making activity of queer life" to that which is understood "from the false vantage point of 'society'" (Warner, 2002, p. 288). It has been my argument that only by continuously critiquing and problematizing the center—even in cases, such as that of Harvey Milk, in which LGBTQ subjects become the center—can we exercise the disruptive and productive power that can potentially lead to real changes for equality and emancipation.

Notes

1. For example, some lesbians, especially lesbians of color, broke away from the white, male-centered Gay Liberation Front, and from the straight, white feminist movements due to conflict of interests; these lesbians of color then proceeded to establish lesbian-centered organizations, movements, and theories.
2. For the purposes of this chapter, I do not intend to reiterate the dominant discourse on Harvey Milk. For more information, please reference the documentary, *The Times of Harvey Milk* (Epstein, 1984) and *Milk* (Van Sant, 2008).
3. I borrow the term "shadow" from Martin Manalansan's article, "In the Shadow of Stonewall: Examining Gay Transnational Politics and the Diasporic Dilemma." *GLQ*, 2(4), No. 4
4. Feminists have advocated for the right to equal work for equal pay and the right against sexual harassment and pornography (Brown & Halley, 2002); lesbians and gay men advocate the right to military service and adoption, and the right to same-sex marriage; bisexual and transgender (BT) groups demand the right to their membership within established gay/lesbian and male/female identities, and the right against BT-phobic violence (Valentine, 2007); newly constructed identities based on various differently abled/disabled individuals seek the right to particularized accommodations in education and sports and the right against ridicule out of ignorance (Brown & Halley, 2002); consumers demand the right to satisfaction of products or services of their purchase and the right against customer experience otherwise; property owners demand the right to proper and the right against vandalism; etc.
5. The early feminist movement of "women-identified women" is an example of such an identity formation that presumes a common experience among all women (Brown & Halley, 2002; Seidman, 1993). Gays and lesbians were similarly assumed to share a fixed, natural identity based on their same-sex desire (Brown & Halley, 2002; Seidman, 1993).
6. In an editorial comment on November 4, 1976, the editor wrote that even though Moscone received many gay votes, when he was elected, "every gay district has had the worst Halloween violence in our history," and that violence showed Moscone's "inept lack of leadership of the city." (Editorial, 1976, Nov. 4).
7. Another example was in an article from the *San Francisco Chronicle* on November 7, 2008. Michael Wong recalled an incident in which Milk, the newly elected supervisor declared his intention to endorse Wong's political nemesis, an old-school leader of the Chinatown machine. Wong felt betrayed while Milk told him that "you gotta look at the big picture, Michael." Another article, "Death of Dreams," in the *Advocate* on November 25, 2003, reported that in the time when coalition politics were strong, Harvey Milk supported and gained support from Rev. Jim Jones and People's Temple despite Milk's ambivalent feeling about them.
8. It continued, "In an area where gay interests are hammered into a broader agenda of progressive strategy, success for gays has relied heavily on effective and charismatic politicizing by Democratic Party insiders working more as Democrats than as gays and lesbians."
9. The *LA Times* also suggested that Milk reflected the grassroots flavor of "Obama-mania" (Abramowitz, 2008, Nov. 21). The *LA Times* also stated that the film *Milk* "capitalizes on

the current U.S. political mood and its call for change, especially among younger people who were galvanized by the recent presidential election" (LATWP News Service, 2008, Nov. 24).
10. Moreover, an article in *New York Times* stated that Obama had spoken out against Proposition 8 as a legal rights issue but maintained his opposition to same-sex marriage for religious reasons (Healey, 2008, Nov 1).
11. For more examples that demonstrate similar sentiments, reference "When Your Beliefs" (2008, Dec. 13) and "A Setback" (2008, Nov. 7).

References

1978—The Year. (1978, December 29). *San Francisco Sentinel*, p. 2.
A setback for same-sex marriage. (2008, November 7). *New York Times*, p. 34.
Abramowitz, R. (2008, November 21). After delay, 'milk' may be right on time. *Los Angeles Times*. Retrieved from http://infoweb.newsbank.com.proxy2.library.uiuc.edu/iwsearch/we/InfoWeb?p_product=AWNB&p_theme=aggregated5&p_action=doc&p_docid=1249CBDEEDB27898&p_docnum=1&p_queryname=210.
Brown, W., & Halley, J. (2002). *Left legalism/left critique*. Durham, NC; London: Duke University Press.
Buchanan, W. (2008, May 22). Milk's spirit felt as bust finds a home. *San Francisco Chronicle*, p. B1.
Butler, J. (1990). *Gender trouble: Feminism and the subversion of identity*. New York: Routledge.
Cole, R. (1979, June 2). Explosion of violence after the stone verdict. *Los Angeles Times*, p. B4.
Comments. (1978, December 1). *San Francisco Sentinel*, p. 6.
Davis, J. (1979, January 12). On the left. *San Francisco Sentinel*, p. 7.
Davis, J. (1979, March 9). On the left: Democracy? *San Francisco Sentinel*, p. 7.
Derrida, J. (1982). *Margins of philosophy*. Chicago: University of Chicago Press.
Drescher, J. (2008, November 7). A setback for same-sex marriage. *New York Times*, p. 34.
Editorial. (1976, November 4). *San Francisco Sentinel*, p. 5.
Editorial Desk. (2008, November 6). Equality's winding path. *New York Times*, p. 32.
Epstein, R. (1984). *The Times of Harvey Milk*. (film).
Ferguson, R. (n.d.). "Administering sexuality." Unpublished Manuscript.
Foucault, M. (1990). *The history of sexuality: Vol.1 An introduction*. R. Hurley (Trans.). New York: Vintage.
Foucault, M. (1995). *Discipline and punish: The birth of the prison*. A. Sheridan (Trans.). New York: Vintage.
Gamson, W. (1992). The social psychology of collective action. In A. Morris & C. McClurg Mueller (Eds.). *Frontiers in social movement theory*. New Haven, CT; London: Yale University Press.
Gamson, J. (1995, August). Must identity movement self-destruct? *Social Problems*, 42(3), 390–407.
Gold, H. (1977, November 6). Homosexuals step out of the closet, into politics. *Los Angeles Times*, p. F1.

Hall, S. (1989). New ethnicities. In K. Mercer. (Ed.). *Black film, British cinema*. London: BFI/ICA Documents 7. 27–31.

Hall, S. (1996). Minimal selves. *Black British cultural studies: A reader*. Chicago: University of Chicago Press.

Hall, S., & Du Gay, P. (Eds). (1996). Introduction: Who needs 'identity'? *Questions of cultural identity*. London: Sage.

Hardman, P. (1977, September 8). Deluded democracy. *San Francisco Sentinel*, p. 6.

Hardman, P. (1978, January 12). Power, politics, and people. *San Francisco Sentinel*, p. 6.

Healey, P. (2008, November 1). Hopefuls defer as they reject gay marriage. *New York Times*, p. 1.

Hopkins, B. (2008, November 7). A setback for same-sex marriage. *New York Times*, p. 34.

Knight, H., Heredia, C., Jones, C., Fimrite, P., Cote, J., & May, M. (2008, June 18). Wholly matrimony: Gays and lesbians from all over the state, some of whom have been together for decades, finally get the chance to say "I do." *San Francisco Chronicle*, p. A9.

Kunig, R. (1977, October 6). Letter: Milk endorsement serious error. *San Francisco Sentinel*, p. 5.

LATWP News Service. (2008, November 24). Studio hopes that audiences get 'milk.' *Los Angeles Times*. Retrieved from http://infoweb.newsbank.com.proxy2.library.uiuc.edu/iwsearch/we/InfoWeb?p_product=AWNB&p_theme=aggregated5&p_action=doc&p_docid=124AC8FFCCF371E8&p_docnum=4&p_queryname=4

LATWP News Service. (2009, January 20). Now, about gay marriage. *Los Angeles Times*. Retrieved from http://infoweb.newsbank.com.proxy2.library.uiuc.edu/iw-search/we/InfoWeb?p_product=AWNB&p_theme=aggregated5&p_action=doc&p_docid=125DC7199F8A3030&p_docnum=1&p_queryname=5

Manalansan, M. (1995). In the shadows of Stonewall: Examining gay transnational politics and the diasporic dilemma. *GLQ*, 2(4), 425–438.

Mariana. (1977, February 24). From under the dome. *San Francisco Sentinel*, p. 6;

Mariana. (1978, December 1). From under the Dome. *San Francisco Sentinel*, p. 6.

McKinley, J. (2008, December 10). Marriage ban inspires new wave of gay rights activists. *New York Times*, p. 23.

Milk, H. (1974, February 28). Waves: From the left. *San Francisco Sentinel*, p. 5.

Milk, H. (1978, December 1). *San Francisco Sentinel*, p. 3.

Milk sworn in as new district supe. (1978, January 12). *San Francisco Sentinel*, p. 1.

Milk wins easy victory. (1977, November 17). *San Francisco Sentinel*, p. 1.

Morris, C. (1978, December 1). Harvey Milk. *San Francisco Sentinel*, p.1.

Morris, C. (1979, January 12). Comment: A little too hasty? The deed is done. *San Francisco Sentinel*, p. 5.

Nagel, J. (1994). Constructing ethnicity: Creating and recreating ethnic identity and culture. *Social Problems*, 41(1), 152–176.

Pickets exorcize hall of justice. (1974, February 28). *San Francisco Sentinel*, p. 5. p. A1.

Sentinel Endorses. (1977, October 6). *San Francisco Sentinel*, p. 4.

Sentinel Endorses. (1977, November 3). *San Francisco Sentinel*, p. 12.

Shectman, L., & Smith, D. (1978, November 8). We did it! *San Francisco Sentinel*, p. 1.

Seidman, S. (1993). Identity politics in a 'postmodern' gay culture: Some historical and conceptual notes. In M. Warner (Ed.), *Fear of a queer planet*. London: University of Minnesota Press.

Smith, D. (1978, December 1). Harvey Milk. *San Francisco Sentinel*, p. 3, 6.

Smith, D. (1979, January 12). Britt sworn in as supervisor. *San Francisco Sentinel*, p. 1.
Valentine, D. (2007). *Imagining transgender: An ethnography of a category*. Durham, NC; London: Duke University Press.
Van Sant, G. (2008). *Milk*. (film).
Warner, M. (2002). Beyond gay marriage. In W. Brown & J. Halley (Eds.), *Left legalism/left critique*. Durham, NC; London: Duke University Press.
Weizl, J. (1984, November 21). Rainbow coalition. *San Francisco Sentinel*, p. 5.
West, C. (2001). *Race matters*. New York: Vintage.
When your beliefs and my civil rights collide. (2008, December 13). *New York Times*, p. 20.
Wildermuth, J. (2008, October 9). Milk club rejects Sheehan, votes to keep backing pelosi. *San Francisco Chronicle*, p. B3.
Winn, S. (2008, January 30). Filming of movie evokes memories, emotions in the Castro. *San Francisco Chronicle*, p. A1.
Yes, Stonewall 2.0. (2008, December 12). *New York Times*, p. 40.
Zacchino, N. (1978, November 28). Gay community mourns for man they called 'leader': Supervisor Milk credited for creating tolerance among varied San Francisco political faction. *Los Angeles Times*, p. B3.

SECTION III
Reterritorializing Bodies

· 9 ·

From Masculinity to Cybermasculinity

Marginalizing the Other in "DCinside"

JUNGMIN KWON

In 2002, an anonymous participant uploaded a picture of a woman on DCinside, a popular cyber community. She had a weird and rather frightful expression (see Figure 1), and so participants of this cyber community named her the *Gwangnyeo*—insane (*gwang*) woman (*nyeo*)—and begun photoshopping her image as a source of parody and sexual humor. In August 2003, after becoming aware that her image was being mocked, the woman in the picture petitioned the administrators of this cyber community and requested that participants stop using her image. The administrators obliged and deleted a considerable amount of *Gwangnyeo* themed pictures. Yet, despite the prohibition of the *Gwangnyeo* theme, this has not stopped participants from creating and parodying other *nyeos*.

Figure 1: The original picture of Gwangnyeo

By conducting a textual analysis of the images and discourses of DCinside, this chapter seeks to understand how masculinity rearticulates itself in the online public sphere. This analysis is necessary as the digital realm has frequently been spoken of as a utopian space that exists outside of the problematic of race, class, gender, sexuality, et cetera (Ergin Bulut, this volume). In contrast, I argue that the online public sphere is frequently policed by masculine norms which function to disenfranchise gender and sexual minorities, such as women and homosexuals. DCinside represents an ideal site for analysis, as it is currently amongst the most popular websites within South Korea, and South Korea incidentally is regarded as possessing one of the most well-developed Internet infrastructures. Begun as an online space concerned primarily with digital camera purchase and photography, DCinside has quickly grown to include a place where participants can upload images and discuss social issues of relevance. This expansion paved the way for the digital manipulation of those images, for both political and entertainment purposes, and hence an active parody community has come to take hold. Given the predominance of men in this computer-related subculture, it has become popular to procure and manipulate provocative images of women; with the increased presence of gays in Korean culture, homosexuals have also come to be targets of this online parody culture. Hence, DCinside offers insight as to how masculinity as a material and ideological construct is able to sustain itself even when its material foundation (i.e., the flesh) appears absent. My contention is that due to protections of the freedom of expression and the depoliticizing effect of "fun" culture, masculinity is able to rearticulate itself online: from masculinity to cybermasculinity.

Cybermasculinity

In struggling through the theoretical idealism of the Habermasian public sphere, Fraser (1990) argues that in actually existing democracies, "the development of powerful informal pressures [. . .] marginalize the contributions of members of subordinated groups" (p. 64). Hence, due to these pressures to conform, subordinate groups, such as that of women, "sometimes cannot find the right voice or words to express their thoughts, and when they do, they discover they are not heard" (Fraser, 1990, p. 64). This disciplining of the public sphere in cultural terms further entrenches dominant voices as subordinate groups are denied practical familiarity with the material substructures of contemporary democracy. In other words, as Cassell and Jenkins (1999) argue, if media literacy is a necessary prerequisite to contemporary democracy, then to construct a new technology as the domain of men, "informally" works to discourage women from developing the necessary technological fluency to participate. And, as a result, the ideological form of masculinity crystallizes into a political economic structure in which men dominant the material means necessary for participating in the public sphere (Fraser, 1990).

In the twenty years since Fraser's initial critique, a plethora of new communications technologies have been developed; perhaps most importantly, the Internet. The development of the Internet has garnered intense debate as to what type of public sphere this new communications infrastructure will support. Optimistically, many feminist scholars have conceived of the online public sphere as a gender free space (Fernback, 1997; Fredrick, 1999; Hall, 1996; Herring, 1996; Kramarae & Taylor, 1993; Scott, Semmens & Willoughby, 2001; We, 1994). This hope is grounded in the belief that "the lack of social cues and hierarchy in the structure of the Internet provide the potential for equality in the digital realm" (Fredrick, 1999, p. 187). These liberal cyberfeminists, as Hall (1996) argues, "imagine the computer as a liberating utopia that does not recognize the social dichotomies of male/female and heterosexual/homosexual" (p. 148). In contrast, radical cyberfeminists contend that issues of power do not dissipate upon entry into cyberspace (Hall, 1996; Nakamura, 2002).

An obvious concern amongst radical cyberfeminists has been that of the digital divide. The critique is that the material and ideological substructures of the Internet—i.e., computers, software, webspace, etc.—have traditionally been dominated by males, and, due to this technological familiarity, men "have comprised the majority of [Internet] users [...] since its inception" (Herring, 1996, p. 144). As a result, "women are underrepresented in their use and ownership of computers" (Cooper, 2006, p. 321). This point has been readily accepted by cyberfeminists of various political extremities, and much work has gone into the alleviation of this digital divide. As such, thanks to the efforts of cyberfeminists and the spread of computer literacy education, the digital divide between genders has been somewhat assuaged.

The debate regarding the digital divide, however, has functioned somewhat as a red herring of sorts, as increased access has not alleviated the structural challenges women continue to face in cyberspace (Nakamura & Haraway, 2003). These problems derive from the fact that "gender is not erased in the virtual world, but intensified discursively" (Hall, 1996, p. 148). As Benwell and Stokoe (2006) argue, in their discussion about online identity, sex is strongly rooted in the virtual world despite the opportunities to transcend the physical body. Even when gender crossing/passing occurs, the preoccupation with gender is still strongly binary in its orientation and essentialized in its themes and performances. Herring (1996) further insists that the Internet cannot be "gender-blind" because of the persistence of gendered styles of writing in online space. As such, the Internet is merely "relatively" freer than an offline world because, while absent of physical markers of identity, a discursive link to reality still remains (Fernback, 1997); often, those discursive links replicate "the biases, contradictions, and prejudices of our offline life" (We, 1994, para. 1).

The fact of material anonymity, however, does work to distinguish the online world from that of offline society. To an extent, this anonymity does function positively in cyberspace. For instance, Internet participants can straightforwardly critique the government via online political debate. As Doran (this volume) notes, in places with heavy state censorship, the Internet has become the only viable means for oppositional views to be heard: "online utilities [i.e., Twitter, YouTube, and Facebook] that are extremely flexible in their modes of access and thus more difficult to block, become the primary venues" of political unrest (Doran, p. 13). When it comes to notions of gender, however, "the cloak of anonymity has allowed for men to express sexual desires that they would not otherwise present in 'real life'" ([my translation], M. Lee, 2003, p. 42). In addition, the physical anonymity which may function to positively encourage attempts at "cross-expressing," also works to encourage a kind of online overcompensation; without the presence of a physical body, flaming (i.e., verbally abusive online behavior) becomes an alternative sign of one's masculinity (Hall, 1996). Hence, these aspects of anonymity make virtual space violent, especially when women confront hostile and inhospitable sites (S. Lee, 1999). That is, anonymity often enables online masculinity to emerge more offensively and aggressively than offline. Thus, it seems fair to conclude that not everyone is equal in cyberspace.

In addressing this "new" form of masculinity that has emerged with the Internet, Hall (1996) identifies several configurations of its deployment: conversational dominance, textual harassment, heterosexism and physical hierarchies, and the "talking penis." First, conversational dominance refers to the fact that "men talk more in mixed-sex electronic discussions" (Hall, p. 154). Hall found that male participants tend to ignore "the topics which women introduce, [. . .] [dismiss] women's responses as irrelevant, and [contribute] a much higher percentage of the total number of postings and text produced" (p. 154). Second, textual harassment is an ever-present reality for women on the Internet, as there have been:

> Ongoing reports of aggressive sexual harassment within private e-mail and bulletin board systems. The masculine discursive style witnessed on the Internet is a kind of

verbal violence that only rarely occurs between strangers in the non-virtual world, where its employment in casual interaction would be perceived as the exception and not the rule. (Hall, p. 155)

As a result, a significant number of women have been victimized by sexist jokes, obscene language, and unsolicited pornographic pictures. Third, and closely intertwined with the second point, the dominance of masculinity is completed through displays of heterosexism: "a prejudice realized on the Internet through the proliferation of 'anti-homosexual' discursive threads" (p. 155). Fourth, internal competition amongst "men" is settled through "violent and sexualized verbal compensation among male participants" (Hall, p. 157). These four distinct phenomena of cybermasculinity are all interconnected, as it is through the last component of the "talking penis" that the hierarchy of heterosexual masculinity is maintained: with "real" men at top and women and "abnormal" men at the bottom.

To understand the appearance of cybermasculinity in South Korea, we need to first explore the transnational discourses on the crisis of masculinity. Heterosexual masculine identity, according to Cook (2006), is performed against the anxiety of "the (failed) repression of femininity that is central to the production of male identity" (p. 48). In our contemporary society, this anxiety has "has been intensified by feminism" (Cook, p. 50). Put simply, as the status of women rises, and conventional masculinity continues to be challenged, men experience a sense of impending crisis. The various manifestations of feminism have typically functioned as internal pressures to masculine authority; but, in addition, as Walzer (2002) argues, the advent of contemporary globalization and the subsequent cultural pluralism it brought about have functioned externally to undermine the notion of a "unitary national culture," which men so depend upon for their cultural authority (p. 221). A similar phenomenon can be found in South Korea. Murphree (2008) has traced "the disappearance of the masculine subject" in Korea to the annihilation of traditional national values (pp. 684–685). As the entry of women into public affairs and the awareness of gender equality have increased, the traditional patriarchal system in Korean society has weakened. Women have experienced tremendous success in the social, economical, and legal arenas. In fact, as more and more women begin to work in male-dominated fields, men may feel threatened, and as a result, experience anxiety. To alleviate this anxiety and boost their self-confidence, men have attempted to maintain their dominance in the public sphere by constructing male-centered spaces. But, it has become difficult to preserve and construct traditional masculinity openly in the existing public sphere. Therefore, they have found an alternative space, overflowing with anonymity, where they can freely express their masculinity without constraint. In this new public sphere, the Internet, men have sought to reassert their masculinity and estrange women and others by performing cybermasculinity.

In this chapter, I argue that the parody culture of DCinside functions as one such example of the cybermasculinity that pervades the Korean online public sphere. This is insofar as it offers a venue for the four aspects of cybermasculinity to manifest: conversational dominance, textual harassment, heterosexism, and the "talking penis." DCinside sustains cybermasculinity in that: it is difficult to find female participants on the parody bulletin board; women are frequently harassed through the construction of highly sexualized parody pictures; participants explicitly ridicule certain homosexual celebrities; and, participants enjoy mocking the "penis" of those "inferior" men. In other words, even when granted relatively equal access to this new public sphere, subordinate groups are not likely to find the Internet to be a utopian democratic space. Hence, I believe that we must examine sites such as DCinside if we are to locate possible means of combating the gendered inequalities that have come to manifest in the online world.

DCinside: A Powerful Cyberspace in South Korea

DCinside is a well-known online community in South Korea.[1] It started in 1999 as an online space where people could share information on digital camera technology. But since there had yet to be any other spaces for the sharing of users' digital creations, DCinside quickly expanded to include a venue for such purposes. At first, DCinside participants—primarily young adults, such as university students and entry-level employees in their 20s to 30s (C. Lee, 2003)—merely shared information regarding digital cameras and/or uploaded and parodied the images that they took. As these parodied images spread, however, DCinside began to attract more online users and became socially powerful. For instance, during the 2002 national elections in South Korea, parodied pictures of certain candidates affected the public sentiment and were used by their opponents. Additionally, the bulletin board in DCinside functions as an online public sphere among young Internet users. Due to this, it has long attracted significant attention, with more recent estimates at about 800,000 hits daily (M. Kim, 2006).

Participants of DCinside are popularly called the "Pae-in," which conventionally means a disabled person or a bum.[2] However, DCinside users have appropriated the word to mean people who are frequent users, and appear to be addicted to the website—in a positive sense; and thus, the Pae-in refers to an exclusively online social network held together by a shared passion for parody pictures (Pang, 2002). In this sense, the concept of a Pae-in implies a similar meaning as the terms "geek" in the United States and "otaku" in Japan, and other subcultures built upon a common passion for new media culture. It is worth noting, however, that even though the Pae-in are obsessed with DCinside, they do have personal lives independent from the website. Namely, the Internet does not dominate their entire lives, but it is one tool for performing their identity.

DCinside culture can broadly be considered as both politically resistant and playful. Some research has been done examining the political aspects of DCinside (Hwang, 2003; J. Lee, 2009; Pang, 2002; Song, 2005). Initially, the parody culture of DCinside was criticized as rendering politics superficial (Song, 2005). Song (2005) points out, "it was not until 2002 that the Pae-in began to mobilize as a political force, playing an active role in two later events: the election for the 16th president and bringing attention to the death of two female teenagers run over by a US military vehicle" ([my translation], p. 134). Since that time, participants of DCinside frequently produce political parody pictures and actively participate in online debates about current issues. Moreover, their online behavior carries with it particular material consequences: first, they organize to have a tremendous number of Pae-in visit an "enemy's" website, thereby causing the server to collapse; second, the Pae-in will often organize an offline protest/demonstration that includes non-DCinside participants (Pang, 2002).

In addition, much scholarly attention has been paid to the playful side of DCinside as well (J. Kim, 2005; Kim & Park, 2005; C. Lee, 2003; H. Lee, 2006; H. Lee, 2008; Pang, 2002). This research is significant as the vast majority of online activity is conducted for apolitical purposes (H. Lee, 2006): 78.7% of Internet users reported that they used the Internet for leisure purposes, second only to checking email and/or chatting (86.9%). Hence, it is reasonable to believe that some people access the Internet only for entertainment purposes. Like the Internet, Pang (2002) argues, so too has DCinside shifted from being a technical, market-based space (i.e., camera hardware) to that of a social, leisure-based space (i.e., sharing photoshopped images).

The Pae-in, as members of an online, leisure-based community, create and sustain their culture through the commenting on and parodying of images as well as by developing specialized insider language. For them, the parodied images function as a unifying aspect of their culture, and commenting on these posted images is a huge part of the fun. Yet, what is significant about these comments is not just what participants write but also how many people leave comments for a particular image or who comments first. As one Pae-in confessed: "Lots of comments for my photo make me think I am cared for and loved" ([my translation], J. Kim, 2003, para. 4). As DCinside has matured, the Pae-in have begun to construct a new symbolic system as a prerequisite for participation. This is important as Ross (2005) notes, "the use of shorthand symbols and abbreviations and the continuing development of symbols and words to fit the forms of the Internet [is a key part of] textual interaction on the Internet" (p. 344). This new language system (which is rarely used offline) allows for the Pae-in to express feelings and ideas that they could not otherwise articulate through formal language (Kim & Park, 2005). Moreover, it not only helps users connect and express their feelings amongst one another but also works to subvert established cultural norms. This subversive aspect is important as parody culture has become a central feature of the DCinside community (Kim & Park, 2005). All aspects of life—politics, entertainment, social, and cultural issues—are considered fair game for being parodied; frequently, even contemporary issues are parodied as soon as they occur (Ham, 2002).

While DCinside has become famous thanks to their parody culture, their creations have also been troubling for those concerned with the tension between the freedom of expression and the respect for personal well-being. As such, this chapter is concerned with the problematic of parody culture and its implications for the realization of a more democratic public sphere. Particularly, I am concerned with how cybermasculinity and parody culture work hand in hand to both mutually reinforce one another and disenfranchise gender and sexual minorities.

Doing Research on DCinside

There are many sections in which participants can post on DCinside. Those sections are mostly divided between "galleries" and "bulletin boards." Galleries are spaces where participants mainly post images (and comment upon them); whereas, in bulletin boards, people primarily write messages. Amongst the galleries, the "Composite Gallery" differs from the others, in that to post an image within it, one must incorporate a "requisite" (*hap seong yo so*). The notion of a requisite refers to an original image, considered to be so humorous or impressive, that it is targeted as an object of parody. Within the Composite Gallery, these initial images are manipulated and combined with other (non-requisite) images, such as movie posters and photos of sporting events. For example, an image of a very cute dog became targeted by the Pae-in as a requisite for the Composite Gallery (see Figure 2). The Pae-in then took this dog and abstracted it from its original context, and placed it within a pre-existing movie poster. Marked as a requisite, parodied images of this dog have been posted throughout the Composite Gallery. At any given time, there are roughly 30 to 40 requisites within the Composite Gallery and if a composited image does not contain at least one of them, that posting is removed by an administrator.[3] As of May 2009, there were approximately 22,000 images posted in this gallery, with about 15 to 20 additional images uploaded every day. The average number of comments associated with each image is around ten; if the post is really popular, however, it often receives over 100 comments. Regardless of the amount of comments left, each posting typically shows at least 1000 hits. This gallery is of particular interest in that, while parodied images can be found in other galleries, those images and associated comments which resonate most

Figure 2. (from left-right). The cute dog from the first image (left) was photoshopped into a movie poster (right).

heavily with the characteristics of cybermasculinity are frequently found within the Composite Gallery. Not surprisingly, the vast majority of requisites consist of images of women and sexual minorities. Therefore, the Composite Gallery will serve as my primary site of analysis.

To conduct this analysis, I follow the lead of Rose (2001) and employ a critical visual methodology. This framework combines the data management capabilities of content analysis with the structural insights of semiology. Hence, the first step, as outlined by Rose (2001) is to begin by identifying only those images relevant to my research questions. Thus, I focused exclusively on postings with titles pertaining to female and/or homosexual content. I then classified them into subgroups according to their respective topics: *Gwangnyeo* (insane woman), *Ddalnyeo* (strawberry woman), etc. Some images were deemed not worthy of analysis because they were poorly produced, and as such do not attract much user attention. For the sake of this analysis, I selected as representative examples images that were frequently exposed to the general public through the press and, as such, held the most comments. Presumably, frequent exposure and many comments suggest that the posting resonates with the core elements of the online community.

The next step of Rose's (2001) critical visual methodology builds upon the categorical impulses of content analysis by infusing it with the analytical skill set of semiology. Whereas content analysis would be satisfied with placing the coded images within conversation amongst each other (e.g., according to the categories of cybermasculinity as identified by Hall [1996]), semiology pushes further and deconstructs the manifest content in order to tease out the ideological substructures that keep the categorical system itself intact (Rose, 2001).[4] In this regard, the parodied images found within DCinside do not just reference cybermasculinity, as an already pre-existent classificatory system, they also reconstruct, and therefore reinforce, cybermasculinity by deploying an array of cultural signifiers. Hence, by elucidating what each sign in the postings represent, semiology offers a means of revealing how the parody culture of DCinside works to sustain the unequal power relations embedded within the South Korean gender system.

While the images found within the postings on DCinside operate as the organizational and analytical center of my analysis, we cannot forget that the comments each image generates functions as a powerful ideological anchor for subsequent visitors. The original posting may have emerged from an already existing sign system, but as Fairclough (2003) asserts, new signs "can bring about changes in our knowledge, our beliefs, our attitudes, values and so forth" (p. 8).

Therefore, I also concentrate on reviewing the comments that accompany each posting as important textual formations. Online participants post with the general expectation that others share the ideological systems embedded within their writings and images. Also, Internet users enjoy giving feedback to writers regardless of subsequent praise or criticism. Moreover, this interaction between producers and consumers of online contents has played a key role in the formation of cyber-culture. Hence, it is tremendously important to study these comments. In particular, the comments play a huge part in the parody culture of DCinside in that participants produce images expecting feedback and hence construct their images with that audience participation in mind. In investigating these comments, I try to identify what unsaid (i. e., assumed) ideological structures operate to support the said (Fairclough, 2003). The images act as ideological referents to the comments left behind. In this regard, the images and comments work in conjunction to discipline the gender-identity of its participants in accordance with the cultural logic of cybermasculinity. The next section explores the result of the analyses of these images and comments.

Cybermasculinity in the Parody Culture of DCinside

Hall (1996) argues that cyber-masculinity manifests across four interlocking categories: conversational dominance; textual harassment; heterosexism and physical hierarchies; and the enactment of the "talking penis." The postings found within DCinside display a strong affinity for cybermasculinity and, hence, their particular enactments of this ideology are discussed below.

Conversational Dominance

The conversational dominance of cybermasculinity (Hall, 1996) is not so different from the behavior of conventional masculinity in the off-line public sphere (Fraser, 1990); in both cases, women are typically silenced. Kramarae and Taylor (1993) argue that in just about any "open" network, the cultural dictates of masculinity mean that men will monopolize the conversation. The gendered space of DCinside does not appear to be different. The Internet Matrix group (as cited in Y. Kim, 2006) reports that 40% of DCinside visitors are women. However, the content of the postings (e.g., anti-women) suggests that whether women visit these galleries or not, they are not amongst the participants—this is true of other galleries and bulletin boards as well.[5]

It is clear that much of the content within DCinside is explicitly aggressive towards women. Three patterns of posting illustrate the dominance of men over women in this gallery. First, the Pae-in create what are called "before and after plastic surgery" composites: these are modifications of female requisites that are considered to be ugly (see Figure 3). Then, malicious comments regarding the "excellent" work or the impossibility of the task are frequently left behind. Second, the Pae-in enjoy posting images that denigrate the accomplishments of the Ministry of Gender Equality. And third, certain female groups, such as that of women colleges or clubs, are often referenced as being made up of "beautiful fools." Collectively, these aspects of DCinside suggest that the main participants are male.[6]

The problem, however, is not that most of the users are men, but rather that 3hese males participate in a masculine culture that is contingent upon the degradation of women. This is demonstrated in the following parody picture and its associated comments (see Figure 4):

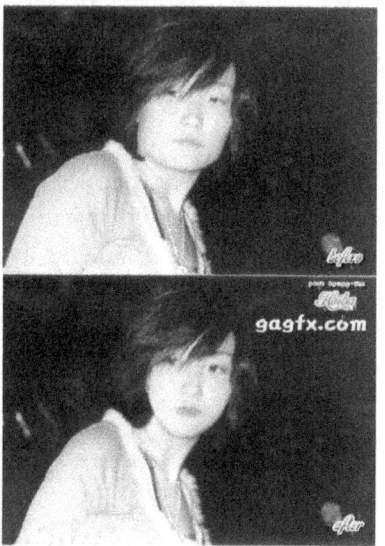

Figure 3. The woman from the original photo (top) has been remade as a "plastic beauty" (bottom).

WRITER:	Before sleeping, I tried to create one.
QUICK MOVE:	I wish I just slept without seeing this.
AHEH:	I need the original work as well.
KIM CHANG RYUL:	What is your sin? [said to the woman in the picture]
FWY:	Every woman is the same in the darkness~
OH, DAMN!:	I can do ddr..... (x▽ x)(x▽ x)
HENGH:	hard to make it [penis] stand...DDR

YESTERDAY:	Really the same even after lights-out!!!!!!!!!!
NO MISTAKE:	Is it fun? Is it? Really? Is it really fun? Is it? Yes, it is.
SONGSONGSONG:	My hand unconsciously positions in DDR posture -.-;; excellent work~

"DDR" (short for *DdalDdaRi*) is commonly used amongst men as slang for masturbation. As this posting illustrates, conversations that would otherwise be conveyed in private or masked through the use of sexual puns are considered publicly acceptable in cyberspace. Unfortunately, whenever female pictures are posted onto the Composite Gallery, "DDR" conversations always arise. In essence, masculinity assumes that when online, its private interests become public goods—thereby reconfiguring the digital public sphere as a male-only space, even when access remains open.

In order to understand the Pae-in's sexual jokes, such as DDR, it is necessary to expand our comprehension of "flaming." This is because as Herring (1996) claims, "it is virtually only men who flame" (p. 149); and as such, flaming can help to explain why it is that men attack or sexually objectify women. Flaming is "the expression of strong negative emotion, through the use of derogatory, obscene, or inappropriate language, and personal insults" (Herring, 1996, p. 149). Male flaming in this gallery naturally creates a hostile environment for women. As a result, women avoid visiting the Composite Gallery or posting on it

Figure 4. DDR Assistant

(Kang & Jeon, 2004). Therefore, women must choose either to conceal their gender or to avoid posting in the online world. Even if they post, they might "worry about being attacked and/or hit on by men" (We, 1994, para. 27). Even when flaming is not directed at women, it commonly leads female users to leave that online space (Barak, 2005). To address this issue, DCinside opened a women-only space on March 2008 (Chae, 2008). However, this is not a space where users can upload parody pictures. As such, parody culture is deemed strictly the domain of masculinity.

Textual Harassment

So far, a great number of women have been parodied in the Composite Gallery. Of them, "Sophitia," *Gwangnyeo*, and *Ddalnyeo* are amongst the oldest and most popular.[7] While most other parodied women are famous peoples, such as Hillary Clinton, the four women just mentioned are notable in that they were just unidentified ordinary people. This anonymity, combined with the candidness of their photographs, presumably aroused people's curiosity. Additionally, since these women were not yet identified, the Pae-in may have felt less restrained in parodying them; pictures of other "*Nyeos*" (women) who recognized themselves being parodied are often removed. However, it took a while for the women of *Gwangnyeo*, *Halnyeo*, *Ddalnyeo*, and "Sophitia" to become aware that their photos were being exploited and to ask for the removal of those images. As a result, a considerable amount of parodied images and comments about them still remain. Therefore, I primarily deal with pictures of these four women.

Parody culture in the Composite Gallery can be bisected into the mutually reinforcing themes of mocking appearance and sexual objectification. As Pang (2002) notes, "since most of the Pae-in are male, when they mock a female's appearance, they are in essence sexualizing them" ([my translation], p. 63). The first parodied female was "Sophitia," or Sophie. Sophitia is a well-known character from *Soul Caliber*, a fighting-genre video game. In the game, the physical appearance of the character is very attractive. However, a Japanese woman, whom the Pae-in believed was

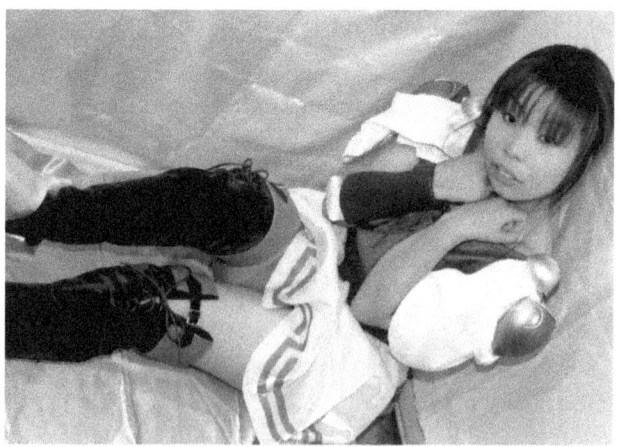

Figure 5. The original image of the woman posing as Sophitia

not attractive, "ruined" the image of the original character through a *costume* role play (see Figure 5). Therefore, the Pae-in made sarcastic remarks about her because they felt that only pretty women should be able to masquerade as a Sophitia. Amazed at her "shamelessness" and boldness, they satirically pretended to admire her beauty; while at the same time, they aggressively parodied her images:

SURD NUMBER:	I saved this image as a desktop background since I am lost in her beauty.
DBDBDBDB:	Long time no see Sophie! What a beauty! She is surely a rarebeauty. Her skin is transparent and bright and her lip is as lovely as a cherry.
SOOHEH:	Did she intend to make her lips like that? Or she can't close by reason of oral structure? Either way, she is attractive.
ALREADY CRAZY	Woman: Frankly, she is not that ugly except that she cannot close her mouth.
-_-;:	not that? -_-;; then you marry her. [To Already Crazy woman]
BEGINNERHEH:	Instantaneously, a murderous impulse. . .! The way to control myself is hard.
BEGINNERHEH. .:	How could you find a really ugly women if Sophitia is not that ugly -_-; [To Already Crazy woman]

Surd Number and Dbdbdbdb feign admiration for the beauty of Sophitia. Reading within the framework of the larger discussion, however, suggests that when the Pae-in mock a woman's appearance, it is because they have reduced a woman's essence to being solely that of sexual pleasure, and, should her appearance deny the possibility of sexual objectification, then it is enough to cause "murderous impulses" (BeginnerHeh).

On June 30, 2002, a user by the name of Nagari uploaded a picture, titled "Since Sophitia looks poor" (see Figure 6) He made her face prettier using graphic tools. He left lines detailing the reason why he created the image, saying:

I tried to make her beautiful because Sophitia has always been parodied by the Pae-in...but...[the job to make her beautiful was] impossible. Even though I cut her thick legs and changed her face to another woman...she is still ugly...

For this image, commentators rejected the "new Sophitia," writing: "Sophitia is the best when she is just herself. So don't change anything for her" (Huhm); "Boo. ..Sophitia.. ;;; Save her" (A Huge Fan of Sophitia); "This is not what we wish for Sophitia. Ahehheh~" (Cigarette in the Morning); "No beauty cannot take in the curvaciousness of Sophitia. . .haha" (Merely Insect). Their negative responses suggest that they cannot accept a "really" pretty Sophitia because once beautified she functions as a useless object of parody and derision.

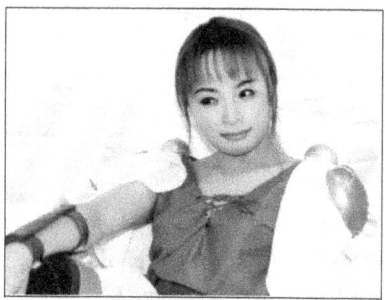

Figure 6. Nagari's "Since Sophitia looks poor"

Extreme comments mocking the female body have also emerged from the parody photos of *Gwangnyeo* (see Figure 7):

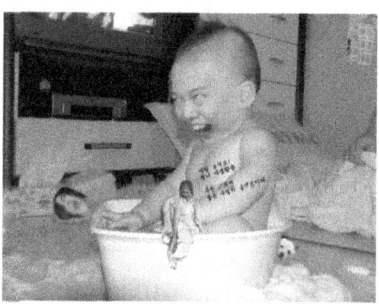

Figure 7. Titled, "Urgent Acquisition," this image is a photoshopping of the Gwangnyeo's face onto a baby's body

KKOHEH: So funny.. . .Honestly, a little creepy though.

—^: Everyone guesses her real appearance is prettier enough to oppress the beauty of Eugene Prince [who is another parodied woman in the Composite Gallery]. It would be appreciated if she uploaded her real face now...^^(—^),

DYEUS: I must not be able to sleep tonight.

As in the case of Sophitia, the Pae-in pretend to think *Gwangnyeo* is beautiful, but actually confess that she is so "creepy" that they "are not able to sleep." In contrast to the other *neyos* who are parodied as sexual objects, however, in the images of *Gwangnyeo*, it is the men who have become the object of desire; in other words, the *Gwangnyeo* is portrayed as a demonic figure believed to be capable of raping men (see Figure 8). In these images, the *Gwangnyeo* is portrayed as threatening the penises of the surrounding men. In the first, she is shown as purposely kicking a ball towards the crotches of terrified soccer players (see Figure 8 [top]). In the second, she is grabbing a guy's penis, as other male swimmers look helplessly on (see Figure 8 [bottom]). In both instances, the appearance of *Gwangnyeo* is utilized as a means of suggesting that unattractive and sexually aggressive women pose a physical threat to men; this is in contrast to the amicable posture of "Sophitia," which allows for her and "ugly" woman like her to remain in the conversation of sexual desire.

Figure 8 (from top to bottom). Titled as "Gwangnyeo, playing free kick" (top) and "Gwangnyeo Debate" (bottom) respectively, both parodied images portray the Gwangnyeo as a demonic figure that terrorizes men.

As representative examples, Sophitia and *Gwangnyeo*, are mocked by the Pae-in as worthy and/or capable of rape precisely because of their ugly faces. This is because the Pae-in deem ugly women both as sexually threatening (e.g., "giving nightmares") and incapable of finding a sexual partner on their own (e.g., New Sophitia)—hence, the "favor" of rape. This ridiculing of appearance and practice of sexual objectification are representative of how the Pae-in consume parody pictures. Unfortunately, this brand of masculinity has only intensified since the advent of *Ddalnyeo* within DCinside.

When *Ddalnyeo* appeared in the middle of 2003, she was received enthusiastically by the DCinside community. Men found her image irresistible, as she possesses a sensual look: she is holding strawberries near her breasts and appears to be moaning (see Figure 9 [left]). As such, since *Ddalnyeo*'s initial appearance, nearly all parody pictures in DCinside have contained her image—and she is always shown having sex (see Figure 9 [middle and right]). These parodied images have generated a great deal of excitement from the community, with most comments overflowing with sexual references:

  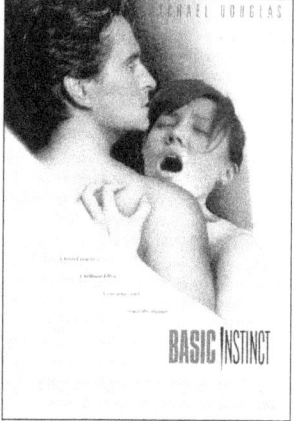

Figure 9 (from left-right). The initial image of *Ddalnyeo* (left) has generated a vast amount of sexually charged images. For instance, in "Bewitching" (middle), her face is composited onto the image of a woman in a skirt being taken from behind; and, in "*Ddalnyeo* is the best" (right), her head is pasted on top of Sharon Stone, as she is engaged in a passionate embrace with Michael Douglas. It is important to note that while much could be parodied within the initial image (e.g., strawberries could be replaced), it is the sexual expression of her face that has garnered the most attention.

Writer:	I bought it [*Ddalneyeo*] as an accessory. My *Ddalnyeo* is living on the backspace key. It makes a sensational sound when I hit the key. *Ddalnyeo* on my keyboard looks very lovely. >0< //
Pervert:	Any other [sexual] positions?
Tyranno:	I have it as well. Whenever hitting the ESC key, I reluctantly do sexual harassment.
Uhm:	I saw a mouse that looks like a boob. So hard to avoid pushing a nipple. .;

These images of sexualized women have been circulated over the Internet at-large without any filtering. While pressure from the press and petitioning by the women parodied have resulted in the pictures being removed, in cyberspace these often-belated measures are useless. To begin with, it is still easy to find these images in search engines, as many Internet users have already copied them to their own blogs. As such, once published online, the images never truly disappear. On top of that, this belated removal does not alleviate the humiliation and ridicule that these women must have already suffered at the hands of these images. For these reasons, the textual harassment of cybermasculinity can have a detrimental impact on women. But, unfortunately, women are not the only targets; the ensuing two sections argue that the masculinity of DCinside is violent not only for women but also for men, particularly for those men who are deemed "abnormal," such as homosexuals and eunuchs.

Heterosexism

Since the turn of the millennium, the quantity of homosexual-related media content in South Korea has proliferated; under the term "queer," homosexual culture has become a social phenomenon in Korea, with gay characters found in movies, television, and literature (Ko, Kim, Kipkoech, Lee, & Chang, 2008). As such, one would think that Korean society is incredibly generous towards homosexuals. However, such a judgment is hasty in that most consumers of this content are young women, and homosexuals in South Korea still experience high amounts of discrimination from others.[8] In addition, these queer cultural products market gay identity as "pretty and tender," playing into the sexual desires of woman to find a "sweet and handsome" guy (J. Kim, 2008). In contrast, men often refuse to engage homosexual content, and hence are more likely to hold negative attitudes towards gay men (J. Kim, 2008).

This anti-homosexual sentiment has gained increased popularity within DCinside parody culture. In the past, it was only women who were objectified and sexualized in the Composite Gallery. Recently, however, actor Sukcheon Hong, who came out in 2000, became a requisite. Considering that, after coming out, Hong was informally banned from just about every television program in Korea, his appearance on DCinside suggests that cybermasculinity is just conventional masculinity performed via other means.

With titles such as "The eye of Hawk on Jongsoo" (see Figure 10 [left]) or "Hong, Never picky for men" (see Figure 10 [right]), the *Pae*-in fused the photos of Hong with other male celebrities and sport players.[9] In doing so, they suggest that all homosexuals regard every man as a potential sexual partner. When later Hong was attacked by a cheetah and seriously injured, the Pae-in took this as an opportunity for further parody. In these later images, and their subsequent comments, they depict Hong as "being raped" by the Cheetah (see Figure 11):

Figure 10 (from left-right). Composited images of Sukcheon Hong always portray him in the act of sexually assaulting another male. For instance, in "The eye of Hawk on Jongsoo" (left), Hong is portrayed groping another player; in "Hong, never picky for men," he is shown thrusting his pelvis into another man. It is important to note that unlike the *Ddalnyeo* images, this act of passion is posited as clearly unwanted.

Figure 11. This image is titled "The eyes of cheetah look on as Hawk observes his prey."

> DIVING BEETLE: kk. In fact, he didn't make any mistake, but is always parodied and criticized kk. This is why our country cannot be amicable for minorities. kk.
>
> Qlffl: That's because we have a pity for him.
>
> AH: Son of a bitch pretends to worry him. What an evil. Don't come over here again, fucker! [To Qlffl]
>
> LIONEL APRICOT: Hawk [Hong] deserves criticism, though.
>
> ADSF: It is from heart for his fast recovery!
>
> DD: kkkkkkkkkk such a contradiction! Do you think one can parody him even though s/he really hopes his recovery?

As seen, those commenting are very aware that Hong is a sexual minority and that their parodies of him are prejudiced. To be sure, there are some users who seem reasonable, such as Diving beetle or dd. In another posting, a user by the name of Seasplayer commented: "Fortunately, Hong was only wounded without danger for his life, but he was still badly hurt. It is heartless to parody his wound and make fun of him, isn't it?" However, the vast majority of participants in this online space leave little room for the expression of ethical concerns; they instead poke fun and facetiously write that they have much "pity" and "heart" for him. Moreover, they justify their behavior by suggesting that he "deserves criticism" for being a homosexual.

In addition to Hong, the Pae-in have been very active in parodying pictures of Billy Harrington, a male-to-male pornographic actor. Since this actor is very muscular, the Pae-in position him as capable of "raping any man" through the sheer use of his physical power. In the pornographic posting titled "The drifting story of Billy" (2009), in which the user OtakuBilly pasted the face of Billy, the following comments were found:

SAPPHIRE: f...fuck!!! D...dirty kkkkkkkkk but you made it great...

OH MY GOD: Me got used to gay unconsciously...fuck Snake Ugh! Disgusting!

These comments and responses hold a similar attitude as those toward Sukcheon Hong's pictures. It is common to describe homosexuals by using the expression "dirty or disgusting" and to treat them as abnormalities and perversions against whom "normal" men must always be on their guard. For this reaction of heterosexual men to homosexuals, Herek (1986) argues that heterosexual men respond in this way because "homophobia is an integral component of heterosexual masculinity" (p. 572), and their antagonism, they believe, helps them to "win approval from important others and thereby increase self-esteem" (Herek, p. 573). By purposely othering and abnormalizing homosexuals through the use of parody, the Pae-in try to maintain and enhance their already established masculinity. This tendency also exists in how they parody eunuchs.

Physical Hierarchies and the Talking Penis

Since mid-2008, the most popular and provocative requisite in the Composite Gallery may be that of the actor Sim Young. He gained notoriety among the Pae-in after his character in the popular drama, *Yain Sidae* (2002–2003), was castrated by a rifle. Upon learning this fact from his doctor, he made a very shocked facial expression. One of the Pae-in captured the moment and uploaded it to the Composite Gallery. The response of the Pae-in to this photo was so passionate that most of the later parody pictures featuring this image included his dialogue from the drama: "unbelievable that I am a eunuch!"[10]

At first, merely this line accompanied by his pained expression generated a significant amount of parody. However, the emphasis soon shifted into a discussion of his castration, as the Pae-in begin to ridicule him for not having a penis. For instance, one picture describes him as looking at a young man's penis sadly (see Figure 12). Another posting portrays him as furiously masturbating in front of a nurse after he regains his penis. In addition, the Pae-in frequently composite his shocked face alongside images of Sukcheon Hong and/or Billy Harrington; in these postings, Young is depicted as being sexually harassed by one of these men (see Figure 13):

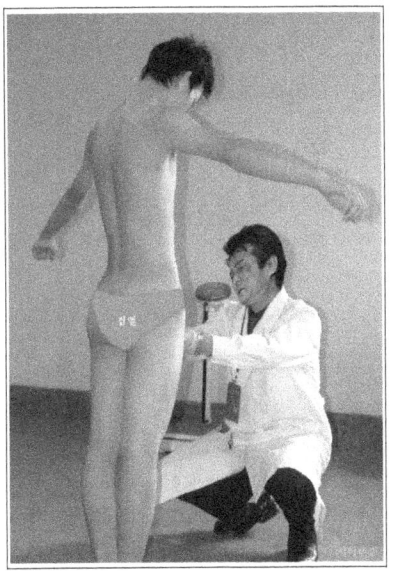

Figure 12. In this image, Sim Young's face is pasted onto the head of a doctor checking the body of another male for the army physical exam.

Figure 13. In this posting by Khaichel, titled "Sim Young as raped by Hong," Sukcheon Hong (man on top) can be seen groping Sim Young (man on bottom).

SIM YOUNG: ah. .No. My purity TT [On behalf of Sim Young]

KIM DOO HAN: Hhhhhh it is not that important at all kk

SAMDEOTAKER: Ah fuck,, relevant [means great and point taken in Composite Gallery] kkkkkkkkkkkkkkkk you got it right which is soft (penis).[11]

As "Sim Young as raped by Hong" and its associated comments illustrate, the Pae-in usually connect homosexuals with eunuchs. This is because homosexuals are considered perverse and thus desperate to find any sexual partners—even if that means a eunuch. Moreover, once an individual loses his penis, it is believed by the Pae-in that he, by extension, has become physically incompetent.

As a result, the masculinity of a eunuch is also castrated, and, as such, he is unable to compete in the patriarchal sexual economy—meaning he can only be victimized. Sexual power for men, according to Khan et al. (2008) is "the most potent asset in men's lives and is needed to win women" (p. 39) as a demonstration of a robust male performance. Put simply, men who cannot have sex with women are not men at all.

Hall's (1996) notion of the talking penis offers a compelling account for the ways in which men mention their phallus as a means of asserting their masculinity. Through the ritual of the talking penis, men transform a biological organ into a symbolic marker by which in-group status is maintained. To maintain this cultural space, masculine men flaunt their symbolic penises as a means of demonstrating contempt for those outside their community. However, whereas Hall (1996) spoke of the talking penis as symbolic manifestation of a biological organ, presuming that merely having one was tantamount to having the other, the Pae-in of DCinside prove otherwise: having a biological penis is not enough; rather, one must use it, or otherwise be at risk of falling into the category of "abnormal." In this regard, the Pae-in also utilize their symbolic penises as a means of creating an internal class among men.

The Internet and Masculinity

On April 28, 2004, a Pae-in by the name of KIN wondered, "If DCinside adopted the membership system, would people still make malicious comments like they do now?" This self-criticism identifies a major reason for the ruthlessness of online parody culture: anonymity. Danet (2001) argues that with the absence of nonverbal and other social or material cues for identification, the anonymity of the Internet encourages the development of a masculine playfulness: users can behave recklessly and express their hidden personality without fear of repercussion. Kim and Park (2005) point out that, "DCinside does require that users create a nickname and password in order to access the system" ([my translation], p. 88), but since no personal information is needed to set up an account, its online community is able to operate with a relatively secure amount of anonymity. In a comparative analysis of three online communities, Hwang (2003) argues that DCinside's lack of a robust membership system contributes to its status as the most tasteless site amongst the three.

On the one hand, this anonymous system encourages people to freely state their opinion and upload whatever images they may find relevant; as a result,

DCinside ranks as one of the most vibrant public spheres within cyberspace. On the other hand, such anonymity helps "the interactants to find themselves freed not only from the politeness expectations of face-to-face interaction, but also from the identifying physical characteristics of vocality" (Hall, 1996, p. 156). In this regard, while DCinside may function as a vibrant democratic space, the anonymous membership system functions in such a way as to allow its users to police the borders of participation; DCinside is a male-centered space that encourages other men to spout their "repressed" masculinity.

In a strange twist, "in online interactions the lack of physical markers does not weaken gender identity but rather strengthens it" ([my translation], M. Lee, 2003, p. 44). In focus group interviews, M. Lee (2003) found that "men wished to express online their sexuality which could not be exhibited offline" ([my translation], p. 42). This resonates somewhat with Yoosik Kim's findings that the Pae-in were just "normal" students and workers, despite their DCinside affiliation (as cited in Hwang, 2003).[12] But in Kyuchan Kim's (2006) formulation, "normal" people produce provocative pictures and make indecent jokes in real life. Instead, we cannot let masculinity continue to position itself as "normal," and rather must remember that, while operating under the shield of anonymity, certain bodies (men) are harming others (women and "abnormal" men); cybermasculinity is but another incarnation of masculinity.

As cybermasculinity further establishes itself as the online norm, the Internet will continue to be what Benwell and Stokoe (2006) contend is a playful, creative, impressive, and limitless place. Yet, it can only function as such to the extent that we ignore that virtual identities are not necessarily detached from physical identities. So while, virtually, the Pae-in express their ulterior desires through the construction of new identities (i.e., a creative act), these new identities are contingent upon the victimization of offline people (e.g., the *nyeos*). In this sense, the illusion of an immaterial Internet is rather that of a voyeuristic fantasy for men.

The Internet has become this space of masculine fantasy, at least in Korea, according to H. Lee (2006) because of the historical development of a coercive nationalistic military culture. In this sense, the Internet provides the Pae-in with a free space in which they can get away from this hierarchical order (Kim & Park, 2005). This is possible, for as Ross (2005) argues, on the Internet, "a participant can experiment with a sexual behavior not by just thinking about it, but by engaging in it online and with another person without actually 'doing' it" (p. 344). But instead of the creation of new masculinities, this space is being used by the Pae-in as a means of reversing the hierarchy: from repressed men at the bottom to repressed men at the top—with women and other "abnormal men," of course, at the bottom. Indeed, the Pae-in frequently produce eccentric sexual images and use coded language as a means of fulfilling (online) their unfulfillable (offline) masculine cravings. This parody culture, expressed in the virtual, lets them experience a cathartic breakaway.

Moreover, the Pae-in expect others to agree with them and enjoy making fun of the persons in images. This fun culture has been the driving force of DCinside, and has worked to make it a male-centered space. Sexualizing women and deriding "abnormal" men, have helped the Pae-in confirm their masculinity by clarifying a common bond amongst "normal" men (Kim & Choi, 2007). According to Kendall (2000), this bluff of masculinity is "an important element of masculine identities and [source of] connection with other men" (p. 265). Therefore, so as to affirm and reinforce their own masculinity: men sexualize women more and more. Additionally, they satirize "fallen" men, such as homosexuals and eunuchs, all while asking for other men's approval of their masculinity. Through jokes targeting sexual minorities as sexual objects, male participants in DCinside demonstrate a root appeal for hegemonic masculinity (Kendall, 2000). As men experience a sense of impending crisis, they try to firm up their dominant position by constructing male-centered spaces. In addition, through othering homosexuals and eunuchs who deviate from the dominant male image, they aim to maintain a hegemonic masculinity.

Issues Derived from Cybermasculinity

Many problems exist in parody culture in that it enforces hegemonic masculinity. Here, I locate these issues as falling into two interrelated spaces: sexual harassment and the reproduction of gender inequality. First, DCinside's parody pictures and comments often function as sexual harassment which should be a crime. Virtual harassment obviously violates personal rights. For instance, sexualized people might not be able to restore their honor and/or recover from the trauma, especially when they are ordinary people unused to public exposure. For instance, the *Gwangnyeo* woman petitioned for her image to be removed after she realized her photo was being parodied. She must have been devastated seeing the Pae-in construct sensational images with her picture and ridicule her appearance. Moreover, even those not individually targeted in an image may still find offense in the symbolic functioning of the pictures. For instance, gay men may not be happy to find that homosexuality, via the parodies of Sukcheon Hong, is portrayed as a sexually insatiable deviant practice.

As Barak (2005) insists, even though the harasser does not submit harassing messages directly to a particular person or group but, rather, submits the images into a cyberspace of potential receivers, it is still sexual harassment. Namely, not only are cyberstalking and cyberthreatening forms of sexual harassment, but so too is textual harassment a form of sexual assault. This harassment could be even more dangerous than that in real life in that it is widely disseminated through the Internet, thereby casting a greater net of impact.

Many men, however, do not seem to recognize that their parody culture could be a crime. They remain ignorant of its violence against women because of the different perceptions of men and women about sexual harassment. According to K. Lee (2005), men answered that "access to a sexual joke free of malice would enhance the quality of their life" ([my translation], p. 304). But as Biber, Doverspike, Baznik, Cober, and Ritter (2002) suggest, men generally are not self-reflective enough to judge which behaviors are sexually harassing. It is a significant issue that men are not conscious about the sexism and violence embedded within masculine parody culture. Considering that sexual harassment is not about sex but about power, male-centered parody culture subverts female access to the Internet and deepens the anxiety and fear experienced by women in new media environments (Woo, 1999). In the long run, this segregation of women from the informatized space and the reproduction of masculine culture stifle the possibility of using cyberspace as a means for creating a gender-equal world (K. Lee, 2005).

This second problem of reproducing gender inequality is especially worrisome because many of the DCinside Pae-in include students from elementary to high school. Although it is not clear to what extent media usage affects the behavior of adolescents, Woo (1999) argues that sexual images, such as those including pornography, certainly influence the formation of one's viewpoints about women. Namely, it is a possibility that members of the Pae-in look down upon women and possess harmful ideas regarding gender relationships. As such, cybermasculinity strengthens offline gender stereotypes (Kim & Choi, 2007), and therefore the social disparity between men and women is reified both in online and offline worlds. Put simply, the ironic sexism of DCinside discourse sustains what Kendall (2000) calls, "the order of gender domination" (p. 264).

Parody Culture and the Freedom of Expression

When it comes to discussing parody culture, the most problematic issue arises over the debate regarding the freedom of expression. So far, sexual parody pictures and comments have not received any legal sanction under the name of the freedom of expression. In the case of political parody pictures, producers of them were punished on charge of violating honor or election law if their description was excessively insulting. That said, it has not been the legal realm, but rather the social sphere which has produced the most criticism of the parody culture of DCinside. As such, most of the parodied images and comments persist online unless the person in the photo demands they be deleted. Even the administrators of both DCinside and related portal sites often do not attempt to interrupt the production and distribution of any sexualized pictures in advance.

Some advocates of parody culture insist that the regulation of parody culture will result in an infringement of the freedom of expression, so that the autonomy of the Internet culture at-large would suffer (J. Kim, 2005). While it is necessary to ask if parody culture is worthy of protection from the standpoint of the freedom of expression, as a matter of fact, most of the pictures created in the Composite Gallery of DCinside deviate from the essence of parody. Certainly, parody is a form of imitation. Imitation should be, however, characterized by ironic reversal. Therefore, when we speak of parody, we do not mean the simple combination of two texts; rather, we convey "an intention to parody another work (or set of conventions)" and make explicit both a recognition of that intent, as well as provide the ability to find and interpret the original source material in relation to its parody (Hutcheon, 2000, p. 22). That is, parody should be deeply engaged with the meaning or the expression of the original work, not just borrowing it.

Considering it from this respect, the parody pictures of DCinside do not look meaningfully into the ironies of the original image. Their goal seems only to make the person in the picture a laughingstock through photo manipulation. Kim and Park (2005) point out that "the parody photos of DCinside are not art but rather mimicry in that the Pae-in only intend to produce futile communication without sincere support and interest for parody culture" ([my translation], p. 95).[13] In other words, the making of sexual pictures and meaningless jests purely for the alleviation of boredom constructs a depoliticized notion of fun, which works to sustain the status quo: masculine culture. Accordingly, when the question is of gender equality rather than that of other political issues, it is hard to believe that parody culture plays a critical function beyond the maintenance of fun culture, which becomes a code word for masculine hegemony. That is, the discussion that the parody culture of DCinside deserves protection under the freedom of expression is not valid even if we allow the Pae-in access to the freedom of expression, the deriding of certain persons for their ugly appearance and/or marginalized sexuality cannot or should not be undertaken.

Conclusion

South Korea is believed to have one of the most well-developed Internet infrastructures. Within the past several years, unfortunately, South Korea has also witnessed the suicide of several female and gay-male celebrities due to malicious comments on the Internet. This is in conjunction with the widespread popularity of "joke-websites" that target women and other gendered and sexual minorities. Looking into the website, DCinside, as a case study, I argued that the Internet is not the technological manifestation of a utopian public sphere, but rather an enabling space for the performance of a digital form of cybermasculinity. In a representative website lying at the root of parody culture in South Korea, participants of DCinside have produced massive composite images for years. Some of them, in their particular handling of political issues, have helped to make our society more democratic and open to public debate. But others, especially in their depictions of women and homosexuals, continue to reproduce a hegemonic heterosexual masculinity that outshines the potentiality of the Internet as a liberating space.

Cybermasculinity precisely captures this phenomenon of male online users continuing to sexualize and objectify people of marginalized gendered identities. I analyzed the cybermasculinity of DCinside with Hall's four categories: conversational dominance, textual harassment, heterosexism and physical hierarchies, and the phenomenon of the "talking penis." Cybermasculinity towards women and homosexuals was found to be more extreme than expected. I had difficulty finding female users in the Composite Gallery and found most issues to be framed from a masculine perspective. Consequently, the postings of female photos and accompanying comments consisted of pleasure and *sexuality-ridden* jokes. The target of male users is not limited to women, however, as even homosexuals and eunuchs are sexually harassed and mocked for the sole reason that they are different from the notion of a "typical" man.

The presence of cybermasculinity in parody culture suggests that conventional masculinity has found a way to exploit the anonymity afforded online in order to sustain itself. This has resulted in virtual segregation, in that sexual minorities are being excluded from certain spaces of the Internet. What is more, attitudes expressed in the virtual world towards women and homosexuals could influence perspectives in the offline world. The defenders of parody culture refute this concern by asserting that parody culture should be guaranteed by the freedom of expression. However, the parody postings of DCinside are against the original purpose of the very notion of parody and instead violate personal rights.

It, of course, should not be overlooked that cybermasculinity is merely one part of DCinside culture and that there are lots of positive functions that the website has carried out. As such, I would argue that it is necessary that we continue in our effort to make DCinside a more desirable cyberspace for gender equality. We (1994) insists that the Internet is full of virtual spaces where women and men can meet and talk. As one of the top cyber communities, DCinside has the capacity to reach a wide range of audiences. With such a critical reach and political potential, DCinside should stand at the forefront of gender equality rather than continuing to reinforce masculinity through the guise of parody culture.

Notes

1. According to the ranking site 100hot (2010), DCinside is the most popular website among the hardware information category. DCinside has kept the lead among websites which review digital devices for years (H. Kim, 2006).
2. The labeling of DCinside participants as the *Pae-in*, originated shortly after its users parodied a random Telecommunication Company's commercial. The commercial's catchphrase was: "You are a 'Main' [i.e., a person/thing of extreme significance] who never leaves work." A participant of DCinside co-opted the slogan as, "You are the 'Pae-in' who never leave the Internet" ([my translation], Kim & Park, 2005, p. 88).
3. At first, the Composite Gallery was restricted to pictures but now even sound and video can become a requisite.
4. Here it is important to note that Rose (2001) uses ideology to refer to interests of power rather than the conventional understanding of false consciousness.
5. For instance, the Nude Gallery is full of female nude picture and the Girlfriend Gallery is a space where men upload images of their "girl" and ask others to evaluate her appearance (Chae, 2008). These are just a few examples of how much male-centered content exists on DCinside.
6. The term "beautiful fools" refers to those women who seem to only care about their physical appearance without also cultivating the cultural capital deemed necessary in order to marry men of high status (economically or politically).
7. Other popular parodies of women have included: *Halnyeo*, Eugene *Hehnyeo*, Jihyun maiden, Euna Chung, Bin, *Hyok*, Hillary Clinton, and *Seo-rilla*.
8. There have been several events that illustrate difficulties that homosexuals go through in

Korea. First, one male model and actor, Jihoo Kim, killed himself. After he came out, he reportedly had a hard time dealing with the criticism of his sexuality (Seo, 2008). Additionally, upon coming out to her mother, one high school girl was sent to a mental hospital by her mother. Her mother preferred sending her daughter to the hospital to prevent others from learning of her child's 'abnormal' status. This choice of her mother directly shows the whole atmosphere toward homosexuals in South Korea (J. Lee, 2008). Hence, it is not surprising that "popular sentiment towards homosexuals is still negative" ([my translation], D. Lee, 2008, para. 4).
9. The Pae-in call Hong a "hawk" due to the shape of his eyes.
10. Jeong's (2008) study found the following amongst Internet participants voting for hot key words in 2008, the line in the drama, *Yain Sidae* "unbelievable that I am a eunuch!" (my translation) ranked second, getting 15.4%. The scene which became a topic in those days of broadcasting described Sim Young's grief. Although he survived the attack by Kim Doo Han, he could not help crying out because he was a eunuch. This year, it continued to attract attention as DCinside participants parodied his line by inserting it into a variety of background music.
11. Kim Doo Han is the name of the character that shot the gun at the penis of Sim Young in the drama.
12. Yoosik Kim is a representative of DCinside. He came to the conclusion that the Pae-in were just typical people after having met several of them in person (Hwang, 2003).
13. Most of the images and related comments are malicious or meaningless (C. Lee, 2003a). As such, they function as mimicry insofar as mimicry is a copy of the original but without the intentions of the original; mimicry is an attempt to emulate the act of a given communicative event without any of the original's authenticity. In this regard, mimicry as used by the Pae-in is that of an attempt to depoliticize the communicative intent of the original.

References

Barak, A. (2005). Sexual harassment on the Internet. *Social Science Computer Review, 23*(1), 77–92.

Benwell, B, & Stokoe, E. (2006). *Discourse and identity*. Edinburgh, UK: Edinburgh University Press.

Biber, J., Doverspike, D., Baznik, D., Cober, A., & Ritter, B. (2002). Sexual harassment in online communications: Effects of gender and discourse medium. *Cyberpsychology & Behavior, 5*(1), 33–42.

Cassell, J., & Jenkins, H. (1999). Chess for girls? Feminism and computer games. In J. Cassell & H. Jenkins (Eds.), *From Barbie to Mortal Kombat: Gender and computer games* (pp. 3–45). Cambridge, MA: MIT Press.

Chae, H. (2008, March 21). [인터뷰] 박유진 디시인사이드 뉴스팀장: 남성중심 인터넷 공간에 '여성전용' 개설 주도. 여성신문. [(Interview) Park Eugene, DCinside News Manager: Initiate to Make 'Women-Only Space' in Male-Centered Internet Space. Womennews], 973. Retrieved from http://www.womennews.co.kr/news/view.asp?num=35943&page=1&ns_id=A0&wno=97

Cook, I. (2006). Western heterosexual masculinity, anxiety, and web porn. *The Journal of Men's Studies, 14*(1), 47–63.
Cooper, J. (2006). The digital divide: The special case of gender. *Journal of Computer Assisted Learning, 22,* 320–334.
Danet, B. (2001). *Cyberplay: Communicating online.* Oxford: Berg.
Fairclough, N. (2003). *Analysing discourse: Textual analysis for social research.* London, New York: Routledge.
Fernback, J. (1997). The individual within the collective: Virtual ideology and the realization of collective principles. In S. G. Jones (Eds.), *Virtual culture: Identity and communication in cybersociety* (pp. 36–54). London, Thousand Oaks, CA: Sage.
Fraser, N. (1990). Rethinking the public sphere: A contribution to the critique of actually existing democracy. *Social Text, 25/26,* 56–80.
Fredrick, C. (1999). Feminist rhetoric in cyberspace: The ethos of feminist Usenet Newsgroups. *The Information Society, 15*(3), 187–197.
Hall, K. (1996). Cyberfeminism. In S. C. Herring (Eds.), *Computer-mediated communication: Linguistic, social, and cross-cultural perspectives* (pp. 147–170). Philadelphia, PA: John Benjamins.
Ham, Y. (2002). [*A Study on Societal Connotation of the Digital Parody and Its Forecast* (Doctoral dissertation)]. Hanyang University, Seoul.
Herek, G. (1986). On heterosexual masculinity: Some psychical consequences of the social construction of gender and sexuality. *American Behavioral Scientist, 29*(5), 563–577.
Herring, S. C. (1996). Bringing familiar baggage to the new frontier: Gender differences in computer-mediated communication. In V. Vitanza (Eds.), *CyberReader* (pp. 144–154). Boston, MA: Allyn & Bacon.
Hutcheon, L. (2000). *A theory of parody.* Champaign: University of Illinois Press.
Hwang, J. (2003). [*The study of collective identity and actions about cyber-communities* (Master's thesis)]. Dongguk University, Seoul.
Jeong, J. (2008, December 25). [The Hot Keyword this Year, 'Ddong Ddeong Uh Ri,' 'Unbelievable I am a Eunuch!' *Joynews*]. Retrieved from http://joynews.inews24.com/php/news_view.php?g_menu=700100&g_serial=381581
Kang, Y. & Jeon, H. (2004, July 21). [Dreaming between Digital and Analog. *Pressian*]. Retrieved from http://www.pressian.com/article/article.asp?article_num=30040720140530&section=04
Kendall, L. (2000). Oh no! I'm a nerd: Hegemonic masculinity on an online forum. *Gender and Society, 14*(2), 256–274.
Khan, S. I., Hudson-Rodd, N., Saggers, S., Bhuiyan, M. I., Bhuiya, A., Karim, S. A., & Rauyajin, O. (2008). Phallus, performance and power: Crisis of masculinity. *Sexual & Relationship Therapy, 23*(1), 37–49.
Kim, H. (2006, May 8). [DCinside Ranks First among Digital Device Information Website. *Inews24*], (1) 24. Retrieved from http://itnews.inews24.com/php/news_view.php?g_serial=203315&g_menu=020100
Kim, J. (2003, April 27). [신세대 신풍속] 신주류로 뜨는 '찰칵족.' 경향신문. [(New Generation and New Customs) Click Tribe as a Rising Mainstream. Kyunghyang Sinmun]. Retrieved from http://www.khan.co.kr/

Kim, J. (2005). [*A study of the transformation in Internet cultural contents through the entrance of digital cameras: Based on the personal homepage media providers Cyworld and Blog* (Master's thesis)]. Sogang University, Seoul.

Kim. J. (2008, November 28). 영화 속 男男 커플이 뜬다. 매일경제. [Gay couple in movies is getting popular. Maeil Business Newspaper]. Retrieved from http://news.mk.co.kr/newsRead.php?year=2008&no=725953

Kim, K. (2006). [*The process and implication of Internet witch-hunt: Focusing on the "Dog-poop girl" case in Korea* (Master's thesis)]. Seoul National University, Seoul.

Kim, M. (2006, November 14). [DCinside "We will compete with all the Internet Service." *Etnews*]. Retrieved from http://www.etnews.co.kr/news/detail.html?id=200611130153

Kim, R. & Park, S. (2005). [A study of 'digiholics' from the perspective of postmodernism. *Journal of Consumer Studies*], 16(4), 81–102.

Kim, S., & Choi, S. (2007). [Construction and re-production of masculinities in Korean Cyberspace: Comparative study on the difference between community board and discussion board. *Media, Gender & Culture*], 8, 5–41.

Kim, Y. (2006, June 16). [(Kim Yoo Sik Column) Female Internet participants, inevitable to pretend to be male. *Ohmynews*]. Retrieved from http://www.ohmynews.com/nws_web/view/at_pg.aspx?CNTN_CD=A0000338598

Ko, E., Kim, S., Kipkoech, D., Lee, E., & Chang, M. (2008, July 21). [Homosexuals, a new stimulus? Or another reality? *Maeil Business Newspaper*]. Retrieved from http://news.mk.co.kr/newsRead.php?year=2008&no=435887

Kramarae, C., & Taylor, J. (1993). Women and men on electronic networks: A conversation or a monologue? In C. Kramarae, J. Taylor, & M, Ebben (Eds.), *Women, information technology and scholarship* (pp. 52–60). Urbana, IL: University of Illinois.

Lee, C. (2003). [*A study about cultural aspects of virtual community members* (Master's thesis)]. Korea University, Seoul.

Lee, D. (2008, November 25). [(Special homosexuals) popular culture, overcoming homophobia. *Weekly Hankook*]. Retrieved from http://weekly.hankooki.com/lpage/coverstory/200811/wk20081125155423105410.htm

Lee, H. (2006). [Internet and play: Swimming in the sea of wit and humor. *National Internet Development Agency of Korea*], 1–17.

Lee, H. (2008). [A study of the different play of digital images: Focused on Internet communities. *Illusology*], 11(4), 123–130.

Lee, J. (2008, December 7). ['Cool gay' is OK, 'terminal gay' is NO? *Ohmynews*]. Retrieved from http://www.ohmynews.com/NWS_Web/view/at_pg.aspx?CNTN_CD=A0001025179

Lee, J. (2009). [*A study of 'Media 2.0' phenomenon in the 2008 Korean candlelight protest over mad cow disease* (Master's thesis)]. Hanyang University, Seoul.

Lee, K. (2005). [Various issues of cause and the real situation on a cyber sexual violence, *National Ethics Study*], 60, 285–316.

Lee, M. (2003). [Gender identity and online communication. *Informatization policy*], 10(3), 33–45.

Lee, S. (1999). 사이버스페이스에서의 여성배제 구조와 저항에 관한 연구 -PC통신을 중심으로-. 이화여자대학교 석사학위논문. [A study on patriarchal order in the cyberspace]. Ewha Womans University, Seoul.

Murphree, H. J. Y. (2008). Transnational cultural production and the politics of moribund masculinity. *Position, 16*(3), 661–688.

Nakamura, L. (2002). *Cybertypes: Race, ethnicity, and identity on the Internet.* New York, London: Routledge.

Nakamura, L., & Haraway, D. (2003). Prospects for a materialist informatics: An interview with Donna Haraway. Retrieved from http://www.electronicbookreview.com/thread/technocapitalism/interview

Pang, H. (2002). [*Cyber democracy based on minority culture: Focusing on minority culture of 'Cyber Pe–In'* (Master's thesis)]. Sogang University, Seoul.

Rose, G. (2001). *Visual methodologies.* London; Thousand Oaks, CA: Sage.

Ross, M. (2005). Typing, doing, and being: Sexuality and the internet. *The Journal of Sex Research, 42*(4), 342–352.

Scott. A., Semmens, L., & Willoughby, L. (2001). Women and the internet: The natural history of a research project. In E. Green & A. Adam (Eds.), *Virtual gender: Technology, consumption and identity* (pp. 3–22). London: Routledge.

Seo, M. (2008, October 8). [The suicide of Kim Jihoo, who suffered from internet bullying after his coming out. *Seoul Sinmun*]. Retrieved from http://nownews.seoul.co.kr/news/newsView.php?id=20081008603019

Song, K. (2005). 네트워크 시대의 인터넷 정치 참여. 담론. [Political participation in the IT based network age. *Discourse* 201], 8(3), 123–160.

Walzer, A. (2002). Narratives of contemporary male crisis: The (re)production of a national discourse. *The Journal of Men's Studies, 10*(2), 209–223.

We, G. .(1994). Cross–gender communication in cyberspace. *Arachnet Electronic Journal on Virtual Culture, 2*(3). Retrieved from http://serials.infomotions.com/aejvc/aejvc–v2n03–we–crossgender.txt

Woo, J. (1999). 포르노그라피 규제에 대한 담론을 통해 본 사이버스페이스와 여성문제. 한국언론학회. [A study on discourse regarding the regulation of pornography. *Korean Journal of Journalism & Communication Studies*], 44(1), 244–286.

· 1 0 ·

Displaced Bodies and Governmentality

Lessons from the CHA Website

CRYSTAL THOMAS

> Now we get to see and feel how the middle class and the upper class live, and vice versa, they get to see how we live...We all on the same page.
> —BETTY FLAKE, "RESIDENT STORIES"[1]

Eleven years in progress and almost two billion over projections but still pushing to re-house thousands of residents, the City of Chicago's "Plan for Transformation" is a model case for examining how neoliberal hegemony, New Urbanism ideals, and the performance of governmentality shape our discourses about bodies and citizenship. Under the umbrella of Hope VI legislation, the "Plan for Transformation" targets 25,000 public housing units for demolition or rehabilitation and purports to be the most ambitious overhaul of housing in the country due to the sheer volume of construction and relocation inherent in the project (Chicago Housing Authority, 2010) as well as the concentrated turnaround of Chicago's housing authority. But the "Plan" doesn't just promise public housing renovation or bureaucratic accountability; it aims at the inscription of mixed-income, ethnically diverse communities as the wave of the future—and the recuperation of public housing renters as respected members of those communities and essential elements of the Chicago work force. "No other city is doing more [. . .] to ensure that everyone—regardless of income—share in its success," the Chicago Housing Authority (CHA) website touted in 2007. Like all Moving to Work (MTW) programs instituted under the Clinton Administration, the Chicago plan equally affirms the value of self-sufficiency and mandates some level of participation in the labor market. Like acclaimed New Urbanism trends, the "Plan for Transformation" emphasizes the private development of greenways and predominantly low-rise housing with improved access to retail and public services (New Urban News, 2000). At issue, however, is that the Plan buttresses the larger agenda of the Commercial Club of Chicago—which many revile for inequities such as its hand in disproportionate school closings in communities of color, the enabling of gentrification through property tax hikes, and limited democratic participation (Blocks Together, "Housing," 2010; Lipman & Hursh, 2007). Moreover, the "Plan for Transformation" is highly contested and has been criticized for insufficient eviction and relocation notices, slow or stalled construction on replacement units, and its contribution to resegregation and criminalization (Bensing & Caputo, 2010; Ihejirika, 2010; Venkatesh et al, 2004). But for such a messy movement of thousands of people from one home to another—and for many, more moves than that—the rhetoric of the Plan is strikingly neat, scrubbed of the gaps between its policies and practice. Almost.

This chapter focuses on the transformation of public housing residents into "good citizen bodies" (Brandzel, 2005, p. 179) through discourse; in particular, the metonymic language and imagery of the CHA that for a specific period of time worked to construct seamlessness between ideas of rehabilitated buildings, reformed government, and middle class neighborliness all the while displacement strategies heightened residents' subjectivity as lower class and black. Housing is at the heart of how we are perceived in America, and our potentiality as prospective homeowners is central to the way we are governed and understood ideologically, socially, and culturally. This symbol of the American Dream is also political because of its relationship to the economy: its "infrastructure includes developers, the financial services industry, the real estate industry, planners, road builders, and the like" (Schlay, 2006, p. 512). Not only does homeownership connote stability, it helps in stimulating revenue for the state. Housing is a cornerstone of the Commercial Club's *Metropolis 2020* prospectus (Chicago Metropolis 2020 (1999a). Its offshoot committee, the Chicago Metropolis 2020 organization, cites that where one lives is "the core of opportunity" (Chicago Metropolis 2020, "Housing," 2010, para. 1) and the key to promoting a viable region for businesses and employees. As such, housing has been constructed as integral to the making of a global capitalist utopia in Chicago. This could not be made any clearer than by the cover of *The Metropolis Principles* document (1999b) which shows a white man and woman embracing in front of a white house next to a "Sold" sign, the woman's single lifted leg signaling the stereotype of heterosexual contentment and her thick-soled shoes indicating the two's labor position. Such an ideological dream codes the ultimate working class family as white and reinforces the hierarchy of owners over renters, which explicitly places public housing and its leaseholders, if not transitional, at the bottom of the capitalist scale. So does *Metropolis 2020*'s (1999a) labeling of the demographic body of public housing (predominantly African American) as the "urban" and "minority" poor (p. 42, 89). Thus, the role of the "Plan for Transformation," and by extension of the CHA, becomes to literally and symbolically inscribe low-income residents into the capitalist map by dispersing them throughout "opportunity areas" where it is presumed mixed income communities will inspire them to emulate their neighbors and blend more into the city's landscape (Chaskin & Joseph, 2010).

The reduction of people into metonymic signs of the built environment (especially the ghetto or slum) is not new nor is the often accompanying justification for spatial separation and urban clearance (Dowling, 2007; Osofsky, 1971). What, perhaps, is new that this chapter tries to stake out is the incredible visibility of governmentality underlying the "Plan for Transformation" and similar plans in their effort to be global models. The CHA website reflects an increasingly reflexive clustering of technology and power-knowledge within a neoliberalism that conceals the material and psychic costs to those most disciplined by its rationale. Consistent for at least six years, the CHA website from 2003–2008 represented a visual manifesto for the "Plan for Transformation," elaborately displaying the plan's attempts to create the "new culture of success and hope" ("Plan for Transformation: Reform," 2007). [2] The website has since been redesigned for a simpler user interface per its CEO ("Message from the CEO," 2010) that will also be briefly discussed, but even the latter's more forthright presentation is evidence of the governmental performance of public confidence and the need to keep people believing in the Plan (Clarke, 2004). Despite the recent makeover, a critical discourse analysis of the CHA's analogous *and* counter-texts, also on the web, indicates a significant attempt at narration of bodies and their movement, all while the material effects of displacement are happening on the ground.

Methodology

The "Plan for Transformation" has and continues to be studied for its impact on social and cultural processes such as gang activity, neighborhood development, the formation of public spheres, and uses of human rights language (Chaskin and Joseph, 2010; Fleming, 2008; Pfeiffer, 2006; Venkatesh et al., 2004). A project affecting so many on the macro and micro level merits multiple theoretical, sociological, and urban planning analyses since these principles are so intertwined in the *Metropolis 2020* venture. My analysis, however, pertains to the specific *discursive* representations constructed by the CHA in an attempt to point out the use of its rhetoric as a form of governmentality. Such an investigation might be useful to Cultural Studies in elucidating the paradoxes of neoliberalism in both the represented and lived experience of urban housing. By discursive, I refer to visual, written, and verbal enunciations (website copy, videos, brochures, etc.) that may reify actual practices and serve to construct a revelatory picture of relationships between social signs and structures of power. I rely on the critical discourse approach that concerns itself with the "opacity of these relationships [. . .] itself a factor securing power and hegemony" (Fairclough, 1993, p. 135), and I position myself as a critic vested in the exposure of representation and policy detrimental to the lower class (van Dijk 1993). The distance between a governmental website and the actual bureaucratic office/property in which one may find herself subject to more overt forms of control may seem wide or opaque. However, rhetorical conventions cross genres and contexts and, by doing so, can illustrate what ideologies might be at work in multiple sites. By looking at discourse primarily made public on the Internet, I am not necessarily marking a different legitimization of power-knowledge concerning housing and welfare but a unique location where we can spy acts of spatial and cultural discipline.

As mentioned above, I consider the websites discussed a sign and practice of governmentality. Foucault (1984, 1986) has drawn our attention to the ways in which discourse formations (institutions, norms, and forms of subjectivity) shape our understanding of ourselves in the world, as well as how the individual's relationship to the state and its associated apparatuses reflects a form of bio-politics. Bio-politics' today (that is, the range of concerns over the body's welfare, movement and reproduction) may be rationalized in concert or even in tension with neoliberal government, depending on whether the state's various techniques and outcomes support a liberalized economy (Dean, 2010). Public housing currently occupies a particularly awkward position on this tightrope because while, legitimized as a federally regulated space, it is also quickly becoming privatized by corporate entities, which inflicts a special and often unfair vulnerability on those who live there. The CHA and the discourses deployed by CHA reflect this neoliberalist shift.

Though primarily interested in face-to-face texts, or speech acts, Fairclough (1989) provides a way of analyzing and discussing the ideologies embedded behind bureaucratic discourses such as that of housing authority websites. As method, he (1989) suggests examining vocabulary, metaphor, and grammar to tease out the "value" or kinds of meaning texts may have underlying their textual structures. He outlines a set of ten questions designed to help critics discuss the features, intertextuality, and implications of discourse (1989, see pp. 110–111). Rose (2007) extends this method to visual texts and iterates the importance of also looking for complexity and contradictions. Since both affirm their syntheses of discourse analysis as "blueprints" requiring selectivity, I will borrow from them liberally in order to discuss the representational issues in the CHA website. Taken together, *Metropolis 2020* discourse, of which the "Plan for Transformation" forms a part, is an example of how neoliberal housing strategies are not only enforced but how they become discursively persuasive.

CHANGE: Redevelopment and Opportunity Rhetoric in CHA Discourse

More overtly than the websites of other large housing authorities at the time of this study, the 2003–2008 CHA website displayed a virtual metaphor of neoliberal governmentality and its paradoxes. Designed in the sharp colors of bright orange and white, it contained a proliferation of information to choose from: videos, annuals reports, brochures, meeting minutes, applications, newsletters, FAQs, issue logs, a photo gallery, and more. Intriguing graphics faded in and out on the front page, and documents of interest announced their accessibility in English and Spanish via html or pdf. The website was chic and highly imitative of robust corporate websites. Yet it was not its sophistication that distinguished it from Detroit's, New York's, or Washington, DC's housing authority websites at the time but the *visibility* of its concentration of tactics to promote the "Plan for Transformation's" content. This was most obvious from the CHANGE advertisements dispersed throughout the site and the site's extensive archiving, some features of which are still present in the

2010 redesign. The content of the 2003–2008 design, in conjunction with the technologies that advanced it, promoted an idea of change as cutting edge and inevitable. Redevelopment, it seemed to suggest, goes hand in hand with opportunity, and its own extreme visuality implied that nothing could be left out.[3]

If you typed in the CHA web address in 2006, a graphic immediately unfolded at the top of the page requiring Adobe Flash Player. It depicted a small cityscape in which a red, shiny building towered over two white buildings against a bright blue sky. Then the block letters, "WE LOOK GOOD IN RED," suddenly appeared. And here, irony peeks through. Like public housing residents, the CHA was moving to a new location at the time. The positive reference to the color red does the doubled duty of recuperating the agency's notoriety as a landlord, and also plays on the lyrics of "Lady in Red," indicating an image of renewed desirability.[4] It could also be read as an allusion to the red of the Robert Taylor Homes and the "Cabrini Reds:" two of the most maligned public housing developments for crime and social ills. The "WE" personifies the CHA as well as the building, emphasizing a parallel or *seamless* identity between the agency, public housing, and residents that is a motif of that period's literature. Under the paragraph welcoming you to the site, what caught the eye next was a montage of alternating graphics that appeared first as blurry tableaus and then sharpened into actual photographs. A scene of quaint row houses flashed first, then a trio of photos of smiling residents. Next came the green space of a small park where a mom in medical uniform strolled with her son. Then three photographs of living rooms came into focus, one with a large pool table near the black marble countertop of a sparkling kitchen. Between each set of graphics, a "Plan for Transformation" ad flashed with the caption "Vision for Change: Building Hope."[5] By juxtaposing imagery of buildings with residents, with persuasive marketing language sandwiched in between, this oscillation of photos, like the red banner's allusion, I would argue, metonymically implied a transition into the CHA's glossy future. Out with the old, and in with the new.

There were ten tabs on the former website's navigation bar and twenty-six hyperlinks to the left of the page hailing different audiences. These included forms for vendors to become involved, resources for residents preparing to move, announcements for summer camp, press release titles, and a listing of sister agencies. Compared to the current web design that only boasts six drop-down tabs on its navigation bar, the 2003–2008 site may just sound "busy." But I would argue the busyness of its design reflects a statement within the discourse that the CHA was trying to make visible its transparency and that it had and has nothing to hide. If one scrolled through the FAQs in 2008, for example, bulky paragraphs with embedded links, addressed questions such as "Is the Plan for Transformation a land-grab for developers?" (This reflexivity is also apparent in the current website, but the former website's concern with instructiveness and display made CHA's governmentality that much more visual.) The former website did not assume, for example, that visitors understood that they had to use the mouse to link to new pages. Its multiple taglines directing one to "click here" under promo videos and forms make the agency appear eager to share information and politically aware of the digital divide. The denseness of the 2003–2008 CHA website, in fact, with its clickable maps, graphs, and tables, its status reports of at least 18 housing sites, and its 1128 pdf pages of reports from 2000 to 2006, is mirrored by the current website, though the latter is more navigable.[6] Both sites illustrate an agency working to ensure stakeholders who include residents, prospective investors, and HUD that it is striving to stay on track.

Although any aspect of the website would be intriguing for a case study, the 2003–2008 CHA media pages and short videos (twelve in total) are perhaps most representative of its discourse. To stay within the scope of the chapter, I will only highlight three ads on the former media pages and the "Plan for Transformation" video. The ads are from a 2005 campaign that ran on billboards at bus stops and other locations around Chicago (Chicago Housing Authority, 2005). The video is short but comprehensive, telling the story of public housing and the motivation behind the "Plan."

On the CHA media pages labeled "In the News," "Newsletters," and "Brochures," *photo-like* ads accompanied the text describing the agency's communication vehicles. One ad features a Hispanic woman sitting in front of a desk. There is a calendar and adding machine behind her. In the left quadrant of the picture, it reads, "Everything Is New. Even My Outlook." A second ad shows an older African American man standing in front of a building. He is in profile, wearing a suit, and the text above him reads, "Public housing is coming to a point I hoped it would—full circle." Finally, the third ad positions an elderly African American woman in a white blouse above a panorama of low-rise homes—whether public or privately owned we don't know. The caption reads, "I feel just like the buildings. All brand new." The invocation of "newness," full circle, and the juxtaposition of human subjects with physical spaces asks viewers of the ads to read a connection between the redevelopment of buildings and the transformation of individuals. In fact, the CHA states this connection explicitly in the outline of the "Plan for Transformation."

Redevelopment is not just "bricks and mortar"; it is an opportunity for human hope ("Plan for Transformation: Reform," 2007). Thus, what is interesting about the above ads is not their promotion of successful communities, but their (re)characterization of public housing residents as an outcome of and justification for an elaborate building project.

In contrast, the 2003–2008 "Plan for Transformation" video (available in dial up and broadband) characterizes the resulting communities as the main benefit; personal results for individual residents are a sub-theme (Chicago Housing Authority (Producer), 2007). "Across the city of Chicago, communities are being reborn," CHA Press Secretary Derek Hill narrates, "Residents are getting new homes and a new lease on life [. . .] and it's all happening under the innovative Plan for Transformation." Except for a few segments featuring photographs, the 2003–2008 video is composed of pixilated graphics with hardly any people. In varying historical detail, the narrator reiterates the end of the era of isolated housing while bird's eye angles fly over roofs and pan past neighborhoods. The scenic emphasis is on the independence of the buildings (sprouting between green spaces, reconnecting to city grids, bowing before the skyline of the Magnificent Mile), while rare clusters of pixilated people walk by on the street. In fact, in the early "Plan for Transformation" video, the only *human* footage is of construction workers bulldozing and hammering walls and one inserted cameo of the former Central Advisory Council President. The rest of the video unfolds like a virtual condo tour. In fact, it is a tour of a projected community. Viewers are told Chicagoans "from all walks of life [will share] the same sidewalks and parks," that the view from mixed-income housing will stretch "as boundless" as the new opportunities for public housing residents.

But something rings oddly (at least to me) about this rhetoric. Given that one celebratory feature of public housing communal life is residents' congregation outside, each time I watched one of the twelve 2008 promos, I found myself asking, where are the people? At the end of each video, the implied audience is more informed, perhaps even excited about the changes in public housing. Surely the *absence* of one of the more unfortunate and visible conditions of low-income housing—vulnerability to drug and gang traffic—was and is still welcome. However, even the utopian neighbor interactions of New Urbanism are missing from the video. The streets are quiet and clean, and there's something about the visual primacy given to buildings that makes one wonder even more about the thousands of people associated with them. Where have they gone? The video that promoted Cabrini-Green's renovation ends with the narrative that "For CHA families, a new day is dawning," yet the smiling "face" and last image of the clip is that of a townhouse complex (Chicago Housing Authority (Producer), 2007). The pixilated "feel" of the 2003–2008 videos reinforced the dreamy quality of the home page's tableaus. Those impressionist portraits of better living, along with the computer animation of public housing's future, rendered the "Plan for Transformation" vision as if it really were a dream. The question, of course, is whose?

I am reminded of the real estate truism that houses sell best when their owners are absent. Similarly, opportunity may be more willingly extended when the bodies of its recipients are mediated. Fleming (2003, 2008), having studied hundreds of policy documents, news media, and development plans, found that discourse concerning public housing residents often defines them in "highly partisan ways," using techniques such as "reduction, omission, and juxtaposition" (2003, p. 210). These techniques in discourse can be intentional but also formulated through the unconscious use of ideological language. Ideology hides within language and masks the particular power relations in play; or, contrarily, when identified, can reveal the widespread assumptions that help legitimize both coercion and consent (Fairclough, 1989). Rose (2007) further reminds us that visual culture, such as advertising, often highlights "(*or renders invisible*) social difference" through associative images (p. 12). Because language conceals and wields power, the rhetoric of reduction and displacement should raise eyebrows; it implies cultural and political beliefs about what has been displaced, in this case, the often aversive relation to those on public welfare.

According to Lodge (1977), we naturally rely on "selection and combination," otherwise known as metaphor (comparison) and metonymy (substitution/association). Whereas metaphor involves the comparison of similar and dissimilar things, Willerton (2005) explains rather clearly, "Metonymy involves substituting some attributive or suggestive word for what is actually meant, as a means of showing associations between the word and its referent" (p. 11). Metonymy is reducing a thing or concept to its related parts or ideas, and its counterpart, synecdoche, is not much different. I have already asserted the way the CHA website used language and imagery to associate change with buildings and people-less sidewalks with a community dream. As the discourse highlights the "Plan for Transformation's" positive effects by comparing the rehabilitation of public housing residents to the buildings themselves (metaphor), it also subordinates these same residents' images to the images of buildings, and even to the CHA itself (metonymy). By enacting the reform of negative associations (the color red is only one example), the CHA personifies itself as a good-looking organization and, through synecdoche, is thus able to "stand in" as the representation of public housing neighbors who might not be as accepted because of perceived social difference.

This associative language works in many ways to create seamlessness between imagery and ideas. Grammatically, the parallel between buildings, bodies, and the CHA is also evidenced in active voice construction. In the 2007 "We are CHANGE" brochure accessed from the website, active voice and agency in the first three pages are given mostly to the CHA, the "Plan for Transformation," or the City of Chicago (i.e., "The Plan for Transformation guarantees [...] Chicago creates the new national model"). Bold captions reference these entities in active tense: "We are Chicago"; "We are all living together"; "We are building new communities." In the next three pages, however, agency shifts to the residents of public housing ("We are your new neighbors and friends" . . ."We are improving our own lives" . . ."We are smart managers"), so that the repetition of "we" runs together and becomes associatively interchangeable. Thus, certain equality is implied between the state and citizen, between CHA and its renters, as "the other" being introduced. Conversely, by the CHA and the City of Chicago literally being a synecdoche for government and not just a metaphor, this alignment, we know, is really a hierarchy. In spite of the seeming rhetorical agency given public housing residents here, they are the objects being advertised in this brochure; they are not its producers, nor its audience.

This analysis is complicated by the CHA website's redesign to a look and feel that is much more realist, much more personable, and seemingly less "concentrated." On the new homepage, for example, a photo of a smiling little girl is centered prominently between two photos of developments in progress. The language of the first two paragraphs is strikingly benign. In them, the CHA, without any subjective superlatives, announces itself as "the largest owner of rental housing in the city of Chicago" ("Welcome to the Chicago Housing Authority," 2010, para. 1). It commendably claims to "[support] healthy communities in neighborhoods all across the city" (para. 1). And five minutes into the new twenty-minute video, the contrast from the earlier promotion of building plans is immediately evident. The 2010 video is full of people: interview clips, snapshots, meeting footage, live families. The "Plan for Transformation" is acknowledged on the homepage but not too boastfully; it does not even get a first level link on the navigation side bar.[7] In fact, on the "Plan at 10" page, the text is incredibly sparse in comparison to the 2003–2008 site's seventeen-plus paragraphs. The caption under the page's memorial video states, "As with any good plan, the Plan for Transformation continues to evolve" ("Plan at 10," 2010, para. 2). Seemingly gone is the concentrated campaign to prove the CHA's success through a techno-business model. Organizations, after all, are fallible just like people.

A quick perusal of May 2010 news stories, however, exposes that the current website may still package the "Plan for Transformation" too succinctly, too neatly.[8] In the current discourse, the Plan is ambitious but still manageable; it has only had to be extended for another five years. And the CHA is just another landlord of 50,000 tenants, never mind a quickly dropped headline from its press links on the homepage about a thirty-day eviction given to Cabrini high-rise residents.[9] The CEO Statement ("Message from the CEO," 2010) affirms both the CHA and its leaseholders are "part of the fabric of the city" with the goal of "nothing less than to support active, stable families in taking part in all of Chicago's vibrant communities" (para. 4). A respectable goal worded with only slightly metonymic language, except that in the "Brief History of CHA" (2010) a reliance on passive voice construction blurs the CHA's contribution to the *instability* and segregation of those same families (see Lawrence, 2003). The 2003–2008 website admitted such faults, even bulleted them ("The CHA's Plan for Transformation: Reform," 2007). Two years later, on the current website, the same ongoing issues are subsumed within the language of "challenges and lessons learned" ("Plan at 10," 2010, para. 1).

By looking at some of the pervasive and subtle ways in which the CHA has exerted itself as a champion of the "Plan for Transformation," I am attempting to synthesize an outgrowth of a larger paradox within both neoliberalism and governmentality. One way to understand modern government is to observe how late- or neo-liberalism evolves the natural freedom and individualism of man into a *collective* understanding required for individual participation in markets (Hayek, 1979; Dean, 2010). In fact, this understanding does not "evolve" but is constructed through an elaborate set of persuasive acts concomitant with both external regulation and *self*-regulation, the "conduct of conducts," which is Foucault's idea of governmentality (Foucault, 1982). Public housing, particularly under Hope VI legislation, is an example par excellence of neoliberalism *and* governmentality in that many residents are not only encouraged, they are circumstantially forced to transition into the private housing market by the decrease in public housing stock. However, because welfare discourse has for so long stigmatized these residents as both haplessly and willfully dependent, they may seem incapable of freedom on their own and, thus, rationalize both intrusive and "hands off" regulation, even as the CHA website suggests it is submitting itself to the same conduct. One of the effects of this double discourse, then, is the rhetorical replacement of non-enterprising bodies by a body of neoliberal language, as well as the performance of government as the ultimate citizen. The CHA's rhetoric of redevelopment and opportunity gives the impression that it too is undergoing change but leaves out the unevenness of its discipline.

Signs of the Times: Governmentality Modeled as Good Citizenship

Rose (1999) maintains that the fact of governmentality should be thought of as an analytic that alerts us to new productions of truth and truth regimes. He summarizes governmentality as "a kind of catch-all to refer to any strategy, tactic, process, procedure or programme for controlling, regulating, shaping, mastering, or exercising authority over others in a nation, organization or locality" (p. 15). But governmentality also names the processes by which "actors" submit to these strategies *or* imitate controlling techniques to exert power or suasion over others (Rose, 1999). Governmentality is thus a system of complicity in a great network of techniques and technologies that construct, and are conducted through, ways of knowing. Dean (2010) reminds us that Foucault's concept of governmentality always-already includes the freedom of the actor as well as the acted upon, and so the production of knowledge, a form of power, may be dispersed amongst various nodes. These concepts are useful for articulating the various ways in which truth is deployed against and authored *by* public housing residents, as well as how knowledge attached to multiple disciplinary technologies continues to cling to a sign (the public housing high rise) quickly being effaced.

Rose (1999) hypothesizes that governable spaces are effectively constructed "to distribute attraction and repulsions, passions and fears across it, to bring new facets and forces, new intensities and new relations into being" (p. 30). These spaces are structured temporally because of both economic and social stratifications and may merge lived experience with representations of them.[10] To take the historic case of public housing, this particular space originated at a very specific moment in time. A sign of federal goodwill in the 1930s, public housing originated as multi-family developments designed to attract and house the white working poor (Stoloff, 2004). Shortly after, however, these families were incentivized to buy homes through VA and FHA mortgage benefits, and over the next fifty years, racially discriminatory housing policies and middle class suburban flight led to a demographic shift in public housing from an ethnically white, working class base to a predominantly African American, low-income or welfare-dependent tenant population. Furthermore, income-based rental requirements discouraged upward mobility as well as cohesive family structures in this latter population, causing African American households to languish at a time when the unemployment rate for blacks averaged in the double digits (Last year, it was still 15%).[11] Equally unhelpful, the liberalization of control and funding for local housing authorities could not outpace infrastructure costs and property maintenance, which led to increased social isolation and neglect. New subjectivities and representations were ascribed to the space of public housing: "the welfare queen," the beleaguered caseworker; and because infrastructural isolation promotes criminal activity, the "gang banger," and the racist, overzealous "po-po." Each of these subjectivities, similar to Foucault's homosexual, presented new opportunities for discourse production and governmentality with varying degrees of autonomy and privilege. Each presented a new "body" to be disciplined.

In his "Panopticism" essay, Foucault (1984) posits the theory of discipline to include any technology of power created to "[assure] the ordering of human multiplicities" (pp. 206–213). The objective of discipline, particularly that of the state, is to reduce inefficiency in extracting use from bodies by characterizing "targets" in the most beneficial way possible (p. 206). Discipline has a long history, beginning with the eighteenth century sovereign. It aggregates human beings through the exercise of power over their bodies, which may be done by "[disqualifying] or [invalidating] the bodies themselves" (p. 212). While contemporary governmentality utilizes these same strategies, Dean (2010) tells us "it also departs from them [in that] the new object of government [. . .] regards these subjects, and the forces and capacities of living individuals [. . .] as resources to be fostered, to be used and to be optimized" (p. 29). Delineating a governmentality specific to the welfare state, Clarke (2004) argues that welfare policies in particular (such as public housing regulations) instate the everyday norms of the nation—"the boundaries between states, markets and families [. . .] who the people are, what they should be doing and how they should [live]" (p. 40). In other words, we do not define ourselves, but our relationship to social welfare constitutes our citizenship. How productive we are for the nation determines how well we are treated.

This equation reiterates the contradiction in neoliberal governmentality in the previous section, and the CHA website discourse shows its application. Through its opus of information and echoing of Chicago Metropolis 2020 principles, the CHA works to aggregate public housing bodies, to reterritorialize them rhetorically and spatially as well as to recover its own reputation. To accomplish this, it has had to engage in an incredible amount of accounting, campaigning, and reflexive evaluating "there and not there" in the discourse. Clarke (2004) points to the frenetic quality of the vigilant evaluation of public service agencies as a cultural trend that stems from twentieth century conservatism in the UK and from perhaps Al Gore's "Reinventing Government" initiatives in the 1990s in the U.S. Organizations now have a disciplinary impetus to demonstrate good faith through transparency and efficiency, to essentially "perform" as corporate citizens. This fits right in with the reliance of the CHA on metonymy so as to lend public housing residents its own performativity as a "good citizen body."

I borrow the notion of "good citizen bodies" from Brandzel who, in synthesizing M. Jacqui Alexander (1994), argues that the United States as a nation requires citizens to be "married, heterosexual, reproductive, and white" in order to sustain the institution of the American family (Brandzel, 2005, p. 179). From Chicago Metropolis 2020's (1999) problematic of the "minority poor," exemplified as African American and its emphasis on making the region productive for global business, I would extend Brandzel and Alexander's qualifications of good citizen bodies to being employed and "ambitiously" middle class. The 2003–2008 "Plan for Transformation" videos illustrate that good citizen bodies in urban America are sanitized of uncomfortable markers of race or poverty; they congregate in small clusters in manufactured green spaces and don't draw attention to themselves. Good citizen bodies are fully trained to act as good neighbors, and housekeepers.[12] For instance, sample tenant leases confirm that CHA's redevelopment sites stipulate a home visit for applicants so that the ability to care for units can be monitored ("Tenant Selection Plan-Roosevelt Square," 2010; "Tenant Selection Plan-Parkside of Old Town," 2010). Public housing residents are also reminded of the discriminatory CHA rule that "other than husband and wife, persons of the opposite sex will not occupy the same bedroom" ("Tenant Selection Plan-Mahalia Place," 2010). Such measures constitute a severe form of discipline and bio-power that unequally penalizes low-income African Americans as the most hyper-concentrated and, therefore, most visibly potential *non-citizen* bodies in Chicago's governable spaces.

The "Plan for Transformation" is the continuation of the liberal project to create a society of ethical, well-behaved human beings able to preside over their own conduct through shared goals, rules, and competition (Rose, 1999). But since white *and* black middle class residents have historically eschewed living next to public housing because of presumptions about behavior and impacted property values (Kofie, 1999; Patillo, 2007), public housing residents are symbolically asked to "look and act like" their more ideal class counterparts. This is not to deny efforts at cross-cultural education (Fleming, 2008), but overwhelmingly integrating black bodies into white space, i.e., the nation, demands converting those bodies into a predetermined manageable, marriageable, work-ready group even when this conversion is indicative of performativity. This particular deployment of an ideal subjectivity informs social relations and is not only connected to citizenship but to survival. Consequently, the paradox of governmentality spied in CHA discourse can also be observed in discourse produced by public housing residents about themselves.

At the heart of the nation's current public housing policy, which mandates the destruction of over 100,000 units, including fifty-one high-rise buildings in Chicago, is the concern that not enough replacement units are being built or subsidized, and particularly not on the same housing sites (Popkin, 2006; Smith, 2006). This means that many residents will have to transition to the private housing market, voluntarily and involuntarily, where they must compete for affordable housing without guarantee of being able to remain in their home neighborhoods. Given the speed of the "Plan for Transformation's" demolition schedule and even Chicago Metropolis 2020's (1999) acknowledgment of "the widely and strongly held belief throughout the region that [low-income] rental housing brings in an unsavory element" (p. 43), housing advocates have rightly feared that hasty displacement shuffles families to equally poor and racially concentrated areas, newly isolated from prime real estate.[13] Admittedly, HOPE VI studies show that residents often report better living conditions and a raise in income, but often rental barriers for large families, those with mental and physical disabilities, or troubled rental histories counterweigh these statistics (Popkin, 2006). Moreover, the push to attract private developers and market rate homebuyers to finance the city's new mixed-income developments has compelled the prioritization of these interests, leaving public housing residents to fight for their inclusion in the redevelopment planning process and the city's geographic and cultural landscape.

Over the past ten years, collaborating variously with social justice organizations, civil rights lawyers, city aldermen, journalists, local and national organizers, and religious and educational institutions, Chicago public housing residents have engaged in the following resistance strategies to the "Plan for Transformation's" displacement of the poor: formed the Coalition to Protect Public Housing (CPPH), a community alliance once composed of seventy supporting organizations that since 1996 has proactively drawn attention to the

Plan's imbalances and exclusions, as well as general housing practices in Chicago, including foreclosures; organized "Saturday Schools," prayer vigils, and sit-ins in the tradition of the Civil Rights movement; initiated relocation studies that have aided in the lodging of class action suits against "the Plan's" contribution to the continued segregation of current and former residents; produced video documentaries with counter-testimonials and policy recommendations; organized to get public housing supporters elected to the Chicago Housing Authority's Central and local advisory councils; held annual Juneteenth demonstrations to remind the city of public housing's presence and importance; gained a voice in the allocation of Chicago TIF grants in key areas; testified in front of the United Nations and brought not one, but two UN Special Rapporteurs to Chicago to observe and make recommendations on the city's housing and racial discrimination; and, summarily, worked to reframe housing injustice as a violation of Article 25 of the Universal Declaration of Human Rights.[14] Alongside these considerable feats, public housing residents in Chicago (and elsewhere) maintain a prolific virtual presence that articulates a citizenship premised more on the universality of rights to democratic inclusion, safety, and basic shelter apart from class while sustaining awareness of the particular vulnerability of lower income people and bodies of color to be rendered invisible.

A prime example comes from the Chicago-based group, We the People Media, a 501c3 not-for-profit organization that formed in 1999 in the wake of the CHA's withdrawal of support from its resident-authored publication, the *Residents' Journal* ("We the People Media," 2008). The newspaper, available in print and online, features investigative concerns and human-interest stories related to public housing. Its website banner features the upper segment of a black and white negative of a smiling, multigenerational group whose race and class are not completely determinable, albeit a quick perusal of the journal's covers shows a focus on blacks as Chicago's largest public housing demographic. Some of the journal covers display reporters' consternation with the "Plan for Transformation's" effects through images of high rises and wrecking balls. Other covers celebrate public housing life and history such as youth participation in the Bud Biliken parade and the Jesse White gymnastic tumbling team. Of interest is the way in which this discursive activity projects and interpellates the public housing subject without need of any mediation. Contributors frequently write in first person and easily distinguish their identities attached to and apart from their address. By debating the pros and cons of the Plan's relocation and redevelopment promises, reporters and interviewees express the same concerns of any Chicagoan while questioning the constitutionality of practices that have accompanied the Plan which seem to disproportionately stigmatize CHA leaseholders.[15] Similar models of online reporting, memorials, and protest to the nation's public housing policy have been sprouting up everywhere the past ten years and are worthy of more concerted study.[16]

Through the mounting of their own discursive space in the virtual sphere, a tactic surely influenced by the rise of the Internet and of social media but also as opposition to negative cultural representation, public housing residents and their allies illustrate themselves to be a modern, liberal body politic able to resist panoptical techniques through the strategies of self-reporting and counter-surveillance. This discursiveness effectively provides a more accurate picture of the "Plan for Transformation" and other such plans, but it also exposes the constraints and ironies of market-oriented forms of governmentality that subjects in this day and age operate within.

The key pressure behind neoliberalism is available capital, which is able to organize all of us into acceptable incentivized roles. For instance, behind both the "Plan for Transformation's" considerable agenda and the social platforms of some of its critics is a shared pot of funding, including but not limited to the Catherine T. MacArthur, Chicago Community Trust and Robert R. McCormick Foundations. We the People Media receives funding from some of these large donors, which on the one hand could be seen as the promotion of a democratic forum but on the other implies the centralization of the city's competing interests. Tangentially, We the People's Media Bus Tours, which received a full ad page in its Winter 2007 journal, reveal a decentralization of the interests of public housing residents but, also, the ambivalence I would say is endemic to neoliberalism. The Bus Tours, according to the copy and aligning snapshots, welcomed media and the general public into housing developments and willing families' living rooms on tours led by staffers and local residents. The copy promised, "to provide [. . .] facts and figures about life in the inner city," or the real story, if you will. These tours seem to have run in tandem or competition with the deceased Beauty Turner's "Ghetto Bus Tours," which openly critiqued the "Plan for Transformation" and garnered national attention.[17] A resident-run neighborhood tour is reflective of a population using its available technologies of agency to mitigate the production of knowledge about itself and divert capital to perhaps more useful ends. However, by working within recognizable forms of service agreements and market niches, i.e., the tourist and tour guide, it is also apparent how the economy persuades us to perform and manage our own conduct, even at risk of exploitation or misunderstanding

(Associated Press, 2007; Dean, 2010). Access to capital, and by extension, policymaking, most certainly equate into true social equality, but when it comes to dispersing rhetoric, public housing residents show they are indeed enterprising citizen bodies and can exhibit a similar reflexivity to the CHA when the need arises.

Lessons Learned and Questions to Answer

The 2003–2008 CHA website is an instance of governmentality that displays a "full body" of power-knowledge about public housing residents and through the effective use of metonymic language and graphics distracts from the presence of poor (black) bodies in Chicago's cityscape, thereby presenting them as acceptable neighbors and workers. This discourse, analyzed here as mainly visual rhetoric, also manifests as a material form of power in community space through the management of thousands of people who have become subject to where they live. Interestingly, a parallel displacement of bodies in favor of buildings is evident on the website of the Commercial Club of Chicago. In lieu of photographs of diverse, happy Chicagoans, watermarks and blue saturated images of the skyline border its pages, particularly illuminating the cityscape's verticality and its downtown financial center. One might observe, then, that like the 2003–2008 CHA website the Commercial Club's visual focus on city form, reflective as it is of the twentieth century's modernist aesthetic, downplays the unpredictability of Chicago's citizenry and upholds the primacy of viewing Chicago as an open container for the economy.

Visuals, ergo language, point to a complex mythology that sheds light on a culture's overall meaning system (Rose, 2007). Fairclough affirms (2000) that the ways representations take shape and are interpreted also influence the production and enactment of diverse cultural imaginaries, which in turn may lead to divergent, even oppositional social practices. If an intense visibility of governmentality models good citizenship for the public sector but also suggests the narrowing of freedom, one can see why contradictions and paradoxes within public housing discourse might be troubling and not easily resolved. The overriding myths of American success, equal opportunity, and individual choice are necessary to the understanding of class as flexible and impermanent, even while debates over the obligations of the welfare state fix class subjectivities as rigid and haunting (Clarke, 2004). Housing is a basic human right, but for those capital puts on the last rung of wealth generation, affording access to housing means subjecting oneself to the vagaries of state regulation, at least for as long as public housing exists. The alternative is to place oneself at the mercy of the vagaries of the market, and as the 2009 foreclosure panic has shown us, this is an equally uncertain place to be for homeowners and non-public housing tenants.

Because public housing high rises and its residents have been so spatially demonized, what does it mean that one of the symbols of capitalism's abject (social welfare) is being torn down? Will we understand the artificiality of class and cultural assumptions any better when our neighbors are of higher or lower income? How significant are virtual representations of contemporary housing struggles? And how do government created, mixed-income developments, as opposed to organic ones, affect social relations and spatial imaginaries? Do they, for example, reify residents' perceptions of race, ethnicity, cultural practice, or reproductive norms? These questions, while beyond the scope of this chapter, might be partially addressed by conducting ongoing critical discourse analysis to accompany social science research (Fairclough, 2000). A cultural studies approach might parse out an analytic for the genre of public housing discourse and trace patterns of ideological language attached to practice. It might, for example, regard the Atlanta Housing Authority's website and its CEO's use of religious rhetoric to illuminate how cultural difference within state policy influence or is overridden by economic concerns.[18] If, as Clarke (2004) puts forth, "welfare states 'produce the people' in trying to put the national-popular imaginary into practice" (p. 48), then buying into a more idealized subject as the proper body of the home and workplace reinforces an exclusive citizenship and naturalizes *Metropolis 2020* goals and objectives in spite of their possible costs.

The CHA's website rhetoric is just one case study of the flattening out of city space for the marching forward of a global economy. The powerful image of green, newly designed mixed-income communities implies that everyone living in them will be healthy, employed, and working to hold the social fabric together. However, assuming that some of the poor are included in this image, Smith points out:

> Not everyone who is poor can work, and even if they can, working does not guarantee that a poor family will get out of poverty [. . . .] Stepping back from the image of immaculate new homes [for public housing residents], we can see what continues to exist outside these new developments: the larger systemic problems of racism and classism and a long-standing cultural bias against cities that continues to push [some] people farther out. (2006, p .277)

In fact, Chicago's poverty level was 21.2% in 2004 compared to the country's level of 13.2%.[19] As structurally unsound and often dangerous as the high rises were, they at least reminded us that inequities in American society are impossible to deny and that capitalism, in fact, exploits them.

I don't think many would argue for the continuance of the *conditions* of the nation's former high rises, but what the proposed transformation of America's public housing does is crystallize a conjuncture in which the ideologies of neoliberalism and new urbanism are influencing a heavy investment in spatial amnesia. The renaming of former public housing sites testifies to this (e.g., the property the Robert Taylor Homes once sat on is now called Legends South, and the torn-down homes of Cabrini Extension North are under the auspice of Old Town Square). Since only a third of the units in CHA's redeveloped communities have been designated for public housing and two-thirds for market rate housing, some averaging half a million in price, the real "new neighbors" to this land are presumably the young gentrifiers Chicago will attract to its growing financial base, the unwitting "urban colonists" (Behr, 2008). The new names, like CHA discourse, signal a benignity and availability to different consumers, different modes of consumption, and new income. It signals that the virtual sphere might be the only trace of what used to be home for very different people. Public housing residents challenge this amnesia by asserting their own consumption patterns, by hosting building reunions at or near former sites, and through commemorative blogs and Facebook fan pages.[20] As the publisher of the *Residents' Journal* puts it, "Robert Taylor Homes still exists—on the Internet" (Michaeli, 2010, para. 1). It is as if to say, no matter that some bodies have moved, we are still here and claim this space. Within public housing discourse, this is a powerful way of thinking of mobility.

Notes

1. Ms. Flake's quote is extracted from a video clip posted to the CHA's redesigned website in October of 2003, which is the primary website under discussion in this chapter. The website remained consistent until at least 2009, and the "Resident Stories" could be found by clicking the top navigation bar's Relocation tab and then scrolling down the left navigation bar to "Resident Success Stories." Two other videos and accompanying narrative summaries are excerpted there from *A Better Place* cable access program, produced by the CHA. (Videos may or may not be accessible now through Internet archiving). Chicago Housing Authority (Producer). (2002). *A Better Place*. Chicago: Chicago Cable Access Network.
2. Old editions of the CHA website dating back to 1998 can presently be located through

"Wayback Machine," an Internet archive. The CHA website was consistent from 1998–2003, with a notable change in its top navigation bar September 29, 2003: under a collage of photographs of public housing buildings, reads the slogan "Changing the *face* of public housing" (emphasis mine). By October 27, 2003, the website was redesigned to reflect the site that forms the basis of this analysis, although at three different dates in 2006 (Oct 3, Oct 18, and Nov 17) it underwent design changes that I argue eventually de-emphasized the presence of bodies: the CEO's headshot on the home page was replaced by the juxtaposition of resident and building photos; the same oscillating photos become impressionistic tableaus that blur into one another; finally, a striking graphic of the CHA's office exterior, a stark red high rise was added to the homepage and was still there in 2009. Retrieved from http://www.archive.org/web/web.php)
3. "Visuality" is a term Gillian Rose (2007) defines as "The way in which vision is constructed in various ways" (p. 2).
4. This reputation consists not only of decades of gross property neglect and dehabilitating housing practices that have been settled in court, but the CHA's Hope VI grant was also taken over by HUD in 1995 due to mismanagement. The agency was only removed from the HUD "troubled list" in 1998 and just this year regained receivership over public housing in Chicago after a twenty-three year court mandate. So the CHA is overcoming a so-called double-stigma, that of its own and that sometimes lofted at public housing residents.
5. There is significance to the use of impressionism-styled tableaus crystallizing into an actual photograph. A more extensive critique could be done of modernist v. postmodernist models of visuality and their effect on user perception. This seems to be behind current CEO Lewis Jordan's announcement of the shift to a site that "make[s] it easier than ever to find information on CHA."
6. Each report is about 188 pages in length.
7. For Chicagoans, the most exciting aspect of the 2010 redesign is likely the announcement that the public housing waiting list has finally opened up. In 2007, there were 90,000 people still on it (Saulny, S. (2007, March 18), "At Housing Project, Both Fear and Renewal," *The New York Times*. Retrieved from http://www.nytimes.com/2007/03/18/us/18cabrini.htm)
8. Belying the smoothness of this rhetoric are the following top headlines that appeared during the time this chapter was being drafted: "Chicago Housing Authority emerges from receivership" (Hutson, 2010); "A wish for more community in mixed income units" (Fitzsimmons, 2010)"; "CHA issues eviction notices, cites safety at Cabrini-Green: Residents get 30 days to leave" (Ihejirika, 2010); "Slow housing market impacting public-housing seekers" (Bensing & Caputo, 2010).
9. According to journalism reports, residents of this high rise at Cabrini-Green were recently taken off guard by the short notice, especially since the remaining families had been living with squatters and other worrisome conditions since the Plan's beginning. Note that the link to this May 18 press release was dropped from the CHA home page within days of its posting while a May 4 census notice remained. This prioritization strategy for press releases on the website comes across as rather ironic given that residents immediately contested the notice as an unjust expectation (Ihejirika, 2010).
10. Rose somewhat presents something of an either/or notion of "abstract space," his alter-

nate term for the governable zone coined by Henri Lefebvre. He reads Lefebvre as saying that abstraction and experience are oppositions, but I believe, not only do these spaces "make new kinds of experience possible" (Rose, 1999, p. 32), the actual lived experience can be concealed by abstract representation even while that representation is shaping how one experiences the space.

11. United States Department of Labor, (2009). "Economic News Release," Table A-2: Employment status of the civilian population by race, sex, and age. Bureau of Labor Statistics Retrieved from http://www.bls.gov/news.release/empsit.t02.htm
12. Relocation counseling was once called "Good Neighbor Training," as cited by Press Secretary Derek Hill in a 2007 phone interview (D. Hill, personal communication, March 29, 2007).
13. In 2003, for example, current and former CHA residents filed a class action lawsuit against CHA charging that the agency had failed to move families into racially and economically mixed areas, despite CHA's claims of relocation success (Smith, 2006; see also C. Lawrence, "CHA Failing to Help Families, Suit Alleges," *Chicago Sun-Times*, January 23, 2003).
14. The articulation and continuation of these resistance strategies were personally observed by the author during an internship with the Coalition to Protect Public Housing in 2008. At the beginning of her internship, the second Special Rapporteur, Doudou Diene, had just come to tour Cabrini-Green and listen to testimony about poor housing and neighborhood conditions. The UN's expert on housing, Miloon Kothari, visited in April of 2004. For detailed accounts of community resistance and usage of human rights discourse see J. Smith, 2006, and D. Pfeiffer, 2006.
15. The Winter 2008 issue, in particular, alerts readers to the apartheid reminiscence of "CPD contact cards" used indiscriminately by Chicago police in low-income neighborhoods to gather addresses and personal information on tenants' visitors (See Turner, B. (Winter 2008). Are CPD Contact Cards Unconstitutional? *Residents Journal*. 44 Retrieved from http://wethepeoplemedia.org/Archive/2008_Winter/Articles/ContactCards.html). And a recent CHA policy requiring parents to sign a release for schools to report on their children's conduct is highly contested, as it should be (Johns, M.C. (Spring 2010). Tenants Protest New CHA School Reporting Policy. *Residents Journal*. Retrieved from http://wethepeoplemedia.org/uncategorized/tenants-protest-new-cha-school-reporting-policy/)
16. Examples include http://www.invisibleinstitute.org, http://housingisahumanright.org/, http://tellingourstory.org/, http://www.limits.com/cpph, http://www.maydaynolahousing.org/, and such Facebook fan groups for the Robert Taylor and Lathrop Homes.
17. The former award-winning journalist, reporter for the *Residents' Journal*, university research assistant, Ms. Beauty Turner, conducted these tours at $20 a person under the name of the Poor People's Millennium Movement. As of June 2010, her blog on the tours was still available online: http://beautysghettobustours.blogspot.com/.
18. One of CEO Renee Glover's exact quotes is, "When I decided to take on the challenges at the Atlanta Housing Authority, I knew that the only way to address the myriad problems was to call on my faith and follow my belief that all people are children of God, with unlimited human potential." Glover, R.L., (2010, June 13). Looking back 15 years, *Lessons Learned*, Blog, Retrieved from http://ahalessonslearned.blogspot.com/. The AHA

site represents another excellent case study for the visuality of governmentality, particularly as situated within a Protestant ethic of man as subject to God and capital (see Weber, 1958).
19. U.S. Census Bureau, "Housing and Household Economics Statistics Division," *Housing and Household Economic Statistics*, www.census.gov/hhes/www/poverty.html November 17, 2009. See also "2008 Report on Illinois Poverty: Chicago Area Snapshot," *Mid-America Institute on Poverty of Heartland Alliance*, http://www.heartlandalliance.org/whatwedo/advocacy/reports/chicagosnapshot2008.pdf. November 17, 2009.
20. Similar to other media vehicles, the *Residents' Journal* provides such demographic expenditures like grocery and fast food preferences for potential advertisers.

References

Alexander, M. J. (1994). Not just (any) body can be a citizen: The politics of law, sexuality and postcoloniality in Trinidad and Tobago and the Bahamas. *Feminist Review, 48*, 5–23.

Associated Press. (2007, July 22). Ghetto bus tour' glorifies Chicago's projects: City officials say tour guide paints unrealistic view of troubled tenements. MSNBC. Retrieved from http://www.msnbc.msn.com/id/19902528/

Behr, R. (2008, November 9). Is there a new class war? *The Guardian*. Retrieved from http://www.guardian.co.uk/society/2008/nov/09/class-war-mosaic-database

Bensing, A., & Caputo, A. (2010, May 13). Slow housing market impacting public-housing seekers. *The Chicago Reporter*. Retrieved from http://www.chicagonow.com/blogs/chicago-muckrakers/2010/05/vacancies-in-public-housing.html

Blocks Together. (2010). *Affordable housing*. Retrieved from http://www.blockstogether.org

Brandzel, A. L. (2005). Queering citizenship? Same-sex marriage and the state. *GLQ, 11*(2), 171–204.

Chaskin, R. J., & Joseph, M. L. (2010). Building 'community' in mixed-income developments: Assumptions, approaches, and early experiences. *Urban Affairs Review, 45*(3), 299–335.

Chicago Housing Authority and Chicago Cable Access Network (Producers). (2002). *A better place* [Video].

Chicago Housing Authority. (2005). *FY2005 Annual Report*.

Chicago Housing Authority. (Producer). (2007). *Cabrini-Green Homes* [Video]. Retrieved from earlier http://www.thecha.org

Chicago Housing Authority. (2007). Plan for transformation: Reform. CHANGE. Retrieved from http://www.thecha.org

Chicago Housing Authority. (Producer). (2007). *The plan for transformation* [Video]. Retrieved from earlier http://www.thecha.org

Chicago Housing Authority. (2007). *We are CHANGE*. Retrieved from http://www.thecha.org

Chicago Housing Authority. (2007). *Welcome to the CHA*. Retrieved from http://www.thecha.org

Chicago Housing Authority. (2010). Message from the CEO Lewis Jordan. CHANGE. Retrieved from http://www.thecha.org/pages/ceo_statement/122.php

Chicago Housing Authority. (2010). *Tenant selection plan—Mahalia place*. Retrieved from http://www.thecha.org/filebin/pdf/MixedIncome/Web%20Info%20TSP%20Legends%20South%20Phase%20C-1%20-%20Mahalia%20Place.pdf

Chicago Housing Authority. (2010). *Tenant selection plan—Parkside of Old Town*, Retrieved from http://www.thecha.org/filebin/pdf/MixedIncome/Lease%20and%20TSP%20-%20Parkside.pdf

Chicago Housing Authority. (2010). *Tenant selection plan—Roosevelt square phase I*. Retrieved from http://www.thecha.org/filebin/pdf/MixedIncome/ RS1%20 TSP % 20from%20closing%20binder.pdf

Chicago Metropolis 2020. (1999a). *Metropolis 2020*. Retrieved from http://www.chicagometropolis2020.0rg/25_3.htm

Chicago Metropolis 2020. (1999b). *The metropolis principles*. Retrieved from http://www.chicagometropolis2020.0rg/25_3.htm

Chicago Metropolis 2020. (2004). *The metropolis index: Housing as opportunity*. Retrieved from http://www.chicagometropolis2020.0rg/documents/housingindex_000.pdf

Chicago Metropolis 2020 (2010). Housing. Retrieved from http://www.chicagometropolis2020.0rg/10_20.htm.

Clarke, J. (2004). *Changing welfare, changing states: New directions in social policy*. London: Sage.

Dean, M. (2010). *Governmentality: Power and rule in modern society*. London: Sage.

Dowling, R. M. (2007). *Slumming in New York*. Urbana and Chicago: University of Illinois Press.

Fairclough, N. (1989). *Language and power*. London: Longman.

Fairclough, N. (1993). Critical discourse analysis and the marketization of public discourse: The universities. *Discourse and Society, 4*(2), 133–168.

Fairclough, N. (2000). Language and neo-liberalism. *Discourse and Society, 11*(2), 147–148.

Fitzsimmons, E. G. (2010, May 20). A wish for more community in mixed-income units. Retrieved from www.nytimes.com/2010/05/21/us/21cnchousing.html

Fleming, D. (2008). *City of rhetoric*. New York: State University of New York Press.

Fleming, D. (2003). Subjects of the inner city: Writing the people of Cabrini-Green. In M. Nystrand & J. Duffy (Eds.), *Towards a rhetoric of everyday life: New directions in research on writing, text, and discourse* (pp. 207–244). Madison, WI: University of Wisconsin Press.

Foucault, M. (1982).The subject and power. In H. Dreyfus & P. Rabinow (Eds.), *Beyond structuralism and hermeneutics*. Chicago: University of Chicago Press.

Foucault, M. (1984). The order of discourse. In M. Shapiro (Ed.), *Language and politics*. Oxford: Blackwell.

Foucault, M. (1984). Panopticism. In P. Rabinow (Ed.), *The Foucault reader*. New York: Vintage.

Foucault, M. (1986). The right of death and power over life. In P. Rabinow (Ed.), *The Foucault reader*. New York, NY: Pantheon.

Hayek, F. A. (1979). *Law, legislation and liberty*, vol. 3: *The political order of a free people*. London: Routledge.

Hutson, W. (2010, May 26). Chicago Housing Authority emerges from receivership. *Chicago Defender*. Retrieved from http://www.chicagodefender.com/article-7845-chicago-housing-auth.html

Ihejirika, M. (2010, May 20). CHA issues eviction notices, cites safety at Cabrini-Green. *Chicago Sun-Times*. Retrieved from http://www.suntimes.com/news/metro/2295308,CST-NWS-cabrini20.article

Kofie, N. F. (1999). *Race, class, and the struggle for neighborhood in Washington, D.C*. New York: Garland.

Lawrence, C. (2003, January 23). CHA failing to help families, suit alleges. *Chicago Sun-Times*. Retrieved from Lexis Nexus.

Lipman, P., & Hursh, D. (2007). Renaissance 2010: The reassertion of ruling-class power through neoliberal policies in Chicago. *Policy Futures in Education*, 5(2), 160–178.

Lodge, D. (1977). *The modes of modern writing: metaphor, metonymy, and the typology of modern literature*. Ithaca, NY: Cornell University Press.

Michaeli, E. (2010, April 1). Robert Taylor on line. *Residents' Journal*. Retrieved from http://wethepeoplemedia.org/tag/Spring-2010-Issue/

New Urban News (2000). *New urbanism and traditional neighborhood development: Comprehensive report & best practices guide*. Ithaca, NY: New Urban News

Osofsky, G. (1971). *Harlem: The making of a ghetto*. New York: Harper Torchbook.

Patillo, M. (2007). *Black on the block*. Chicago, IL: The University of Chicago Press.

Pfeiffer, D. (2006). Displacement through discourse: Implementing and contesting public housing redevelopment in Cabrini-Green. *Urban Anthropology*, 35(1), 39–74.

Popkin, S. J. (2006). The Hope VI program: What has happened to the residents? *Where are poor people to live? Transforming public housing communities*. L. Bennett, J. L. Smith, & P. A. Wright (Eds.), Armonk, NY: M.E. Sharpe.

Rose, G. (2007). *Visual methodologies*. London: Sage.

Rose, N. (1999). *Powers of freedom: Reframing political thought*. New York: Cambridge University Press.

Schlay, A. B. (2006). Low-income homeownership: American dream or delusion. *Urban Studies*, 43(3), 511–531.

Smith, J. L. (2006). Mixed-income communities: Designing out poverty or pushing out the poor? *Where are poor people to live? Transforming public housing communities*. L. Bennett, J. L. Smith, & P. A. Wright (Eds.). Armonk, NY: M.E. Sharpe.

Stoloff, J. A. (2004). A brief history of public housing. *Paper presented at the annual meeting of the American Sociological Association, Hilton San Francisco & Renaissance Parc 55 Hotel, San Francisco, CA, Online*. Retrieved from http://www.allacademic.com/meta/p_mla_apa_research_citation/1/0/8/8/5/p108852_index.html

United States Department of Labor, (2009). "Economic News Release," Table A-2: Employment status of the civilian population by race, sex, and age. Bureau of Labor Statistics Retrieved from http://www.bls.gov/news.release/empsit.t02.htm

van Dijk, T. A. (1993). Principles of critical discourse analysis. *Discourse and Society*, 4(2), 249–283.

Venkatesh, S. A., Celimli, I., Miller, D., Murphy, A., & Turner, B. (2004). *Chicago public housing transformation: A research report*. New York, NY: Center for Urban Research and Policy. Retrieved from http://www.curp.columbia.edu/publications2/PH_Transformation_Report.pdf

We the People Media (2008). *Residents' Journal*, 8(44), 1–23.

Weber, Max (1958). *The protest ethic and the spirit of capitalism*. New York: Scribner.

Willerton, R. (2005). Visual metonymy and synecdoche: Rhetoric for stage-setting images. *Journal of Technical Writing and Communication*, 35(1), 3–31.

· 1 1 ·
Body/Flesh of the Teacher in the Digital Age

HEATHER GREENHALGH-SPENCER

Have You Ever Thought About What Your Body Does in the Classroom?

I sit in a hard chair in front of a table with my students arrayed in a circle before me. Today, I'm planning on doing a lot of discussion, so I'll spend most of my time sitting down. I could always stand up and walk around the classroom, but for some reason, the very act of standing seems to initiate a different kind of discussion, a different kind of disciplinarity. Today, I want the students to lead. I take a sip from my Diet Coke, paste on a smile, adjust my "professional" looking blouse, and hope that my outward bodily performance can fool the students into believing that I'm completely confident in their ability to discuss tough topics without my intervention. I throw out the first question and am met by that moment of silence. They sense the absence of coercion: *my body is not* standing at the chalkboard, ready to write down what is said; my body is not encircling the classroom, making sure that I am the focus. There is only my body, staring out at the students, smile on my face, and. . .the void of silence. But then, someone feels compelled to answer. From there the discussion flows fairly easily. The students know each other, and they debate back and forth without much intervention on my part. For the moment, I need only sit here, on my hard chair and with my smiling face, and wait for the next moment of silence.

Does the Body Hange When Moving from the Physical to the On-line Classroom?

I sit in a hard chair in front of a table with my laptop stationed before me. Today, I'm planning on a lot of student-led discussion, and I've asked the students to come prepared with critical questions of their own. I agree to start our discussion, so I throw out the first question. I am met again by that moment of silence. Is it silence in anticipation? Silence in thought? Silence in fear? Confusion? What is the quality of this silence? I become aware that the *inability to see* my students, prohibits me from utilizing their body language to interpret this silence. And again, they sense the absence of coercion: my body is not standing at the chalkboard, ready to write down what is said; my body is not encircling the classroom, making sure that I am the focus. *There is not even my body*, staring out at the students, smile on my face, to combat this void of silence. Should I turn on the camera? Would the projected image of my face somehow encourage the students to begin talking? I'm only wearing comfy clothes and a pony-tail; would my less-professional image provoke more discussion or less? I do what I can: I take a sip of Diet Coke, stare at the computer, and...am silent. But then, it begins. Two people begin talking on their mics. One of them must wait, and there is the awkward exchange of two people trying to negotiate speaking-turns when they cannot see or really even hear each other. The chat-box also comes to life. I become a multi-tasker: I must listen to what one class member is audibly saying; I must read the textual responses that other class members are writing in reply; *I must create* multiple responses in my head to the simultaneous audible and textual "talking"; and, I must be prepared to call on the next person who raises their virtual hand.[1] I can feel the slight adrenaline rush as I try to keep track of everything. From here, the discussion flows quite easily. There are so many ways to interact. For the moment, I need only sit here, on my hard chair and with my smiling face, and wait for the next moment of silence.

For the Moment

I would not be the first person to argue that changes in technologies create changes in the ways we perceive ourselves and in the ways we labor in our lives.

In trying to make sense of his historical moment, Walter Benjamin (1968) argued that the ability to massively reproduce art and artifacts changed our perceptions of value and labor:

> The mode of human sense perception changes with humanity's entire mode of existence. The manner in which human sense perception is organized, the medium in which it is accomplished, is determined not only by nature but by historical circumstances as well. (p. 222)

Years later, Arjun Appadurai (1996) would echo Benjamin's claims and state that ubiquitous media, along with other factors, have changed the ways we experience the "here and now."

I am also in strong company when I argue that the very act of living in a world of computer-mediated-reality possibilities has changed the ways we perceive and work (Greenhow, Robelia, & Hughes, 2009; Lantham, 2004; Ross & Sennyey, 2008). Through virtual avatars, we now have the ability to interact in alternate realities on *Second Life* or other MMORPGs, MUDs / MOOs. We can have on-line friendships with people whom we've never actually seen face to face. Some of us spend more time communicating via computer than any other medium of communication. We attend classes on-line or we watch YouTube videos when we want to quickly learn how to do something.

These new technologies have changed our modes of existence and have changed our perceptions. As James Carey (1992) has pointed out, in moments of flux, our rituals become destabilized. The rituals that we use for the sake of maintaining society in time are themselves vulnerable to shifts (Carey, 1992). As our "sacred ceremonies" that are the backdrop of societal commonality begin to change, the need to map out or enshrine other rituals of commonality increases (Carey, 1992). We begin to need new rituals in order to, once again, create "an artificial though nonetheless real symbolic order that operates to provide not information but confirmation, not to alter attitudes or change minds but to represent an underlying order of things" (Carey, 1992, p. 15) And so, rather than using this paper to make a theoretical argument that in this digital age there *are* differences in the ways we labor and perceive, I would like to use my body as a means of *showing* some of the ways in which this digital age has changed the way *I* labor and perceive myself as a body.

Specifically, I aim to parse out the multiple modalities of my body as a teacher. I want to pay close attention to both what my body means and what my body does, and how these influence each other. I attempt to explore the tensions and intricacies of my teaching body as a stubbornly solid and highly physical entity—not as opposed to, but in addition to—my body as code: virtual code, discursive code. I also intend to draw attention to the ways that "theory" is bereft of capturing the moment. It seems to me that so many theories *either* focus on the body as a discursive production *or* as a stable, knowing, agential, perceiver. But the body is always multiple. In this chapter, I will use both phenomenologists and discourse theorists to help me articulate both what my body does and what my body means in various contexts. Yet I also intend to point out the ways that these theories do not adequately account for the body across its variegated and manifold forms.

I divide this paper according to "scenes." The word "scene," for me, adequately connects to the theatricality of the body and the body as physical territory (scenery). In this way, I focus on the body as both a territory, which takes up real space, and also a performative accomplishment. My task is to explore the scenes/scenery of the body both as flesh and discursively interpellated domain. I want to show what the body does and what the body means in various scenes in order to talk through various theories of the body and, hopefully, to better understand the ways that laboring in the virtual may be different from other types of labor. In order to more fully *show my labor*, I choose to take a more auto-ethnographic approach to this paper. I choose to tell stories. As many scholars have pointed out, it is often in story-telling that we can better get at new formations of identity and practice (Anzaldúa, 1987; Ellis, 2004; Goodall, 2000; Hall, 1996; Sarup, 1996; Weedon, 2004). As I spend a good deal of my labor as a teacher, this paper will walk through the body and labor of teaching.

Scene 1: In Front of a Classroom

I don't take up that much space. I am only 5'4," and even in my grown-up-girl-heels, I'm only about 5'6." This means that most of my students stand at my height or taller. So, when a student comes up to me to talk at the end of class, I regularly feel short or little. I think I place my hands on my hips when this happens as a way to compensate. My height also means that, at times, I have to reach up, on toes and with arm out-stretched, to write on the chalkboard. When reaching for the top of the board, I wonder if my dress has managed to show a little too much leg.

In some of the classrooms, there is a small rope used to pull down the projection screen. Sometimes, the rope gets placed on the top lip of the chalkboard so as not to obscure the teacher's writing when the screen is up. I hate this, because it means I have to jump up to try and fish the rope off the chalkboard lip whenever I want to pull the screen down. For some reason, jumping makes me feel like a child. Then, if one of my taller male students volunteers to get it down for me, I become hyper-aware of my status as female.

There is also the fact that I'm blonde. I'm not really sure what this means or how this translates. I will only say that, being blonde, I tend to be a little sensitive about the ditzy, naïve, hyper-sexual stereotypes that come along with it. Whenever I make a dumb mistake in front of my students, I wonder, did I just get encoded as a ditzy blonde? This also means that I stand in front of the mirror and internally debate about whether or not I should undo that second button on my shirt.

And then, in contrast to my small-ish, blonde, female body, there is my voice. Somehow, subconsciously, I have developed this lower, confident, perhaps a bit intimidating, professor-voice. I use it in all of the classes I teach: on campus and on-line. I'm not sure to what lengths I can characterize my own voice. I can only say, I notice a definite difference between the voice I use to teach academic classes and the voice I use to teach yoga. Then, both of these voices are different from the one I use with friends and family. I have a rather female-coded body and this rather male-coded academic voice. I wonder how this seeming-dichotomy affects my students.

I'm also completely aware that my body bears all the marks of middle-class whiteness. I *look* the part of the oppressor. So, when I talk about social justice issues, dialogue, and counter-hegemonic practice—do I come off as insincere? Am I nothing but a *poseur*? Will my body allow me to be anything but the enemy? I feel gazed-at whenever I, as a white body, try to talk about oppression and emancipation; hegemony and counter-hegemonic stances. Quite literally, I *feel* the gaze of my students.

I feel this gaze on my physical body, as a physical body—and because my physical body stands in particular spatial and power relationships vis-à-vis my students. It doesn't seem to matter whether I arrange the desks in my classroom in rows, in tables, or in a circle—the eyes and even bodily gestures reference me as the object of their gaze or attention. Even when I am having my students give presentations or having them talk to each other in groups, there are always the quick eye movements that look to me to see. . .where I am?. . .if I approve? I become the axis around which their gazes orient. Like the North Star, my students seem to look to my body to exhibit some sort of fleshy direction.

And my body is not the only object that exerts polarity. My body moves in orbit around, in between, and in front of, the bodies/objects in my class. When the chairs are in rows, I tend to stand at the front of the class. When the chairs are in a circle, I tend to sit. When the desks are in tables, I tend to wander around the room. When a group of people are disrupting the discussion or activity, I tend to go over in that direction. My body moves and my postures vary depending on the other bodies/objects in the room.

Sometimes, as a way to symbolically give up my power and create an equal and equally shared space, I sit with the students and try to encourage other bodies to take charge of discussions or presentations within the space of the class. Symbolically, I make the move to undercut my power in the classroom. Perhaps even, intellectually, I believe this symbolic move creates a feeling of equality. However, as I've noted before, my symbolic power is revealed in the way the students' gaze follows me. I'm always/already "in front," even while my physical body does the labor of moving from place to place, sitting, standing, jumping, moving, still.

There are several theories that can help us parse out this moment, this scene. We can start with performativity theories that draw attention to the ways that bodies perform and are encoded by discourse. One of the strongest attributes of this type of theorizing is that it allows us to articulate the hybrid process of discursive production. De Beauvoir (1949), Butler (2006), Byrne (2006) and Tate (2005) all give excellent accountings of the ways that discourses are both read onto the skin and also enacted on/by the flesh toward particular aims.

Performativity theories allow me to focus on the ways that discourses can be recruited and deployed in the way I enact the body but can also discipline and define my body, regardless of the way I attempt to fashion it. These theories allow me to talk about my whiteness in particular ways. I am able to articulate the ways that my whiteness, regardless of what I wear or how I stand or how I pose my body, encodes me as an oppressor. I am also able to talk about my body as always/already coded as the authority. Elyse Lamm Pineau (2005) writes about the always accumulating and circulating power relations between teachers and students. She suggests:

> Our performing bodies inevitably carry the inscription of differentiated status. We cannot enter our classrooms as learners, nor can we empower our students to experience themselves as teachers until we more fully understand the ways in which educational institutions have already politicized our bodies. (Pineau, 2005, p. 35)

This idea allows me to better understand why my students orient their gaze toward me, regardless of my attempts to undercut my power. Performativity theories help me to talk about what the body means; but they don't really allow me to foreground what the body does—and how that doing is limited or bounded by the actual body—not just the discourses deployed by or amassed onto the body. Performativity theories do not allow me to focus on the body's own processes and limits.

In order to talk about the body as delineated by the physical, I turn to thinkers like Dreyfus (1992), Foster (1995), Giddens (1991) Gumbrecht (2004), Merleau-Ponty (2002), and Tilley (2008). For example, Gumbrecht (2004) contends that there are things which "meaning cannot convey" (p. xix). Specifically, he interrogates the idea that phenomena can/should only be known though interpretation, that phenomena only matter when we interpret or point to the meaning (symbolic, representational) of said phenomena (Gumbrecht, 2004). He tries to work against the "perspective that gives a higher value to the meaning of phenomena than to their material presence; the world view that always wants to go beyond (or below) that which is 'physical'" (Gumbrecht, 2004, p. xiv). Tilley (2008) also wants to advance the theorizing of the physical body. He focuses on the ways that bodies are defined, delineated by their own physicality. Tilley (2008) advocates for a theoretical understanding that stresses

> the role of the carnal human body: perception is regarded as being both afforded and constrained by the sensuous human body. The general claim is that the manner in which we perceive [. . .] is fundamentally related to the kinds of bodies we have. (p. 19)

These types of claims allow me to pay closer attention to what *my body does as a teacher*. In a physical classroom, I am required to jump and stretch to reach the top of the chalkboard of the projection screen. No matter how my height gets interpellated within cultural contexts, I will always be 5'4". No matter what my height *means*, it bounds my body in particular ways which require particular types of actions.

Because I am a physical body, with other physical bodies, in a physical space, we labor in specific ways. I walk from my office to the classroom. I have a student who is in an electric wheelchair and has an assistance dog with him. He takes a special bus and then the elevator to get to the classroom. When I am walking around the rather small classroom, I have to be careful not to physically trip over or step on the dog. When I sit at one of the tables, my legs fit neatly on the seat and under the table. I have a student, however, who bumps his knees on the table every time he moves his body in the chair. Our bodies—

the ways they move and how they look—conjure different contextual meanings. But regardless of what our bodies mean, their physicality requires specific ways of moving through the world. Yet, even discursivity theories and phenomenology do not adequately address what it means to labor as a teacher.

I am not sure that any of these theories adequately portray the ways that discursive bodily meanings and physical boundings interact with each other. Perhaps disability theories would help here. However, even this line of inquiry has seemed to focus on the social production of disability—rather than physicality (Goodley, 2009; Thompson, 2009). And, of course, what happens to these theories of the body when we move to the on-line classroom? How do we talk about bodily meanings and bodily doings when the bodies of the students and the teacher may or may not physically manifest themselves to each other?

Scene 2: In Front of the Computer

I don't worry too much about what I'm wearing. No one can see me. I've been asked why I don't turn on the camera; I always give evasive answers. The truth is, at times I find comfort in invisibility. Also, I am somehow uncomfortable with the idea of my students being able to look at me without me having the ability to look back at them. I am, of course, aware that it is due to my positioning within power (the authority of teacher) that I am sought out as an object of the gaze, and it is this same positioning which allows me to make the choice not to be seen.

This invisibility allowed by the on-line environment nurtures a different sort of player within me. When teaching on-line classes, I feel a greater need to "show" that I am competent and ready for this fast, virtual environment. For this reason, I tend to foreground my male-coded professor-voice. While I am aware that my students can look at my avatar and, perhaps, guess at what my body might look like in a material classroom, it still feels like my small-ish, female, white, blonde body isn't quite so obvious. Am I taken more seriously because the students don't always have my body in front of their gaze? Of course, by losing the ability to all gaze at each other, distinct losses are incurred.

Teaching in an on-line environment, at least for me, makes me aware of how much I rely on bodily cues for the pacing of the class. In a physical classroom, I watch the students' eyes. I look to see if they're nodding. I try to gauge interest and understanding by noticing the ways they sit in their chairs. So, even if some students aren't actively engaging in the discussion, I feel like I can usually tell whether or not they are listening and learning. When I ask a question and there is a long-ish wait time before answering, I look to their facial expressions to determine whether they are thinking about their answers or they don't understand the question. All of these visual cues are lost to me in an on-line environment. On-line, when there is a long wait time after a question, I am forced to wonder, did they understand the question, are they thinking deeply, or is there something really good on television that has diverted their attention? Do I need to repeat the question, rephrase, or just wait a little longer? Suddenly, the physical bodies of the students become glaring in their absence from my sight.

I notice my physical body in different ways too. I realize that I am accustomed to a lot of bodily movement in a physical classroom. After two hours of sitting in a chair with my laptop in front of me, I start to fidget a little more. I start doing calf stretches. I move my neck side to side, releasing the cricks that have developed. I notice my posture, and I try to sit up a little straighter (pull my abs in) so my back won't hurt.

My eyes feel noticeably tired after teaching on-line. I pay close and prolonged attention to the computer screen. In the teaching program I use, there is the possibility for students to vocally ask a question or simply type a question that will appear in a text box. The teacher keeps track of who wants to verbally ask a question by looking at an altogether different box where the students are listed in the order that they raised their virtual hands. So, I can be listening to one student's question and also reading a different student's question. I have to read fast, otherwise, the typed question will be lost from the box as it becomes filled with other class members' textual responses to the typed question. I sometimes have to choose, do I respond to the question thread that I'm seeing or the one that I'm hearing?

There are also these oddly voyeuristic moments for me as an on-line teacher. In the teaching program I use for on-line classes, students can vocalize a comment, type a comment to the whole group, or send private messages to any one person or group in the class. The other class members cannot see these private messages, but I, as the teacher, can see them pass back and forth. They are made aware of my special capabilities as far as this feature goes. Still, multiple private conversations move back and forth, all within my view. I sit in the virtual dark, where they cannot see me, and I am able to learn who went out with whom, who is pregnant, whose wife is ill, and who is going out for drinks after class.

I have also noticed that the on-line environment positions the teacher as confessor in some interesting ways. Sometimes, those private messages are directed to me, and I am required to read these personal notes and respond to them, while still doing the other reading, listening, typing, and talking required of an on-line teacher. Other times, the virtual confession comes in the form of an email or on-line Moodle posting.[2]

I have noticed that my students are more intimate when they talk to me on-line than in a physical classroom. The "distance" created by using an on-line space works in interesting ways. While there are times when the "distance" of a "distance-learning" classroom creates a lack of connection, there are also times when that distance enables a greater level of intimacy, a whole new level of "closeness" and communion. While there are students who will share personal experiences when in the physical classroom, I am always amazed at how many more personal stories I get through posts or e-mail. In the physical space of the classroom, I get more questions about and responses to the assigned texts. The text becomes foregrounded. In the Moodle postings, I get more personal experiences related to the texts. The personal becomes foregrounded. For example, in class, I will hear students discuss the consequences of inequitable school funding. On Moodle, I will read personal experiences (several paragraphs long) of how inequitable funding affected the life of one student or another.

This move to the personal is also obvious in the mundane communication that goes on between student and teacher. In class, for example, I may have a student who lets me know that they will be absent for the next class. And that's how it is said: "I just want you to know. I won't be in class next time. I'll be out of town." That same student (or one of many like her/him) will say something altogether different in email. In the email version of the "please excuse me from class" request, I get more details. I hear that they will be out of town for their brother's wedding and the wedding is in Texas and they have to drive there. The student is really not looking forward to that kind of drive. However, the student has to go because everyone has to go to their brother's wedding.

I have asked my on-line students about what makes their experiences in an on-line classroom different from their experiences in a material classroom. I was amazed by how many students confessed that they never talk in "normal" classrooms. They feel far more comfortable giving their opinion and attempting to answer questions in a virtual space. In fact, as Burbules (2002) notes:

> Educationally, it can be extremely useful to have the distance and impersonality that online interaction affords. Some students speak up *more* under such circumstances; there is more time to reflect on what one is writing or reading in an online discussion. (p. 389)

Some students seem to like the invisibility.

There are also times where I get amazingly personal information. I hear about illnesses and family tragedies in pleas for understanding and leniency where grading is concerned. In my experience, I hear far more details about personal affect in an email, than I do in a face-to-face chat. And this is where I really begin to feel like a novice or underling version of the confessor.

I believe that the faceless-ness of on-line communication lends itself to the practice of the confessional. I can understand the desire to give the details of a life, and how the giving becomes easier when you don't have to look at the person who is hearing the details. However, I do sometimes wonder about what my students would think if they saw me as I read their posts, emails, and private messages. Would they feel like they had been adequately "heard" if they saw the amount of multi-tasking I have to do when I'm in the middle of teaching an on-line class? Would the experience of "telling" be cheapened if they saw that I read and respond to emails while I am in my pajamas, with a snack, and in the middle of the *30 Rock* I TiVoed the night before? What does my body mean to these students and does it matter to them that they cannot see it? What does my body do as an online teacher, and does it matter that I can't see the students and that I know I won't be seen?

Once again, there are multiple theories that can help me to parse out this scene. For example, it is Merleau-Ponty (2002) who urges us to "attend to the experience of perception" instead of overlooking it "in favor of the object perceived" (p. 4). I like Merleau-Ponty because he draws attention to the physical nature of the body, draws attention to what the body does and how the body works as the entity which actually does the perceiving. This is helpful because, I think, often we believe that on-line teaching does not involve the body *doing* anything. However, the body still must labor in very specific ways. Usually, the body is sitting. Often, the hands are poised above the keyboard, typing, or at the ready. The eyes must focus in particular ways, noticing and reading multiple text boxes. Different text boxes often include variable font sizes, and the eyes must grow accustomed to that. Allowing the eyes to rest, for just a moment, usually means that you, as the teacher, have missed multiple comments or questions. This charge to focus on the physical makes me aware that, when I teach on-line, there is an adrenaline rush that is similar to, but not quite the same as, the one I get when I'm teaching in a physical classroom. Multi-tasking usually gives me a bit of adrenaline and on-line teaching requires a lot of multi-tasking. Not only that, but when I can tell that my students understand and desire to interact with the concept I'm teaching, there is the adrenaline rush of feeling like you have a good discussion going. This happens in on-line environments just like it happens in tangible environments.

It is focusing on the physical body that also allows me to talk about what I miss when I teach on-line. As I said earlier, teaching on-line makes me more fully aware of how much I rely on the bodies of my students. I look to the body in order to tell if my students are paying attention. I look to the body in order to tell if my students understand or if they have any questions. In fact, I look to the bodies of my students to find approbation. I get joy out of seeing for myself the "ah-ha" moments that happen for my students—the eyes get bigger, the eyebrows raise, the head raises slightly, and the lips sometimes begin to form the word "oh." I miss that production when I teach on-line. So, focusing on the physical body allows many aspects of on-line teaching to be brought to the fore, but focusing exclusively on the physical body also obscures some of the other aspects of on-line teaching.

For Merleau-Ponty (2002) and others like him, time and space can only be experienced through the physical body. We experience a world only through the "kinaesthetic residua" we touch or perceive with our bodies (Merleau-Ponty, 2002, p. 124). In fact, for Merleau-Ponty (2002), learning, knowledge, and the very creation of, and understanding of, space involves the interaction between a physical body and other physical phenomena (pp. 142–162). The interaction between physical bodies is paramount. Benjamin (1968) continues along a similar theme when he suggests that the loss of visceral tangible bodies standing in relation to each other causes a sort of loss of power or force of the body. Benjamin (1968) contrasts actors on a theatrical stage with actors in a movie. For Benjamin (1968), when the bodily interaction comes via an image or virtual production, then the body loses its aura—its force:

> For aura is tied to presence; there can be no replica of it. The aura which on the stage emanates from Macbeth, cannot be separated for the spectators from the actor. However, the singularity of the shot in the studio is that the camera is substituted for the public. Consequently, the aura that envelops the actor vanishes, and with it the aura of the figure he portrays. (p. 229)

So given this, how would Merleau-Ponty and Benjamin talk about an on-line space?

In on-line teaching our interactions are in the virtual. We, of course, labor as physical bodies, but we labor as both physical and on-line enunciations of ourselves. And yes, we rely on cues given by kinaesthetic residua in order to habituate the bodies to using the technology, but the mutual creation/imagination/understanding of a virtual classroom relies on more than kinaesthetic cues. Furthermore, to charge that the loss of physical presence and physical interaction creates a loss of aura, neglects to tell how this loss of the physical presence *enables* the confessional space of on-line communication—the creation of a new kind of aura. The logic of the confessional relies on the belief that you will be heard, but that you won't have to see or be seen by the confessor. In fact, on-line spaces are the ultimate confessional. You neither have to see nor hear nor smell the confessor. And so our physical bodies become the *referent*—our bodies are both physically and symbolically referenced in the virtual. It is this type of interaction that allows students to be more talkative or more intimate in an on-line space. Theories of discourse allow us to talk about the habituation of interaction in more depth.

Discourse theorists, like Foucault and others, do a good job of showing how relationships are habituations of discourse. The teacher is discursively constructed or produced as an authority figure. The teacher is discursively posed as confessor and the student is discursively fashioned and habituated as penitent. It is discursive habituation that allows on-line students and on-line teachers to interact in an on-line classroom and still understand what is considered expected and appropriate behavior from both parties. The very fact that the on-line teaching software I use creates "virtual hands" for the students to raise when they want to vocalize a thought, is evidence of discursively habituated behavior. How do students know how to act in an on-line classroom? They rely on the codes they know about physical classroom life and they transfer those codes into the on-line space. Discursive codes create the matrices of meaning through which we understand our lives. So, understanding discursive constructions allows me to articulate and understand the moments when I feel like a voyeur or like a confessor—rather than just a teacher. While discourse theories do a lot of work toward thinking about the role of the teacher, they make it more difficult to tease out specific ways that the physical and the discursive interact in on-line worlds.

Reading Butler (2006), Tate (2005), Byrne (2006), Foucault (1990), and Althusser (1970), one sees discourse as always circulating but also needing to interpellate bodies (phenomena) as instantiations or reifications of discourse. And naturally, as Lisa Nakamura (2002) points out, when people go on-line, they carry with them all of the discursive habituations, positionalities, and markers that frame them in tangible spaces. However, this does not get at the ways that discourse surrounds, frames, delineates, and contours the virtual body. In other words, discourse encodes and enfleshes the tangible body as a reification of discourse. Discursively encoded bodies go on-line and try to interact with others in a virtual space. However, do discourses encode the virtual body (the avatar, who is not completely *referent* nor completely *sign*, not just the symbol of the tangible person or object who/which is on-line) in exactly the same ways and with exactly the same force as they encode a tangible body (phenomena)? Do discourses surround, and stick to, and delineate the "mutual hallucination" of virtual worlds in exactly the same ways that they encode the tangible world (Gibson, 1984)? Do the discourses that produce what it means to be a teacher or a classroom operate in the same ways and with the same coercive force in an on-line space as in a tangible space? If there is a weaker sense of discursive disciplinarity in virtual spaces, what implications does this have for on-line teaching? Does my body *mean* something different depending upon where and how it is *doing* what it does? Again, I feel like Theory is bereft of the ability to fully capture what it means to labor as a teacher on-line. Perhaps we need a way to talk about strong and weak discursive force: a quantum mechanics of discursivity—focused more explicitly on the multiple modalities of the body.

Scene 3: Learning to Fly

My on-line students told me that, in one of their other on-line classes, they were required to create avatars for Second Life and actually meet together as a class. I asked them if it made a difference to see something/someone who represented their fellow classmates and teacher as they met together as a class. Did they like having a visual referent of a physical body to look at and interact with as a fellow classmate? Most of them really enjoyed the experience. Some of them thought it was really fun to create bodies/avatars that looked nothing like them. They all thought it was fun to experiment with creating a virtual body that represented the self. I think it is amazing to see the ways that a virtual space allows us to *be* someone else, not just "pretend" to be, but actually *be* multiple versions of the "self." Then, a few of my students started talking about how difficult it was to learn how to move in Second Life. They did not like that their virtual bodies did not seem to move very naturally. I thought this was an interesting expectation. Why would you enjoy the idea that your virtual body does not need to look like your physical body but then expect that your virtual body was supposed to move in the same ways as your physical body? ("Be different. Be Yourself." says the front page for Second Life.) Either way, I thought this was an interesting assignment from a pedagogical standpoint: Assign your students to create avatars and meet in a virtual classroom in order to talk about the act of Teaching writ large. This inspired me to try out Second Life, and see whether or not I might do something similar in a future class.

Once I'd entered Second Life, I began to see what my students were talking about: the way my avatar body moves creates an odd sense of reality. In Second Life, bodies can fly. They can also walk, sit, and go through most gestures that you see as you go about your daily life. For me, the odd moment came when I noticed what my avatar did when I/she/it wasn't moving. When my avatar is stationary, she puts one hand on her hip and then shifts her weight from one hip to the next. I do not control this movement nor do anything to make it happen. This is how the avatar moves when I am not giving me/her/it some sort of command or direction. And, it is quite ingenuous really. Most humans do not stand completely still in one place for very long. They shift their weight from side to side. They move their gaze. My avatar was doing the same thing—but not in the ways I would do it. Years of ballet, gymnastics, and yoga training have made me quite aware of how my body moves. I have become attuned to what my body does. Suddenly, watching my stationary avatar, I felt a disjuncture of identity. When my avatar is stationary, she shifts her weight by swishing her hips from one side to the other. I don't know if my body could be that saucy if I tried. My avatar suddenly seemed like a different person; a "not-me."

Physical bodily discipline and habituation also bring with them certain expectations. I can usually walk down a street with the expectation that I will not run into walls. I can usually assume that I will not trip on something like a stair. However, especially as a beginner in Second Life, I regularly run into things and trip over things. While I intellectually understand that this is because I am still getting use to the control keys—I am a beginning avatar body—I cannot help but feel that something has been taken away from me. My physical body experiences the corporeal effects of embarrassment, chagrin, and even a little pain when my avatar body runs into a stair rather than stepping onto it. There is a haptic relationship, a tactile feedback loop, between my physical body and the body of my avatar. Somehow, I feel like this developing coordination between my physical body and my avatar body should entitle my avatar to the accumulated disciplinarity of my physical body. I *should* be more graceful.

This sense of the *avatar as me*, develops more fully when I communicate with other people in Second Life. Having a conversation with another avatar creates a stronger tie between my physical body and my avatar body. There are brief moments when I feel like I *am* my avatar. Still, those moments are brief.

I have this schizophrenic relationship with my avatar where, at times, I think of her as a sort of symbol of me; a particular instantiation of me, one of the multiple "I"s that my post-modern leanings allow me to articulate. At other times, I think of her as an "other"; a character I control but not really me. So I am curious, when on-line classmates come together as avatars in Second Life, exactly who is interacting? Who shows up to class, and does it matter?

As with my other scenes, there are several theories I can apply to come to a fuller understanding of this experience. Many academics are doing work on haptics and telepresence in/for on-line spaces. Welch (1999), Witmer and Singer (1998), Garau et al. (2008) and Alcaniz, Rey, Tembl, and Parhutik (2009) have shown that our physical bodies manifest some very physical reactions—physical effects—due to stimulus in on-line worlds. Hove (2008) articulates some of the ways that interpersonal synchrony develops in on-line spaces. Because of this connection, Hove (2008) argues that the "self/other distinction can be blurred" between the avatar and material body (p. 29). Alcaniz et al. (2009) and Garau et. al. (2008) believe that they can show that on-line stimuli can affect the body to a greater degree than other media, and that on-line stimuli can affect the body, in much the same way and to similar degree, as stimuli in the material world.

This type of work attempts to prove that there are connections between the physical body and the virtual. This allows me to articulate the connections between the physical and the virtual as being corporeal—bodily—connections, not just connections generated by emotions or expectations. I can talk about the ways my body physically manifests shame when my avatar bumps into a wall. I can talk about a physical sensation of warmth when a friend/avatar hugs me/avatar in a virtual space. Affect theories also allow me to talk about connections between body and code but in a slightly different way.

For example, Brian Massumi (2002) develops a theory of Affect that directly tries to take up the ways that code can inhabit and affect the physical body. Massumi (2002) believes that the digital age "requires a new understanding of the body in its relation to signification and the ideal or incorporeal" (p. 44). Massumi (2002) makes a doubled move in order to talk about the corporeal body as more than just a tabula rasa for significations, codes, discourse—but also as a space that is very much habituated by discourse. He wishes to put "what seemed most directly corporeal back into the body" (Massumi, 2002, p. 4). So, he calls for an understanding of the body as a highly sensitive and phenomenal (phenomenological sensing) entity that is also sensitized, acclimatized, and disciplined within discursive matrices. Massumi (2002) hopes:

> Movement, sensation, and [. . .] matter in its most literal sense (and sensing) might be culturally-theoretically thinkable, without falling into either the Scylla of naïve realism or the Charybdis of subjectivism and without contradicting the very real insights of poststructuralist cultural theory. (p. 4)

In fact, Massumi (2002) makes a very interesting theoretical move by suggesting that discourses map onto and coerce the body in specific ways *in relation to* the body's physicality. It is the ability to sense, to feel sensations, "the *perception of one's own vitality,* one's sense of aliveness, of changeability (often signified as 'freedom') [. . .] the distinction between the living and the nonliving," which makes the body react to and be penetrated with discourse in particular ways ([emphasis in original] Massumi, 2002, p. 36). For Massumi (2002), discursive power exists only insofar as it affects/infects the physical. The virtual, on the other hand, is a multiplication of images as discourse—felt by the physical body (Massumi, 2002).

Once again, I like the ways that this theory draws attention to the physical. I think Massumi (2002) does important work when he focuses on the very corporeal entity that limits and delineates the ways that the virtual is felt. Focusing on the physical allows me to more thoroughly trace out what it means to labor as an on-line teacher. However, I take issue with the way that Massumi (2002) seems to collapse discourse and the virtual. Virtuality gets defined using some of the same metaphors used to define discourse. Discursive code seems to become the same thing as virtual code (see Massumi, 2002, pp. 132–143). While this theoretical move creates space for Massumi (2002) to talk about the dynamic range of virtuality, it fails to capture the unique moment of avatar interaction.

Interacting as an avatar provides a sort of "me/not-me" moment that is neither and both a "me" and a "not me" juncture. Massumi's (2002) conception seems to posit a thesis/antithesis binary where the two infect each other but without synthesis. Massumi (2002) advocates a parallax—a productive tension between two ends. While, undoubtedly, this model sums up a lot of interaction as a physical body in a virtual space, it does not capture the moments where the physical, the virtual, and the discursive all blend. It does not capture the recognition of the avatar as both/neither the self and/nor the "other." Also, as this model collapses the virtual and the discursive, it does not allow us to capture the ways that discourse might surround and mold virtual productions/performances/bodies in different ways than physical productions/performances/bodies. Does discursive disciplinarity hold the same sway and work in the same ways in Second Life as in our physical world? How can it, when people experiment with on-line identities in such unique ways. Once again, is there a strong/weak force element to discursivity? What implications does this have for the on-line teacher? Once again, I find that Theory is unable to contain the moment.

End Scene: False Dichotomies and Blended Flows

As I have attempted to trace out the labor of a teacher, more particularly the labor of an on-line teacher, I have found myself beset by a lack of theoretical language. I feel the force of a language that seems to operate in dichotomies. I have found myself implicated in and coerced by the power of language, which tends toward binaries. I have seen the positioning of the physical in opposition to the virtual, the physical in opposition to the discursive, the virtual as an extension of discourse or the virtual as an extension of the body. It seems incredibly difficult to stay away from dichotomies when one is trying to parse out similarities and differences—when one is using comparison as a methodology of definition or delineation. So, I tell my stories and I attempt to take stock of them. Yet, I find that in my attempt to trace out the body, and the labor of the body, and the virtual, that I, at times, also fall victim to dichotomies. Even my positioning of what the body *means* as juxtaposed to what the body *does* creates a binary where one stands in opposition to the other. I reject these dichotomies as unable to capture the nuance of on-line labor. How does one find a theory of "both/and"?

And even the idea of "both/and" is lodged in a binary. The "both" implies the acceptance of the two poles and the "and" implies the joining them together: synthesis. I'm not sure that dichotomies nor syntheses adequately capture the interplay of the corporeal, the discursive, and the virtual. I want a theoretical language that captures the multiple modalities of the body and the leakage of meaning and doing. I have tried, in this chapter, to convey the multiplicity of the body, along with its corporeality, as a laborer. However, by the very act of parsing out the body's meanings and actions in various contexts, I have set one idea against another. How can one talk about the multiple in a language system and theoretical landscape that seems to rely on binaries?

Deleuze and Guattari (1987) sought to overcome this system through their notion of "flow": a movement that desires only expansion and multiplicity; it is without primogeniture and without specific destination; it is rhizomatic in its reproduction; a flow of desire, people, capital, objects, bodies—swings "between the surfaces that stratify it and the plane that sets it free" (Deleuze & Guattari, 1987, p. 161). Existence conceived as flow would contain "the whole art of poses, postures, silhouettes, steps, and voices" that make up bodies, virtuality, and discourse (Deleuze & Guattari, 1987, p. 320). To understand the body as a flow means to see the "pure and immeasurable multiplicity" of the body; the body as importantly physical, conspicuously a discursive production, and necessarily other things as well (Deleuze & Guattari, 1987, p. 352). While Deleuze and Guattari (1987) do a good job of defining flow and what it looks like in its movements, they do not come up with a methodology of flow. How does one apply an understanding of "flow" to the act of tracing out what it means to be a body and to labor as a physical body in a virtual space?

More work will have to be done as we come up with better ways of talking about the materiality of laboring in landscapes and forums that are highly shifting, contingent, virtual, and multiplying. I urge us to come up with new tools and new language in order to more thoroughly account for the meanings of labor in the digital age.

Notes

1. This does not even include the myriad of other distractions that are unique to this particular mode of pedagogical engagement, such as the "private" textual exchanges that are not remotely on target—as the instructor, I am able to see all private and public communication that occurs within the program.
2. Moodle is the name of an open source online learning environment that the University of Illinois utilizes. For more information, see: http://moodle.org/about/

References

Alcaniz, M., Rey, B., Tembl, J., & Parhutik, V. (2009). A neuroscience approach to virtual reality experience using transcranial Doppler monitoring. *Presence. 18*(2), 97–111.
Althusser, L. (1970). Ideology and ideological state apparatuses. *Lenin and Philosophy and Other Essays.* New York" Monthly Review Press.
Anzaldúa, G. (1987). *Borderlands/la frontera: The new mestiza.* New York: Aunt Lute.
Appadurai, A. (1996). *Modernity at large.* Minneapolis, MN: University of Minnesota Press.
de Beauvoir, S. (1949). *The second sex.* H. Parshley, (Trans.). New York: Penguin.
Benjamin, W. (1968). *Illuminations.* New York: Random House.
Burbules, N. (2002). Like a version: Playing with online identities. *Educational Philosophy and Theory. 34*(3), 387–393.
Butler, J. (2006). *Gender trouble.* New York: Routledge.

Byrne, B. (2006). *White lives*. London: Routledge.
Carey, J. (1992). *Communication as culture*. New York: Routledge.
Deleuze, G., & Guattari, F. (1987). *A thousand plateaus: Capitalism and schizophrenia*. B. Massumi (Trans.). Minneapolis, MN: University of Minnesota Press.
Dreyfus, H. (1992). *What computers still can't do*. Boston, MA: MIT Press.
Ellis, C. (2004). *An ethnographic I: A methodological novel about autoethnography*. Walnut Creek, CA: Altamira.
Foster, S. (1995). *Corporealities: Body, knowledge, culture, and power*. New York: Routledge.
Foucault, M. (1990). *History of sexuality, volume 1*. New York: Vintage.
Garau, M., Friedman, D., Widenfeld, H., Antley, A., Brogni, A., & Slater, M. (2008). Temporal and spatial variations in presence: Qualitative analysis from an experiment on breaks in presence. *Presence, 17*(3). 293–309.
Gibson, W. (1984). *Neuromancer*. New York: Ace.
Giddens, A. (1991). *Modernity and self-identity: Self and society in the late modern age*. Stanford, CA: Stanford University Press.
Goodall, H. L. (2000). *Writing the new ethnography*. Lanham, MD: AltaMira Press/Rowman & Littlefield.
Goodley, D. (2009). Bringing the psyche back into disability studies: The case of the body with/out organs. *Journal of Literary and Cultural Disability Studies, 3*(3), 252–272.
Greenhow, C., Robelia, B., & Hughes, J. (2009). Learning, teaching and scholarship in a digital age: Web 2.0 and classroom research: what path now? *Educational researcher, 38*(4).
Gumbrecht, H. (2004). *Production of presence: What meaning cannot convey*. Stanford, CA: Stanford University Press.
Hall, S. (1996). The question of cultural identity. *Readings in contemporary political sociology*. Oxford, UK: Blackwell.
Hove, M. (2008). Shared circuits, shared time, and interpersonal synchrony. *Behavioral and Brain Sciences, 31*, 29–30.
Lantham. S. (2004). New age scholarship: The work of criticism in the age of digital reproduction. *New Literary History, 35*(3).
Massumi, B. (2002). *Parables for the virtual: Movement, affect, sensation*. Durham, NC: Duke University Press.
Merleau-Ponty, M. (2002). *Phenomenology of perception*. New York: Routledge.
Nakamura, L. (2002). *Cybertypes: Race, ethnicity, and identity on the Internet*. New York: Routledge.
Pineau, E. L. (2005). Teaching is performance: Reconceptualizing a problematic metaphor. In B. Alexander, G. Anderson, & B. Gallegos (Eds.), *Performance theories in education*. Mahwah, NJ: Lawrence Erlbaum.
Ross, L., & Sennyey, P. (2008). The library is dead, long live the library! The practice of academic librarianship and the digital revolution. *The Journal of Academic Librarianship, 34*(2).
Sarup, M. (1996). *Identity, culture and the postmodern world*. Edinburgh, UK: Edinburgh University Press.
Tate, S. (2005). *Black skins, black masks*. London: Ashgate.
Thompson, R. (2009). *Feminist theory, the body, and the disabled figure*. New York: McGraw-Hill, Humanities/Social Sciences.
Tilley, C. (2008). *Body and image*. Walnut Creek, CA: Left Coast.

Weedon, C. (2004). *Identity and culture: Narratives of difference and belonging*. Oxford, UK: Oxford University Press.

Welch, R. (1999). How can we determine if the sense of presence affects task performance? *Presence: Teleoperators and virtual environments*, 8(5), 574–577.

Witmer, B., & Singer, M. (1998). Measuring presence in virtual environments: A presence questionnaire. *Presence: Teleoperators and virtual environments*, 7(3), 225–240.

Section IV

Global Regimes and Local Transformations

· 1 2 ·
Understanding Neoliberalism and Its Implications for Contemporary Educational Policies

VIVIANA PITTON

Over the last two decades the term 'neoliberalism' has been used extensively in the social sciences literature (Sparke, 2006). In the field of education, for instance, just in the last year, an important number of books with the word 'neoliberalism' on their title have been published in English (Rutz & Balkan, 2009; Hill & Kumar, 2009; Hill & Rosskam, 2009; Canaan & Shumar, 2008; Hill, 2008; Torres, 2008). The fact that neoliberalism has become an object of academic interest among education scholars may be explained in relation to the widespread recognition of its ideas and practices informing educational policies at the state, federal, and regional level, as well as international policy recommendations. In relation to this, there is plenty of literature assessing the effects of neoliberal-driven policies on schools and universities around the world (Hill & Kumar, 2009; Hill & Rosskam, 2009; Erkiliç, 2008; Olssen, 2002; Puiggrós, 2002; Apple, 2001). Yet, there are fewer efforts trying to assess to what extent the concept of neoliberalism allows us to explain the content and processes of education policies within the context of globalization.

National governments around the world have restructured their education systems along the lines of the private sector through changes in the financing, management, and delivery of education services (Mukhtar, 2009). Under the pressure of the global economy, policy initiatives have come to define the aims of education in economic terms. These changes have implied a major break with the tradition of the post-war era where education had come to signify shared values relating to national identity, community aspirations, and citizenship rights, and whose provision had been mostly regarded as a social responsibility of the state. There is a new discursive policy order very much informed by the language and economic rationalism of neoliberalism. This new language has had a major influence in legitimating reform agendas in many countries and defining the parameters of public debate on education in an era of globalization.

It is my contention that one needs to understand what 'neoliberal' means in order to grasp to what extent policies in education are informed by it. Also, it is necessary to unpack the link between the policy language associated with the marketization of education—permeated by terms such as "free market," "efficiency," "deregulation," "privatization," "decentralization"—and the concept of neoliberalism. In addition, it is worthwhile to explore how the language of neoliberalism interprets globalization and informs policies in agreement with this interpretation. Finally, it is useful to address how this concept is being understood and used by its commentators and critics.

With this purpose in mind, this chapter starts by exploring different definitions of neoliberalism as a way to show the extent of its use across different disciplines and the different emphases and interpretations of this term. Secondly, there is an analysis of the extent to which the concept and ideas associated with neoliberalism allow us to understand the content and processes of educational policy within the context of globalization. Thirdly, there is a brief reference to some implications of the marketization of education. The chapter concludes by discussing some recent contributions that, in spite of criticizing the promiscuousness, omnipresence and omnipotence of the concept of neoliberalism (Clarke, 2008), advocate for a nuanced understanding of the term, rather than to abandon its use.

Defining Neoliberalism

Over the last two decades the concept of 'neoliberalism' has become quite widespread in the social sciences literature. Indeed, the references to neoliberalism are as plentiful as the foci of its commentators. For instance, many critics of neoliberalism focus on its coercive and detrimental aspects: they refer to it as "a mode of domination based on the institution of insecurity, domination through precariousness" (Bourdieu, 2003, p. 29), a form of terror (Brennan, 2003; Giroux, 2004), a source of chaos and increasing conflict (Amin, 2001) and a destructive form of capitalism (Klein, 2007). In line with these criticisms, neoliberalism has been associated with the exploitation of labor, mounting inequality, acute economic strife for all but the well-off individuals and the vanishing of all things public (Aronowitz, 2001; Aune, 2001; Saad-Filho & Johnston, 2005).

According to Thorsen and Lie (2006), critical scholarship along those lines has turned neoliberalism into a catchphrase or "a generic term of deprecation describing almost any economic and political development deemed to be undesirable" (p. 9). This critique is particularly aimed at some critical literature whose main goal it is to denounce a powerful tendency which goes under the name of 'neoliberalism' (cf. e.g., Bourdieu, 1998, 2003; Chomsky, 1999; Campbell & Pedersen, 2001; Touraine, 2001; Plehwe, Walpen, & Neunhöffer, 2006) but which often seems at ease leaving the concept of neoliberalism completely undefined, claiming along with Saad-Filho and Johnston (2005), that it defies definition.

An exception to this tendency is David Harvey's critical work, *A Brief History of Neoliberalism* (2005), which provides a comprehensive definition of this concept:

> Neoliberalism is in the first instance a *theory of political economic practices* that proposes that human well-being can best be advanced by liberating individual entrepreneurial freedoms and skills within an institutional framework characterized by strong private property rights, free markets and free trade. The role of the state is to create and preserve an institutional framework appropriate to such practices. The state has to guarantee, for example, the quality and integrity of money. It must also set up those military, defense, police and legal structures and functions required to secure private property rights and to guarantee, by force if need be, the proper functioning of markets. Furthermore, if markets do not exist (in areas such as land, water, education, health care, social security, or environmental pollution), then they must be created, by state action if necessary. But beyond these tasks the state should not venture. State interventions in markets (once created) must be kept to a bare minimum because, according to the theory, the state cannot possibly possess enough information to second-guess market signals (prices) and because powerful interest groups will inevitably distort and bias state interventions (particularly in democracies) for their own benefit. ([emphasis added], p. 2)

Against the idea that neoliberalism is a mere economic doctrine (Cohen & Kennedy, 2000),[1] Harvey considers it as a political economic theory which regards individual liberty and freedom as essential to human well-being. According to this theory, Harvey suggests, individual liberty and freedom can best be protected and achieved by an institutional structure—made up of strong private property rights, free markets, and free trade—in which individual initiative can flourish. From this follows that the state should not be involved in the economy too much, but it should use its power to preserve private property rights and the institutions of the market and promote those on the global stage if necessary. Harvey views neoliberalism not as the revival of liberalism in general but as a distinctive political economic theory which: has replaced Keynesian approaches to macroeconomic governance, has counteracted the "dependency culture" of the welfare state (Cerny, 2008a); and has succeeded in fixating the public on a particular definition of 'freedom' that has served to conceal a project of upper class wealth accumulation. According to his view, the main goal of neoliberal reforms is the restoration of capitalist class power in the context of global economic pressures (Harvey, 2003).

Another definition comes from political scientist Anna-Maria Blomgren, whose concept of neoliberalism overlaps to some extent with Harvey's definition, though it stresses more clearly the internal diversity of neoliberal thinking:

> Neoliberalism is commonly thought of as a *political philosophy* giving priority to individual freedom and the right to private property. It is not, however, the simple and homogeneous philosophy it might appear to be. It ranges over a wide expanse in regard to ethical foundations as well as to normative conclusions. At the one end of the line is 'anarcho-liberalism,' arguing for a complete laissez-faire, and the abolishment of all government. At the other end is 'classical liberalism,' demanding a government with functions exceeding those of the so-called night-watchman state. ([emphasis added] Blomgren, 1997:224, as cited in Thorsen & Lie, 2006)

Neoliberal political philosophy promotes a certain way of organizing society that places a great emphasis on individuals being 'free to choose' (cf. Friedman 1962; 1980). In this framework, the so-called 'free' individual is the basic unit of political order, and the state's main responsibility consists of guaranteeing the individuals' security, liberty and property (Peters, 2001). Wherever it appears, and under whatever guise, neoliberalism promises 'freedom,' defined almost exclusively in terms of the rights of individuals to participate in markets and for markets themselves to act free from any governmental intervention (Clarke, 2004). From this viewpoint, then, social well-being rests on individual choice and can only take place within a freely operating market.

Different scholars, however, have pointed out that under neoliberalism the state has a continued "intimate and ubiquitous" (Pierson, 1996) involvement in regulating the minutiae of the market economy and have emphasized its central role in implementing free market policies. Indeed, the contemporary consensus is that the 'retreat of the state' argument is inaccurate,[2] and that consideration about states and markets being somehow intrinsically opposed to each other emerges as something of a myth (Kingfisher & Maskovsky, 2008). In order to be efficient, the market needs the protection of the state and its power of enforcement. Its existence and functioning depend on certain political, legal, and institutional conditions that are provided by the state (Burchell, 1996). As Andrew Barry, Osborne, and Rose (1996) contend, neoliberalism "involves less a retreat from governmental 'intervention' than a re-inscription of the techniques and forms of expertise required for the exercise of government" (p. 14). The neoliberal state has been reorganized and restructured but without losing its traditional regulatory functions. What makes it different is the fact that it has transferred its historical responsibility for social welfare to the individual (Klees, 2002). At issue, therefore, are analyzing the critical shifts in the ways that the contemporary state intervenes in the market and addressing to what ends and in whose interests the state operates.

Rather than seeing neoliberalism as an ideology that presents itself as the necessary withdrawal of the state through practices like privatization, deregulation and free markets, Foucault defines neoliberalism as a form of *governmentality* that changes the techniques by which states and individuals govern and are governed (Foucault, 2008). The advantage of this approach is that it focuses on the rationality upon which government practices are based. Such an approach reveals that neoliberalism differs from earlier forms of liberalism in that it conceives of the market as something that the government needs to actively construct by establishing particular political, legal and institutional conditions. The state is then faced with the additional dilemma of needing to encourage the development of the particular forms of 'autonomous' and 'free' individuals that neoliberal styles of government depend upon (Johnson, 2000).

Building upon Foucault's ideas, there is a rising amount of research and writing focused on neoliberalism as a new form of governance or governmentality.[3] According to this line of work, neoliberalism functions by creating self-regulated mechanisms to bring about governmental results through the devolution of risk onto the enterprise or the individuals—now regarded as "entrepreneurs of themselves" (Foucault, 1979, as cited in Lemke, 2001, p. 198)—and the responsibilization of subjects who are increasingly empowered to discipline themselves (Barry et al., 1996; Burchell, 1996; Rose, 1996). In their view, the state under neoliberalism instead of retreating or rolling back has been transformed into a modality of government whose operations have been autonomized (Barry et al., 1996) and adjusted to an entrepreneurial model via the fabrication of techniques that emphasize "the greater individualization of society and the 'responsabilization' of individuals and families." (Peters, 2001, p, 85)

In line with these ideas on neoliberal governmentality, Ong (2006) addresses the all-too-common view of neoliberalism as a market ideology which limits the scope and activity of governing by suggesting:

> Neoliberalism can also be conceptualized as a new relationship between government and knowledge through which governing activities are recast as nonpolitical and nonideological problems that need technical solutions. Indeed, neoliberalism considered as a *technology of government* is a profoundly active way of rationalizing governing and self-governing in order to 'optimize.' The spread of neoliberal calculation as a governing technology is thus a historical process that unevenly articulates situated political constellations. An ethnographic perspective reveals specific alignments of market rationality, sovereignty, and citizenship that mutually constitute distinctive milieus of labor and life at the edge of emergence. ([emphasis added] p. 3)

In her view, neoliberalism as a 'malleable technology of government' is adopted in different ways by different regimes—be they authoritarian, democratic, or communist—and produces new forms of sovereignty and citizenship in which rights and benefits are distributed in accordance with entrepreneurial capacity (not necessarily according to nation-state membership). Ong sees neoliberalism as a political rationality that introduces 'exceptions' to established governing practices. For instance, she says, East and Southeast Asian states are making 'exceptions' to their traditional practices of governing in order to position themselves and to better compete in the global economy. The neoliberal exception, she argues, "allows for a measure of sovereign flexibility in ways that both fragment and extend the space of the nation state.[. . .] Market-driven strategies of spatial fragmentation respond to the demands of global capital for diverse categories of human capital, thus engendering a pattern of non-contiguous, different administered spaces of 'graduated' or variegated sovereignty." (2006, p. 7)

Other conceptualizations of neoliberalism refer to it as a dominant ideology and policy paradigm that assumes the superiority of market mechanisms to face the diverse challenges brought about global processes to nation-states and civil society. Along these lines, Cerny (2008a) posits that, in recent years,

> Neoliberalism has turned out to be the framework of intellectual and political debates as economic doctrine, public policy agenda, descriptive framework, analytical paradigm and social discourse. It has become deeply embedded in 21st century institutional behavior, political processes and understandings of socio economic 'realities.' In this way it has superseded "embedded liberalism" (Ruggie, 1982) as the common sense and key "shared mental model" (Roy, Denzau and Willett, 2007) of the evolving "art of governmentality" in a globalizing world (Burchell, Gordon and Miller, 1991; Cerny, 2008a). Embedded neoliberalism has become the common sense of the 21st century. (p. 2)

In a similar fashion, Rizvi (2007) states that neoliberalism can be better understood if regarded "as a social imaginary that implies a tacit and implicit understanding of current global processes" (p. 76). Building upon Taylor's ideas on 'social imaginary'—a socially shared way of thinking, a framework of common understandings that give sense and legitimize everyday practices—Rizvi suggests that the neoliberal social imaginary of globalization

> represents a range of ideas concerning new forms of politico-economic governance based on a pervasive naturalization of market logics and the extension of market relationships. (p. 8)

In line with Rizvi's assertion, Pick and Taylor (2009) argue that the policy reforms brought about by neoliberalism in developed and developing countries alike are closely linked to a particular vision of globalization promoted by the Washington Consensus.[4] According to this vision, shared by OECD nations and major financial institutions, the principles of free market, free trade, competition, deregulation and privatization were the answer not only to economic, but also to political and social global challenges (Held & McGrew, 2007). These principles, it is argued, have assumed "the status of an alleged precondition for the survival and the welfare of nations within a rapidly changing environment." (Dakopoulou, 2009, p. 85) Not surprisingly, the neoliberal interpretation of globalization brings about new policy requirements in different social areas, especially in relation to education. For instance, educational policies around the world seem to be conspicuously reshaped in response to the pressures and requirements of the global economy. I will analyze in the next section the extent to which the concept and ideas associated with neoliberalism allow us to understand the content and processes of educational policy within the context of globalization.

Educational Polices under the Neoliberal Interpretation of Globalization

A constellation of core ideas stands out from all of the definitions of neoliberalism presented in the prior section: 1) market fundamentalism; 2) emphasis on free trade; 3) relevance of competition; 4) entrepreneurialism and managerialism; 5) deregulation and privatization; 6) redefinition of the role and responsibilities of the state; 7) replacement of the public good with individual responsibility (Martinez & Garcia, 1996, 8) importance of individual choice. Over the last decades, these neoliberal ideas or principles have been ingrained in educational policy discourses and have transformed the way one comes to think about education, about its purposes, and about the ways in which it is organized and administered. By no means am I implying that neoliberal principles are articulated globally in the same way. On the contrary, the use of neoliberal ideas in the development of policy is historically specific, multivocal, and is in a constant state of struggle. As Hartman (2005) highlights, "key values associated with neoliberalism are not uniformly applicable across all neoliberal regimes" (p. 59), while Albo (2002) recognizes "unevenness in the universalisation of the neoliberal project." (p. 46) So while the actual dynamics and pace of educational policy change differ across national systems according to their historical traditions and economic, social, political and cultural characteristics (Schugurensky, 1999), the direction of change appears to be conspicuously similar and informed by neoliberal principles.

More often than not, a failing and inefficient public education system has been presented by national governments as the rationale for restructuring their systems along the lines of deregulation, cost-efficiency, consumer choice and competition (Basu, 2004). As public resources for education have decreased, there has been a growing emphasis on increasing the role of the private sector in the financing, management, and delivery of education services (Mukhtar, 2009). The restructuring of education systems has also involved a shift from central administration to managerial decentralization coupled with new forms of performance management and accountability (Peters, 2007). Furthermore, educational institutions are not only expected to behave like the market does, but also are being transformed into one (Hirtt, 2009, p. 214). Moreover, inscribed in the new globalized space of services, education has become subjected to a logic of commoditization (Rizvi, 2007).

These changes in the way goals, organization, and delivery of education are thought out within policy reforms, constitute a major break with the discursive tradition of the post-war era—a tradition in which education had come to signify shared values relating to national identity, community aspirations, and citizenship rights, and whose provision had been mostly regarded as a social responsibility of the state. In the new discursive order, the language and economic rationalism of neoliberalism have acquired doctrinal prominence, entailing the emergence of a new set of key words, such as "decentralization," "choice," "efficiency" and "accountability." This new language has had a major influence in legitimating reform agendas in many countries and defining the parameters of public debate on education in an era of globalization. In relation to this, it is argued that international organizations such as the OECD and the World Bank have played an instrumental role in shaping and promoting an educational agenda mostly oriented to respond to the imperatives of the global economy (Dakopoulou, 2009; Hirtt, 2009; Carnoy, 2002; Henry et al., 2001).

Considering the global economy as a knowledge economy, under the neoliberal gaze education and training become regarded as key sectors in promoting national economic competitiveness and future national prosperity. Concomitantly, international organizations' policy recommendations tend to suggest governments from developed and developing countries alike should invest in education and training as a basis for national economic growth. For instance, a World Bank (1995) report summarizes the priorities and strategies of education by saying:

> Education is critical for economic growth [...]. Changing technology and economic reforms are creating dramatic shifts in the structure of economies, industries, and labor markets throughout the world. The rapid increase in knowledge and the pace of changing technology raise the possibility of sustained economic growth with more frequent job changes during individuals' lives. These developments have created two key priorities for education: it must meet economies' growing demands for adaptable workers who can readily acquire new skills, and it must support the continued expansion of knowledge. (p. 1)

Along the same lines, a 1999 report emphasizes that

> Education has become more important than ever before in influencing how well individuals, communities and nations fare. The world is undergoing changes that make it much more difficult to thrive without the skills and tools that a high quality education provides. Education will determine who has the keys to the treasures the world can furnish. [...] Those who can best engage in competition (with more advanced literacy, numeracy and other skills) have an enormous advantage over their less prepared rivals in a changing economic environment." (World Bank, 1999, p. 1)

Similarly, a report by UNESCO and the OECD (2002) points out:

> It has become clear that educational attainment is not only vital to the economic well-being of individuals but also for that of nations. Access to and completion of education is a key determinant in the accumulation of human capital and economic growth. (p. 5)

Michael Peters (2001) posits that these organizations' ideas about the importance of investment on education are informed by a new theory of human capital. New human capital theory, a rejuvenated version of Becker's (1964) tenets, assumes that investing in education and training will benefit not only the individual but also will be conducive to economic growth and competitiveness in the global economy. With an economic, industrial and technological environment growing more unstable, volatile and chaotic than ever due to global economic competition, the acquisition of knowledge, and consequently, of education, becomes more crucial than ever (Hirtt, 2009). As it is increasingly difficult to predict which specific qualifications will be needed in ten or fifteen years time, the argument goes, education is required to focus less on formal knowledge or 'general culture' and emphasize more skills that guarantee flexibility and adaptability to the changing conditions of the global economy. Two different OECD reports formulate this very clearly:

> It is more important to aim at educational objectives of a general character than to learn things which are too specific. In the working world, there exists a set of basic competences—relationship qualities, linguistic aptitudes, creativity, the capacity to work in a team and to solve problems, a good understanding of new technologies—which have today become essential to possess to be able to obtain a job and to adapt rapidly to the evolving demands of working life. (OECD, 1998, p. 5)

As complexity [in economic systems] increases, more and more 'bits' of information are required to specify interactions and changes within the structured system. To cope with increasing complexity in an economy, higher levels of skill and adaptability are required of citizens. (Hogdson, 2000, p. 90)

In a constantly changing environment where technologies continually evolve, products keep changing, and competition leads to job insecurity, this rhetoric sustains that workers are expected to undergo continual training to remain productive and employable (OECD, 1998). From this follows that policy reforms need to transform methods, objectives and instruments of training in order to create the conditions required for 'learning to change' (flexibility) and 'learning to learn' (Pérez, 2001), the latter understood here as the mere ability to adapt quickly to changing technological and workplace conditions (Hirtt, 2009). Under this rhetoric, education is circumscribed to its economic ends; it becomes essential to human capital development and economic self-maximization.

This instrumental view of education is further advanced by policy documents that acknowledge the relevance of life-long learning, "the magic spell in the discourse of educational and economic policymakers, as well as in that of the practitioners of both domains." (Lambeir, 2005, p. 350) In these documents, life-long learning is presented as a key component for developing workforce versatility, something which is allegedly needed to accommodate the needs of flexible production in the global economy. In relation to this, some commentators add that besides seeking to minimize the 'time lag' between individual skills and the ever-increasing economic and technological innovations, life-long learning represents a form of biopower that aims to discipline subjects under neoliberalism (Olssen, 2008). In relation to this it is being said that "the life-long learning discourse identifies a broad need to teach individuals to become autonomous learners." (Tuschling and Engemann as cited in Olssen, 2006, p. 42) Life-long learning discourses contribute to shape individuals to become self-determined and self-responsible in educational tasks, including their financial aspects. Being prepared for participating in the global economy, the argument goes, is now more the individual's responsibility (particularly in financial terms) as opposed to a social obligation of the state.

The assumption underlying this discourse, Olssen claims, is that learners need "to become the entrepreneurs of their own development. What the states provide are the tools that facilitate and audit the process. Not only must individuals learn, but they must learn to recognize what to learn, and what and when to forget [what they had learned] when circumstances demand it." (p. 42) However, some have argued, "the problem with this is that this apparent freedom carries responsibilities to make oneself continually employable through life-long learning, endless flexibility, and viewing what happens to oneself as the product of individual, autonomous choices." (Phoenix, 2004) In a similar vein, Bansel (2007) claims that the neoliberal discourse of choice—which positions the rational, self-managing, self-promoting subject engaged in life-long learning as able to choose among, and consume, multiple options—"assumes that all subjects are equally positioned to recognize, mobilize and consolidate productive or successful choices. There is no space in this discourse for any consideration of the different and inequitable locations of subjects in terms of familial, cultural or socioeconomic privilege or disadvantage, or of age, education, gender, class and ethnicity." (p. 298) Underlying this discourse is the assumption that all subjects are able to choose equally from identical sets of options.

The conditions of increasing complexity and uncertainty not only have implications in terms of the preparation of students as future workers but also face educational institutions with the need for managing those conditions. One of the main policy responses to those challenges has been decentralization and the increasing autonomy of schools and higher education institutions. Influenced by the so-called 'new contractualism' and 'new public management,' those processes often involve the increasing recourse to contractualism—understood here as the use of contracts as the main resource for regulating public relations (and in some cases private ones as well)—and managerialism, which broadly refers to the closer alignment of public sector governance with its private sector counterpart (Ramia & Carney, 2000). The basic assumption underlying these processes is that turning formally regulated bureaucratic units into autonomous agencies and letting them be directed by contracted managers instead of career bureaucrats contributes to an increased capacity to manage complexity and uncertainty.

It is necessary to point out that managerialism in education borrows heavily from public choice theory (Buchanan & Tullock, 1962), which offers a framework applying economic rationality in decision making as the key criterion. Public choice theorists contend that since public schools are input-driven organizations accountable to bureaucratic structures (Peterson, 1990), they lack the structural incentives to respond appropriately to the students' families' demands (Chubb & Moe, 1988, 1990). That is, as legislatures and school boards establish and enforce compliance through a bureaucratic hierarchy, public schools end up being more responsive to the demands of exogenous political constituencies than to their students' needs. On the contrary, they believe private schools seem to be less constrained by political pressures and more receptive to the demands of those families willing to pay tuition in exchange for better opportunities and educational quality. Based on these arguments, public choice theorists propose replacing state control with a competitive education marketplace in which parents are able to select a school on the basis of academic quality and to choose another if that school fails to meet their expectations, producing competitive incentives for schools to improve.

Informed by these theories, many former state-run centralized education systems around the world have been transformed into networks of flexible, competitive schools, often managed by local authorities or nongovernmental groups (EURYDICE, 1997; Rhoten, 2000; Gershberg, 1999; Tatto, 1999). Fiske

(1996), for instance, claims that decentralization of schools is truly a global phenomenon:

> Nations as large as India and as tiny as Burkina Faso are doing it. Decentralization has been fostered by democratic governments in Australia and Spain and by an autocratic military regime in Argentina. It takes forms ranging from elected school boards in Chicago to school clusters in Cambodia to vouchers in Chile. [...] This global fascination with decentralization has manifold roots. Business leaders have discovered the limitations of large, centralized bureaucracies in dealing with rapidly changing market conditions. The collapse of the Soviet Union and the struggles of other socialist states have weakened faith in centralized states and increased the pressure for democratization. The worldwide recessions of the late 1980s and early 1990s have drawn attention to the crucial role of education in building sound economies, and experience has shown that many centralized systems of education are simply not working. A global debate about the proper role of the state has led to more emphasis on the concepts of free markets, competition, and even privatization. (p. v)

Given its strategic value to be competitive in the global economy, the neoliberal state is unlikely to abdicate fully the responsibility for shaping education either to a 'marketized' public sector or even an entirely privatized system (Gordon & Whitty, 1997). Despite their rhetoric, neoliberal states maintain a continued interest in ensuring that educational institutions remain accountable to them. Consequently, they introduce macro steering mechanisms such as evaluation and accreditation regimes or legislation. In line with this, one can observe that contemporary education systems embarked in policy reforms seeking the decentralization of management control away from the central administration to individual schools often have paired this process with new accountability structures (Peters, 2001). New accountability measures in education include monitoring techniques and incentives to performance enhancement. With consumer-managerial forms of accountability, education institutions need to demonstrate the quality of their provision (educators also are subjected to accountability measures of their teaching), which is measured against some sort of established parameter. The problem with the emphasis on accountability and performance measures, Harris (2007) points out, is that it is mainly concerned with performativity in terms of effectiveness and efficiency. In her view, the neoliberal governance of education is connected to a new positivistic regime of accountability that strictly follows an economic imperative. Not surprisingly, then, life-long learning policy initiatives are mainly linked to the construction of the learner as a subject capable of efficient self-management: an entrepreneur rather than a citizen.

Alongside decentralization initiatives and counting on the support (or pressure via conditionalities and other mechanisms) of key international agencies such as the World Bank and the OECD as well as by the International Trade Centre of the UNCTAD and the WTO, different countries have implemented privatized forms of educational 'delivery' in an effort to solve the issues inherited from inefficient, bureaucratic and deteriorated publicly state-run education systems. Pro-privatization initiatives in general broadly assume that 1) markets are more flexible and efficient than the bureaucratic structures of the state; 2) the private provision of services is more efficient and cost-effective than the public one; 3) market competition will produce more accountability for social investments than bureaucratic policies (Torres, 2002). When these ideas are transferred to the educational arena, the argument explaining the movement towards privatization is often that the state can (and should) no longer be responsible for the growth of the education sector, and, therefore, there should be greater reliance on private investment and practices. Besides, it is argued, the entrance of private operators to the system may not only widen the supply of educational services but also may contribute to improve their quality.

Another argument has been provided by the World Bank, which has funded diverse private education initiatives (IFC, 2001)[5] across Latin America toward the goal of fostering 'equity of choice' (Davidson-Harden & Schugurensky, 2009). Broadly, the argument contends that by privatizing education at various levels, 'subsidies' for wealthier families are eliminated as they transfer their education 'investment' into the private sector, thus, leaving state funding for the rest of the public school system. Some educational researchers suggest that extant evidence seems to go against this claim. For instance, evidence from Latin American countries such as Chile suggests that the increased levels of private (including for-profit) education provision at all of its levels is accompanied by an unequal access to better quality schools based on social class, despite compensatory measures from international financial institutions intended to defray the stratification effects of privatized voucher systems (Carnoy & McEwan, 2003; Carnoy, 2002, 1998). A corresponding dilemma of this dynamic is the phenomenon of private schools 'cream-skimming' of children from wealthier families who are better prepared to succeed at school, with a corresponding burden on the public system to absorb students with greater educational needs and long histories of social exclusion and oppression. Far from overcoming equity issues in education systems with rampant social polarization, market style restructuring efforts seem to exacerbate the social gap in terms of access to quality schools and colleges; a dynamic observable not only in Latin America but also in other international contexts (Gewirtz, Ball, & Bowe, 1995; Whitty, Power, & Halpin, 1998).

In relation to the privatizing trends in education across countries, one cannot overlook the capacity of international trade regimes such as the WTO's GATS to reinforce those trends. According to Schugurensky and Davidson-Harden (2003), the WTO/GATS educational agenda has the potential to further the project of privatization to a higher level by transforming education into a service that can be traded on a commercial basis in the global economy. The consideration of education as a commodity that can be traded across borders needs to be considered as part of a neoliberal discourse that points to the virtues of free trade and that recognizes the (economic) opportunities and competitive advantages for national governments associated with the increasing mobility of students, programs and ideas. Facilitated by the advances in transport, information and telecommunications, international education—often referred to also as cross-border, transnational, offshore or borderless education—has grown exponentially over the last years. It seems that this trend is far from decreasing; it has been projected that the demand for international education will augment from 1.8 million international students in 2000 to 7.2 million international students in 2025 (Bohm, Meares, & Pearce, 2002). This is a staggering increase that presents enormous opportunities (not only economic but also in terms of cross-cultural experiences and academic institutional cooperation). Nevertheless, as global economic competitiveness forces investors to search constantly for new profitable markets, one should not be surprised that international education appears to have become a 'new El Dorado' not only for the private corporate sector but also for national governments that are keen to maximize the export potential of their educational services (Hill & Kumar, 2009). The implications of the commoditization of international education remain to be seen, but one may speculate that its projected growth may continue to exacerbate already extant differences in relation to the job and career opportunities available to those students who graduate abroad and those who do it in their home country (see Mok & Lo, 2009).

Discussion

After having addressed processes such as marketization, vocationalization, managerialism, deregulation, privatization, and internationalization of education, I would like to argue that the concept of neoliberalism—that I define in this chapter as a set of ideas pertaining to new forms of governance underwritten by market theories and practices and pushing towards an increased presence of market dynamics in social life—allows us to understand the undergoing changes and the prevailing orientation of educational policies under globalization. The terms that circulate in neoliberal rhetoric and the practices that follow from them were shown to have important implications for educational policy. Based on an understanding of globalization "as a process denoting the universal, boundless and irreversible spread of market imperatives" (Colás, 2005, p. 71), neoliberal-driven reforms have repurposed the aims and the governance of education to meet its demands. Assuming that a country's competitiveness rests on its people's knowledge and ability to respond and adapt to the increasing complexity of technological and productive processes and the concomitant uncertainty of working conditions brought about by the global economy, neoliberal reorientations of education seem to be conspicuously directed towards human capital development. Therefore, vocationalization is a ruling logic in current policy discourses of international organizations and national governments pertaining to education. This vocationalization is advanced by the policy mantra of life-long learning.

Assuming the efficiency of the market as a superior allocative mechanism for the distribution of scarce public resources (one of neoliberalism's main claims), national governments in different parts of the world have promoted educational policy reforms including privatization and decentralization initiatives oriented to reduce the state's participation in terms of funding, provision, and administration. In light of these initiatives, user-pay fees, new providers (non-profit, and particularly, for-profit) and management technologies that include increased exposure to competition, increased accountability measures and the implementation of performance goals and quality assurance measures (Davies & Bansel, 2007) have become common features in many education systems around the world. These initiatives can be better understood when considered in relation to the shifts in the relationships among state, economy and civil society driven by neoliberalism's understanding of economic rationality as encompassing all aspects of human action and behavior (Gordon, 1991). Underlying neoliberal thinking is the idea that the economic is optimized through the entrepreneurial activity of autonomous agents who are regarded as best able to assess the benefits of their actions, make rational choices and be responsible for their consequences. The state simply needs to guarantee the conditions necessary for the efficient functioning of the market. Thus, education reforms informed by neoliberalism position economic ends at the center and value the idea of choice as being exercised and dependent on a rational assessment of costs and benefits in order to maximize investment. In this way, responsibilities for education and other social services become the individual's responsibility; they become privatized.

Ruled by the economic imperatives of the private sector, social services such as education are redefined as part of the market. Concomitantly, they become like any other service that can be traded, even in the global market. The implications of the commodification of education at the global level are still to be seen. However, many scholars have already shown concern regarding the marketization of education by arguing that encouraging greater school autonomy and competition among schools may intensify not only "the disparities between schools in terms of social outcomes, but also social inequalities." (Tan, 1998, p. 47) In relation to this it has been said that in an education market where parents and students do not have the freedom to create the choices, but only the freedom to choose from whatever the authorities supply to them (Marginson, 1997), those who can 'choose' (afford) to go to elite private schools obtain positional goods,[6] while less privileged students are left with public education as a choice-of-better-than-none. Far from being an equalizer, competition tends to make it more difficult for disadvantaged groups to access quality education. Another criticism is that a marketized education "lacks concern for the humanistic issues of equal opportunity, social justice and the social contract." (Sullivan, 1998, p. 15) One could say instead that these issues are still relevant to education, but that they need to be understood in relation to the broader framework of its economic ends (Rizvi, 2007).

When educational policies are considered in relation to the set of ideas and practices that neoliberalism represents one is likely to gain a general understanding about their content and processes. One needs to keep in mind, though, that this is a concept whose meaning needs to be explained in reference to particular peoples, territories, states and cultural formations (Kingfisher and Maskovsky, 2008). Similarly to what happens with the concept of 'globalization,' one needs to avoid using the term neoliberalism as if it explains anything in and of itself. Moreover, one needs to be aware that the concept of neoliberalism is not univocal and that its use is somewhat problematic. In fact, there are many definitions of this term (as shown in the first part of this chapter), and there is much discussion about the all-encompassing nature of its use, which for some weakens the explanatory power of this concept.

Some of the criticisms target the use of neoliberalism as a monolithic ideology. Against this conception, Ayers and Carlone (2007) refer to Peck and

Tickell's (2002) 'phases of neoliberalism' as a challenge to the standing view of neoliberalism as a homogeneous ideology and suggest that neoliberalism is rather a fragmented ideology whose ideas have been translated into policy in different ways at different points in history. In the same vein, Kjaer and Pedersen (2001) contend that neoliberal ideology takes on meaning through "a process whereby concepts and conceptions from different social contexts come into contact with each other and trigger a shift in the existing order of interpretation and action in a particular context" (p. 220). This process of meaning-making is referred to as *translation*, whereby institutional actors "select various relevant neoliberal concepts and conceptions from ideas available to them and use them in ways that displace the existing order of interpretation and action and trigger a shift in [. . .] opportunities for political action." (Ayers & Carlone, 2007, pp. 462–463)

In a different direction, Clarke (2008) presents his criticism by saying he fears that the concept of neoliberalism "has been stretched too far to be productive as a critical analytical tool" (Clarke, 2008, p. 135). Clarke summarizes this point as follows:

> Neo-liberalism suffers from promiscuity (hanging out with various theoretical perspectives), omnipresence (treated as a universal or global phenomenon), and omnipotence (identified as the cause of a wide variety of social, political and economic changes). (p. 135)

In addition, he claims that attempting to define a "core or essential neoliberalism" implies dealing with three problems: "the variations of neoliberal discourses, technologies, and interventions; the changing repertoire of neo-liberalism over time and the effects of strategies of appropriation/articulation." (p. 140) He proposes, then, a way of thinking about neoliberalism that diminishes its density and totalizing weight. Keeping neoliberalism "open"— to the contradictions, antagonisms and contested political projects that characterize the social field with which neoliberalism engages—"announces the possibility of thinking about what is *not* neo-liberal. . .and thus the possibility of living *without* neo-liberalism." (p. 145)

Kingfisher and Maskovsky (2008) provide another interesting approach to thinking about neoliberalism. They suggest treating neoliberalism, "as an unstable, incomplete and limited governmental regime; [. . .] both as a project with totalizing desires [. . .] and as a project whose totalizing desires are rarely fully realized" (p. 117) Furthermore, they comment on the need for avoiding references to neoliberalism as an external force—understood either as a set of economic policies or discourses—forced upon states, civil society institutions, populations or individuals whose agency is conceived narrowly in terms of either accommodation or resistance. For them, those representations of neoliberalism risk describing it "as something that is perhaps more powerful and all-encompassing than it really is, ignoring in the process its contradictions, fractures, partialities, contingencies, and both dialectics with and determinations by other social forces" (Kingfisher, 2002, pp. 164–165).[7] Then, they suggest to question, locate and problematize (rather than overstate) neoliberalism's power to reshape the world (p. 119).

Although they are concerned with the diversity of 'actually existing' neoliberalisms (Gledhill, 2004), their interest is focused on considering the limitations of those neoliberalisms and on questioning what Gledhill refers to as their 'apparent successes.' To facilitate the task of disentangling the nature and limits of neoliberalism, they draw attention to the use of three interrelated concepts: culture, power and governing practices. Departing from an idea of culture as "disarticulating and rearticulating, disjunctive and contradictory" (p. 120), they challenge the view of neoliberalism as a homogeneous cultural system in which fixed definitions of personhood, state-civil society relations and market relations are thought to exist. Instead, they consider neoliberalism "as a cultural formation [. . .], a set of cultural meanings and practices related to the constitution of proper personhood, markets and the state that are emergent in a contested cultural field." (p. 120) Based on Wolf's (1999) conceptualization of power as a relational term rather than as a unitary, independent and omnipotent force and drawing from his distinction of four modalities of power, Kingfisher and Maskovsky (2008) propose to explore neoliberalism by focusing on its tactical or organizational power, that is, on its ability to instrumentally circumscribe the actions of others within a setting or domain. By engaging in this kind of situated analysis, they argue, one may be able to avoid falling on fetishized theorizations of neoliberalism as a foreign and external set of fixed policies or a coherent governmental rationality that pervades globally and to address questions such as 'who does what, by what means, to what ends and with what institutional effects" (p. 121). They add that this type of analysis on neoliberalism draws attention to its governing practices, understood as something different than governance and government.[8] In their view, focusing on governing practices allows them to tackle the exercise of power as a dynamic and contested process both in its organizational and structural modalities.

In their view, a focus on culture, power and governing practices provides a framework for mapping the articulation of neoliberalism with established practices and policies, and for assessing how new hegemonic relations of power arise in different contexts due to these articulations. In addition, they contend that their perspective promotes a more sophisticated approach to the study of new patterns of class division and inequality. They also add that although some of the most notorious forms of inequality, poverty, exploitation and oppression in today's world are related to the rise of neoliberalism, it is also true that in most cases this is not all that they are. As they put it, "new patterns of inequality and class division are in many senses continuous with established relations of power and coercion." (p. 121) For them, analyses of current neoliberalism need to incorporate this dynamic of old and new, as well as top-down and bottom-up relations.

Critical analyses of neoliberalism imply defying its "transparence," "naturalness," and "inevitability," which, according to Gounari (2006), was achieved through a powerful discourse of "universality" and "Truth." As Bauman (1999) put it, "what [. . .] makes the neoliberal worldview sharply different from other ideologies—indeed, a phenomenon of a separate class—is precisely the absence of questioning, its surrender to what is seen as the implacable and irreversible logic of social reality." (p. 79) Challenging neoliberalism, thus, implies defying its discourse—a private discourse "allowing us consumers to speak via our currencies of consumption to producers of material goods but preventing us from speaking as citizens to one another about the social consequences of our private market choices." (Barber, 2001, p. 59) One needs to abandon this language, stripped of any ethical referent, that keeps people enclosed as consumers and keeps them from articulating political projects that link education with the broader society.

Notes

1. According to Cohen and Kennedy (2000), "neo-liberalism is an economic doctrine that insists states should never interfere with or constrain free markets, competition or private enterprise" (p. 127).
2. The idea of the "retreat of the state" has been formulated by Strange (1996), who among others, argues that the lack of regulation and increased capital mobility has "hollowed out" the state authority.
3. For more recent work focusing on neoliberalism as a regime of governance, see Sparke, 2006; McCarthy & Prudham, 2004; Miraftab, 2004; De Angelis, 2003; Weiner, 2001. Of interest are also Lemke (2001) and Larner's (2000)'s contributions dealing with Foucault's ideas on neoliberalism as a form of governmentality.
4. Globalization is broadly characterized in this chapter as the intensification and speeding

up of the mobility of people, capital, ideas and cultures mostly driven by the improvement of communication, information and transportation systems.
5. Further information on the type of projects through which the IFC supports private initiatives in education can be found at www.ifc.org
6. Simon Marginson refers to positional goods as "places in education which provide students with relative advantage in the competition for jobs, income, social standing and prestige" (Marginson, 1997, p. 38). The relevance of positional goods, Thrupp (2007) argues, "is that they are scarce in absolute terms so that only some people can benefit from them. If they were available to all they would lose the relative advantages they bring and hence their positional value" (p. 80). He illustrates this by pointing out that middle class schools are often seen to offer positional advantage, and thus, are predominantly more popular than low socioeconomic schools, which have little positional value.
7. See also Clarke, 2004; Maskovsky and Kingfisher, 2001.
8. It is argued that *governance* draws attention to the traditions, institutions and processes that shape how power is exercised, whereas *government* leads the organization of political units or rationalities.

References

Albo, G. (2002). Neoliberalism, the state, and the left: A Canadian perspective. *Monthly Review*, 54(1), 46–55.

Amin, S. (2001). Capitalism's global strategy. In F. Houtart & F. Polet (Eds.), *The other Davos: The globalization of resistance to the world economic system* (pp. 17–24). London: Zed Books.

Apple, M. W. (2001). Comparing neo-liberal projects and inequality in education. *Comparative Education*, 37(4), 409–423.

Aronowitz, S. (2001). *The last good job in America: Work and education in the new global technoculture*. Lanham, MD: Rowman & Littlefield.

Aune, J. A. (2001). *Selling the free market: The rhetoric of economic correctness*. New York: Guilford.

Ayers, D. F., & Carlone, D. (2007). Manifestations of neoliberal discourses within a local job-training program. *International Journal of Lifelong Education*, 26(4), 461–479.

Bansel, P. (2007). Subjects of choice and lifelong learning. *International Journal of Qualitative Studies in Education*, 20(3), 283–300.

Barber, B. (2001). Blood brothers, consumers, or citizens? Three models of identity—ethnic, commercial, and civic. In C. Gould & P. Pasquino (Eds.), *Cultural identity and the nation state*. Lanham, MD: Rowman & Littlefield.

Barry, A., Osborne, T., & Rose, N. (1996). *Foucault and political reason: Liberalism, neoliberalism and rationalities of government*. Chicago: University of Chicago Press.

Basu, R. (2004). The rationalization of neoliberalism in Ontario's public education system, 1995–2000. *Geoforum*, 35, 621–634.

Bauman, Z. (1999). *In search of politics*. Stanford, CA: Stanford University Press.

Becker, G. S. (1964). *Human capital: A theoretical and empirical analysis, with special reference to education*. Chicago: University of Chicago Press.

Bohm, A. D., Meares, D. D., & Pearce, D. (2002). *The global student mobility 2025 report: Forecasts of the global demand for international education*. Canberra, Australia: IDP.

Bourdieu, P. (1998). *Utopia of endless exploitations: The essence of neoliberalism.* Le Monde Diplomatique, December 1998. Retrieved from http://mondediplo.com/1998/12/08bourdieu

Bourdieu, P. (2003). *Firing back: Against the tyranny of the market II.* New York: New Press.

Brennan, T. (2003). *Globalization and its terrors: Daily life in the West.* New York: Routledge.

Buchanan, J., & Tullock, G. (1962). *The calculus of consent: Logical foundations of constitutional democracy.* Ann Arbor, MI: University of Michigan Press.

Burchell, G. (1996). Liberal government and techniques of the self. In A. Barry, T. Osborne, & N. Rose (Eds.), *Foucault and political reason* (pp. 19–36). Chicago: University of Chicago Press.

Burchell, G, Gordon, C. & Miller, P. (Eds.) (1991). *The Foucault effect: Studies in governmentality.* Chicago: University of Chicago Press.

Campbell, J. L., & Pedersen, O. K. (Eds.). (2001). *The rise of neoliberalism and institutional analysis.* Princeton, NJ: Princeton University Press.

Canaan, J. E., & Shumar, W. (Eds.). (2008). *Structure and agency in the neoliberal university.* New York: Routledge.

Carnoy, M. (1998). National voucher plans in Chile and Sweden: Did privatization reform make for better education? *Comparative Education Review, 42*(3), 309–337.

Carnoy, M. (2002). Latin America: The new dependency and educational reform. In H. Daun (Ed.), *Educational restructuring in the context of globalization and national policy.* New York: RoutledgeFalmer.

Carnoy, M., & McEwan, P. (2003). Does privatization improve education? The case of Chile's national voucher plan. In D. N. Plank, & G. Sykes (Eds.), *Choosing choice: School choice in international perspective* (pp. 24–44.). New York: Teachers College Press.

Cerny, P. G. (2008a). Embedding neoliberalism: The evolution of a hegemonic paradigm. *The Journal of International Trade and Diplomacy, 2*(1), 1–46.

Cerny, P. G. (2008b).The governmentalization of world politics. In G. Youngs & E. Kofman (Eds.), *Globalization: Theory and practice* (pp. 221–237). London: Continuum International Pub. Group, 3rd ed.

Chomsky, N. (1999). *Profit over people: Neoliberalism and global order.* New York: Seven Stories.

Chubb, J., & Moe, T. (1988). Politics, markets and the organization of schools. *American Political Science Review, 82,* 1065–1089.

Chubb, J., & Moe, T. (1990). *Politics, markets and America's schools.* Washington, DC: Brookings Institution.

Clarke, J. (2004). *Changing welfare, changing states: New directions in social policy.* London: Sage.

Clarke, J. (2008). Living with/in and without neo-liberalism. *Focaal—European Journal of Anthropology, 51,* 135–147.

Cohen, R., & Kennedy, P. (2000). *Global sociology.* New York: New York University Press.

Colás, A. (2005). Neoliberalism, globalization and international relations. In A. Saad-Filho, & D. Johnston (Eds.), *Neoliberalism: A critical reader* (pp. 70–79). London: Pluto.

Dakopoulou, A. (2009). The appropriation of the global discourse in the formulation of national education policies: A case of continuing education of teachers in Greece. *Globalisation, Societies and Education, 7*(1), 83–93.

Davidson-Harden, A., & Schugurensky, D. (2009). Neoliberalism and education in Latin America: Entrenched problems, emerging alternatives. In D. Hill, & E. Rosskam (Eds.), *The*

developing world and state education: Neoliberal depredation and egalitarian alternatives (pp. 13–33). New York: Routledge.
Davies, B., & and Bansel, P. (2007). Neoliberalism and education, International Journal of Qualitative Studies in Education, 20(3), 247–59.
De Angelis, M. (2003). Neoliberal governance, reproduction and accumulation. The Commoner, 7, 1–28.
Erkiliç, T. A. (2008). A discussion on effects of neo-liberal globalization on Turkish higher education. World Applied Sciences Journal, 4(3), 356–362.
EURYDICE. (1997). A decade of reforms at compulsory education level in the EU: 1984–1994. Brussels.
Fiske, E. B. (1996). Decentralization of education: Politics and consensus. Washington, D.C.: The World Bank.
Foucault, M. (2008). The birth of biopolitics: Lectures at the college de France, 1978–1979. New York: Palgrave Macmillan.
Friedman, M. (1962). Capitalism and freedom. Chicago: University of Chicago Press.
Friedman, M. (1980). Free to choose. New York: Harcourt Brace Jovanovich.
Gershberg, A. (1999). Education "decentralization" processes in Mexico and Nicaragua: Legislative versus ministry-led reform strategies. Comparative Education, 35(1), 63–80.
Gewirtz, S., Ball, S. J., & Bowe, R. (1995). Markets, choice, and equity in education. Buckingham, UK: Open University Press.
Giroux, H.A. (2004). The terror of neoliberalism: Authoritarianism and the eclipse of democracy. Boulder, CO: Paradigm Publishers.
Gledhill, J. (2004). Neoliberalism. In D. Nugent & J. Vincent (Eds.), A companion to the anthropology of politics (pp. 332–348). Malden, MA: Blackwell.
Gordon, L., & Whitty, G. (1997). Giving the 'Hidden Hand' a helping hand? The rhetoric and reality of neoliberal education reform in England and New Zealand. Comparative Education, 33(3), 453–467.
Gordon, C. (1991). Governmental rationality: An introduction. In G. Burchell, C. Gordon, & P. Miller (Eds.), The Foucault effect: Studies in governmentality (pp. 1–51). London: Harvester Wheatsheaf.
Gounari, P. (2006). Contesting the cynicism of neoliberal discourse: Moving towards a language of possibility. Studies in Language & Capitalism, 1, 77–96.
Harris, S. (2007). The governance of education: How neo-liberalism is transforming policy and practice. London: Continuum.
Hartman, Y. (2005). In bed with the enemy: Some ideas on the connections between neoliberalism and the welfare state. Current Sociology, 53(1), 57–73.
Harvey, D. (2003). The new imperialism. Oxford: Oxford University Press.
Harvey, D. (2005). A brief history of neoliberalism. Oxford: Oxford University Press.
Held, D., & McGrew, A. (2007). Globalization/anti-globalization. (2nd ed.). Cambridge: Polity.
Henry, M., Lingard, B., Rizvi, F., & Taylor, S. (2001). The OECD, globalization and education policy. Oxford: Pergamon.
Hill, D., & Rosskam, E. (Eds.) (2009) The developing world and state education: Neoliberal depredation and egalitarian alternatives New York: Routledge,
Hill, D. (2008). Contesting neoliberal education: Public resistance and collective advance. New York: Taylor & Francis.

Hill, D., & Kumar, R. (2009). Neoliberalism and its impacts. In D. Hill & R. Kumar (Eds.), *Global neoliberalism and education and its consequences* (pp. 12–29). New York, NY: Routledge.

Hirtt, N. (2009). Markets and education in the era of globalized capitalism. In D. Hill & R. Kumar (Eds.), *Global neoliberalism and education and its consequences* (pp. 208–226). New York, NY: Routledge.

Hogdson, G. M. (2000). Socio-economic consequences of the advance of complexity and knowledge. In OECD (Ed.), *The creative society of the 21st century* (pp. 89–112). Paris: OECD.

International Finance Corporation, Health and Education Group (2001). *Investing in private education: IFC's strategic directions*. Washington, DC: IFC.

Johnson, C. (2000). *Governing change: From Keating to Howard*. St. Lucia: University of Queensland Press and API Network.

Kingfisher, C. (Ed.) (2002). *Western welfare in decline: Globalization and women's poverty*. Philadelphia: University of Pennsylvania Press.

Kingfisher, C., & Maskovsky, J. (2008). Introduction to special issue on yhe limits of neoliberalism. *Critique of Anthropology, 28*, 115–126.

Kjaer, P. & Pedersen, O. K. (2001). Translating liberalization: Neoliberalism in the Danish negotiated economy. In J. L. Campbell & O. K. Pedersen (Eds.), *Neoliberalism and institutional analysis* (pp. 219–248). Princeton, NJ: Princeton University Press.

Klees, S. J. (2002). Privatization and neo-liberalism: Ideology and evidence in rhetorical reforms. *Current Issues in Comparative Education, 1*(2), 19–26.

Klein, N. (2007). *The shock doctrine: The rise of disaster capitalism*. New York: Metropolitan Books/Henry Holt.

Lambeir, B. (2005). Education as liberation: The politics and techniques of lifelong learning. *Educational Philosophy and Theory, 37*(3), 349–355.

Larner, W. (2000). Neo-liberalism: Policy, ideology, governmentality. *Studies in Political Economy, 63*, 5–25.

Lemke, T. (2001). The birth of bio-politics: Michel Foucault's lecture at the College de France on neo-liberal governmentality. *Economy and Society, 30*(2), 190–207.

Marginson, S. (1997). *Markets in education*. St. Leonards, NSW.: Allen & Unwin.

Martinez, E., & Garcia, A. (1996). *What is neoliberalism?* Retrieved from: http://www.corpwatch.org/article.php?id=376

Maskovsky, J., & Kingfisher, C. (2001). Introduction to special issue on global capitalism, neoliberal policy and poverty, *Urban Anthropology and Studies of Cultural Systems and World Economic Development, 30*(2–3), 105–21.

McCarthy, J., & Prudham, S. (2004). Neoliberal nature and the nature of neoliberalism. *Geoforum, 35*, 275–283.

Miraftab, F. (2004). Making neo-liberal governance: The disempowering work of empowerment. *International Planning Studies, 9*(4), 239–259.

Mok, K. H., & Lo, Y. W. (2009). From the state to the market?: China's education at a crossroads. In D. Hill & Rosskan, E. (Eds.), *The developing world and state education* (pp. 216–231). New York: Routledge.

Mukhtar, A. (2009). The neoliberalization of education services (not including higher education): Impacts on worker's socioeconomic security, access to services, democratic accountability, and equity—A case study of Pakistan. In D. Hill & Rosskan (Eds.), *The developing*

world and state education (pp. 125–139).
OECD (1998). *Education policy analysis 1998.* Paris: OECD.
OECD (2002). *Mechanisms for the co-finance of lifelong learning.* Paper presented at the 2nd International Seminar: Taking Stock of Experience with Co-finance Mechanisms. London.
Olssen, M. (2002). The restructuring of tertiary education in New Zealand: Governmentality, neoliberalism, democracy. *McGill Journal of Education* (Winter).
Olssen, M. (2006). Understanding the mechanisms of neoliberal control: Lifelong learning, flexibility and knowledge capitalism. *International Journal of Lifelong Education*, 25(3), 213–230.
Olssen, M. (2008). Understanding the mechanisms of neoliberal control: Lifelong learning, flexibility and knowledge capitalism. In A. Fejes & K. Nicoll, K. (Eds.), *Foucault and lifelong learning: Governing the subject* (pp. 34–47). New York: Routledge.
Ong, A. (2006). *Neoliberalism as exception: Mutations in citizenship and sovereignty.* Durham, NC; London: Duke University Press.
Peck, J., & Tickell, A. (2002). Neoliberalizing space. *Antipode, 34*, 380–404.
Pérez, C. (2001). Technological change and opportunities for development as a moving target. *Cepal Review, 75*, pp. 109–130.
Peters, M. A. (2001). *Poststructuralism, Marxism and neoliberalism.* Oxford, England: Rowman & Littlefield.
Peters, M. (2007). *Knowledge economy, development and the future of higher education.* Rotterdam: Sense Publishers,
Peterson, P. E. (1990). Monopoly and competition in American education. In W. H. Clune & J. F. Witte (Eds.), *Choice and control in American education* (pp. 47–78). Bristol, PA: Falmer.
Phoenix, A. (2004). Neoliberalism and masculinity: Racialization and the contradictions of schooling for 11- to 14-year-olds. *Youth Society, 36,* 227–246.
Pick, D., & Taylor, J. (2009). 'Economic rewards are the driving factor': Neo-liberalism, globalisation and work attitudes of young graduates in Australia. *Globalisation, Societies and Education, 7*(1), 69–82.
Pierson, C. (1996). *The modern state.* London: Routledge.
Plehwe, D., Walpen, B., & Neunhöffer, G. (Eds.). (2006). *Neoliberal hegemony: A global critique.* London: Routledge.
Puiggrós, A. (2002) The consequences of neo-liberalism on the educational prospects of Latin American youth. *Current Issues in Comparative Education, 1*(2), 35–41.
Ramia, G., & Carney, T. (2000). Contractualism, managerialism and welfare: The Australian experiment with a marketised employment services network. *Policy & Politics, 29,* 59–80.
Rhoten, D. (2000). Education decentralization in Argentina: A "global-local conditions of possibility" approach to state, market, and society change. *Journal of Education Policy, 15*(6), 593–619.
Rizvi, F. (2007). Rethinking educational aims in an era of globalization. In P. D. Hershock, M. Mason, & J. N. Hawkins (Eds.), *Changing education: Leadership, innovation and development in a globalizing Asia Pacific* (pp. 63–91). Dordrecht: Springer.
Rose, N. (1996). Governing "advanced" liberal democracies. In A. Barry, T. Osborne, & N. Rose (Eds.), *Foucault and political reason* (pp. 37–64). Chicago: University of Chicago Press.
Roy, R., Denzau, A. T., & Willett, T. D. (Eds) (2007). *Neoliberalism: National and regional experiments with global ideas.* London and New York: Routledge.

Ruggie, J. G. (1982). International regimes, transactions and change: Embedded liberalism in the Post-War economic order. In S. D. Krasner (Ed.), *International regimes* (pp. 195–231). Ithaca, NY: Cornell University Press.

Rutz, H. J., & Balkan, E. M. (2009). *Reproducing class education: Neoliberalism and the rise of the new middle class in Istanbul.* London: Berghahn.

Saad-Filho, A., & Johnston, D. (2005). *Neoliberalism: A critical reader.* London: Pluto.

Schugurensky, D. (1999). Higher education restructuring in the era of globalization: Towards a heterogeneous model? In R. Arnove & C. A. Torres (Eds.), *Comparative education: The dialectic of the global and the local* (pp. 257–276). Lanham, MD: Rowman & Littlefield Publishers.

Schugurensky, D., & Davidson-Harden, A. (2003). From Córdoba to Washington: WTO/GATS and Latin American education. *Globalisation, Societies and Education, 1*(3), 321–357.

Sparke, M. (2006). Political geography: Political geographies of globalization (2)—governance. *Progress in Human Geography, 30*(3), 357–372.

Strange, S. (1996). *The retreat of state: The diffusion of power in the world economy.* Cambridge: Cambridge University Press.

Sullivan, K. (Ed.). (1998). *Education and change in the Pacific rim: Meeting the challenges.* Oxford: Triangle.

Tan, J. (1998). The marketization of education in Singapore: Politics and implications. *International Review of Education, 44*(1), 47–63.

Tatto, M. (1999). Education reform and state power in Mexico: The paradoxes of decentralization. *Comparative Education Review, 43*(3), 251–282.

Thorsen, D. E., & Lie, A. (2006). *What is neoliberalism?* Retrieved from http://folk.uio.no/daget/What%20is%20Neo-Liberalism%20FINAL.pdf

Thrupp, M. (2007). Education's 'inconvenient truth': Part one—persistent middle class advantage. *New Zealand Journal of Teachers' Work, 4*(2), 77–88.

Torres, C. A. (2002). The state, privatisation and educational policy: A critique of neo-liberalism in Latin America and some ethical and political implications. *Comparative Education, 38*(4), 365–385.

Torres, C. A. (2008). *Education and neoliberal globalization.* New York: Taylor & Francis.

Touraine, A. (2001). *Beyond neoliberalism.* Cambridge: Polity.

UNESCO/OECD (2002). *Financing education: Investments and returns analysis of the world education indicators.* Paris: UNESCO/OECD.

Weiner, J. (2001). Globalization and disciplinary neoliberal governance. *Constellations: An International Journal of Critical and Democratic Theory, 8*(4), 461–479.

Whitty, G., Power, S., & Halpin, D. (1998). *Devolution and choice in education: The school, the state and the market.* Melbourne: ACER.

Wolf, E. R. (1999). *Envisioning power: Ideologies of dominance and crisis.* Berkeley: University of California Press.

World Bank (1995). *Priorities and strategies for education: A World Bank review.* Washington, D.C.: World Bank.

World Bank (1999). *Education sector strategy.* Washington, D.C.: World Bank.

· 1 3 ·

Traveling Policies

Mobility, Transformations and Continuities in Higher Education Public Policy

RODRIGO BRITEZ

Concerns about the quality of higher education are not new in Paraguay. There have been recurrent discussions on the need for national policy reform for decades without any apparent resolution; hence Paraguay still lacks a well-defined higher education act, especially with respect to private institutions. However, these debates are now occurring not simply at the national level but within a context characterized by the increased *global* circulation of policy ideas. Furthermore, these global policy flows are now crucial to understanding conditions at the level of local policy environments. In order to illustrate this point, I will present the case of policy developments related to the dramatic private expansion of Paraguay's higher education sector since the 1990s.

In point of fact, global patterns of transformations are generating diverse and complex outcomes in different countries, in ways that may preclude a simple or direct relationship between international policy prescriptions and policy change in higher education at the national or local level. In this way, the different processes that constitute globalization within local spaces demand recognition of the importance of specificities in their constitution. In short, the starting point to understanding these processes seems to require, as Saskia Sassen suggests, "detecting/constructing the social thickness and specificity"

(Sassen, 2000, p. 216) of the dimensions in which the dynamic interaction between global and local takes place. Indeed, I argue in what follows, for a fuller consideration of the impact of the global context and the ways in which global-local dynamics shape developments in public policy at the national context.

The context of a country is usually described in relation to a bounded territory organized by the nation-state. In this sense, Paraguay is a small, landlocked country in South America possessing a territorial extension of 406, 752 km^2 with a population of 6.12 million. As of 2002, 2.6 million live in below globally defined poverty levels (Fazio, 2005, p. 7). Paraguay's economy is characterized by a large informal sector, with a GDP of 14.668 billion US dollars in 2009 (International Monetary Fund, 2010). In contrast with other countries in the region, a large percentage of Paraguayans still live in rural areas, where many are relegated to subsistence agriculture. This is still a fundamentally agricultural and cattle-raising production economy (see Borda, 2007), "with over 40 percent of the population living in rural areas" (International Monetary Fund, 2009, p. 16); while most of its urban population now live in areas that are in close proximity to the capital city of Asuncion. Paraguayan society and economy have been greatly affected by processes of rapid urbanization and social change since the 1970s, provoking, among other developments, a dramatic quantitative expansion of its higher education system.

In recent years, much has been written about the notion of policy transfer (Evans, 2004; Ladi, 2005; Dolowitz & Marsh, 2000). This term is widely used in order to understand the international dimensions of national policy processes. In short, it is used in reference to globalizing dynamics in policy making. According to Sklair (2007), generic globalization in the contemporary world refers to a number of moments (forces) affecting each sector of society across nation states. Capitalist globalization, on the other hand, refers to dominant projects of transnational integration fostering and organizing (generic globalization), as part of a capitalist global system. In this way, as Sklair (2007) points out, globalization can be understood as "a contested world-historical project with capitalist and other variants." (Sklair, 2007, p. 94)

Furthermore, globalization itself is now constituted through a multiplicity of flows and networks of communication facilitating different types of mobilities in ways that seem to destabilize notions of national boundaries and territorial authority in public policy (Castells, 2000, 2005; Urry, 2007; Sassen, 2003, 2007; Aneesh, 2006). If this is so, then, how is policy production at the national level shaped by global processes? It is important to remember that a state's claim to public policy authority is derived in large measure by their ability to allocate values (such as resources) in order to pursue specific objectives that fulfill certain public expectations. But where does this authority come from, especially if authority as a type of power is exercised and not possessed? This exercise is becoming increasingly complex, contested and contingent, and deeply affected by international dynamics.

For instance, as international policy arenas have become places of global production and communication of knowledge and policy advice, it has become increasingly evident that across Latin America, educational policies seem to follow global models of educational change promoted by the World Bank and other international organizations (IOs). International agents are also increasingly providing strategic structures and helping to generate and communicate diagnostics and prescriptions about policy change at the national level. This has resulted in a certain convergence of higher education policies across countries that have widely differing cultural, economic and political traditions.

The recognition of this convergence has resulted in a rich literature (see Castells, 2005; Evans, 2004; Marginson & Rhoades, 2002) using a set of ideas and concepts that suggests increasing global mobilities, including policy mobility: transfer, translation, flows, circulation, borrowing, lending and so forth. These terms are widely used to describe, and possibly also explain, different aspects of the complex system of interactions and relationships across transnational, regional, national and local spaces. They are designed to underline the contemporary dynamics of policy ideas being produced in one space but transferred in application and utilization in another.

Accordingly, the study of transfer processes in educational policy is assumed to be increasingly important because of the ways in which an emergent set of organizational patterns (a mixture of bureaucratic practices and networks) is thought to be shaping an increasingly globalized policy agenda in education. These patterns include the increasing advocacy of transnational institutions for the adoption of distinctive policy orientations regarding the role of higher education in society by local, national and states entities. These global patterns and agendas for transformation have been described as "travelling policy" (Ozga & Jones, 2006) or "international models of systemic change" (Jones, 2003, p. 11).

Today, policy change in education becomes embedded in an overlapping web of policy narratives and discourses of capitalist globalization, including those directly affecting our notions on the purposes and values of higher education. An example in the literature showing some effects of these shifts of values in Latin America is presented by Miguel de la Torre Gamboa (2004), in his work *Del humanismo a la competitividad*. Gamboa applies a critical discourse analysis approach in his assessment of relevant policy documents. Specifically, he explores recent shifts in the understanding of values and principles affecting the practices and perspectives about higher education in Mexico. He points to ways in which ideas of change in public policies have begun to be linked to global narratives of a neoliberal project for educational change as circulated through international organizations. He argues that a neoliberal discourse is used to inform new perspectives and beliefs on the role of the national system of education. Thus, political actions and higher education institutional responses, since the 1980s, have begun to be linked to a discursive legitimating vision that renders educational purposes as subordinate assets wedged to economic ends, including the need to improve the global competitiveness of individuals and national institutions (see Maldonado-Maldonado, 2004; Torres, 2002).

All in all, the growing spread of international conventions and agreements also seems to express the emergence of a complex international institutional structure, consisting of networks facilitating the flow, and subsequent implementation of policy ideas among nation states and policy actors. Now, ideologies, including those containing neoliberal ideas, and different types of educational discourses are moving across borders in an array of complicated ways.

Here I am using the term "neoliberal" in a very generic manner, as related to a set of market-driven, for-profit ideologies. Hence, I am not addressing this notion directly. Neither do I explore its specific meaning within the local case. Rather, I intend to recognize how extensive externalities, among these neoliberal ideas, have affected policy debates and shifts in higher education in Paraguay. I am interested in shifts in governance practices, together with the recognition of their international inspiration.

In the first part of the chapter, I will introduce the context and the many-sided ways in which a set of public policy mobilities in education operates in the Paraguayan higher education system. I seek to provide an account of some aspects of the political, social and economic dimensions, relevant to the description of Paraguay's policy environment and its system of higher education. At the same time, I provide here a partial understanding of the role that intergovernmental organizations (IGOs) and local actors play in the configuration and adoption of specific global narratives about the need for policy change, and the interactions that steered the development of a national system of higher education. This analysis particularly focuses on providing an historical account that shows the crucial specificity of Paraguay's policy environment.

The Context of Paraguayan Higher Education

In Paraguay's national context, policy transfer could be shown as a constant feature of the changing interaction between local and international dynamics in the development of Paraguay's higher education institutions. For instance, the origins of the university in Paraguay lay in various regional transfers and local adaptations of a European organizational framework of the university "translated" or emulated by newly independent countries in Latin America at the beginning of the 19th century. The collapse of the Spanish and Portuguese colonial empires in South America gave birth to a number of independent nation-states, including Paraguay. These states sought to build their own institutional capacities to train their national bureaucracies. Therefore, trained local bureaucrats were required for the building and running of the independent national administrative structures. Not surprisingly, Latin American nation-states borrowed heavily from various European institutional models of university organization, interpreting the idea of the university in their own particular ways.

In the same manner, the idea of the university in Paraguay was also historically influenced by the policy transfer of the educational ideologies of successive waves of regional reforms (Rama, 2006) even if the introduction of reforms in terms of substantial changes in the higher education system has been often constrained by limits in the local and national organizational capacities, institutional resistances and particularly narrowly-focused private interests.

It was not until the beginning of the twentieth century that the phrase "University Reform" was used in Paraguay, though not in today's sense. In Latin America, the use of this expression, as Simon Schwartzman (2001) indicates, started with the Cordoba Manifest, and the first wave of regionally located reforms affecting Latin American countries. The demands of students at Cordoba University in Argentina led to a wave of regional reforms, which transformed the university systems in the region by establishing "a peculiar type of university autonomy." Basically, the notion was that "...governments have to pay for the maintenance of the universities, but have little say in the way universities are managed" (Schwartzman, 2001, ¶ 11). The social imaginary of a specific type of institutional autonomy as a desirable feature of university governance still resonates in current debates about the transformation of Paraguay's higher education. In Paraguay, this results in the emergence of a self-governing university system outside the control of any specific ministry or state institution. The Ministry of Education, *Ministerio de Educación y Cultura* (MEC), was, until very recently, primarily in charge of the primary and secondary education sector.

However, the most important element to understand the historical trajectory of Paraguay's higher education developments in the twentieth century is the prevalence of a policy environment hostile to the idea of public policy change in higher education. The political instability of the first part of the twentieth century, including a short but violent civil war and the policies of dictatorial regimes, favored an approach resistant to any substantial change in the governance structures of Paraguay's higher education institutions.

The crisis of Paraguay's liberal model of the nation-state in the 1930s, and a long period of political instability, presented conditions that encouraged politicization of the only university institution in the country: the National University of Asuncion, *Universidad Nacional de Asunción* (UNA). In the 1940s, the military government acquired control of the university, and by 1954, under the Stroessner regime, the Colorado Party assumed a key role in subordinating tertiary institutions to authoritarian rule. For the next thirty-five years, the possibilities of graduates securing employment in state bureaucracies became linked to an affiliation with the Colorado Party—the political arm of the regime (Serafini, LaFuente, & Rivelli, 1989).

In the 1960s, the regime allowed a very limited and highly controlled expansion of the system with the creation of the Catholic University of Asuncion, *Universidad Católica "Nuestra Señora de la Asunción"* (UCA) (Law 663, September 1960). The main function of the UCA was to mimic the institutional and academic model of the UNA (see Universidad Católica, 2000, p. 20). A radical expansion and diversification of the system were discouraged and were only possible after the end of the dictatorial regime in 1989. The authoritarian state lacked any interest in the provision of social services at all levels, with a very low level of investment in education. It should be noted that "the stable level of investment in education by the authoritarian regime was, for a quarter of century, around 1 % of the GDP, well below the Latin American average of investment in education" (CONEC, 2005, p. 22, my translation). This shows the scarce support for higher education policy reform and partially explains the adverse conditions for introducing educational policy initiatives without international support.

It is clear that the Paraguayan state, for most of the second half of the twentieth century, was militarily strong but socially weak. As a result, it failed to build the institutional capacities to evaluate and expand its educational system. As Andrew Nickson and Peter Lambert (2002) contend, quoting the former director of a European Union-funded State Modernization Project in Paraguay: "the state had been extremely weak throughout most of this period and social provision was minimal. Here there was no 'over-developed state' and no 'crisis of the welfare state' to contend with" (p.163).

After 1989, Paraguay, as a transition state, sought to expand social services and the capacities of the country but could only do so with international assistance and expertise. This made it into a state highly dependent on international aid agencies. Thus, even after 1989, Paraguay, as a transitional society, remained extremely vulnerable to a process of coercive, voluntary coercive, or even "inappropriate forms of policy transfer" (Ivanova & Evans, 2004, p. 98). Thus, it came under a tremendous amount of local and regional pressures to introduce changes in its higher education system. However, the country now experienced these pressures within a global context in which external actors, with their own agendas for transformation, provided resources, expertise and guidelines that informed policy priorities for educational reform, sometimes ignoring the local historical trajectories and traditions. For example, financial intergovernmental organizations, such as the World Bank and the *Inter-American Development Bank*, overlooked some local demands in setting policy priorities for change in the 1990s. In the case of the development of the national higher education system, a mixture of local, regional and global pressures generated calls for unprecedented levels of expansion through autonomous, and mostly for-profit institutions.

However, it is important to note that, in the complex and highly politicized context of Paraguay, the introduction of new policies, or even laws, does not necessarily imply their effective implementation. One of the most salient characteristics of Paraguay's policymaking processes over the last 50 years is the difficulty of making any major modification to national public policies; "many areas of reform identified as crucial by key stakeholders have been stalled" (Molinas, Pérez-Liñán, Saiegh & Montero, 2006, p. 41). Among others, a crucial problem persists in relation to the uneven and arbitrary allocation of financial and human resources for public reform. Local resources often are insufficient to make viable the introduction of new institutional frameworks. Past experiences of policy reform, for example, have been characterized by inefficiency, inhibiting any project aimed at transformation of the university system.

Policy resistance by main stakeholders and lack of clarity and contradictory positions about the responsibilities of the state are part of Paraguay's policy environment. The crucial point is that, in current debates of reform, the meaning of those responsibilities for higher education is a consequence of a complex and extended period of public policy interactions in education between international organizations and the Paraguayan state.

International Organizations and the Transfer of Policy

Although the notion of *transfer* is a perennial object of interest in the comparative policy studies literature, the concept of policy transfer itself (and related notions) began to appear with an increasing frequency since the 1980s, often associated closely with the literature on lesson drawing. In comparative policy studies, the idea of policy transfer became associated with the increasing international movement of policy or traveling policy, associated, in diverse and descriptive ways, with globalization processes.

Today, prescriptive models of policy reform in higher education have striking similarities across countries. These patterns appear to suggest a form of "ideational convergence" (Radaelli, 2004) of public policies, often promoted by intergovernmental organizations, such as the World Bank, the United Nations Educational, Scientific and Cultural Organization (UNESCO) and the Organisation for Economic Co-operation and Development (OECD). Yet, according to the literature in educational policy studies, the spread of initiatives of change generates contradictory processes generating, not only actual convergence of policies and institutions towards global or regional models of transformations but also divergent and hybridizing outcomes or no specific changes in national settings.

This raises an important question: what agencies and mechanisms have led to the introduction of similar policies and the development of increasingly common structures across one national system to the next? In other words, how has the convergence of patterns of policy development, at least at the rhetorical level, across many different countries and regions and localities emerged? In short, the way in which similar policies have become part of the educational agendas of countries across the planet has underlined the importance of understanding how educational reform is interpreted, negotiated and takes place. For instances, Marginson and Rhoades (2002) point to the need in the literature of comparative higher education to address those global dimensions that, at times, help to provide a better and more extensive understanding of the dynamics and interactions operating at national states. Considering this issue, Stephen Ball (1998) points to the necessity of exploring this basic problem in contemporary educational policy analysis: how do international policies influence national and local educational policies?

Ball (1998) argues that contemporary global policy ideas on education have become a new belief system, an orthodoxy that links education to the concerns related to the economic wealth of nations. Thus, education now seems to have become colonized by the supposed imperatives of the global economy. This "vision of the future" has spread globally, in a diversity of complex ways. The most significant among these are the activities of multilateral agencies in promoting a particular set of educational policy ideas.

Ball (1998) points out, however, that these policy ideas are never translated in the same way. Nor can the resistance and negotiation to the pressures of multilateral agencies be explained in universal terms. Policy ideas, he maintains, are subject to the processes of re-contextualization.

There are divergences, as well as convergences, of objectives across these organizations. On this point, I am arguing that international organizations exercise influence as creators of global educational spaces; thereby "steering" different aspects of national public policies on education. They represent spaces where ideas are communicated and negotiated but often in ways that are asymmetrical.

In this way, IGOs and international non-governmental organizations promote international policy communication of ideas through complex processes of framing, steering and re-contextualization of policy problems and policy solutions. Their discourses, linking ideas of education to economic development, contain diverse arrays of narratives: about globalization, the relevance of world market economy, the knowledge economy, the crisis of education, democracy, social inclusion, among others.

Today, in developing countries in particular, national policies on education are increasingly made with the participation of IGOs at the global, regional and national level; the global agenda of public education is articulated through these institutions. Multilateral agencies have promoted the transfer of a particular set of education policies, associated with neoliberal ideologies, that merges education within programs of national development. However, it is often the case that policy transfer refers to the adoption of a common policy language (ideas or priorities of policy change) rather than to the development of concrete programs or models (Radaelli, 2004). This discursive convergence occurs through policy networks, bringing "together representatives from international organizations and state agencies with politicians, the media, business groups, trade unions and sometimes grass-roots associations" (Stone, 2001, p. 14), constituted around specific parameters, knowledge resources, information, and issues.

Policy convergence, however, is not the only outcome of global policy interactions. Various modalities of transfer are also leading to a divergence in policy outcomes. For example, while there may be considerable convergence of discourses, it is also often the case that the mobility of policy ideas generates different types of adoptions and interpretations, which are very difficult to define due to the specific types of contexts and institutional frameworks.

Shifts and Continuities in Paraguayan Higher Education

In Paraguay's higher education sector, policy initiatives, narratives and research in education supported and promoted by IGOs and implemented by the state in the 1990s indirectly created and continue to influence a set of policy dynamics that at least partially explain the current policy environment for the higher education sector. As a former member of the Advisory Council for the Education Reform, *Consejo Asesor de la Reforma Educativa* (CARE), suggested, the lack of attention to higher education as public policy, especially in the university, is a result of several local factors, but it is also related to the agendas of international agencies. In a newspaper article entitled "*¿Quien pagara por los platos rotos?*" Domingo Rivarola argued that the current state of the higher education sector in Paraguay is a direct outcome of the lack of attention paid to it in the 1990s when higher education was excluded from the agenda for public policy reform, largely due to external pressures. He added that the negotiations on education reform with "international cooperation" involved a complete alignment with the policy priorities of international financial institutions (Rivarola, 2000, p. 11), which were designed to leave higher education at the mercy of private operators.

It is important to recognize, however, that the capacity of IGOs in steering policy change is limited. The transfer of policy advice and material resources is always contingent on the intentions of local policy actors as well as on the existing, appropriate state structures that enable a relationship of receptivity to the international policy advice. So what was the nature of the relationship between IGOs and the Paraguayan state with respect to proposals for reform of the Paraguayan educational system at the beginning of the 1990s? It is certainly true that the Paraguayan state representatives participated fully in various world educational forums for the emerging global agenda for education reforms related to their needs and conditions. At the same time, however, as a developing country, the financing of such reforms was always dependent on the line of credit provided by financial IGOs.

More importantly, in the 1990s, the local promoters of reform used a diverse array of global narratives to justify and generate a consensus around education reforms that they argued, were essential for the modernization and democratization of Paraguayan society after the fall of a long dictatorial regime. In other words, they used international discourses on the purposes of education as a way to legitimize a particular set of changes that were aligned to the expectations generated around the process of political and economic transition. In this way, international discourses about Paraguay's participation in the global economy became inextricably tied to the local discourses about democratic transition.

Examples of this rhetorical interplay can still be observed in all official policy documents, including a recent policy proposal for higher education reform produced by the National Commission for the Reform of Higher Education, *Comisión Nacional para la Reforma de la Educación Superior* (CNRES). For example, in a document of discussion on the university reform it is argued that:

> Since the beginning of the so-called democratic transition in 1989, educational reform has been constructed as one of the more firmly shared aspirations of Paraguayan society, this attribution was in large degree the result of a very simple reflection, only educational improvement of the population is capable of guaranteeing the future solidity of a democratic order. (CNRES, 2006, p. 19, my translation)

This local narrative is aligned to a web of interrelated discourses embraced and promoted by various international agencies, such as the agendas for educational change recommended at the World Conference on Education for All (WCEFA) at Jomtien, Thailand, in March 1990 that eventually became transmogrified into the Millennium Goals by the United Nations. The international legitimacy that such narratives provide do not only serve local policy actors in their efforts to secure lines of credits for the project of reform but also imply the transfer of discourses and stories of educational reform linked to specific agendas for economic development.

The Jomtien declaration, as Reimers (1995), Buchert (1995), and others have pointed out, contains a number of recommendations that have informed key changes in the policy priorities in Latin America. As Reimers notes, the Jomtien declaration involved a general consensus among the major IGOs involved in the education sector to increase international support for basic education, with the goal of entitling every child in the world to primary education by 2015. Reimers quotes a United Nations Children's Fund (UNICEF) executive director who maintained the following:

> UNICEF, the World Bank, UNESCO, and the UNDP [United Nations Development Programme] are in agreement that a special effort should be made to ensure that by the year 2000 virtually all children are achieving a common early level of achievement, in literacy, numeracy and basic life skills. (Reimers, 1995, p. 36)

Basically, this opened the possibility for international support for major reforms in basic education systems throughout the region. As Lene Buchert (1995) notes after Jomtien,

> many national and multinational donor organizations have showed renewed concern for the Basic Education level. This is expressed in the focus on Basic Education in numerous policy documents, whether they are individual subsector documents, part of education sector documents, or integrated in[to] broader development strategy documents. (Buchert, 1995, p. 546)

International conferences around this agenda played a crucial role in the process of transfer of ideas about educational change. Narratives presented at these conferences were later used by local policy players to convey a specific rhetoric, even a sense of urgency for action. In this sense, the stories framed a particular logic to justify local priorities in the name of international cooperation.

However, the role that these international stories of reform play in the implementation of policy actions is complex. One the one hand, they serve to justify the international support for policy initiatives put forward by national actors, and on the other, they become a legitimizing factor in creating local consensus that justifies the need for "change." However, this does not imply that individual countries follow a homogenous or predictable pattern of international reform. Even as all countries and institutions appear to use a pool of international stories and common rhetoric to justify the need for change, they do so in ways that are different according to different national context and policies. For instance, this can be observed when one reads different country reports addressing the notion of quality, during the current regional wave of initiatives to ensure the quality assurance mechanism in higher education (Lamarra, 2009).

Stories rather than official discourses are more important in articulating a particular logic about the "social purposes" of transformation and their possible consequences. It is in these stories that education became central to economic policies implemented in developing countries in the 1990s. At the same time, these policies were aligned to a body of research that sustained a pervasive logic about the nature of human beings as subordinated to a global pattern of economic development. More importantly, policy priorities become aligned with particular assumptions about development, education and the role of the state in a global context. These assumptions were further supported by the research produced by international organizations, which often articulated a general set of priorities for educational change and paid little attention to the specificities of the local context in developing countries.

These generalized principles, as I have already argued, largely ignored the tertiary sector contributing to conditions that led to the private unregulated expansion of Paraguay's higher education system. It is in the context of a policy vacuum that the state, in a sense, allowed the expansion of private initiatives. Therefore, a symbolic policy promoted by IGOs towards the privatization and deregulation of higher education became effectively translated, in Paraguay, into an ad hoc expansion of the tertiary system; quality and the public good were largely sacrificed. This analysis suggests that recent changes in higher education in Paraguay are in effect the hybrid outcome of the continuation of past policy trajectories and ideas and newer policy suggestions emanating from IGOs.

Policy Challenges

A direct translation of the term "challenge" in the Spanish language is *desafío*. An understanding of the term can itself convey the idea of a number of pressures and dilemmas confronting policy-makers. In the case of educational policy this has connotations of both risks and opportunities. Aware of this connotation, the word *desafío* was inserted into the title of an important policy report during the initial planning period of the Paraguayan educational reform of the 1990s: *El Desafío Educativo*.

The document was written with the advice and support of the Harvard Institute for International Development (HIID) in 1995 and is important for an understanding of the way in which challenges and educational opportunities were initially framed by local policy actors, following the profound transformations that affected Paraguay society after 1989. The proposals in this document were not merely linked to the theme of reform in the basic and secondary sectors but viewed such reform as part of the political process of democratic transition. The document also mentioned suggestions for changes to the higher education system. These suggestions responded to a set of external demands associated with an accelerated process of transformation of the Paraguayan society, which include the desire, among a group of policy actors, for a planned integration of Paraguayan higher education into the work the state needed to do in strategic planning for the future. It is important to point out that HIID's vision for education, as presented in *El Desafío Educativo*, and later in a planning document, shares a similar set of assumptions about the challenges confronted by Paraguay's educational system as those presented in a diagnostic document of the Paraguayan educational system elaborated by HIID and a local non-governmental organization: the Paraguayan Center of Sociological Studies, *Centro Paraguayo de Estudios Sociologicos* (CPES).

This study was made with members linked to the CARE and financed by the United States Agency for International Development (USAID), as part of the Advancing Basic Education and Literacy (ABEL) project (HIID & CPES, 1993, p. 10) and was published in 1993 with the title, *Análisis del Sistema Educativo en el Paraguay. Sugerencias de Políticas y Estrategia para su Reforma*.

Each of these documents contains a combination of descriptions of Paraguayan education and a set of prescriptions that are driven by an implicit international ideology of education that I will outline later in this section. The first pages of the document on strategic planning, for example, state that the key challenges in Paraguay were to consolidate its democracy, increase productivity and reduce poverty, while preserving a sense of national identity within the framework of the process of regional and global integration, in order to enable a path towards sustainable development (MEC, CARE & HIID, 1996a, 1996b).

Yet, in reading policy documents relating to the diagnosis and planning of the educational reform in Paraguay, produced by HIID, it is hard to see how the recommended objectives of education and its strategies of reform were not, in fact, more suited to the introduction of changes at the level of higher education.

The report, *El Desafío Educativo* articulates a broad vision of policy change that can easily be shared by any important segment of key stakeholders in the educational system that recognizes readily that the legacy of the dictatorial regime needs to be overhauled. For, indeed, this was a legacy that left the education system unable to address the social and international challenges confronting the country.

To express the challenges in international terms implies that the role of local stakeholders who were in fact a part of the dictatorial system has not been revisited in a fuller description of what needs changing. The language of international challenges was also considered appropriate in relation to the entrance of Paraguay into the Common Market of the South, *Mercado Común del Sur* (MERCOSUR), which defined a new reality for the nation, without revisiting its past. In Paraguay, the project of regional integration has had profound, though indirect, implications for policy planning in education by creating a forum of regional cooperation that has proposed the harmonization of the educational systems among its members. The protocols and agreements signed at MERCOSUR have thus become an important element of educational planning in Paraguay.

MERCOSUR's proposals for change have been defined in terms of global economic competition. As such, one has to compare Paraguay with other countries in the region. *El Desafío Educativo* has indicated, for example, that the Paraguayan higher education system is weak in comparison with other systems in the region, and this has major implications for its economic competitiveness. Essentially, the document suggests three basic problems: (a) low quality; (b) low relevance of programs; and, (c) low number of graduates needed to meet the labor demands of the country. This report provides data of low coverage of the system, low percentage of high school graduates seeking access to higher education, and low levels of university retention. Against such a bleak description, ironically, most of the educational reforms proposed in the report relate to the basic and secondary levels of education, with only minor attention paid to the higher education sector.

This is in part explainable due to the leading role of the Ministry of Education in this process of education reform. A characteristic of the Paraguayan educational system is its dual nature. In short, as a dual system, educational policies in Paraguay are formulated by two distinct bodies: the Ministry of Education and the universities. There is very little in the way of policy coordination across these two sectors. In its policy documents, the CNRES describes this system arrangement as fragmented. It has stated that:

> A characteristic of the educational system is its segmentation into two sectors which are functionally disconnected. On one hand, university education is constitutionally autonomous [from state control] and self governed. On the other hand, secondary education is organized under the supervision of the Ministry of Education and Culture. Both sectors lack institutional mechanisms to ensure a functional articulation between them. In these circumstances, there is no unity of purpose between those two levels, such as their respective policies might operate in an integrated manner to define, at least in theory, a national education system. (CNRES, 2006, p. 33, my translation)

Thus, in the introduction of educational reforms in Paraguay, universities were excluded from the process of reorganization of the Paraguayan education as a whole. Excepted from this exclusion were the teacher education institutes. Those institutes were in charge of the professional formation of teachers and operated under the jurisdiction of the Ministry of Education. As a result, university institutions became isolated from the reform process (as if no connection existed between secondary and tertiary education).

Thus, the terms of educational challenges facing Paraguay became framed by the need to prioritize basic education, consistent with a global vision of the educational reform articulated by major IGOs. So even as the document, *Paraguay 20/20 Enfrentemos Juntos el Desafío Educativo: Plan Estratégico de la Reforma Educativa* (1996b), stated that programs of reform needed to take place at the four levels of human resource formation—secondary education, technical education, professional formation and higher education—little was said about how these levels worked with each other, and how the proposals for reform could constitute an "articulated" national system. The strategies elaborated in the report suggested that "the global program of reform for the four systems of human resources formation of Paraguay were to advance gradually and by stages" (MEC, CARE, & HIID, 1996b, p. 13, my translation). In this sense, basic education was to take precedence over other educational sectors.

Similarly, the HIID technical advisors had argued, even before the arrival of the mission that, "while the idea of a reform seemed to receive much lip service by internal and external stakeholders, few, including members of the advisory reform commission and the senior managers for the ministry, could formulate a vision of the reform" (Reimers & McGinn, 1997, p. 168). For them, the objective of the mission was "to help to create a common language and a shared vision of the education system about the goals of reform, and about specific projects which could be implemented to support it" (Reimers & McGinn, 1997, p. 168). Yet this language was largely a borrowed global language that focused on basic education at the expense of other sectors of education.

It is important to understand that educational challenges are defined in the documents of educational reform in terms of serious deficiencies in human resource formation in Paraguay. Basically, the descriptions provided by the HIID and MEC stressed that the national education system was unable to offer adequately skilled workers a plan for initiating a process of industrial development and economic transformation. This severe structural problem was further accentuated by the prevailing context in which rapid changes in the global economy were affecting Paraguay's own relationships with the region and the world. As mentioned previously, after 1989, Paraguay became part of the Common Market of the South, thereby participating in a regional process of economic integration that generated a series of external pressures for transforming the educational system.

This presented a number of challenges for the country but also opportunities in the sense of the emergence of a policy environment favorable to the introduction of educational reforms in the country. Thus, these developments not only augured well for the emerging democratic transition, but they held out, as well, the promise of Paraguay's entry into a new era of economic modernization. All this however has to be set against a troubling reality: the low level of public investment according to international parameters and the absence of available international financing for expanding the public system leave few options but private expansion.

According to critics such as Melquíades Alonso, the process of elaboration of the planning and implementation of reforms was strongly dependent on the framework established by the international organizations, such as the World Bank. In his article, "La propuesta educativa del Banco Mundial," Alonso (2000) points out that the priority of the reform in the 1990s towards basic and general basic education leaves the rest of the sectors of the system without any operative changes. In these terms,

> Secondary education, technical education, university education, and even adult education are absent from the project of reform and are operating in the same manner established by the educational innovations—elaborated in the 1970s—or through initiatives organized by sectores empresariales [business sectors] (Alonso, 2000, ¶ 2 ,my translation).

Basically, educational policies elaborated in the 1970s were sustained with little modification in the 1990s due to the absence of policy innovations. According to Alonzo (2000), the World Bank and the Inter-American Development Bank (IADB) proposals were highly influential during the initial period of planning and subsequent implementation of the educational reform. The project of reform that the World Bank supported for implementation in the country was basically, according to Alonso (2000), one of

> increased coverage of the basic education until the 9th grade, improvements on the efficiency of the system in terms of cost-benefits, and the privatization of university and secondary education (Alonso, 2000, ¶ 6, my translation).

In other words, this was a proposal of educational reform that saw as priority the formation of human capital, following the criteria of cost-benefits analysis, and economic projects of development. This implied in practical terms, that the priorities of the loans available for reforms in the 1990s for Paraguay were mainly destined for basic education.

The subsequent massification of the university system and the effects of the educational reform favored the emergence of a complex and very diverse system of higher education in which the boundaries of the university system and higher education in general became less clear than in the past. This is observed in the ambiguity in the position and precise place that teacher preparation now has. According to the general law of education, teacher training centers are situated within the higher education system, but it seems that the institutes of teacher preparation, though at the tertiary level of education, are still closely associated with the idea of secondary education rather than university education.

According to Crista Weise (2007), the key elements common to the regional agendas of transformation of higher education supported by IGOs (World Bank, IADB, UNESCO, etc.) in the 1990s were:

> (a) reduction of state financial investment in higher education or diversification of sources of financing; (b) linking of universities to the market and the productive system; (c) selectivity in the access; (d) control, regulation and evaluation by state, transparency (accountability by universities, and (e) Institutional reform linked to standards of productivity, efficiency and efficacy as elements of institutional quality (Weise 2007, p. 122, my translation).

Paraguay seems to have adopted most of the elements of this regional agenda. However, this has been done within a policy environment characterized by a weak state without the capacities or institutions to organize or monitor the university system as a whole. This has meant rapid expansion but also diversification and stratification of Paraguay's university system around autonomous commercially oriented institutions. In other words, the system has become self-regulated, but lacks any coherent national purpose, or any significant measure of coordination.

Therefore, in the 1990s, innovations introduced to expand the university system responded to the increasing local demand for tertiary education as well as regional pressures generated in the form of an agenda of regional integration; expressed through the idea of a Common Market of the South. A year after the promulgation of the new national constitution (1992), in line with this regional agenda, Paraguay introduced a law for universities (law 136/93) which formalized a minimalist role for the state in the governance of its National University—the "flagship" institution of the system. The 1992 legislation did not seek to introduce substantial positive changes but, instead, to remove any past restrictions for the creation of new university (private) institutions. The state effectively withdrew initiatives to govern the national system of higher education. The only regulatory measure left was the creation of a Council of Universities, *Consejo de Universidades* (CU), whose members, as it turned out, were the rectors (and often the owners) of the new universities themselves. Among its functions were the coordination and formulation of a national university policy and the evaluation of university institutions. More important, the CU was established with scarce technical and financial resources to operate effectively.

Between 1989 and 1999, 17 new institutions were recognized as universities, 14 of them private (Rivarola, 2004, p. 47). In 1998, the New General Law of Education created the National Council of Education and Culture, *Consejo Nacional de Educación y Cultura* (CONEC). This became the main public advisory body in charge of all reform efforts at all levels of education policy. Universities now became nominally integrated into an education system, over which CONEC was given oversight. Yet, this legal reform only tangentially addressed some of the more pressing issues facing higher education institutions. Nevertheless, the creation of CONEC did indicate a shift in policy that suggested the need for an increased attention to higher education reform.

This attention, however, cannot merely be explained by endogenous factors. A number of externalities affecting Paraguay's policy development must be considered, including increased pressures for the harmonization of Paraguay higher education with a set of minimal requirements on educational quality and student mobility agreed to at MERCOSUR forums as well as the implicit adoption of a regional discourse on the need for higher education reform around those issues. Moreover, international agendas of change are not static, but rather refer to extended periods of times. In the second half of the nineties, there was a policy shift in the international agenda of education reform in relation to the higher education sector. For instance, at the beginning of the twenty-first century, the World Bank and UNESCO were establishing a new common regional agenda for higher education. Rodríguez-Gómez and Alcántara (2001) describe this agenda in the following terms:

> an attitude more favorable to the strengthening of the higher education, science and technology systems of developing countries would be expected providing projects are

congruent with the 'hard' lines of the proposal: pragmatism, reinforcement of private participation, insistence on quality and efficacy, formulas of social compensation, use of distance education options, lifelong education approach, among the principal aspects (519).

Table 1. Number of Higher Education Institutions in Paraguay by Institutional Type and Sector (2009)

Type of Institution	Private	Public	Total
Universities	38	7	45
Institutes of Higher Education	23	7	30
Teacher Training Colleges/ Institutes of Professional Teacher Formation	59	41	100
Institutes of Technical Education	228	20	248

Note. Adapted from DGES (2010) *Cantidad de Instituciones de Educación Superior, por Tipo y Sector*. Available from, DGES Web site, http://educacionsuperior.mec.gov.py/v4/index.php/instituciones.html

Hence, the World Bank, and other financial IGOs shift priorities and recommendations about higher education and knowledge production investment in terms of national innovation initiatives in science and technology.

It is important to understand that, in the case of Paraguay, the regulation of "market" institutions is now perhaps one of the most urgent issues in public debates. In 2004, the national congress introduced the law 2529/04. This legislation diluted the minimal requirements demanded by the Law Universities by removing even the limited criteria that had been formulated for the authorization of new universities. Pedro Gerardo González (Caballero, 2007), the rector of the National University, has observed that the national congress can approve the opening of new institutions without the input of the Council of Universities, while universities are free to open faculties, campuses, and new professional schools without constraints. In this context, the expansion of the system is acquiring a dramatic character in recent years (see Table 1).

As observed, in Paraguay, the state usually meets political demands about the university system through legislative reforms. However, attempts to create a regulatory framework for university education have been paralyzed due to the lack of consensus on several points. Among these is the disagreement over issues of autonomy and the demands of accountability. This is of course a crucial point of contention for many owners, of the newly created private universities in particular, who fear their profit margins evaporating.

Moreover, as mentioned before, as an effect of its recent dictatorial past, Paraguay has experienced recurrent cycles of political instability, generating a sense of extreme uncertainty among policy makers, thus creating a reluctance to act decisively and impartially. The implementation of the regional agenda of educational development in Latin America in the 1990s, for example, created problems for Paraguayan policy makers, in having to juggle local and regional demands. In the current context, new global and regional discourses of reform are, thus, useful to Paraguay's policy makers. To solve a local problem they can always point to the need to borrow IGOs' ideas and pursue regional agreements in relation to priorities for reforming the educational system. However, the conundrums confronting the higher education sector are not simple questions or problems awaiting solutions. They require a more complex treatment of issues than what is provided by IGOs and cannot be expressed in legislative responses to local pressures or merely as global challenges.

At this point, what Jürgen Habermas calls "knowledge constitutive interests" (Habermas, 2005, p. 318) and Michel Foucault calls "power-knowledge" (Foucault, 1980) constantly operate as part of the process of production and negotiation of policy movements and adoption at international and local spaces. But, influence itself is not necessarily exclusively a function of exogenous factors.

What is clear, then, is that international and local networks have affected various discourses of higher education in Paraguay around such issues as private expansion, poor quality and, most crucially, privatization. These discourses have expressed a range of opportunities and expectations of education within the broader narrative of globalization. Basically, education is seen as an important ingredient in national economic development within a competitive global economy. These economic perceptions have generated demands for the transformation of higher education in Paraguay. These demands for change have been characterized both as a challenge as well as an opportunity.

However, all this is not entirely "new"; such challenges have always existed for higher education. Since education institutions in Paraguay have historically been dependent on international cooperation, they have had to take external pressures into account. What is "new" now is the systematic way in which global and regional influences are articulated in an attempt to shape the vision of the changes to follow. The systematic nature of processes of communication, and promotion of those general narratives, points to universalizing visions of reform. At the same time, local state characteristics and policy environments mediate the borrowing and implementations of agendas of change. In Paraguay, the lack of substantial changes in higher education during the long dictatorial regime (1954–1989) resulted, for the most part, in the absence of policy change and the exclusion of Paraguay from regional reforms in higher education. However, since the 1990s, Paraguay's higher education system has followed a common regional and global pattern of transformation characterized by rapid massification, institutional differentiation, growth of the private sector, emergence of new providers, institutional and legal innovations, as well as regional integration and internationalization (Larrechea & Chiancone Castro, 2009).

Yet, change so far has been largely cosmetic, trapped within the historical patterns of inertia and resistance by elite interests to a well-structured and coordinated system of higher education. Changes *are* occurring but with a virtual absence of an articulate and coherent set of policy initiatives by state institutions and of reforms in the institutional model of university and by the slow development of state capacities for the coordination of the system.

Conclusion

There are several reasons for international borrowing, mimicking, emulation, etc., of a policy solution or priorities of changes. The circulation of a specific policy-export, or recommendation of policy change, are usually linked to a vision of change. However, centers of reception for these policy recommendations, or ideas, are confronted with external and internal constraints to change in often different ways according to the content of the policy and the objective of the policy export.

At first glance, the activity of international organizations on public policy in higher education continues to be weak or marginal. Attempts to provide technical assistance, forums of discussion, or financial support are still limited at the local level while debates occur within communities of discussion. They use many of the same references and are constituted by a reduced number of the same policy actors and local referents but often do not communicate between and among each other very well. Processes of policy circulation and their up-take by states are always contingent on local realities.

The international priorities of policy change are transformed through time, but the outcome of ongoing processes of transfer constantly modify the conditions in which changes in narratives and priorities of public policy are discussed by local actors. In these situations, it is more methodologically useful to read transfer as an assemblage of ideological strategies, instead of rational processes of policy making. Therefore, the intensity of interactions between local and global policy actors on a specific policy field (i.e., public policies related to higher education) can also be read in terms of the type of power strategically implemented at different instances of transfer, and the interactions of specific institutional settings that lead to those transformations.

Proposals for reform do not necessarily imply change. At the same time, changes can sometimes occur even in the absence of specific reforms. Changes, in terms of the growth and diversification of a system of higher education institutions, do not necessarily imply substantial transformation in the ways in which institutions in a national system operate. In the same way, transfer and the implementation of specific modifications in public policy may represent only a symbolic adoption—resulting from policy inertia or political resistance to innovation in public policy—as observed in the case of Paraguay.

As shown through descriptions of the context, contingency is relevant to any modification in a system. The initial introduction of policy innovations, the promulgation of new legislations, or the effective constitution of new institutions, is contingent on local policy environments. This analysis points to the importance of historical approaches to the study of policy mobility in creating conditions for the developments of educational systems in each country. This development of policy is often related to common patterns of historically constituted public policy response, where approaches to reform—both old and new—are based, for example, on long-held beliefs about university autonomy. However, as this chapter indicates, global or regional patterns, are not irrelevant, but are contingently applied.

Similarly, the significance attached to the activities of intergovernmental organizations in public policy seem contingent on particular economic and political interests, local policy trajectories, and past processes of international transfer. This is the Paraguayan case.

References

Alonso, M. (2000, April). La propuesta educativa del Banco Mundial (I): Notas para la reflexión y discusión [The educational proposal of the World Bank (I): Notes for reflection and debate]. *Revista Acción, 202*, online. Retrieved from http://www.uninet.com.py/accion/
Aneesh, A. (2006). *Virtual migration*. Durham, NC: Duke University Press.
Ball, J. S. (1998, June). Big policies/small world: An introduction to international perspectives

in education. *Policy Comparative Education, 34*(2), 119–130. Retrieved from EBSCO
Borda, D. (Ed.). (2007). *Economía y empleo en el Paraguay* [Economy and employment in Paraguay]. Asunción: CADEP.
Buchert, L. (1995). The concept of education for all: What has happened after Jomtien? *International Review of Education, 41*(6), 537–549.
Caballero, W. (2007, May 28). Hay desorganización y caos en la educación superior del Paraguay: Entrevista con Pedro Gerardo González [There is disorganization and chaos in Paraguayan higher education: Interview with Pedro Gerardo González]. *ABC digital*. Retrieved from http://www.abc.com.py/2007-05-28/articulos/332648/hay-desorganizacion-y-caos-en-la-educacion-superior-del-paraguay
Castells, M., (2000). *The information age: Economy, society and culture: Volume 1: The rise of the network society*. Oxford: Blackwell.
Castells, M. (2005). Global governance and global politics. *PS: Political Science & Politics, 38*(1), 9–16.
CNRES. (2006). *Paraguay: Universidad 2020, documento de discusión sobre la reforma de la educación superior*. Asunción: MEC-CONEC-CU.
CONEC. (2005). Situación y perspectivas de la educación paraguaya: Análisis prospectivo y acciones prioritarias para el bienio 2006/2007 [Situation and perspectives of Paraguayan education: Prospective analyses and priorities of action 2006/2007]. Asunción.
DGES. (2010). *Cantidad de Instituciones de Educación Superior, por Tipo y Sector*. Retrieved from DGES Web site, http://educacionsuperior.mec.gov.py/v4/index.php/instituciones.html
Dolowitz, D. P., & Marsh, D. (2000). Learning from abroad: The role of policy transfer in contemporary policy-making. *Governance: An International Journal of Policy and Administration, 13*(1), 5. Retrieved from EBSCOHOST
Evans, M. (Ed.). (2004). *Policy transfer in global perspective*. Aldershot, England: Ashgate.
Fazio, M. V. (2005). *Monitoring socio-economic conditions in Paraguay* (Rep. No. 32949). Working paper. CEDLAS-The World Bank.
Foucault, M. (1980). *Power/knowledge: Selected interviews and other writings, 1972–1977*. (C. Gordon, Ed.), (C. Gordon, L. Marshall, J. Mepham, & K. Soper, Trans.). New York: Pantheon.
Gamboa, M. (2004). *Del humanismo a la competitividad: El discurso educativo neoliberal* [From humanism to competitiveness: The neoliberal educational discourse]. México: Universidad Nacional Autónoma de México.
Habermas, J. (2005). Knowledge and human interests: A general perspective. In G. Gutting (Ed.), *Continental philosophy of science* (pp. 310–321). Oxford: Blackwell.
HIID & CPES. (1993). Análisis del sistema educativo en el Paraguay. Sugerencias de políticas y estrategia para su reforma [analysis of the educational system in Paraguay: Suggestions of Policy and Strategy for Its Reform]. Asunción: HIID/CPES.
International Monetary Fund. (2009, July). *Paraguay: Detailed assessment report on anti-money laundering and combating the financing of terrorism* (Country Report No. 09/235). Washington, D.C.: International Monetary Fund. Retrieved from http://www.imf.org/external/pubs/ft/scr/2009/cr09235.pdf
International Monetary Fund. (2010). World economic outlook database, 2010 [Data File]. Retrieved from International Monetary Fund, http://www.imf.org

Ivanova, V., & Evans, M. (2004). Policy transfer in a transition state: The case of local government reform in the Ukraine. In M. Evans (Ed.), *Policy transfer in global perspective* (pp. 95–112). Aldershot, England: Ashgate.
Jones, K. (2003). *Education in Britain: 1944 to the present*. Cambridge, UK: Polity.
Ladi, S. (2005). *Globalisation, policy transfer and policy research institutes*. Northampton, MA: Edward Elgar.
Lamarra, N. F. (2009). Higher education quality assurance processes in Latin America: A comparative perspective. *Policy Futures in Education, 7*(5), 486–497.
Larrechea, E., & Chiancone Castro A. (2009). New demands and policies on higher education in the Mercosur: A comparative study on challenges, resources, and trends. *Policy Futures in Education, 7*(5), 473–485.
Maldonado-Maldonado, A. (2004). An epistemic community and its intellectual networks: The field of higher education in Mexico. Ph.D. dissertation, Boston College, United States—Massachusetts.
Marginson, S., & Rhoades, G. (2002). Beyond national states, markets, and systems of higher education: A glonacal agency heuristic. *Higher Education, 43*(3), 281–309. Retrieved from Professional Development Collection database.
MEC, CARE, & HIID. (1996a). *El desafío educativo: Una propuesta para el diálogo sobre las oportunidades educativa en el Paraguay* [The educational challenge: A proposal of debate on educational opportunities in Paraguay]. Asunción: MEC/CARE.
MEC, CARE, & HIID. (1996b). *Paraguay 2020 enfrentemos juntos el desafío educativo: Plan estratégico de la reforma educativa* [Paraguay 2020: Strategic plan for education reform]. Asunción: MEC.
Molinas, J., Pérez-Liñán, A., Saiegh, S., & Montero, M. (2006). *Political institutions, policymaking processes, and policy outcomes in Paraguay, 1954–2003*. Research Network Working paper R-502. Washington, D.C.: IADB Research Department.
Nickson, A., & Lambert, P. (2002). State reform and the 'privatized state in Paraguay.' *Public Administration and Development, 22*, 163–174.
Ozga, J., & Jones, R. (2006). Travelling and embedded policy: The case of knowledge transfer. *Journal of Education Policy, 21*(1), 1–17.
Radaelli, C. M. (2004). Europeanization: Solution or problem? European Integration online Papers (EIoP), 8(16). Retrieved from http://eiop.or.at/eiop/texte/2004-016a.htm
Rama, C. (2006). La tercera reforma de la educación superior en América Latina y el Caribe: Masificación, regulaciones e internacionalización. IESALC, Informe sobre la educación superior en América Latina y el Caribe 2000–2005.
Reimers, F. (1995). Education for all in Latin America in the XXI century and the challenges of external indebtedness. In C. A Torres (Ed.), *Education and Social Change in Latin America* (pp. 27–46). Australia: James Nicholas.
Reimers, F., & McGinn, N. (1997). *Informed dialogue: Using research to shape education policy around the world*. Westport, CT: Praeger.
Rivarola, D. (2000, March 18–19). ¿Quien pagara por los platos rotos? [Who will pay for the broken dishes?] *Ultima Hora-Correo Semanal*, p. 11.
Rivarola, D. (2004). La Educación Superior Universitaria en Paraguay. MEC-UNESCO-CONEC.
Rodríguez-Gómez, R., & Alcántara, A. (2001). Multilateral agencies and higher education

reform in Latin America. *Journal of Education Policy*, 16(6), 507–525.
Sassen, S. (2000). Spatialities and temporalities of the global: Elements for a theorization. *Public Culture*, 12(1), 215–232.
Sassen, S. (2003, February). Globalization or denationalization? *Review of International Political Economy*, 10(1), 1–22.
Sassen, S. (2007). *Territory, authority, rights: From medieval to global assemblages*. Princeton, NJ: Princeton University Press.
Schwartzman, S. (2001). Higher education reform: Indonesia and Latin America. This text is an elaboration of the presentation made at the International Higher Education Reform, Jakarta, Indonesia, organized by the board of higher education of Indonesia, August 14–16, 2001. Retrieved from http://www.schwartzman.org.br/simon/jakarta.htm
Serafini, O., LaFuente, C. L., & Rivelli, D. (1989). *La Universidad Paraguaya y sus egresados*. Asunción. CIDSEP.
Sklair, L. (2007). A transnational framework for theory and research in the study of globalization. In I. Rossi (Ed.), *Frontiers of Globalization Research* (pp. 93–108). New York: Springer.
Stone, D. (2001). Learning lessons, policy transfer and the international diffusion of policy ideas. CSGR Working Paper No. 69/01. Centre for the Study of Globalisation and Regionalisation (CSGR), University of Warwick, Coventry.
Torres, C. A. (2002). The state, privatisation and educational policy: A critique of neo-liberalism in Latin America and some ethical and political implications. *Comparative Education*, 38(4), 365–385.
Universidad Catolica. (2000). Anuario 1999. Asunción: UCA.
Urry, J. (2007). Global complexities. In I. Rossi, (Ed.), *Frontiers of Globalization Research* (pp. 151–162). New York: Springer Science/Business Media.
Weise, C. V. (2007, March). Visiones de país, visiones de universidad políticas universitarias: ¿cambio real o cambio aparente? *Umbrales*, 15. Retrieved from http://bibliotecavirtual.clacso.org.ar

· 1 4 ·
M
A Critical Analysis of a Cultural Artifact

JAMES GEARY

I'm investigating things that begin with the letter M.
THE MAD HATTER

The Golden M

Around the world the letter M represents golden arches, an entry to heaven on earth, the gateway to happiness, and an emblem of success in a world dominated by market rationale and capitalist logic. However, this same M also represents exploitation of labor, degradation of the environment, the inhumanity of a corporate entity, and an absurd proposal that pleasure is a commodity to be marketed, sold and consumed. For our purposes here, M stands as a text in itself to be analyzed, interpreted and theorized as a ubiquitous icon in a global context; a symbol used and abused by various political factions, representative of a place, a time, and a way of thinking. These various perspectives illustrate that M is not just a simple letter, and we would do well to recognize it as a text infused and laden with a variety of meanings across the globe, manipulated and propagated through various forms of media everywhere. In this chapter, I attempt to understand how M might reveal a struggle for explanations as to the way our world is configured, the shape a local community might assume as well as the social and economic framework within which people construct their thoughts and individual identities. But, what is this M and whence came its myriad meanings? How can the letter "M" be more than simply a letter in the English alphabet, more than just the beginning of a family name, more than the neon sign outside a restaurant, and more than a dominant global corporation?

This chapter conducts a critical analysis of a single letter, not just as an exercise in the deconstruction of language, nor as a practice in employing theory for the sake of academic justification. Rather, power runs so deep that even the tiniest unit of communication, the phoneme, has become an area of contestation that has a direct impact upon the daily lives of real people. Hence, an analysis of M can help us move towards a deeper understanding of how one particular cultural artifact can play a role in the creation, maintenance, and transformation of social and economic structures. This analysis could have been conducted otherwise, as there are other equally powerful signs and symbols that operate on a global scale, but a red and yellow M has a certain ubiquity and market dominance that gives it a distinct standing in the world; our 'new times' require continued investigations into such pervasive symbols. Given that M marks the beginning of McDonald, the family name of two brothers who ran a hamburger joint in California more than fifty years ago, and that this single letter has become emblazoned in a neon sign that shines yellow and bright above more than 31,000 restaurants in 119 countries around the world, the M has come to represent the McDonald's corporation, both revered and reviled around the world. The pervasiveness of this symbol, which transcends the boundaries of both national and linguistic borders, marks the M as an ideal case study for analyzing the ideological and material effects of communication. An analysis of the letter is not intended to simply shed light on the multiplicity of meanings possible in a single phoneme but strives towards a deeper understanding of how a certain symbol serves as a site of struggle for a number of forces at work in our world.

In order to move toward a deeper understanding of this cultural sign, Arthur Asa Berger (2005) offers four helpful methodologies for an analysis of M, which may assist in understanding how meanings are produced and disseminated. These methodologies (semiotic, Marxist, psychoanalytic, and sociological) might enable us to resist some of the forces that perpetuate inequity and injustice in our current global systems, dominated as they are by persistent neoliberal ideology. A multi-pronged approach to methodology, as offered by

Berger, promises to reveal the complexity of a seemingly simple sign—like that of the letter M. In this chapter, I will draw on multiple theorists as I explore the letter M in its semiotic, Marxist, psychoanalytic, and sociological contexts. To begin with, the semiotic approach of Stuart Hall attempts to make sense of the conceptual maps that are required to understand the signs of language as different meanings are communicated, received, and interpreted. Second, a Marxist analysis notes the role of the economic structures in society that have significant power in shaping human consciousness, while Zygmunt Bauman warns against the acceptance of supposed truths that arise from this consciousness-shaping process. Third, the construction of myths serves as one way to understand human consciousness, and a Freudian perspective argues for a psychoanalytic approach to help individuals interpret meaning. Finally, Arjun Appadurai offers a dynamic sociological analysis of the letter M, examining the role of different media forms, patterns of human migration, and the deployment of a social imagination. While any one of these methodological approaches may yield helpful analysis on its own accord, the combination of Berger's suggested methods illuminates much more of the letter M. For now, allow M to stand for 'Mixed-Methodology,' an approach based in multiplicity, to expropriate this symbol for a cause that looks beyond the continued celebration and accumulation of profit and power that dominates our times.

The Semiotics of M

As a start to this mixed-methods approach, the use of semiotics can be extremely constructive in analyzing the realm of human communication and our attempts at producing and sharing knowledge, a social practice embedded in structures of power. Berger (2005) teaches us that knowledge is social, and we must keep this in mind as we talk about our collective consciousness, shared ideas and common dreams that share space with the deceptively simple M. As we examine the construction of cultural knowledge, we might subscribe to Stuart Hall's notion of 'culture' as the shared conceptual maps, the shared language systems, and the shared codes that enable us to make meaning out of complex signs such as M. It is important to recognize the dynamic interplay in this social practice: what Hall (1993) calls the relationships of translation. Symbols and signs are open to perpetual interpretation, nowhere is it more obvious than M, which by some may be seen as efficient, productive, and profitable, while others may view it as deficient, repulsive, and reprehensible. The system of possible interpretations is under constant revision from a place of power to ensure that the dominant meanings remain: eat here, buy now, be happy. A system of semiotics assists us in interpreting and understanding the multiple meanings that exist in signs, as they shift and transform within particular contexts of time and place. M has no meaning by itself. We construct meaning—a life's work that entails continually pushing back against the historically dominant interpretations of symbols and signs.

Perhaps it is helpful to think of M as 'a language' of its own, employing the notion of language asserted by Hall (1997) as "any sound, word, image or object which functions as a sign and is organized with other signs into a system which is capable of carrying and expressing meaning" (p. 19). Hall argues that meaning depends on a relationship between things and a common conceptual system: a shared language that makes communication possible, if the necessary conceptual 'maps' are available to decode the encountered signs. While the letter M is obviously part of the English language, it also functions as a vital sign within a global, neoliberal language that communicates the importance of efficiency, continual corporate expansion, and growing profits. Representation is the process of linking things, concepts and signs (Hall, 1997), and without this arrangement of representation, humans could not communicate. So the M can be linked to the consumption of hamburgers, to a model of food production, and to a system of capitalist dominance. Thus, we may begin to see the importance of understanding M as a language that communicates and works to shape meanings around the world, through a variety of media forms. At the same time, we are not simply dry sponges soaking up these meanings, but rather, we engage with the concepts and signs that surround us, with which we make meaning of our world and our lives.

Signs, signifiers and signifieds can aid us in coming to grips with the semiotics of M. The golden M begins as a signifier of the place, while the ideas that it represents stand as the meaningful 'signifieds.' These dynamic and dialectical signs, with their concurrent acts of signification, become more enlightening (or perhaps confounding) when we frame them within the context of 'hyper-reality.' Jean Baudrillard (1983) suggests the concept of "hyper-reality" as a way to understand the moment when a sign becomes more important than that for which it stands: "it is no longer a question of a false representation of reality (ideology), but of concealing the fact that the real is no longer real, and thus of saving the reality principle" (p. 25). French fries are not really potatoes, hamburgers are not really meat, and a visit to the red and yellow funhouse is not really that fun; all of this non-reality is concealed by an 'imaginary.' That is, the M no longer simply represents the letter, the name, the restaurant, or the corporation; the 'real' M has become hyper-real, no longer just a red and yellow sign pointing to a hamburger joint. Now, M represents an ideology that celebrates capitalism, Americanization, and imperialism. Simultaneously, M represents happiness, success, profit, domination and accumulation.

As an ideology, M is produced and reproduced so many times (billions and billions served) that its simulation of reality becomes detached. Ultimately, as Baudrillard (1983) warns, simulations become more real and important than reality itself. In fact, the real seems no longer possible, as simulation has become an accepted reality, as power rejects the notion of realness, which Baudrillard (1983) argues is true in the realm of work:

> It is no longer a question of the ideology of work—of the traditional ethic that obscures the 'real' labour process and the 'objective' process of exploitation—but of the scenario of work. . . .Ideology only corresponds to a betrayal of reality by signs: simulation corresponds to a short-circuit of reality and to its reduplication by signs. It is always the aim of ideological analysis to restore the objective process; it is always a false problem to want to restore the truth beneath the simulacrum. (p.21)

Baudrillard's discussion of hyper-reality, as fascinating as it may seem, threatens to take us farther away from the world in which we live, where real people do struggle and suffer with a reality represented by powerful signs and disseminated by pervasive media outlets. Sadly, real people eat this unreal food disguised by a letter and its promises. This symbolic meal, at its worst, represents acquiescence to domination and acceptance of a social system that depends upon mass production, consumption and exploitation. However, the notion of hyper-reality need not necessarily lead to fatalistic conclusions; an awareness of the dangerous implications of a simulated reality may be a crucial step in reinterpreting the signs of our times.

What if we 'misinterpret' these signs, or what if there are, as is apparent, numerous available codes and interpretations? Does M mean hamburgers and fries with Mom and Dad as well as representing labor exploitation and environmental degradation by the ruling class? The polysemic impulse of language evades the confines of a prefigurative reality, and meaning expands, shifts, floats, and fragments. What if the possible interpretations are infinite, depending on human individuals living in the context of particular temporally situated places?

Umberto Eco (1976) warns that the truth becomes increasingly doubtful as a goal: "semiotics is in principle the discipline studying everything which can be used in order to lie. If something cannot be used to tell a lie, conversely it cannot be used to tell the truth; it cannot be used 'to tell' at all" (p.7). Signs can be misrepresented, intentionally or accidentally, but this seems to be inherent in the system of signs, the system of 'telling' the world. Signs can carry paradoxical meanings, meanings in direct opposition to one another as is evidenced by M. Is it happiness or misery? Is it freedom or bondage? Is it delicious or poisonous? We work hard to understand others' perceptions, and we strive to communicate our personal interpretations to enable others to understand us as we intend. The context of our lives, the historicity of particular times and places, determines the different codes that bring different meanings to signs, and these codes and signs are everywhere shifting and reshaping. Hence this exercise in semiotics is not just an academic practice but becomes essential to our understanding the world, vital to understanding ourselves, crucial to understanding the structures put in place to maintain a particular social organization. If we accept Baudrillard's (1983) exposure of betrayed reality at the hand of simulation, along with Eco's (1976) doubtful truth, the real no longer seems possible. What remains for us to do? Such theoretical assertions threaten a fatalistic conclusion that reality is not possible, but it remains quite evident that human suffering remains as real as the corporate profits signified by the letter M.

As we begin to understand the importance of language, viewed here in its broadest terms, we begin to comprehend the importance of M in our lives. To borrow the words of Ferdinand de Saussure (1966), "Language is a system of signs that expresses ideas" (p.16); these ideas shape our world, but this system is likewise manipulated by active subjects, twisted into truths and falsehoods in a continuous process of meaning-making and remaking. It becomes increasingly important to examine how these signifiers generate meanings, determined by and determining certain contexts and particular people. How has M come to signify so much, ranging from happiness to hate? Human construction of knowledge is a complex process, entangled in every aspect of humanity, currently saturated with market rationale and capitalist logic. M might mean efficiency, cleanliness, convenience and speed. At the same time, M might mean exhaustion, pollution, homogeneity and monotony. We need to remember that M adjusts and transforms itself according to time and place, further altered by us, depending on the codes we use or the conceptual maps we carry.

These systems of representation are not universal truths or biological components; they are perpetually learned, constructed, demolished, and transformed. By learning and using them, we belong to a group or multiple groups, both by our own self-designation and through processes of assignation beyond our individual control. Hall (1997) suggests, "to belong to a culture is to belong to roughly the same conceptual and linguistic universe" (p. 22), but this does not explain the range of interpretations that infuse M with so much meaning. So, it is our responsibility to infer meaning from signs; to examine M and recognize the potential range of interpretation. Furthermore, we must help one another to recognize the forces that produce these different meanings, to make an informed analytical decision about M, and to respond to the dominant meaning-makers in kind. As one of the most globally prevalent corporate symbols or icons, M is used across the spectrum of political affiliation as a symbol of success or as a symbol of oppression. Every medium that carries M has limitations, and every sign can be decoded in multiple ways. We educate each other to further interpret and understand the world that we inhabit, as one step in challenging the many institutions that serve to oppress humanity. As our understanding grows, as our codes develop, as our maps increase their scope and depth, ideally we find a voice to speak out and we begin to find a place to stand and participate in building a more equitable global organization of people, to challenge and deconstruct the meaning of M.

Marx & M

Semiotic analysis can be helpful in understanding how meanings are produced, consumed, and interpreted, but we can also look at the systems of production that occur on a material economic level. Again we commandeer M for something other than it may have been originally intended, to signify some of the ideas attributed to Karl Marx (1963), who argued that the economic system of a society has the power to shape thought, as knowledge is a social construct set in a particular context. Furthermore, this production of meaning is connected to the mode of material production, affecting our collective consciousness and the material existence of all humans: "The production of ideas, of conceptions, of consciousness, is at first directly interwoven with the material activity and the material intercourse of men [and women], the language of real life" (Marx, p. 74). For Marx, human consciousness is shaped by our positioning as social beings in particular contexts. So, M is involved in making us who we are as humans, involved in shaping our material world, involved in shaping our thoughts, operating within class structure and varying social configurations. The letter itself operates as a powerful sign, constantly feeding us meals made of deceptive meanings. We must acknowledge the pervasive presence of different media that perpetuate M as a sign, as well as acknowledging the power of the institutions that utilize M to perpetuate a system that maintains our current global organization. It is necessary to understand both the semiotic tension that functions within a text such as M, in addition to grasping the material structures and forces of production. Then, we may begin to unite in a struggle to re-envision and rebuild our world, to re-shape our thoughts and identities, as we resist dominant meanings and rewrite the letter M.

We can apply a Marxist analysis to public media forms that use M as a sign of the capitalist system; this system shapes our cultural selves, affects our conceptual cartography, and maintains the social arrangement of a dominant ruling class. Such an analysis recognizes that communication is not simply a system of transmitting pure information directly between a 'sender' and 'receiver,' but that there is an overwhelming array of media outlets forcing imagery and discourse upon us at increasing rates and with multiplying effects. An oppressive worldview is perpetuated through the daily media forms, and the domination of knowledge-production affects our collective consciousness; the result is not simply the domination of an individual, but has broad effects upon different communities around the world, but all the while we can simultaneously resist the oppressive systems that have been constructed.

Berger asserts "that the consciousness of people has important social, economic, and political implications" (p. 47); this consciousness is always forming from within and being formed from without, confronting the continual tension of subjectivity and objectivity. What is at stake here is both individual and collective consciousness-construction. There are real people involved in this dynamic, multilayered interplay of social structures and institutions, real people affected by the social construction of knowledge and perceived commonsense truths. Zygmunt Bauman (1998) warns us of the suggestion of commonsense declarations that claim to be "self-evident truths which serve to explain the world while themselves need no explanation" (Bauman, p. 7). This 'common sense' affects real people who are influenced by the many forms of media, real people oppressed by the power of M, seduced by the false allure of M. That said, people are not passive recipients of media messages but rather are involved in the constant creation of meanings, responding with their own acts of communication and interpretation.

For those involved in a theoretical examination of M, it is essential to be aware that the dominant material forces are connected to the dominant intellectual forces of our time. Intellectuals are products of the class into which they are born, if we follow the argument put forward by Antonio Gramsci (2001):

> Though all humans are intellectuals, not all humans are granted the public function of intellectuals. Every human "carries on some form of intellectual activity, that is, he is a "philosopher," an artist, a man of taste, he participates in a particular conception of the world, has a conscious line of moral conduct, and therefore contributes to sustain a conception of the world or to modify it. (p. 1141)

Intellectuals are thus involved in the organization of social hegemony and the domination of particular ideologies such as those embodied in M. The ideas of the ruling class affect us in our inquiry, affecting the way we approach knowledge and the essence of our understanding, and so we need to be cognizant of these forces which serve the perpetuation and strengthening of a ruling class. The ideology of M becomes more apparent, as we begin to see that the dominant meaning-makers assume the position of knowledge, proclaim truths, determine what is right and declare the common sense of our world. Ideology, here, is simply understood as "any system of logically coherent and widely applicable sociopolitical beliefs" (Berger 2005, p. 48). M might represent the ideology of global capitalism, the expansion of corporate power, the requirement of increased profits, and the continued social domination by a small group of people, perpetuated through various media forms and intellectuals who are implicated in this ideological perpetuation.

The prevalent ideology of global capitalism is epitomized in the dominant significations of M, and a closer look at the dynamics of ideology seems helpful. In his collection of articles entitled *For Marx*, Louis Althusser (1979) endeavors to reinterpret some of Marx's early work, arguing that Marx, along with Engels and Lenin, struggled against humanist ideological interpretations that seemed to threaten Marxist theory. For Althusser, ideology is an objective social reality, an organic part of class struggle, but he criticizes the theoretical effects of ideology that potentially hinder knowledge. Ideology can be seen as a system of representations endowed with historical existence, with a role in society, and thus human societies depend upon the formation of ideologies: "Ideology is indispensable in any society if humans are to be formed, transformed, and equipped to respond to the demands of their conditions of existence" (Althusser, p. 235). While we may recognize M as representative of inequitable economic and social conditions, our disdainful focus on the M alone may distract us from the macro-ideological system it represents. While ideology may be necessary for social organization, it can also impede our movement towards real social and economic change in the world, and in moving towards our goal of human liberation, we must understand the structural conditions in which thought and language are dialectically framed. Even a critical analysis of the letter M, such as this one, may unwittingly serve the purposes of the dominant ideology at work in the world, unless such an analysis manages to unveil the multiplicity of signs and furthermore move towards re-signifying the M in a move towards greater human emancipation. "The objective of revolutionary struggle has always been the end of exploitation and hence the liberation of [humans]" (Althusser, p. 221). Whereas Marx's analytical method was rooted in a social-economic perspective, a form of "class humanism" formed around his work, distinct from a "social humanism" focused on the individual. In such a conception, "Socialism" is a scientific idea, while "Humanism" is an ideological one, prompting an important question: What is the theoretical value of an ideological concept like humanism (Althusser, 1979)? A similar question needs to be asked of any ideological formation and as historically situated humans, we are capable of the necessary self-reflection; capable of challenging the predominant themes of our era, capable of restructuring and re-creating our worldview. As conscious beings, we exist in numerous dialectical relationships; we exist within interdependent tensions between subjectivity and objectivity, oppression and liberation, reflection and action.

We must be aware of our role in the public debate and question the discourse we employ to articulate ourselves as we become embroiled in the theoretical discussions that surround the letter M. Zygmunt Bauman (1998) derides the language of cosmopolitan chatter that serves to represent the thoughts of a global intellectual as opposed to a local individual. The intellectual force is tightly connected to both the dominant material force and the dominant media forms (despite proclamations of autonomy and objectivity), further serving the interests of a dominant hegemony. The local experience is not so liberating as the cosmopolitan chatter sometimes suggests, despite the celebration of hybrid cultures and successful 'Global Diasporas.' Cosmopolitan intellectual discourse does not necessarily represent the reality of people struggling against oppression on a daily basis; "the cultural hybridization of the globals may be a creative, emancipating experience, but cultural disempowerment of the locals seldom is" (Bauman, p. 100). Intellectuals must remain alert to the perpetuation of assumed 'truths,' as the dominant social forces often hold the leashes upon which we tug and bay at the moon. Bauman suggests that the intelligentsia has become disconnected from the reality of most people, in effect serving the interest of M that represents corporate ideology, as communication fails to serve humanity. It is not enough to critically analyze M, if the system sustaining the dominance of M never changes, and it seems worse still if the discourse just adds to cosmopolitan chatter.

Furthermore, and perhaps most importantly, there are real people who can unite with each other to resist these institutions, these dominant constructs, these media forms and this systematic oppression. The history of humans, Marx contends, is a history of such struggle against domination, "an uninterrupted, now hidden, now open fight, a fight that each time ended either in a revolutionary reconstitution of society at large, or in the common ruin of the contending classes" (Marx, p. 200). Marx maintained the possibility of a revolution, or even the necessity of one, to challenge and defeat the oppressive class structure that maintains global inequities and human degradation. We will return later to this idea of united resistance, in an examination of collective imagination and the possibility of new social constructions that occur both conceptually and institutionally.

Myth & M

We can see that different media forms play a critical role in disseminating the discourse of market ideology and we begin to understand how this discourse controls and limits the debate involved in developing or challenging our social structures. But what can we understand by examining our psychological development as individuals and as a collective group? How does M function as a mythical force in the world? Berger tells us "myths are an important component of our psyches, our media and popular culture, and our everyday lives" (p. 85). The powerful myth of M involves multiple themes, including the myth of Manifest Destiny, the myth of limitless money, and the myth of a 'self-made man.' The myth of M also includes a sense of nostalgia: for things we never knew, for the tenuous present, or even for a future that has yet to be imagined. Arjun Appadurai (1996) argues that "pastiche and nostalgia are central modes of image production and reception" (p. 30), another aspect of the many signs which we confront in media. We are modern, we are connected to a better history, and we create a mythical future to inhabit, and all of these myths are for sale beneath the M. Perhaps the M stands for another time in America, when the hamburger joint was a real place on the road across the country, when two brothers could make a living there, a place where families gathered and ate a meal together with some of their community, or perhaps this nostalgia is just a longing for a time and place that never existed.

Sigmund Freud (1972) offers the myth as a way of understanding our consciousness, the same consciousness that Marx claimed was linked to the material mode of production. The economic, the political, and the social become further entangled in the creation of an individual, making the formation of identity a complex process. As individuals, and as a group of humans living together, we interpret the world around us, and this type of mythical investigation lies at the root of psychoanalysis. There are conscious and unconscious processes that interact to shape our minds, in turn shaping our view of the world and the possibilities for participation in transforming that place where we live. Mental acts were full of meaning, and psychoanalysis could help subjects discover deeper meanings that remained hidden within the unconscious mind:

> It was a triumph for the interpretative art of psychoanalysis when it succeeded in demonstrating that certain common mental acts of normal people, for which no one had hitherto attempted to put forward a psychological explanation, were to be regarded in the same light as the symptoms of neurotics: that is to say they had a meaning which was unknown to the subject but which could easily be discovered by analytic means. (Freud, 1972, p. 235)

These revelations of meaning that are hidden within the unconscious mind can expand our mental lives, but more importantly, they can allow us to actively participate in practices of resistance against the subconscious mechanisms at work in the various forms of media around us. The awareness of our previous unawareness becomes a vital aspect of our investigation; as we admit to a lack of awareness concerning activity in our own minds, we admit to an ignorance of ourselves. With this admission and increased self-awareness, we might begin to examine some of the forces that shape our unconscious, maybe examine the underbelly of M, to dissect these nuggets of meaning.

Remembering the function of M as a text, we can use psychoanalytic theory as an approach to analyzing M, to understand the work of symbolism, as well as understanding how these symbols affect our consciousness. Forms of media are similar to dreams, in that they can be interpreted and analyzed in an attempt to locate meaning; some media productions could be analyzed as if they are the dreams of a collective unconsciousness. Lacan (1977) argued that the unconscious is structured like a language and Hall (1997) saw all images as languages, so we now see a further complexity in the conceptual maps that we use to make meaning of M. Different forms of media influence our dreams; media affect our conscious thoughts and these media shape our actual lives. A tall clown with red hair and red shoes, dressed in a yellow suit, greets us at the door but also stands as a plastic symbol of childhood and happiness. M infuses various media with meaning and in turn is further infused with more meaning, with additional implications as M works within the unconscious and conscious mind, interpreted and reconfigured indefinitely.

Psychoanalytic theory offers another particular idea that may assist us in our attempts to understand M and its power to influence our lives, and this is notion of the archetype in relation to human instincts, as put forward by Carl Jung (1964).

> Instincts are physiological urges perceived by the senses. They also manifest themselves in fantasies and often reveal their presence only by symbolic images. These manifestations are what I call the archetypes. They are without known origin; and they reproduce themselves in any time or in any part of the world. (Jung, p. 69)

The archetype can be understood as a universal theme in myth, life and media, connected to history and to our unconscious. Archetypes seem to exist independently of the personal unconscious of individuals, functioning as collective thought patterns and manifestations that might work to steer us in particular directions. Two of Jung's archetypes are 'the golden age' and 'the hero,' a time of peace and prosperity embodied by human figures of mythological stature. The golden M shines as a symbol of this bygone era to which we might return someday as well as representing the work of heroes who have succeeded in the capitalist mode of profit and exploitation. Of course, this 'hero' stands in stark contrast to Marx's ideas of a hero, a real person that Berger suggests is one who fights for a more just and equitable social order. Our age's archetypal hero stands out as a human capable of capital accumulation, regardless of the modes of exploitation necessary for such relentless accrual of profits. It may be helpful here to lay Marxism on the psychoanalytic sofa for a moment and investigate its longing for fantastical futures and hero-worshipping. As Harry Harootunian (2007) notes,

> What yoked capitalist and Marxian versions together was the allure of a better future, the fantasy destiny of the perfect future toward which the present was being asked to direct its energies; there is of course a difference between revolution and evolution, but perhaps in retrospect not as great as it once was made to seem (p. 489).

It may be that capitalist and Marxist dreams are shaped in the same collective consciousness, resulting in a similar archetypal hero and craving a golden future, but surely the hero is not Ronald McDonald, nor will the perfect future be served up like fast food on a plastic tray.

Another important Jungian concept is the dark side of the psyche, or the 'shadow,' that usually remains hidden from consciousness. Berger writes of "a battle for deliverance" (2005, p. 100) that occurs between the shadow and the ego, in the struggle for dominance. Jung argued that we must all confront this shadow within ourselves, if we are to gain a better understanding of who we are, but it can be an especially interesting exercise to apply this notion of the shadow to M. Behind the glowing, happy, successful smirk of M lies the dark, exploitative, greedy and destructive shadow. We resist the urge to partake in the myth of M, fight the desire for fatty, sugary, salty food, and deny the impulse to consume packaged happiness. Our golden age of the future must not be the one promised by M, our heroes must not be those proffered by the dominant hegemony of M, and our myths need not be the simplified ones represented by M. Myths are central to meaning-making in life, with both archetypal and rhetorical aspects, and communities are shaped by the communication of myths. To borrow the suggestion of Janice Hocker Rushing (1989), "the new myth for humankind needs to be a quest, not a conquest; its purpose, to search rather than to search and destroy" (p. 21). Myths require an integrated critical framework to offer deeper and broader interpretations, as the combined power of archetypal and ideological narratives have enormous potential within the formation of myths. A psychoanalytic understanding of myth-making enriches our theoretical conceptualization of M approached from a semiotic perspective or a Marxian angle, shining more light on our triangulated grasp of this shadowy letter that can hold so much sway in our collective imagination.

The Media, Migration & Imagination of M

Media and migration impel and compel the work of the imagination, posits Arjun Appadurai (1996), and this collective imagination serves as the basis for a plurality of imagined worlds; "ordinary people have begun to deploy their imaginations in the practice of their everyday lives" (p. 5). We create new mythologies, new conceptual maps, new heroes, new codes and new interpretations of old signs that promise us new social projects. Social imagination, despite being involved in the world of mass consumption, has the potential to lead us to a new stage for action, locate a new voice to articulate ourselves, and create a new social agency that encourages participation and imagination from varied, multiple sources. M is not simply an American icon or a symbol of Americanization, although America has certainly been heavily involved in the production and dissemination of M in various media forms. America is only "one node of a complex transnational construction of imaginary landscapes" (Appadurai, p. 31): landscapes that collectively work to influence the collective, social imagination. The ubiquity of M situates this symbol at the gateway of such a global landscape, the golden arches leading to a world of promise and prosperity.

Appadurai (1996) identifies five scapes that are involved in global cultural flows, which, for us, means the creation and spread of M throughout the world. A cursory look at these landscapes might assist us in understanding the power of M as it represents a dominant ideology, and what is more important, Appadurai's ideas offer us the optimism of resistance against such oppressive global systems. 'Ethnoscapes' recognize migration as an essential feature in our world, as shifting people assume particular roles, some as consumers, some as exploited labor, and others as the dominant mobile class. 'Technoscapes' allow for the production of food on a global scale, processing and distributing goods to be consumed, dependent on systematic, computerized efficiency, ordered by market rationale. 'Financescapes' make possible the unlimited movement of capital around the world, accumulating profits for a limited few, at the expense of many, perpetuating an unbalanced economic system. 'Mediascapes' are essential to the commercial success of M, as the icon represents ideas everywhere, designed to target people in certain locations, speaking directly to us, affecting the way we think. 'Ideoscapes' are more directly political in nature, inextricably linked to mediascapes (as all of these landscapes overlap, entwine each other, and meld into various shapes), a chain of ideas that shift with geographical and temporal context. These five landscapes, at work in the production of M, require a global analysis that recognizes the difficulty of understanding such disjunctive cultural flows.

Media and migration are linked, as more people move to more places, represented by more media forms, which means the possibility of more people seeing the potential and necessity of systematic and institutional transformation. More of us recognize alternative social configurations exist within our collective imagination, and we must work to make these alternatives a reality. As Appadurai (1996) writes, "Many lives are now inextricably linked with representations" (p. 64), and the media continually bombard us with these representations. We must struggle to make sense of our world, to comprehend the multiple, fragmented modes of production and consumption that require a theoretical framework similarly fragmented. Furthermore, Appadurai (1996) recommends that social imagination and participation embrace the fractal forms and diversity of thought available through these new theoretical frameworks. People living in very different settings will need to cooperate to resist against the powerful system represented by M. Working within the paradoxical forms of globalization, we seek unity and cohesion amidst the fragments, as we must find a common ground upon which to stand and challenge the dominant hegemony.

Membership & M

Berger (2005) offers a final approach to media through a sociological analysis, focusing on the social relationships that exist between people, affecting how groups and institutions function. We are members of a collective group, or perhaps a number of different groups, occupying shared spaces, vying for resources, involved in various systems of power and privilege. We live in society and society dwells in us, and media formations play a role in situating us in a particular place at a particular time. We need one another to exist, we depend on one another to make our world, and we assume a certain position in relation to one another. We make meanings as members of society, and the media configurations have enormous power in socializing us. A sociological perspective enables us to see how the collective whole interacts with the letter M through various media forms and how the whole is further influenced through new understandings.

While the transnational appeal and power of the media are enormous (and the concentrated ownership of media translates into concentrated power and capital for a very few corporate entities), we must remember that resistance against this power is possible. Resistance begins with a sharpened awareness of the ways in which global media messages infiltrate communities, and such an awareness can inform and inspire group action that is necessary to counter the concentrated power of corporate M. A sociological analysis unveils the importance of cultural studies as an academic discipline that has increased in recent years, and we deepen our understanding of M with such an analysis of the cultural practices and meanings at work behind such an apparently eternal and infinite icon. This particular manifestation of M, the corporate entity, has been around for just less than a century, yet it appears to maintain a monumental status around the world. We can demystify the M with a close sociological analysis that reveals how such artifacts and ideas gain this eternal quality and how seemingly simple signs affect our sense of membership in particular groups.

Earlier, we looked at Hall's notions of language and our belonging to a particular cultural universe that depended on our sharing signs and codes with other people, and he adds to this idea of membership: "Primarily, culture is concerned with the production and the exchange of meanings. . .between the members of a society or group" (Hall, 1997, p. 2). As a member of society, each of us has a responsibility to closely analyze the signs that surround us, to examine the codes we use to make meaning, and to challenge our assumptions about the world that may be based on socially constructed 'truths.' A multi-pronged analysis (semiotic, Marxian, psychoanalytic, and sociological) best serves us in understanding the signs that surround us, and this is not simply an academic exercise; as Gramsci (2001) reminds us, all humans are intellectuals, though not all are granted this public function, and thus each of us can engage with M in an intellectual and sociological struggle. The M is a complex sign that needs to be deconstructed, devalued and perhaps ultimately demolished in its role as a construct of power and domination.

We need to continually ask what it means to be a member of society, what we expect from each other, what we require in return for membership. Bauman (1998) argues that the primary practice in a capitalist society is to consume, and to accept the norm as an individual's "ability and willingness to play" (p. 80) this role of consumer. Living becomes consuming, until we grow dissatisfied and move on to consume something else. We consume particular foods and particular environments, until we are bored or agitated, and we look elsewhere for gratification. Always, M represents desire, even though we believe in our freedom of choice. Bauman speaks of "the disguise of a free exercise of will" (p. 84), and he suggests that mature consumers reveal the practice at work in society and resist against it. M is not simply one restaurant. It represents the requirement to choose from a selection within the narrow confines of a capitalist configuration of society, supposedly an endless amount of choice, but all of it strictly regulated within a global system that perpetuates inequity and oppression. Not everybody can be a consumer, as the system demands a certain amount of Bauman's 'vagabonds' who must move to survive, a growing group of marginalized souls, exploited humans, discarded and disregarded people wearing M as a badge of dishonor, representing their failure to succeed in the established social and economic organization that dominates our world.

Multidimensionality of M

An examination of M began here with full recognition of the golden arches associated with a restaurant corporation; bending the M where we found it necessary to apply some different theories to the corporate phenomenon as representative of a much larger set of global processes. The M means very different things in varying contexts but informs so much of how we consider other signs, co-constitutive of one another, layering upon one another, intersecting with one another. M continues to represent a place that serves fast food and promises happiness, but the M also stands as an icon of global capitalism. The multidimensionality of the icon functions so effectively around the world due to a combination of signs that shift their signifying practices depending on a particular context and particular people. Douglas Kellner (2003) persuades us to locate a similar context for resistance against the phenomenon of M, opposing the situation of hegemonic ideology at every turn in public space, challenging the signs that we meet. We need to ask whether M simply represents a burger stand, good times and fair value. We need to further ask whether M also symbolizes the dynamics of social change, political dominance and economic manifestation. We need to decode M and recognize the multidimensionality of such an icon, and then perhaps we can begin to resist its power, resist its manipulative meanings, and invest it with meanings of our own that serve to devalue it simply as an icon of global domination.

However, our times demand that resistance against M must work on a number of levels, just as M manages to function in particular contexts, through particular media. Kellner (2003) tells us that opposition requires "a more contextual and dialectical approach that evaluates specific phenomena, articulates negative and/or positive dimensions, and then makes nuanced judgments" (p. 46). Of course, this is no easy task that Kellner has put forth, and we must critically and optimistically educate one another if we are to involve ourselves in such an approach. The dominating aspects of globalization spawn resistance and opposition to the forces that maintain an inequitable social organization, and M has become a symbol used by the resistance movement against a powerful cultural ideology that demands continued domination of the world, accumulation of profits and the desired control of the signs with which we produce and interpret knowledge.

We have the ability and the responsibility to add further dimensions to M, to challenge the dominant representations that have been assigned to it and reproduced in various media. We locate ourselves in a particular place and a certain time, recognize the possible effects of these signs upon our psyches, discern the different institutions and dynamic processes throughout the world that maintain a dominant social structure, and resist the perpetuation of oppression. We oppose the limited meaning of M. M is more than money, more than market manipulation, more than legal maneuverings that benefit corporations, more than the mythologies and meta-narratives that feed us fairy tales of capitalist success, and more than mass media conglomerates that strive to sell us our lives. Let M stand for our conscious mind, fed and nourished by an infinite number of sources, a mind willing and able to take part in an act of resistance against oppression, a mind prepared to face the daunting task of structural reorganization on a global scale, a mind dedicated to imagining and manufacturing a more equitable world, and a mind that demands alternatives to exploitation and degradation. These 'new times' require us to rewrite, rethink, re-imagine, and re-signify the multiple meanings of M.

References

Althusser, L. (1979; 1977). *For Marx* [Pour Marx.]. London: Verso.
Appadurai, A. (1996). Diversity and disciplinarity as cultural artifacts. In, C. McCarthy et al. *Race, Identity and Representation in Education* (pp. 427-438). New York: Routledge.
Baudrillard, J. (1983). *Simulations*. New York: Semiotexte.
Bauman, Z. (2000). *Liquid Modernity*. Cambridge, UK: Blackwell.
Berger, A. A. (2005). *Media analysis techniques* (3rd ed.). Thousand Oaks, CA: Sage.
de Saussure, F. (1966). Introduction. In C. Bally, A. Sechehaye & A. Reidlinger (Eds.), *General course in linguistics* (W. Baskin Trans.). (1st ed., pp. 1–34) McGraw-Hill.
Eco, U. (1976). *A theory of semiotics*. Bloomington, IN: Indiana University Press.
Freud, S. (1972). *Character and culture*. New York: Collier.
Gramsci, A. (2001). The formation of intellectuals. In V. Leitch (Ed.), *Norton anthology of theory and criticism* (1st ed., pp. 1135–1143). New York: Norton.
Hall, S. (1993). Encoding, decoding. In S. Durning (Ed.) *The cultural studies reader* (pp. 90-103). London: Routledge.
Harootunian, H. (2007). Remembering the historical present. *Critical Inquiry, 33*(3), 471–494.
Jung, C. G. (1964). *Man and his symbols*. New York: Doubleday.
Kellner, D. (2003). *Media spectacle*. London; New York: Routledge.
Lacan, J. (1977). *Écrits: A selection* [Écrits.]. New York: Norton.
Marx, K. (1963). *Selected writings in sociology and social philosophy* (2nd ed.). Harmondsworth: Penguin.
Rushing, J. H. (1989). Evolution of 'the new frontier' in Alien and Aliens: Patriarchal co-optation of the feminine archetype. *Quarterly Journal of Speech, 75*(1), 1–24.

AFTERWORD
Manifesto for Education in the Age of Cognitive Capitalism

Freedom, Creativity and Culture

MICHAEL A. PETERS

Transform the world, said Marx, change life, said Rimbaud. These two watchwords for us one only.

ANDRÉ BRETON

The social revolution of the nineteenth century cannot derive its poetry from the past, but only from the future. It cannot begin with itself, before it has shed all superstitious belief in the past. Earlier revolutions needed to remem¬ber previous moments in world history in order to numb themselves with regard to their own content. The revolution of the nineteenth century must let the dead bury the dead in order to arrive at its own content. There, the phrase exceeded the content. Here the content exceeds the phrase.

KARL MARX, THE 18TH BRUMAIRE OF LOUIS BONAPARTE

Manifestos, Art and Politics

In *Le Manifeste du Surréalisme* [The Surrealist Manifesto] André Breton defines Surrealism as 'pure psychic automatism with which one proposes to express, either orally or in any other manner, the real process of thought, in the absence of any control exercised by reason, outside any aesthetic or moral concerns.'[1] Surrealist poetics revalues and reconsiders the irrational element in human creativity and the will to express itself through art at a subconscious level. Freud, Marx and Rimbaud are the guiding lights for Breton as he derives a form of ('fleeting') modernity after Baudelaire that is truly revolutionary and which is based upon total freedom of expression that goes beyond (bourgeois) reality to uncover the super real. In this revolutionary overthrow Breton and his surrealist compatriots utilize all the aspects of the unthought and unconscious, including dream, madness, hallucination and irrationality all of which allegedly bring us closer to *life* and reveal the superior reality of certain forms of association in dream making that manifest the true function of thought.

In *Poetry of the Revolution* Martin Puchner (2005: 2) argues that Marx had invented a poetry of the future revolution in the *Communist Manifesto* which 'seeks to produce the arrival of the "modern revolution" through an act of self-foundation and self-creation: we, standing here and now, must act!' As Puchner notes 'manifestos weave together social theory, political acts, and poetic expression' (2). The manifesto itself is an act of creation, a creative practice that seeks to prefigure and realize the future. The interesting fact is that the *Manifesto* became part of "world literature" and entered the world of art in the twentieth century through its acts of reception, transportation and translation. In this sense Puchner (2005) argues that in the twentieth century we should read avant-garde manifestos alongside political manifestos because they were intimately self-referencing and involved—among others, the Italian and Russian Futurists, Dadaism, Surrealism, and Debord's revolt against the spectacle. Thus, the study of manifestos requires not only a poetics of the form but also an understanding of the politics of speech acts. Puchner argues that the *Communist Manifesto* forms the genre and then undergoes a process of temporal, linguistic and geographical diffusion, drifting into the realm of aesthetics as well as politics with the appearance of the avant-garde manifesto.

Manifesto, from the Italian, means to 'make clear' (in English, 'manifest'). Manifestos are declarations. They often shape intentions and political actions. It is not remarkable that politics and art should be expressed in a kind of poetry that constitutes a kind of speech act or performance. Resistance often first registers itself in a form of poetics that expresses the emotions and feelings associated with exploitation and other forms of oppression before it is 'translated' into theory or narrative (Peters & Besley, 2006).

In *The Theory of the Avant-Garde* (first published in Italian in 1962) Renato Poggioli (1981) attempted to demonstrate that avant-garde artists existed in a critical relationship to tradition, fashion and the public, united across the arts in their alienation and opposition to the bourgeoisie. Clement Greenberg (1939) in his famous article argued that the avant-garde, distinctively bohemian, repudiated both bourgeois ('high art') and revolutionary politics and developed in opposition to the mass produced culture of kitsch to preserve the living culture we still have. This avant-garde opposition to mass consumerism and its kitsch culture has been taken up by leading members of the Frankfurt School. Peter Bürger (1974) in his *Theory of the Avant-garde* distinguishes the historical avant-garde—Dada, Surrealism, Russian avant-garde after the October Revolution—from the 'neo' avant-garde (Abstract Expressionism, Pop Art, Nouveau Réalism, Fluxus) which simply recycles earlier strategies. The historical avant-garde involves a radical break with tradition and opposition to art as an institution such as it has developed in bourgeois society with its insistence on the autonomy of the aesthetic. Its main tendency is the sublation of art in everyday praxis, and it reacts against aestheticism which is detached from the praxis of life. Bürger also engages in an extended discussion of Bertolt Brecht (1898–1956) who experimented with Dada and Expressionism but developed a style more suited his own unique vision in his later work that rejected the commodification of the world.

One of the major questions is whether the avant-garde still exists or is still possible—whether its energy, opposition to mainstream culture, and its formal innovation have been totally recuperated by capitalist culture (Habermas) or whether the avant-garde still has the spirit of criticism that enables it to break the rules of art and go beyond what is accepted (Lyotard). Irmelia Hautamaki (2003) indicates the concept of the avant-garde has both a political and a cultural dimension which are closely intertwined: the concept applied to art was first mentioned in the political programs of French utopian socialists and later used to describe the 'most advanced and stylistically innovative art' based on the work of the poets Arthur Rimbaud, Paul Verlaine, Stephane Mallarmé and Charles Baudelaire. As Matei Calinescu (1987: 114) indicates, Marxists used avant-garde as a political term in the 1880s—the party is the avant-garde of the working class. Yet Marxist critics also referred to avant-garde literature as 'modernist' or 'decadent' in contrast to 'socialist realism,' a discussion reflected in the so-called realism (expressionism) debate that took place between György Lukács (1885–1971) and Bertolt Brecht, characterized by Bela Kiralyfalvi (1990) as 'primarily a broad discussion of disagreements among Marxist artists and theorists about the values and characteristics of classical, bourgeois and socialist art.'[2]

The idea that the classical realist tradition should be followed by modern writers is a problem that arose out of Lukács' attempt to remain faithful to Marxist aesthetics but in view of the development of modernist fiction, art or theatre ultimately unsatisfactory and a kind of assertion that totalizes realism as the objective perspective on the world. Pike (1985) intelligently suggests that 'their commitment to a dogmatized and dogmatic political credo was the prime source of their artistic and philosophical inspiration; the dogma inspired them in their quest for aesthetic solutions appropriate to the contemporary political age, the transition from capitalism to socialism, and they both used it to claim exclusivity for their respective theoretical approaches' (xi).

This debate is part of the wider meeting of Marxism and Modernism that took place in Germany and elsewhere in Europe that took place in a struggle over the very meaning of the avant-garde and its relation to capitalist society. Marxism provided a trenchant critique of capitalist economy, and yet its attempt to provide an aesthetics based on the dogma of a 'copy' theory of consciousness as a straightforward reflection of objective processes impugns its usefulness and consigns most of the intelligent thought-provoking, challenging and experimental art, theatre and music to the dustbin of history while aggrandizing the palpably meagre achievements of 'socialist realism.' It is also to rob Marxist aesthetics of its vitality and openness.

In this brief postscript I want to run together art, politics and education. In particular, I want to argue that the future of education is a matter of aesthetics, in particular, of the *design of systems*. Insofar as the future of education is a question of the *design* of knowledge and learning systems—communication and data networks that promote participation and collaboration—then design is also a matter of politics for who owns and designs education, and new media systems are critical to what kinds of systems architectures and platforms are promoted and what kind of knowledge and learning cultures are possible.

Designing Educational Futures and Knowledge Cultures[3]

It was Nietzsche who said 'The future influences the present just as much as the past' and Paul Valery, the French poet and critic, who said 'The future isn't what it used to be.' In the past philosophers have attempted to lay down principles for a philosophy of the future: I am thinking not only of Nietzsche but also Feuerbach's (1843) *Principles of Philosophy of the Future* and Bloch's (1970) *A Philosophy of the Future*.[4] My starting point is Nietzsche, Wittgenstein and Heidegger—'prophets of postmodernity' (as I call them)—who provide some ground on which to stand. Nietzsche, of the three, perhaps most explicitly addressed questions of the future. In a work that was to have been his second book, *On the Future of Our Educational Institutions*,[5] portions of which appear in *Untimely Meditations*,[6] he called for radical educational reform presented in the form of a prolonged narrative dialogue. *Beyond Good and Evil*[7] was subtitled *A Prelude to a Philosophy of the Future*, and he often talked of 'philosophers of the future' who have a specific task:

> All sciences are now under the obligation to prepare the ground for the future task of the philosopher, which is to solve the problem of value, to determine the true hierarchy of values. (Neitzsche, 1907)

In the Preface to *The Will to Power*, Nietzsche describes himself as the 'perfect nihilist of Europe' but one, at the same time, who had 'lived through the whole of nihilism, to the end, leaving it behind, outside himself' (p. 3). As he writes, again in the Preface, the title—*The Will to Power: Attempt at a Revaluation of All Values*—is formulated as a *countermovement* that will take the place of nihilism, but which at the same time logically and psychologically presupposes it in the sense that only after the advent of nihilism can we realize that nihilism is the logical extension of our values. Only after our experience of nihilism can we discover for the first time what these values really meant and what real value they had. Only at that point, will we realize that we require new values.

Knowledge cultures is an approach to philosophy of education that ties it to contemporary debates about knowledge and the value of knowledge, especially those accounts that draw on the concepts of 'postindustrialism,' 'postFordism,' 'knowledge economy,' 'creative economy' and open source models of scientific communication, scholarship and science. In this afterword I do not have the space to defend this broad approach to the philosophy of education[8] as I need to be programmatic in setting out an agenda which is concerned not only with the idea of creating or designing futures but also that is critical in an accepted sense. Such an approach needs to be non-deterministic, especially in relation to technology, sensitive to cultural difference, and radically interdisciplinary. Most importantly, it needs to accept there is a logical as well as temporal asymmetry between the future and the past.[9]

Philosophy of the future is a platform for rethinking the philosophy of education and policy futures in education. Although policy futures may draw on the techniques and methodologies of futures studies, it is not reducible to this field or to its siblings—futurology, scenario planning, foresight, or science fiction. I am much more inclined to see *futures* in an applied philosophical framework that is akin to what Foucault, after Nietzsche, calls 'histories of the present,' which is driven by a genealogical investigation of value and guided by the epistemological question of how the historical awareness of our present circumstances affect what and how we know and can know.[10] Consider 'histories of the future' a separate but parallel critical activity. It is an approach that I have attempted to develop and exemplify over the past few years through the establishment of journals and books series, and through various books and courses.[11]

In this afterword I want to draw attention to one aspect of this program that I have called 'Knowledge Cultures' which I have addressed in terms of three specific aspects—'Open source, open access, and free science' (Peters & Besley, 2006). In Nietzsche's terms I am trying to determine the true hierarchy of values in relation to knowledge futures, and, on some indicative evidence I want to assert the value of *freedom* to relation to the future of knowledge.[12] 'Freedom' on the standard account has been defined as *freedom from the dependence on the will of others*—which is the classic statement by the tradition of nineteenth-century British liberalism stated first by Locke, then elaborated by Mill, Bentham, Green and others, and later adopted in the twentieth century by Hayek (1960) in his influential *The Constitution of Liberty*. This notion of liberty, which is at the heart of liberalism in both its Protestant and Catholic forms, is also historically tied to democracy and to the development of free intellectual inquiry, the modern university and the value of openness. Academic freedoms, stemming from freedom of speech, refer to alleged rights of students, teachers and institutions to pursue the truth or persuade, without political suppression.[13] The U.S. Supreme Court in *Regents of the University of California v. Bakke*, 438 U.S. 265, 312; 1978 states that academic freedom means a university can 'determine for itself on academic grounds: who may teach; what may be taught; how it should be taught; and who may be admitted to study.'

This is not the place to pursue the full genealogy of freedom in its educational forms but let us state some significant aspects of its continuing importance. I state these propositions in the language of the manifesto form (with some irony).

Freedom

1. Today the value of freedom in relation to the distribution, access and exchange of knowledge is under threat at an historical moment that also provides unparalleled opportunities for the establishment of open

global architectures for knowledge, science, learning and education.
2. The study of education should concern itself in a critical way with the historical forms of freedom and their uneven development—freedom of expression and of speech, of freedom to learn, of freedom to teach, and of freedom to publish.
3. The assertion and establishment of these freedoms take different historical forms and pose different technical, political and ethical problems for knowledge and learning futures, including those of copyright, intellectual property, and plagiarism.
4. The lesson I take from Marx, and from Nietzsche, Wittgenstein and Heidegger based on a materialist and historicist approach is that *knowledge and the value of knowledge are rooted in social relations*. In order to investigate the genealogy of the value of knowledge in relation to its freedoms, its *freedoms-to-come*, and their educational significance, we must critically examine its various emergent institutional and networked forms as well as the obstacles to them.
5. In the practical context this program means an investigation of the value of openness and the mode of open production. Openness has emerged as an alternative mode of *social production* based on the growing and overlapping complexities of open source, open access, open archiving, open publishing and open science. It has become a leading medium and source of creativity and innovation in the world global digital economy.
6. The Free Software and 'open source' movements constitute a radical non-proprietarian alternative to traditional methods of text production, distribution and reception and we need to develop a radical political economy of distributive knowledge and learning to promote intercultural exchanges between and among the North and South so that knowledge and access to knowledge are evenly shared.
7. This alternative non-proprietary method of cultural and knowledge exchange threatens traditional models and the legal and institutional means used to restrict creativity, innovation and the free exchange of ideas. In terms of a model of communication there has been a gradual shift from content to code in the openness, access, use, reuse and modification, reflecting a radical personalization that has made these open characteristics and principles increasingly the basis of the cultural sphere. So open source and open access have been developed and applied in open publishing, open archiving, and open music constitut-

ing the hallmarks of 'open culture.'
8. The values of freedom and openness are the metavalues that will determine knowledge cultures in the future and, therefore, also the production of knowledge and the design of knowledge and learning systems.
9. Today increasingly we must talk of the freedom to use, to make and distribute copies, and to make changes and improvements; that is, anything represented in digital form permits the growing globalization of *open works* and for a growing part of humanity to *access, create, modify, publish and distribute* various kinds of works.[14]
10. Today, intellectuals—academics, students, teachers, editors, critical media journalists—must become aware of the changing historical and material conditions for the reproduction and development of their own thought, discourse and digital labor, and, thereby, against the monopolization and privatization of knowledge and culture by the new capitalist info-utilities, to win back the ownership of the means of intellectual production and distribution.

Freedom, Openness and Creativity[15]

Every aspect of culture and economy is becoming transformed through the process of digitization that creates new systems of archives, representation and reproduction technologies that portend Web 3.0 and Web 4.0 where all production, material and immaterial, is digitally designed and coordinated through distributed information systems.

Digitization transforms all aspects of cultural production and consumption favouring the networked peer community over the individual author and blurring the distinction between artists and their audiences. These new digital logics alter the logic of the organization of knowledge, education and culture, spawning new technologies as a condition of the openness of the system. Now the production of texts, sounds and images is open to new rounds of experimentation and development, providing what Felix Stalder (2004) calls 'a new grammar of digital culture' and transforming the processes of creativity, which are no longer controlled by traditional knowledge institutions and organizations but rather permitted by enabling platforms and infrastructures that encourage large-scale participation and challenge old hierarchies.

The shift to networked media cultures based on the ethics of participation, sharing and collaboration, involving a volunteer, peer-to-peer gift economy has its early beginnings in the right to freedom of speech that depended upon the flow and exchange of ideas essential to political democracy, including the notion of a 'free press,' the market and the academy. Perhaps, even more fundamentally free speech is a significant personal, psychological and educational good that promotes self expression and creativity and also the autonomy and development of the self necessary for representation in a linguistic and political sense and the formation of identity.

Openness has emerged as a global logic based on free and open source software, constituting a generalized response to knowledge capitalism and the attempt of the new mega-information utilities such as Google, Microsoft, and Amazon.com to control knowledge assets through the process of large-scale digitization, of information often in the public domain, the deployment of digital rights management regimes (May, 2008) and strong government lobbying to enforce intellectual property law in the international context.

The Internet is a dynamic, changing, open ecosystem that progressively changes its nature towards greater computing power, interactivity, inclusiveness, mobility, scale, and peer governance. In this regard and as the overall system develops, it begins to approximate the complexity of the architectures of natural ecosystems. The more it develops, one might be led to hypothesize, the greater the likelihood of not merely emulating Earth as a global ecosystem but becoming an integrated organic whole. Open cultures become the necessary condition for the systems as a whole, for the design of open progressive technological improvements and their political, epistemic and ontological foundations.

The other side of the state and corporate digital reproduction of identity is a tendency that emphasizes the relation between openness and creativity as part of a networked group. The "open self" is self-organizing and is formed at the interstices of a series of membership of online communities that shaped spontaneous self-concept and self-image.

Openness to experience is one of the five major traits that has shaped personality theory since its early development by L.L. Thurstone in the 1930s and is strongly correlated with both creativity and divergent thinking (McCrae, 1987). Sometimes referred to as the "big five" personality traits or "the five factor model," trait theory emerged as a descriptive, data-driven model of personality based on openness, conscientiousness, extraversion, agreeableness, and neuroticism. Openness is associated with creativity and the appreciation of art, emotionality, curiosity, self-expression and originality. Meta-analysis reviewing research that examines the relationships between each of the five-factor model personality dimensions and each of the 10 personality disorder diagnostic categories of the *Diagnostic and*

Statistical Manual of Mental Disorders (4th ed. DSM-IV) reveals strongly positive (with neuroticism) and negative associations (with the other factors) (Saulsman & Page, 2004). One of the limitations of personality theory is its focus on the individual, and in the age of networks this centeredness might seem somewhat misplaced. There are close links between open content, open science and open collaboration that makes collaborative creativity sustainable.

Openness to experience is probably the single most significant variable in explaining creativity, and there is some evidence for the relationship between brain chemistry and creative cognition as measured with divergent thinking (Jung et al., 2009). Openness also can be defined in terms of the number, frequency, and quality of links within a network. Indeed, the mutual reinforcement of openness and creativity gels with Daniel Pink's (2005) contention that right-brainers will rule the future. According to Pink, we are in the transition from an 'Information Age' that valued knowledge workers to a 'Conceptual Age' that values creativity and right-brain-directed aptitudes such as design, story, symphony, empathy, play, and meaning.

Creativity as the New Development Paradigm

The contemporary politics of creativity rests on the intersection between art and politics, tracing the influence between art and labor in the form of co-creativity and peer collaboration and within the new mode of social production. This much, at least in its nascent form, has been recognized now by the United Nations (2008), which acknowledges that there is another reality and narrative emerging that provides an interpretation of 'globalization as connectivity' rather than economic integration or free trade and is 'reshaping the overall pattern of cultural production, consumption and trade in a world increasingly filled with images, sounds, texts and symbols' (.iii).[16] As the 'Overview' of the UN *Creative Economy Report* (2008) clarifies:

> In the contemporary world, a new development paradigm is emerging that links the economy and culture, embracing economic, cultural, technological and social aspects of development at both the macro and micro levels. Central to the new paradigm is the fact that creativity, knowledge and access to information are increasingly recognized as powerful engines driving economic growth and promoting development in a globalizing world. "Creativity" in this context refers to the formulation of new ideas and to the application of these ideas to produce original works of art and cultural products, functional creations, scientific inventions and technological innovations (3).

Rather than accept this mainstream neoclassical economic orientation that endeavors to understand the economic aspect of creativity through its contributions to entrepreneurship, and the ways in which it fosters innovation, enhances productivity and promotes economic growth, one might follow the debates in the literature on 'cognitive capitalism' to focus on labor struggles and begin to interpret this in the light of 'biopolitics' and see it signaling ' the moment that the traditional nation/State dichotomy is overtaken by a political economy of life in general,' where 'power has invested life' to create 'sites of the production of subjectivity,'privileging the 'the transformation of work in the organization of labor'(Negri, 2008: 13–14). Antonio Negri, drawing on both Foucault and Deleuze, investigates the organization of labor under neoliberal globalization and the radical transformation of the production process though new processes of self-regulation and expressive creativity unleashed by information and communication technology that facilitates the rise of what Negri and others call 'immaterial labor' (after Marx's 'general intellect') as the dominant productive force that take place with the development and cultivation of new laboring subjectivities.

A manifesto for education in the age of cognitive capitalism must address the question of new laboring subjectivites and their cultivation, socialization and education. In this case we can take as our starting point the 'creative energy of labor' as Negri (2008: 20) argues:

> In the Fordist era, temporality was measured according to the law of labor value: consequently it concerned an abstract, quantitative, analytic temporality, which, because it was opposed to living labor time, arrived at the composition of the productive value of capital. As it is described by Marx, capitalist production represents the synthesis of the living creativity of labor and of the exploitive structures organized by fixed capital and its temporal laws of productivity. In the era of post-Fordism, on the contrary, temporality is no longer—nor totally—enclosed within the structures of constant capital: as we have seen, intellectual, immaterial, and affective production (which characterizes post-Fordist labor) reveals a surplus. An abstract temporality—that is to say, the temporal *measure* of labor—is incapable of understanding the *creative energy of labor itself* (my emphasis).

Notes

1. Two surrealist manifestos were issued in 1924, written by André Breton, and in 1929, a version supervised by him. There are various online versions including: http://www.tcf.ua.edu/Classes/Jbutler/T340/F98/SurrealistManifesto.htm; and, http://www.tcf.ua.edu/Classes/Jbutler/T340/SurManifesto/ManifestoOfSurrealism.htm.

2. Kiralyfalvi (1990) provides the following genealogical and bibliographical footnote: 'The debate originated with Lukacs's critique of the work of Willi Bredel in *Linkskurve* (1931) and his comments on Ernst Ottwalt's documentary novel (*Denn Sie wissen, Was Sie tun*) in 1932. Lukacs's 1934 essay, "Expressionism: Its Significance and Decline," published in *Internationale Literatur*, sparked a long debate conducted mostly in *Das Wort* until 1939. Those participating in the early debate included Klaus Mann, Alfred Kurella, Klaus Berger, Bêla Balazs, Ernst Bloch, Anna Seghers, Bertolt Brecht and Walter Benjamin. Contributions to the debate by Theodor Adorno, Walter Benjamin, Ernst Bloch and Frederic Jameson can be found in *Aesthetics and Politics* (London: NLB, 1977).'
3. This draws on my paper 'Futures of Philosophy of Education' (Peters, 2009).
4. Feuerbach writes: 'The culmination of modem philosophy is the Hegelian philosophy. The historical necessity and justification of the new philosophy must therefore be derived mainly from a critique of Hegel's.' For his *Principles of Philosophy of the Future* (1843) see http://www.marxists.org/reference/archive/feuerbach/works/future/.
5. See The Project Gutenberg EBook at http://www.gutenberg.org/files/28146/28146-h/28146-h.htm. Translator J. M. Kennedy, February 20, 2009 [EBook #28146].
6. See http://www.geocities.com/thenietzschechannel/um.htm.
7. See e.g., http://www.marxists.org/reference/subject/philosophy/works/ge/nietzsc1.htm.
8. I have addressed this theme a number of times and progressively over the years: see Peters (1998, 2002, 2006), Peters & Marshall (1999), Peters, Marshall & Smeyers (2001).
9. This issue is fundamental to future studies and also my own take: is the 'flow' of time subjective? The philosophy of time has been dominated by disagreements between two views of the nature of temporal reality: one side argues, after John McTaggart, that there is an objective distinction between past, present and futures and the other side argues that there is an objective distinction between earlier and later, but that the experience of the flow of time is an illusion. See e.g., http://plato.stanford.edu/entries/time-thermo/ and http://plato.stanford.edu/entries/time-experience/ . Recently chaos theory has returned to Boltzmann's problem to suggest that 'dynamical chaos is the rule, not the exception, with our world . . . the past is fixed [but] the future remains open and we rediscover the arrow of time' (Coveney and Highfield 1990, pp. 37–8) but see http://www.usyd.edu.au/time/price/preprints/ISST.html.
10. Foucault, following Heidegger, reconceptualises space and time in non-Cartesian terms. The Cartesian mathematical conceptualisation of space and time (as aggregates of points and instants respectively) is replaced by an experiential and ontological understanding of space and time. Foucault goes beyond the traditional dichotomy to speak of these concepts relationally ('spatial time' and 'temporal space') and develops a spatialized history that can no longer be seen as an assemblage of events in linear sequence. He rejects both romantic and teleological history to conceptualise the present in terms of both past and future. As Deleuze (1988: 119) puts it "Thought thinks its own history (the past), but in order to free itself from what it thinks (the present), and be able finally to 'think differently' (the future)."
11. See, for example, the journal *Policy Futures in Education* (established in 2003) http://www.wwwords.co.uk/pfie/index.html (with issues on the knowledge economy, university futures, and Marxist futures); the book series, *Educational Futures: Rethinking*

Theory and Practice http://www.sensepublishers.com/books/edfu/edfu.htm; and, the books, *Futures of Critical Theory: Dreams of Difference* (with Colin Lankshear and Mark Olssen) (2003) and *Edutopias: New Utopian Thinking in Education* (with John Freeman-Moir) (2006).

12. See Lessig's (2001) *The Future of Ideas* and his homepage http://www.lessig.org/, which has useful links to Creative Commons, Electronic Frontier Foundation, Public Knowledge etc. Lessig makes the case for the value of freedom in relation to the future of ideas. As he remarks in his blurb:

    The explosion of innovation we have seen in the environment of the Internet was not conjured from some new, previously unimagined technological magic; instead, it came from an ideal as old as the nation. Creativity flourished there because the Internet protected an innovation commons. The Internet's very design built a neutral platform upon which the widest range of creators could experiment. The legal architecture surrounding it protected this free space so that culture and information—the ideas of our era—could flow freely and inspire an unprecedented breadth of expression. But this structural design is changing–both legally and technically.

    In this regard see also the work of Yochai Benkler at http://www.benkler.org/. He states his research interests in terms of two theoretical problems: Commons-based information production and exchange; and, freedom, justice, and the organization of information production on nonproprietary principles.

13. The history of the concept of academic freedom, basically liberty of thought, while asserted by Socrates, has a recent modern history beginning with the founding of the university at Leiden in 1575 and contemporaneous with the rise of economic liberalism in the sixteenth and seventeenth centuries. Thus, the liberal propietarian concept of freedom has a very complex relationship to the freedom of thought and speech, especially as it was established in relation to the medieval university.

14. See http://freedomdefined.org/Definition.

15. This section draws on 'Open Works, Open Cultures, and Open Learning Systems' (Peters, 2010).

16. See *Creative Economy Report 2008* at http://www.unctad.org/en/docs/ditc20082cer_en.pdf.

References

Bloch, E. (1970) *A Philosophy of the Future*. Translated by John Cumming. New York, Herder & Herder.

Bürger, P. (1984) *Theory of the Avant Garde*. Translated by M. Shaw. Minneapolis: University of Minnesota Press.

Calinescu, M. (1987) 'AvantGarde.' In *Five Faces of Modernity: Modernism, AvantGarde, Decadence, Kitsch, Postmodernism*. Durham: Duke University Press.

Coveney, P. and Highfield, R. (1990) *The Arrow of Time*, London: W. H. Allen.

Deleuze, G. & Guattari, F. (1994) *What Is Philosophy?* New York: Verso.

Deleuze, G. (1988) *Foucault* Translated by Dean Hard, Minneapolis: University of Minnesota Press.

Elden, S. E. (2001) *Mapping the Present: Heidegger Foucault and the Project of a Spatial History*, London: Continuum Press.
Feuerbach, L. (1966) *Principles of the Philosophy of the Future*, translated with an introduction by Manfred H. Vogel, Library of Liberal Arts. Indianapolis: Bobbs-Merrill.
Greenberg, C. (1939) Avant-Garde and Kitsch. *Partisan Review*, 6 (5): 34–49. At http://www.sharecom.ca/greenberg/kitsch.html.
Hayek, F.A. (1960) *The Constitution of Liberty*. Chicago: University of Chicago Press.
Jung, J. (1998) The Future of Philosophy, Twentieth World Congress of Philosophy, Boston, August 10–15, at http://www.bu.edu/wcp/MainCont.htm.
Jung, R. E., Gasparovic, C., Chavez, R. S., Flores, R. A., Smith, S. M., Capriha, A., & Yeo, R. A. (2009) Biochemical Support for the "Threshold" Theory of Creativity: A Magnetic Resonance Spectroscopy Study. *The Journal of Neuroscience*, 29(16): 5319–5325.
Kiralyfalvi, B. (1990) The Aesthetic Effect: A Search for Common Grounds Between Brecht and Lukacs, *Journal of Dramatic Theory and Criticism*, Spring.
Lessig, L. (2001) *The Future of Ideas: The Fate of the Commons in a Connected World*, New York: Random House.
Marginson, S., Murphy, P. & Peters, M. A. (2009) *Global Creation: Space, Connection and Universities in the Age of the Knowledge Economy*. New York: Peter Lang.
May, C. (2008) Globalizing the Logic of Openness: Open Source Software and the Global Governance of Intellectual Property. In A. Chadwick & P. N. Howard (Eds.), *Handbook of Internet Politics*. London: Routledge.
McCrae, R. R. (1987) Creativity, Divergent Thinking, and Openness to Experience. *Journal of Personality and Social Psychology*, 52, 1258–1265.
Murphy, P., Peters, M. A. & Marginson, S. (2010) *Imagination: Three Models of Imagination in the Age of the Knowledge Economy*. New York: Peter Lang.
Negri, Antonio (2008) The Labor of the Multitude and the Fabric of Biopolitics. Translated by Sara Mayo, Peter Graefe and Mark Coté. Ed. Mark Coté. *Mediations* 23.2 (Spring 2008), 8–25. Retrieved from www.mediationsjournal.org/the-labor-of-the-multitude-andthe-fabric-of-biopolitics.
Nietzsche, F. (1907). *Beyond Good and Evil*. Trans. H. Zimmern. London: Macmillan.
Nietzsche, F. (1966) *Beyond Good and Evil*. Trans. W. Kaufmann. New York: Viking Press.
Nietzsche, F. (1989) *Human, All-Too-Human*. Translated by R. J. Hollingdale. Cambridge: Cambridge University Press.
Peters, M. A. (2000) Nietzsche, Nihilism and the Critique of Modernity: Post-Nietzschean Philosophy of Education, *Proceedings of 7th Biennial Conference of the International Network of Philosophers of Education*, University of Sydney, 2000: 88–96. Translated into Polish, *Kwartainik Pedagogiczny*, Warsaw University, 191–192, (1–2), 2004: 103–118.
Peters, M. A. (2001) Gilles Deleuze's 'Societies of Control': From Disciplinary Pedagogy to Perpetual Training, *The Review of Education/Pedagogy/Cultural Studies*, 23, 4.
Peters, M. A. (2002) Geofilosophia, Educação e Pedagogia do Conceito, *Educação & Realidade*, 27 (2) July-December: 77–88. Translated from the Portuguese by Tomaz Tadeu da Silva.
Peters, M. A. (2002) Nietzsche's Educational Legacy Revisited. A Response to Professor Rosenow *Studies in Philosophy and Education* 23 (2–3): 203–209.
Peters, M. A. (2006) Lyotard, Nihilism and Education, *Studies in Philosophy and Education*, 25(4): 303–314

Peters, M. A. (2009) Futures of Philosophy of Education, *Analysis and Metaphysics*, 7:13–25
Peters, M. A. (2010) Open Works, Open Cultures, and Open Learning Systems, in Timothy W. Lukes & Jeremy Hunsinger (eds.), *Putting Knowledge to Work and Letting Information Play: The Center for Digital Discourse and Culture*, Blacksburg: Virginia Tech, Center for Digital Discourse and Culture: 75–99.
Peters, M. A. & Besley, A.C. (2006) Postscript: Freedom and Knowledge Cultures. In: *Building Knowledge Cultures: Education and Development in the Age of Knowledge Capitalism*, Lanham, Boulder, New York, Toronto, Oxford: Rowman & Littlefield.
Peters, M. A. & Besley, T. (2006) *Building Knowledge Cultures: Education and Development in the Age of Knowledge Capitalism*. Lanham, Boulder, New York, Oxford, Rowman & Littlefield.
Peters, M. A. & Besley, T. (2010) The Narrative Turn and the Poetics of Resistance: Towards a New Language for Critical Educational Studies, in *The Possibility/Impossibility of a New Critical Language in Education*, Ilan Gur-Ze'ev (ed.), Rotterdam: Sense, pp. 261–274.
Peters, M. A., J. Marshall & P. Smeyers (2001) (Eds.) *Nietzsche's Legacy for Education: Past and Present Values*, Westport, CT. & London: Bergin & Garvey.
Peters, M. A., Murphy, P. & Marginson, S. (2009) *Creativity and the Global Knowledge Economy*. New York: Peter Lang.
Peters, M. A. & Roberts, P. (2010) *The Virtues of Openness*. Boulder: Paradigm Publishers.
Pink, D. (2005) *A Whole New Mind: Why Right-Brainers Will Rule the Future*. New York: Penguin.
Poggioli, R. (1981). *The Theory of the Avant-Garde*. Translated from the Italian by Gerald Fitzgerald. Cambridge, New Haven: Belknap Press of Harvard University Press.
Puchner, M. (2005) *Poetry of the Revolution: Marx, Manifestos and the Avant-Gardes*. Princeton: Princeton University Press.
Saulsman, L. M. & Page, A. C. (2004) The Five-factor Model and Personality Disorder Empirical Literature: A Meta-analytic Review. *Clinical Psychology Review*, 23, 1055–1085.
Staler, F. (2004) *Open Cultures and the Nature of Networks*. Retrieved from http://felix.openflows.com/pdf/Notebook_eng.pdf.
United Nations (2008) *Creative Economy Report*. At http://www.unctad.org/en/docs/ditc20082cer_en.pdf.

Contributors

Ergin Bulut is a doctoral student at the University of Illinois at Urbana-Champaign in the department of Educational Policy Studies. He received his Bachelor's degree from the Department of Translation and Interpreting and gained his Master's from The Ataturk Institute for Modern Turkish History, both at Bogazici University. His research interests broadly include critical theory, political economy, labor and education. He has published on subjects including education and cultural studies, cognitive capitalism, and child labor in Turkey. He has translatied of people including Michael Apple and Aijaz Ahmad among others. He is currently working on an edited volume about digital labor and cognitive capitalism.

Rodrigo G. Britez is a doctoral student in Educational Policy Studies at the University of Illinois at Urbana-Champaign. His major research interests include globalization and education policy, higher education policy in South America, and networks of governance in higher education policy. He is currently working on issues relating to social networks and the role of transnational agencies in policy processes in higher education.

Matthew Crain is a doctoral candidate in the Institute of Communications Research at the University of Illinois, Urbana-Champaign. His research centers on political and cultural economies of media and communications with a focus on the Internet and emerging technologies. His work has been published in the *International Journal of Communication* and the *Rocky Mountain Communication Review*. A departmental steward for the Graduate Employee's Organization, he was an organizer in the union's successful work action to secure a more equitable labor contract for Illinois graduate employees in late 2009. At Illinois, Matthew teaches courses in digital media and media economics and is a researcher with the Project on Public Policy and Advanced Communications Technology. In summer 2009 he was a participant in the Annenberg-Oxford Summer Institute on Global Media Policy.

Steven Doran is a doctoral candidate in the Institute of Communications Research at the University of Illinois Urbana-Champaign. He received a BA in Psychology from the University of Calgary as well as an MA in Humanities from York University. Steven's research looks at questions that fall broadly within technology studies, critical theory, cultural studies, and social theory. He presented on the cultural production of mobile telephony at the 2009 National Communications Association annual convention and is presently concerned with how communications technologies figure into contemporary forms of rule with a focus on neoliberalism and Foucauldian governmentality. Steven is currently a fellow with the Humanities, Arts, Science and Technology Advanced Collaboraty (HASTAC), an inter-university scholarly initiative centered on research in the digital humanities.

James Geary is a doctoral candidate in Educational Policy Studies at the University of Illinois at Urbana-Champaign. He received his M.Ed. from the same university in Global Studies in Education, writing extensively about education and culture in Taiwan where he lived and taught for ten years. His current research interests include the theory of secularization, spirituality in education, and concepts of global humanity and global citizenship.

Heather Greenhalgh-Spencer is the Harry F. Broudy Scholar in the Department of Educational Policy Studies at the University of Illinois in Urbana-Champaign. She is currently a Ph.D. candidate within the Philosophy of Education track and is also working towards a Ph.D. Certification in Gender and Women's Studies. Heather has also obtained Bachelor's Degrees in English and Education Studies. She earned a Master's Degree in Education, Culture, and Society from the University of Utah. Heather is a certified teacher and has taught at the secondary level for several years. Heather's work on identity construction and performance of the White Expert has appeared in *Borderlands*, an international peer-reviewed journal. Heather has also presented work on identity performativity and on performativity in educational coalition-building at several international conferences. Heather's current work focuses on the body; the way the body performs, the ways the body takes up knowledge/learning in various spaces/modalities but also on the body as a phenomenological concern. Her work draws from performativity theory, post-humanism, Continental phenomenology, and technology studies. Heather draws inspiration for her work on learning and the body both as an Instructor for the Social Foundations of Education Course and as a yoga teacher.

Stephen Hocker is a doctoral candidate in the Institute of Communications Research at the University of Illinois Urbana-Champaign. He received a BA in American Studies and Psychology from the University of New Mexico as well as an MA in Communication from Annenberg School for Communication at the University of Pennsylvania. He is currently the managing editor for the journal *Communication Theory* as well as The *Encyclopedia of Identity* due out from Sage in 2010. Stephen's research addresses the representation of non-normative gender identities in media as well as the tactics and strategies deployed by various movements in order to resist them. He is both a scholar and an activist interested in understanding the intersections of gender non-conformity in relation to racial, class, sexual, disability and national social formations within an increasingly global and digital media environment.

Douglas Kellner is George Kneller Chair in the Philosophy of Education at UCLA and is author of many books on social theory, politics, history, and culture, including *Camera Politica: The Politics and Ideology of Contemporary Hollywood Film*, co-authored with Michael Ryan and an Emile de Antonio reader co-edited with Dan Streible. Other works include *Critical Theory, Marxism, and Modernity; Jean Baudrillard: From Marxism to Postmodernism and Beyond*; works in cultural studies such as *Media Culture and Media Spectacle*; a trilogy of books on postmodern theory with Steve Best; and a trilogy of books on the media and the Bush administration, encompassing *Grand Theft 2000, From 9/11 to Terror War*, and *Media Spectacle and the Crisis of Democracy*. Author of *Herbert Marcuse and the Crisis of Marxism*, Kellner is editing the collected papers of Herbert Marcuse, four volumes of which have appeared with Routledge. Kellner's *Guys and Guns Amok: Domestic Terrorism and School Shootings from the Oklahoma City Bombings to the Virginia Tech Massacre* won the

2008 AESA award as the best book on education. In 2010, he published with Blackwell *Cinema Wars: Hollywood Film and Politics in the Bush/Cheney Era.* Kellner's website is at http://www.gseis.ucla.edu/faculty/kellner/kellner.html

Jungmin Kwon holds a Bachelor of Arts in International Relations and Communication and a Master's degree in Communication from Seoul National University. She is currently researching media and cultural studies at the Institute of Communications Research at the University of Illinois, Urbana-Champaign. At Illinois, she has worked on projects dealing with the relationship of the cultural industries to Korean women in their 20s and 30s. She is particularly interested in how women's media use and consumption culture has been commodified by the media industries. For this work, her project is situated in their consumption of queer media artifacts. She aims to historicize a process of how media capital transforms young females from voluntary producers of queer contents to passive audiences of those mediated texts, and she hopes to produce an institutional approach to gender culture. With Professor Yeran Kim, she has co-authored "Identification in Mobile Visualization—A Cultural Approach," which appeared in the journal *Media and Society*, as well as the book chapter, "Identity as Everyday 'Taking' and 'Being': A Cultural Approach to Production and Management of Digital Images," which appeared in *Gender, Migration, the Mobile Play* (Hanul Publishing Company, 2008).

Alice Liao received her BA in English from National Taiwan University and her MA in Film Studies from Boston University. She is the editorial assistant of *Critical Studies in Media Communication*. Her current research focuses on identity formation in media, both popular and independent. Specifically, she analyzes the discourses of queer identities and politics during historically representative moments, including the Stonewall riot, the assassination of Harvey Milk, the AIDS epidemics, the murder of Matthew Shepard, and the melée surrounding California's Proposition Eight, et cetera. Her work on these cases reveals that discourse functions paradoxically to advance queer visibility and rights-oriented political campaigns but simultaneously to privilege mainstream gay politics over alternative and grassroots queer politics. The overall goal of these projects is to reconceptualize identities and their effects and thereby to make imaginable alternative cross-group coalitional strategies and non-legal-based political efficacy. Her other areas of interest include queer theory, film theory, post-humanism, new media, and avant-garde cinema.

Cameron McCarthy teaches mass communications theory and cultural studies at the University of Illinois at Urbana-Champaign. He is University Scholar and Communications Scholar in the Department of Educational Policy

Studies. Cameron also holds appointments in the Institute of Communications Research and in the Unit for Criticism and Interpretive Theory at the University of Illinois. He has been a visiting scholar and lecturer at Jesus College, the University of Cambridge, York University, the University of Western Ontario, the University of Newcastle, Monash University, the University of Salamanca, Spain, and the University of Queensland. He has published widely on topics related to postcolonialism, problems with neoMarxist writings on race and education, institutional support for teaching, and school ritual and adolescent identities in journals such as *Harvard Educational Review, Oxford Review of Education, The British Journal of the Sociology of Education*, and the *European Journal of Cultural Studies in Education* among many others. Cameron has authored or co-authored many books such as: *Race and Curriculum* (Falmer Press, 1990), *Multicultural Curriculum: New Directions for Social Theory, Practice and Policy* (Routledge, 2000), and *Reading and Teaching the Postcolonial: From Baldwin to Basquiat and Beyond* (Teachers College Press, Columbia University, 2001). With his graduate students, Cameron has published a number of books such as *Foucault, Cultural Studies and Governmentality* (SUNY Press, 2003) and *Race, Identity and Representation in Education* (Routledge, 2005). He co-edited the collection, *Globalizing Cultural Studies*, which was published by Peter Lang (2007). His most recent book (co-edited with Cathryn Teasley of the University of A Coruña, Galicia) is *Transnational Perspectives on Culture, Policy, and Education: Redirecting Cultural Studies in Neoliberal Times* (Peter Lang, 2009). With Angharad Valdivia, Cameron is co-editor of the "Intersections in Communication and Culture" book series at Peter Lang and the Institute of Communications Research at the University of Illinois. He is also one of the Senior Editors of Lang's Global Studies in Education book series. Last academic year, Cameron was a distinguished visiting professor in the Department of English and Communications Studies at the Saint Louis University of Madrid, Madrid, Spain.

Robert Mejia is a doctoral candidate in the Institute of Communications Research at the University of Illinois, Urbana-Champaign. His research interests coalesce around problems of the epistemological-ontological relationship. In essence, he is concerned with how epistemological claims work to bring about their own materiality and, in turn, how the excess of the ontological marks all knowledge claims as an exercise in struggle. He has published in the *Rocky Mountain Communication Review* on the topic of performance ethnography, as a place where the ontological and epistemological meet in the triangulated gaze of the performer, subject, and audience to create a potent space for activism. He considers himself an instructor first, and a researcher second; his passion for scholarly work is driven by his love for his students. He has taught courses in argumentation, public speaking, popular culture, and currently the introduction to media studies course at Illinois.

Michael A. Peters is Professor of Education at the University of Illinois at Urbana-Champaign and Adjunct Professor in the School of Art, Royal Melbourne Institute of Technology (RMIT). He is the executive editor of *Educational Philosophy and Theory* and editor of two international ejournals, *Policy Futures in Education* and *E-Learning and Digital Media*. His interests are in education, philosophy and social policy and he has written over fifty books, including most recently the trilogy *Creativity and the Global Knowledge Economy* (2009) *Global Creation: Space, Connection and Universities in the Age of the Knowledge Economy* (2010), *Imagination: Three Models of Imagination in the Age of the Knowledge Economy* (2010) (with Simon Marginson & Peter Murphy); *Subjectivity and Truth: Foucault, Education and the Culture of the Self* (2008) (AESA Critics Book Award 2009), and *Building Knowledge Cultures: Educational and Development in the Age of Knowledge Capitalism* (2006), both with Tina (A.C.) Besley.

Viviana Pitton is a doctoral student in Educational Policy Studies at the University of Illinois at Urbana-Champaign. She holds a BA in Sociology from the Universidad Nacional de Cuyo and an Ed.M. in Educational Policy Studies from the University of Illinois at Urbana-Champaign. Viviana has published on topics related to neoliberalism, globalization and higher education in journals such as *Policy Futures in Education, Discourse: Studies in the Cultural Politics of Education* and *Critical Studies in Education*. Her main research interest is focused on the effects of global processes on education, with a particular emphasis on the neoliberalization of educational policy discourses and practices in Latin American countries. She is also interested in comparative and international education, critical policy analysis and discourse theory.

Carolyn A. Randolph is a doctoral student in the Institute of Communications Research at the University of Illinois, Urbana-Champaign where she instructs Popular Culture and Sex & Gender in Media. She holds a B.A. in English and Communication & Culture from Indiana University. Her interdisciplinary scholarship significantly contributes to the fields of communications research, gender and women's studies, and Africana studies. Specifically, her work foregrounds the intersectionality of race, gender, class, and sexuality with an emphasis on representation and identity. Carolyn is currently working on an interpretive qualitative study that explores the contemporary representation of Black American women living with HIV and AIDS. Specifically, her project intervenes in the under-representation of Black American women living with HIV/AIDS in the popular imaginary while broadly adding to our understanding of how human actors—interacting with/in various institutions—define and redefine social reality.

Crystal Thomas holds a MFA in Fiction from Indiana University-Bloomington and is currently a doctoral student in English at the University of Illinois at Urbana-Champaign. Her research and creative work focus on the relationship between representation and resistance in literature and housing justice struggles, and particularly how neoliberal policies and metaphors impact the strategies of the displaced. Her interests include African American, immigrant, and "city" fiction; critical theory; and film. She has published an essay on Cabrini Green and Chicago's *Plan for Transformation* in *Ninth Letter* literary magazine and is currently assisting with an ethnographic project to interview men affected by housing displacement.

Index

Abbate, J., 110
Abramowitz, R., 183, 188
Academia, 10, 33, 37, 39–40, 42–44, 52, 58, 64–65, 70–76, 81, 110, 152, 258, 277, 291, 354, 356–357, 361
   Adjunct Faculty, 25, 40–41, 46
   Concept-Fetishism, 41–43, 46, 295
   Departments, 41, 96–98, 151
   Graduate Students, 25, 40–41, 46
   See also Educational Policy
Adam, G. S., 38–39, 110
Adorno, T. W., 27, 30, 45, 62, 66, 360
Advancing Basic Education and Literacy Project (ABEL), 316
Aesthetics, 8, 30, 53, 61–62, 87–88, 164, 246, 349–352, 360
African Americans, 81, 91–92, 153–154, 156, 168, 174, 176–177, 183–184, 230–231, 235, 241–244, 246
   See also Blacks
Agency, 30–32, 52–61, 63–65, 74, 77, 238–240, 245–246, 248, 295, 342
   See also Resistance

Ahmed, S., 168
Aizura, A. Z., 153
Albo, G., 284
Alcaniz, M., 269
Alcántara, A., 321
Alexander, M. J., 242
Alonso, M., 319
Alpert, J., 111
Althusser, L., 44, 266, 337–338
Amazon (Company), 2, 357
Ambinder, M., 139
America's Next Top Model, 162
Andrejevic, M., 58, 66
Aneesh, A., 304
Anyon, J., 92
Anzaldúa, G., 150, 167, 257
Appadurai, A., 256, 331, 339, 342–343
Apple, M. W., 277
Araujo, G., 162
Arnold, M., 28–30
Aronowitz, S., 279
Arvidsson, A., 61
Associated Press, 246

American Telephone & Telegraph (AT&T), 66, 120, 129
Audre Lorde Project (ALP), 149, 156, 160–161, 164–166
Aune, J. A., 279
Australia, 96, 289
Ayers, D. F., 293, 304

Báez, J. M., 76
Balibar, E., 39
Balkan, E. M., 277
Ball, S. J., 291, 310–311
Balzac, H., 94
Bansel, P., 9–11, 287, 292
Barak, A., 207, 221
Barber, B., 296
Barboza, D., 125
Bar-Ilan, J., 108
Baron, N. S., 117
Barry, A., 135, 281–282
Basu, R., 284
Battelle, J., 111, 121
Baudrillard, J., 332–334
Bauman, Z., 7, 9, 16, 56, 87, 93, 99, 101, 296, 331, 336, 338, 345
Baznik, D., 221
Bealieu, A., 150
Beauchamp, T., 162
Beck, G., 96
Beck, U., 1, 89
Behr, R., 248
Beller, J., 61
Ben-Amos, I., 51
Benjamin, W., 26, 30, 45, 59, 64, 66, 256, 265
Benkler, Y., 2, 361
Bensing, A., 230, 249
Benwell, B., 197, 219
Berger, A. A., 330–331, 336–337, 339, 341, 344, 347
Berman, M., 65
Bérubé, M., 41
Biber, J., 221
Birkerts, S., 117

Bitzer, L., 23
BlackBerry (cell phone), 130, 137–138
Black Entertainment Television, 78
Blacks, 8, 91
　Black Americans, 71, 73–82, 88
　See also HIV/AIDS
Bloch, E., 352, 360
Bobo, J., 76
Bodroghkozy, A., 36, 40
Body, the, 5, 12, 26, 32, 59, 65, 71, 76, 78, 151, 154–155, 157, 159, 197–198, 210, 232, 240, 245, 247
　Biology, 51, 71, 74, 78–79, 164
　Discipline, 72–73, 151, 155, 241–242
　Performance, 218, 254–272
Bohm, A.D., 291
Bolivia, 120
Bonsu, S., 57
Booth, D. L., 108
Borda, D., 304
Borders, 7, 9, 115, 148–149, 157–160, 166–167, 219, 291, 306, 330
　Theorizing the, 150–151, 166–167
Bourdieu, P., 152, 279
Bowe, R., 291
boyd, d., 56, 59, 65
BP, 115
Brah, A., 71
Brandzel, A. L., 230, 242
Braverman, H., 125
Brin, S., 120, 125
British Cultural Marxism, 27, 31–32
　Communist Party Historians Group (CPHG), 30–31
　See also Cultural Studies
British Literary Theory, 27–30
　See also Cultural Studies
British Popular Front, 30–31, 44
Bronzeville, 92
Brown, M., 77–78
Brown, W., 5, 9, 25, 163, 173–174, 179, 188
Buchanan, J., 288
Buchanan, W., 171
Buchert, L., 313–314

Buck–Morss, S., 66
Bui, D.-M., 76
Burbules, N., 263
Burchell, G., 281–283
Bürger, P., 351
Burke, K., 25
Burnett, V., 101
Bush, G. W., 115
Butler, J., 151, 172, 259, 266
Byrne, B., 259, 266
Byther-Smith, I. W., 80

Caballero, W., 322
Caballero-Munoz, D., 130
Cabral, A., 41
Calhoun, C., 152
Calinescu, M., 351
Campbell, C., 55, 60
Campbell, J. L., 279
Canaan, J. E., 277
Canadian School, the, 37–38
   See also Innis, H.; McLuhan, M.
Cantor, N., 96–98, 101
Capital/Capitalism, 28–29, 45, 54–59, 62, 64–66, 121–122, 125, 150–152, 158, 161, 163, 166, 173, 231, 245–248, 271, 304–305, 329, 332–334, 336–337, 341, 345–346
   Cultural, 334, 336–337, 341, 345–346
   Digital/Informationalized, 53–63, 66, 107–109, 119–124, 130, 349–361
   Finance, 6–9, 11, 87, 92, 152–153, 158, 343–344
   Flexible, x, 3, 7–10, 12, 87, 89–90, 99, 163, 296–297
   Human, 12, 14, 66, 122, 151, 158, 343–344
   Late, 11, 13, 62, 88, 90, 279–292, 296
   Social, 11, 41–42, 98, 152, 158, 154
   Symbolic, 41, 152, 158, 162, 167, 171, 231, 247
   See Neoliberalism
Caputo, A., 230, 249
Carby, H., 79

Carey, J., 1–2, 16, 25, 33, 36–40, 42–43, 46, 109–110, 116, 256
Caribbean, 8, 91–92
Carlone, D., 293–294
Carney, T., 288
Carnoy, M., 285, 290
Cassell, J., 61, 196
Castells, M., 55, 110, 148, 304–305
Census (U.S.), 73, 251
Center for Disease Control and Prevention (CDC), 70, 77, 79
Centro Paraguayo de Estudios Sociologicos (CPES), 316
Chae, H., 207, 224
Chakrabarty, D., 12
Chang, M., 114, 213
Chaskin, R. J., 231–232
Chen-Chuan Chang, K., 114
Chester, J., 122
Chiancone Castro, A., 324
Chicago, City of, 80, 88, 90–95, 229–251
   Department of Cultural Affairs, 92–92
   Housing Authority (CHA), 92, 229–250
   Legends South, 91–92, 248
   Millennium Park, 86, 96
   Mixed–Income Housing, 229–230, 236–237, 243–244, 248
   "Plan for Transformation," 233–239, 242–245
   Public Schools (CPS), 86, 91, 101
   Robert Taylor Homes, 91, 101, 234, 248, 250
   Southside, 91–92
Chicago, Commercial Club of (Commercial Club) 86, 91, 100, 230–231, 246
   Chicago Metropolis 2020, 91, 100, 230–233, 241–243, 247
   Left Behind, 86, 91, 100
   Renaissance 2010, 86, 91, 101
Chicago, University of Illinois (UIC), 94–95
   Strategic Plan Version 1.3 ("Access to Excellence"), 94–95

Chicago School, the, 34, 36, 45–46
  See also Dewey, J.
China, 115, 125, 139
Choi, S., 220–221
Chomsky, N., 279
Chubb, J., 288
Citizenship, 8, 10–12, 14, 70, 73–74, 94, 97, 99, 118, 138–146, 148, 229–230, 238, 244, 246, 278, 285, 296
  and the Body, 151, 157–163, 165–166
  Neoliberal, 130–135, 136–140, 142–146, 163, 240–243, 246–247, 278, 282, 285–286, 289, 296
  See also REAL ID Act
City, theorizing the, 87–94, 96, 99, 238, 247
  "Knowledge City," 87, 96
  See also Chicago, City of
Civil Rights, 38–39, 75, 80, 95, 172–174, 180, 185–187, 243–244
  See also Movements
Clarke, J., 10, 231, 241–242, 246–247, 278, 280, 294, 297
Class, x–xi, 1, 11–12, 28, 30–32, 51–52, 54, 56, 64, 71–76, 78, 80, 81, 87–90, 98, 125, 150, 153, 155, 166, 167, 173, 175, 179, 196, 244, 246–247, 288, 296, 333, 335–339, 343
  Middle, 11, 54, 66, 80, 89, 91–92, 94, 96, 100, 122, 152–153, 155, 158, 160, 167, 168, 229–230, 240, 242–243, 297
  Upper, x, 71, 160, 229, 280
  Working, 4–6, 8, 27–32, 39, 52, 71, 88, 91–92, 96, 101, 153, 159, 168, 177, 231–232, 240, 242–243, 246–247, 250, 351
Clinton, H., 184, 208, 224
Cober, A., 221
Cohen, R., 279, 296
Colás, A., 292
Cold War, 110
Cole, N. K., 92
Cole, R., 185
Collins, P., 73, 78

Comaroff, J, 7, 89, 91, 96
Comaroff, J. L., 7, 89, 91, 96
Comisión Nacional para la Reforma de la Educación Superior (CNRES), 313, 317–318
Commodities, 54, 59, 61–64, 78, 96, 329
  Audience, 36, 120–122
  Commodification, 8, 53–56, 59–60, 66, 90, 109, 124–125, 163, 284, 291, 293, 351
  Fetish, 62–64
  User, 108, 118–122, 124
Communications Research, 1–5, 33–36, 38–40, 45, 61, 107, 148, 197, 256, 291, 304
Communications Technologies, 2–4, 33–34, 38, 107, 148, 256, 291, 304
  Broadcasting, 5, 7, 29–30, 58, 66, 100, 111–114, 116, 121, 135, 162–163, 213–214
  Internet, 2–3, 14, 54, 57–58, 63, 65, 100, 107–126, 139, 145, 196–202, 205, 218–224, 232, 245, 248, 255, 261–272, 357, 361
  Photography, 87–88, 98, 139–140, 195–196, 201–203, 206–208, 210–212, 214–217, 220, 222–223, 234–236, 238, 246, 249
  Print, 33, 66, 112–114, 244
  Telegraph, 33–34
  Telephony, 5, 129–131, 135–146
Communism, 6, 29–30, 36, 115, 139, 157, 160, 282
  Russian Communist Party, 29
  See also British Cultural Marxism; Marxism
Consejo Asesor de la Reforma Educativa (CARE), 312, 315–318
Consejo de Universidades (CU), 321
Consejo Nacional de Educación y Cultura (CONEC), 308, 321
Coalition Politics, 44, 149, 155–157, 159–162, 164–167, 172–188, 243–244, 250

Consumerism, 27, 53–58, 60–61, 63, 65, 91, 96, 117, 120, 145, 164, 188, 205, 213, 248, 284, 287, 289, 296, 343, 345, 351
    Consumption, 5, 8, 11, 29, 36, 45, 52–58, 61–62, 64–65, 78, 91, 118, 121, 130, 134, 212, 248, 296, 329, 332–333, 335, 342–343, 345, 356, 358
Cook, I., 199
Cooley, C., 33, 45
Cooper, J., 197
Cote, M., 59
Courant, P., 96–98, 101
Coveney, P., 360
Cultural Studies, x–xi, 5–6, 13, 24–26, 39–44, 61, 63–65, 76, 88, 149, 232, 247, 344
    British Cultural Studies, ix, 26–33, 38–39, 44–45, 52–53, 64
    U.S. Cultural Studies, 33–39, 46
Culture, defined, 71, 152, 295, 331, 335, 344–345
    Convergence, 57
    as Ritual, 37
    and Society, 28–30, 44
    as Strategy, 87, 100
    Subcultures, 52–53
    See also DCinside
Curran, J., 2, 6, 25, 38, 40, 53
Cyberspace, 14, 125, 197–198, 200–202, 207, 213, 219, 221, 224
    Community / Culture, x, 7, 63, 195–196, 200–202, 204–205, 212, 218–219
    Cyber–Masculinity, 196–225
    Dark Web, 114
    Digital Divide, 197, 235
    See also DCinside; Virtual
Czitrom, D., 33, 35

Dakopoulou, A., 283, 285
Dale, R., 10
Daley, R. M., Mayor, 86
Danet, B., 218

Darmody, A., 57
Datamonitor (Company), 120
Daumier, H., 94
Davidson–Harden, A., 290–291
Davies, B., 10–11, 292
Davis, D. A., 11
Davis, J., 177, 180
DCinside, 195–196, 200–225
    Composite Gallery, 202–203, 214, 216, 222
    Ddalnyeo, 204, 208, 212–213
    Gwangnyeo, 195, 204, 208, 211–212
    Halnyeo, 208, 224
    Harrington, B., 216–217
    Hong, S., 214–217, 220, 225
    Nyeo, defined, 195, 208
    Pae-in, 201–203, 206–225
    Requisites, defined, 203
    Sophitia, 208–212
    Young, S., 216–217, 225
de Beauvoir, S., 259
de Certeau, M., 166
de Peuter, G., 55
de Saussure, F., 334
Dean, M., 133, 232, 239–241, 246
DeCarava, R., 87–88, 98–99
Deleuze, G., 99, 271–272, 359–360
Dell (Company), 120
Democracy, 3, 8, 14, 33, 36, 58, 64, 75, 81, 114, 130, 140, 144, 183–186, 196, 200, 230, 245, 279, 282, 289, 311, 313, 315–316, 319, 354
    Critical, 34–37, 97, 202, 219, 223, 244, 356–357
    See also Citizenship
Dening, G., 24, 26
Derrida, J., 175, 186
Deuze, M., 7, 97, 111, 148
Dewey, J., 36–37, 42–43
Diaz, J., 141–142
Dill, B. T., 75
Dilthey, W., 99
Dimitriadis, G., 64, 99
Dirlik, A., 58, 61

Dixon, T., 80
Dolby, N., 7, 64, 96
Dolowitz, D. P., 304
Doverspike, D., 221
Dowling, E., 66
Dowling, R. M., 231
Downes, D., 52
Downing, J. D. H., 41–42
Doxtader, E., 24
Drescher, J., 183
Dreyfus, H., 260
Du Bois, W. E. B., 36
Du Gay, P., 16, 175
Duggan, L., 11–12
Durham, A., 76
Durham, M.G., 76
Dworkin, D., 27–31, 44–45, 64
Dwyer, J., 139
Dyer-Witheford, N., 54–55, 60, 66
Dyson, M., 74

Eco, U., 333–334
Educational Policy
    See Pedagogy; Policy
Eliot, T. S., 28–30
Ellis, C., 257
Ellul, J., 3
Employment Non–Discrimination Act (ENDA), 155
England
    Tyneside, Newcastle, 8, 91
Entman, R., 80
Erkiliç, T. A., 277
Esposito, J., 159
Ethnicity, 7–8, 11–12, 70–82, 89, 91–92, 98, 100, 150, 155, 157, 164–165, 177, 180, 229, 240–241, 247, 287–288
    New Ethnicities, 172, 174–175, 180, 183–185
    See also Race
Ethnography, 150, 153–155, 282
    Auto-, 257
E-Trade, 137–138
European Union Directive Number 24 of 2006, 140–142
Evans, M., 304–305, 309

Fairclough, N., 150, 152, 204–205, 232–233, 237, 246–247
Fallows, D., 112, 122–123
Fazio, M. V., 304
Feinstein, D., 181
Fellow Traveler, 156–157, 160, 164
    Website, 157
Ferguson, R., 152, 154, 167, 175
Fernback, J., 197–198
Fiske, E. B., 288
Fiske, J., 52
Fitzsimmons, E. G., 249
Fleming, D., 232, 237, 243
Ford, F., 33
Fortune 500, 90
Foster, S., 260
Foucault, M., 7, 25–26, 43, 63, 72–73, 149, 323, 354, 359–360
    Bio-Power, 232, 241, 287, 359
    Discipline, 72, 171–173, 241–242, 266–267
    Governmentality, 131–135, 232, 239–241, 281–283, 296
Frank, T., 61
Frankfurt School, 27–28, 30, 35, 44–46, 55, 351
Franzen, B., 4
Frasca, G., 2
Fraser, N., 24, 196–197, 205
Fredrick, C., 197
Freedom of Speech/Expression, 196, 202, 221–224, 350, 354–357, 361
Freud, S., 331, 339–340, 350
Friedman, E., 115
Friedman, M., 280
Friedman, T. 94
Fuchs, C., 58, 66
Fukuyama, F., 57
Fun/Parody Culture, 2, 59, 195–196, 200–205, 208, 214–215, 218, 219–224
    See DCinside

INDEX

Gadamer, H., 99
Gamboa, M., 305
Gamson, J., 162, 172, 174
Gamson, W., 174
Garau, M., 269
Garber, M., 151
Garcia, A., 284
Garcia-Montes, J. M., 130
Garnham, N., 40–41
General Agreement on Trade in Services (GATS), 291
Geertz, C., 36–37, 46
Gender, x–xi, 11–12, 51, 56, 61–62, 71–82, 90, 115–116, 148, 150–152, 155–156, 160, 162, 164, 167, 173, 175, 179, 196–200, 202, 204–225, 287–288
    Non-Conformity, 149–151, 153–157, 159, 162–164, 166–168
    See also Cyberspace; Transgendered
GenderPAC (GPAC), 155
Gentrification, 87, 89, 177
    Gentrifiers, 230, 248
Gershberg, A., 288
Geser, H., 130
Gewirtz, S., 291
Giardina, M., 88
Gibson, W., 267
Giddens, A., 260
Gillespie, T., 66
Gilman, S., 78
Gilroy, P., 32, 76
Ginzburg, C., 24
Gitelman, L., 4
Gledhill, J., 295
Globalization, 6, 8–10, 53, 64, 70, 77, 87–97, 99–101, 108, 111, 116, 132, 148–149, 152, 163, 199, 277–278, 283–297, 303–306, 310–325, 343–344, 347, 356–359
    Defined, 296, 304
    See also Transnationalism
Gold, H., 176–177
Goodall, H. L., 257
Goodley, D., 261

Google (Company), 2, 58–59, 111, 113–118, 120, 122–123, 125–126, 357
Gordon, C., 283, 292
Gordon, L., 289
Goss, B. M., 5
Gounari, P., 296
Gramsci, A., 53, 64–65, 336–337, 345
    Organic Intellectual, 38, 337
Great Depression, the, 34
Greenberg, A., 115
Greenberg, C., 351
Greenhow, C., 256
Griffin, C., 51
Griffin, P., 11
Grossberg, L., 12, 27, 38, 40, 99
Guattari, F., 271–272
Gumbrecht, H., 260

Habermas, J., 196, 323, 351
Haines, N., 87
Hajaj, N., 111
Halavais, A., 107, 114–115, 120–121
Halberstam, J., 75, 151
Hall, G. S., 51
Hall, K., 197–199, 204–205, 218–219, 223
Hall, S., 5, 24–26, 32, 38–46, 52, 63, 71, 77, 175, 257, 331–332, 335, 340, 344
Halley, J., 173–174, 179, 188
Halpin, D., 291
Ham, Y., 202
Hammonds, E. M., 78, 81
Haney-López, I., 72
Hanson, A. F., 118–119
Haraway, D., 197
Hardman, P., 178
Hardt, M., 60, 63
Harewood, S., 73, 88
Hargittai, E., 108, 125
Hargreaves, D., 52
Harootunian, H., 341
Harris, D., 53
Harris, S., 289
Harvard Institute for International Development (HIID), 315–318

Harvey, D., 65, 92, 94, 163, 166, 279–280
Hawkins, C., 92
Hayek, F. A., 239, 354
He, B., 114
Healey, P., 189
Hebdige, D., 32, 39, 52
Hedge, R.S., 148, 151–152, 154
Held, D., 283
Helft, M., 125
Henderson, M, 168
Henry, M., 285
Herek, G., 216
Hernandez, D., 76
Herring, S. C., 197, 207
Heteronormativity, 74, 152, 162, 164, 173
  Heterosexism, 198–200, 205, 213–217, 223
  Homophobia, x, 74, 79–80, 184, 199, 216, 220
Higgins, J., 10, 16
Highfield, R., 360
Hill, D., 277, 291
Hill, D. (CHA Press Secretary), 236, 250
Hinman, L. M., 125
Hip Hop, 75, 80
Hirtt, N., 284–287
Historiography, xi, 3–5, 12, 15, 23–28, 31–32, 44, 72–75, 110, 324–325, 339, 349, 353–354
  See also Marxism
HIV/AIDS, 70–71, 73, 77
  Black Americans with, 77–81
Hoad, N., 154
Hogdson, G. M., 286
Hoggart, R., 28, 30, 32, 38
hooks, b., 72, 74, 76
Hope IV legislation, 229, 239
Hopkins, B., 184
Horkheimer, M., 27, 30, 45
Hove, M., 269
Hughes, J., 256
Hughes, L., 88
Human Rights, 80, 180, 232, 244, 246, 250
Human Rights Campaign (HRC), 155–156

Human Rights Watch, 115
Hursh, D., 90–91, 230
Hutcheon, L., 222
Hwang, J., 201, 218–219, 225

Iceland, 120
Identity, ix–x, 7–12, 14–16, 32, 55–56, 59, 70–71, 74–75, 81, 98–99, 130, 150–160, 164–168, 197–199, 201, 205, 213, 219, 223, 234, 244, 257, 271, 330, 336, 340, 357
  Hybridity, x, 7, 62, 76, 164, 259, 338
  Intersectionality, 70–73, 75–78, 80–81, 152
  Politics, 39, 171–175, 179, 183–188
  Rupture, 71–81, 87–90, 94–96, 268
Ideology
  12–13, 31, 43, 52–53, 72–73, 80, 96, 131–132, 134–137, 142, 161, 168, 174, 179, 196–197, 204–205, 230–233, 237, 247–248, 282, 293–294, 296, 306–307, 325, 330, 332–333, 337–339, 342–343, 346
  Defined, 152–153, 224, 281
Ihejirika, M., 230, 249
Immigrants, 6, 8, 72, 88, 91, 93, 95, 101, 149, 151, 157–158, 160–161, 164–165
  Asylum-Seekers, 149, 160–161, 164–166
  Anti-Immigration, 70, 161–162, 165–166
India, 8, 73, 91, 168, 289
Information Saturation, 107, 110–112, 116, 119–120
Innis, H., 36–37, 109
InterActiveCorp, 120
International Association of Media and Communication Research (IAMCR), 36, 45
International Finance Corporation, Health and Education Group (IFC), 290, 297
International Monetary Fund (IMF), 120, 304
International Telecommunication Union

(ITU), 111
Introna, L., 125
Iran, 138–139, 144
Ivanova, V., 309

Jameson, F., 39, 62–63, 360
Jansen, B.J., 108
Jansen, S. C., 26, 35, 39, 42
Jay, M., 24, 27, 62, 66
Jeanneney, J., 114
Jefferson, T., 52
Jenkins, H., 7, 57, 60–61, 65, 196
Jeon, H., 207
Jeong, J., 225
Jerry Springer Show, 162–163
Johnson, C., 281
Johnson, M., 164
Johnson, P. E., 168
Johnson, R., 27, 30, 64–65
Johnson, S., 139
Jones, J., 188
Jones, K., 305
Jones, R., 305
Jordan, L., 249
Joseph, M. L., 231–232
Journal of Communication, the, 74
Journalism, 3, 33–34, 38–39, 74, 112–114, 117, 138–139, 243, 356
    Citizen, 139–140, 144–145, 244–245, 248, 250–251
Jung, C. G., 341
Jung, R., 358
Jurgenson, N., 55, 59–60, 65
Juul, J., 2

Kahn, R., 54, 65
Kaiser Family Foundation, 78
Kaiser, S., 39
Kane, M., 115
Kang, Y., 207
Kant, I., 1, 27, 45
Kellner, D., 6, 54, 57, 65, 346
Kelly, J., 7
Kendall, L., 220–221

Kennedy, P., 279, 296
Kennedy, R., 88
Khan, S. I., 218
Kim, H., 224
Kim, J., 201–202, 213–214, 222, 225
Kim, K., 219
Kim, M., 200
Kim, R., 201–202, 218–219, 222–224
Kim, S., 213, 220–221
Kim, Y., 204, 219, 225
King, S., 133
Kipkoech, D., 213
Kiralyfalvi, B., 362, 351
Klees, S.J., 281
Klein, N., 7, 9, 90–91, 279
Knight, H., 171
Ko, E., 213
Kofie, N. F., 243
Kramarae, C., 197, 205
Kumar, R., 277, 291
Kunig, R., 181

Lacan, J., 340
Ladi, S., 304
Ladson-Billings, G., 72, 74, 76
LaFuente, C., 308
Lamarra, N. F., 314
Lambert, P., 308
Lantham, S., 256
Larrechea, E., 324
Latin America, 92, 152, 290–291, 303–310, 312–325
Lawless, K. A., 160
Lawrence, C., 239, 250
Leavis, F. R., 28–30
Lee, C., 200–201, 225
Lee, D., 225
Lee, E., 213
Lee, H., 201, 219
Lee, J., 201, 225
Lee, K., 198, 221
Lee, M., 219
Lee, S., 198
Legalism, 173–174, 177, 179, 182–186

Lemke, T., 281, 296
Lesko, N., 64
Leslie, E., 66
Leslie, S. W., 125
Lessig, L., 361
Lewis-Thornton, R., 78
LGBTIQ, 80, 93, 155–157, 164–165,
    171–171, 175, 181–184, 187, 197, 241
  Butch Queen, 153–154, 167
  Gay Economy, 176–177, 187
  Gays, 74, 79, 151–154, 156–157, 160,
    164–165, 167–168, 171, 176–189,
    196, 200, 204, 213–217, 220,
    223–225
  Intersexed, 73, 156, 162
  Lesbians, 74, 152, 154, 156, 171, 176,
    181, 188
  Marriage, 152, 156, 160, 165, 171, 173,
    182–185, 187–189
  Queer (identity), 73, 153–154,
    156–157, 161, 164–167, 171, 173,
    175, 182, 185–187, 213
  See also Heteronormativity; Movements;
    Queer; Transgendered
Liberalism, 63, 354, 361
  See also Neoliberalism
Lie, A., 279–280
Ling, R. S., 130
Linz, D., 80
Lipman, P., 87, 90–91, 230
Lippmann, W., 35–37, 42–43
Lipsitz, G., 75
Lloyd, D., 152
Lo, Y. W., 291
Logue, J., 6
Los Angeles Times, 177, 182, 184, 188
Lovegreen, N., 51
Lowe, L., 152
Lowenthal, D., 24–25
Lubiano, W., 76
Lugo, A., 151, 166
Lugones, M., 72
Lycos (Company), 112–114, 117

MacCabe, C., 41, 44
MacLeish, A., 35
Maldonado-Maldonado, A., 306
Manalansan, M., 154, 188
Mandel, E., 57
Marginson, S., 293, 297, 305, 310
Marsh, D., 304
Marshall, J. D., 360
Martin, C., 78
Martinez, E., 284
Marvin, C., 3, 5
Marx, K., x, 30–31, 54, 65–66, 335,
    338–339, 341, 349–350, 355, 359
Marxism, 5, 27–32, 36, 39, 52, 59–60, 62,
    66, 92, 121–122, 124–125, 157, 330–331,
    335–339, 341–342, 345, 351–352, 360
  Historical Materialism, 28, 30–31
  Neo-, 6–7
  Totality, 61–65
Masculinity, 11, 52, 64, 71, 73, 153,
    195–196, 223–224
  Eunuch, 213, 216–218, 220, 223, 225
  See also Cyber-Masculinity
Massumi, B., 269–270
Mastro, D. E., 80
Mattelart, A., 148
May, C., 357
McCarthy, C., 6, 45, 88, 96, 296
McCarthyism, 36
McChesney, R. W., 2–3, 5, 34–35, 38–41,
    46, 113
McCrae, R. R., 357
McCulloch, K., 51
McElroy, W., 144
McGinn, N., 318
McGrew, A., 283
McGuigan, J., 53
McKinley, J., 183
McLuhan, M., 109, 118
McNichol, T., 115
McRobbie, A., 52, 64, 76
Meadow, S., 8, 91
Meares, D. D., 291
Media Studies

See Communications Research
Meehan, E., 36, 39–40
Melody, W., 36
Mercado Común del Sur (MERCOSUR), 317, 321
Merleau-Ponty, M., 260, 264–265
Metaphor, 7, 77, 94, 168, 233, 237–238, 270
   Metonymy, 237, 242
   Synecdoche, 237–238
Michaeli, E., 248
Microsoft, 9, 90, 120, 122–123, 357
Miklaucic, S., 62
Milk (film), 182–183
Milk, H., 171–188
Miller, P., 283
Miller, T., 58
Mills, C. W., 36–37
Mills, S., 150
Min-ha, T., 76
Ministerio de Educación y Cultura (MEC), 307, 316, 318
Miyoshi, M., 91
Moe, T., 288
Mok, K. H., 291
Molina-Guzmán, I., 76
Molinas, J., 309
Montero, M., 309
Moodle (Website), 263, 272
Moorti, S., 74–76
Moraga, C., 73, 76
Morley, D., 25, 40
Morris, C., 179, 181
Mosco, V., 3–4
Moscone, G., 176–178, 185, 188
Movement/Mobility (Populations), 6, 8–9, 60, 90, 149–150, 153, 156–157, 160, 166, 230–232
   Tourism, 86–97, 92–93, 101, 156–161, 245
   Vagabond, 93, 101, 345
   See also Immigration
Movements (Political), 5, 30, 41, 44, 80, 157, 173–175, 179–180, 186, 250, 346, 355

Civil Rights, 38, 75, 80, 172, 174, 185, 244
   Feminist, 53, 75, 80, 188
   Grassroots, 80, 182–183, 188
   New Social Movements, 165, 172, 179–182, 185
   Women's Suffrage, 38, 172
Mukhtar, A., 277, 284
Multiculturalism, 63, 75–77, 81, 101
   Strategic, 87–89, 91, 95–96, 98–100
Mungham, G., 51–52
Murdock, G., 40
Murphree, H. J. Y., 199
Muslims, 157–159
Myth, 14, 24, 27, 108, 112–114, 116, 123, 246, 281, 331, 339–342, 346
   See also Ideology

Nadesan, M. H., 132
Nagel, J., 174
Nairn, K., 10, 16
Nakamura, L., 61, 125, 197, 266
Napoleon III, L., 94
National Center for Transgendered Equality (NCTE), 149, 155–156, 158–161, 165–166
National Public Radio (NPR), 88
National Transgender Advocacy Coalition (NTAC), 149, 155–161, 165–166
Nationalism, 33, 39, 72–73, 75, 148, 219
Nayak, A., 5, 12, 89, 91
Negri, A., 60, 359
Nelson, C., 39, 41
Neoliberalism, 6, 11–15, 25, 70, 88–100, 118, 130–145, 157, 163, 166, 229, 231–233, 239–242, 245, 248, 277–297, 306, 311, 330, 332, 359
   Defined, 42, 89, 131–132, 277–283, 293–294, 306
   Fiscalization, 97–98
   Virtualization, 96–97
   Vocationalization, 97
Neuendorf, K., 80
Neunhöffer, G., 279

New York City, 90, 92, 141, 156, 160, 163, 165–166, 233
   Harlem, 88
New York Times, 182, 183, 189, 249
Newton, J., 39
Nichols, J., 3
Nietzsche, F., 26, 352–355
Nike, 7, 9, 90
Ninja, W., 162–163
Nissenbaum, H., 125
Nokia, 120
Nord, D. P., 16, 37–39

Obama, B. H., President, 96, 182–184, 188–189
Oliver, M. B., 80
Olssen, M., 277, 287, 361
Ong, A., 282
Ono, K. A., 39, 45
Organisation for Economic Co-operation and Development (OECD), 283, 285–286, 290, 310
Osborne, T., 281
Osofsky, G., 231
Ozga, J., 305

Page, A., 358
Page, L., 120, 125
Pakistan, 8, 91
Pang, H., 201, 208
Paraguay, 303–304, 306–309, 312–325
Parameswaran, R., 76
Parascandola, R., 141
Parhutik, V., 269
Paris Is Burning, 168
Park, J.-K., 88
Park, S., 201–202, 218–219, 222, 224
Pearce, D., 291
Pearson, G., 51–52
Peck, J., 293–294
Pedagogy, 58, 61, 66, 96, 98–99, 132, 254–269, 271–272, 287, 354–355
   Knowledge Cultures, 352–359
   See also Policy

Pedersen, O. K., 279, 294
Pérez, C., 286
Perez-Alvarez, M., 130
Pérez-Liñán, A., 309
Peters, M. A., 280, 282, 284, 286, 289, 350, 354, 360
Peterson, P. E., 288
Pew Internet and American Life Project, 112
Pew Project for Excellence in Journalism, 117, 121
Pfeiffer, D., 232, 250
Philippines, 164
Phoenix, A., 287
Pick, D., 283
Pierson, C., 281
Pineau, E. L., 259
Pink, D., 358
Plant, S., 130
Plehwe, D., 279
Poggioli, R., 350
Policy
   Education, 10, 25, 86–91, 94–101, 277–280, 283–293, 303, 305–324, 352–359
   Resistance, 309, 315–316, 319, 323–325
   Transfer / Traveling, 304–305, 307, 309–315, 324–325
   Political Economy, 2, 25, 30, 36–41, 46, 54, 62, 95, 110, 119, 130, 150, 163–164, 196–197, 279–280, 355, 359
   See also Communism; Liberalism; Marxism; Neoliberalism;
Pooch, U., 108
Popkin, S. J., 243
Portugal, 101
Postcolonialism, 73, 76, 97, 151
Postman, N., 2, 65, 109, 116
Power, S., 291
Proctor, J., 77
Proposition 6, California, 178–180, 185, 187
Proposition 8, California, 171, 182–187,

189
Prosser, J., 151
Prudham, S., 296
Psychoanalytic Theory, 330–331, 339–342, 345
Puar, J. K., 158
Public Choice Theory, 288–289
Public Housing, 229–250
Public Sphere, 3, 16, 195–202, 205–207, 219, 223, 232
Puchner, M., 350
Pybus, J., 59

Queer
    of Color Criticism, 73, 78, 150–152, 154–155, 167
    Politics, 172–175, 185–187
    Theory, 73, 151
    See also LGBTIQ
Quiroz, P.A., 12

Race, x–xi, 7, 11–12, 51, 56, 66, 70–81, 87–90, 95–96, 99–100, 151–156, 167–168, 173, 175, 195–196, 242, 244, 247, 250
    See also Ethnicity
Racism, x, 11–12, 74, 79–80, 95–96, 164–165, 183–184, 241–242, 247
    See also Whiteness
Radaelli, C. M., 310–311
Rai, A., 158
Rama, C., 307
Ramia, G., 288
Real ID Act, 149, 156–157, 160–164, 166–167
Reddy, C., 151, 158
Rehman, B., 76
Reimers, F., 313–314, 318
Resistance, x, 7–8, 15–16, 28, 32, 52–53, 60–61, 72, 144–145, 152, 154, 167–168, 173–174, 187, 201, 243–245, 250, 295, 307–309, 311, 324–325, 330, 336, 339–340, 342–347, 350–352
    See also Agency

Revolution, 8, 26–28, 30–31, 38, 45, 66, 139, 338–339, 341, 349–351
    See also Marxism
Rey, B., 269
Rezai-Rashti, G., 88
Rhoades, G., 305, 310
Rhoten, D., 288
Rieger, O. Y., 108
Ritter, B., 221
Ritzer, G., 55, 59–60, 65
Rivarola, D., 312, 321
Rivelli, D., 308
Rizvi, F., 283–284, 293
Robelia, B., 256
Robertson, C., 151, 158
Robertson, S., 10
Rodríguez-Gómez, R., 321
Rogers, E., 34–35, 45
Rojas, V., 76
Rojecki, A., 80
Roman, L., 5
Rosaldo, R., 39, 41
Rose, G., 204, 224, 233, 237, 246, 249
Rose, N., 11, 133, 240, 242, 249–250, 281–282
Ross, L., 256
Ross, M., 158, 202, 219
Rosskam, E., 277
Rubin, G., 148
Ruby, A., 95
RuPaul, 162–164
Rushing, J. H., 342
Rutz, H. J., 277

Saad-Filho, A., 279
Saiegh, S., 309
San Francisco Gay Democratic Club, 178, 181
San Francisco Sentinel, 172, 175–181
Sandoval, C., 76
Santa Ana, O., 76
Sarup, M., 257
Sassen, S., 92, 303–304
Saulsman, L. M., 358

Saussure, F., 334
Saxton, A., 33
Schiller, D., 9, 54, 58, 90, 111, 119, 124
Schiller, H., 36
Schlay, A. B., 230
Schmidt, E., 123
Schramm, W., 35, 45
Schugurensky, D., 284, 290–291
Schwartzman, S., 307
Scott, A., 197
Search Engines, 107–126
    Advertising, 115, 119–122
    Gender, 115–116
    See also Google; Lycos
Seidman, S., 179–180, 188
Semiology/Semiotics, 32, 53, 95, 204–205, 330–336, 342, 345
Semmens, L., 197
Sennett, R., 7, 9–10, 12, 87, 92, 94, 99
Sennyey, P., 256
Seo, M., 225
Serafini, O., 308
Shectman, L., 180
Shohat, E., 71, 76
Shome, R., 148, 151–152, 154
Shumar, W., 277
Silicon Valley, 119–120, 125
Singer, M., 269
Sloop, J., 76
Smith, D., 179–180
Smith, J. L., 243, 247, 250
Smith, T., 72
Smythe, D., 36, 45, 120–121, 125
Somerville, S., 151, 158
Song, K., 201
South Korea, 195–196, 199–204, 213–214, 218–219, 223–225
    Ministry of Gender Equality, 206
Spade, D., 156
Sparke, M., 277, 296
Sparks, C., 52
Speers, L., 111
Spink, A., 108–109
Spivak, G. C., 43, 73
Sprint (Company), 3
    Palm Centro/Pre, 3, 130
Staff, L., 72
Stam, R., 71, 76
State, the, x, 1, 5, 8, 13, 25, 33, 36, 53, 72–73, 80–81, 87, 90, 94, 111, 115, 120, 131–134, 140–146, 149, 150–152, 157–161, 163, 165, 167, 172–175, 181, 184–187, 198, 230, 232, 238, 241, 246–247, 277–296, 304–325, 357, 359
    Welfare, 9–10, 12, 70, 78, 241, 246–247, 281
    See also Neoliberalism
Steinberg, M., 24
Stern, S. R., 80
Sterne, J., 4–5
Stewart, A., 51
Stokoe, E., 197–219
Stoler, A., 73
Stoloff, J. A., 240
Stone, D., 311
Stonewall, 156, 172, 183, 188
Strange, S., 296
Sullivan, K., 293
Surveillance, 122, 130–131, 140–145, 149–151, 157–161, 164–167, 172, 245
Sylvia Rivera Law Project (SRLP), 149, 156, 160–162, 164–166

Tan, J., 293
Tapscott, D., 58, 65
Tate, S., 7, 266
Tatto, M., 288
Taylor, H. J., 197, 205
Taylor, J., 283
Teasley, C., 88
Telus Mobility, 135–137
Tembl, J., 269
Terranova, T., 60
Terrorism, 79, 141–143, 148–149, 157–159, 161–162, 166–167, 279
    September 11th (9/11), 79, 149, 161–162, 166
Thatcherism, 39
This Is England, 8, 91
Thobani, S., 159

Thompson, E. P., 4, 28, 30–32, 38–39, 45–46, 52
Thompson, R., 261
Thorsen, D. E., 279–280
Thrift, N., 57, 65
Thrupp, M., 297
Tilley, C., 260
Time Warner, 120
Times of Harvey Milk, 188
Tomlinson, J., 7, 116
Torres, C. A., 277, 290, 306
Touraine, A., 279
Transgendered People, 73–74, 148–168, 171
    Advocacy, 149–150, 152–162, 164–167, 181, 188
    Defined, 153
    See also Fellow Traveler
Transnationalism, 6–9, 38, 75–76, 151, 160, 163–164, 199, 304–305, 342, 344
    Defined, 291
    See also Globalization
Treichler, P. A., 79
Tullock, G., 288
Turow, J., 122
Tuschling, A., 287

United Nations, 244, 313, 358
United Nations Children's Fund (UNICEF), 313–314
United Nations Educational, Scientific and Cultural Organization (UNESCO), 286, 310, 314, 320–321
United States, 11, 33–39, 45–46, 62, 65, 70–75, 77–82, 87–88, 91–97, 110, 112, 120, 141, 144, 149–168, 172–174, 176–189, 201, 229–251, 316, 333, 339, 342, 354
United States Agency for International Development (USAID), 316
Universidad Católica "Nuestra Señora de la Asunción" (UCA), 308
Universidad Nacional de Asunción (UNA), 308
Urry, J., 304

Valdivia, A. N., 72, 74–76, 152, 158
Valentine, D., 153–154, 188
Van Couvering, E., 125
van Dijk, T. A., 232
Venkatesh, S. A., 230, 232

Walker, J., 64
Wallace, M., 89
Wallerstein, I., 91
Walpen, B., 279
Walzer, A., 199
Warner, M., 179, 187
We the People Media, 244–245
We, G., 197–198, 207, 224
Weber, M., 24, 46, 251
Weedon, C., 257
Weeks, K., 63
Weis, L., 99
Weise, C. V., 320
Weizl, J., 181
Welch, R., 269
Wellman, B., 130
West, C., 26, 99, 117, 172
Westbrook, L., 162
Whiteness, 11–12, 73–76, 79–81, 152–155, 158, 161, 242–243, 258–259
    See also Race; Racism
Whites, 5–6, 8, 52, 71, 73–76, 78–80, 91, 95–96, 101, 153–155, 161, 167–168, 188, 231, 240–242, 258, 261
Whitty, G., 289, 291
Wildermuth, J., 181
Wilken, R., 130
Willerton, R., 237
Williams, A. D., 58, 65
Williams, R., 1, 25, 28–32, 38, 110, 119
Willis, P., 5, 7, 52–54, 64, 90, 99
Willoughby, L., 197
Wilson, D., 96, 101
Wilson, R., 25
Winn, S., 171
Wintle, G., 142
Witmer, B., 269
Woo, J., 221
World Bank, 11, 285, 290, 305, 309–310,

319–322
World Conference on Education for All (WCEFA), 313
World Trade Organization (WTO), 290–291
World War II, 35–36, 45, 88

Yahoo (Company), 111, 113
Yates, J., 125

Zacchino, N., 177
Zambrana, R. E., 75
Zeman, E., 112
Zhang, Z., 114
Zimmer, M., 108–109, 118
Zizek, S., 63
Zwick, D., 57–58, 60–61

GLOBAL
STUDIES IN
EDUCATION

A.C. (Tina) Besley, Michael A. Peters,
Cameron McCarthy, Fazal Rizvi
General Editors

Global Studies in Education is a book series that addresses the implications of the powerful dynamics associated with globalization for re-conceptualizing educational theory, policy and practice. The general orientation of the series is interdisciplinary. It welcomes conceptual, empirical and critical studies that explore the dynamics of the rapidly changing global processes, connectivities and imagination, and how these are reshaping issues of knowledge creation and management and economic and political institutions, leading to new social identities and cultural formations associated with education.

We are particularly interested in manuscripts that offer: a) new theoretical, and methodological, approaches to the study of globalization and its impact on education; b) ethnographic case studies or textual/discourse based analyses that examine the cultural identity experiences of youth and educators inside and outside of educational institutions; c) studies of education policy processes that address the impact and operation of global agencies and networks; d) analyses of the nature and scope of transnational flows of capital, people and ideas and how these are affecting educational processes; e) studies of shifts in knowledge and media formations, and how these point to new conceptions of educational processes; f) exploration of global economic, social and educational inequalities and social movements promoting ethical renewal.

For additional information about this series or for the submission of manuscripts, please contact one of the series editors:

A.C. (Tina) Besley: tbesley@illinois.edu
Cameron McCarthy: cmccart1@illinois.edu
Michael A. Peters: mpet001@illinois.edu
Fazal Rizvi: frizvi@unimelb.edu.au

Department of Educational Policy Studies
University of Illinois at Urbana-Champaign
1310 South Sixth Street
Champaign, IL 61820   USA

To order other books in this series, please contact our Customer Service Department:

(800) 770-LANG (within the U.S.)
(212) 647-7706 (outside the U.S.)
(212) 647-7707 FAX

Or browse online by series:
www.peterlang.com